T0190330

Lecture Notes in Computer Science 14322

The series Lecture Notes in Computer Science (LNCS), including its subseries Lecture Notes in Artificial Intelligence (LNAI) and Lecture Notes in Bioinformatics (LNBI), has established itself as a medium for the publication of new developments in computer science and information technology research, teaching, and education.

LNCS enjoys close cooperation with the computer science R & D community, the series counts many renowned academics among its volume editors and paper authors, and collaborates with prestigious societies. Its mission is to serve this international community by providing an invaluable service, mainly focused on the publication of conference and workshop proceedings and postproceedings. LNCS commenced publication in 1973.

Halimah Badioze Zaman · Peter Robinson ·
Alan F. Smeaton · Renato Lima De Oliveira ·
Bo Nørregaard Jørgensen · Timothy K. Shih ·
Rabiah Abdul Kadir · Ummul Hanan Mohamad ·
Mohammad Nazir Ahmad
Editors

Advances in Visual Informatics

8th International Visual Informatics Conference, IVIC 2023
Selangor, Malaysia, November 15–17, 2023
Proceedings

 Springer

Editors
Halimah Badioze Zaman
Universiti Tenaga Nasional
Kajang, Selangor, Malaysia

Alan F. Smeaton
Dublin City University
Dublin, Ireland

Bo Nørregaard Jørgensen
University of Southern Denmark
Odense, Denmark

Rabiah Abdul Kadir
Universiti Kebangsaan Malaysia
Bangi, Selangor, Malaysia

Mohammad Nazir Ahmad
Universiti Kebangsaan Malaysia
Bangi, Selangor, Malaysia

Peter Robinson
University of Cambridge
Cambridge, UK

Renato Lima De Oliveira
MIT Sloan School of Management
Asia School of Business
Cambridge, MA, USA

Timothy K. Shih
National Central University
Jhongli, Taiwan

Ummul Hanan Mohamad
Universiti Kebangsaan Malaysia
Bangi, Selangor, Malaysia

ISSN 0302-9743 ISSN 1611-3349 (electronic)
Lecture Notes in Computer Science
ISBN 978-981-99-7338-5 ISBN 978-981-99-7339-2 (eBook)
https://doi.org/10.1007/978-981-99-7339-2

This Springer imprint is published by the registered company Springer Nature Singapore Pte Ltd.
The registered company address is: 152 Beach Road, #21-01/04 Gateway East, Singapore 189721, Singapore

Paper in this product is recyclable.

Preface

The International Visual Informatics Conference (IVIC) 2023 once again brought together experts from academia and industries in a multidisciplinary field that encompasses Computer Science, Information and Communications Technology and Computing Engineering. The conference took place amidst tremendous challenges of the post-COVID-19 pandemic, Energy Transition, Climate Change, Digital Transformation, Wars, Security, low education standards, unemployment and corruption. Despite these challenges, nations are braving it through and embracing opportunities that come their way. Emphasizing its multidisciplinary nature, this time the conference returned to its original home, Universiti Kebangsaan Malaysia (UKM) and was hosted once again by the Institute of Visual Informatics (IVI). Together with other institutional partners of this conference, research findings in various specialized areas of Visual Informatics integrated into various fundamental domains were shared together at this conference. We have seen the areas of Visual Informatics grow since the conference first began in 2009. We are grateful to all our partners, locally and internationally, for making this 8th IVIC a specially exciting and meaningful one.

The Eighth International Visual Informatics Conference (IVIC 2023) was conducted for the first time face-to-face after more than three years of not being able to have physical meetings but only virtual ones. For the first time after a long time too, participants could meet co-researchers from different institutions and different countries; and interact with potential partners from different institutions and industries physically. Participants were also able to appreciate exhibitions and discuss with the respective researchers the works exhibited to get first-hand explanations on matters that they did not understand or were concerned about. Like the previous conferences, the main objective of this conference was to bring together experts and researchers from academia and industry to discuss and share new knowledge, ideas and innovations through internationalization and industrialization. Like the previous IVIC conferences, this conference was organized collaboratively by the Visual Informatics fraternity from various public and private universities, professional institutions and industry players from various parts of the world (their names are listed in the proceedings). The conference was co-sponsored by the Malaysian Information Technology Society (MITS), Malaysia Chapter MyAIS, Institute of Informatics and Computing for Energy (IICE), UNITEN, ARB Berhad and MatrixStreams Sdn. Bhd. The conference was co-chaired by six (6) Professors from Cambridge University, MIT Sloan Management School/ABS, Dublin City University, University of Southern Denmark, National Central University and Universiti Tenaga Malaysia (UNITEN).

The theme of the conference mentioned earlier reflects the importance of the need for organizations and nations to create innovations to achieve Energy Transition efforts and digital transformation for societal well-being. All these innovations were undertaken at a time when disruptive technologies, Climate Change, Sustainability and Generative

AI had brought about interesting emerging visual technologies such as Electric Vehicles; Autonomous and semi-autonomous vehicles, Smart Energy Efficient Chat-bots, as well as Internet of things (IoT) and Blockchain for various domains such as smart buildings, healthcare, agriculture and education. The human-centric future smart society and citizenry of the various nations required new digital innovations that were adopting advanced AI such as Generative Artificial Intelligence (GAI) and data-driven AI and secured AI; they also required digital transformation through strategic digital adoption and sustainable technologies for better technological and economic growth of their respective countries. Thus, the theme of the conference was relevant, apt and timely.

The conference focused on six (6) tracks: *Modeling & Simulation, Mixed Reality & HCI, Systems Integration & IoT, Cybersecurity, Energy Informatics* and *Intelligent Data Analytics,* which lasted for two days (15th and 16th November 2023) and ended with four (4) half-day workshops (17th November 2023) that ran concurrently online entitled: *Data Development for Information Visualisation; Designing Questionnaires for Product, Process, Organizational & Marketing Innovation; Introduction to Deep Learning;* and *Advanced Techniques in Cybersecurity- Safeguarding your Digital Assets* respectively. There were five keynote speakers and 51 paper presentations based on topics covered by the six (6) main tracks. The reviewing of the papers was conducted by experts who represented the Programme Committee locally and internationally from Asia, Europe, and Oceania. Each paper was single-blind by three reviewers and the acceptance rate was 50%. The reviewing process was managed using the system Conference Bay. The conference also included an exhibition portraying research and innovations by academia and industry.

On behalf of the organizing and program committee of IVIC 2023, we thank all authors for their submissions and camera-ready copies of papers, and all participants for their thought-provoking ideas and active participation at the conference. We also thank the Vice-Chancellor of UKM (host university), and Vice-Chancellors and Deans of all Computer Science & IT and Business faculties and Research Institutes of the IHLs and Industry for their support in organizing this conference. We also acknowledge the sponsors, members of the organizing committees, program committee members, support committees and individuals who gave their continuous help and support in making the conference a success. We believe that IVIC will grow from strength to strength and will one day be hosted by not only different institutions in Malaysia but also in different host countries around the world.

November 2023

Halimah Badioze Zaman
Peter Robinson
Alan F. Smeaton
Renato Lima De Oliveira
Bo Nørregaard Jørgensen
Timothy K. Shih
Rabiah Abdul Kadir
Ummul Hanan Mohamad
Mohammad Nazir Ahmad

Organization

The 8th International Visual Informatics Conference (IVIC 2023) was organized by the Institute of Visual Informatics, Universiti Kebangsaan Malaysia (UKM), in collaboration with local public and private Universities in Malaysia, Multimedia Development Corporation (MDEC), and ICT Cluster of the National Professors' Council (MPN).

Local Executive Committee

General Chair

Halimah Badioze Zaman	UNITEN, Malaysia

Deputy Chairs

Rabiah Abdul Kadir	UKM, Malaysia
Zainab Abu Bakar	AeU, Malaysia

Secretaries

Ummul Hanan Mohamad	UKM, Malaysia
Nazrita Ibrahim	UNITEN, Malaysia
Siti Nor Umi Khalilas	UKM, Malaysia

Treasurers

Shafrida Sahrani	UKM, Malaysia
Chaw Jun Kit	UKM, Malaysia
Siti Norazimah Ahmat	UKM, Malaysia

Program Committee

Program Co-chairs

Halimah Badioze Zaman	UNITEN, Malaysia
Peter Robinson	University of Cambridge, UK

Alan F. Smeaton	Dublin City University, Ireland
Renato Lima De Oliveira	Asia School of Business (in collaboration with MIT Sloan), USA
Bo Nørregaard Jørgensen	University of Southern Denmark, Denmark
Timothy K. Shih	National Central University, Taiwan

Technical Program Committee

Mohammad Nazir Ahmad (Head)	UKM, Malaysia
Ely Salwana Mat Surin	UKM, Malaysia
Muhamad Firdaus Abdull Razab	GAE, Malaysia
Rabiah Abdul Kadir	UKM, Malaysia
Ummul Hanan Mohamad	UKM, Malaysia

Sponsorship

Azlina Ahmad (Head)	UKM, Malaysia
Halimah Badioze Zaman	UNITEN, Malaysia
Mohammad Nazir Ahmad	UKM, Malaysia
Rahmat Hidayati	JOIV, Indonesia
Wan Fatimah Wan Ahmad	UTP, Malaysia

Publicity (Web Portal)

Mohamad Hidir Mhd Salim (Head)	UKM, Malaysia
Hafizhah Suzana	UKM, Malaysia
Norazlin Binti Othman	UKM, Malaysia
Nur Adilah Binti Shahli	UKM, Malaysia
Zarul Azham Bin Amin	UKM, Malaysia
Marina Ng	University of Nottingham (Malaysia Campus), Malaysia
Nur Intan Raihana	USM, Malaysia
Mohd Almuiet	Irbid National University, Jordan
Norizan	UiTM, Malaysia
Nur Intan Raihana Ruhaiyem	USM, Malaysia
Syed Nasir Alsagoff	UPNM, Malaysia
Dahlan	UniKL, Malaysia
Nizam	UTHM, Malaysia
Suhaidi Hassan	UUM, Malaysia
Suraya Yaacob	UTM, Malaysia
Rosalina Abdul Salam	USIM, Malaysia

Mohd Hafiz Faizal	UniKL, Malaysia
Ibrahim Mohamed	UKM, Malaysia
Wong Seng Yue	UM, Malaysia
Nur Hanani Binti Azami	UNITEN, Malaysia
Yazeed AlSayed Ali Al Moayed	MEDIU, Malaysia
Titik Khawa Abdul Rahman	AeU, Malaysia
Joshua Thomas	UOW, Malaysia
Amelia Ritahani Ismail	IIUM, Malaysia
Angela Lee	Sunway University, Malaysia
Robiatul A'dawiah Jamaluddin	IUKL, Malaysia
Munir	UPI, Indonesia
Aliza Sarlan	UTP, Malaysia
Suziah Sulaiman Sarlan	UTP, Malaysia
Choo Wou Onn	INTI, Malaysia
Noramiza Hashim	MMU, Malaysia
Muzaffar Hamzah	UMS, Malaysia
Azreen Azman	UPM, Malaysia
Rabiah Ahmad	UTHM, Malaysia
Faaizah Shahbodin	UTEM, Malaysia

Logistics

Mohamad Taha Ijab (Head)	UKM, Malaysia
Syed Nasir Syed Zakaria Alsagoff	UPNM, Malaysia
Hafizhah Suzana Hussien	UKM, Malaysia
Aziah Ali	MMU, Malaysia
Mujahid Abu Bakar	UKM, Malaysia
Nur Adilah Binti Shahli	UKM, Malaysia
Zarul Azham Bin Amin	UKM, Malaysia
Abdul Mutalib Omar	UKM, Malaysia

Workshop

Ang Mei Choo (Head)	UKM, Malaysia
Juhana Salim	MITS, Malaysia
Md. Mahidur Rahman Sarker	UKM, Malaysia
Joshua Thomas	UOW, Malaysia
Mohd Almuiet	Irbid National University, Jordan
Esmadi Abu Abu Seman	UMS, Malaysia
Kasturi Dewi Varathan	UM, Malaysia
Dhanapal Durai Dominic	UTP, Malaysia
Wong Seng Yue	UM, Malaysia

Conference Management System

Ely Salwana Mat Surin (Head)	UKM, Malaysia
Muhamad Firdaus Abdull Razab	GAE, Malaysia
Mohammad Nazir Ahmad	UKM, Malaysia

Tour

Prasanna Ramakrisnan (Head)	MITS, Malaysia
Hajah Norasiken Bakar	UTEM, Malaysia
Azreen Azman	UPM, Malaysia

Exhibition

Riza Sulaiman (Head)	UKM, Malaysia
Hanif Baharin	UKM, Malaysia
Arif Roslan	UKM, Malaysia
Zarul Azham Amin	UKM, Malaysia
Zaina Nabila Binti Zainol Mahdzir	UKM, Malaysia

Special Task

Norshita Mat Nayan (Head)	UKM, Malaysia
Mohd Syahmi Shahril	UKM, Malaysia
Nor Zakiah Binti Gorment	UNITEN, Malaysia
Eddren Law Yi Feng	UNITEN, Malaysia
Low Loi Ming	UNITEN, Malaysia
Nur Aimi Syaqilah Binti Aziz	UNITEN, Malaysia
Nor Nashrah Binti Azmi	UNITEN, Malaysia
Rajeshkumar A/L Sugu	UNITEN, Malaysia
Bavani Ramayah	University of Nottingham Malaysia Campus, Malaysia
Siti Nor Umi Khalilas	UKM, Malaysia

Floor Managers

Syed Nasir Alsagoff Syed Zakaria (Head)	UPNM, Malaysia
Hafizhah Suzana	UKM, Malaysia
Mujahid Abu Bakar	UKM, Malaysia

Registration

Chaw Jun Kit (Head)	UKM, Malaysia
Prasanna Ramakrisnan	UiTM, Malaysia
Marizuana Mat Daud	UKM, Malaysia

Technical Committee

International

Alan F. Smeaton	Dublin City University, Ireland
Timothy K. Shih	National Central University, Taiwan
Sergio Velastin	Queen Mary Univ. of London, UK
Terutoshi Tada	Toyo University, Japan
Emanuele Trucco	University of Dundee, UK
Hang-Bong Kang	Catholic University of Korea, South Korea
Marta Fairén	Universitat Politècnica de Catalunya, Spain
Erich Neuhold	University of Vienna, Austria
Theng Yin Leng	Nanyang Technological University, Singapore
Tony Pridmore	University of Nottingham, UK
Neil A. Gordon	University of Hull, UK
Hyowon Lee	SUTD, Singapore
Jianguo Zhang	University of Dundee, UK
Jing Hua	Wayne State University, USA
Nick Holliman	Durham University, UK
Qingde Li	University of Hull, UK
Wenyu Liu	Huazhong Univ. of Science and Technology, China
Malcolm Munro	Durham University, UK
Huang Jiung-yao	National Taipei University, Taiwan
Li Kuan-Ching	Providence University, Taiwan
Khider Nassif Jassim	University of Wasit, Iraq
Kamal Badr Abdalla Badr	Qatar Foundation, Qatar
Yunis Ali	Simad University, Somalia
Furkh Zeshan	University of Islamabad, Pakistan
Kamarul Faizal Hashim	University of Dubai, UAE
Omar Ahmed Ibrahim	University of Mosul, Iraq
Sommai Khantong	Mahasarakham University, Thailand

Malaysia

Azlina Ahmad	UKM
Afzan Adam	UKM
Amalina Farhi Ahmad Fadziah	UPNM
Asama Kuder Nseaf	UKM
Aslina Baharum	Sunway University
Azreen Azman	UPM
Ang Mei Choo	UKM
Anusha Achuthan	USM
Bahari Belaton	USM
Bavani Ramayah	University of Nottingham Malaysia Campus
Chiung Ching Ho	MMU
Chaw Jun Kit	UKM
Dahlan Abdul Ghani	UNIKL
Dayang Rohaya Awang Rambli	UTP
Ely Salwana Mat Surin	UKM
Eddren Law Yi Feng	UNITEN
Falah Y. H. Ahmed	MSU
Fauziah Zainuddin	UMP
Halimah Badioze Zaman	UKM
Hanif Baharin	UKM
Hajah Norasiken Bakar	UTEM
Hoo Meei Hao	UTAR
J. Joshua Thomas	UOW
Jamaiah Yahaya	UKM
Khairul Shafee Kalid	UTP
Magiswary Dorasamy	MMU
Mahidur Rahman Sarker	UKM
Marizuana Mat Daud	UKM
Marwan D. Saleh	MSU
Noor Afiza Mat Razali	UPNM
Mohamad Taha Ijab	UKM
Mohd Fairuz Iskandar Othman	UTeM
Mohammad Nazir Ahmad	UKM
Mohammad Hidir Mhd Salim	UKM
Mohd Afizi Mohd Shukran	UPNM
Mohd Nadhir Ab Wahab	USM
Mohd Nizam Husen	UNIKL
Mohd Rizal Mohd Isa	UPNM
Nor Hidayati Zakaria	UTM
Nazlena Mohamad Ali	UKM

Noor Hafizah Hassan	UTM
Noor Hayani Abd Rahim	IIUM
Noorminshah Iahad	UTM
Nor Zakiah Gorment	UNITEN
Nor Zairah Ab. Rahim	UTM
Norizan Mat Diah	UiTM
Norshahriah Abdul Wahab	UPNM
Norziha Megat Mohd. Zainuddin	UTM
Nur Azaliah Abu Bakar	UTM
Nur Fazidah Elias	UKM
Nurulhuda Firdaus Mohd Azmi	UTM
Noor Afiza Mat Razali	UPNM
Norshita Mat Nayan	UKM
Nor Fatimah Awang	UPNM
Prasanna Ramakrisnan	UiTM
Puteri Nur Ellyza Nohuddin	UKM
Rabiah Abdul Kadir	UKM
Rahayu Ahmad	UUM
Rahmah Mokhtar	UMP
Rasimah Che Mohd Yusoff	UTM
Razatulshima Ghazali	MAMPU
Ridzuan Hussin	UPSI
Riza Sulaiman	UKM
Robiatul A'Dawiah Jamaluddin	IUKL
Roslina Ibrahim	UTM
Rahayu Ahmad	UUM
Savita K. Sugathan	UTP
Siti Nurul Mahfuzah Mohamad	UTEM
Stephanie Chua	UNIMAS
Suraya Hamid	UM
Suzaimah Ramli	UPNM
Suziah Sulaiman	UTP
Syed Nasir Alsagoff	UPNM
Syahaneim Marzukhi	UPNM
Ummul Hanan Mohamad	UKM
Wan Fatimah Wan Ahmad	UTP
Zahidah Abd Kadir	UNIKL
Zarul Fitri Zaaba	USM
Zuraini Zainol	UPNM
Zahidah Zulkifli	IIUM

Strategic Partners

Yayasan Canselor UNITEN (YCU)
Tenaga Nasional Berhad (TNB)
National Council of Professors (MPN)
Malaysia Digital Economy Corporation (MDEC)
Malaysian Information Technology Society (MITS)
Malaysia Association for Information Systems (MyAIS)
ARB Berhad

Co-organizers

Universiti Kebangsaan Malaysia (UKM)
Universiti Pertahanan Nasional Malaysia (UPNM)
Universiti Sains Islam Malaysia (USIM)
Universiti Teknikal Malaysia Melaka (UTeM)
Universiti Teknologi PETRONAS (UTP)
Universiti Sains Malaysia (USM)
Infrastructure University Kuala Lumpur (IUKL)
Universiti Kuala Lumpur (UniKL)
Universiti Teknologi Malaysia (UTM)
Universiti Malaya (UM)
Universiti Teknologi MARA (UiTM)
Al-Madinah International University (MEDIU)
International Islamic University Malaysia (IIUM)
University of Malaysia, Sarawak (UNIMAS)
Universiti Pendidikan Sultan Idris (UPSI)
Universiti Tenaga Nasional (UNITEN)
Universiti Utara Malaysia (UUM)
University of Nottingham, UK (Malaysia Campus)
UOW Malaysia
Sunway University

Contents

Mixed Reality and Human-Computer Interaction

Systems Integration and IoT, Cybersecurity, Energy Informatics

Intelligent Data Analytics

Keynote

Managing Personal Information

Alan F. Smeaton[(✉)][ID]

Insight Centre for Data Analytics, Dublin City University,
Glasnevin, Dublin 9, Ireland
`alan.smeaton@dcu.ie`

Abstract. There is an increasing awareness of the potential that our own self-gathered personal information has for our wellness and our health. This is partly because of our increasing awareness of what others – the major internet companies mainly – have been able to do with the personal information that they gather about us. The biggest hurdle to us using and usefully exploiting our own self-gathered personal data are the applications to support that. In this paper we highlight both the potential and the challenges associated with more widespread use of our own personal data by ourselves and we point at ways in which we believe this might happen. We use the work done in lifelogging and the annual Lifelog Search Challenge as an indicator of what we can do with our own data. We review the small number of existing systems which do allow aggregation of our own personal information and show how the use of large language models could make the management of our personal data more straightforward.

Keywords: Personal information · Personal data · Lifelogging · Data integration · Information search

1 Introduction

Most of us regard ourselves as consumers rather than creators of information. We watch TV and streamed media, we listen to music, radio and podcasts, we view the images and videos of others and we read the from websites of major content producers. Yes we also take and share our own photos and videos and perhaps we blog or post on social media and we create and share emails and all these are forms of personal information but the vast majority of our interaction with media is to digest rather than to create our own. To help us navigate through all the available content we would like to believe that we use recommender systems and search engines which put us in control of our own information bubbles but in fact a lot of our information feed is controlled by factors other than our own interests.

This research was conducted with financial support of Science Foundation Ireland [12/RC/2289_P2] at Insight the SFI Research Centre for Data Analytics at Dublin City University.

Almost by stealth we are also becoming creators of some forms of personal information. Since the early days of search engines we have unwittingly been leaving behind the digital footprints of our searches, our queries and clickthroughs [16] and this data has become the "oil" which has powered the very successful advertising revenue stream for the large internet companies worldwide. We have very little control or even awareness of this information that we create, though we are becoming more conscious of its value and there are options available to us through trace-free services like DuckDuckGo [9], Startpage, searX, ECosia[1] and others, to limit that information creation, but only if we want and make the effort to do so.

In addition to the hidden forms of personal information creation that we do, we have also become creators of personal information which is very visible to us. Many of us use devices and/or services which passively capture data about us, about what we do, where we do it, with whom and about how are bodies are reacting to those activities. In its most extreme form this is known as lifelogging [3] and can include capturing data from physiological sensors which monitor our heart rate and HRV, stress, blood pressure, body temperature, to wearable cameras and sound recorders, to location trackers and activity monitors, to wearable cameras from which we can deduce our activities and the company we keep. Lifelogging can also include recording the footprints of our online activities on our phones and computers including pages browsed, emails sent/read, documents written or read, even the timing of our keystrokes as we type [13]. We have shown in some of our previous work, this data, when cleaned, integrated and analysed can be used to indicate shifts in our everyday behaviour [5], as a memory prosthetic for our forgetfulness [12] or to generate a visual summary or reflection on past events in our lifetimes [6].

The aggregated accumulation of our online activities which is scatted across our email logs, browser logs and elsewhere but which is integrated and connected together, could provide an incredible resource to help us to re-find personal information that we once found but cannot re-find. Re-finding information is known to take a huge amount of our time [8, 10] yet few systems have been built and none are globally used, to help address this task.

The closest we ever came to a system to help us to re-find information which is scatted across different places is *Stuff I've Seen* [1] developed more than 2 decades ago. However the cost for search engines to create personal indices for each individual person where each index covered just the unique online information that person had encountered was too prohibitive, or more likely there was not a strong enough business case to make doing so economically worthwhile. Instead we have one-size-fits-all search services which have become extremely profitable.

In this article we focus on personal information which we ourselves, individually, gather about our everyday activities. Rather than focus on the extreme versions of this known as lifelogging, we dial this down and address the popular forms of data gathered about everyday activities by millions of everyday people, us though we are guided by the developments from those trailblazers in visual

---

[1] https://www.startpage.com/ https://searx.thegpm.org/ https://www.ecosia.org/.

and other forms of lifelogging. In the next section we define the scope of this everyday personal information that we address and following that we examine some of the trends that the extreme lifeloggers have shown to see what lessons we can take away. We then examine the main problem associated with current personal information data, the lack of integration and accessibility and we show some possible ways in which this can be overcome.

2   Definition of Personal Information Management

A digital footprint is the electronic evidence of our actual existence [11], since most of the things we do are now digital and so much of these activities are logged by third parties. Our digital footprints were initially gathered by search engines, social networks and e-commerce platforms but now every interaction with every website, on a fixed or mobile device now forms part of that footprint.

There are some aspects of this footprint we know about because it is obvious such as the adverts we are presented based on the searches we execute, and we accept and we may even like it. This is the Faustian pact we have with the internet service providers . . . they give us free content, we give them our access data. Some other aspects of our footprint we do not realise and are surprised at when we realise, but we are still OK with it because we benefit from better quality targetted advertising. Our awareness of our footprints varies hugely and the vast majority of people do not realise the size or what can be leveraged from this data including our demographics [4], gender, political persuasion, marital status, and more.

Our digital footprint also includes self-generated activity and behaviour data and this can come from online activities and from wearable devices. Examples of self-generated online behaviour data includes keystroke timing information [13] which can be processed to indicate mood and stress though this remains a niche and specialist application whose benefits have not yet been really proven.

Other types of self-generated personal data from wearables and from in-situ sensors typically measure raw indicators of the state of our bodies' physiology. These include heart rate, activity and movement, blood pressure, body temperature and stress level from galvanic skin response sensors. From these raw measures we can infer the number of steps taken, sleep quality, duration and start/end times, energy levels, caloric energy expenditure, and more. When combined with location from a GPS device we can also infer activity type (run, walk, cycle, swim, etc.) activity intensity, speed, distance, quality, etc. When the devices that gather this data upload it to an online platform it is then compared with data from our past so we can gave our progress measured and trends determined, is our sleep improving or getting worse over the last few months, is our fitness level improving and are we back to where we were before a COVID-19 infection. Some activity platforms such as Strava and Garmin allow our data to be shared with others so we can see if our run/walk/bike ride was solo or in a group with others and if so then whom which allows a social dimension to be added to our exercise routines and can give us additional motivation.

Our reasons for capturing such data about our everyday activities are primarily to allow us to better understand ourselves by getting insights into our behavioural patterns and habits. This has a longer-term goal to maintain or improve our wellbeing and health though we can only do this when we have the tools available to help us analyse this data. Such data also creates a personal record of our lives, allowing us to look back on our experiences and achievements.

In this paper we limit our coverage of personal information to just that self-generated and recorded behaviour data though we acknowledge that personal information has a much wider remit.

3   Lifelogging: Extreme Personal Information Gathering

Before we look at the available and possible ways to process that subset of personal information that we address here, it is worth looking at the broader field of lifelogging and its current status and challenges [7]. The best source of up-to-date progress on information access to lifelogs is the most recent of the annual lifelog search challenges (LSC), held in 2023 [2]. This is the sixth of the annual comparative benchmarking exercises for interactive lifelog search systems. In the spirit of several decades of comparative benchmark evaluations in information retrieval including TREC, TRECVid, FIRE, NTCIR and others, LSC measures the capabilities of different lifelog search systems to access large multimodal lifelogs. Each of the participants in the LSC, 12 in 20023, developed an interactive lifelog retrieval system which was used in a live setting, against the clock, to locate information from a large lifelog based on information needs (queries) which were shared with participants for the first time in the live setting. This mode of comparative evaluation in a live setting has been present for all previous editions of the LSC workshop.

The workshop proceedings from LSC'23 and the previous editions provide a collective summary of the system engineering aspects of the lifelog search tools developed over the years and cover design, architecture, interfaces, backend pre-processing and response formats. The most interesting aspects of the LSC and the lesson we can take away for this paper, is the functionality that the challenge tasks participants with implementing. The LSC challenge now requires participants to address three types of information seeking, namely:

1. Known Item search where an incident from the past, captured in the lifelog, is known and is described and participants have to locate that single known incident in as fast a time as possible. An example of a KI search from LSC'2023 is "In disaster prepper-mode, I was buying an oversized tin of beans, in case of emergencies when COVID was starting. I had looked at many large food items in a warehouse store called Musgrave MarketPlace, including honey and breakfast cereal and tuna fish. It was in February 2020."
2. Ad-Hoc search where there may be zero, one or many incidents which match the query and an example of an ad-hoc query from LSC'2023 is "I like cake. Find examples of when I was looking at cakes for sale in a cafe or restaurant (but not in a shop)."

3. Question Answering (QA) where the information need is posed as the opening line for an interactive conversation. An example of a QA topic from LSC'2023 is "What type of dog does my sister have?"

What we learn from the LSC challenge and from the performances of the top-performing participating teams is that these 3 types of queries satisfying different types of information need, can be executed on large, unstructured, multimodal lifelogs and can give fast and accurate responses. With this in mind we can now examine some of the relevant the challenges for managing personal information.

4   Problems, Challenges and Opportunities for Personal Information

The LSC has shown that the ways in which we want to access our personal information, lifelogs in the case of the LSC, is that we want to do the following:

- Single item identification and retrieval which is essentially a form of data lookup. Examples would be when did I do something? Where was I for some activity? What was my highest HR when I did some activity?
- Aggregate item identification and retrieval involves counting, summing, averaging or otherwise combining multiple instances of the same form of personal information, possibly with some temporal or spatial or other limiting constraints. Examples include how many times did I do a particular kind of activity? Where is the most popular place for me to do some activity which is within the city I live in? What is the average number of steps I take over weekends?
- Cross item aggregation involves combining different sources of personal information in ways to allow us to query for insights which do not exist in any source alone. Examples of this include is my sleep quality improved or worse after I do more than 10,000 steps in a day? Is my resting heart rate at night impacted by my stress levels at work during weekdays?

When we look for examples of systems to support wearable lifelogging we find that they exist in silos. We may use an app or a website to query just one source of self-generated personal data at a time and even these are sometimes quite limited.

There are few examples of systems which aggregate across sources of self-generated personal data and of those which do exist include the following commercial offerings.

Apple Health is an app running on iOS which collects health and activity data from the built-in sensors smartphones and on Apple Watch and allows data from compatible third party devices such as heart rate monitors and third party apps such as Strava, Garmin, Oura ring, sleepScore, Wahoo, Zwift and others. WHile it can present some nice summary visualisations, Apple Health does not allow a user to query across data sources.

Datacoup was a US-based company that shut down in 2019 but while operational it allowed a user to upload their personal information from multiple sources including their interactions with social media as well as from wearables and they would anonymise and aggregate tat data and sell trends and summaries to third party firms. Users were paid a monthly fee and were offered visual analytics which spanned across their personal information sources in return for sharing. Ultimately the service ended because users were not being paid enough but it showed the interest in visualising across personal information sources.

The **dacadoo** health platform invites users to share some of their personal information including demographics and physical characteristics and physiology indicators from wearables, responses from a quality of life questionnaire and data from physical activity, nutrition, sleep, self-control and mindfulness. It combines all this data into a wellness core for the user and uses motivation techniques from the gaming industry as well as data analytics and a reward system to incentivise and sustain changes in behaviour. Users are only allowed to see the output of the process, the wellness score and access is based on a paid monthly subscription but it once again shows the interest in cross-pollinating our individual sources of personal information though in this case how this is done is opaque to users.

An alternative approach to allowing users to explore their own personal information drawn from across individual sources is our proof of concept work described in [14,15]. Here, the data owner collaborates with a data analysis expert where they find one another, communicate and share datasets and analysis results with one another in a secure and anonymised way. Although the software to support this is developed and used in a user trial demonstrating collaborative analysis of sleep data, the business case for making this self-sustaining is lacking.

The most interesting recent development in the area of supporting cross-source querying of personal data, comes from the recent widespread use of large language models and in particular the ability of the larger models to ingest sources of structured data. The most popular of these, ChatGPT, has the facility to have its input tokens consist of data as text or in CSV format which it can parse. Even though there are limitations on the numbers of input tokens allowed (at the time of writing GPT-3.5-turbo-16k allowed a maximum of 16,000 input tokens or prompts) with the correct prompt engineering to direct the model on how to interpret the columns of data in the input CSV files.

Using the ChatGPT Chat Completion API we have taken personal information from the Strava app which records exercise activities like running, biking, etc. and from the Oura ring, a wearable which records heart rate, movement, body temperature and sleep metrics and imported this in CSV format into ChatGPT through an API. This required a detailed description of the CSV columns to be provided as part of the prompt engineering as shown in Fig. 1.

```
messages = [{'role': 'system', 'content': """I am a fitness instructor and an expert in providing insights about
        My instructions which I should adhere to at all cost are:
        1. All the questions asked are in reference to the dataset provided in the previous conversation.
        2. Whenever a question is asked regarding the dataset, you should refer to the column description provide
        3. You should never provide code in your responses.
        4. You are required to answer questions, you should not provide me with steps or methods for calculations
        5. You should be able to perform calculations on your own and should only provide results.
        6. All the questions where I ask you about the activities I performed like 'when was my last ride?', you
        7. For questions where it requires you to consider multiple columns and rows like 'what was my highest av
        8. For questions like 'which run had the highest average speed?', you should never answer with this respc
        9. You should not include this in your answers 'Let me retrieve that information for you.', instead you s
        10. You should provide the serial number of the record in all your answers.
        11. Calculations must be accurate and must be recalculated before providing the answers.
        12. You should directly tell me the answer without telling me how you are retrieving that information.

        Here is a brief description about all the columns present in the dataset.
        1. "serial number": The unique identifier for each activity.
        2. "activity name": The name or type of the activity recorded.
        3. "activity summary": A brief description of the activity.
        4. "distance": The distance covered during the activity in meters.
        5. "moving time": The duration of the activity while in motion, in seconds.
        6. "elapsed time": The total duration of the activity, including rest breaks, in seconds.
        7. "total elevation gain": The total elevation gained during the activity in meters.
```

Fig. 1. Detailed descriptions of columns in prompting used with ChatGPT

Once this was done then the model had been configured to support the three types of personal information queries which we had identified earlier from the Lifelog Search Challenge workshops, namely single item identification and retrieval, aggregate item identification and retrieval and cross item aggregation. An illustration of this is shown in Fig. 2.

```
import openai
openai.ChatCompletion.create(
    model="gpt-3.5-turbo",
    messages=[
        {"role": "system", "content": "You are a fitness assistant. "
        "Your job is to to provide insights from the {dataset} provided"},

        {"role": "user", "content": "How much distance did I run on 26/05/2022?"},

        {"role": "assistant", "content": "Distance ran is 8.5 kilometers"},

        {"role": "user", "content": "Did I sleep better after the run"},

        {"role": "assistant", "content": "Yes the sleep score is better than "
        "on 22/05/2022 when you ran 2 kilometers"},
    ],
    temperature=0.5,
)
```

Fig. 2. Example of promoting used with ChatGPT

While this is just an illustrative example and operating on only a small dataset (there is a 16,000 token limit on the version of ChatGPT we used and that includes all the prompts and all the data points), it is sufficient to indicate the possibilities that this approach holds.

5   Future for Personal Information and Its Management

There is an increasing awareness of the potential that our own self-gathered personal information has for our wellness and our health. This is partly because of our increasing awareness of what others – the major internet companies mainly – have been able to do with the personal information that they gather about us. The biggest hurdle to us using and usefully exploiting our own self-gathered personal data are the applications to support that.

In this paper we have highlighted both the potential and the challenges associated with more widespread use of this data and we have pointed at possible ways in which we believe this might happen. Ultimately whether this actually happens and we do get unfettered and supported access to the insights from our own data, like everything else on the internet will depend on the economics. If a business case emerges where we pay for it ourselves, directly, or our anonymised data is used by somebody else to benefit from, then this will determine whether we get to use our own data for our own benefit.

References

1. Dumais, S., Cutrell, E., Cadiz, J., Jancke, G., Sarin, R., Robbins, D.C.: Stuff I've seen: a system for personal information retrieval and re-use. In: Proceedings of the 26th Annual International ACM SIGIR Conference on Research and Development in Informaion Retrieval, SIGIR 2003, pp. 72–79. Association for Computing Machinery, New York, NY, USA (2003)
2. Gurrin, C., et al.: Introduction to the sixth annual lifelog search challenge, LSC'23. In: Proceedings of the 2023 ACM International Conference on Multimedia Retrieval, ICMR 2023, pp. 678–679. Association for Computing Machinery, New York, NY, USA (2023). https://doi.org/10.1145/3591106.3592304
3. Gurrin, C., Smeaton, A.F., Doherty, A.R., et al.: Lifelogging: personal big data. Found. Trends Inf. Retr. 8(1), 1–125 (2014)
4. Hinds, J., Joinson, A.N.: What demographic attributes do our digital footprints reveal? A systematic review. PLoS ONE 13(11), e0207112 (2018)
5. Hu, F., Smeaton, A.F.: Periodicity intensity for indicating behaviour shifts from lifelog data. In: 2016 IEEE International Conference on Bioinformatics and Biomedicine (BIBM), pp. 970–977. IEEE (2016)
6. Hu, F., Smeaton, A.F.: Image aesthetics and content in selecting memorable keyframes from lifelogs. In: Schoeffmann, K., et al. (eds.) MMM 2018. LNCS, vol. 10704, pp. 608–619. Springer, Cham (2018). https://doi.org/10.1007/978-3-319-73603-7_49
7. Ksibi, A., Alluhaidan, A.S.D., Salhi, A., El-Rahman, S.A.: Overview of lifelogging: current challenges and advances. IEEE Access 9, 62630–62641 (2021)

8. Meier, F., Elsweiler, D.: Going back in time: an investigation of social media re-finding. In: Proceedings of the 39th International ACM SIGIR conference on Research and Development in Information Retrieval, pp. 355–364 (2016)
9. Parsania, V.S., Kalyani, F., Kamani, K.: A comparative analysis: DuckDuckGo vs. Google search engine. GRD J. Glob. Res. Dev. J. Eng. **2**(1), 12–17 (2016)
10. Sappelli, M., Verberne, S., Kraaij, W.: Evaluation of context-aware recommendation systems for information re-finding. J. Am. Soc. Inf. Sci. **68**(4), 895–910 (2017)
11. Sjöberg, M., et al.: Digital me: controlling and making sense of my digital footprint. In: Gamberini, L., Spagnolli, A., Jacucci, G., Blankertz, B., Freeman, J. (eds.) Symbiotic 2016. LNCS, vol. 9961, pp. 155–167. Springer, Cham (2017). https://doi.org/10.1007/978-3-319-57753-1_14
12. Smeaton, A.F.: Lifelogging as a memory prosthetic. In: Proceedings of the 4th Annual on Lifelog Search Challenge, LSC 2021, p. 1. Association for Computing Machinery, New York, NY, USA (2021). https://doi.org/10.1145/3463948.3469271
13. Smeaton, A.F., Krishnamurthy, N.G., Suryanarayana, A.H.: Keystroke dynamics as part of lifelogging. In: Lokoč, J., et al. (eds.) MMM 2021. LNCS, vol. 12573, pp. 183–195. Springer, Cham (2021). https://doi.org/10.1007/978-3-030-67835-7_16
14. Tuovinen, L., Smeaton, A.F.: Remote collaborative knowledge discovery for better understanding of self-tracking data. In: 25th Conference of Open Innovations Association (FRUCT), pp. 324–332. IEEE (2019)
15. Tuovinen, L., Smeaton, A.F.: Privacy-aware sharing and collaborative analysis of personal wellness data: process model, domain ontology, software system and user trial. PLoS ONE **17**(4), e0265997 (2022)
16. Zhou, G., et al.: Deep interest network for click-through rate prediction. In: Proceedings of the 24th ACM SIGKDD International Conference on Knowledge Discovery & Data Mining, pp. 1059–1068 (2018)

Modeling and Simulation

A Visual Real-Time Mobile E-Logbook System to Capture Design Activities, Decisions, and Ideas for Engineers

Kok Weng Ng[1], Yun Ching Tan[1], JianBang Liu[2], and Mei Choo Ang[2(✉)]

[1] University of Nottingham Malaysia, Jalan Broga, 43500 Semenyih, Selangor, Malaysia
[2] Universiti Kebangsaan Malaysia, UKM Bangi, 43650 Bangi, Selangor, Malaysia
amc@ukm.edu.my

Abstract. Logbook is one of the important tools to engineers, which is used to capture engineers' design activities, decisions, and ideas. It is useful to engineers in accomplishing project designs, organising, tracking, and providing post-design evaluation. However, the lack of digitalization of logbooks had made the engineers' design activities heavily dependent on human intervention. Therefore, this research work explores the potential of digitalization of logbooks by redesigning and developing the paper-based logbook into a visual real-time mobile application. The focus of the developed visual e-logbook is to move the old-fashioned way of capturing design activities and decisions into a more systematic and effective way which allows engineers to capture and access logs at any point of time. The visual e-logbook application uses Swift programming language, SwiftUI framework and XCode as the main Integrated Development Environment (IDE). The implemented visual e-logbook is then tested with case studies and results show that the visual e-logbook has good potential for engineering design projects by replacing the paper logbook. Feedback is thus collected from the case studies for future implementation such as search and filtering function, enable collaboration, and reminder function.

Keywords: Design Methodology · Product Design · Logbook

1 Introduction

Logbook, also an important document, which is defined in Collins dictionary as "a book in which someone records details and events relating to something". Logbooks are utilised in different disciplines and serve various purposes. For example, a vehicle logbook can commonly be found to record service logs or safety files in Ireland that are prepared by an architect to record information outlining health and safety risks. Electronic Lab Notebook (ELN) is another example in the pharmaceutical industry that appears to be at the forefront of the development of digital logbook. The usage of ELN not only constricted on data collection but also served multi purposes such as asset monitoring, instrument calibration, order management and so much more. The market of ELNs is challenging and huge, as of 2020, the Electronic Lab Notebook (ELN)'s

H. Badioze Zaman et al. (Eds.): IVIC 2023, LNCS 14322, pp. 15–25, 2024.
https://doi.org/10.1007/978-981-99-7339-2_2

market size was valued as USD 551.12 Million and is projected to reach USD 794.53 Million by 2028 [1]. This shows that a well-designed data collection tool is having high demand in the market due to multiple facts as discussed and required by companies. One of the reasons for these high-value software is due to its high customizable features by developer and can solve critical issues required by customers, conversely, this is thus shown by [2] that they lack fluidity and flexibility for design tasks. For engineers, logbooks have been contributing as a main tool to record, track and analyse design decisions. It served as a dynamic tool that proved to be helpful to engineers.

Study [3] showed that logbooks are an effective method to direct both alumni in their study onto the right track of learning. The guide in the logbook has motivated them to learn what they are unable to obtain from textbooks and online resources. By using a logbook, they can consolidate their existing knowledge and reflect on their past experiences. In the longitudinal study of 'design journals' from graduate-level product design course by study [4], also showed keeping a logbook support reflection. It is important in supporting thinking and making a series of design recommendations. While enabling reflection is the main benefit of keeping a logbook which also further enhances decision making and improves the design process, it also serves as a reminder for engineers to remind them of their work-in-progress [5]. Few researchers have shown the benefits of having a logbook to capture engineer design activities, decisions and ideas in real-time. However, several problems are found on the current systems and implementation can be done to better serve engineers as a useful tool. First, the problem with the current logbook is that it is not efficient in recording and documenting their inputs. Often, engineers find it hard to maintain the habit of documenting with a paper logbook, as it is time consuming to arrange and document in real time and is mistake prone. Someone forgetful will even feel overwhelmed when a large amount of data needs to be recorded.

Besides that, there exist few limitations to the paper logbook, where only word description and sketching is available to record their design activities, decisions and ideas real-time. Following the fast evolution of the world, most of the information is only available digitally both online and offline, and it is hard to transform information into descriptive text for documentation purposes. The flexibility of a paper logbook is deemed in doubt.

As mentioned previously, logbooks proved to be useful as a reflective dialog for design engineers, however, a paper logbook is tricky to use as a study material. This is mainly due to lack of flexibility in graphical representation of the information collected. Recorded design decisions in a paper logbook are hard to link and represent their relationship with each other. Often, engineers need to spend more time redrawing them in a mind- mapping or similar illustration to better study the possibility of improvement on design decisions.

Post-processing the data collected by a logbook is also found significant in visualising the design activities, decisions and ideas of engineers. This is helpful by filtering unwanted information or prioritising significant information from a large amount of collected data. Data analytics is also used by most engineers nowadays to carefully analyse all important findings.

2 Literature Review

Data these days is notoriously more complex than ever before, with the significant growth of the digital world, digitalisation of data collection is crucial to engineers. A digital building logbook is nothing new to designers and available in different disciplines as mentioned in study [6]. However, the digitalisation of engineers' logbooks is still underdeveloped in comparison to other industries. Some research has been done in the past to study the potential of software to replace logbooks and support designers' work in various design projects. An overview of the research is given in Table 1, which also describes the functionalities and features of e-logbooks found in the literature.

Table 1 above shows different features and functionalities of an e-logbook could have. It is generally agreed that the main building blocks of an e-logbook is their role in supporting recording of various data types such as video recording in studies [8] and [10]. Existing studies as shown in Table 1 have shown features and functionalities such as cloud sync and task management could provide additional support to design thinking. However, this study will focus on the fundamental and critical building blocks of e-logbook while saving the additional function on future implementation.

Table 1. Overview of the Functionalities and Features of e-logbook

No	Author	Key Findings	Functionalities and features of their e-logbook
1	Joshua, Alao, Ogbudje, Ogundipe [7]	The paper shows the development of an android-based e-logbook for the administration of SIWES	• Support file attachment • Support image • Time-based notifications and reminder • Cloud backup
2	Foley, Charron and Plante [8]	In the research, interviewers do come up with a lot of useful suggestions for the features in e-logbook. Following shows features that being discussed	• Data linking to calendar • Fast memo (closer to the speed of opening a paper logbook and jotting something down) • Without the need to login every time • Basic sketch function • Files sync from cloud • Videos capturing • Tables • Contact information • Hypothesis • Comments • Task management

(continued)

Table 1. (*continued*)

No	Author	Key Findings	Functionalities and features of their e-logbook
3	Buler [9]	Authors address the complexity of developing an e-notebook when experimental protocols are continually changing, this mean redesigning the structure of the underlying database is needed. Various factors such as skilled database engineer and limited funding is the main concern	• Automatically capture and stored experiment • Can be hyperlinked • Secured with timestamp and signature • Instantly shared with collaborators • Need to include user-friendly tools allowing customisation but without demanding computing skills
4	Pedgley [10]	E-logbook is addressed as "diary" in the research, the diary writing process is concurrent with the case study and each of the diary entry consists of annotated sketches and few lines of text	• Two systems are used to refer to simple artwork and marked up letter 'X' for complex artwork • Video recordings were made to gather evidence on the duration and frequency of diary writing

The objective of this study is to develop a mobile application to capture design activities, decisions and ideas real-time, manage the captured data, show in an interactive timeline and enable users to check their captured history. Furthermore, a qualitative research strategy is chosen to study the potential of developed e-logbook to replace the paper logbook by understanding how engineers utilised the various features of e-logbook to support their design projects. This research strategy verified the viability of the proposed mobile application that fulfilled the objective of this study by conducting case study on the usability of the developed e-logbook.

In the following section of the paper, a design methodology of the waterfall model is selected and followed to document the design and development process. Test plan and result of case study are described and presented in Sect. 3. Finally, Sect. 4 discusses, concludes, and describes possible future research directions.

3 Methodology

There are different software development methodologies commonly available, the mostly used models are agile development model and waterfall model. In this project, the waterfall model is used to break down the project activities into stages that follow linear sequential phases as it is simpler and clearer to use in implementation, usage and management [11]. By using the waterfall model, the project is separated into phases from beginning to the end of the project which are requirement and analysis, design, implementation, test plan and results as shown in Fig. 1.

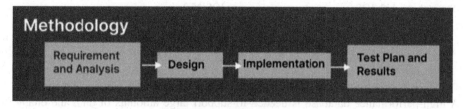

Fig. 1. Methodology

3.1 Requirement and Analysis

In the requirement and analysis phase, analysis on the existing problems is carried out through detailed literature review as discussed in the literature review section. Hence, this section will focus on the requirements that are needed to solve each of the problems listed. This is then divided into three main parts which are data requirement, functional requirement as shown in Table 2 and hardware requirement as shown in Table 3.

Table 2. Functional Requirement

Functional Requirement	Description
Capture design activities, decisions and ideas real-time	The system shall enable users to enter their design activities, decisions and ideas in 5 different data types 1. Image 2. Text 3. Video 4. Document 5. Voice Recording
Real time data management	The mobile application shall be able to upload, edit, and download the data committed by users in real time which should also be stored, removed or edited instantly in the database
Check design activities, decisions and ideas history	The system shall enable users to view their recorded design activities, decisions and ideas history through the mobile application
Provide interactive design decisions timeline	The system shall be able to process and detect the data committed and thus illustrate the design decisions in an interactive timeline

Table 3. Hardware Requirement

Hardware Requirement	Description
Smartphone with IOS	IOS 15.2, Camera Enable, Microphone Enable

The design activities, decisions and ideas are recorded by users as data in the system. A high-performance database is needed to support large amounts of data and enable multiple access concurrently. Firebase, which is a platform developed by Google, is chosen to store all the input data, and enable real-time access. It is highly rated by most software engineers for its simple manageable backend infrastructure and limited free storage for their new project.

3.2 Design

In the design phase, the requirements collected in the previous phase served as the input to the system design. In this section, it will focus on system architecture design and user interface design, this includes the design of system flow, functionality, and specification. For a mobile application system architecture, it is represented by 3 layers which are presentation layer, business layer and data layer as shown in Fig. 2. These 3 layers are critical as the presentation layer provides services that are based on the Swift user interface framework, the business layer facilitates services related to management such as project management, versions management, logs management, media management including management of audios, videos, images, and documentations. Four main functional requirements and the required specification for the e-logbook system design are described in Table 4.

3.3 Implementation

The e-logbook was implemented based on the tools and software as stated in Fig. 2. A toolbar for the e-logbook was then designed and developed to support the user input data types and it is shown in Table 5. Several user interface screens were captured to illustrate the workflow of the e-logbook case study and they are shown in Fig. 3.

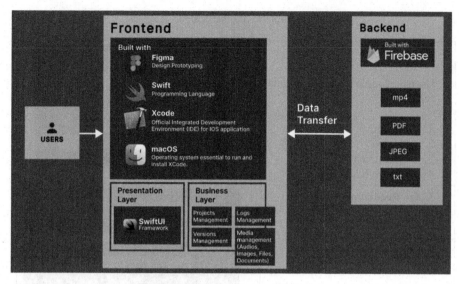

Fig. 2. System Architecture Illustration

Table 4. E-Logbook System Design

Functional Requirement	Specification
Capture design activities, decisions and ideas real-time	Bottom toolbar with different data type input
Real time data management	Cloud database
Check design activities, decisions, and ideas history	Interactive user interface
Provide interactive design decisions timeline	Graphical illustration of captured logs arranged by creation time

3.4 Test Plan and Results (Verification with a Case Study)

In a case study, a designer was invited to design a home use water purifier. The task of redesigning an existing and commonly used water purifier that is expensive and is difficult to carry around. The details of design activities, decisions and ideas were captured in real-time and are documented using the prototype e-logbook (running on a mobile phone) designed and developed in this research work.

Table 5. Toolbar design

Default Mode	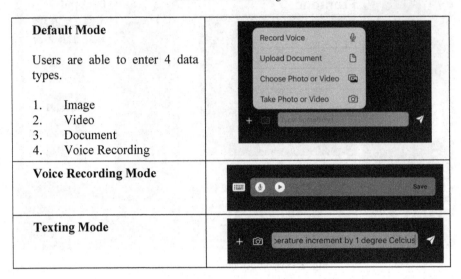
Users are able to enter 4 data types. 1. Image 2. Video 3. Document 4. Voice Recording	
Voice Recording Mode	
Texting Mode	

The project started by opening a new project (shown in Fig. 3, screen 1 to 3) where the name, descriptions and purposes of the project can be captured while screen 4 provides information about the versions of the project log. The task of identifying the design requirements for the water purifier and these requirements can then be captured as different logs into the application as shown in Fig. 3, screen 5 and then can be further decomposed into components which are linked to each requirement as shown Fig. 3., screen 6. The design activities can be later captured based on each of the design requirements. The design decisions are expected to change during the water purifier design process as the designer tinkers about the best possible solutions for each design requirement. Therefore, the design activities, decisions or ideas will be captured during each input or change where any changes to an existing design idea will be captured as a new version by the e-logbook.

Table 6 shows the test results from the case study. The results above clearly show that 4 of the functional requirements stated earlier are satisfied as well as the objective of this study. Firstly, the mobile application is able to check design activities, decisions and ideas history and provide interactive version history timeline.

The inputs and changes made on the log will create a new version in your project detail screen which allows engineers to access, restore, or make a copy of an older version. The new version of history appears in a new column on top of each older version as shown in Fig. 3, screen 3.

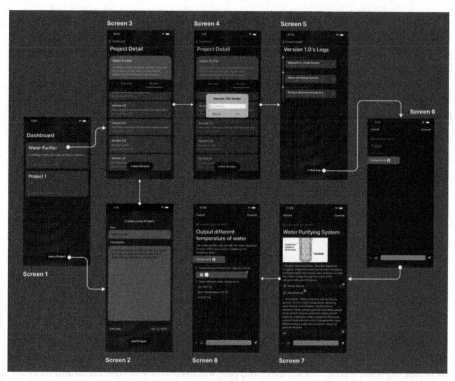

Fig. 3. Application Workflow

Table 6. Test result for each functional requirement

Functional Requirement	Test Result by Designer (Pass/ Fail)
Capture design activities, decisions and ideas real-time	Pass
Real time data management	Pass
Check design activities, decisions and ideas history	Pass
Provide interactive design decisions timeline	Pass

Figure 3 also showed how users can log their design process and similarly allows the user to track back their previous versions and expand to see more granularity. The result of the case study showed that the interface is simple to understand and can better visualise the logs for each version history, however, it was suggested that the scroll view will be complicated to visualise when the timeline becomes longer and longer as the project can go bigger than expected.

Moreover, the mobile application allows users to capture design activities, decisions and ideas in real-time. They are captured in five different input data types which are images, text, videos, documents and voice recordings as shown in Fig. 3, screen 7 and 8. The bottom toolbar is bundled with four specific icons for five different data creation tools. The interface was generally intuitive enough to use and no issues have been raised. Important feedback from the participants is that a linking element such as hashtag or '@' can be added to the bottom toolbar to link to another item or logs. It could help to discover and organise relevant information quickly.

Lastly, the backend firebase is checked with the data input by users to confirm the concurrency of data storage. This also thus enables real-time access of the data input through different devices.

Fig. 4. Firebase console

Figure 4 shows the real-time updated cloud database from Google Firebase. Also, participants suggested a few implementations can be added to the mobile application, this including search function which could provide instant keywords search and filtering. In-app reminders are also mentioned to be useful when they need to maintain engagement with project progress.

Overall, the research has demonstrated the importance of using digital applications to assist engineers in storing and retrieving ideas, images, data, etc., remembering deadlines and tasks, evaluations on decisions made, providing alternative options for available for materials selections, suppliers, designs, etc. as well as the directions and progressions of their designs towards meeting all design requirements.

4 Conclusion

This paper discussed the potential of digitalization of logbooks as a supportive tool to engineers in their design process. The design and development of the e-logbook process is described across the paper and is successfully built which is then validated by the case study. The results are concluded that the e-logbook:

- Able to replace the traditional paper logbooks.
- Capable of capturing design activities, decisions and ideas real-time.
- Able to manage the data in real-time.
- Able to check design activities, decisions and ideas history.
- Provide interactive design decisions timeline.
- Loads faster and requires fewer resources than other logbooks.
- The display is clear, easy to use and can be carried out in less time than a complex website.

However, the system does come with a few weaknesses and future improvement is needed. The weaknesses of the system and proposition of future improvement include:

- When the usage of the backend database reaches a limitation, it requires a better backend system to manage the database record as it will become complicated and huge.
- Better graphical illustration is needed for the history timeline when the list goes too long.
- Add collaborative functionalities to the app to enable real-time feedback between different users.
- Add search function.
- Reminder function on different events such as project deadlines.
- Finally, the e-logbook would require longer and more rigorous trials with practicing engineers to ensure all the bugs of the application is detected and rectified.

References

1. Electronic Lab Notebook (ELN) Market Size By Product (Cross Disciplinary, Specific), By License (Proprietary, Open), By Application (Chemical Industry, CROs, Environmental Testing Labs), By Geographic Scope And Forecast. 2021 [cited 2021 2 December]; Available from:. Research, V.M. Global (2021)
2. Oleksik, G., Jetter, H.-C., Gerken, J., Milic-Frayling, N., Jones, R.: Towards an information architecture for flexible reuse of digital media. In: Proceedings of the 12th International Conference on Mobile and Ubiquitous Multimedia, pp. 1–10 Article 12. Association for Computing Machinery, Luleå, Sweden (2013)
3. Akhtar, R., Neo, E.Y.L., McDonald, J., Teo, S.S.S.: A paediatric logbook: millstone or milestone? J. Paediatr. Child Health **56**, 1500–1503 (2020)
4. Oehlberg, L., Lau, K., Agogino, A.: Tangible interactions in a digital age: medium and graphic visualization in design journals. AI EDAM **23**, 237–249 (2009)
5. McAlpine, H., Hicks, B.J., Huet, G., Culley, S.J.: An investigation into the use and content of the engineer's logbook. Des. Stud. **27**, 481–504 (2006)
6. Volt, J., et al.: Definition of the digital building logbook: report 1 of the study on the development of a European Union framework for buildings' digital logbook. Eur. Comm., Executive Agency for Small and Medium-sized Enterprises (EASME) Competitiveness of the enterprises and small and medium-sized enterprises (COSME), B-1049 Brussels (2020)
7. Joshua, J.V., Alao, O.D., Ogbudje, E., Ogundipe, O.K.: eLogbook: an android-based logbook system. IUP J. Comput. Sci. **13**, 47–56 (2019)
8. Foley, D., Charron, F., Plante, J.S.: Potential of the CogEx software platform to replace logbooks in capstone design projects. Adv. Eng. Educ. **6**, 1–25 (2018)
9. Butler, D.: A new leaf. Nature **436**, 20–21 (2005)
10. Pedgley, O.: Capturing and analysing own design activity. Des. Stud. **28**, 463–483 (2007)
11. Lawal, A., Chukwu Ogbu, R.: A comparative analysis of agile and waterfall software development methodologies. Bakolori J. Gen. Stud. **11**, 1–2 (2021)

A Virtual Reality Development Methodology: A Review

Mohd Amran Md Ali[1], Mohammad Nazir Ahmad[1(✉)], Wan Salwina Wan Ismail[2],
Nur Saadah Mohamad Aun[3], Mohd Akif Farhan Ahmad Basri[2],
Shima Dyana Mohd Fazree[3], and Nor Hidayati Zakaria[4]

[1] Institute of Visual Informatics, Universiti Kebangsaan Malaysia, 43600 Bangi, Selangor, Malaysia
mnazir@ukm.edu.my
[2] Department of Psychiatry, Faculty of Medicine, Universiti Kebangsaan Malaysia, Cheras, Kuala Lumpur, Malaysia
[3] Centre for Research in Psychology and Human Well-Being, Faculty of Social Sciences and Humanities, Universiti Kebangsaan Malaysia, Bangi, Selangor, Malaysia
[4] Azman Hashim International Business School, Universiti Teknologi Malaysia, Kuala Lumpur, Malaysia

Abstract. This paper presents several appropriate methodological approaches to the development of virtual reality (VR) in several fields to meet the needs of today's industry. It is based on the proposed several selected methodologies, including the important phases such as design, creation, implementation and evaluation of individual courses implemented in a VR environment. Many VR applications have been developed and recommended to the public. However, there is little research that specifically examines the role of a development methodology in the field of VR. The progress of VR development methodology is still slow; the proposed methodologies are mostly immature and used on an ad-hoc basis; and therefore, more issues need to be explored. This paper attempts to provide the latest updates in VR development methodology using a selected narrative review method on related articles between 2000 until 2023. Our study shows that VR development methodologies still need more improvement, and most methodologies are defined according to the development purpose and its context. There is no consensus among researchers about the similarities that should exist in VR development methodologies.

Keywords: Virtual Reality · Methodology Development · Research Design

1 Introduction

Following the rise of Virtual Reality (VR) in the past decade, there has been a surge of hype surrounding the use of in-depth technology in various fields such as health [1], education [2] and training [3]. In just a few years, the number articles discussing this topic have grown exponentially; some are even starting to suggest that VR is the best medium for learning. Nevertheless, the lack of rigorous empirical assessment, as well as

H. Badioze Zaman et al. (Eds.): IVIC 2023, LNCS 14322, pp. 26–39, 2024.
https://doi.org/10.1007/978-981-99-7339-2_3

conflicting preliminary evidence, suggests that we still know little about how we learn in VR, especially the method of developing such learning experiences VR.

VR is an everyday real-world simulation built using computer immersive 3D graphics and 360-degree video. Deep VR environments can benefit educators and therapists, by offering them the opportunity to access a protected, custom-made and repeatable learning environment [4]. In recent years (since 2016), there has been some exploration on this topic through literature reviews conducted on VR treatment in psychiatry. VR is also increasingly being used for informal learning, and for exploring individual passions and hobbies [5]. At the same time, we have also begun to witness the emergence of virtual learning tools in planned and institutionalized educational initiatives that encompass schools, universities, and organizational settings [5]. The field of health also acknowledges that VR technology can help in a large part of a treatment effectively [6].

The advent of Virtual Reality (VR) is not a new concept and has roots dating back to the 1950's. From Weinbaum's science fiction exploration of VR to Mattel's rudimentary Power Glove in the 1970's, the virtual world has been a topic on of interest for many years [4]. From 1990 to 2000, the emergence of the Sega VR headset although still infantile in terms of technical prowess, demonstrated the potential of what was to come. With 2016 looming, VR headsets are on a collision course with all other mediums in becoming the next medium of choice. By reviewing the literature regarding VR currently, an extrapolation is feasible in order to anticipate applications and implications with VR in Pedagogy.

Unfortunately, existing VR development methodologies are still lacking important characteristics or requirements. For example, Benferdia et al. [7] highlighted that major VR development methodologies do not pay much attention to having knowledge-based models explicitly, throughout the VR methodologies or development life cycle. Majority of the focus is given to recent methodologies, such as proposing the methodologies specifically applicable to 3D content development. The fact that 3D content methodologies are only a small part of the whole set of VR development methodologies, makes it obvious that there are common or explicit domain knowledge involved or mentioned to support these activities.

A methodology has been suggested and applied to vascular Ehlers-Danlos syndrome (VEDS). A patient's quality of life (QOL) is greatly decreased by VEDS, a rare genetically caused disease that causes premature death and other medical problems. This methodology is the result of many years of experience building virtual environments [6]. The number of activities identified here is higher than the previous methods, due to the details that this methodology uses in describing the process. Specification of requirements, the separation between general and detailed design, and the suggested proactive tools for the designer are all given emphasis. Therefore, this research paper aims to examine the methods used in developing VR modules by incorporating appropriate phases to complete the method process. This will help certain parties improve the process of study and their findings. VR modules designed from a combination of existing methods will be able to produce better methods.

2   Several Virtual Reality Development Methodologies (VRDM)

The systematic literature review was the methodology used to perform the review conducted in this study. In the first stage, on related articles between 2000 until 2022 were identified from 11 different databases. The following databases were used to search keywords in the 'search terms' section: Science Direct; Business Source Premier; Inspec; Springer Link; AIS (Association for Information System) Electronic library; Scopus; ProQuest Science Journals; Google Scholar; ISI Web of Science; ACM Digital library; IEEE Explore. Assessing and analyzing the various virtual reality development methodologies (VRDM), this work formulates and uses research methods, which are seen as most suitable for the purpose of this research as described in the following ten research papers.

2.1   Model – Driven Architecture (MDA)

The video game and entertainment industry has been growing in recent years, particularly in areas related to VR. Therefore, in order to increase customer pleasure, video game developers are looking for ways to provide and improve realism in their products. In this work, [7] present a model to improve the user experience in a personal way through reinforcement learning (RL).

The model design is based on the Model-Driven Architecture (MDA) approach and consists of three main phases: analysis phase, design phase, and implementation phase. In order to demonstrate the transitions between undesirable and desired satisfaction states while considering a personal approach, a simulation experiment is presented. The proposed model is composed of the following phases: The Computation-Independent Model (CIM) established as an analysis phase; in this phase the system and user tasks, as well as the context tools are defined. The Platform-Independent Model (PIM) is described as a design phase.

2.2   360° Immersive Video Applications

Applications for Head Mounted Displays (HMD) [8] that deliver 360-degree immersive video have a lot of potential for creating compelling types of experiential media solutions, particularly for teaching about cultural heritage. However, because to the 2D resources employed for their production, the absence of depth, the limited interaction, and the requirement to address the sense of presence, design issues arise with this new type of immersive media. Additionally, using VR headsets frequently has the side effect of making users feel queasy or motion sick, which has further concerned for work involving moderate motion.

The problem and technique classification used in this paper's methodical introduction to the design of 360° immersive video apps. In accordance with the design strategy described, a testbed application that functions as an immersive interactive virtual tour of Rethymno's historical district in the Greek island of Crete has been developed and put through user testing. A set of design principles for the execution of 360° immersive video virtual tours is suggested based on the analysis of the study's findings.

2.3 Virtual Reality Clinical Trials

Therapeutic VR has become a successful treatment option for a variety of medical issues. It is necessary to get agreement on the optimal method for creating and analyzing VR treatments within a scientific framework, notwithstanding the promising results of early-stage research [9]. This study's goal was to create a methodological framework with input from a global working group to direct the planning, execution, analysis, interpretation, and reporting of trials that create and test VR treatments. Based on their contributions to the literature on virtual reality, a group of 21 foreign specialists was chosen. Iterative meetings were held by the resultant Virtual Reality Clinical Outcomes Research Experts to try and reach agreement on the best procedures for creating and evaluating VR medicines.

Due to the transcription of the interactions and the identification of significant themes, a scientific framework supporting best practices in methodology of clinical VR studies was created. A framework for three rounds of VR clinical trial designs VR1, VR2, and VR3 emerged using the Food and Drug Administration Phase I–III pharmacotherapy model as guidance. Through the use of human-centered design concepts, VR1 studies concentrate on developing content in collaboration with patients and healthcare professionals [10]. Early testing is done in VR2 studies, and it focuses on initial clinical efficacy, acceptability, and feasibility. VR3 trials are randomized, carefully monitored investigations that assess effectiveness in comparison to a control condition.

2.4 Knowledge Oriented Medical Virtual Reality (KOMVR)

A significant issue is the lack of effective medical and biomedical engineering education. Traditional techniques are time-consuming and expensive. Because of this, virtual reality is frequently employed for this purpose. Virtual reality for education in medicine is a well-established IT industry with a wide range of hardware and software options. The preparation of current solutions lacks a methodical approach. Because there is no standardization, each VR system used for medical applications is distinct, which increases development time and expenses [11].

In this research, a novel methodology for creating immersive virtual reality (VR) apps for medical skill training is presented. The approach is known as "knowledge-oriented medical virtual reality" (KOMVR), as it makes use of fundamental knowledge-engineering tools for developing and evaluating interactive educational solutions [12]. The methodology's steps and the tools used to carry them out are demonstrated in the paper. An easy example using a human body atlas serves as an illustration of the effectiveness of the suggested methodology. Using the methodology, significant time savings can be made; in the presented scenario, the time savings were 50 to just 14 working days. The novel strategy suggested can improve the efficiency of developing instructional VR solutions in the fields of medicine and other professions.

2.5   Knowledge Engineering Methodologies

The author provides a novel method for developing knowledge-based VR apps for corporate purposes. Virtual reality is being used more frequently in engineering applications. The majority of solutions, particularly in maintenance, are, nonetheless, inflexible and immediate. In typical VR application development, all product or process knowledge is hard-coded, making it impossible to access the data from outside the programming environment. Additionally, the process is prolonged and less effective when new solutions are developed without employing any technique at all.

In order to increase the efficiency of creating VR applications and assure their flexibility and access to stored knowledge even after an application is launched, the author suggests using general rules of existing knowledge engineering approaches. Practical case studies are used to support the methodology that is being taught. The creators of the MOKA divided the work of building a KBE system into six distinct stages [13]:

- Identification – determination of purpose and range of building of the KBE system;
- Justification – approximation of resources, costs and business risk;
- Acquisition – gathering the knowledge from selected sources;
- Formalization – formal recording of the gathered knowledge;
- Application – implementation of knowledge in computer software;
- Implementation – launching of the KBE system.

2.6   Designing Virtual Reality Applications – Development IDEs

In this study, a brand-new methodology for building virtual reality environments is proposed, using game development IDEs as a base. The approach is built on prior expertise with both traditional and virtual reality programming as well as on a combination of other approaches. The technique was developed in preparation for the creation of a virtual therapeutic serious game and proven on other projects. The description of the virtual environment scenario, the list of required objects, their states, and actions to modify these states are the method's outputs, which result in the formation of a state machine and asset lists [14].

In this paper, the researchers gathered all this expertise and proposed a new methodology after several sessions of brainstorming and revision with their colleagues who had been involved in previous virtual reality projects and studied the methodology mentioned in the sources mentioned above. After using the initial project, the author made certain adjustments, which significantly improved this process.

2.7   Virtual Reality Simulation (VRS)

An interprofessional team is needed to create virtual reality simulations, but there aren't many formalized mechanisms for exchanging information, which makes it difficult to communicate effectively. There aren't many tools available for developing virtual reality storyboards, according to an assessment of the literature. The goal of this work is to give a general overview of the storyboard method created by an interprofessional research team looking at Neonatal Intensive Care evacuation. The researchers created procedures and templates for storyboarding using the Jeffries model and Standards of Best Practices in Simulation as a framework. The results gave way to the creation of simulations based on best practices.

The interprofessional team was able to create a virtual simulation that is reflective of best practices and the Neonatal Intensive Care evacuation scenario thanks to the storyboard structure, which contains objectives, scenes, actions, difficulties, redirection, and opportunity to debrief. Objectives, scenes, actions, difficulties, and redirection were the content categories of the storyboard format, which was presented in a table format (formative feedback and facilitation). In the storyboard's first column were the learning objectives. All simulation content had to be driven by the identified learning objectives while the VR evacuation scenario was being developed [15]. The storyboard format gave the connections between the content in these particular regions structure and support. The researchers were able to create a virtual simulation that is representative of simulation best practices thanks to the storyboard structure, which incorporates objectives, scenes, actions, difficulties, redirection, and opportunity to debrief.

2.8   Design – Based Research (DBR)

This research emphasizes the necessity for a research model that takes the social environment into account as part of its unit of analysis instead of only the individual's cognitive process and learning due to the peculiarities of educational virtual worlds. Because the methodology used by the DBR perspective fully addresses the challenges related to understanding how learning occurs within a complex context of activities and interactions, like those that typically take place inside an educational virtual environment, the author of this paper proposed that such a research approach could be design-based research (DBR) [16].

The DBR uses an iterative methodology—repeating cycles of design, implementation, analysis, and redesign—to achieve this. Using DBR, a researcher can not only learn how to improve the quality of a specific virtual environment, but also address questions about the theoretical framework on which the design was built, modify it, and extend it. This methodical procedure allows theory to arise during the process. The major goals of this article are to outline the research process in detail and to advocate the adoption of design-based research as an effective approach for doing research in a virtual environment like Second Life.

2.9   TRES-D Methodology

Only experts and technicians with the requisite skills and expertise should create VR applications because the process might be exceedingly difficult. However, there is a growing need for tools that enable non-technical people to produce or contribute to the production of these apps. One argument for this is that using these technologies will allow domain experts to communicate with VR professionals more efficiently and reduce the number of development cycles. As a result of the media's contribution to virtual reality's appeal, there is also a need for tools that let average people create their own virtual worlds. We may compare this to the WIMP user [17].

This paper introduces the TRES-D technique for building VR applications and high-lights prospects for building tools that are user-friendly to non-VR experts. This way of creating virtual worlds is based on earlier approaches, both on observed practice and suggested methods, as well as on methodologies and techniques from the fields of software engineering and human-computer interaction. In-depth research is also done on pertinent prior work. The goal of the TRES-D (Three-dimensional user interface Development) methodology is to combine the best elements of those earlier methods into an incremental, iterative development process that can be adjusted to the varying complexity of various developments [18]. A set of activities, for which we wish to specify the roles involved, a set of tools to carry out the tasks in varied degrees of detail, and rules and directives to help developers complete the jobs make up the methodology's core.

2.10   Virtual Reality Interface Design (VRID)

VR interfaces contain a larger range and more complicated forms of objects, behaviors, interactions, and communications when compared to traditional interfaces. In order to a) think broadly about the overall design of the VR interface, b) break the design task down into smaller, conceptually distinct, and easier tasks, and c) explain the structure of the design to software developers, designers of VR interfaces must overcome significant conceptual and methodological challenges. [19] Suggests a Virtual Reality Interface Design (VRID) Model and an associated VRID methodology to assist designers in overcoming these difficulties.

Researcher highlight object images, object behaviors, object interactions and object communications as the major constructs that designers should consider when creating VR interfaces, building on our analysis and synthesis of the prior work on the subject. As a result, Table 1's multi-component object design serves as the foundation for how we structure the VRID model. To conceptually define and address the distinctive features of VR interfaces, components such as graphics, behaviors, interaction, and communication are included. In order to organize communications amongst the other four components of an object, the mediator component is included. These five elements are the main building blocks of our design model.

Table 1. A List of VR Development Methodologies.

VRMet	Research Problem	Model Use
Model- Driven Architecture (MDA) Reyes et al., (2021)	This proposed model has the purpose of producing virtual environments where the user's personal adjustment of parameters can be considered by means of a reinforcement learning technique, so that these environments can be adapted to the consumer's preferences	Reinforcement Learning (RL) Model-Driven Architecture (MDA)
360° Immersive Video Applications Argyriou et al., (2020)	Design challenges emerge through this new kind of immersive media due to the 2D form of resources used for their construction, the lack of depth, the limited interaction, and the need to address the sense of presence	-
Virtual Reality Clinical Trials Birckhead et al., (2019)	Therapeutic virtual reality (VR) has emerged as an efficacious treatment modality for a wide range of health conditions. However, despite encouraging outcomes from early-stage research, a consensus for the best way to develop and evaluate VR treatments within a scientific framework is needed	Food and Drug Administration Phase I-III pharmacotherapy model
Knowledge Oriented Medical Virtual Reality (KOMVR) Górski, F., et al. (2017)	Effective medical and biomedical engineering education is an important problem	MOKA (Methodology and tools Oriented to Knowledge-based engineering Applications)
Knowledge Engineering Methodologies Górski (2017)	-	CommonKADS (Common Knowledge Acquisition and Documentation Structuring)
Designing Virtual Reality Applications Polcar et al., (2016)	This paper suggests a new virtual reality environment creation methodology using game development IDEs as a platform	-
Virtual reality simulation (VRS) Farra et al., (2016)	Development of virtual reality simulations requires an interprofessional team, but effective communication is inhibited by a lack of structured methods for sharing information	Standards of Best Practices in Simulation and Jeffries model

(continued)

Table 1. (*continued*)

VRMet	Research Problem	Model Use
Design-Based Research (DBR) Santos (2010)	Concerns about the low impact of educational research on educational practice	-
TRES-D Methodology Molina et al., (2005)	-	OVID (Object View Interaction Design), based on the object model-view paradigm
Virtual Reality Interface Design (VRID) Tanriverdi et al., (2001)	Designers of VR interfaces face significant conceptual and methodological challenges in: a) thinking comprehensively about the overall design of the VR interface; b) decomposing the design task into smaller, conceptually distinct, and easier tasks; and c)communicating the structure of the design to software developers	-

3 Discussion

In just a few years, the number articles discussing the topic of virtual reality have grown exponentially, where some are even starting to suggest that VR is the best medium for learning [20]. Expressing the uniqueness of VR and recognizing its capabilities to change traditional ways of representation and interaction, this paper highlights the importance centered on the unique capabilities of this new medium in its design. In this study, it was found that not VR alone, but the way it has been designed and combined with several other aspects such as process phases, reference models, and language modeling, that will ultimately determine the success of VR in education and other domains.

3.1 No Consensus on Standard of VRDM

Based on this paper, there is a phase of developing VR that is often used by past researchers. It is a sequence of six different stages – introduction, justification, acquisition, formalization, application, and implementation [21]. In the rapid and advanced development in the field of medicine, the application of VR methodology still has a gap. For example, no standard VR development methodology is used in the development of current VR applications for the orthopedic domain [13–15]. This situation occurs because there is no gold standard VR application development methodology from the ICT domain. Such VR methodologies are very limited to specific applications as well as ad-hoc methodologies.

3.2   Importance of Knowledge on Domain or Reality to Support VR Development

There are still open questions and ongoing research to reach a common ground on what should be shaped in any VR development methodology. Additionally, a large gap exists between domain specialists and IT experts that want to replicate, due to a lack of awareness of the domain's knowledge. For example, VR development is knowledge – intensive task and therefore, an understanding of the domain, thinking or thinking of content experts is very important to be made explicit, and the structure of their knowledge of something that requires virtualization or visualization is also important. However, the use of this methodology is incomplete in its processing layout to guide the development of VR, for example in a domain like ASD and particularly, HFASD [17].

3.3   The Importance of Virtual Reality Development Methodology

The proposal of a new methodology in this study emphasizes the importance with the aim of gathering the best from previous approaches on an iterative basis, and additional development processes that can be adapted to the developmental complexity of different variables [22]. The core components of this methodology are a list of activities for which we want to identify the roles involved, tools for doing tasks at different levels of detail, and guidelines and instructions for developers. According to the analysis that was conducted in the last section, the researchers saw that there are several important key points in developing a methodology for VR.

3.3.1   Inconsistencies in Past Research VR Methodologies Developed

No methodology is fully mature if we compare it with all the previous methodology lists. It can be seen that there are phases that are not used in the development of each of the methodologies. There are certain strategies that are completely different from others [23]. This may imply that having multiple widely used approaches rather than one standardized methodology is most desirable. However, integration between methodologies for collaborative work and other methodologies would be very interesting.

3.3.2   Key Components in Developing VR Methodology

There are key components that are considered crucial for designing a methodology for VR. The methodologies proposed define the objectives for a solution and design their second activity respectively. These two activities are considered to be similar activities, as the aim of both is to define what is going to be done as a result of the research – defining the specific research problem and justifying the value of a solution [20]. Since the problem definition will be used to develop an effective art factual solution, it may be useful to atomize the problem conceptually so that the solution can capture the problem's complexity.

3.3.3   Criteria for Analysis Virtual Reality Methodologies

Details of the criteria for analyzing and comparing virtual reality methodologies are defined below. The first six aspects of the criteria are type of model used, phases of methodology, type of application domain, and approaches for conceptual model support, tools, and modeling language used. They do not discuss specific and technical details. They help the reader quickly understand the technical point of view of a methodology.

Criteria 1: Model Use: The literature reveals that VR methodological development can refer to several original models divided into three major categories namely, stage -based models, evolving prototype models, and guidelines, depending on the type of development model that needs to be followed. Different approaches have their respective pros and cons. Level -based methodologies may be appropriate for scenarios where the purpose and needs are clear [26]. On the other hand, an evolving prototype may be the best option when the needs are initially unclear and require improvement over time.

Criteria 2: Phases of Methodology: To develop a systematic VR model of methodology in VR interface design, this document contains a summary of the stages that have been employed in VR methodology. The process of developing a VR interface is conceptualised as an iterative one in which the specifications for an interface are transformed into design principles that software developers may put into practise. As the design is divided, the technique moves into a tiered design phase [24].

This design phase's objective is to conceptually use multi component object architecture while defining design solutions at a high level of abstraction. During the high-level design phase, VR interface input is employed, according to the functional description. Graph model, internal and external behaviors, interactions and communications, and the characteristics of the interface object are identified and defined on a high degree of abstraction.

Criteria 3: Application Domain: Virtual reality (VR) is seen as a framework that holds promise for the development of unique applications in a variety of fields, including business, entertainment, science, and healthcare [1, 17]. Despite the potential advantages of VR applications, we have yet to see their widespread development and use. One of the reasons why VR applications haven't gained much traction is because they can be challenging to develop [2].

Virtual reality application interfaces are more complicated and challenging to develop, especially when compared to interfaces of traditional desktop-based programmes. The visual, behavioural, and interactional characteristics of virtual reality interfaces are distinctive.

Criteria 4: Conceptual Model Support: Virtual reality (VR) is one of the newest technological applications in a number of significant fields, including education, tourism, and health. Virtual reality-based training (VRT), which enables complicated visualisation processes for diagnosis, treatment, illness analysis, and prevention [25], is a crucial component of VR applications in this field.

The amount to which domain information is shared and taken into account when developing VRT applications, however, is not well understood. Ontologies, a related mechanism, have aided in the improvement of domain knowledge clarity. The use of ontologies in the creation of VRTs for medical education and training in the healthcare domain is not explicitly stated anywhere, hence this study fills in the clear overview gap to explain fundamental concepts.

Criteria 5: Tools: There are a variety of virtual reality creation tools available on the market, therefore there are possibilities. The virtual reality development environments Blender, Quest3D, UDK, and Unity3D are described and compared in references [1]. In terms of licencing, usability, and compatibility with VR hardware such different HMDs, haptic interaction devices, etc., we discovered that Unity3D would be the ideal option. Reference [15] supports the usage of Unity3D for web-based depiction of college campuses for educational technologies. The tools for developing the methodology described in this article are more focused on creating an asset for the environment than its logic and development.

Criteria 6: Modeling Language: The international standard for virtual reality, the virtual reality modelling language (VRML), has expanded quickly. By incorporating Java programmes and scripts written in the java scripting language, VRML increases the capabilities of script nodes. A programming language called VRML was also developed for creating 3-D and Web-based models, textures, and illusions.

4 Conclusion

In this paper, we can conclude that there are important things that can be researched in developing the methodology, namely the use of models as a reference, the phases in developing the methodology, the appropriate application domain, equipment, whether hardware or software, and its use.

A combination of previous research methodologies has been introduced with the aim of gathering the best of previous approaches iteratively, and an additional development process that can be adapted to the complexity of the development of different variables. Until now there is no clear process or model that aims to guide researchers in producing a complete and orderly process in the development of methodologies for virtual reality.

VR development usually has two issues: (i) they do not describe the activities involved in the virtual environment (VE) in a more comprehensive and systematic educational way, and (ii) they are usually not reusable because they are only designed for a specific domain. Therefore, further research can be done in obtaining a complete process in developing a VR methodology that is appropriate to the application domain.

Acknowledgment. This research is supported by Transdisciplinary Research Grant Scheme (TRGS), Ministry of Higher Education (MOHE) and Universiti Kebangsaan Malaysia (UKM), Vot. No: TRGS/1/2020/UKM/02/6/2.

References

1. Didehbani, N., Allen, T., Kandalaft, M., Krawczyk, D., Chapman, S.: Virtual Reality social cognition training for children with high functioning autism. Comput. Hum. Behav. **6**(2), 703–711 (2016)
2. Mishkind, M.C., Norr, A.M., Katz, A.C.: Review of virtual reality treatment in psychiatry: evidence versus current diffusion and use. Curr. Psychiatry Rep. **19**, 80 (2017)

3. Liu, X.Y., Wu, Q., Zhao, W.B., Luo, X.: Technology-facilitated diagnosis and treatment of individuals with autism spectrum disorder: an engineering perspective. Appl. Sci. **7**, 1051 (2017)

4. Forbes, P.A.G., Hamilton, A.F.D.C.: Moving higher and higher: imitators' movements are sensitive to observed trajectories regardless of action rationality. Exp. Brain Res. **235**(9), 2741–2753 (2016). https://doi.org/10.1007/s00221017-5006-4

5. Gal, A., Agam, N., Alchanatis, V., Cohen, Y., Zipori, I., Presnov, E., et al.: Evaluating water stress in irrigated olives: correlation of soil water status, tree water status, and thermal imagery. Irrig. Sci. **27**, 367–376 (2019). https://doi.org/10.1007/s00271-009-0150-7

6. Bellani, M., Fornasari, L., Chittaro, L., Brambilla, P.: Virtual reality in autism: state of the art. Epidemiol. Psychiatr. Sci. **20**(3), 235–238 (2016)

7. Benferdia, Y., Ahmad, M.N., Mustapha, M., Md Ali, A.: The role of ontologies through the lifecycle of virtual reality based training (VRT) development process. Int. J. Adv. Comput. Sci. Appl. **12**(9), 122–131 (2021)

8. Cardona-Reyes, H., Munõz-Arteaga, J., Mitre-Ortiz, A., Villalba-Condori, K.O.: Model-driven approach of virtual interactive environments for enhanced user experience. Appl. Sci. **11**, 2804 (2021). https://doi.org/10.3390/app11062804

9. Mesa-Gresa, P., Gil-Gómez, H., Lozano-Quilis, J.-A., Gil-Gómez, J.-A.: Effectiveness of virtual reality for children and adolescents with autism spectrum disorder: an evidence-based systematic review. Sensors **18**, 24–36 (2018). https://doi.org/10.3390/s18082486

10. Den Brok, W.L.J.E., Sterkenburg, P.S.: Self-controlled technologies to support skill attainment in persons with an autism spectrum disorder and/or an intellectual disability: a systematic literature review. Assist. Technol. **10**, 1–10 (2015)

11. Parsons, S.: Authenticity in Virtual Reality for assessment and intervention in autism: a conceptual review. Educ. Res. Rev. **19**, 138–157 (2016)

12. Grossard, C., Palestra, G., Xavier, J., Chetouani, M., Grynszpan, O., David Cohen, D.: ICT and autism care: state of the art. Curr. Opin. Psychiatry **31**, 474–483 (2018)

13. Birckhead, K., Calnan, D., Simmons, N., MacKenzie, T.A., Kakoulides, G.: Effect of an immersive preoperative virtual reality experience on patient reported outcomes: a randomized controlled trial. Ann. Surg. **265**, 1068–1073 (2019)

14. Bekele, E., et al.: Multimodal adaptive social interaction in virtual environment (MASI-VR) for children with autism spectrum disorders (ASD). In: Virtual Reality (VR), pp. 121–130. IEEE, Piscataway, NJ, USA (2016)

15. Blyth, C.: Immersive technologies and language learning. Foreign Lang. Ann. **51**(1), 225–232 (2019). https://doi.org/10.1111/flan.12327

16. Brereton, O.P., Kitchenham, B.A., Turner Budgen, D., Khalil, M.: Lessons from applying the systematic literature review process within the software engineering domain. J. Syst. Softw. **80**(4), 571–583 (2007)

17. Botella, C., Fernández-Álvarez, J., Guillén, V., García-Palacios, A., Baños, R.: Recent progress in virtual reality exposure therapy for phobias: a systematic review. Curr. Psychiatry Rep. **19**(7), 1–13 (2017)

18. Bird, M.L., et al.: Randomized controlled trial investigating the efficacy of virtual reality in inpatient stroke rehabilitation. Arch. Phys. Med. Rehabil. **98**, 27 (2019)

19. Burke, S.L., Bresnahan, T., Li, T.: Using virtual interactive training agents (ViTA) with adults with autism and other developmental disabilities. J. Autism Dev. Disord. **48**, 905–912 (2019)

20. Burdea, G.C., Coiffet, P.: Virtual Reality Technology. John Wiley & Sons, Inc. (2003)

21. Caruana, N., MacArthur, G., Woolgar, A.: Detecting communicative intent in a computerised test of joint attention. Peer J. **5**, e2899 (2016)

22. Chan, C.L., Ngai, E.K., Leung, P.K., Wong, S.: Effect of the adapted virtual reality cognitive training program among Chinese older adults with chronic schizophrenia: a pilot study. Int. J. Geriatr. Psychiatry **25**, 643–649 (2017)

23. De Luca, R., Leonardi, S., Portaro, S.: Innovative use of virtual reality in autism spectrum disorder: a case study. Appl. Neuropsychol. Child **10**(1), 90–100 (2021). https://doi.org/10.1080/21622965.2019.1610964

24. Seth, A., Vance, J.M., Oliver, J.H.: Virtual reality for assembly methods prototyping: a review. Virtual Reality **1**(15), 5–20 (2011). https://doi.org/10.1007/s10055-009-0153-y

25. Stansfield, S., Shawver, D., Sobel, A., Prasad, M., Tapia, L.: Design and implementation of a virtual reality system and its application to training medical first responders. Presence, IEEE **9**(6), 524–556 (2000). https://doi.org/10.1162/105474600300040376

26. Kim, J., Kim, K.-S., Ka, J., Kim, W.: Teaching methodology for understanding virtual reality and application development in engineering major. Sustainability **15**, 27–35 (2023). https://doi.org/10.3390/su15032725

Deep Learning and Sentiment Analysis-Based Cryptocurrency Price Prediction

Jia Ming Low, Zi Jian Tan, Tiong Yew Tang[(⊠)], and Narishah Mohamed Salleh

Sunway Business School, Sunway University, 47500 Subang Jaya, Selangor, Malaysia
tiongyewt@sunway.edu.my

Abstract. The rapid growth of Cryptocurrency dramatically influences the social and economic climate that has developed the trends for investors to seek opportunities for generating income from cryptocurrency investment trading. Cryptocurrency is volatile in nature due to the interdependence of cryptocurrency, market noise and many dependent factors. This has gained the attention of investors to rely on prediction models to forecast prices. Researchers proposed and implemented prediction models that utilized machine learning, deep learning algorithms and sentiment-based algorithm hybrid models. Researchers deduced that deep learning algorithms can capture the dependency features of cryptocurrency to increase accuracy in price prediction. In this paper, we proposed a system framework namely, DLCFS (Deep Learning Cryptocurrency Forecasting considering Sentiment), for cryptocurrency price prediction that considers the market features, trading volume, and interdependency between cryptocurrency and market sentiments. We conduct price forecasting for Bitcoin, Ethereum and Litecoin using their price history, and Reddit Submissions of cryptocurrency. Additionally, we have inferred the results for the performance of prediction models comparing DLCFS against machine learning. Results show that DLCFS outperformed the regression machine learning in predicting the price of Bitcoin, Litecoin, and Ethereum, considering market sentiment, with Correlation Coefficient (R) being 99.18%, 96.82% and 99.05% respectively.

Keywords: Cryptocurrency · price prediction · VADER · TextBlob · Flair · deep learning · sentimental analysis · predictive analysis · LSTM

1 Introduction

Cryptocurrency is a digital currency that was designed to replace traditional currency and has been influencing the perceptions of communities in the generation nowadays. Cryptocurrencies differ from modern currencies as modern currencies are regulated in the sense of whether financial transaction is executed through the involvement of a third-party organization such as banks [1]. Cryptocurrencies operate on decentralized networks and leverage blockchain technology for security and tamper-resistant transactions. Bitcoin, being the first cryptocurrency introduced in 2009, used a proof of work algorithm (PoW) to ensure system integrity and consistency [2]. Nowadays, newer

H. Badioze Zaman et al. (Eds.): IVIC 2023, LNCS 14322, pp. 40–51, 2024.
https://doi.org/10.1007/978-981-99-7339-2_4

digital currencies, namely Ethereum, BNB, Cardano and much more, have adopted a variety of algorithms such as Proof-of-Stake (PoS) to reduce carbon footprints. The cryptocurrency was designed to replace the current centralized financial system with a more transparent, secure and distributed decentralized system. In the current market, 8685 cryptocurrencies are being developed and traded actively and the global market cap for cryptocurrency is at 1.023 trillion USD (until February 2023) [3, 4].

The main objectives of this study are addressed in the following points:

- To develop a system model that can predict prices and performances of cryptocurrency based on social and market sentiment.
- To compute the performance metrics in terms of prediction such as Root Means Squared Error (RMSE), Mean Absolute Error (MAE) and correlation coefficient (R) for the cryptocurrency.
- To compare implemented system model against state-of-the-art regression machine learning models.
- To analyze the forecasted price with the actual price that is capable of mitigating risk for investment firms.

2   Related Work

Cryptocurrency is currently a new and trending digital asset with popular currencies like Bitcoin thus the development of various predicting models has existed. Due to the high volatility nature associated with cryptocurrencies, prediction models have become increasingly challenging for investors to accurately forecast future investment decisions. The authors of [9] utilized the method of classical time series techniques namely the Autoregressive Integrated Moving Average (ARIMA) analysis model to predict time series data such as price prediction for Bitcoin and compared with classification algorithms such as Random Forest (RF), Logistic Regression, Linear Discrimination Analysis (LDA), and Empirical Conditional (EC). Addressing the importance of data size, those algorithms emphasized the need for an adequately substantial dataset to ensure the predictive model's effectiveness and precision. Additionally, due to the algorithms and techniques selected, it only predicted ternary values between (-1 to 1) for the price movement and did not provide an actual price prediction on the value of the cryptocurrency. [10] presented price prediction using a traditional machine learning model namely Reinforcement Learning (RL) prediction model for Litecoin and Monero which includes used features such as market volume, block-chain-based data mining and hash rate, transaction confirmation, and social sentiments from Twitter and Google trends. The prediction model resulted within the price prediction in 3-days, 7-days, and 30-days while achieving high accuracy and less error rate in performance error metrics.

Deep learning algorithms can offer advantages in capturing intricate patterns and features within the data, surpassing traditional regression machine learning algorithms, albeit with longer execution periods. In a comparative study [11], several prediction models, including regression machine learning algorithms such as Linear Regression (LR), Huber Regression, and Theil-Sen Regression, and deep learning algorithms such as Gated Recurrent Unit (GRU) and Long Short-Term Memory (LSTM), were evaluated. Huber Regression, Theil-Sen Regression, and the deep learning algorithms were outperformed by Linear Regression, which had the shortest execution time at 0.01167 s, according to the experimental findings. However, despite differences in execution time, all models obtained the same 0.99 accuracies when only market factors were considered as features. The study done by [12] compared the efficacy of deep learning models (LSTM and Recurrent Neural Network (RNN)) and the Autoregressive Integrated Moving Average (ARIMA) model for Bitcoin price forecasting. The deep learning models demonstrated superior accuracy and Root Mean Squared Error (RMSE), with LSTM obtaining the highest accuracy (52.78%) and RMSE (8%), despite the lengthy training process caused by optimization issues.

In contrast, a study [13] found that machine learning using the Support Vector Machine (SVM) classifier out-performed the Artificial Neural Network (ANN) and deep learning models, with a performance accuracy of 95.5% and a Mean Absolute Percentage Error (MAPE) of 0.31%. Researchers [14] implemented deep learning algorithms, such as GRU, LSTM, and bi-directional LSTM, to forecast the prices of Bitcoin, Ethereum, and Litecoin in pursuit of more accurate and efficient prediction systems. The research demonstrated the efficacy of deep learning algorithms, highlighting their efficiency and dependability. In addition, a hybrid prediction model employing GRU and LSTM outperformed the individual deep learning models with Mean Squared Error (MSE) values of 0.02103 for Litecoin and 0.00482 for Zcash with a three-day latency [15].

Notably, social sentiments, which refer to the collective emotional tone and opinions communicated across social media platforms and online communities, have a significant impact on the prices of cryptocurrencies. Intriguingly, [12, 14], and [15] have omitted the incorporation of these sentiments into their research, opening the door for future studies to investigate and give due weight to the significant factor of social sentiments. This gap in their analysis paves the way for future research to exhaustively investigate and clarify the profound influence that social sentiment factors can exert in the cryptocurrency domain.

The researchers of [16] analyzed the sentiments from social media such as Tweets and Google Trends positively correlated with the price of the cryptocurrency and they presented their system model designed with the stochastic neural network using Multilayer Perceptron (MLP) and LSTM on Bitcoin, Ethereum, and Litecoin. The author analyzed that the selected neural network models can effectively capture the non-linear dependency between market factors, block-chain data, and social sentiments. The author in [17] presented a sentiment-based hybrid model with a deep learning algorithm utilizing GRU and LSTM models for the Bitcoin cash and Dash. The sentiment-based hybrid model resulted in performance error metrics in terms of MSE, MAE, and MAPE with 0.0185, 0.0805 and 4.7928% respectively for dash and 0.0011, 0.0196, and 4.4089% for Bitcoin-cash. Nevertheless, none of the authors from [16, 17] performed future price forecasting despite their successfully implemented prediction model for the cryptocurrency.

3 Methodology

This section layouts out the architecture process of the predictive model considering cryptocurrencies and Reddit sentiments.

Figure 1. Displays the architecture process phases of the DLCFS system model. The DLCFS (Deep Learning Cryptocurrency Forecasting considering Sentiment) system

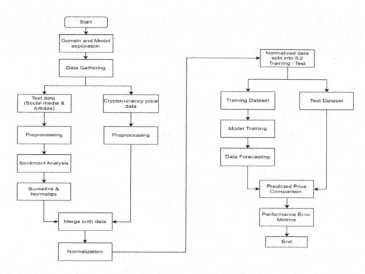

Fig. 1. Deep Learning Cryptocurrency Forecasting considering Sentiment (DLCFS): System Model.

model started with the domain and model exploration phase. During this phase, types of learning algorithms were taken into consideration to solve the supervised learning regression problem. The requirements for the system model are identified to fit the designation of the model to construct the prediction on the cryptocurrency price while considering sentiment aspects.

In the data gathering phase, the types of data required to utilize for the model were the cryptocurrency historic price data for Bitcoin, Ethereum and Litecoin, and the social media text related to cryptocurrency for sentiment analysis retrieved from Reddit. The Reddit submissions were used as social media data. The collected data were analyzed to ensure that the data fit the requirements, and it proceeded into the pre-processing phase to clean the data by removing unwanted data. The cleaned text data was further processed into the sentiments analysis utilizing the hybrid natural language processing (NLP) as referred to in Algorithm 2. Each Reddit submission consists of the score value as positive, neutral, and negative sentiments with their respective terms after processing with the proposed hybrid NLP models.

After Reddit text data was processed to the sentiments and polarity values, the values were passed into the bucketize and normalize phase as referred to in Algorithm 1. Bucketize process refers to categorizing the sentiment values and polarity scores according to the timestamp. The sentiment counts were increased based on the times bucketized. The sentiment values were normalized utilizing the median if there is no bucketized count else sentiment values were normalized using the mean. After that, the normalized sentiment values are merged with cryptocurrency price data. Following the normalization phase where the normalization was applied to the merged data using the min-max scaler and the normalized data was performed train-test splitting.

The training dataset was assigned as input to perform training for the supervised learning regression model and data forecasting. Then, the forecasted price and actual price are utilized to perform the price comparison and performance error metrics.

3.1 Data Description

The data for the price of Bitcoin, Ethereum and Litecoin were collected via the Binance API for research purposes, and it provided real-time data for the analysis of the cryptocurrency market. The data has the following features:

- Open: The opening price of each cryptocurrency.
- Close: The closing price of each cryptocurrency.
- High: The highest price of each cryptocurrency.
- Low: The lowest price of each cryptocurrency.
- Volume: The average trading volume of each cryptocurrency.
- Timestamp: The date and time in the hour of each cryptocurrency.

The social media data was obtained from Reddit submissions to analyze the sentiment, trends, and discussions of the cryptocurrency market. To collect relevant data, the pushshift API was utilized to extract Reddit submissions about cryptocurrency, given the importance of Reddit submissions in providing valuable insights into the cryptocurrency market [18].

The proposed model used Bitcoin, Litecoin, and Ethereum to train and predict the respective prices of these cryptocurrencies. The prediction of cryptocurrency prices was based on historical price data for these crypto-currencies, as well as market sentiment extracted from the Reddit dataset, which was an essential component of the model. The data collection period extended from January 1, 2020, to November 20, 2022, and included every hour of each day. The dataset contained a total of 5022 data points, which included Bitcoin, Ethereum, and Lite-coin price data in addition to Reddit sentiment data.

The selection of this data collection period was intended to capture long-term market trends and patterns and their correlation with Reddit discussions. The model could provide reliable insights into these long-term trends by incorporating a vast array of events that occurred during this period. Furthermore, this period encompassed significant events, such as controversies surrounding cryptocurrency investment trading platforms and the pre and post-COVID-19 pandemic's global economic impact. The purpose of this study was to examine, through a comprehensive analysis, the impact of these events on cryptocurrency prices and the associated Reddit discussions. This method enabled a greater comprehension of the interplay between market conditions, external factors, and investor sentiment in determining the price dynamics of cryptocurrencies.

The extended period of data collection provides a solid basis for analyzing the effects of both macroeconomic events and specific controversies on the cryptocurrency market. The proposed model provides a comprehensive analysis that enhances our comprehension of the relationship between cryptocurrency prices and Reddit discussions by incorporating these variables.

3.2 Pre-processing

The preprocessing of the cryptocurrency price data was undergone by replacing the null value with zero, removing the not a number (NaN), and duplicated values. Due to the significant differences in terms of price range among Bitcoin, Litecoin, Ethereum and sentiment values, the training time and performance of the forecast model can be affected. Therefore, to address this, a min-max scaler is applied to normalize the merged dataset with the range of 0 to 1 as a minimum to maximum respectively as shown in Eq. (1).

$$Xsc = \frac{X - Xmin}{Xmax - Xmin} \tag{1}$$

where X_max and X_min are the maximum and minimum values, 1 and 0, respectively.

The Reddit submission data were gathered directly from Reddit thus the data were performed pre-processing before the data can be processed into the sentimental analysis. The Reddit submissions included a variety of symbols such as ASCII characters, emojis, special symbols and Unicode which may hinder the analysis. Algorithm 1 shows the process of bucketize and normalizing sentiment values.

As the input with the sentiment values included positive, negative, and neutral and the timestamp of the publish time of the Reddit submission text. The sentiment values were bucketized according to the timestamp and the sentiment counts increased based on the times bucketized. The normalization process was applied after bucketized on the sentiment values using Eq. (2) if there is no bucketized count else sentiment values are normalized using Eq. (3).

$$\operatorname{med} x = (\frac{n + 1}{2})^{th}. \tag{2}$$

$$\bar{x} = \Sigma x / n. \tag{3}$$

where Eq. (2) refers to the median and n. is the number of values in the dataset and divide by 2 while Eq. (3) refers to the mean and Σx is the sum of the sentiment value and divided by n as the count of the bucketize.

3.3 Sentiment Analysis Model

Extraction of the polarity of positive, negative, and neutral sentiments was performeusing a mix and match of Valence Aware Dictionary and Sentiment Reasoner (VADER), Flair, and TextBlob [20, 21]. With this hybrid NLP model using VADER [22], Flair [23] and TextBlob [24], the collected Reddit submissions were then fed into the main algorithms and produced the larities for each submission. The outputs of sentimental scores were processed into bucketized and normalized and further con-catenated with the prices of the respective cryptocurrencies. Table 1 shows the type of algorithm of the model with their polarity term.

Table 1. Model and the algorithms

Model	Type of Algorithms	Polarity term return
VADER	Rule-based sentiment analyzer	Positive, Negative, Neutral, Com-pound
Flair	Pre-trained sentiment models	Polarity
TextBlob	Pattern analyzer	Polarity and Subjectivity

The sentiment of the VADER returns with the polarity term and values add up to a total maximum of 100% given with text input. The sentiment of the Flair return with the value of each polarity value lies between $(-1, 1)$ given the input on its polarity score where a polarity value of -1 indicates the negative statement, a polarity value of 1 indicates the positive statement and a polarity value of 0 indicates of the neutral statement. The TextBlob sentiment returns with properties of polarity and subjectivity where the polarity value lies between $(-1, 1)$ which the polarity value of -1 indicates the negative statement, a polarity value of 1 indicates the positive statement and a polarity value of 0 indicates of the neutral statement. Whilst the subjectivity lies within the range of $(0, 1)$ and refers to opinion, emotion, or judgement where 0 indicates the text being objective and 1 is subjective. Algorithm 2 shows the working process of the proposed sentiment models to convert the Reddit text to sentiment value.

The cleaned Reddit submission text data was fed as input into Algorithm 2 for each NLP model including VADER, Flair and TextBlob. Each NLP model can produce different types of output due to the different language processing algorithms that were trained on the models as discussed above. Then the output as sentiment scores and polarity scores for VADER, Flair and TextBlob were concatenated. The concatenated sentiment scores were processed to bucketized and normalized as referred to in Algorithm 1.

3.4 Proposed System Model

This subsection depicts the type of learning algorithms of the Deep Learning Cryptocurrency Forecasting considering Sentiment (DLCFS) system model utilizes to perform the prediction. LSTM is a deep learning algorithm model that is designed to learn long-term dependencies and is capable avoiding of long-term dependency problems while effectively capturing the non-linear dependency between the market factors, block-chain data, and social sentiments [16, 25]. LSTM was developed utilizing the Deep Learning-Keras library [26, 27].

Algorithm 1 Bucketize and Normalize Sentiment Values

Input: S_x: Sentiment values $\in$ {Positive, Negative, Neutral, Polarity, Subjectivity}

Input: T: Timestamp $\in$ {Publish time of Reddit submission}

Output: S $\in$ {Bucketized & normalized sentiment values according to timestamp}

```
1:    Sc ← Ø {Sentiment count}
2:        for each i in Sx then
4:            if i in range T then
5:                Sc ← Sc += 1
6:            if Sc = 0 then
7:                S ← median (Sx)  ▷ refer Eq.1
8:            else
9:                S ← Sx / Sc  ▷ refer Eq.2
10:       end for
11    end procedure
```

Algorithm 2 Reddit Text Conversion to Sentiment Values

Input: T $\in$ {Cleaned Reddit text data}

Output: S $\in$ {Sentiments score & polarity for VADER, Flair, TextBlob}

```
1:    procedure PROCESS_DATA(T)
2:        VP, VN, VNg, Vc ← Ø {Positive, Neutral, Negative,
                                 Compound}
3:        for each i ∈ T:
4:            SS ← VADER(i)   ▷ SS is temporary variable
5:            SS ∈ P, Ng, N, C {Positive, Negative, Neutral,
                                 Compound}
6:            Vp ← P;
7:            VNg ← Ng;
8:            Vn ← N;
9:            Vc ← C
10:       end for
11:       Fx ← Ø {Flair}
12:       for each i ∈ T:
13:           Fx ← Flair(i)
14:       end for
15:       TBp, TBs ← Ø {Polarity, Subjectivity}
16:       for each i ∈ T:
17:           SS ← TextBlob(i)   ▷ SS is temporary variable
18:           SS ∈ p, s {Polarity, Subjectivity}
19:           TBp ← p
20:           TBs ← s
21:       end for
22:       S ← Vp + VNg + Vn + Vc + Fx + TBp + TBs
23:   end procedure
```

The first layer of the LSTM model is the input layer, which is propagated to 64 units of LSTM neurons and followed by a dense layer with 64 units of neurons. As mentioned, the cryptocurrency price data type is a time series, and the regression is suitable for solving the predictive problem of time series. The output layer is using the linear activation function. To fine-tune the model, the numbers of the epoch for the model training were determined by utilizing the regularization approach of early stopping to solve the problem of overfitting and underfitting and achieve the best fitting for the model training.

Additionally, the LSTM model was compared with the state-of-the-art regression machine learning models as following Support Vector Regressor (SVR) [29], Bayesian Ridge (BR) [30], Theil-Sen Regressor [11], and Linear Regression [11]. The scikit-learn library was utilized to create the regression machine-learning model [31].

3.5 Performance Error Metrics

This subsection discusses the methods of performance evaluation for the proposed DLCFS system model compared with regression machine learning models. The performance error metrics such as RMSE, MAE and R were used to evaluate the prediction outcomes and price trends of the models.

3.6 Model Comparison

Table 2 presents the performance error metrics for the DLCFS system model as compared to the proposed regression machine learning models including with and without the sentiment elements. The values highlighted in bold are the best performance accuracy in terms of performance error metrics achieved as the comparison between the models.

The DLCFS system model designed with LSTM achieved a higher accuracy score in RMSE, MAE and R compared to the regression machine learning models regardless of whether sentiment analysis was included, for all three cryptocurrencies. For instance, the highest RMSE accuracy score obtained by the DLCFS system model was 0.005 for Litecoin with sentiment analysis, and the lowest accuracy score was 0.0174 for Ethereum with sentiment analysis. Nevertheless, the lowest accuracy score for DLCFS was still relatively higher than that of all regression machine learning models, indicating that DLCFS is a better fit overall. Similarly, when comparing the models using MAE, the highest accuracy score was 0.102 for Bitcoin with sentiment analysis, lowest accuracy score was 0.14 for Ethereum without sentiment analysis. It can be said that DLCFS consistently outperformed regression machine learning models. The same trend was observed when comparing the models based on the correlation coefficient, with the highest accuracy score of 99.37% for Ethereum without sentiment analysis, and the lowest accuracy score being 96.82% for Litecoin with sentiment analysis, which was still marginally better than regression machine learning models.

Table 2. The architecture of the LSTM model and hyperparameter

Bitcoin							
Model		RMSE		MAE		R (%)	
		Include Sentiments					
		Yes	No	Yes	No	Yes	No
DLCFS	**LSTM**	**0.0054**	**0.0200**	**0.1020**	**0.1350**	**99.18**	**98.85**
Regression	SVR	0.0483	0.0469	0.3457	0.1490	98.31	98.48
Machine	Bayesian Ridge	0.0730	0.0755	0.1697	0.1680	96.11	95.92
Learning	Theil-Sen Regressor	0.0784	0.0800	0.1497	0.1468	95.72	95.45
Model	Linear Regression	0.0761	0.0755	0.1700	0.1682	95.90	95.92

Litecoin							
Model		RMSE		MAE		R (%)	
		Include Sentiments					
		Yes	No	Yes	No	Yes	No
DLCFS	**LSTM**	**0.0050**	**0.0139**	**0.1740**	**0.2160**	**96.82**	**97.26**
Regression	SVR	0.0590	0.0620	0.4360	0.2590	94.08	93.94
Machine	Bayesian Ridge	0.0680	0.0689	0.5750	0.4530	91.96	91.85
Learning	Theil-Sen Regressor	0.0752	0.0718	0.0334	0.7521	90.43	91.21
Model	Linear Regression	0.0686	0.0689	0.850	0.4550	91.96	91.85

Ethereum							
Model		RMSE		MAE		R (%)	
		Include Sentiments					
		Yes	No	Yes	No	Yes	No
DLCFS	**LSTM**	**0.0174**	**0.0040**	**0.1490**	**0.140**	**99.05**	**99.37**
Regression	SVR	0.0955	0.0893	0.7650	0.298	93.62	94.71
Machine	Bayesian Ridge	0.1090	0.1135	0.4960	0.572	91.61	90.90
Learning	Theil-Sen Regressor	0.1106	0.1166	0.9740	1.260	91.57	90.66
Model	Linear Regression	0.1090	0.1135	0.4763	0.613	91.61	90.89

4   Conclusion

This paper explored and analyzed the existing system model for price prediction. Cryptocurrency prices will remain unpredictable and challenging due to their volatile nature. The reliance on sentiments, interdependency and trading factors is insufficient for making accurate predictions, particularly in the face of unforeseen events. However, leveraging the short-term prediction model can be made reliably using a deep learning algorithm that captures the non-linear dependency between the market factors. In this paper, we presented a framework, DLCFS for cryptocurrency price prediction that considered Bitcoin, Ethereum and Litecoin using their price history and Reddit Submission of cryptocurrency. We evaluated the performance of DLCFS using performance error metrics and compared the results with regression machine learning. The results show that DLCFS outperformed the regression machine learning in predicting the price of three cryptocurrencies considering market sentiment, with a RMSE of 0.0054, 0.005 and 0.0174 for

Bitcoin, Litecoin, and Ethereum, respectively. The MAE for DLCFS was 0.102, 0.174 and 0.149 for Bitcoin, Litecoin, and Ethereum, respectively. The Correlation Coefficient for the DLCFS was presented with 99.18%, 96.82% and 99.05% for Bitcoin, Litecoin, and Ethereum, respectively.

Acknowledgement. This work was supported in part by Sunway University and Sunway Business School under Kick Start Grant Scheme (KSGS) NO: GRTIN-KSGS-DBA[S]-02–2022. This work is also part of the Sustainable Business Research Cluster and Research Centre for Human-Machine Collaboration (HUMAC) at Sunway University.

References

1. Lotfi, M., Monteiro, C., Shafie-khah, M., Catalão, J.P.S.: Transition toward blockchain-based electricity trading markets. In: Blockchain-based Smart Grids, pp. 43–59 (2020)
2. Milutinović, M.: Cryptocurrency. Ekonomika **64**(1), 105–122 (2018)
3. Statista. Number of crypto coins 2013–2023. https://www.statista.com/statistics/863917/number-crypto-coins-tokens/
4. CoinMarketCap.:Global Cryptocurrency Market Charts. https://coinmarketcap.com/charts/
5. Brown, G.W.: Volatility, Sentiment, and Noise Traders. Financ. Anal. J. **55**(2), 82–90 (1999)
6. Sun, Y., Kong, X., Chen, T., Su, H., Zeng, X., Shen, Y.: Measuring investor sentiment of cryptocurrency market – using textual analytics on chain node. Procedia Comput. Sci. **187**, 542–548 (2021)
7. Hassan, M.K., Hudaefi, F.A., Caraka, R.E.: Mining netizen's opinion on cryptocurrency: sentiment analysis of Twitter data. Stud. Econ. Finance **39**(3), 365–385 (2022)
8. Zhang, X., Fuehres, H., Gloor, P.A.: Predicting stock market indicators through Twitter "I hope it is not as bad as I fear." Procedia – Soc. Behav. Sci. **26**, 55–62 (2011)
9. Amjad, M., Shah, D.: Trading bitcoin and online time series prediction. In: Neural Information Processing Systems, pp. 1–15 (2016)
10. Shahbazi, Z., Byun, Y.-C.: Improving the cryptocurrency price prediction performance based on reinforcement learning. IEEE Access **9**, 162651–162659 (2021)
11. Shankhdhar, A., Singh, A.K., Naugraiya, S., Saini, P.K.: Bitcoin price alert and prediction system using various models. IOP Conf. Ser.: Mater. Sci. Eng. **1131**(1), 012009 (2021)
12. McNally, S., Roche, J., Caton, S.: Predicting the price of bitcoin using machine learning. In: 2018 26th Euromicro International Conference on Parallel, Distributed and Network-based Processing (PDP), Cambridge (2018)
13. Hitam, N.A., Ismail, A.R.: Comparative performance of machine learning algorithms for cryptocurrency forecasting. Indonesian J. Electr. Eng. Comput. Sci. **11**(3), 1121 (2018)
14. Hamayel, M.J., Owda, A.Y.: A Novel Cryptocurrency Price Prediction Model Using GRU, LSTM and bi-LSTM Machine Learning Algorithms. AI, pp. 477–496 (2021)
15. Tanwar, S., Patel, N.P., Patel, S.N., Patel, J.R., Sharma, G., Davidson, I.E.: Deep learning-based cryptocurrency price prediction scheme with inter-dependent relations. IEEE Access **9**, 138633–138646 (2021)
16. Jay, P., Kalariya, V., Parmar, P., Tanwar, S., Kumar, N., Alazab, M.: Stochastic neural networks for cryptocurrency price prediction. IEEE Access **8**, 82804–82818 (2020)
17. Parekh, R., et al.: DL-GuesS: deep learning and sentiment analysis-based cryptocurrency price prediction. IEEE Access **10**, 35398–35409 (2022)
18. Wooley, S., Edmonds, A., Bagavathi, A., Krishnan, S.: Extracting cryptocurrency price movements from the reddit network sentiment. In: 2019 18th IEEE International Conference on Machine Learning and Applications (ICMLA). Boca Raton, FL, USA (2019)

19. Gemici, E., Polat, M.: Relationship between price and volume in the Bitcoin market. The J. Risk Finan. **20**(5), 435–444 (2019)
20. Maqbool, J., Aggarwal, P., Kaur, R., Mittal, A., Ganaie, I.A.: Stock prediction by integrating sentiment scores of financial news and MLP-regressor: a machine learning approach. Procedia Comput. Sci. **218**, 1067–1078 (2023)
21. Bonta, V., Kumaresh, N., Janardhan, N.: A comprehensive study on lexicon based approaches for sentiment analysis. Asian J. Comput. Sci. Technol. **8**(S2), 1–6 (2019)
22. Hutto, C., Gilbert, E.: VADER: a parsimonious rule-based model for sentiment analysis of social media text. ICWSM **8**(1), 216–225 (2014)
23. Akbik, A., Bergmann, T., Blythe, D., Rasul, K., Schweter, S., Vollgraf., R.: FLAIR: an easy-to-use framework for state-of-the-art NLP. In: Proceedings of the 2019 Conference of the North, Minneapolis, Minnesota, pp. 54–59 (2019)
24. Manguri, K.H., Ramadhan, R.N., Mohammed Amin, P.R.: Twitter sentiment analysis on worldwide COVID-19 out-breaks. Kurdistan J. Appl. Res. **5**, 54–65 (2020)
25. Hochreiter, S., Schmidhuber, J.: Long short-term memory. Neural Comput. **9**(8), 1735–1780 (1997)
26. Ketkar, N.: Introduction to Keras. In: Deep Learning with Python, pp. 97–111. Apress, Berkeley, CA (2017)
27. Team, K.: Keras documentation: LSTM layer. https://keras.io/api/layers/recurrent_layers/lstm/
28. Arshi, S., Zhang, L., Strachan, R.: Prediction using LSTM networks. In: 2019 International Joint Conference on Neural Networks (IJCNN). Budapest, Hungary (2019)
29. Ali Alahmari, S.: Predicting the price of cryptocurrency using support vector regression methods. J. Mech. Continua Math. Sci. **15**(4), 313–322 (2020)
30. Soni, K., Singh, S.: Bitcoin price prediction- an analysis of various regression methods. In: 2022 IEEE 12th Symposium on Computer Applications and Industrial Electronics (ISCAIE), pp. 271–276. Penang, Malaysia (2022)
31. Scikit-learn: 1.1. Linear Models. scikit-learn. https://scikit-learn.org/stable/modules/linear_model.html

A Comparative Study of Univariate and Multivariate Time Series Forecasting for CPO Prices Using Machine Learning Techniques

Juz Nur Fatiha Deena Mohd Fuad, Zaidah Ibrahim, Noor Latiffah Adam[✉],
and Norizan Mat Diah

School of Computing Sciences, College of Computing, Informatics and Mathematics, Universiti Teknologi MARA, Shah Alam, Malaysia
latiffah508@uitm.edu.my

Abstract. The Malaysian palm oil sector has significantly contributed to developing the domestic economy and the global palm oil market. However, the fluctuation in Crude Palm Oil (CPO) prices poses a significant risk to farmers, producers, traders, consumers, and others involved in CPO production and marketing. An accurate CPO price forecasting technique is required to aid decision-making in risky and unpredictable scenarios. Hence, this project aims to compare the performances of four-time series forecasting models, including Multilayer Perceptron (MLP), Convolutional Neural Network (CNN), Long Short-Term Memory (LSTM), and CNN-LSTM, in the context of univariate and multivariate analysis for CPO prices in Malaysia. This research methodology is based on five phases: research understanding, data understanding, data preparation, modeling, and evaluation. Monthly CPO prices, the production and export volume of CPO, selected vegetable oil prices, crude oil prices, and monthly exchange rate data from January 2009 to December 2022 were utilized. The metrics evaluation of Root Mean Square Error (RMSE) and Mean Absolute Percentage Error (MAPE) were then performed to compare and evaluate the performance of the models. Experimental analysis indicates that the CNN model trained on a multivariate dataset with carefully selected significant independent variables outperformed other models. With a configuration of 500 epochs and early stopping, it achieved remarkable results compared to models trained using a univariate approach, boasting an RMSE of 245.611 and a MAPE of 7.13.

Keywords: Convolutional Neural Network · Long Short-Term Memory · Multivariate · Multilayer Perceptron · Time series forecasting · Univariate

1 Introduction

Crude Palm Oil (CPO) is an important commodity in Malaysia, as the country is one of the world's largest producers and exporters of palm oil. Massive expansions in production and export capacities have made Malaysia the global leader in palm oil production

H. Badioze Zaman et al. (Eds.): IVIC 2023, LNCS 14322, pp. 52–62, 2024.
https://doi.org/10.1007/978-981-99-7339-2_5

and export. In addition, it is currently utilized in over 150 nations worldwide [1]. The palm oil industry significantly contributes to Malaysia's economy, employing hundreds of thousands of people and generating billions of dollars annually. This emphasizes the importance of this sector to the Malaysian economy. However, according to prior research, the price of palm oil fluctuates, and the instability of palm oil prices will indirectly affect various industries, including the country's earnings [1].

Previous studies only evaluated a few variables in their research without considering other crucial aspects that may significantly impact palm oil prices [2]. Some researchers suggested that information on the trends of total production and export of palm should be included in determining the palm oil price [3, 4]. Therefore, the relevant determinants, such as the total production and export of CPO, the Brent crude oil prices, and the exchange rate by month, were included to understand the Malaysian CPO price movement. In addition, the selected vegetable oils selected that are included in the forecasting CPO price are soybeans, sunflower, rapeseed, and coconut oil. Therefore, this study employs and compares multivariate approaches, wherein several new explanatory variables are included in CPO price forecasting, in contrast to most previous literature, which used a univariate approach.

Numerous models, including machine learning techniques, have been employed to forecast the future prices of oil [5] and CPO [6]. Some machine learning techniques used for forecasting CPO prices include Multilayer Perceptron (MLP) [6, 7], Convolutional Neural Network (CNN) [8], Long Short-Term Memory (LSTM) [9, 10], and CNN-LSTM [11–13]. Thus, this research aims to determine which of these four time-series models is the best for forecasting. To enhance the model's performance, a few hyperparameters are fine-tuned to find the optimal values that minimize the loss function.

2 Background Study

Crude Palm Oil (CPO) forecasting is handled mostly by economists; thus, most CPO price forecasting research employs statistical methods [6]. She also mentioned that some recent studies that employed artificial intelligence techniques in forecasting CPO prices have utilized univariate time series analysis for forecasting without considering the impact of other commodity prices. Understanding the CPO price behavior and its affecting factor is also crucial. Moreover, [24] mentioned that even though the fundamental analysis, technical analysis, and time series analyses were carried out for forecasting the movement of oil prices, the accuracy of such forecasting is still questionable. Thus, it is necessary to identify better methods to forecast crude palm oil prices as accurately as possible.

Time series forecasting has attracted a great deal of interest due to its extensive spectrum of applications in numerous fields, including finance, economics, meteorology, and marketing, among others. Time series forecasting enables us to make informed predictions and decisions for the future by analyzing past observations and identifying patterns [14–16]. Univariate analysis examines and describes individual variables, whereas multivariate analysis investigates the relationships and interactions between several variables [17]. Both approaches are helpful in data analysis because they allow researchers and analysts to acquire insights into various aspects of the data they are analyzing.

MLP models have been widely used in time series forecasting because they can capture nonlinear correlations and patterns in sequential data [7]. MLP models are suited for smaller datasets and easy forecasting jobs due to their simplicity and ease of implementation. However, high-dimensional, or complicated time series datasets may struggle to capture long-term dependencies and are prone to overfitting [6].

Convolutional Neural Networks (CNNs) have demonstrated potential in time series forecasting tasks by leveraging local dependencies and extracting relevant features from sequential data [8]. CNNs excel at capturing local dependencies and can handle large-scale datasets, making them robust to variations in data length or sampling rates. However, they may struggle to capture long-term dependencies or global patterns in longer sequences due to their fixed-size receptive fields.

Long Short-Term Memory (LSTM) networks, a type of recurrent neural network (RNN), have shown exceptional capability in modelling long-term dependencies and capturing temporal patterns, making them ideal for time series forecasting applications [10]. LSTMs are meant to capture long-term dependencies and perform well in various domains. They are, however, computationally expensive, particularly for large-scale or high-dimensional time series data and may suffer from disappearing or inflating gradient difficulties [11].

CNN-LSTM hybrid models, which combine the strengths of CNNs and LSTMs, have emerged as a viable strategy for time series forecasting. The CNN-LSTM architecture allows for the extraction of spatial and temporal characteristics, which leads to improved forecasting accuracy [11]. CNN-LSTM models can capture both spatial and temporal patterns, which improves forecasting accuracy. They are, nevertheless, more sophisticated, and computationally intensive, necessitating meticulous hyperparameter tuning and architecture design [9].

3 Methodology

The research method involves several phases, starting with the data description, exploratory data analysis, data pre-processing and predicting the model, and evaluating model performance.

3.1 Data Description

The historical dataset consists of data from January 2009 until December 2022 with 168 instances or rows and 11 variables. Table 1 shows the data description and its data type. The highlighted row is the selected variable that this research needs to forecast, which is CPO prices. All these variables are manually retrieved from websites such as Malaysia Palm Oil Council [18], Index Mundi [19] and investing.com [20].

Table 1. Data Description and its Data Type.

Variables	Data Description	Data Type
Date	By month	Date
Time	Time	Time
CPO	CPO monthly average price	Float
PCPO	The volume production of CPO	Integer
EXPO	The volume export of CPO	Integer
SBO	Soybean oil monthly average price	Float
RSO	Rapeseed oil monthly average price	Float
CCO	Coconut oil monthly average price	Float
SFO	Sunflower oil monthly average price	Float
BCO	Brent Crude oil monthly average price	Float
ExchangeRate	USD/MYR	Float

3.2 Exploratory Data Analysis

The Pearson correlation test is conducted to assess the significance of the correlation between the variables, utilizing a p-value for evaluation. This test involves the formulation of two hypotheses:

i. H0: There is no significant correlation between the independent variable and dependent variable.
ii. H1: There is a significant correlation between the independent variable and dependent variable.

Based on the provided hypothesis testing scenario, where the null hypothesis (H0) states that there is no significant correlation between the independent variable and the dependent variable, and the alternative hypothesis (H1) states that there is a significant correlation between the independent variable and the dependent variable, with a significance level of 0.001, the decision rule is to reject H0 if the computed p-value is less than 0.001.

Table 2 shows that EXPO has a statistically significant negative correlation, while SBO, RSO, CCO, SFO, and BCO have statistically significant positive correlations with the dependent variable. However, PCPO and ExchangeRate do not exhibit statistically significant correlations. Hence, the experiments were conducted using different datasets with varying numbers of variables. Table 3 shows the three datasets and their corresponding variables.

Based on Table 3, including the various variables in the multivariate datasets allows for a more comprehensive understanding of the factors influencing CPO, while the univariate dataset provides a focused analysis of CPO specifically.

Table 2. Correlation between Independent Variables and CPO.

Independent Variables	Pearson Correlation between Independent Variables and CPO	P-Value
PCPO	−0.220593	0.004062
EXPO	−0.290201	0.000136
SBO	0.904036	3.65E−63
RSO	0.923699	4.56E−71
CCO	0.699301	5.51E−26
SFO	0.905665	9.45E−64
BCO	0.547212	1.66E−14
ExchangeRate	0.224967	0.00337

Table 3. Constructive Datasets and its Corresponding Variables.

Datasets		Variables
Multivariate	A	Date, Time, CPO, EXPO, SBO, RSO, CCO, SFO, and BCO
	B	Date, Time, CPO, EXPO, SBO, RSO, CCO, SFO, and BCO, PCPO, ExchangeRate
Univariate	C	Date, Time, CPO

3.3 Data Pre-processing

Pre-processing plays a crucial role in preparing the data for further analysis and modelling, which includes data loading, duplicate and missing value checks, variable selection, data normalization, sequence preparation, and data splitting. Once the data is loaded, the next task is identifying duplicate rows or missing values. These checks are essential for data quality assurance and to ensure accurate analysis.

After selecting the input and output variables, we normalize the data using the *MinMaxScaler*. Normalization ensures that all the input and output variables are scaled within a consistent range, typically between 0 and 1. This step is necessary to prevent certain variables from dominating the analysis due to their larger magnitude.

Next, define the number of input-output time steps. In this case, the input has 48 time steps, representing the past 48 time steps of input data, while the output has 12 time steps, representing the next 12 time steps of output data to be predicted.

The next task involves preparing the input and output sequences by creating sliding windows of the specified lengths. This process involves iterating through the data and extracting the subsequence of the input and output variables based on the defined time steps.

Finally, as listed in Table 3, all three datasets are split into training and testing sets with a ratio of 80:20, implying that 80% of the cleaned dataset is used for training while the other 20% is used for testing.

4 Experimental Results and Analysis

This study aimed to determine the most effective time series machine learning algorithm for forecasting CPO prices among MLP, CNN, LSTM, and CNN-LSTM models, considering different three types of datasets as listed in Table 3, employing both univariate and multivariate approaches. These are the models that will be used for forecasting CPO (Crude Palm Oil) prices:

i. MLP: Hidden Layers: The MLP model includes a dense layer with 100 units and a ReLU activation function.
ii. CNN: The CNN model includes a 1D convolutional layer with 64 filters, a kernel size of 3, and ReLU activation;
    Max Pooling Layer: A max pooling layer with a pool size of 4 is added to reduce the spatial dimensions of the output from the convolutional layer.
iii. LSTM:The LSTM model includes an LSTM layer with 100 units and a ReLU activation function.
    Dropout regularization with a rate of 0.2 is applied after each LSTM layer to prevent overfitting.
iv. CNN-LSTM: Convolutional Layers: A 1D convolutional layer with 64 filters, a kernel size of 3, and ReLU activation is added;
    A max pooling layer with a pool size of 4 is added to reduce the spatial dimensions of the output from the convolutional layer;
    An LSTM layer with 100 units and ReLU activation;
    Dropout regularization with a rate of 0.2 is applied after the LSTM layer to prevent overfitting.

As for the compilation, epochs, batch size and validation split are the same for all models. The hyper-parameters for each model were tuned to identify the optimal configuration based on RMSE and MAPE of each model. The hyper-parameters that were fine-tuned for each model during training are as follows:

i. Epochs: The model is trained for [50, 500, 500 + Earlystopping].
ii. Batch Size: The training data is divided into batches of size 128 for each gradient update.
iii. Validation Split: 20% of the training data is used for validation during training

Early stopping is a technique where training is halted if the model's performance on a validation set does not improve after a certain number of epochs. It helps prevent overfitting [21] and saves the model's weights when the validation loss is minimized. Other than that, the number of epochs defines how often the model is exposed to the full dataset, and it is critical to achieving effective generalization while avoiding overfitting or underfitting [22].

Table 4. Summary of Results

Machine Learning	Dataset	Epochs: 50		Epochs: 500		Epochs: 500 + EarlyStopping	
		RMSE	MAPE (%)	RMSE	MAPE (%)	RMSE	MAPE (%)
MLP	A	344.394	9.62	290.167	8.11	320.105	8.62
	B	340.104	9.78	283.543	7.9	296.43	8.56
	C	601.979	18.28	554.700	16.19	547.861	16.2
CNN	A	450.418	12.84	309.492	8.29	245.611	7.13
	B	412.416	12.10	265.800	7.48	258.769	7.26
	C	727.970	21.19	417.866	12.26	414.55	12.41
LSTM	A	405.066	10.86	272.578	7.19	324.435	8.7
	B	423.959	12.54	273.864	7.32	463.733	13.17
	C	619.461	18.81	287.743	8.13	343.164	9.55
CNN-LSTM	A	609.033	18.94	294.484	8.56	489.686	12.17
	B	423.319	12.29	286.151	7.9	554.023	15.61
	C	813.112	23.62	305.278	7.86	345.952	9.35

The findings and results include the evaluation of three different epoch configurations: 50 epochs, 500 epochs, and 500 epochs with early stopping. Table 4 summarizes the overall results by comparing the selected evaluation metrics, RMSE and MAPE.

Based on Table 4, increasing epochs generally improved the forecasting performances for the MLP, CNN, LSTM, and CNN-LSTM models across different datasets. The MLP model showed improved results with decreased MAPE values for all datasets, ranging from an initial MAPE of 9.62% to 8.11% for Dataset A, 9.78% to 7.9% for Dataset B, and 18.28% to 16.19% for Dataset C. Utilizing early stopping further improved the performance.

Moreover, for the CNN model, increasing the epochs from 50 to 500 consistently improved the results in terms of RMSE and MAPE for all datasets. The best overall performance was achieved with the 500-epoch configuration and early stopping. Dataset A, the 50-epoch configuration had an RMSE of 450.418 and MAPE of 12.84%, while the 500-epoch configuration achieved an RMSE of 309.492 and 8.29%. The best performance was observed with the 500-epoch configuration and early stopping, resulting in an RMSE of 245.611 and MAPE of 7.13%.

Next, the LSTM model also demonstrated improvements with increased epochs for Datasets A and B. For Dataset A, the MAPE decreased from 10.86% to 7.19% with increasing epochs. However, the 500-epoch configuration with early stopping resulted in a slightly higher MAPE of 8.7%. For Dataset B, the MAPE decreased from 12.54% to 7.32% with increased epochs. Surprisingly, the 500-epoch configuration with early stopping resulted in higher errors, with a MAPE of 13.17%.

The CNN-LSTM model's performance varied across datasets. While Datasets A and B improved with increased epochs, Dataset C consistently exhibited higher errors. The best overall performance for the CNN-LSTM model was achieved with Dataset A using the 500-epoch configuration and early stopping. At the same time, Dataset C had the highest errors regardless of the configuration.

Figures 1, 2, 3 and 4 provide insights into the optimal hyper-parameter configurations for each machine learning model in achieving the best forecasting results.

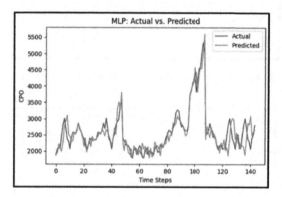

Fig. 1. MLP: Actual vs. Predicted (Dataset B with 500 epochs)

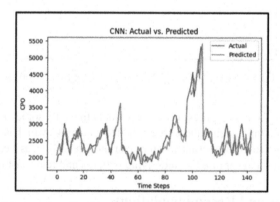

Fig. 2. CNN: Actual vs. Predicted (Dataset A with 500 epochs + EarlyStopping)

Comparing the results illustrated by Figs. 1, 2, 3 and 4, we can see that the CNN model, utilizing Dataset A and 500 epochs with early stopping, outperformed the LSTM, MLP, and CNN-LSTM models, achieving the lowest values of RMSE and MAPE.

Among the figures, the CNN-LSTM model, utilizing Dataset B and 500 epochs, exhibited the lowest performance, indicating its relative inefficiency in capturing the patterns and features in the time series data. Hence, Fig. 4 demonstrates lower accuracy, as the predicted line does not align closely with the actual values, further emphasizing the advantage of the CNN model with Dataset A and 500 epochs in achieving superior forecasting performance.

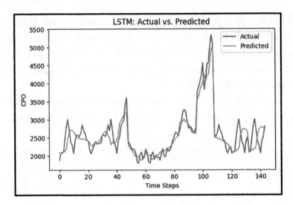

Fig. 3. LSTM: Actual vs. Predicted (Dataset A with 500 epochs)

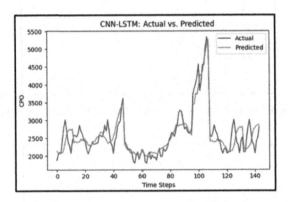

Fig. 4. CNN-LSTM: Actual vs. Predicted (Dataset B with 500 epochs)

Other than that, from the figures above, it is evident that only some of the best models for each machine learning technique were applied to Dataset C, which is univariate. This observation emphasizes the importance of multivariate forecasting, as it can provide more accurate predictions and capture the underlying patterns and relationships in the data.

5   Conclusions and Recommendations

The primary objective of this study is to conduct a comparative analysis between univariate and multivariate time series forecasting models. The findings indicate that datasets A and B, incorporating relevant independent variables, outperform dataset C regarding forecasting accuracy and overall model performance. This suggests that considering significant variables or a comprehensive set of predictors improves forecasting outcomes.

Based on the experimental results, the CNN model consistently outperformed the MLP, LSTM, and hybrid CNN-LSTM models regarding forecasting accuracy, demonstrating its superior capability in capturing relevant features and patterns from time series data. Besides, the CNN model on dataset A_multivariate, with a 500-epoch configuration and early stopping, stood out as the best-performing model, while the CNN-LSTM model on dataset C_univariate showed the poorest performance. Including early stopping and longer training epochs generally contributed to improved performance across the models and datasets. Increasing the number of epochs generally led to improved results, as observed in datasets A_multivariate and B_multivariate. However, careful monitoring is necessary to avoid overfitting, especially when using many epochs. Techniques such as early stopping can help prevent overfitting and optimize the model's generalization capabilities. Other than that, conducting robust sensitivity analyses by varying hyperparameters, such as learning rates or batch sizes, could provide insights into the stability and robustness of the models. Out-of-sample validation or cross-validation techniques could be included in extending the analysis to enhance the reliability of the results. The study emphasizes that multivariate forecasting generally performs better than univariate forecasting as it considers additional relevant variables that contribute to improved accuracy.

Furthermore, it is essential to acknowledge that the current analysis was based on monthly data. Consider incorporating daily data to enhance forecasting accuracy and capture more nuanced patterns. Daily data would provide a higher-resolution perspective on CPO price dynamics, allowing for a more detailed understanding of short-term trends, intra-day patterns, and potential market anomalies. By expanding the dataset to include daily observations, the models can capture additional insights and improve forecasting accuracy.

Moreover, it is suggested that future researchers conduct a comparative analysis with traditional time series forecasting methods, such as ARIMA or Exponential Smoothing, to evaluate the performance of machine learning models concerning these established techniques. According to [23], the most popular and widely used model to forecast CPO prices is the Autoregressive Integrated Moving Average (ARIMA) model. By including traditional methods in the analysis, researchers can establish a benchmark against which the performance of machine learning models can be evaluated. This comparative analysis can also help identify scenarios where one approach may be more suitable based on the characteristics of the data or the specific forecasting task.

Acknowledgment. The authors would like to thank the School of Computing Sciences, College of Computing, Informatics and Mathematics, Universiti Teknologi MARA, for sponsoring this research.

References

1. Rahim, N.F., Othman, M., Sokkalingam, R., Abdul Kadir, E.: Forecasting crude palm oil prices using fuzzy rule-based time series method. IEEE Access **6**, 32216–32224 (2018). https://doi.org/10.1109/ACCESS.2018.2846809
2. Khalid, N., Ahmad Hamidi, H.N., Thinagar, S., Marwan, N.F.: Crude palm oil price forecasting in Malaysia: an econometric approach. J. Ekonomi Malaysia **52**, 263–278 (2018). https://doi.org/10.17576/JEM-2018-5203-19
3. Nambiappan, B., Mohd Hassan, N.A.: Examining the long-term relationships between the prices of palm oil and soyabean oil, palm oil production and export: cointegration and causality. Oil Palm Ind. Econ. J. **16**, 31–37 (2016)

4. Zaidi, M.A.S., Abdul Karim, Z., Zaidon, N.A.: External and internal shocks and the movement of palm oil price: SVAR evidence from Malaysia. Economies **10**, 7 (2021). https://doi.org/10.3390/economies10010007
5. Abang Shakawi, A.M.H.: Crude palm oil price modelling: a comparison of time series model. Menemui Matematik **43**(1), 9–20 (2021)
6. Kanchymalay, K., Salim, N., Sukprasert, A., Krishnan, R., Hashim, U.R.: Multivariate time series forecasting of crude palm oil price using machine learning techniques. IOP Conf. Ser. Mater. Sci. Eng. **226**, 012117 (2017). https://doi.org/10.1088/1757-899X/226/1/012117
7. Amal, I., Tarno, Suparti: Crude palm oil price prediction using multilayer perceptron and long short-term memory. J. Math. Comput. Sci. **11**, 8034–8045 (2021). https://doi.org/10.28919/jmcs/6680
8. Torres, J.F., Hadjout, D., Sebaa, A., Martínez-Álvarez, F., Troncoso, A.: Deep learning for time series forecasting: a survey. Big Data **9**, 3–21 (2021). https://doi.org/10.1089/big.2020.0159
9. Zhang, K., Hong, M.: Forecasting crude oil price using LSTM neural networks. Data Sci. Financ. Econ. **2**, 163–180 (2022). https://doi.org/10.3934/DSFE.2022008
10. Thakur, D.: LSTM and its equations (2018). https://medium.com/@divyanshu132/lstm-and-its-equations-5ee9246d04af
11. Xue, N., Triguero, I., Figueredo, G.P., Landa-Silva, D.: Evolving deep CNN-LSTMs for inventory time series prediction. In: 2019 IEEE Congress on Evolutionary Computation (CEC), pp. 1517–1524. IEEE (2019). https://doi.org/10.1109/CEC.2019.8789957
12. Lu, W., Li, J., Li, Y., Sun, A., Wang, J.: A CNN-LSTM-based model to forecast stock prices. Complexity **2020**, 6622927 (2020). https://doi.org/10.1155/2020/6622927
13. Livieris, I.E., Pintelas, E., Pintelas, P.: A CNN–LSTM model for gold price time-series forecasting. Neural Comput. Appl. **32**, 17351–17360 (2020). https://doi.org/10.1007/s00521-020-04867-x
14. Lim, B., Zohren, S.: Time-series forecasting with deep learning: a survey. Phil. Trans. R. Soc. A **379**(2194), 20200209 (2021). https://doi.org/10.1098/rsta.2020.0209
15. Khamis, A.B., Hameed, R., Nor, M.E., Che Him, N., Mohd Salleh, R., Mohd Razali, S.N.: Comparative study on forecasting crude plam oil price using time series models. Sci. Res. J. (SCIRJ) **VI**(XII) (2018). http://dx.doi.org/10.31364/SCIRJ/v6.i12.2018.P1218588
16. Burba, D.: An overview of time series forecasting models. https://towardsdatascience.com/an-overview-of-time-series-forecasting-models-a2fa7a358fcb (2019)
17. Jin Wee Mah, P., Nanyan, N.N.: A comparative study between univariate and bivariate time series models for crude palm oil industry in peninsular Malaysia. Malaysian J. Comput. **5**(1), 374 (2020)
18. Malaysia Palm Oil Palm Council. https://mpoc.org.my/. Last accessed 5 Jul 2023
19. IndexMundi. https://www.indexmundi.com. Last accessed 5 Jul 2023
20. Investing.com: https://uk.investing.com/. Last accessed 5 Jul 2023
21. Caruana, R., Lawrence, S., Giles, C.L.: Overfitting in neural nets: backpropagation, conjugate gradient, and early stopping. In: Advances in Neural Information Processing Systems, NIPS, vol. 13, pp. 402–408 (2000)
22. Siami-Namini, S., Tavakoli, N., Siami Namin, A.: A comparison of ARIMA and LSTM in forecasting time series. In: 2018 17th IEEE International Conference on Machine Learning and Applications (ICMLA), pp. 1394–1401. IEEE (2018). https://doi.org/10.1109/ICMLA.2018.00227
23. Nathaniel, J.: Introduction to ARIMA for Time Series Forecasting. https://towardsdatascience.com/introduction-to-arima-for-time-series-forecasting-ee0bc285807a (2021)
24. Sivaprakash, J., Manu, K.S.: Forecasting crude oil price using artificial neural network model. Asian J. Manag. **12**(3), 321–326 (2021). https://doi.org/10.52711/2321-5763.2021.00049

Improving Autonomous Robot Gripper Position on Lifting Trash Objects based on Object Geometry Parameters and Centroid Modification

Emil Naf'an[1], Riza Sulaiman[1,2(✉)], and Nazlena Mohamad Ali[1]

[1] Institute of Visual Informatics, Universiti Kebangsaan Malaysia, 43600 Bangi, Malaysia
riza@ukm.edu.my
[2] Faculty of Computer Science, Universitas Putra Indonesia YPTK Padang, Padang 25221, Indonesia

Abstract. Waste management in the modern urban era requires a more advanced and efficient approach. Autonomous robots have emerged as an innovative solution to address this challenge. The robot's success in collecting trash cannot be separated from the ability of the robot's gripper to pick up the trash. This study aims to improve the positioning accuracy of the gripper robot in lifting trash objects. If the geometrical parameters of the objects are different, there is a possibility that the centroid points are in the 2D area so that the gripper robot cannot grip and lift the trash objects. Likewise, if there is a difference in weight, the robot gripper will have difficulty lifting the object because the object is one-sided. For this reason, removing trash objects needs to be improved by considering several parameters, not only the centroid parameter. A method for lifting trash objects is proposed based on several parameters: geometry, centroid and trash object type. The proposed method is Object Geometry Parameters and Centroid Modification (OGP-CM). The test results show that the OGP-CM method can set the centroid position based on the geometric parameters and the type of trash. On the same object geometry, the improvement in accuracy is relatively low, ranging from 0.46% to 1.72%. A relatively great improvement in accuracy occurs for different object geometries, ranging from 11.54% to 13.09%. Thus, improving the position of the autonomous robot gripper in lifting objects using OGP-CM has been successfully carried out.

Keywords: Robot · Gripper Position · Geometry Parameters · Centroid · Type of Trash

1 Introduction

A trash picking robot is a type of robot designed to assist in the process of collecting and transporting trash. These robots usually have navigation systems, sensors and manipulation devices to automatically identify, collect and transport trash [1]. Some examples of the use of trash-collecting robots include: 1. Street Cleaning: Trash-picking robots can

© The Author(s), under exclusive license to Springer Nature Singapore Pte Ltd. 2024
H. Badioze Zaman et al. (Eds.): IVIC 2023, LNCS 14322, pp. 63–75, 2024.
https://doi.org/10.1007/978-981-99-7339-2_6

be used to clean streets or public areas of trash. This robot can be configured to operate autonomously, recognizing and collecting trash scattered along the road. 2. Trash Collection in Public Places: Trash-picking robots can be used in public places such as parks, parking lots, or shopping centres to collect trash thrown away by visitors. This robot can move automatically and collect trash around it. 3. Trash Collector in Industrial Environments: In industrial or factory environments, trash collector robots can collect trash or trash in production areas. This robot can be equipped with sensors to identify certain trash or trash and move it to the appropriate disposal site. 4. Trash Collector in Offices or Households: Trash collector robots can also assist in daily trash collection in offices or households. Robots can be programmed to follow specific routes and collect trash from bins at every point [2].

Using trash-picking robots has several benefits, such as increasing efficiency and cleanliness, reducing the need for human labour in the trash collection, and reducing the potential risk or danger to workers [3]. In addition, they can also be equipped with an automatic grouping or recycling system to separate trash based on its type. In developing a trash-collecting robot, several factors that need to be considered are the reliability of the navigation system, the ability to identify different types of trash, safety in interacting with humans or the surrounding environment, and efficiency in collecting and transporting trash.

Along with the development of Artificial Intelligence (AI) technology, many researches on trash-collecting robots also use AI. Deep learning is a widely used field of AI, especially Convolutional Neural Networks (CNN). The following table summarizes some of the applications implemented over the past years regarding deep learning investigations (CNN) in trash management.

Table 1 shows that CNNs are commonly used in trash classification studies. This is due to the relatively high success rate of trash identification. However, some research combines CNN and sensors to verify this trash. In Table 1 some use ultrasonic sensors and range sensors in combination with CNN, but their use is only to detect the presence of objects in the designed system. Table 1 also has a prototype of a robot arm to collect trash. However, the robot does not yet have a LiDAR sensor that produces 2D and 3D shapes. So if the object is 2D, the robot gripper cannot hold the trash.

This research is focused on trash collection robots in the house compound. To collect trash, it is necessary to determine the accurate position of the gripper in lifting the trash object. Accurate gripper position affects the success of the object-lifting process [18]. In order for gripper placement to be achieved optimally, it is important to pay attention to the dimensions and characteristics of the object to be lifted, as well as consider factors such as weight distribution, gripper strength, and the capabilities of the robotic system used.

There are many techniques in determining the centroid, among others: methods of gravity, moment, thresholding, contour, and area-based segmentation [19]. However, if the object lifting process is based on the object's centroid only, at least three possibilities occur when the robot gripper tries to lift the trash object. This is illustrated in Figs. 1, 2 and 3. In Fig. 1, the trash object can be lifted properly. This is because the weight between the left and right sides of the object is relatively the same so that the gripper can lift the object perfectly.

Table 1. Deep Learning Application in Trash Management, 2005–2022.

No	Author	Contribution	Description
1	(Fuchikawa et al. 2005 [4])	Picking up trash using the Outdoor Service Robot	The robot only collects plastic trash in the form of PET bottles
2	(Salvini et al. 2011 [5])	Picking up trash using the *Dust Cart* robot	This robot collects types of trash based on user input. After the user enters the type of trash, the robot opens the trash store according to the type of trash input
3	(Yang & Thung. 2016 [6])	Trash classification using CNN	The type of trash that can be identified is only up to 6 items of trash
4	(Hulyalkar S., Deshpande R., Makode K. 2018 [7])	SmartBin used CNN	The type of trash that can be identified is only up to 4 items of trash, namely metal, glass, paper, and plastic
5	(Salimi et al. 2019 [8])	Trash classification using CNN on Trash Bin Robot	After the robot sees trash, it makes a sound and invites people to come, collect the trash found by the robot, and throw it into the trash can attached to the robot
6	(Adedeji & Wang. 2019 [9])	Trash classifica-tion using CNN	The type of trash that can be identified is only up to 6 items of trash
7	(Raza et al. 2021 [10])	Trash classifica-tion using CNN	Develop real-time trash detection using CCTV cameras. The type of trash that can be identified is only up to 8 items of trash
8	(Funch et al. 2021 [11])	Classification of metal and glass trash using CNN	Develop a prototype to classify the presence of glass and metal in consumer trash bags

(*continued*)

Table 1. (*continued*)

No	Author	Contribution	Description
9	(Longo et al. 2021 [12])	Trash classification using CNN on Smart Trash Bin	Developed a prototype of a smart trash can, able to classify trash with a hybrid sensor/image classification algorithm and automatically separate different trash materials
10	(Mao et al. 2021 [13])	Trash classifica-tion using CNN	The type of trash that can be identified is only up to 6 items of trash
11	(Ren et al. 2021 [14])	Beach trash classification using CNN	The type of trash that can be identified is only up to 6 items of trash, namely: plastic, glass, paper, butt, metal, and wood
12	(Yuan & Liu 2022 [15])	Trash classifica-tion using CNN	The type of trash that can be identified is only up to 6 items of trash, namely metal, paper, plastic, cardboard, glass, and trash
13	(Faisal et al. 2022 [16])	Detection of plastic trash using Faster R-CNN	Reduce plastic and bottle trash in the ocean with a case for Turtle conservation
14	(Kshirsagar et al. 2022 [3])	Trash classification using CNN and robotic techniques in trash material separation	Developing a prototype of a Robot Arm that can grasp reusable trash
15	(Rahman et al. 2022 [17])	Trash classifica-tion using CNN	Developed a TrashBin prototype for trash sorting. The type of trash that can be identified is only up to 6 items: cardboard, glass, metal, paper, plastic, and trash

In Fig. 2, the trash object cannot be gripped by the gripper because the centroid is in a 2D position. As a result, the main objective, removing the trash object, cannot be carried out.

In Fig. 3, the robotic gripper does not lift the object perfectly due to the object's weight not matching the centroid.

An example of an object being lifted is the screwdriver. In a screwdriver, if the centroid is made in the middle, then the weight between the two sides of the screwdriver is not the same. Because in the plastic package that holds the screwdriver, there is iron

Fig. 1. The robotic gripper is capable of lifting trash objects.

Fig. 2. The robotic gripper cannot grip or lift trash objects.

Fig. 3. Robotic grippers are not able to lift trash objects perfectly.

for other types of screwdrivers. As a result, when lifting the screwdriver, the gripper cannot lift it perfectly. The two sides of the screwdriver are not parallel. One side of the screwdriver is down.

For this reason, lifting trash objects needs to be improved by considering several parameters, not only the centroid parameter. In this study, it is proposed to add parameters to achieve this improvement. Those parameters are object geometry and trash type.

2   Material and Methods

This study begins with creating an autonomous robot to identify trash and navigate the house compound. This has been done in previous research. The trash identification process has been successfully carried out in previous studies. The trash identification process has been successfully carried out in previous research [20]. The method used is Sequential Camera LiDAR (SCL). In this method, identifying and classifying the types of trash uses the Convolutional Neural Network (CNN). This method also generates trash objects in 3D using the LiDAR sensor as a scanner. These two parameters become one of the references in lifting objects. Another parameter that is no less important is the determination of the centroid of the trash object. By obtaining the centroid of the trash object, the process of lifting the trash object is easier to do.

In this study, a method for lifting trash objects is proposed based on several parameters: geometry, centroid and types of trash object. The proposed method is called Object Geometry Parameters and Centroid Modification (OGP-CM) (Fig. 4).

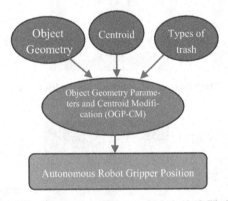

Fig. 4. Block Diagram of Proposed Method (OGP-CM).

The geometry of the object used is the 3D shape of the object. This shape is generated from detailed scanning by the LiDAR sensor on the Sequential Camera LiDAR (SCL) method [20]. Likewise, the type of trash also obtained from the output of the SCL method [20].

In Fig. 5 it can be seen the flowchart of the proposed method (OGP-CM). The flowchart shows that in the early stages, variables and constants were prepared to accommodate geometric object data and trash type data. Then, the Sequential Camera LiDAR (SCL) method is called. The result of the call is stored in the geometry object variable and the trash type. Next, the position of the gripper robot is checked until the position is the same as the Centroid Index (i) value. If they are the same, then the robot lifts the object using the gripper robot.

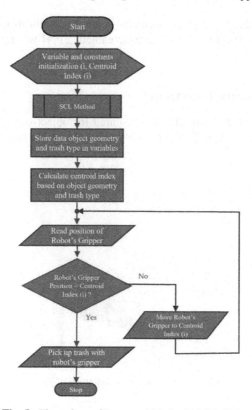

Fig. 5. Flow chart of Proposed Method (OGP-CM).

3   Results and Discussion

3.1   Result of Type Trash

In the previous study [20], a real-time identification test of 11 types of trash was carried out using four CNN architectures, namely AlexNet, VGG16, GoogleNet and ResNet18. The results of the trash identification are in Table 2.

Table 2. The Average Accuracy of 11 Types of Trash Using CNN Architectures.

No	CNN Architecture	Accuracy
1	AlexNet	79.410
2	VGG16	86.588
3	GoogleNet	96.513
4	ResNet18	95.146

Table 2 shows that the highest accuracy in trash identification was produced by GoogleNet, namely 96,513% and AlexNet, namely 79,410%, produced the lowest accuracy.

3.2 Result of Geometry Trash Object

Only the 3D shape of the trash object is required for object geometry. This has been done in previous studies [20]. Figure 6 shows the results of a detailed scan of one of the trash objects.

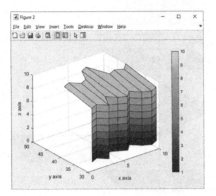

Fig. 6. Result of geometry trash object.

Figure 6 shows the 3D shape of the detected trash object. The more the amount of y-axis and z-axis data, the better the 3D shape of the trash object.

3.3 Result of Centroid

The results of centroid object can be seen in Fig. 7. The left side is the 3D shape of the object, while the right side is the result of calculating the centroid area of trash object.

In Fig. 7, it can be seen that the centroid is marked with a red dot. Determination of the centroid using MATLAB software.

3.4 Result of Object Geometry Parameters and Centroid Modification (OGP-CM)

The test results from the OGP-CM can be seen in Figs. 8, 9 and 10. In Fig. 8, the trash object used has relatively the same two parameters between the left and right sides of the centroid. These parameters include trash object geometry type of trash.

Figure 8 shows that the gripper is right at the centroid, and trash objects can be lifted by the gripper perfectly. In Fig. 9, it can be seen that the centroid is shifted to the side of the 3D object geometry. Calculation of the centroid based on the geometry of the 3D object.

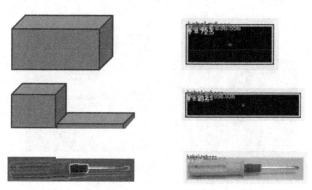

Fig. 7. Result of Centroid.

Fig. 8. Result of OGP-CM, trash object has the same parameters

Fig. 9. Result of OGP-CM, trash objects have different geometry parameters.

In Fig. 10, it can be seen that the centroid is shifted to the position of the screwdriver holder. The displacement of the centroid position is determined based on the type of trash object. This is because the whole trash object has geometry in 3D form.

Tests were carried out for 11 types of trash. Only 1 sample was taken from each trash. The accuracy value is taken from the position of the trash lifted by the robot gripper. If the position is flat, then the accuracy value is 100%. Every 1-degree change in tilt angle this is assessed as a 1 percent reduction in the accuracy value. The test is only carried out when the robot gripper grips the object until the gripper rises approximately 20 cm from

Fig. 10. Result of OGP-CM, trash objects have different types of trash parameters.

the robot's base. The robot gripper is given a delay of 10 s for accuracy measurement time. The accuracy of the gripper position is determined based on the gripper position error from the reference value. This error value is calculated as 1% per 2 mm error. The test results can be seen in Table 3.

Table 3. The Comparison of positioning accuracy of robotic grippers in lifting trash with conventional and OGP-CM methods (Same Geometry Parameters)

No	Type of Trash	Geometry Parameters	Gripper Position (%)		Object Position (%)	
			Conventional	OGP-CM	Conventional	OGP-CM
1	Cardboard	Same	98	99	94	97
2	Food Packaging	Same	96	98	96	95
3	Fabric	Same	98	98	97	97
4	Fruit	Same	95	97	93	95
5	Glass	Same	84	85	83	89
6	Leaf	Same	96	98	97	94
7	Metal	Same	94	96	93	94
8	Paper	Same	97	98	96	95
9	Plastic	Same	92	98	90	93
10	Rubber	Same	95	95	93	90
11	Wood	Same	96	98	96	94
Average			**94.64**	**96.36**	**93.45**	**93.91**

In the geometry parameters, there are the words 'Same' and 'Different'. The word 'Same' indicates that the geometry between the left and right sides of the centre of mass is the same. The word 'Different' indicates that the geometry between the left and right sides of the centre of mass is different. The OGP-CM method shifts the centroid value according to a predetermined value.

Table 4. The Comparison of positioning accuracy of robotic grippers in lifting trash with conventional and OGP-CM methods (Different Geometry Parameters)

No	Type of Trash	Geometry Parameters	Gripper Position (%)		Object Position (%)	
			Conventional	OGP-CM	Conventional	OGP-CM
1	Cardboard	Different	76	97	74	96
2	Food Packaging	Different	85	96	82	93
3	Fabric	Different	78	97	79	96
4	Fruit	Different	76	97	75	93
5	Glass	Different	76	83	78	86
6	Leaf	Different	85	95	87	93
7	Metal	Different	84	93	82	91
8	Paper	Different	84	97	82	93
9	Plastic	Different	82	97	81	92
10	Rubber	Different	90	95	85	88
11	Wood	Different	83	96	82	93
Average			**81.73**	**94.82**	**80.64**	**92.18**

In Table 3, the object geometry used is the same. The accuracy between conventional and OGP-CM is not much improved, only around 1.72% on the gripper position. While in the position of the object, 0.46%. This small increase in value is due to the same geometric object values. This value causes the position of the object's lifting centroid to be the same, which is right in the middle of the trash object.

In Table 4, the geometry of the objects used is different. There is a relatively large improvement in accuracy between conventional and OGP-CM, namely 13.09% in the gripper position. While in the position of the object, 11.54%. This relatively large increase is due to the different geometric object values between conventional and OGP-CM. Conventionally, the centroid position for lifting objects remains in the middle, even though the object's geometry values differ. For example, if there is a trash object whose centre of mass is not at the centre of the object, it will become one-sided on one side when the object is lifted. This is why the accuracy value of the conventional method is relatively low compared to the OGP-CM method. In the OGP-CM method, if the geometric object values are different, then the robot gripper position refers to the centroid index (i) value, as shown in the flowchart in Fig. 5. This value is obtained from collecting data based on the object's parameters. Those parameters are trash type, and object geometry. An example case can be seen in Fig. 10. If the gripper's position is based on the centre point (centroid) of the object, then the screwdriver becomes one-sided when lifted, as shown in Fig. 3. Now, because the geometry values of the screwdrivers are different, the centroid values (i) change, according to the parameters of that object. These changes result in a relatively perfect lifting of the object, where the screwdriver is flat when lifted and not lopsided.

4 Conclusions

Improving the position of the autonomous robot gripper in lifting objects has been successfully carried out using the Object Geometry Parameters and Centroid Modification (OGP-CM) method. The test results show that the OGP-CM method can set the centroid position based on the geometric parameters and the type of trash. On the same object geometry, the improvement in accuracy is relatively low, ranging from 0.46% to 1.72%. A relatively great improvement in accuracy occurs for different object geometries, ranging from 11.54% to 13.09%.

The improvement in accuracy can be even higher if the gripper used is not a standard gripper. In the next research, the gripper's ability must be improved to grip objects better. The gripper used should be adjusted to the object being lifted.

Acknowledgment. This research is fully supported by Research Grant number TAP=K007341 of Universiti Kebangsaan Malaysia (UKM).

References

1. Kulshreshtha, M., Chandra, S.S., Randhawa, P., Tsaramirsis, G., Khadidos, A., Khadidos, A.O.: OATCR: outdoor autonomous trash-collecting robot design using YOLOv4-tiny. Electronics **10**(18), 2292 (2021)
2. Fang, B., et al.: Artificial intelligence for waste management in smart cities: a review. Environ. Chem. Lett. **21**(4), 1959–1989 (2023)
3. Kshirsagar, P.R., et al.: Artificial intelligence-based robotic technique for reusable waste materials. Comput. Intell. Neurosci. **2022**, 1–9 (2022)
4. Fuchikawa, Y., et al.: Development of a Vision System for an Outdoor Service Robot to Collect Trash on Streets, pp. 100–105 (2005)
5. Salvini, P., Teti, G., Spadoni, E., Laschi, C., Mazzolai, B., Dario, P.: The Robot DustCart. IEEE Robot. Autom. Mag. **18**(1), 59–67 (2011)
6. Yang, M., Thung, G.: Classification of Trash for Recyclability Status. In: CS229Project Report, no. 1, p. 3 (2016)
7. Hulyalkar, S., Deshpande, R., Makode, K., Kajale, S.: Implementation of smartbin using convolutional neural networks. Int. Res. J. Eng. Technol. **5**(4), 3352–3358 (2018)
8. Salimi, I., Bayu Dewantara, B.S., Wibowo, I.K.: Visual-based trash detection and classification system for smart trash bin robot. In: International Electronics Symposium Knowledge Creative Intelligent Computing IES-KCIC 2018 – Proceedings, pp. 378–383 (2019)
9. Adedeji, O., Wang, Z.: Intelligent waste classification system using deep learning convolutional neural network. Procedia Manuf. **35**, 607–612 (2019)
10. Raza, S M., Hassan, S.M.G.. Hassan, S.A., Shin, S.Y.: Real-Time Trash Detection for Modern Societies using CCTV to Identifying Trash by utilizing Deep Convolutional Neural Network (2021)
11. Funch, O.I., Marhaug, R., Kohtala, S., Steinert, M.: Detecting glass and metal in consumer trash bags during waste collection using convolutional neural networks. Waste Manag. **119**, 30–38 (2021)

12. Longo, E., Sahin, F.A., Redondi, A.E.C., Bolzan, P., Bianchini, M., Maffei, S.: A 5G-enabled smart waste management system for university campus. Sensors **21**(24), 8278 (2021)

13. Mao, W.L., Chen, W.C., Wang, C.T., Lin, Y.H.: Recycling waste classification using optimized convolutional neural network. Resour. Conserv. Recycl. **164**(July 2020), 05132 (2021)

14. Ren, C., Jung, H., Lee, S., Jeong, D.: Coastal waste detection based on deep convolutional neural networks. Sensors **21**(21), 7269 (2021)

15. Yuan, Z., Liu, J.: A hybrid deep learning model for trash classification based on deep trasnsfer learning. J. Electr. Comput. Eng. **2022**, 1–9 (2022)

16. Faisal, M., et al.: Faster R-CNN algorithm for detection of plastic garbage in the ocean: a case for turtle preservation. Math. Probl. Eng. **2022**, 1–11 (2022)

17. Rahman, M.W., Islam, R., Hasan, A., Bithi, N.I., Hasan, M.M., Rahman, M.: Intelligent waste management system using deep learning with IoT. J. King Saud Univ. – Comput. Inf. Sci. **34**(5), 2072–2087 (2022)

18. Hernandez, J., et al.: Current designs of robotic arm grippers: a comprehensive systematic review. Robotics **12**(1), 5 (2023)

19. Ni, J., Chen, J., Wu, Y., Chen, Z., Liang, M.: Method to determine the centroid of non-homogeneous polygons based on suspension theory. ISPRS Int. J. Geo-Information **11**(4), 233 (2022)

20. Naf'an, E., Sulaiman, R., Ali, N.M.: Optimization of trash identification on the house compound using a convolutional neural network (CNN) and sensor system. Sensors **23**(3), 1499 (2023)

A Web Application to Recommend Songs Based on Human Facial Expressions and Emotions

Qhairun Nisa' Mohd Hanafi, Suziah Sulaiman[✉], and Saipunidzam Mahamad

Universiti Teknologi PETRONAS, 32610 Seri Iskandar, Perak, Malaysia
suziah@utp.edu.my

Abstract. Facial expressions are a common non-verbal way of how humans show and express their emotions to others. Emotions can be categorized as positive and negative emotions, derived from facial expressions, in which negative emotions can affect a person's behavior and thinking. Music is a common remedy for people to cope with both positive and negative emotions. The use of deep learning to identify emotions based on human expression can be an effective and efficient way to provide solutions for humans because it can mimic the way humans think while requiring less time and effort. By creating a solution that encompasses recommending songs from emotion detected using deep learning, it can benefit society health and entertainment-wise. This paper presents a project that focuses on developing such a solution and testing its performance and effectiveness to users, in improving their emotions via songs. The method used for this web application is OpenCV and DeepFace as face detector and emotion recognition system, respectively; while the song recommendations are pulled via Spotify API, where all these elements are deployed in a web application using Streamlit. DeepFace has been stated to have an accuracy of around 97% for its facial recognition functionality, along with their facial attribute analysis, which can be considered reliable enough to recognize emotions. For future work, other factors that can help to identify emotions are to be put more focus on, as it is envisaged to improve the emotion recognition system in this web application.

Keywords: Facial Emotion Recognition · Song Recommender · DeepFace

1 Introduction

Facial expression is one of the common ways of how humans show their emotions or feelings to other people. It is a type of nonverbal communication as it expresses countless types of emotions without saying a word. Facial expression is important in one's life to regulate interpersonal relationships and it also helps one to make decisions in their life. Emotions can be classified into two categories; positive and negative emotions, in which positive emotions bring pleasure or positive affects in situational responses [1]. On the other hand, negative emotions are feelings that humans usually do not find pleasurable to experience, where it leaves a negative effect towards an event or person such as stress or even cause them to lose self-love and focus in their everyday surroundings.

© The Author(s), under exclusive license to Springer Nature Singapore Pte Ltd. 2024
H. Badioze Zaman et al. (Eds.): IVIC 2023, LNCS 14322, pp. 76–86, 2024.
https://doi.org/10.1007/978-981-99-7339-2_7

Another important aspect of this project besides facial expression and emotion is music, where it is a known remedy to listeners to help calm their mood and control their emotions, especially negative emotions. Bono, a singer, and author of a book called On the Move, once said "Music can change the world because it can change people". Deep Learning (DL), a subset of Machine Learning (ML), is a computer neural network which imitates the behaviour of the human brain. As of today, ML and DL in the emotion recognition industry is widely being utilized by companies and developers globally and is actively being explored by researchers to expand their capabilities.

Referring to past research conducted on developing an emotion-based song recommendation system, it can be argued that a lot of them focused on implementing an emotion recognition system through building and training models from scratch, in which some of them only include a limited choice of emotions. The building process includes gathering appropriate datasets, coding the machine learning or deep learning algorithm, running the dataset, and conducting validation tests. All these activities mentioned are time-consuming as well as require a lot of knowledge and computing skills. Not to mention, it also takes a lot of computing power and space because it is basically creating a virtual intelligent agent capable of identifying what expressions belong to which emotions.

Realizing the problems mentioned, this project aims to create a web application for users to improve, cope or explore with their emotions by recommending songs based on their emotions, effectively and efficiently.

2 Literature Review

2.1 Facial Expression and Emotions

There are various types of emotions that can be deduced from the facial expressions being made by humans, all of which brings meaning in a conversation among each other as it helps to comprehend others' intentions [2]. According to a well-known American psychologist and professor, Dr Paul Ekman, he stated that there are six universal or basic emotions; anger, surprise, disgust, enjoyment, fear, and sadness, all of which are shared around the world. In other words, Dr Ekman stated that these six emotions share similar human facial expressions around the world. On the other hand, it was stated in Nature news article that researchers are split over the conclusion made by Dr Ekman, highlighting that facial expressions can vary widely in context and cultures, which responses to different emotions [3]. There is no denying that emotions shown do not always tally with what is being expressed by the human faces, which shows the naturality of human emotions and expressions. However, it is not to be discarded the facts and effort made by not only Dr Ekman on his research, but other researchers as of today as well, who are actively researching on this topic to improve the results being gathered.

2.2 Music and Emotions

Music is known as a remedy to help cope with emotions, especially negative emotions. This can further be supported by Raney et al., where their findings conclude that for many people, music is denoted as the number one media source for feeling moved, touched, and inspired [4]. This is possible because the brain stem reflex is activated by changes in basic acoustic events [5]. Elaborating more, Gabrielsson and Lindstrom, and Juslin et al. also state that any unexpected change of tempo, loudness, pitch, or timbre in music can fundamentally trigger an arousal response or give a pleasant effect to the listeners [6]. Relating to negative emotions, the choice of song to cope with negative emotions can differ based on preferences. Some people might prefer to choose upbeat songs to alter their sad emotions, and some might choose to listen to slow, melancholy songs to suit and cope with their sad feelings. To understand more about subjective experiences requires gathering responses or feedback from a various array of rich and diverse stimuli [7].

2.3 Facial Emotion Recognition Technology

The Facial Emotion Recognition (FER) is a type of technology that implements the concept of machine learning or deep learning that is used to analyze facial expressions from both static images and videos as sources of input, to produce useful information such as in this case, one's emotional state. It comprises of three important steps which are: 1) Facial detection, 2) Facial Expression Detection, 3) Expression classification to an emotional state [8]. When it comes to data accuracy, the FER analysis may not be accurate because facial expressions can vary for some individuals, or that the expressions shown might represent a different emotion instead.

Not only that, a person's skin color or ethnic origin can also affect the analysis where algorithms that implements the FER are found to biased for certain emotions just because the facial expression in one region are normally represented that way but interpreted wrongly. Telford in their news article mentioned that it is important to train systems with a lot more data, comprising of other factors that affect the display of emotion such as vocal characterization and body positioning [9].

One company called Affectiva, is heading towards the right path in which it has trained its software with over 7 million faces from 87 countries which gives around 90% result accuracy. However, definitely to work with millions of data, requires a top-notch computer system that can handle massive data, and for the sake of this web application project, the focus is more on the implementation of computer vision and deep learning as a subset of machine learning, to analyse the facial points in images, recognize the emotions from those inputs, which is less complex than using various and massive data.

As for emotion recognition system, DeepFace is focused on more for this topic, which is a lightweight face recognition system, created by a group of researchers at Facebook. This system can be mainly used to identify human faces in images. It also has additional functions that can be used to complement the function of identifying faces from images, such as facial attribute analysis. This feature enables the system to analyze and recognize human attributes such as age, gender, race, and emotions. This lightweight package makes it even easier for beginners to jump into deep learning and working on projects on facial recognition system because it only requires just a few lines of codes to implement its library and start analyzing images given, compared to coding, or setting up a whole Convolutional Neural Network (CNN) from scratch to then feed images into the model. DeepFace works based on deep convolutional neural networks

(DCNN) which uses a three-dimensional neural network to process the red, green, and blue elements of an image. In other words, a DCNN is basically a CNN but with deeper layers. The team that created DeepFace, trained on the largest dataset at that time with four million facial images of four thousand identities which goes through a nine-layer deep neural network [10]. Its facial recognition system achieves an accuracy of 97.35% on the Labeled Faces in the Wild (LFW). By having such high accuracy on detecting faces from images, it has made their facial attribute analysis, especially in this case (to identify emotions from facial expressions), perform much better.

2.4 Existing Systems

There are many existing systems available that could recommend songs based on humans' emotions. One particular example is DJRunning, a mobile application that uses Internet of Things (IoT) wearables to detect users' emotion and their current location or environment to recommend songs as they conduct physical activities [11]. Another example is Moodify, a web application to recommend music to users by considering user's current emotion state and the emotion that they want to be in, implementing reinforcement learning (RL) [12]. The one which is closer to what we are developing is Music Heals the Soul. This is a smart application developed by Vedanth et al. [13] for HackOn Hackathon 2021. The application is about emotion-based music recommendation system for happy and non-happy emotion state. Their work has influenced how we designed and developed our system for this project. We differ from theirs by including more emotions to be detected, and more playlists for each emotion. These features are to address the problem described in the earlier section.

3 Methodology

The objective of this project is to create a web application that can detect emotions from users' facial expressions, and then recommend songs based on it, as well as testing its performance in relation to the users' satisfaction and rating of the application. The processes in developing this web application can be divided into sections as follows:

3.1 Developing the Web Application Base

Since web application was chosen as the platform for this application, a base must be created where all the functions and features will lay. Streamlit is used as a 'web host' or a web framework base to power the web application in a local host environment. It is a Python open-source framework commonly used by developers to visualize machine learning projects. Sections are created in Streamlit to be able to break down and run through the process of the application easily, where the first section focuses on capturing the expressions. The images captured will be stored first for it to be called by then the next function to analyse the emotion from it. Then, the last section will be recommending users songs based on the emotions identified.

3.2   Face Detection and Emotion Recognition

A popular algorithm that is used by developers to detect faces from images is called the Haar Cascade algorithm, where its XML repository files can be accessed using OpenCV, an open-source Python library, to detect and return the faces that were able to be identified from images captured.

In the application, a user will press the Spacebar to capture their expression, and the image taken will be stored in a.jpg format, for it to be passed to the emotion recognition function, which is done via a well-known lightweight facial recognition and facial attribute analysis module, DeepFace. The module identifies up to seven emotions: happy, sad, neutral, anger, disgust, surprise and fear. As mentioned earlier, DeepFace has an accuracy of 97.35% in facial recognition, where it has trained around four million images pulled from Facebook. Figure 1 shows the actual user interface design of the expression capture and emotion recognition section in the web application.

Fig. 1. Actual user interface design for Expression Capture and Emotion Recognition Section

Dr Ekman's six basic emotions theory does not include neutral but for this web application, it includes neutral emotion because it is a very common and easy to express emotion shown by human at most times while disgust emotion is discarded to focus on only six emotions, as there are not many songs that can suit or improve disgust as an emotion, generally. DeepFace is beginner-friendly where in this case, only one line of code is needed to implement the function that will analyse the emotions from the image that is processed and stored by OpenCV. In DeepFace, it can show all the emotions that were identified and its confidence percentage, but for the sake of this application, the function was altered to only show the most dominant emotion to retrieve one particularly designed playlist.

3.3 Recommending Songs Based on Emotion Identified

Once DeepFace has analysed the emotion from the image, the application will communicate with Spotify via its own API. At the beginning of the development, a client ID must be obtained from Spotify's own Spotify for Developers website, where a developer must firstly be subscribed to Spotify Premium, in order to use their services.

Moving on, six playlists for six emotions stated earlier, were created from a Spotify account, where these playlists will be called out, when their respective emotion is identified. A randomizer function will output five random songs picked from the respective playlist, for users to choose to listen to, on the web application interface. For example, if a user's emotion is identified as 'Happy', then the system will retrieve five randomized songs from the Happy playlist created prior. A randomizer helps to prevent the same songs from playing every time user gets the same emotion identified. While randomizing five songs only instead of showing all the songs simply helps to make the web application look neater, and it also helps with the performance. To grasp a better understanding of how the application works, Fig. 2 and Fig. 3 illustrate the system architecture and flowchart diagram, respectively, to visualize the overall flow from user to the internal part of the web application and returning a playlist of songs back to the user.

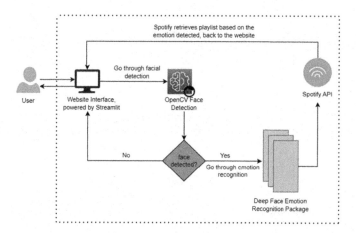

Fig. 2. System architecture diagram of the web application

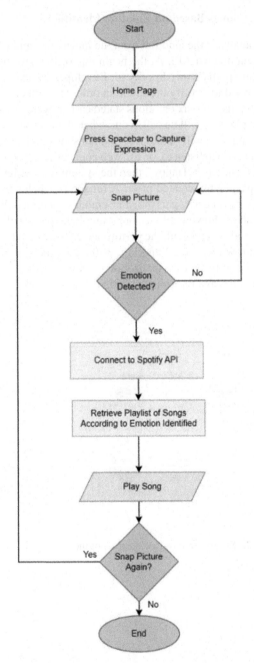

Fig. 3. Flowchart of the web application

4 Experiments and Results

4.1 Experiments

A group of 20 people from Universiti Teknologi PETRONAS (UTP) were invited to evaluate the web application's functionality and usability. The participants' perception was used to analyze the effectiveness of the application in order to improve the user's emotion when they interact with it. The participants involved were Undergraduate students and Master's degree Graduate Assistants. Each participant was given about five minutes to interact with the application.

After they have evaluated the web application, they were invited to answer a Google Forms survey of 16 questions on their usability feedback to give their ratings on the application. This user's usability feedback survey can be divided into a few sections, covering the user experience (UX) aspects in Likert scale structure. The sections are Perceived Ease to Use, Perceived Enjoyment, Perceived Usefulness and Overall Performance. Mental health related questions were also included in this survey to gain their feedback on the effectiveness of the application towards this particular topic.

Lastly, a reliability analysis was constructed using the results gathered from this survey, using Cronbach's Alpha. The purpose is to determine the reliability of the questions used as a measurement tool in this study. Cronbach's Alpha is a common method used to measure consistency or reliability of the scales in multiple Likert questions. The formula for Cronbach's Alpha is shown below. K represents the number of items in the survey for each section, S2y is the sum of the items' variance and S2x is the variance of total score.

$$\alpha = \frac{K}{K-1}\left[1 - \frac{\sum S^2 y}{S^2 x}\right]$$

4.2 Results and Analysis

Some of the questions in the feedback survey involve asking the respondents the emotions that they wish to express, and then asking them what emotion was identified by DeepFace. In this way, a general accuracy checking can be deducted from counting the number of times the two emotions asked tally each other and the times they did not. Figure 4 shows a bar chart on the results of the count of tally.

Referring to Fig. 4, there is a difference between the emotion the participants tried to express, versus the emotion that was identified by the application. On the 'tally' column, the emotion of that the users tried to express, and the one the web application identified does tally for 65% (13) of the respondents, while the remaining 35% (7) did not tally. Although this is a not a great indicator to examine the accuracy of DeepFace overall in this case, it can be a good way to show that DeepFace is able to identify emotions of a person based on the positively inclined results.

A possible reason why DeepFace is not always able to detect emotions could be from the lighting in the testing environment conducted, which can disrupt recognizing the facial points in an image. The sample size used for this testing session might also be too small, which does not give much justice to the count of tally as in Fig. 4. Not to

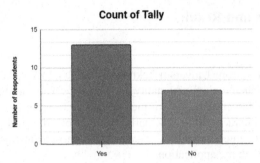

Fig. 4. Count of Tally on the emotion to be expressed and emotion identified by DeepFace

mention, this is a 'side' functionality to carry out facial attribute analysis, where it is much more successful in recognizing faces as it is its main functionality. The accuracy of 97% in the facial and emotion recognition industry is considered quite low, as models trained from scratch can obtain an accuracy of 99% and above. However, it cannot be denied that DeepFace performs well for a lightweight library package, which means in this case, it is reliable enough as an emotion recognition system, especially for beginners who would like to start off their first emotion recognition project application using this library package.

For the reliability analysis conducted from the results of the survey, Table 1 shows the results of the Cronbach's Alpha value for all 16 questions from the four sections in the questionnaire combined.

Table 1. Results of Reliability Test Using Cronbach's Alpha.

Variables	Description	Values	Level of Reliability
K	No. of items	16	Excellent
$\sum S^2y$	Sum of the Item Variance	6.69	
S^2x	Variance of Total Score	44.15	
a	Cronbach's Alpha	0.9	

Table 2 can be referred to as a rule of thumb to conclude whether the value given is acceptable or not in terms of reliability or internal consistency.

Based on the Cronbach Alpha value of 0.9 as presented in Table 1, and by referring to the information in Table 2, it can be interpreted that all 16 questions that were given in the questionnaire have excellent reliability in measuring latent variables – unobservable variables such as the respondent's openness and consciousness. Thus, this questionnaire is reliable enough to be distributed to people for larger testing purposes in the future.

It can be said that DeepFace does not always accurately identify emotions correctly, as from observations being made from testing, it often detects neutral emotion, for sad, fear, and surprise. Another point worth mentioning is that users might also have to put a lot of effort into expressing their expressions, since the emotion identification will make

Table 2. Cronbach's Alpha Value and Its Level of Reliability

Cronbach's Alpha Value	Level of Reliability
$a \geq 0.9$	Excellent
$0.9 > a \geq 0.8$	Good
$0.8 > a \geq 0.7$	Acceptable
$0.7 > a \geq 0.6$	Questionable
$0.6 > a \geq 0.5$	Poor
$0.5 > a$	Unacceptable

use of all the facial points it can get from faces. However, in terms of usefulness, based on the questionnaire, 45% for both strongly agree (5) and agree (4), respectively, were rated by the respondents, suggesting that the songs that were recommended to them based on their emotion did make them feel better, while 10% of the respondents feel that the songs did not make them feel better or worse as they rate a 3 out of 5. Furthermore, 90% of the respondents agree that this application can help people to improve their mental health. Consequently, this can be concluded that the web application developed has potential to become a solution to help users improve their emotions through listening to the songs that were recommended to them, despite having slight difficulties in emotion recognition accuracy.

5   Conclusion and Future Work

This web application was created to recommend songs based on emotions identified by users, as a way for them to improve or cope with their emotions, especially negative emotions. Negative emotions can bring negative effects to humans such as stress and losing focus in their surroundings. Using the methods elaborated in this paper, it can be deduced that emotions are able to be classified and identified using deep learning algorithm. DeepFace is able to identify emotions from expressions accurately, for most of the respondents that participated. On top of that, the usefulness aspect in user's experience also has a positive outcome where most of the respondents agree that listening to the songs recommended made them feel better emotionally, and that the application has potential to improve other people's mental health.

As for future work, more focus is to be put in considering other factors that can help identify emotions from human such as their heart rate, voice recognition, as well as improving the reliability of the recognition system by using other available algorithms. Besides that, song recommendation can also be improved by asking the respondents their preference of music genre prior to using the application. This is to ensure the recommended songs fit according to the respondents' emotions. The classifications of songs such as happy, sad, and neutral songs will also have to be decided earlier using another set of study that involves experts in the field. Lastly, since this web application was implemented on a local host, deploying the application for public use can also be part of the future work or goals, to help increase participation.

References

1. Sullivan, G.S.: Positive emotions. In: Servant Leadership in Sport. PSWSF, pp. 145–157. Springer, Cham (2019). https://doi.org/10.1007/978-3-030-11248-6_8
2. Ko, B.: A brief review of facial emotion recognition based on visual information. Sensors (Switzerland) 18(2), 401 (2018)
3. Heaven, D.: Why faces don't always tell the truth about feelings. Nature, 26 Feb 2020 [Online]. Available: https://www.nature.com/articles/d41586-020-00507-5?error=cookies_not_suppor ted&code=e898d3a1-f432-469d-8f7e-87a7666370e5 (2020)
4. Raney, A.A., Janicke, S.H., Oliver, M.B., Dale, K.R., Jones, R.P., Cox, D.: Profiling the audience for self-transcendent media: a national survey. Mass Commun. Soc. 21(3), 296–319 (2018). https://doi.org/10.1080/15205436.2017.1413195
5. Juslin, P.N., Liljeström, S., Västfjäll, D., Lundqvist, L.: How does music evoke emotions? Exploring the underlying mechanisms. In: Music and Emotion: Theory, Research and Applications (2010)
6. Gabrielsson, A., Lindstrom, E.: The role of structure in the musical expression of emotions. In: Juslin, P.N., Sloboda, J.A. (eds.) Handbook of Music and Emotion: Theory, Research, Applications. Oxford University Press, New York, NY, pp. 367–400 (2010)
7. Cowen, S., Fang, X., Sauter, D., Keltner, D.: What music makes us feel: at least 13 dimensions organize subjective experiences associated with music across different cultures. Proc. Natl. Acad. Sci. 117(4), 1924–1934 (2020)
8. TechDispatch #1/2021 – Facial Emotion Recognition. European Data Protection Supervisor, 21 Nov 2022. https://edps.europa.eu/data-protection/our-work/publications/techdispatch/tec hdispatch-12021-facial-emotion-recognition_en (2022)
9. Telford, T.: Emotion detection' AI is a $20 billion industry. New research says it can't do what it claims. Washington Post, 31 July 2019. [Online]. Available: https://www.washingtonpost.com/business/2019/07/31/emotion-detection-ai-is-billion-industry-new-research-says-it-cant-do-what-it-claims/
10. Taigman, Y., Yang, M., Ranzato, M., Wolf, L.:DeepFace: Closing the Gap to Human-Level Performance in Face Verification. In: Computer Vision and Pattern Recognition (2014)
11. Álvarez, P., Zarazaga-Sofia, F., Baldassarri, S.: Mobile music recommendations for runners based on location and emotions: the DJ-Running system. Pervasive Mob. Comput. 67, 101242 (2020)
12. De Prisco, R., Guarino, A., Malandrino, D., Zaccagnino, R.: Induced emotion-based music recommendation through reinforcement learning. Appl. Sci. 12(21), 11209 (2022)
13. Vedanth, V., Aaditya, G., Prateek, R.: Song Recommendation Based on Emotion [Online]. Available: https://github.com/vedanthv/MusicHealsTheSoul

Understanding Text Messages for Anxiety Therapy Through Topic Modeling

Teh Faradilla Abdul Rahman[1(✉)] and Norshita Mat Nayan[2]

[1] Centre of Foundation Studies, Universiti Teknologi MARA, Cawangan Selangor, Kampus Dengkil, 43800 Dengkil, Selangor, Malaysia
tehfaradilla@uitm.edu.my
[2] Institute of Visual Informatics, Universiti Kebangsaan Malaysia, 43600 UKM, Bangi, Selangor, Malaysia

Abstract. Digital health platforms such as text messaging and mobile therapy are being increasingly embraced by patients as a valuable source of anxiety treatment. This mobile therapy-generated treatment comes in the form of text messages, and is normally known as short text and sparse. Since many real-world text-based data need semantic interpretation to reveal meaningful and relevant latent topics, research in Short Text Topic Modelling (STTM) was conducted. The current study examines the topics included in anxiety mobile therapy using STTM, particularly from the text messages sent by mental health professionals. Prior to the actual experiment, initial study was conducted using four topic modelling techniques with 28 text messages from anxiety therapy datasets and different hyperparameter settings. The performance evaluation includes classification accuracy, purity, normalized mutual information, and topic coherence. Based on the performance, Latent Feature Dirichlet Multinomial Mixture (LFDMM) with $\alpha = 0.1$, $\beta = 0.01$, and $K = 8$ is found to be the most suitable hyperparameter setting for the anxiety text messages dataset and is used further in the actual experiment with 53 sample text. The findings from the actual experiment show that the anxiety text messages dataset comprises 8 interpretable topics that are classified under the domain of energy recharge, locus of control, mutual respect, activity scheduling, handling uncertainty, medium of communication, managing thoughts and health, and hope and readiness.

Keywords: Topic Modeling · Text Message · Mental Health Therapy · Message Content · Short Text Therapy

1 Introduction

Anxiety is a health condition that can be diagnosed, and it is a set of distinguishable feelings of worry or fear that everyone can occasionally experience. A person may experience occasional anxiety when dealing with a difficulty at work, before taking a test, or when making a significant decision. However, anxiety disorders go beyond common concerns or fears. Anxiety can get worse over time when it is not well treated and the anxious feeling doesn't go away [1].

H. Badioze Zaman et al. (Eds.): IVIC 2023, LNCS 14322, pp. 87–97, 2024.
https://doi.org/10.1007/978-981-99-7339-2_8

Implementation of text-based mental health therapy via mobile phone could guarantee the accessibility to mental health care services especially during the pandemic context. Other than accessibility to the service, the topics included in the text messages as part of anxiety treatment are also essential. Although some topics used in anxiety mobile therapy have been mentioned by previous scholars in their interventions [2–5], topic exploration on a big corpus of text messages sent by mental health professional as a therapy is still limited. A manual approach to analyze and categorize a big corpus of text messages to discover latent topics would takes a long time and is prone to mistakes. Fortunately, many topic modeling methods are in hand to discover latent topics in short text. To the best of the authors' knowledge, there is no topic modeling analysis conducted to explore the hidden topics inside text messages for anxiety therapy. Thus, the current study aims identify topics contain in anxiety-therapy text messages by first comparing the performance of four topic modeling.

2 Topic Modeling

Being able to rapidly theme topic of text messages can help mental health professionals provides content of therapy in nature of the patients' concerns and better understand the patients' problems. It is important for mental health systems to begin to prepare for an increased volume due to the ease of texting via mobile therapy. Given the massive amount of texts that mental health experts sent to anxiety patients, a thorough investigation of the topics of text-based treatment has the potential to provide valuable information on specific concerns. The creation of automated tools to help programmers categorize short text content by topic and provide decision makers with broad overviews of themes as they emerge has been made possible by advancements in Natural Processing Language (NLP), which have opened up alternatives to hand-coded, framework-driven categorizations [6]. As far many types of topic modelling has been introduced [7–12].

The topic-word multinominal distribution is drawn using a combination of the Dirichlet Multinominal Model (DMM) component and the word embedding component by Latent Feature Dirichlet Multinomial Mixture (LFDMM) [9]. Topics are projected into the same vector space as word embeddings when using the embedding component. The drawback is that the computational process is expensive in nature and it limits the utility of LFDMM. A Generalized Polya urn (GPU) was later included to expand DMM [8]. By encouraging semantically related terms under related subjects, the GPU leverages word embeddings to produce more coherent and pertinent results. Other scholar [13] discussed on Poisson distribution (PDMM) which expanded on the idea of having one to three connected issues per short sentence rather than just one. Although Generalized Polya urn Poisson-based Dirichlet Multinomial Mixture Model (GPUPDMM) performs better, the Gibbs sampling method causes it to have a high time complexity [14].

3 Experimental Design

This study is divided into two parts; initial experiment and actual experiment.

3.1 Initial Experiment

The initial experiment was conducted on four topic modeling methods namely Latent Feature Dirichlet Multinomial Mixture (LFDMM), Gibbs Sampling Dirichlet Multinomial Mixture (GSDMM), Generalized Polya urn Dirichlet Multinomial Mixture (GPUDMM) dan Poisson-based Dirichlet Multinomial Mixture Model (GPU-PDMM), with 28 text messages of anxiety therapy to examine the best-performing topic modeling by comparing them in classifying text messages of anxiety therapy into different topics. A dataset composed of 53 text messages used by mental health professionals in anxiety therapy were collected from previous published literatures between 2014 and 2021 [2, 15–23]. Prior to this, text pre-processing steps include removing stop words, numeral, punctuation, separator and special characters, converting all text to lowercase, and lemmatization are performed to prepare the text messages for the analysis. A set of hyperparameters combinations, $\alpha = (0.05, 0.1)$ and $\beta = (0.01, 0.1)$ were applied. For LFDMM, λ is set to 0.6, which has shown in the past study that after combines data from bigger external corpus with corpus-specific topic-word multinomials, better word-topic distributions were produced in this way. The number of topics K is set to 8 in the experiment which resulted from manual interpretation process by a group of mental health professionals on the data source. GSDMM, GPUPDMM and GPUDMM were run for 2000 iterations while for LFDMM, the iteration baseline model was run 1500 times followed by further 500 iterations using the sample produced by the baseline model. Next, the best-performing topic modeling and the ideal combination of hyperparameters identified from the initial experiment were used in the actual experiment. The performance is measured using classification accuracy, clustering, and coherence evaluation.

3.2 Actual Experiment

Based on the result from initial experiment (see Sect. 4), it was found that LFDMM performed the best compared to the rest of the topic modeling methods. The combinations of hyperparameters $\alpha = 0.1$ and $\beta = 0.01$ are the most suitable to work with LFDDM and to draw topics for anxiety-therapy text messages. In the actual experiment, 53 text messages of anxiety therapy were included. At this point, the experiment primarily focuses on the words that the algorithms have categorized into several topic groups. In a focus group interview, a group of mental health professionals is given a list of words that was generated from the actual experiment. By analyzing the top 20 words in each topic group, the interview's goal is to make topic labelling. At the end of the interview, a consensus must be achieved on the name given for each topic.

4 Result and Discussion

This section presents the result from initial experiment which includes classification accuracy, clustering and coherence. Next, results from actual experiment and topic labelling are presented.

4.1 Classification Accuracy

The accuracy score of four topic modeling methods with four different hyperparameter settings and eight number of topics are shown in Fig. 1. The line graph shows the maximum average of accuracy score of each method. All methods score close to each other when $\alpha = 0.05, \beta = 0.1$, indicates that they have almost similar ability in classifying the topics. Despite the accuracy scores are close to each other and the differences between values are comparatively small, it is difficult to distinguish the best method for analyzing topics in anxiety dataset when K = 8. Next, GPUPDMM performed inconsistently with steep decrease and sharp increase when $\alpha = 0.1, \beta = 0.01$ and $\alpha = 0.1, \beta = 0.1$ respectively. This indicates that GPUPDMM is not a good method to be considered for the use in actual experiment. In contrast, LFDMM achieves the highest score twice when $\beta = 0.01$. It also outperformed GSDMM and GPUDMM when $\alpha = 0.05, \beta = 0.1$, though it is not the best score.

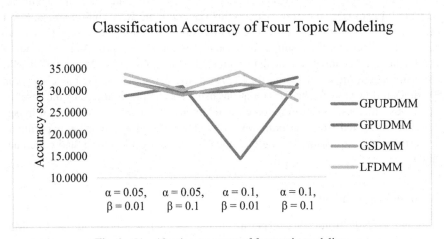

Fig. 1. Classification accuracy of four topic modeling.

4.2 Topic Clustering

Topic clustering evaluation reports the average of Purity and Normalized Mutual Information (NMI) score of four topic modeling used in the initial experiment. A better clustering performance is indicated by scores closer to 1 whereas poorer clustering performance is indicated by a closer value to 0 [9]. Based on Fig. 1 and Fig. 2, it can be observed that all models produced slight difference in purity scores between different combinations of alpha and beta, except for LFDMM where it scores comparatively higher when $\alpha = 0.1$ and $\beta = 0.01$. Overall, LFDMM performed the best in clustering evaluation compared to the other methods. This finding shows that compare to the rest of the methods, LFDMM was able to categorize text messages into topic clusters correctly. On the other hand, among the four topic modeling, GPUDMM is the weakest in labelling the sample of text messages into its cluster correctly (see Fig. 3).

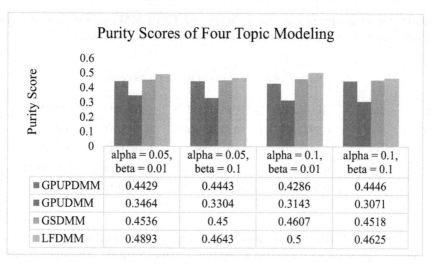

Fig. 2. Purity Scores of Four Topic Modeling

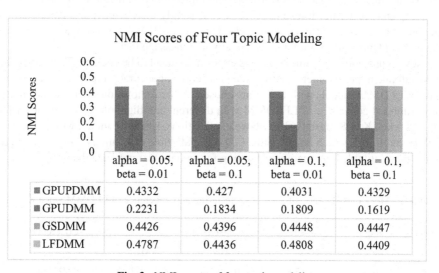

Fig. 3. NMI scores of four topic modeling

4.3 Coherence Score

The overview of coherence scores of each topic method is shown in Table 1. The highest coherence score of each topic modeling is highlighted in bold. Overall, all methods show almost similar coherence scores with comparatively small difference. GSDMM scores the highest in coherence evaluation when $\alpha = 0.05$ and $\beta = 0.1$. It is worth to note that for all four combinations of alpha and beta, coherence scores of LFDMM are very close to each other. This indicate that LFDMM is capable in assessing accurately words related to the same topic in a document. In contrast, GPUDMM scores the lowest for all combinations of hyperparameters compared to the rest of the methods.

Table 1. Coherence scores of four topic modeling

alpha	Beta	GPUPDMM	GPUDMM	GSDMM	LFDMM
0.05	0.01	**0.59439089**	**0.57448266**	0.5918455	0.5973810
0.05	0.1	0.58712026	0.57035823	**0.6037241**	0.5962398
0.1	0.01	0.59288104	0.56964313	0.5957668	**0.5974875**
0.1	0.1	0.59378709	0.57072111	0.5964917	0.5938499

In summary, GPUDMM performed the worst in clustering and coherence indicates that it is not a good choice for further analysis in actual experiment. Although GSDMM performed the best in coherence, it scored lower than LFDMM in accuracy and clustering. Meanwhile, LFDMM outperformed other topic modeling methods in classification accuracy and clustering. It also performed consistently in coherence evaluation across the four combinations of hyperparameters. Therefore, LFDMM is found to be the most suitable in identifying latent topics in anxiety text message therapy.

Next, alpha and beta value for actual experiment need to be decided. To identify the most suitable hyperparameter setting, the best scores of accuracy, clustering and coherence of LFDMM models with K = 8 are chosen. Table 2 shows the scores of accuracy, clustering and coherence of LFLDMM with different combinations of hyperparameter settings when K = 8. Based on the above explanations, LFDMM model with $\alpha = 0.1$, $\beta = 0.01$ and K = 8 which achieved the highest in all three evaluations score is found to be the most suitable hyperparameter setting for anxiety text message therapy.

Table 2. Mean classification of accuracy, clustering and coherence of LFDMM when K = 8

alpha	beta	Accuracy	Clustering		Coherence
			Purity	NMI	
0.05	0.01	33.75000	0.489286	0.478688	0.597381
0.05	0.1	30.00000	0.464286	0.443581	0.596240
0.1	**0.01**	**34.10714**	**0.500000**	**0.480752**	**0.597488**
0.1	0.1	27.50000	0.462500	0.440902	**0.593850**

4.4 Actual Experiment and Topic Labelling

This section reports the interpretability of the topics using a qualitative approach which involves a group of seven mental health professionals. As discussed in the previous section, the topic modeling method used for topic interpretation is LFDMM with the K = 8. In an interview, mental health professionals were initially presented with a list of 8 topics, where each topic has the top 20 words ordered by word probability. Based on the top 20 words, the mental health professionals discussed on the most suitable name for interpretation that would best represent the topic group.

Table 3. Topics in text messages for anxiety therapy produced by LFDMM

Topic	Label	Top 20 Words
1	Energy recharge	feel thing change focus try good activity interest exercise make find emotion week notice help remember bad control today stress
2	Locus of control	start feel time anxiety handle pass drain breath long complete session difficult remember treat alone activate task base extra severe
3	Mutual respect	patience forget forgive assertive aspiration direct backward have respect request advocate need achieve far specific use person look result limit
4	Managing thoughts and health	feel mind great friend control music contaminate enemy now inspiration on kit coping world health healthy number thought include message
5	Activity scheduling	positive anxiety mood treatment live life day help write people activity lead negative events care fair thankful create suffer period
6	Handling uncertainty	goal lie today personal success week mind moment leaves live education work matter relationship visual worry work-related achieve within period
7	Medium of communication	give call media angry go check gift make counselor important continuous social journey feel talk sad put immeasurably keep worry
8	Hope and readiness	today feel better tomorrow success care take fail try opportunity life maintain day make hope discourage social mirror health open

Table 3 shows the 8 topic groups generated from the actual experiment with labelling resulted from experts' group discussion. For instance, the first topic is labelled as "energy recharge" after considering most representative words such as "feel", "change", "focus", "try", "good", "activity", "interest", "exercise", "emotion", "make", "find", "help", "remember", "control" and "stress".

In the Cognitive Behavioral Technique (CBT), patients are asked to match the activity they choose with their energy level [24]. Recharge of lost energy can reduce anxiety and other negative emotions such as anger and frustration. Thus, it is appropriate that the topic "energy recharge" is labelled as the first topic. Next, the topic "locus of control" was chosen based on the opinion of experts who stated that all the words in this topic are related to the locus of control. Locus of control refers to the extent to which a person controls the events that affect his life [24]. One of the control methods via text message is to ask the patient to identify specific unhealthy or polluting thoughts, then isolate them [17]. Many people with anxiety tend to believe that they cannot control their thoughts [24]. However, with the exercises found in CBT, a person can learn to control anxious feelings and situations. If the patient can limit the amount and energy used to worry, the strength and frequency of these unhealthy habits will begin to decrease over time. This finding shows that the topic modeling technique is successful in classifying topics suitable for anxiety therapy. The topic of "mutual respect" was found appropriate because words such as "patience", "forgiveness", "forgetting", "aspiration" and "respect" are among the values taught in therapy. Patients are made aware of the need to respect themselves and others while therapists also are required to show respect to all patients. This value is very important to show patients that they are valued and that everything they share is important [24, 25]. Next, the fourth topic was given the name "managing thoughts and health" because the words listed are clearly aimed at managing thoughts, feelings and health. This topic coincides with psychology principles where patients learn and use thinking and problem-solving techniques to control distressing situations [25]. This also shows that the topic modeling technique is successful in classifying words into one topic well.

The words contained in the next topic such as "positive", "mood", "people", "write", "activity", "event", "care", "create" and "period" contribute to the naming of the topic "activity" scheduling". This topic is one of the behavioral strategies where it includes various pleasant activities such as attending parties, going out to eat with the family, writing poems, short stories and others. Constructing an activity schedule requires the patient to write down the activities they like and the responsibilities that need to be performed during the activity. The topic "handling uncertainty" refers to the technique of handling the patient's feelings of uncertainty about things such as the future, relationships, work, life direction and more. Things related to the future, achievements and tasks that require the patient to manage and handle them wisely. For example, someone who is not sure how to change their thinking and behavior to adapt to a health condition, therapy can help by targeting their thoughts and activities they like [25]. Next, experts agree that it is necessary to introduce to patients a communication medium that can be used to obtain mental health services. Among the communication mediums are communication through the media, seeking help from a counselor, chatting with a friend or making a phone call. Therefore, this topic is seen as compatible with anxiety therapy.

The topic in the last topic group ("hope and readiness") was chosen referring to the words found are related to hope, especially the words "today", "tomorrow", "fail", "opportunity", "life" and "hope". One of the approaches in anxiety therapy is to encourage patients to always be prepared to face future situations whether it is positive or negative. This approach was also used in a text message intervention [26] which was built to teach patients to maintain hope and believe that something good will happen. Patients are also taught to identify positive thoughts and practice positive thinking habits in preparation for facing negative situations in the future [27].

5   Conclusion

Online counselling in addition to in-person counselling can help close the treatment gap for anxiety and may continue to be used as a backup option even after the pandemic-related state of emergency is lifted. Nonetheless, individual needs and the nature of the exact problem are also factors that determine the topic in a treatment, and the same exact wording in text messages reflected that one size does not fit all. Accordingly, text messages for anxiety treatment should be reflective of the diversity of individuals and their needs.

The four topic modeling methods used in this study demonstrate different capabilities in classification accuracy, clustering, and coherence. Although GSDMM and LFDMM both performed well in all three performance measurements, LFDMM outweigh GSDMM in classification accuracy and clustering. Other than that, results from actual experiment exhibits that topic modeling method have the capability in finding latent topic. This paper has few contributions, firstly, it examines the potential of four topic modeling methods in identifying topics in text messages sent by mental health professionals as anxiety therapy. Secondly, the current study also contributes to the hidden content of text messages sent by a mental health professional in anxiety therapy. With suitable text messages crafted targeted to individual needs, ones will generally perceive more positive when they viewed the text messages. It may be important to capture more relevant topics in anxiety therapy text messages to increase buy-in as well as tailoring and personalization. In summary, texting can be a powerful tool to address anxiety problems and symptoms through its ability to connect with people who have constant challenge given the barriers such as the structural discrimination, public prejudice, adverse drug effects, and low accessibility.

References

1. Malaysian Psychiatric Association: Buku panduan kesihatan mental (2020)
2. Agyapong, V.I.O., et al.: Randomized controlled pilot trial of supportive text messages for patients with depression. BMC Psychiatry **17**, 1 (2017). https://doi.org/10.1186/s12888-017-1448-2
3. Agyapong, V.I.O., et al.: Randomized controlled pilot trial of supportive text messaging for alcohol use disorder patients. J. Subst. Abuse Treat. **94**, 74–80 (2018). https://doi.org/10.1016/j.jsat.2018.08.014
4. Aguilera, A., et al.: A Text messaging intervention (staywell at home) to counteract depression and anxiety during covid-19 social distancing: pre-post study. JMIR Ment. Heal. **8**, e25298 (2021). https://doi.org/10.2196/25298
5. Leightley, D., et al.: Evaluating the efficacy of a mobile app (drinks:ration) and personalized text and push messaging to reduce alcohol consumption in a veteran population: protocol for a randomized controlled trial. JMIR Res. Protoc. **9**, 1–15 (2020). https://doi.org/10.2196/19720
6. Fairie, P., Zhang, Z., D'Souza, A.G., Walsh, T., Quan, H., Santana, M.J.: Categorising patient concerns using natural language processing techniques. BMJ Heal. Care Inform. **28**, 1–9 (2021). https://doi.org/10.1136/bmjhci-2020-100274
7. Blei, D.M., Ng, A.Y., Jordan, M.I.: Latent Dirichlet allocation. J. Mach. Learn. Res. **3**, 993–1022 (2003). https://doi.org/10.1016/b978-0-12-411519-4.00006-9

8. Li, C., Wang, H., Zhang, Z., Sun, A., Ma, Z.: Topic modeling for short texts with auxiliary word embeddings. In: SIGIR 2016 - Proceedings of the 39th International ACM SIGIR Conference on Research and Development in Information Retrieval, pp. 165–174. Pisa, Italy (2016)

9. Nguyen, D.Q., Billingsley, R., Du, L., Johnson, M.: Improving topic models with latent feature word representations. Trans. Assoc. Comput. Linguist. **3**, 598–599 (2015). https://doi.org/10.1162/tacl_a_00245

10. Yan, X., Guo, J., Lan, Y., Cheng, X.: A biterm topic model for short texts. In: WWW 2013 - Proceedings of the 22nd International Conference on World Wide Web, pp. 1445–1455 (2013)

11. Zuo, Y., Zhao, J., Xu, K.: Word network topic model: a simple but general solution for short and imbalanced texts. Knowl. Inf. Syst. **48**, 379–398 (2016). https://doi.org/10.1007/s10115-015-0882-z

12. Zuo, Y., et al.: Topic modeling of short texts: a pseudo-document view. In: Proceedings of the 22nd ACM SIGKDD International Conference on Knowledge Discovery and Data Mining, pp. 2105–2114. San Francisco, California, USA (2016)

13. Li, C., Duan, Y., Wang, H., Zhang, Z., Sun, A., Ma, Z.: Enhancing topic modeling for short texts with auxiliary word embeddings. ACM Trans. Inf. Syst. **36**, 1–30 (2017). https://doi.org/10.1145/3091108

14. Tian, T., Fang, Z.: Attention-based autoencoder topic model for short texts. Procedia Comput. Sci. **151**, 1134–1139 (2019). https://doi.org/10.1016/j.procs.2019.04.161

15. Agyapong, V.I.O., et al.: Mental health outreach via supportive text messages during the covid-19 pandemic: improved mental health and reduced suicidal ideation after six weeks in subscribers of text4hope compared to a control population. Int. J. Environ. Res. Public Health **18**, 1–13 (2021). https://doi.org/10.3390/ijerph18042157

16. Aguilera, A., Bruehlman-Senecal, E., Demasi, O., Avila, P.: Automated text messaging as an adjunct to cognitive behavioral therapy for depression:a clinical trial. J. Med. Internet Res. **19**, e148 (2017). https://doi.org/10.2196/jmir.6914

17. García, Y., Ferrás, C., Rocha, Á., Aguilera, A.: Exploratory study of psychosocial therapies with text messages to mobile phones in groups of vulnerable immigrant women. J. Med. Syst. **43**, (2019). https://doi.org/10.1007/s10916-019-1393-3

18. Alfonsson, S., Englund, J., Parling, T.: Tailored text message prompts to increase therapy homework adherence: a single-case randomised controlled study. Behav. Chang. **36**, 180–191 (2019). https://doi.org/10.1017/bec.2019.10

19. Chandra, P.S., Sowmya, H.R., Mehrotra, S., Duggal, M.: "SMS" for mental health – Feasibility and acceptability of using text messages for mental health promotion among young women from urban low income settings in India. Asian J. Psychiatr. **11**, 59–64 (2014). https://doi.org/10.1016/j.ajp.2014.06.008

20. Anstiss, D., Davies, A.: "Reach out, rise up": the efficacy of text messaging in an intervention package for anxiety and depression severity in young people. Child Youth Serv. Rev. **58**, 99–103 (2015). https://doi.org/10.1016/j.childyouth.2015.09.011

21. Fitzpatrick, K.K., Darcy, A., Vierhile, M.: Delivering cognitive behavior therapy to young adults with symptoms of depression and anxiety using a fully automated conversational agent (Woebot): a randomized controlled trial. JMIR Ment. Heal. **4**, 1–11 (2017). https://doi.org/10.2196/mental.7785

22. Furber, G., Jones, G.M., Healey, D., Bidargaddi, N.: A comparison between phone-based psychotherapy with and without text messaging support in between sessions for crisis patients. J. Med. Internet Res. **16**, e219 (2014). https://doi.org/10.2196/jmir.3096

23. Clough, B.A., Casey, L.M.: Will patients accept daily SMS as a communication to support adherence to mental health treatment? Daily SMS: acceptance, feasibility, & satisfaction. Int. J. Cyber Behav. Psychol. Learn. **8**, 24–35 (2018). https://doi.org/10.4018/IJCBPL.2018070103

24. Crane, K.L., Watters, K.M.: Cognitive behavioral therapy strategies (2017)
25. Cully, J.A., Teten, A.L.: A Therapist's Guide to Brief Cognitive Behavioral Therapy. Department of Veterans Affairs South Central MIRECC, Houston (2008)
26. Agyapong, V.I.O., et al.: Cross-sectional survey evaluating Text4Mood: mobile health program to reduce psychological treatment gap in mental healthcare in Alberta through daily supportive text messages. BMC Psychiatry **16**, 1–12 (2016). https://doi.org/10.1186/s12888-016-1104-2
27. Weisel, K.K., Fuhrmann, L.M., Berking, M., Baumeister, H., Cuijpers, P., Ebert, D.D.: Standalone smartphone apps for mental health a systematic review and meta-analysis. npj Digit. Med. **2**, 1–10 (2019). https://doi.org/10.1038/s41746-019-0188-8

Mixed Reality and Human-Computer Interaction

Theoretical Analysis of Research Methodology to Study Emotions Using Emotion AI Among Malaysian E-Learning Tertiary Students for Prototype of Adaptive Interface

Vasaki Seenivasagam[1]([✉]), Zainab Abu Bakar[1], Norshuhani Zamin[2], and Yazrina Yahya[2]

[1] School of Science and Technology, Asia e University, 47500 Subang Jaya, Selangor, Malaysia
c70101200004@aeu.edu.my

[2] Faculty Information Science and Technology, Universiti Kebangsaan Malaysia, 43600 Bangi, Selangor, Malaysia

Abstract. The e-learning method has been in use for more than a decade now. The e-learning method was intensely used during covid-19 pandemic giving an option for learning experiences remotely in various locations. Currently, e-learning optionally facilitates for students from various locations to study even in remote areas. Sustaining the e-learning facilities with improvements becomes essential since the world is moving towards IR4.0 where learning can happen from any part of the world using a diversified technology. This analysis is looking at theoretical concepts to analyze the viability to use emotions to study the requirements analysis for Adaptive Interface Design. This analysis is conducted to identify the emotion and to find appropriateness of using emotions AI tool to study the emotions. It is targeted for Malaysian students' environment. It will be based on current widely used LMS used to identify the methods of analyzing the emotions among Malaysian students of entrepreneurship subject. It is concluded that emotions are an essential feature of User Interface study for further study of influences. Emotions AI can be used with mixed mode method for accuracy. The research will pave the way for Adaptive user interface in e-learning systems. The purpose of Adaptive user interface is to enhance essentially subject-wise and program-wise creativity skills in meeting essential skills of Education 5.0.

Keywords: Malaysian Education 5.0 · e-learning · IR4.0 · humanity technology · education technology · learning emotions · adaptive user interface

1 Introduction

Educational evolution is evident and rampant. The volatility of changes form COVID-19 pandemic is irrepressible than ever. Tertiary education never dimmed to identify unique part our lives [1]. The population of future is based on the education attained from tertiary education. Education has gone through major changes according to eras

© The Author(s), under exclusive license to Springer Nature Singapore Pte Ltd. 2024
H. Badioze Zaman et al. (Eds.): IVIC 2023, LNCS 14322, pp. 101–108, 2024.
https://doi.org/10.1007/978-981-99-7339-2_9

from yesteryears. Initially there were teaching of virtues and life philosophy but now our education system follows the major changes in technology. The syllabus being prepared based on benchmarks. Looking back at educational eras of changes are notable tangled with management of society mounting in complication and social structures. Benchmarking allows educators to identify students' strengths and weaknesses, which can then inform their future instruction.

2 Literature Review

2.1 Changes in Technologies

Currently we are at the verge transformation of way of learning again to new era of revolutions as we move towards IR4.0. The environment of Information technology is creating rapid waves of changes in all form. It is undeniable that that Education system constantly goes thru dynamic changes according to the industrial revolution from yesteryear which dates back to 1800. The education system as enabler of the education started in the first Industrial Revolution dates back 1800. The industrial revolution is constantly influencing of the educational prototype to modernize educational systems. Now the electronic medium education system has to ensure preparation or training towards improvement of job opportunities which itself influenced by the waves of industrial changes. Current factors which determine the successful implementation will be the determinant factors to face the successfulness of eLearning system implementation of Education 5.0 for in preparedness of IR4.0. The study will identify the impact of the factors from the e-learning users' emotions using emotions AI.

2.2 Importance of Tertiary Education

According to the world bank [1] tertiary education refers to all formal post-secondary education, including public and private universities, colleges, technical training institutes, and vocational schools. Tertiary education is instrumental in fostering growth, reducing poverty, and boosting shared prosperity. The importance of tertiary education is not far from essential part of human life. [2] The world bank also states that the history of curriculum development has been characterized and a series of "crises" with the pendulum shifting between traditionalists' call for getting back to the basics and the progressives' focus on the learner. However, tracing this history, one can see a common theme in the criticisms expressed by both parties: the failure of the existing curriculum to meet the demands presented by an increasingly complex society. To add to the complexity the during the outbreak of COVID-19 pandemic beside the impact on human survival it also paved way for more complexities in sustainability of quality education.

In reality the world gone through many industrial revolutions which somehow influence the education. The First Industrial Revolution used power generated by water and steam for producing goods, requiring physical labor. The Second Industrial Revolution used electricity and assembly lines for mass production run by skilled labor educated with higher-learning techniques. Then Third Industrial Revolution used computers, data, and information technology (IT) to automate production through the rise of smart machines and the people who could program them.

Research Objectives

- To understand if emotions is related to enhance e-learning.
- To decide if the student's emotion can be categorized in e-leaning process.
- To identify the emotions that influences eLearning.
- To analyze the stages of analysis to be used to study factors in using online learning.
- To identify theories related to learning What are the factors which creates negative emotions in e-learning?

RO6: What are the positive emotional factors which co-related with motivational intensity?

2.3   Educational Technology for Future

[2] It is detailed by work bank and global philanthropic investment firm that the Education and Technology Readiness Index (ETRI) which is a multi-dimensional easy to use and free of cost global instrument. It was designed and has been tested simultaneously in three different continents to support countries in assessing where they stand on education technologies. ETRI identifies and measures the different enabling factors that are required for EdTech to be effective (e.g., mindset, buy-in, budget, technical infrastructure, and human and technical capacity), which can help governments pinpoint where there is room for improvement, and signal to countries their overall level of readiness to deploy effective EdTech policies.

In his article [3] Vincent Blok, stated that one of the pressing issues in philosophy of technology is the role of human creativity. Humanity cannot be taken away from human. Just like yester-years we are still referring to the virtues and philosophies learned in ancient time which by some means taught is school in current time. But there is a concern if we are deviating from humanity.

2.4   Diverse Impact of Educational Technology

According to the research done on mental front health [4] total of 58% of the students characterized by an increased level of stress. 56% show symptoms of depression and 18% of the participants had suicidal thoughts. The most significant predictor of depression is high stress levels and factors related to e-learning: isolation from friends and acquaintances, negative impact on level of knowledge, reduced motivation to learn, and worsening grades. This predictor may explain about 66% of the variance of depression.

This results in an unsuccessful system and is a waste of universities money. Research on this topic is still at its infancy, where the views and emotions of the students are not fully. Studying e-learning emotions can lead universities to better understand their students' needs, and eventually lead to a successful e-learning.

The study on [5] emotions of students in using e-learning system in Algerian Universities gave an academic understanding of enhancement which is vital for e-learning system in proposing essential subject wise skill as well as transferable skills in University programs (see Fig. 1).

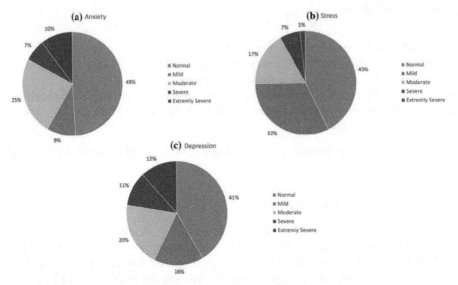

Fig. 1. Overall anxiety, stress and depression scores.

Prevalence, Psychological Responses and Associated Correlates of Depression, Anxiety and Stress in a Global Population, During the Coronavirus Disease (COVID-19) Pandemic. By Shah, Syed Mustafa Ali & Qureshi, Muhammad Fazal & Mohammad, Danish & Abbas, Zain. From Community Mental Health Journal (2021).

Impact of Psychological Pressure in E-Learning

[18] Fahad Alam in his research stated that psychological pressure is the foremost obstruction to academic success. Psychological stress can impact the inspiration, concentration, awareness, and social interactions of students, which are considered critical factors for students to attain academic success. He also stated that Students who are bound with diverse emotionally demanding states, such as homework, assignments, quizzes, examinations, and deadlines, are connected that encompass their psychological intentions we are in the state of adding stress of e-learning system usage of Learning Management systems which is creatin psychological disruption among them.

2.5 Need for Emotional Evaluation Among E-Learning Students

[6] Song and Kim in the research identified hidden emotions in which the facial expression retains a neutral emotion while the bio-signal is active.

[3] Vincent Blok states, with the understanding of deviated responsiveness, we encounter the specific human contribution to human-technology creation. While we could argue that other animals are instinctively absorbed in their responsiveness to affordances in the environment. On the contrary he also mentioned that an animal does not

deviate from its responsiveness to particular affordances in the environment. Humans can deviate willingly or not willingly from their responsiveness to affordances in the environment.

[6] The effective achievement of vast investment in e-learning system depends on students' willingness and acceptance to use the system. Lack of e-learning system usage hampers the realization of emotional impacts can also cause emotional stress.

[3] Emotional experiences are ubiquitous in nature and important and perhaps even critical in academic settings, as emotion modulates virtually every aspect of cognition.

Tests, examinations, homework, and deadlines are associated with different emotional states that encompass frustration, anxiety, and boredom.

According to Emotional experiences are ubiquitous in nature and important and perhaps even critical in academic settings, as emotion modulates virtually every aspect of cognition. Tests, examinations, homework, and deadlines are associated with different emotional states that encompass frustration, anxiety, and boredom. Even subject matter influences emotions that affect one's ability to learn and Frontiers in Psychology I www.frontiersin.org 1 August 2017 I Volume 8 I Article 1454 Tyng et al. Emotional Influences on Learning and Memory remember. The usage of computer-based multimedia educational technologies, such as intelligent tutoring systems (ITSs) and massive open online courses (MOOCs), which are gradually replacing traditional face-to-face learning environments, is increasing.

2.6 Motivational Intensity and Skill Development Among Student

[7] Todays' life is full of challenges and threats. If people do not equip themselves with the necessary abilities, they will face many problems. In the 21st century, a group of psychologists [7] has realized that man must spend his mental energy on the positive aspects of his experience. Thus, one of the topics attracting a lot of attention in recent decades is factors rooted in positive psychology [8] Dewaele, [11] Seligman and Csikszentmihalyi supported the alternation in the focus of psychology by solving undesirable and challenging life issues to improve constructive qualities. In describing positive psychology, it is "the scientific study of what goes right in life, from birth to death and at all stops in between."

[12] In recent years, the number of studies on the role of the affective domain in education and in teaching and learning has increased. As such, research in education has focused on the emotions of students (Emotion recognition is the process of identifying people's emotions). The accuracy with which people would recognize the feelings of others varies considerably. The use of machine learning and artificial intelligence to assist people with emotion recognition is a relatively new research area. [last] Emotions, which affect both. The study of emotional psychology allows researchers to dive into what makes humans react as they do to certain stimuli and how those reactions affect us both physically and mentally.

[13] Identifying Motivational intensity will lead to understanding overall thought pattern or brainwave among e-learning system users. This will preserve the human's essential mystical capability and to preserve life itself in oncoming IR4.0 era.

[14] Human physiological and psychological status, play a very important role in human life. Positive emotions help improve human health and work efficiency, while

negative emotions may cause health problems. Artificial Intelligence (AI) currently used as formal method of studying the e-learning students' emotions. Emotion recognition has been applied in many areas such as safe driving health care especially mental health.

2.7 Adaptive User Interface

According to [19] Selma Medijen Human Computer Interaction (HCI) is one of the active fields in computer science. The main research in HCI revolves around providing means of communication between humans and computers through UI. Knowing that humans and computers do not share the same language, the UI should be designed with a concise understanding of its users as well as their needs. The design process of a UI is carried out with an objective to minimize users' invested efforts during the interaction, both in providing the input and understanding the output. This optimization is reflected through the usability of the UI and the quality of the user experience (UX) during the interaction.

Furthermore, [19] Selma Medijen stated Automatic AUI allows the adaptation via the user's emotions through multiple modalities and offers an active adaption with the context of the task performed via speech based on the emotion, such that the user does not need to manually adapt the system. The complete Manual AUI that allows the user to customize the user interface using manual interactions. And finally, a Hybrid AUI that combines the elements of both Automatic and Manual AUIs. A comprehensive user study is performed using mixed-methods approach to test each AUI and validate its usability and UX both quantitatively and qualitatively. The quantitative measurements allowed the computation of effectiveness, productivity, efficiency, and error safety of the interfaces.

3   Research Methodology

Stage 1: Understand behavior and emotions

[17] Emotion has a substantial influence on the cognitive processes in humans, including perception, attention, learning, memory, reasoning, and problem solving. Emotion has a particularly strong influence on attention, especially modulating the selectivity of attention as well as motivating action and behavior. This attentional and executive control is intimately linked to learning processes, as intrinsically limited attentional capacities are better focused on relevant information.

Emotions are not conscious. They are reactions that are produced in your physical body. They can be triggered by experiences that you're having, as well as by thoughts and memories. It has also found that when it comes to facial expressions, there is little difference between anger and disgust, along with fear and surprise. This leaves us with the most basic list of emotions: happiness, fear, anger, and sadness.

It has found when it comes to facial expressions, there is little difference between anger and disgust, along with fear and surprise. This leaves us with the most basic list of emotions: happiness, fear, anger, and sadness.

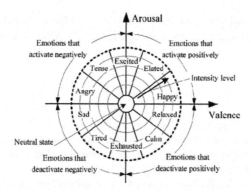

Stage 2: Analysis of emotions and intensity for e-learning experience

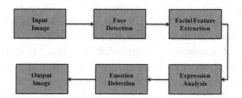

STAGE 3: Plan to Develop conceptual framework

A conceptual framework is a visual representation in research that helps to illustrate the expected relationship between cause and effect. The relationship between the e-learning environment behaviors positive and negative intensity will be recognized.

4 Discussion

In the proposed study Interface for holistic approach in human interaction. With enhanced interface with adaptability with recognition of emotional categorization the creative skill enhancement will be viable. It is essential that the emotions are analyzed to understand the issues involved in multiinvolved in multi-device interactive applications as well, where e-learning system can be accessed through mobile and stationary devices, even exploiting different interaction modalities (graphical, vocal, etc.). Adaptive interface besides paving way for creativity skill it needs to assure socialization, safety and environmental sustainability in a domestic day-by-day living space or learning environment. With Adaptive user interface is anticipated to enhance interaction in e-learning system.

5 Conclusion

The research suggests emotional analysis of the user and system interface Design to be done to understand and corelate the user with behavior pattern of user Interaction with e-learning system. It is essential to understand how the variables are co-related to study to understand he negative and positive emotions. The effectiveness of the current e-learning system will pave the way to apply holistic approach. The emotions are corelated with behavior pattern too understand the pattern involved for the user interface to add degree of adaptability in user interface. Even though Emotions AI is used for accuracy mixed mode will be used.

References

1. https://www.worldbank.org/en/topic/tertiaryeducation
2. https://www.worldbank.org/en/topic/education/brief/edtech-readiness-index
3. Blok, V.: The role of human creativity in human-technology relations. Philos. Technol. **35**, 59 (2022). https://doi.org/10.1007/s13347-022-00559-7
4. Anna-Rutkowska, Cieślik, B., Tomaszczyk, A., Szczepańska-Gieracha, J.: Mental health conditions among e-learning students during the covid-19 pandemic. Front Public Health **10**, 871934 (2022) Published online 2022 May 17
5. Yahiaoui l, F., et al.: The impact of e-learning systems on motivating students and enhancing their outcomes during covid-19: a mixed-method approach. Front. Psychol. 29 Jul (2022)
6. Ahmed, N., Aghbari, Z.A., Girija, S.: A systematic survey on multimodal emotion recognition using learning algorithms. Intell. Syst. Appl. **17**, 200171 (2023)
7. Rawashdeh, A.Z.A.,, Mohammed, E.Y., Arab, A.R.A., Alara, M., Al-Rawashdeh, B.: Ajman University, Ajman, UAE 2Al Balqaa Applied University, Jordan 3Ain-Shams University, Egypt 4Clemson University, USA, Advantages and Disadvantages of Using e-Learning in University Education: Analyzing Students' Perspectives., The Electronic Journal of e-Learning **19**(3) (2021)
8. Dewaele, J.M., Chen, X., Padilla, A.M., Lake, J.: The flowering of positive psychology in foreign language teaching and acquisition research. Front. Psychol. **10**, 2128 (2019). https://doi.org/10.3389/fpsyg.2019.02128

Human Gesture Recognition for Elderly People Using User Training Interaction Data

Nur Ani[1,2(✉)], Nazlena Mohamad Ali[1], and Vina Ayumi[2]

[1] Institute of Visual Informatics, Universiti Kebangsaan Malaysia, Selangor, Malaysia
nur.ani@mercubuana.ac.id
[2] Faculty of Computer Science, Universitas Mercu Buana, West Jakarta, Indonesia

Abstract. Research on human-computer interaction (HCI) has been widely developed for older people. However, there needs to be more research studies on the deep learning model implementation of human gesture image data to monitor the activities of older people. There are four main stages of research, including data preparation, feature extraction using pre-trained models VGG16 and VGG19, training without and with fine-tuning, and comparing the performance of the deep learning model. This study used the dataset of Ralf Leistad Gesture with data classes as backward, forward, left, right, still, and stop. Then, the data is implemented in the data augmentation method using rotation, brightness, width shift, height shift, horizontal flip, and vertical flip. As a result of the experiment, VGG16 achieved an accuracy of 96.88%, and VGG19 reached an accuracy of 96.88%.

Keywords: Elderly Monitoring · VGG16 · VGG19 · Human Gesture

1 Introduction

Globally, the world's elderly population has increased to 9 million per year. If this number continues, it is predicted that the elderly population in the world will reach 800 million people by 2025. The addition of special health organizations and services for older people must follow this increase in population. This care service is necessary to support the health of older adults and help family members to be able to take care of older adults to the maximum [1–5]. Utilizing a system designed suitability for elderly users can support an excellent aging life and get positive acceptance from elderly users to help maintain a healthy lifestyle [6, 7].

However, the number of organizations and exceptional health services for the elderly has not increased much. The number of human resources serving the elderly is still limited. Access to these health services is now increasingly constrained during the COVID-19. Therefore, the role of local governments is needed to increase the number of health workers needed. This is so that the elderly do not need to queue to get services to referral hospitals at the provincial level or national referral hospitals. To cover the service gap, it is necessary to have an innovation that can be used in general and accommodate many service needs for elderly care. This innovation can be in human-computer interaction (HCI) technology [1, 8–12].

H. Badioze Zaman et al. (Eds.): IVIC 2023, LNCS 14322, pp. 109–118, 2024.
https://doi.org/10.1007/978-981-99-7339-2_10

Research on HCI has been widely developed for the elderly [13–17]. There are many forms of implementing HCI for health service improvement. This research will focus on computer vision technology to monitor the body movements of older adults. This supervision measures the movement function of older people and trains them so that they can continue to function normally [1, 18–26]. This research by Purushothaman and Palaniswamy (2020) used the support vector machine (SVM) method to classify existing movements. The recognized activities are up-down motion, 90-degree rotation, left-right, and Z motion. There are 64 sample images used for this experiment. This experiment obtained an accuracy of 98.44% for movement classification [27].

The study by Alam Yousuf (2019) aimed to identify hand movements in front/forward, rear, left, right, and stop or steady activities. The data collected and processed comes from the MPU 6050 module device. As a result of the research, this research obtained an accuracy of 93.8% [28]. Moreover, the study of Desai (2017) used an image dataset with an image resolution of 640 × 480 pixels. The image used is an image of hand gestures 1–5. The hand gesture classification method used is the k-nearest neighbors (k-NN) and Euclidian distance methods. This study obtained experimental results in a classification accuracy of 88% [8, 29].

Furthermore, this study will represent a deep learning model of human gesture picture data to monitor the activities of older adults as a contribution to research on human-computer interaction (HCI) for the elderly. This paper is structured as an introduction, research methodology, result, discussion, and conclusion. The section explains the research background, phase of research, experiment result, and summary of human gesture image data recognition using a deep learning model to monitor the activities of older adults.

2   Research Methodology

This study aims to implement a deep learning model of human gesture image data to monitor the activities of the elderly to support the contribution of research on human-computer interaction (HCI) for the elderly. With the proliferation of deep learning technology, the HCI research process has accelerated even further. Deep learning research can become even more complicated when devising technology solutions for older adults, who are frequently skeptical of new technologies.

Analyzing human gestures and activities using deep learning to enhance human-computer interaction technology is important. The application status of intelligent HCI in deep learning across various industries, including gesture recognition, speech interaction, and natural language processing, is investigated. This work summarizes and analyzes the comprehension of gesture recognition using user interaction data. There are four main stages of research, including data preparation, feature extraction using pre-trained models VGG16 and VGG19, training without and with fine-tuning, and comparing the model's performance, as shown in **Fig. 1**.

The first phase is data preparation. This study used the dataset of Ralf Leistad Gesture. This dataset was collected with the help of cameras, actors, and greenscreen backgrounds. The actor moves according to a predefined data class in front of a green screen background. The data classes used in this study are backward, forward, left, right, still,

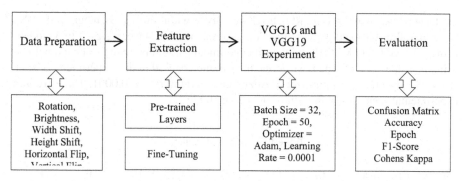

Fig. 1. Research methodology

and stop. The resolution of the image in the dataset is uniformized to 224x224. Then, the data is implemented through the data augmentation method using ImageGenerators. The technique is rotation (RO), brightness (BR), width shift (WS), height shift (HS), horizontal flip (HF), and vertical flip (VF). The result of data augmentation is divided into training data, validation data, and testing data. An example of research data is depicted in **Fig. 2**.

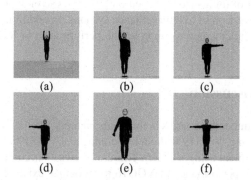

Fig. 2. Example of research data: (a) backward, (b) forward, (c) left, (d) right, (e) still and (f) stop

The second phase is the feature extraction. This stage (using the pre-trained model) performs feature extraction using pre-trained layers VGG16 and VGG19. We use pre-trained layers to extract visual features from the dataset at this stage. Next, we create a fully connected layer and an output layer for the dataset. VGG16 is one of the architectural configurations in a convolutional neural network with an input layer of 224x224. VGG16 has 16-layer convolution with a kernel of 3x3, stride of 1, and ReLu for each hidden layer. VGG19 is one of the architectural configurations consisting of 47 layers that use the concept that more layers have good accuracy. Convolutional layers use 3 × 3 filters, with the number of dimensions increasing in each layer. The dimensions used in the filter are 3, 64, 128, 256, and 512.

At the training without and with the fine-tuning stage, the thing to do is to train the previously described layer with backpropagation using the training data. The technique for data processing is rotation (RO), brightness (BR), width shift (WS), height shift (HS), horizontal flip (HF), and vertical flip (VF). At this training stage, we used two models, namely VGG16 and VGG19, with each experiment using fine tuning (FT) and without using fine-tuning (FT). Then, we define the parameters used in this experiment as batch size = 32, epoch = 50, optimizer = Adam, and learning rate = 0.0001. There are four experimental scenarios in this study, as seen in Table 1.

Table 1. Experiment scenario

No	Experiment	FT	RO	BR	WS	HS	HF	VF
1	VGG16	✗	√	√	√	√	√	√
2	VGG16	√	√	√	√	√	√	√
3	VGG19	✗	√	√	√	√	√	√
4	VGG19	√	√	√	√	√	√	√

The last phase of this research is comparing evaluation models. This research is the first part of developing a deep learning-based application for monitoring elderly activities based on the internet of things (IoT). Based on [30], the use of VGG19 and VGG16 is suitable for implementation in IoT surveillance systems. In addition, according to [31], fine-tuning can be implemented to improve the performance of VGG19 and VGG16 implementations.

3 Result and Discussion

There are four experimental scenarios in this study, namely VGG16 without fine-tuning, VGG16 with fine-tuning, VGG19 without fine-tuning and VGG19 with fine-tuning. The first stage is to experiment using VGG16. This study uses an accuracy model and a loss model to evaluate the performance of VGG16 to recognize existing human movement data. We compare the experimental results of VGG16 & VGG19 without using fine-tuning and fine-tuning as depicted in Fig. 3.

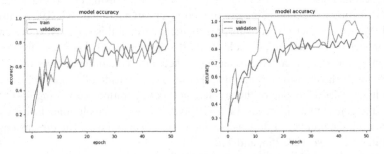

Fig. 3. Accuracy of VGG16 without fine-tuning (left) and VGG16 with fine-tuning (right)

It can be seen that the VGG16 model with fine-tuning obtained a maximum validation accuracy of 1 in the 13th epoch. Meanwhile, VGG16, with no fine-tuning, received a maximum accuracy of 0.96875 at the 49th epoch. This means that VGG16 with fine-tuning found the global maxima faster than VGG16 without fine-tuning. Furthermore, this study also analyzes the results of the loss model for the VGG16 algorithm. The model with VGG16 with fine-tuning finds the minimum loss in the 13th epoch faster is depicted in Fig. 4.

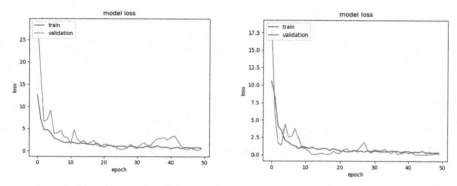

Fig. 4. Loss model of VGG16 no fine-tune (left) and VGG16 with fine-tune (right)

In addition to using a loss model and an accuracy model, this study uses a confusion matrix to see more of the results of the performance of an algorithm. It can be seen that the VGG16 model with fine-tuning can predict all the validation images perfectly, while the VGG16 model without fine-tuning has one wrong image predicted, namely in the forward class. The confusion matrix model VGG16 without fine-tuning and with fine-tuning is depicted in Fig. 5.

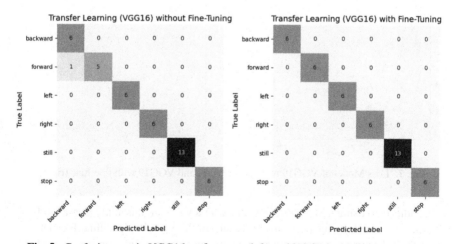

Fig. 5. Confusion matrix VGG16 no fine-tune (left) and VGG16 with fine-tune (right)

The second stage is to experiment using VGG19. This study uses accuracy and a loss model to evaluate the performance of VGG119 for human movement recognition. The comparison of the experimental results of VGG19 without using fine-tuning and fine-tuning is depicted in Fig. 6.

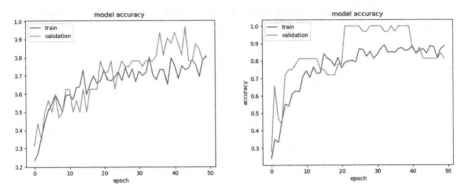

Fig. 6. Accuracy model of VGG16 no fine-tune (left) and VGG16 with fine-tune (right)

The Fig. 6 showed that the VGG19 model with fine-tuning obtained a maximum validation accuracy of 1 at the 22nd epoch. Meanwhile, VGG19, with no fine-tuning, got a maximum accuracy of 0.96875 at the 44th epoch. This means that VGG19 with fine-tuning found the global maxima faster than VGG19 without fine-tuning. Furthermore, this study also analyzes the results of the loss model for the VGG19 algorithm. The model result with VGG19 with fine-tuning finds the minimum loss at the 22nd epoch faster is depicted in Fig. 7.

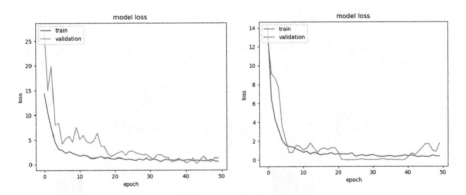

Fig. 7. Loss Model of VGG19 no fine-tune (left) and VGG19 with fine-tune (right)

In addition to using a loss model and an accuracy model, this study uses a confusion matrix to see more fully the performance results of the VGG19 algorithm. It can be seen that the VGG19 model, with fine-tuning, can predict all the validation images perfectly. In contrast, the VGG19 model without fine-tuning has one wrong prediction, which is predicted in the right class. The confusion matrix of VGG19 without fine-tuning and fine-tuning is depicted in Fig. 8.

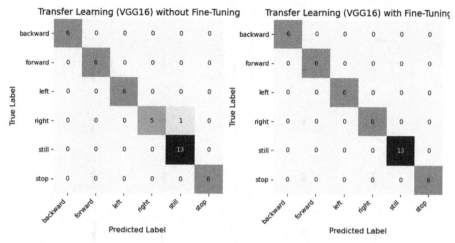

Fig. 8. Confusion matrix VGG19 without fine-tune (left) and VGG19 with fine-tune (right)

As a result of the research, this study also presents a comparison table of metric evaluations for the four experimental scenarios. It can be seen that the VGG16 model with fine-tuning at the 13th epoch has obtained a maximum validation accuracy of 100%, while the VGG19 model with fine-tuning has obtained a validation accuracy of 100% at the 22nd epoch. The comparison table for experimental performance evaluation can be seen in Table 2.

Table 2. Comparison of metric evaluations for the four experimental scenarios

Model	Fine-Tuning	Accuracy	Epoch	F1-Score	Cohens Kappa
VGG16	No	96.88%	49	0.9767	0.9713
VGG16	Yes	100%	13	1.0000	1.0000
VGG19	No	96.88%	44	0.9767	0.9713
VGG19	Yes	100%	22	1.0000	1.0000

Based on the Table 2, the VGG16 with fine-tuning obtained the best value compared to good models. In the 13th epoch, VGG16 with fine-tuning, was able to get 100% accuracy in recognizing existing movements. VGG16 has the advantage of extracting quality features from images with excellent performance. VGG16 architecture with fine-tuning requires the least number of epochs compared to other architectures and requires the least amount of computation time. The experiment result that presented correctly prediction using the VGG16 with fine-tuning is depicted in Fig. 9.

Model predictions (blue: correct, red: incorrect)

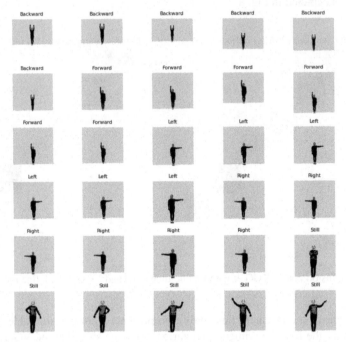

Fig. 9. Prediction results

4   Conclusion

This study focused on human-computer interaction (HCI) technologies to monitor older people's mobility function and train them to continue to operate normally. This research developed a deep-learning model of human gesture images to monitor the activities of older adults. Four primary steps of the study include data preparation, feature extraction using pre-trained models VGG16 and VGG19, training without and with fine-tuning, and model performance comparison. As the result, VGG16 achieved 96.88% accuracy while 100% accuracy with fine-tuning. Moreover, VGG19 achieved 96.88% of accuracy, while with fine-tuning, it achieved 100% of accuracy. In the future, the VGG16 or VGG19 can be implemented by regularization to prevent overfitting. The gesture recognition model becomes complex as the number of features in gesture images rises. Even though some of the features have a minimal impact on the outcome, an overfitting model considers all the features. The recommended regularization methods are L1 regularization, L2 regularization, and dropout.

References

1. Oudah, M., Al-Naji, A., Chahl, J.: Hand gestures for elderly care using a microsoft kinect. Nano Biomed. Eng **12**(3), 197–204 (2020)
2. Mansor, N., Awang, H., Rashid, N.F.A., Gu, D., Dupre, M.: Malaysia ageing and retirement survey. Encycl. Gerontol. Popul. Aging, 1–5 (2019)
3. Wojtyla, C., Bertuccio, P., Ciebiera, M., La Vecchia, C.: Breast cancer mortality in the americas and australasia over the period 1980–2017 with predictions for 2025. Biology (Basel) **10**(8), 814 (2021)
4. Sari, C.W.M., Ningsih, E.F., Pratiwi, S.H.: Description of dementia in the elderly status in the work area health center Ibrahim Adjie Bandung. Indones. Contemp. Nurs. J. 1–11 (2018)
5. Wijaya, S., Wahyudi, W., Kusuma, C.B., Sugianto, E.: Travel motivation of Indonesian seniors in choosing destination overseas. Int. J. Cult. Tour. Hosp. Res. (2018)
6. Ali, N.M., Shahar, S., Kee, Y.L., Norizan, A.R., Noah, S.A.M.: Design of an interactive digital nutritional education package for elderly people. Informatics Heal. Soc. Care **37**(4), 217–229 (2012)
7. Mohadis, H.M., Mohamad Ali, N., Smeaton, A.F.: Designing a persuasive physical activity application for older workers: understanding end-user perceptions. Behav. Inf. Technol. **35**(12), 1102–1114 (2016)
8. Oudah, M., Al-Naji, A., Chahl, J.: Elderly care based on hand gestures using kinect sensor. Computers **10**(1), 5 (2021)
9. Doetsch, J., Pilot, E., Santana, P., Krafft, T.: Potential barriers in healthcare access of the elderly population influenced by the economic crisis and the troika agreement: a qualitative case study in Lisbon, Portugal. Int. J. Equity Health **16**(1), 1–17 (2017)
10. Sensuse, D.I., Kareen, P., Noprisson, H., Pratama, M.O.: Success factors for health information system development. In: 2017 International Conference on Information Technology Systems and Innovation (ICITSI), pp. 162–167 (2017)
11. Ayumi, V.: Mobile application for monitoring of addition of drugs to infusion fluids. Int. J. Sci. Res. Comput. Sci. Eng. Inf. Technol. 48–56 (Nov 2019)
12. Ayumi, V.: Performance evaluation of support vector machine algorithm for human gesture recognition. Int. J. Sci. Res. Sci. Eng. Technol. **7**(6), 204–210 (2020)
13. Ramkumar, S., Emayavaramban, G., Sathesh Kumar, K., Macklin Abraham Navamani, J., Maheswari, K., Packia Amutha Priya, P.: Task identification system for elderly paralyzed patients using electrooculography and neural networks. In: EAI International Conference on Big Data Innovation for Sustainable Cognitive Computing, pp. 151–161 (2020)
14. Meurer, J., Stein, M., Randall, D., Wulf, V.: Designing for way-finding as practices–a study of elderly people's mobility. Int. J. Hum. Comput. Stud. **115**, 40–51 (2018)
15. Shohieb, S.M., El-Rashidy, N.M.: A proposed effective framework for elderly with dementia using data mining. In: 2018 International Seminar on Research of Information Technology and Intelligent Systems (ISRITI), pp. 685–689 (2018)
16. Iancu, I., Iancu, B.: Designing mobile technology for elderly. a theoretical overview. Technol. Forecast. Soc. Change **155**, 119977 (2020)
17. Ani, N.: Evaluation method of mobile health apps for the elderly. Int. J. Sci. Res. Comput. Sci. Eng. Inf. Technol. **3307**, 388–394 (2020)
18. Buzzelli, M., Albé, A., Ciocca, G.: A vision-based system for monitoring elderly people at home. Appl. Sci. **10**(1), 374 (2020)
19. Hbali, Y., Hbali, S., Ballihi, L., Sadgal, M.: Skeleton-based human activity recognition for elderly monitoring systems. IET Comput. Vis. **12**(1), 16–26 (2018)
20. Luo, Z., et al.: Computer vision-based descriptive analytics of seniors' daily activities for long-term health monitoring. Mach. Learn. Healthc. **2**, 1 (2018)

21. Anitha, G., Baghavathi Priya, S.: Posture based health monitoring and unusual behavior recognition system for elderly using dynamic Bayesian network. Cluster Comput. **22**(6), 13583–13590 (2019)
22. Ayumi, V., Fanany, M.I.: Multimodal decomposable models by superpixel segmentation and point-in-time cheating detection. In 2016 International Conference on Advanced Computer Science and Information Systems (ICACSIS), pp. 391–396 (2016)
23. Ayumi, V., Ermatita, E., Abdiansah, A., Noprisson, H., Purba, M., Utami, M.: A study on medicinal plant leaf recognition using artificial intelligence. In: 2021 International Conference on Informatics, Multimedia, Cyber and Information System (ICIMCIS, pp. 40–45 (2021)
24. Noprisson, H., Ermatita, E., Abdiansah, A., Ayumi, V., Purba, M., Utami, M.: Hand-woven fabric motif recognition methods: a systematic literature review. In: 2021 International Conference on Informatics, Multimedia, Cyber and Information System (ICIMCIS), pp. 90–95 (2021)
25. Ayumi, V., Fanany, M.I.: A comparison of SVM and RVM for human action recognition. Internetworking Indones. J. **8**(1), 29–33 (2016)
26. Putra, Z.P., Setiawan, D., Priambodo, B., Jumaryadi, Y., DesiAnasanti, M.: Multi-touch gesture of mobile auditory device for visually impaired users. In: 2020 2nd International Conference on Broadband Communications, Wireless Sensors and Powering (BCWSP), pp. 90–95 (2020)
27. Purushothaman, A., Palaniswamy, S.: Development of smart home using gesture recognition for elderly and disabled. J. Comput. Theor. Nanosci. **17**(1), 177–181 (2020)
28. Alam, M., Yousuf, M.A.: Designing and implementation of a wireless gesture controlled robot for disabled and elderly people. In: 2019 International Conference on Electrical, Computer and Communication Engineering (ECCE), pp. 1–6 (2019)
29. Desai, S., Desai, A.: Human computer interaction through hand gestures for home automation using Microsoft Kinect. In: Proceedings of International Conference on Communication and Networks, pp. 19–29 (2017)
30. Baccour, E., Erbad, A., Mohamed, A., Hamdi, M., Guizani, M.: Distprivacy: privacy-aware distributed deep neural networks in iot surveillance systems. In: GLOBECOM 2020–2020 IEEE Global Communications Conference, pp. 1–6 (2020)
31. Dung, C.V., Sekiya, H., Hirano, S., Okatani, T., Miki, C.: A vision-based method for crack detection in gusset plate welded joints of steel bridges using deep convolutional neural networks. Autom. Constr. **102**, 217–229 (2019)

Virtual Reality for Social-Emotional Learning: A Review

Irna Hamzah[1]([✉]), Ely Salwana[1], Mark Billinghurst[2], Nilufar Baghaei[3], Mohammad Nazir Ahmad[1], Fadhilah Rosdi[4], and Azhar Arsad[5]

[1] Institute of Visual Informatics, Universiti Kebangsaan Malaysia, 43600 Bangi, Malaysia
theirnahamzah@gmail.com
[2] Auckland Bioengineering Institute, The University of Auckland, Auckland 1010, New Zealand
[3] Faculty of Engineering, Architecture and Information Technology, The University of Queensland, St Lucia, QLD 4072, Australia
[4] Faculty of Information Science and Technology, Universiti Kebangsaan Malaysia, 43600 Bangi, Malaysia
[5] Tmn Pulai Utama, V3X Malaysia Sdn Bhd. 87A, Jalan Pulai 7, 81110 Skudai Johor, Malaysia

Abstract. Virtual reality (VR) is an immersive technology that can simulate different environments and experiences. Social-emotional learning (SEL) is a process through which individuals develop the skills, knowledge, and attitudes to understand and manage their emotions, establish positive relationships, and make responsible decisions. SEL promotes healthy emotional regulation in adolescents. However, VR interventions for adolescent emotion regulation have received less attention. The aim of this research is to identify a VR element that includes knowledge in relation to SEL since 2017 through systematic literature reviews (SLRs). A broad review of the current literature was conducted in three databases, namely Scopus, IEEE, and WOS. Data were extracted, including age ranges, year published, and medical procedures, using a search term. The result suggests a requirement list to design a virtual reality for social-emotional learning that promotes a positive impact on emotion regulation for Malaysian adolescents.

Keywords: Virtual Reality · Design · Social-Emotional Learning · Emotion Regulation · Mental Health

1 Introduction

Virtual reality or VR can be best described as user experience, stressing the feeling of being present when immersed in virtual environment (Ip et al., 2018) that has been applied in numerous fields namely medical (Bermúdez et al., 2018) and education (R. Liu et al., 2020). VR has been used widely for social emotional learning (SEL) in education field (Green et al., 2021). SEL can be defined as the mechanisms through which individuals acquire and effectively apply the information, attitudes, and skills required to recognize and control their emotions (Lawlor, 2016). VR has been used in the treatment of anxiety disorders (Bermúdez et al., 2018), autism spectrum disorder (Ip et al., 2018) and psychology (Nararro-Haro et al., 2016). Emotion regulation (ER)

© The Author(s), under exclusive license to Springer Nature Singapore Pte Ltd. 2024
H. Badioze Zaman et al. (Eds.): IVIC 2023, LNCS 14322, pp. 119–130, 2024.
https://doi.org/10.1007/978-981-99-7339-2_11

has been one of the most researched constructs in psychology (Colombo et al., 2019). Hadley described ER as a set of processes for controlling feelings and their expression in order to achieve objectives (Hadley et al., 2019). However current VR development does not focus on specific personalized content to treat mental health for instance, in adolescent (X. Liu et al., 2019). The aim of this research is to identify a VR element that includes the knowledge in relation to SEL since 2017 utilizing a tertiary study to review articles on related field and specifically, we are focused on articles that describe systematic literature reviews (SLRs).

2 Related Work

Cipresso examines the evolution and improvements in the use of virtual reality (VR) in the key areas of application over time, with a focus on potential VR capacities, increases, and challenges (Cipresso et al., 2018). Li discusses the use of student participation in the design of virtual reality educational products (Li et al., 2019). The study generated a series of immersive virtual reality-based science lessons for middle-school students and investigated their impact on learning outcomes (R. Liu et al., 2020). VR is a healthy and well-tolerated instrument for exploring neurocognitive deficits and studying related clinical symptoms (Garety et al., 2017). VR has been widely used in the treatment of mental health disorders over the last two decades (Bermúdez et al., 2018).

Social-emotional learning, or SEL are referred to the mechanisms through which individuals acquire and effectively apply information, attitudes, and behavior (Lawlor, 2016). SEL understanding the skills needed to recognize and control their emotions; comprehend another's point of view and demonstrate empathy towards others (Lawlor, 2016). Murphy focuses on investigating way of technology might facilitate social-emotional learning (SEL) among young children (Murphy et al., 2021). The same study also suggests that in both virtual and physical environments, mixed reality holds promise for children to consciously learn dynamic interpersonal skills alongside peers and with the help of adults (Murphy et al., 2021). Emotions can help or hinder academic participation, work ethic, dedication, and ultimately school success in children (Lawlor, 2016). The study presented a randomized controlled trial of the SPARK (Speaking to the Potential, Capacity, and Resilience Within Every Kid) Pre-Teen Mentoring Curriculum for 357 students from two schools (Green et al., 2021). The findings suggest that students who obtained the program demonstrated substantial gains in comprehension of curriculum content and values, communication, decision-making, and problem-solving skills, emotional control, and resilience (Green et al., 2021). Ip describes a virtual reality-based curriculum for children with ASD to improve their emotional and social adaptation skills (Ip et al., 2018). The findings show substantial improvements in the project's primary measures of emotion regulation in children, as well as social-emotional reciprocity, but not in other secondary measures (Ip et al., 2018). Colombo study evaluates emotion regulation (ER) understanding using virtual reality (VR), wearable biosensors, tablets, and biofeedback techniques (Colombo et al., 2019).

The building phase begins with the development of the first model, which is the design model (Seabrook et al., 2020). Framework can be defined as an essential supporting structure of a building, vehicle, or object (Girvan, 2018). The study of Lawlor stressed on a conceptual framework for how mindfulness practices can improve SEL in educational settings (Lawlor, 2016). Application is referred as a computer software package that performs a specific function (Allcoat & von Mühlenen, 2018). Colombo evaluate emotion regulation (ER) understanding using virtual reality (VR), wearable biosensors, tablets, and biofeedback techniques (Colombo et al., 2019).

3   Method

This study has been undertaken as a systematic literature review based on the original guidelines as proposed by Kitchenham (Kitchenham et al., 2009) and Beecham (Beecham et al., 2008). The study is guided by the research question (RQ); What are the elements to design a social-emotional learning using virtual reality to enhance emotion regulation for mental health? The search terms used are; (Design OR Model OR Framework) AND (Element OR Component OR Characteristic) AND (Social OR Emotion* OR Learn*) AND (Virtual OR Reality OR Artificial OR Intelligence OR Simulat*) AND (Emotion* OR Regulation OR Stress) AND (Mental OR Health OR Wellbeing)". The consistent search terms were used in the three databases that stretch between the year of 2017 until 2021.

Scopus, the Institute of Electrical and Electronics Engineers (IEEE), and World of Science (WoS) are the databases that are utilized in the investigation procedure. The years 2017 through 2021 are included in the data that we extract. The search yielded 589 sources from all databases. The discovering approach included each term and filtered the articles numerous times. The article must contain at least two main keywords: "virtual" and "SEL". We check for repeated research to make sure there is no duplication of work before we accept a paper into the review. For instance, we look to see whether the same study has been published in two separate journals. As a result, we decided not to keep using the WoS database because the filter consistently produced the same items. Following the evaluation of the articles' overall quality, we chose the final piece of literature that was most pertinent to our investigation based on our findings. The data analysis was tabulated to show the number of studied published, the scope and the authors affiliations and their institutions. Table 1 indicates the document retrieval we managed to capture along the process. There are over 589 references were found throughout the search. The final articles found in WoS are all the same articles found in Scopus. We then rejected the WoS database, and we only counted twelve (12) final articles.

Table 1. Document Retrieval.

Database	Filter	Selection	Evaluation	Repeated	Retrieval	Final
Scopus	257	63	12	0	12	12
IEEE	67	21	4	3	4	1
WOS	265	73	7	7	7	0
Total	589	157	23	10	23	13

Table 1 illustrates the documents that were retrieved during the search procedure. The data reveals that out of 589 documents, only 13 made it to the last round of review. There were 257 documents from the Scopus database, and 63 were selected in the first round, then it was finalized into 12 documents. Meanwhile, 67 documents were finalized for the IEEE database, leaving 1 after 3 were excluded for repeated papers and 1 did not match the inclusion criteria. There were 265 documents filtered in the WOS database and finalized to none due to inclusion criteria.

3.1 Final Document

Table 2 presents a summary of the final documents identified in the search process.

Table 2. Final Documents

ID	Title
1	A Virtual Reality Study of Experiential Avoidance, Emotional Experiences, and Hoarding Symptoms
2	Design and Implementation of Virtual Examination System Based on Unity 3D
3	Design of Virtual Reality Scenes with Variable Levels of Fear Evocation
4	Detection of Stress Levels from Biosignals Measured in Virtual Reality Environments Using a Kernel-Based Extreme Learning Machine
5	Does Sharing Your Emotion Make You Feel Better? An Empirical Investigation on the Association Between Sharing Emotions on a Virtual Mood Wall and the Relief of Patients' Negative Emotions
6	Induction and Profiling of Strong Multi-Componential Emotions in Virtual Reality
7	Investigating Age-Related Differences in Spatial Presence in Virtual Reality
8	iSAM: Personalizing an Artificial Intelligence Model for Emotion with Pleasure-Arousal-Dominance in Immersive Virtual Reality
9	Understanding How Virtual Reality Can Support Mindfulness Practice: Mixed Methods Study
10	Using EEG to Decode Subjective Levels of Emotional Arousal during an Immersive VR Roller Coaster Ride
11	Using Emotions in Intelligent Virtual Environments: The EJaCalIVE Framework
12	Virtual eye region: development of a realistic model to convey emotion
13	Creating AWE: Artistic and scientific practices in research-based design for exploring a profound immersive installation

The documents in Table 2 collectively provide a comprehensive perspective on the research topic. The varied sources and content of these documents offer a comprehensive foundation for further analysis and exploration of the chosen research topic. Each document has its own unique identification number (ID), which began with 1.

4 Findings: Virtual Reality Design Framework for SEL

Table 3 indicates the design element of VR for SEL based on the 13 final document in the SLR. The design phase is divided into two major area called VR and SEL. Each element represent each document and it has been identified by the special symbol named Paper ID. Each attributes represented the final papers.

Table 3. The VR design element for SEL.

ID	VR	ID	SEL
2	Interactive	1	Emotional
3	Color	1	Behavioral
3	Sound	4	Stress Level
5	Wall	5	Negative Emotions
4	Physiological Signals	6	Fear
7	Customized	6	Joy
8	personalized image	8	happy
9	Auditory	9	focus
11	Interaction	10	brain activity
12	photographic	12	sadness
12	micro-expressions	12	anger
13	physiological sensors	13	wellbeing

Table 3 presents a comprehensive overview of the design elements inherent in the utilization of Virtual Reality (VR) for facilitating Social and Emotional Learning (SEL), as gleaned from the analysis of the 13 final documents obtained through the Systematic Literature Review (SLR) process. This table encapsulates the collective wisdom of these studies, providing insights into the fundamental characteristics that underpin the integration of VR into SEL contexts. The design elements encompass aspects such as VR environments includes color, wall, sound, image, interactive scenarios, avatar customization and narrative engagement. It also suggests an emotional recognition such as brain activity and negative emotions. Each document sheds light on specific design choices and their implications for fostering SEL competencies among learners. The synthesis of these design elements guides the formation of a comprehensive framework for the effective incorporation of VR in SEL interventions, catering to a holistic developmental experience for learners.

The framework is then defined by including the design components. The study's conclusions, a VR design framework for SEL, are depicted in Fig. 1. The designs fall into two categories: virtual reality (VR) and SEL. We organize the data into a theme called thematic synthesis. Thematic synthesis is the identification of prominent or recurring themes in the text, which has some overlap with narrative summary and content analysis, along with summarizing the findings of various studies (Dixon-Woods et al., 2005).

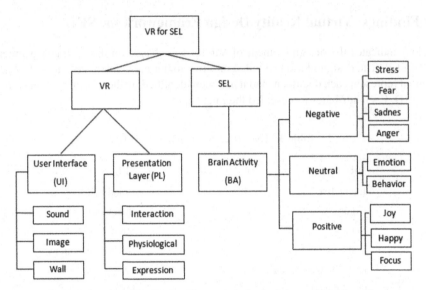

Fig. 1. Virtual Reality Design Framework for Social-emotional Learning

Two main themes were identified, namely, virtual reality (VR) and social-emotional learning (SEL). The VR theme consists of two sub-themes called User Interface (UI) and Presentation Layer (PL). The UI sub-theme includes three attributes: sound, which indicates Paper ID_3, image, which indicates Paper ID_8, and wall, which indicates Paper ID_5. The PL sub-theme includes three attributes: interaction, which indicates Paper ID_11; physiological, which indicates Paper ID_4; and expression, which indicates Paper ID_12. The social-emotional learning (SEL) theme consists of one sub-theme called brain activity (BA). The BA sub-theme is divided into three themes, namely, negative, neutral, and positive. The negative theme consists of stress from Paper ID_4, fear from Paper ID_6, sadness from Paper ID_12, and anger from Paper ID_12. While neutral, consist of emotional and behavioral, both from Paper ID_1. Lastly, positives consist of joy from Paper ID_6, Happy from Paper ID_8 and focus from Paper ID_9.

5 Discussion

Thematic analysis is a qualitative research method widely employed for exploring and understanding the rich complexities of textual data. Central to this analytical approach are themes, which serve as the building blocks to extract meaning, patterns, and insights from the data. Themes represent recurring ideas, concepts, or patterns of meaning that emerge during the process of data analysis, providing a structured framework for interpreting and organizing qualitative information. Our findings suggest two crucial main themes for design element in developing a VR design for SEL and each theme specifically describe the sub themes that is essential in VR design for SEL because each element is related to other elements. Sound, image and wall are crucial to design a VR user interface. Meanwhile, interaction, physiological and expression are highly need in developing the presentation layer for VR design in SEL.

5.1 Virtual Reality (VR)

User Interface (UI). The user interface (UI) in the context of human-computer interaction (HCI) refers to the point of interaction between humans and digital systems. It encompasses all the visual, auditory, and tactile elements that enable users to interact with and control computers, software applications, and other digital devices. A well-designed user interface is essential for creating a seamless and intuitive user experience, facilitating effective communication between users and technology. Figure 2 indicates one of the main themes in designing the VR framework for SEL namely, presentation layer (PL) and user interface (UI). The four attributes for the UI are highly needed in the process of designing the VR for SEL. Paper ID_3 stress that the "sound" with the narrative rhythm should be consider in developing the VR for SEL (Liao et al., 2018). Hohman suggest that VR technology use in the lab for designing complex audiovisual communication environments for hearing assessment and hearing device design and evaluation (Hohmann et al., 2020). Paper ID_8 designed iSAM which successfully learn from user affect to better predict a personalized "image" than static base model (Elor and Song, 2020). Paper ID_5 evaluate whether sharing one's emotions on the virtual mood "wall" is associated with the relief of the patient's negative emotions (X. Liu et al., 2019).

Presentation Layer (PL). The presentation layer is a crucial component within the design process, playing a pivotal role in shaping the user experience and interface of a digital product or application. In the design process, the presentation layer is responsible for translating the raw data and functionalities of the application's core into a visually coherent and user-friendly interface. Paper ID_11 described a robot as a humanoid to ease the "interaction" with the people on its environment (Rincon et al., 2017). Interaction is the degree in which users of a medium can influence the content of the environment, is one of the key features of Virtual Reality. Paper ID_4 described a compact wearable device classifying stress levels using "physiological" signals (Cho et al., 2017). Paper ID_13 involved phenomenological interviews and physiological sensors to evaluate the evoked emotional experiences, which then inform design decisions to improve the system (Quesnel et al., 2018). Paper ID_12 has designed a realistic virtual model of the eye region which can display the "micro-expressions" necessary to transmit an emotional state to an observer (Barrett et al., 2019).

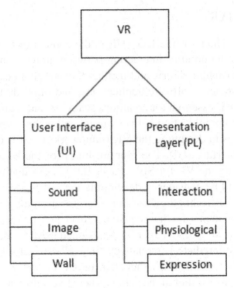

Fig. 2. VR theme

5.2 Social-emotional Learning (SEL)

Themes are not merely descriptive labels; they encapsulate deeper layers of significance within the data. A theme represents a coherent pattern of shared meaning or understanding across various segments of the data set. Thus, the second theme is the one concerned with social-emotional learning (SEL), as depicted in Fig. 3.

Brain Activity (BA). As a result, from the SLR, we found that VR design approaches managed to counter negative brain activity such as stress, fear, sadness and anger. While participant using the VR, the brain activity is in the neutral state which involved both emotional and behavioural. Moreover, we found an output of positive brain activity such as joy, happy and focus which occurred after participants experienced the VR approach which result.

Negative. Paper ID_4 suggests a compact wearable device classifying "stress" levels using physiological signals (Cho et al., 2017). Paper ID_6 stressed that design a virtual environment using HCI (HMD) device with an interactive and immersive realistic 3D graphic scene for exposure therapy of acrophobia that allows patient to sense height and gets used to the "fearful" feelings (Abdullah and Shaikh, 2018). Paper ID_12 suggest a clear relationship between the recognition levels for both photographic and virtual stimuli plus a significant level of emotional perception was found for the virtual eye expressions of "sadness" and "anger" (Barrett et al., 2019).

Neutral. Paper ID_1 examined relationship between hoarding severity and emotional components of HD using a virtual reality (VR) paradigm (McCabe-Bennett et al., 2020). Study also suggest that VR tasks can be used for training and assessment of emotion recognition (Geraets et al., 2021). Paper ID_1 suggest a model provides mixed support for emotional and behavioral components (McCabe-Bennett et al., 2020).

Positive. Paper ID_6 identified joy and fear clusters of responses, each involving changes in appraisal, motivation, physiology, feeling, and regulation (Meuleman and Rudrauf, 2021). Carrying out amusing activities, and experiencing positive emotions within the virtual reality can bring joy to the users of VR glasses (Hartl and Berger, 2017). Paper ID_8 found that users felt iSAM to be interesting and found the final image to feel happy from final images produced by each user (Elor and Song, 2020). Paper ID_9 suggested that the use of VR helped to focus on the present moment by using visual and auditory elements of VR as attentional anchors (Seabrook et al., 2020).

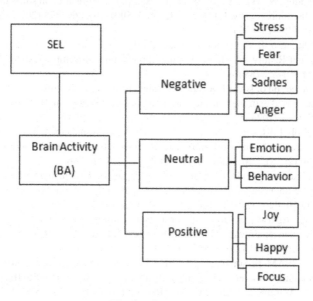

Fig. 3. SEL theme

6 Discussion

The aim of this research is to identify a specific VR element for social emotional learning. As an answer to the RQ, the findings suggest that the element to design a social-emotional learning using virtual reality to enhance emotion regulation for mental health are based on two main themes namely, VR and SEL elements. The result also suggests a require-ment list to design a virtual reality for social emotional learning which could enhanced emotions regulations in Malaysian adolescent's mental health.

Acknowledgment. We would like to express our sincere gratitude to all parties that have sup-ported and contributed to the completion of this research project. This study is fully funded by The Ministry of Education, Malaysia under Trans-disciplinary Research Grant Scheme (TRGS) of the Ministry of Education, TRGS/1/2020/UKM/01/4/3.

References

Abdullah, M., Shaikh, Z.A.: An effective virtual reality based Remedy for acrophobia. Int. J. Adva. Comp. Sci. Appli. **9**(6), 162–167 (2018). https://doi.org/10.14569/IJACSA.2018.090623

Allcoat, D., von Mühlenen, A.: Learning in virtual reality: effects on performance, emotion and engagement. Research in Learning Technology **26**(1063519), 1–13 (2018). https://doi.org/10.25304/rlt.v26.2140

Barrett, S., Weimer, F., Cosmas, J.: Virtual eye region: development of a realistic model to convey emotion. Heliyon **5**(12), e02778 (2019). https://doi.org/10.1016/j.heliyon.2019.e02778

Beecham, S., Baddoo, N., Hall, T., Robinson, H., Sharp, H.: Motivation in software engineering: a systematic literature review. Inf. Softw. Technol. **50**(9–10), 860–878 (2008). https://doi.org/10.1016/j.infsof.2007.09.004

Bermúdez, S., Quintero, L.V., Cameirão, M.S., Chirico, A., Triberti, S.: Towards Emotionally-Adaptive Virtual Reality for Mental Health Applications. November (2018). https://doi.org/10.1109/JBHI.2018.2878846

Cho, D., et al.: Detection of stress levels from biosignals measured in virtual reality environments using a kernel-based extreme learning machine. Sensors (Switzerland) **17**(10) (2017). https://doi.org/10.3390/s17102435

Cipresso, P., Giglioli, I.A.C., Raya, M.A., Riva, G.: The past, present, and future of virtual and augmented reality research: a network and cluster analysis of the literature. Frontiers in Psychology **9**(NOV), 1–20 (2018). https://doi.org/10.3389/fpsyg.2018.02086

Colombo, D., Fernández-álvarez, J., Palacios, A.G., Cipresso, P., Botella, C., Riva, G.: New technologies for the understanding, assessment, and intervention of emotion regulation. Frontiers in Psychology **10**(JUN) (2019). https://doi.org/10.3389/fpsyg.2019.01261

Dixon-Woods, M., Agarwal, S., Jones, D., Young, B., Sutton, A.: Synthesising qualitative and quantitative evidence: a review of possible methods. J. Health Serv. Res. Policy **10**(1), 45–53 (2005). https://doi.org/10.1258/1355819052801804

Elor, A., Song, A.: ISAM: personalizing an artificial intelligence model for emotion with pleasure-arousal-dominance in immersive virtual reality. In: Proceedings - 2020 15th IEEE International Conference on Automatic Face and Gesture Recognition, FG, pp. 572–576 (2020). https://doi.org/10.1109/FG47880.2020.00091

Featherstone, I., et al.: The experience of delirium in palliative care settings for patients, family, clinicians and volunteers: a qualitative systematic review and thematic synthesis. Palliat. Med. **35**(6), 988–1004 (2021). https://doi.org/10.1177/02692163211006313

Flores, A., Linehan, M.M., Todd, S.R., Hoffman, H.G.: The use of virtual reality to facilitate mindfulness skills training in dialectical behavioral therapy for spinal cord injury: a case study. Frontiers in Psychology **9**(APR), 1–7 (2018). https://doi.org/10.3389/fpsyg.2018.00531

Garety, P., Sason, E., Craig, T.J.K., Valmaggia, L.R.: Virtual reality in the assessment and treatment of psychosis : a systematic review of its utility, acceptability and effectiveness (2017). https://doi.org/10.1017/S0033291717001945

Geraets, C.N.W., et al.: Virtual reality facial emotion recognition in social environments: an eye-tracking study. Internet Interventions **25**(December 2020), 100432 (2021). https://doi.org/10.1016/j.invent.2021.100432

Gerry, L.J.: Paint with me: stimulating creativity and empathy while painting with a painter in virtual reality. IEEE Trans. Visual Comput. Graphics **23**(4), 1418–1426 (2017). https://doi.org/10.1109/TVCG.2017.2657239

Girvan, C.: What is a virtual world? definition and classification. Education Tech. Research Dev. **66**(5), 1087–1100 (2018). https://doi.org/10.1007/s11423-018-9577-y

Green, A.L., Ferrante, S., Boaz, T.L., Kutash, K., Wheeldon-Reece, B.: Social and emotional learning during early adolescence: effectiveness of a classroom-based SEL program for middle school students. Psychology in the Schools November 2020, 1–14 (2021). https://doi.org/10. 1002/pits.22487

Hadley, W., Houck, C., Brown, L.K., Spitalnick, J.S., Ferrer, M., Barker, D.: Moving beyond role-play: evaluating the use of virtual reality to teach emotion regulation for the prevention of adolescent risk behavior within a randomized pilot trial. J. Pediatr. Psychol. **44**(4), 425–435 (2019). https://doi.org/10.1093/jpepsy/jsy092

Hartl, E., Berger, B.: Escaping reality: Examining the role of presence and escapism in user adoption of virtual reality glasses. In: Proceedings of the 25th European Conference on Information Systems, ECIS 2017, 2413–2428 (2017)

Hidaka, K., Qin, H., Kobayashi, J.: Preliminary test of affective virtual reality scenes with head mount display for emotion elicitation experiment. International Conference on Control, Automation and Systems, 2017-Octob, pp. 325–329 (2017). https://doi.org/10.23919/ICCAS. 2017.8204459

Hohmann, V., Paluch, R., Krueger, M., Meis, M., Grimm, G.: The virtual reality lab: realization and application of virtual sound environments. Ear Hear. **41**, 31S-38S (2020). https://doi.org/ 10.1097/AUD.0000000000000945

Ip, H.H.S., et al.: Enhance emotional and social adaptation skills for children with autism spectrum disorder: a virtual reality enabled approach. Comput. Educ. **117**, 1–15 (2018). https://doi.org/ 10.1016/j.compedu.2017.09.010

Kitchenham, B., Pearl Brereton, O., Budgen, D., Turner, M., Bailey, J., Linkman, S.: Systematic literature reviews in software engineering - A systematic literature review. Inf. Softw. Technol. **51**(1), 7–15 (2009). https://doi.org/10.1016/j.infsof.2008.09.009

Klotzsche, F., Mariola, A., Hofmann, S., Nikulin, V.V., Villringer, A., Gaebler, M.: Using EEG to decode subjective levels of emotional arousal during an immersive VR roller coaster ride. In: 25th IEEE Conference on Virtual Reality and 3D User Interfaces, VR 2018 - Proceedings, March, pp. 605–606 (2018). https://doi.org/10.1109/VR.2018.8446275

Lawlor, M.S.:. Mindfulness and Social Emotional Learning (SEL): A Conceptual Framework. 65–80 (2016). https://doi.org/10.1007/978-1-4939-3506-2_5

Li, Z., Cheng, X., Wang, L., He, H., Liang, B.: The application of student participation in the design of virtual reality educational products. In: Lecture Notes in Computer Science (including subseries Lecture Notes in Artificial Intelligence and Lecture Notes in Bioinformatics): Vol. 11585 LNCS. Springer International Publishing (2019). https://doi.org/10.1007/978-3-030- 23538-3_34

Liao, D., Huang, Y., Tan, Z., Yang, J., Xu, X.: Design of virtual reality scenes with variable levels of fear evocation. In: Lecture Notes in Computer Science (including subseries Lecture Notes in Artificial Intelligence and Lecture Notes in Bioinformatics): Vol. 10910 LNCS. Springer International Publishing (2018). https://doi.org/10.1007/978-3-319-91584-5_9

Liu, R., Wang, L., Lei, J., Wang, Q., Ren, Y.: Effects of an immersive virtual reality-based classroom on students' learning performance in science lessons. Br. J. Edu. Technol. **51**(6), 2034–2049 (2020). https://doi.org/10.1111/bjet.13028

Liu, X., Pan, M., Li, J.: Does sharing your emotion make you feel better? an empirical investigation on the association between sharing emotions on a virtual mood wall and the relief of patients' negative emotions. Telemedicine and E-Health **25**(10), 987–995 (2019). https://doi.org/10. 1089/tmj.2017.0327

Luo, D., Deng, X.L., Luo, Y.W., Wang, G.X.: Design and implementation of virtual examination system based on unity 3D. In: ACM International Conference Proceeding Series (2019). https:// doi.org/10.1145/3358331.3358404

McCabe-Bennett, H., Provost-Walker, O., Lachman, R., Girard, T.A., Antony, M.M.: A virtual reality study of experiential avoidance, emotional experiences, and hoarding symptoms. J. Obse.-Compul. Rela. Disor. **27**, 100590 (2020). https://doi.org/10.1016/j.jocrd.2020.100590

Meuleman, B., Rudrauf, D.: Induction and profiling of strong multi-componential emotions in virtual reality. IEEE Trans. Affect. Comput. **12**(1), 189–202 (2021). https://doi.org/10.1109/TAFFC.2018.2864730

Murphy, K.M., Cook, A.L., Fallon, L.M.: Mixed reality simulations for social-emotional learning. Phi Delta Kappan **102**(6), 30–37 (2021). https://doi.org/10.1177/0031721721998152

Nararro-Haro, M.V., et al.: The use of virtual reality to facilitate mindfulness skills training in dialectical behavioral therapy for borderline personality disorder: A case study. Frontiers in Psychology **7**(NOV), 1–9 (2016). https://doi.org/10.3389/fpsyg.2016.01573

Quesnel, D., Stepanova, E.R., Aguilar, I.A., Pennefather, P., Riecke, B.E.: Creating AWE: artistic and scientific practices in research-based design for exploring a profound immersive installation. In: 2018 IEEE Games, Entertainment, Media Conference, GEM 2018, December, pp. 200–207 (2018). https://doi.org/10.1109/GEM.2018.8516463

Rincon, J.A., Costa, A., Novais, P., Julian, V., Carrascosa, C.: Using emotions in intelligent virtual environments: The EJaCalIVE framework. Wireless Communications and Mobile Computing (2017). https://doi.org/10.1155/2017/9321463

Seabrook, E., Kelly, R., Foley, F., Theiler, S., Thomas, N., Wadley, G., Nedeljkovic, M.: Understanding how virtual reality can support mindfulness practice: mixed methods study. J. Medi. Inter. Res. **22**(3) (2020). https://doi.org/10.2196/16106

Embodied Narrative: Data Storytelling of Online Artwork Experiences

Hanif Baharin[1](✉), Afdallyna Fathiyah Harun[2], and Noris Mohd Norowi[3]

[1] Institute of Visual Informatics, Universiti Kebangsaan Malaysia, UKM, 43600 Bangi, Selangor, Malaysia
hbaharin@ukm.edu.my

[2] School of Computing Sciences, College of Computing, Informatics and Mathematics, Universiti Teknologi MARA Shah Alam, 40450 Shah Alam, Selangor, Malaysia

[3] Faculty of Computer Science and Information Technology, Universiti Putra Malaysia, 43400 Serdang, Selangor, Malaysia

Abstract. This paper describes a pilot ethnomethodology study of visiting a 3D virtual gallery that exhibits 3D models of physical artworks and of viewing photographs of artworks in a 2D online artist portfolio. Artwork, with its intrinsic information and layers of meaning, is a form of data which narrates a compelling and evocative story to engage audience. The digital landscape is a compelling medium to deliver this storytelling. However, such approach demands a delicate balance between technology incorporation and artistic vision. In an era of converging data and art, this paper explores the aesthetics of data storytelling and immersive online art experiences. Amid CoVID-19 lockdowns, physical art exhibitions migrated online, prompting a study of 3D virtual gallery visits and 2D online artist portfolios. Participants engaged in think-aloud protocols while navigating both formats, revealing insights into rationalizing actions and interpreting artworks online. Challenges emerged, including disrupted responses due to the inability to discern texture in 3D models or artwork photos. Navigational control, viewing distance, detailed artwork descriptions, and stable internet connections further influenced the online viewing experience. This prompts a further exploration on means to curate online exhibitions thoughtfully, where data aesthetics and artistic storytelling is harmonized for realistic interpretation within the digital expanse.

Keywords: 3D Virtual Gallery · Online Artist Portfolio · Ethnomethodology · Think Aloud Protocol

1 Introduction

Digital realm has served as platforms to support execution of tasks in both professional and personal settings. The richness of the digital realm is harnessed through archetyping – how technologies can be reconfigured incorporating social arrangements for contemporary society. This is enabled by mimicking some universal patterns of human nature, enabling a more intuitive participation in the digital realm. The art community

H. Badioze Zaman et al. (Eds.): IVIC 2023, LNCS 14322, pp. 131–141, 2024.
https://doi.org/10.1007/978-981-99-7339-2_12

has also utilized digital platforms for online art exhibition. This allows visitors to not only view art exhibits but to also interact with them. An art exhibition comes in many forms such as photography, paintings, and sculpture, among others. Utilizing the digital realm as an exhibition space, these artworks are digitally captured as images or rendered as 3D virtual contents. This begets several questions that we feel are important to explore. Some artworks require a 360-degree view and come in sensory presentation, are they justifiably presented in terms of its structural or elemental build up? Does the digital realm hinder the honest presentation of these art exhibits due to the present technological constraints?

This paper reports a pilot ethnomethodology study of the experience of viewing artworks in virtual online environments. It also presents the challenges in viewing artworks online and discusses design considerations relating to the development of future online galleries. Restrictions on social contacts and gatherings is the main motivation for this study, as art galleries and museums are forced to close or could only have limited visitors during the Covid-19 global pandemic. As an alternative, museums, galleries, and artists created online exhibitions. Prior to the pandemic, some art galleries, museums, and artists have had virtual exhibitions, but these are usually in conjunction with the exhibitions in their physical spaces. Conversely, the pandemic has abruptly made stand-alone online exhibitions, or online exhibitions without physical counterparts a more viable alternative.

This pilot study was undertaken as a response to a situation faced by a group of artists. A commercial art gallery has had to employ a stand-alone online exhibition as a result of the Covid-19 pandemic. This meant that the work would be displayed online only. The gallery had prior experience in hosting virtual exhibitions using 3D renderings of the gallery space and the artefacts exhibits, but were usually paired with exhibitions in their gallery's physical space. Some of the concerns following the decision by the organizer and the gallery to do the online exhibition only, included that the artworks may not be fully appreciated or understood by visitors if presented via 3D renderings. Thus, this pilot study was conducted as a precursor to future work that will involve participatory design of an online art exhibition with a curator, artists, and members of the audience. The challenges which stemmed from this study are presented in this paper, along with the design considerations for future online exhibitions.

2 Related Work

Web-based or virtual galleries have been researched and developed since the 90's. One of the earliest works on virtual galleries used HTML and VRML [1]. Catton and Smith's temporal analysis of virtual exhibitions for gallery, library, archives, and museum (GLAM) institutions shows that virtual exhibitions have evolved from being websites to fully immersive virtual experiences using VR headsets [2]. Whilst the proliferation of internet use in the 90's provided the catalyst for web-based virtual environment (VE) for exhibitions, it was in the 2000s that the technology for VE in the form of 3D rendering technology was being developed and refined [2]. One example of such development is the Augmented Representation of Cultural Objects (ARCO) project [3]. The project aims to provide 3D archiving of museum artefacts so that artefacts that are costly to maintain or fragile in nature can be observed and appreciated by more audiences without the extra costs of transport and security.

3D representation and Virtual Reality (VR) that enables interactions with 3D artefacts were developed in the 2010's [2]. Virtual exhibition has since been associated with immersive VR experience with the availability for VR headsets in the consumer market [2]. However, when the Covid-19 pandemic hit, GLAM institutions had to quickly create virtual exhibitions [2]. VR or AR have been applied in GLAM context to enhance audience experience at museums and galleries [4, 5]. Despite the availability of VR headsets in the market, they are not widely used compared to mobile phones and computers. With such preference, virtual exhibitions seem to be limited to web browsers (accessible by mobile phones and computers) and very few in between employ VR-based art exhibitions.

In hindsight, online platforms to exhibit art are now fast emerging. This is partly due to the COVID19 pandemic putting a constraint on physical exhibition but also a better embracement to the digital age. What may have begun as a force majeure slowly transformed into a democratization process of sharing artworks that transcend geographical barriers as the conventional means largely means only exhibiting to a particular locality. This pursues convenience and accessibility of an even wider audience [6], leading to higher engagement rates and exposure [7]. Online platforms are also more economically attractive as exhibiting in traditional galleries can be very costly particularly for new artists [8]. Online platforms with engagement features could foster a sense of proximity between the artist and the audience and in turn help gather valuable feedback to the artwork [9] creating a win-win situation for all parties involved. Moreover, online platforms can capture digital trails serving data-driven insights [7] for artists to better understand audience preferences and tailor their artistic endeavors accordingly. In addition [10], argues that, although online exhibitions can facilitate experience not afforded by physical exhibitions, such as interacting with digital copies of artefacts which usually cannot be touched, and the artefacts can be enhanced with digital multimedia contents. However, viewing a digitized representation of a physical artefact reduces "encounter that a physical display can facilitate." This is because people perceive values in the 'real things' that link the objects with the times in the past, or with people admired for their achievements [10].

Despite the advantages an online platform may offer, not all artists are enthusiastic. As art can be in various forms, shapes, textures and dimensions, the lack of a physical platform to appreciate these elements can be a drawback. However, an experiment conducted by Lin [11], that quantitatively measures if viewing artworks physically, on a head-mounted VR display, and on desktop VR differs on a set of subjective feedbacks asked in a questionnaire, shows that there is no significant different in responses in the three settings the artworks are viewed. The study suggests the design of virtual art exhibitions should focus on the readability of texts and the size of the artwork images instead [11]. Besides that, intellectual property protection is a huge concern as there is no clear form of control to unauthorized reproduction of artwork [12]. Curatorial arrangements on an online platform can be challenging due to the vastness and lack of tangible characteristics as usually found in traditional galleries [13, 14]. This is part and parcel of the situation faced by our group of artists, who must exhibit their artworks in a web-based 3D virtual gallery in a virtual exhibition that does not have a physical counterpart.

All of these factors combined could potentially affect the formation of meaningful engagement between the artwork and the audience, as intended by the artist. The fleeting nature of online interactions can hinder deep engagement with artworks [15], making audiences either missing the complex narratives or emotionally disengaged from the full sensory richness of the artwork [16]. Contrary to the finite space offered by a physical gallery, the vastness of online platforms may inadvertently be used to exhibit many artworks. This makes it challenging for individual pieces to stand out making it harder to retain audience attention.

We argue that, in a time of pandemic, encountering digitized versions of physical artefacts is better than not seeing them at all. The need to conduct a fully virtual exhibition is not unique to our group of artists. The 2020 Biennale of Sydney had to close two weeks after it opened and moved the exhibitions to Google Arts & Culture [17]. Meanwhile, Dentro, a Portugal based artist-run space, curated an online exhibition by asking artists to create artworks based on the photos and videos of the physical space sent to them. The produced digital works were then displayed on the artists' Facebook and Instagram pages [17].

We postulate that the transition from physical exhibitions to purely digital exhibitions may take full advantage of the interactivity and information accessibility afforded by a virtual space. In this research, we aim to describe the moment-by-moment actions that people take to make sense of their experience of viewing 3D representations of physical artefacts in a virtual gallery and the experience of viewing photographic images of physical artworks in a 2D online artist portfolio. Research that studies the comparison between 2D and 3D web-based art exhibitions have found advantages and disadvantages for both formats [18]. Communication of information is better with 2D representation compared to 3D representation as the latter distract users by having to focus on navigating the 3D world instead of focusing on the displayed artefacts simulated in it [9]. Despite this distraction, a 3D virtual exhibition provides more enjoyment to the users not afforded by a 2D website [18]. As aforementioned, each medium has its pros and cons. It must be acknowledged that the effectiveness of a virtual exhibition as a form of communication and artefact experience is dependent on the audience background and motivation, the social aspects provided by the exhibition and most importantly, the quality of the content and the robustness of the information system that hosts the exhibition [19]. This research is different from previous research that compares 2D and 3D online exhibitions and the efficacy of the types of media used for virtual exhibitions in the sense that this research looks at how people account for their viewing of digital representations of physical artefacts. By describing these accounts, the contribution of this paper is in the theoretical discussions about the embodied meanings of artworks and the translation of meanings across different media.

3 Implementation

In line with HCI research tradition that uses ethnomethodological approach [20], the aim of this pilot ethnomethodology study is to elicit how people account for their experience of viewing digital representations of artworks in online environments. These behaviors are governed by rationalization of actions displayed and known by the social actors [21]. From these experiences, the challenges which are faced are recorded and design considerations are then suggested.

3.1 Method

Due to the CoViD-19 pandemic, this research was conducted online. Nine participants were recruited (4M:6F), between 18–50 years old of age. Participants and the researcher met online using Zoom. The researcher demonstrated to the participants how to do a think aloud protocol whilst they visited a virtual gallery and a web portfolio. The participants were given the link to the virtual gallery and were asked to share their screen. They were asked to visit the virtual gallery for 30 min, but they could choose to end early. After the participants visited the virtual gallery, they were given a link and asked to visit the 2D online artist portfolio. A post-visit interview was conducted by employing open-ended questions to clarify the comments made by the participants during the think aloud session and for in-depth understanding on the meanings and intentions of their actions in the virtual gallery and the 2D online artist portfolio. Each of the Zoom sessions were recorded and then transcribed. Analysis was done using the same approach by Crabtree et al. [22], which do not follow constructive analysis and documentary interpretation.

3.2 Virtual Gallery

The virtual gallery and artist portfolio used in this research are copyrighted therefore the detailed images of some parts of the gallery and the portfolio were pixelated so that they could not be recognizable in our description. The virtual gallery platform in this research displayed 3D representations of a physical gallery space, while the artworks displayed in this virtual gallery are 3D renderings of the physical artworks. The virtual gallery is accessible through a website. There are the navigation circles placed in front of every artwork on the floor which lit up and pulsated to attract the users' attention (Fig. 1). Users could click on these navigation circles throughout the floor of the virtual gallery to view the artworks. At the bottom right corner of each artwork there is a floating 'i' (information) button which will pop-up a window to display information on the title, artist's name, materials used, and size of the artwork (Fig. 2). Videos will be played automatically in the pop-up.

3.3 Artist Online Portfolio

In the second part of the study, participants were given a link to an artist's online portfolio. Their artworks are displayed as a collage of photographs in the 'Gallery' page of the website. Users could click on a photo, and it will be enlarged to fit the browser. Additionally, users could also click and drag to the left or right to see another artwork in the collection (Fig. 3). An About' page with a short description of the artist and the technique they used was also provided for each artwork.

Fig. 1. The navigation circle on the floor in front of an artwork.

Fig. 2. The "i" button next to a painting

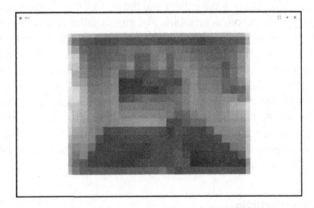

Fig. 3. Artwork viewed in the enlarged view

4 Results

The results obtained are taken from the think aloud sessions and interviews with the nine participants. The data is then analyzed, and the challenges encountered is presented.

4.1 Navigation

The ability to navigate in 3D was the most important feature of the online gallery. In general, users would take some time to figure out how to navigate in the 3D world, but once they knew how to navigate, they could easily jump from artwork to artwork by clicking on the navigation circles on the 3D virtual gallery floor. It was also highlighted that although the navigation circle in front of the artwork had already been animated to pulsate to attract attentions, it was still easily be overlooked, as users tend to place their focus on the visual display first. Another main issue with navigation is relating to the view control. For example, if the camera view had accidentally moved on to areas other than the artwork, it was found that some users had struggled to return to the camera view back to the artwork.

P3: Ok, figure painting exposition of non-figurative art. What shall I do? This, keep on clicking on the circle there. Go to see the painting okay. I am able to move around to see the painting, it's very interesting.

P1: If I look at the display, this is the one that is attracts my attention... But how do I go there? Usually people can click here [the navigation circle], if they are impatient and want to go there straightaway, they won't be able to do it.

4.2 Viewing Distance

Users had reported that there were not able to change the viewing distance between themselves and the artworks. This felt unnatural and rigid to them, as typically, in a real-world setting, they would tend to move to gain different perspectives on the work, i.e. stand further and then move closer to the work. In addition, users also expressed that a zoom-in feature was needed, as they it would enable them to study the materials and certain aspects of the work, enlarged.

P7: But when I go to a (physical) gallery, how is it? Usually, if I go (to physical gallery) sometimes I look (at an artwork) from afar, and then try to interpret. And then I will do near (to see the painting up close).

P6: I don't get the satisfactions when viewing some of the artworks. For some artworks you really have to have a closer look to see and appreciate what the artist did, how they layered the colors, how they layered the things, you know, mixed media, like in mixed media. So, we know what kind of media they used. But when I can't zoom in, I feel a little bit frustrated.

P4: Hm...and I think it's like with some of the paintings, [...] you know paintings are very like textural. [...], I think you can't really get that textural feel if you are not in there personally. Like you're not there physically. You can't really see, like the texture and how certain texture...off the paper sort of thing, are off the canvas. So it's like virtually you can't just replicate.

4.3 3D Online Gallery Versus 2D Online Artist Portfolio

After the participants ended their 3D gallery visit, they were asked to view the artworks of a textile and paint artist on a web portfolio. The same interactions occurred in a 2D website, where the participants switched between navigating the website, viewing, and interpreting the artworks, and reading. In all cases, browsing a 2D website was faster than navigating a 3D gallery. However, the participants felt that the viewing experience was a less explorative, and even compared it to the interactions they had with viewing their phones' photo gallery, Instagram, reading a book or just browsing a website. Hence, although navigation was found to be easier on a 2D website, a 3D virtual gallery provided more values even though it took more effort to navigate.

P3: ...the purpose is to have similar experience as though as we are in an art gallery. If I am to see for example this particular photo gallery, I might as well go to Instagram I can scroll through the Instagram and see the photos. But the experience of actually going into a virtual art gallery [...]. So, I find it's different because if you want to see photos you can just, photos, even photos on Instagram have captions.

P5: In terms of navigation the (2D online portfolio) is easier, but the sense of being in a gallery, the (3D gallery is better).

4.4 Lack of Dimensionality

When a tangible, 3D sculpture in the real-world was represented in a flat, still 2D image online, some participants had difficulties in deciding an artwork was a painting or an image of a sculpture. This was due to the lack of dimensionality that images depicted. This was true for both the 3D gallery and the 2D online portfolio, where participants only identified the materials of the artworks by reading the description of the work. In some cases, participants had zoomed into the photos, but they still could not clearly identify the texture.

P1: Ah, it doesn't look like fabric here...so if I go nearer [zoom in on 3D model]. Maybe this 3D model, has to be more real I think...because the woods, I can see the woods, but to say, fabric, I don't know, maybe I will say that this thing looks like a banner or plastic.

P9: So it's not really a canvas painting. They are actually, textile, put them together. So, so what I'm seeing here is not really paintings. I thought they were paintings. So sorry... But I don't know, I kinda like (their) work.

4.5 Internet Connection

Half of the participants reported that they had experienced slow internet connection at some point during the online gallery tour, which affected the overall experience. Typically, in this setting, fast internet connection is needed to be able to fully enjoy a 3D online gallery. Viewing the 2D online artist portfolio required significantly less internet bandwidth but provided lesser visual support. Most participants agreed that that they preferred 3D gallery but acknowledged that a good internet connection was imperative.

P2: I prefer the [3D gallery]. Because even though...for a (3D Gallery) we need a strong internet connection. When the internet connection is stable than we don't experience lagging when we want to rotate, move forward or backward.

P9: I personally would prefer the virtual art gallery because it, because it made me go round [chuckles] to view...but...at the same time, it also depends on your speed connection et cetera. So, if connection speed is an issue, I would prefer the (2D artist's portfolio).

4.6 Information Scarcity

Half of the participants also expressed that they wanted more information to be provided in the 3D Gallery, in addition to the descriptions provided e.g., artist's name, title of the work, media used, and the size. One participant suggested to have an e-catalogue available, comparing the 3D virtual gallery experience with visiting a physical gallery where catalogues and brochures were common.

P4: So, I think one thing that's sort of missing from, if I compare my experience then and my experience now, it's like I think one is like, what is lacking from this sort of gallery viewing right now is, like each painting like for example, like this one, it doesn't necessarily have a lot of like information on the painting itself.

P1: Because, like when I go to, like the National Art Gallery, there is a bit more description. Who made it? And what are they trying to convey.

5 Discussion

There are two main contributions of this paper – (1) the theoretical discussion on the loss of embodied meanings in the digital representations of some forms of artworks; and (2) the general guidelines in designing an online gallery. The results show that users focused more attention on navigation in a 3D gallery compared to in a 2D website. Although navigating a 3D gallery requires more effort, and the experience can be hampered by a slow internet connection, the participants perceived values in the ability to explore a 3D space. Our work replicated the findings by Kim and Hong [9] which demonstrated that visitors of 3D galleries relate their experience of a 3D world to navigation and manipulation, while browsing a 2D website is like reading a book.

Our findings brought up the theoretical discussion on the loss of embodied meanings in the digital representations of some forms of artworks [17]. Argue that digital representation of a physical exhibition cannot replicate the "aura" of physical works and space. We agree with this view, perhaps, there is something special in being able to see the real thing. However, some forms of arts do not need the "aura of physicality" and can be translated into digital forms better than others, e.g. movies, songs, books, and dance performances. We argue that how well an artwork translates from one medium to another depends on how well its embodied meanings can be translated across media. For instance, a story can be told orally or written in a book. In a book, some aspects of storytelling, such as the orator's voice, tones, and inflections are missing, but the essence of the story, which is embodied in the language, is not lost.

On the other hand, for physical art artefacts, such as paintings, sculptures or installations, the meanings of such artworks are embodied in their materiality, e.g., strokes of a brush, textured patterns on the canvas, etc. As we have shown in our findings, our participants tried to interpret the artworks they saw in the 3D gallery and the 2D online portfolio. This is in line with Grayling's art function to elicit response [23]. However, the response in the audience cannot be completed because the embodied meanings of the artworks in their texture and materials are lost when converted to 3D representations or photographs. This is similar to the findings in the research by Wolf, Reinhardt and Funk [24], which compares user experience of a physical exhibition and a VR version of the exhibition. It was demonstrated that the ability to zoom into digital artefacts is important in order to ascertain the materials of the artwork from the 3D representations and make the experience feel similar to visiting a physical exhibition.

As a general guideline, several design considerations for the development of an online gallery are drafted from the results of this study. This includes:

- Better navigational control.
- The flexibility in adjusting the viewing distance of the artworks.
- The ability to zoom in on the artworks.
- Stable internet connection
- In-depth information relating to the artworks and artists.

6   Conclusion and Future Work

In conclusion, we have conducted a pilot ethnomethodology study on viewing 3D models of physical artworks in a 3D virtual gallery and photos of artworks in 2D online artist portfolio. Using the think aloud protocol we were able to elicit rich accounts that reveal how our participants experience online exhibition. We argue that physical artworks' meanings are embodied in their materiality and texture which do not translate well in 3D models and in photographs and hence disrupt the process of response elicitation that artworks can evoke. Therefore, it is expected by providing the ability to zoom in to see the texture, in addition to stable internet connection and flexibility in controlling the navigation and viewing distance, a better and improved user experience when viewing online exhibition will be formed. In the future, we plan to use the findings from this research to form participatory design with a curator, artists, and audiences to design an online art exhibition.

Acknowledgement. Authors acknowledge the Universiti Teknologi MARA for funding under the Geran Penyelidikan MyRA 600-RMC/GPM ST 5/3 (015/2021).

References

1. Bayraktar, M., Zhang, C., Vadapalli, B., Kipp, N.A., Fox, E.A.: A web art gallery. In: Proceedings of the Third ACM Conference on Digital Libraries. pp. 277–278. Association for Computing Machinery, New York, NY, USA (1998). https://doi.org/10.1145/276675.276727
2. Catton, F., Smith, L.M.: Museums without walls: a temporal analysis of virtual exhibitions in GLAM institutions. Pathfinder: A Canadian J. Info. Sci. Stud. Early Career Profess. **2**, 72–85 (2021)
3. Walczak, K., Cellary, W., White, M.: Virtual museum exhibitions. Computer (Long Beach Calif). (2006). https://doi.org/10.1109/MC.2006.108
4. Hayes, J., Yoo, K.: Virtual reality interactivity in a museum environment. In: Proceedings of the 24th ACM Symposium on Virtual Reality Software and Technology, pp. 1–2 (2018)
5. tom Dieck, M.C., Jung, T.H., tom Dieck, D.: Enhancing art gallery visitors' learning experience using wearable augmented reality: generic learning outcomes perspective. Current Issues in Tourism **21**, 2014–2034 (2018). https://doi.org/10.1080/13683500.2016.1224818
6. Li, W., Huang, X.: The interactive design and user experience of virtual museums: case study of the virtual palace museum. Lectu. Notes Comp. Sci. 400–409 (2022). https://doi.org/10.1007/978-3-031-06047-2_29

7. Giannini, T., Bowen, J.P.: Museums, art, identity, and the digital eco-system: A paradigm shift. Museums and Digital Culture, 63–90 (2019). https://doi.org/10.1007/978-3-319-974 57-6_4

8. Monaghan, D., O'Sullivan, J., O'Connor, N.E., Kelly, B., Kazmierczak, O., Comer, L.: Low-cost creation of a 3D interactive museum exhibition. In: Proceedings of the 19th ACM International Conference on Multimedia (2011). https://doi.org/10.1145/2072298.2072477

9. Kang, X., Chen, W., Kang, J.: Art in the age of social media: interaction behavior analysis of Instagram art accounts. Informatics 6(4), 52 (2019). https://doi.org/10.3390/informatics6 040052

10. Lester, P.: Is the virtual exhibition the natural successor to the physical? J. Soc. Arch. (2006). https://doi.org/10.1080/00039810600691304

11. Lin, C.-L., Chen, S.-J., Lin, R.: Efficacy of virtual reality in painting art exhibitions appreciation. Appl. Sci. 10, 3012 (2020)

12. Hurst, W., Spyrou, O., Tekinerdogan, B., Krampe, C.: Digital art and the metaverse: benefits and challenges. Future Internet 15(6), 188 (2023). https://doi.org/10.3390/fi15060188

13. Bertrand, S.: Curating online collections: towards an authentically digital, mediation protocol for art digitizations. J. Curat. Stud. 11(1), 26–51 (2022). https://doi.org/10.1386/jcs_00054_1

14. Dekker, A., Tedone, G.: Networked co-curation: An exploration of the socio-technical specificities of online curation. Arts 8(3), 86 (2019). https://doi.org/10.3390/arts8030086

15. Liu, K.M.: The attention crisis of digital interfaces and how to consume media more mindfully. Scripps Senior Theses. 1251 (2019). https://scholarship.claremont.edu/scripps_theses/1251

16. Widjono, R.A.: Analysis of user experience in Virtual Art exhibition during pandemic. In: Proceedings of the International Conference of Innovation in Media and Visual Design (IMDES 2020) (2020). https://doi.org/10.2991/assehr.k.201202.059

17. Amorim, J.P., Teixeira, L.: Art in the digital during and after covid: Aura and apparatus of online exhibitions (2021). https://doi.org/10.21659/RUPKATHA.V12N5.RIOC1S1N2

18. Kim, S., Hong, S.: How virtual exhibition presentation affects visitor communication and enjoyment: an exploration of 2D versus 3D. Design J. (2020). https://doi.org/10.1080/146 06925.2020.1806580

19. Kim, S.: Virtual exhibitions and communication factors. Museum Manage. Curators. (2018). https://doi.org/10.1080/09647775.2018.1466190

20. Randall, D., Rouncefield, M., Tolmie, P.: Ethnography, CSCW and Ethno-methodology. Comp. Supp. Coope. Work (CSCW). 30, 189–214 (2021). https://doi.org/10.1007/s10606-020-09388-8

21. Garfinkel, H.: Studies in Ethnomethodology. Prentice-Hall, Englewood Cliffs (1967)

22. Crabtree, A., Nichols, D., O'Brien, J., Rouncefield, M., Twidale, M.: The contribution of ethnomethodologically-informed ethnography to the process of designing digital libraries: Technical Report-CSEG/5/98 (1998)

23. Grayling, A.C.: The Challenge of Things: Thinking Through Troubled Times. Bloomsbury Publishing (2015)

24. Wolf, K., Reinhardt, J., Funk, M.B.: Virtual exhibitions: what do we win and what do we lose? Presented at the (2018). https://doi.org/10.14236/ewic/eva2018.15

Participatory Design Workshop to Create a Virtual Reality Musical Instrument Based on Tumbuk Kalang

Hanif Baharin[1][(✉)], Noris Norowi[2], Khatriza Ahmad Saffian[3], and Yap Eng Sim[3]

[1] Institute of Visual Informatics, Universiti Kebangsaan Malaysia, 43600 UKM Bangi,
Selangor, Malaysia
hbaharin@ukm.edu.my
[2] Faculty of Computer Science and Information Technology, Universiti Putra Malaysia,
43400 Serdang, Selangor, Malaysia
[3] Conservatory of Music, College of Creative Arts, University Teknologi MARA,
40450 Shah Alam, Selangor, Malaysia

Abstract. This paper describes a participatory design workshop to design a virtual reality musical instrument based on Tumbuk Kalang. Originating as a performance for rice harvesting festivals, Tumbuk Kalang as a traditional musical instrument consists of a mortar and pestles. Several players, each holding a pestle will coordinate their movements to pound on the same mortar to create rhythmic sounds whilst singing. These days, Tumbuk Kalang is no longer associated with rice harvest but has been innovated in cultural performances that include songs, dances, and other musical instruments. As machines take over rice production, pestles and mortars are out of use and the tradition of Tumbuk Kalang may be lost. Thus, this research proposes to create a Virtual Reality (VR) Tumbuk Kalang so that it can be preserved and played by future musicians. However, instead of recreating Tumbuk Kalang in VR, we suggest that innovation should be introduced in the design of the new VR Tumbuk Kalang. Hence, we have conducted a participatory design workshop with 12 musicians to design the new VR Tumbuk Kalang. The findings from the workshop produces six new designs of VR musical instruments based on Tumbuk Kalang. The contributions of this paper include the new designs of VR Tumbuk Kalang and the participatory design method used which may be replicated by other researchers who are aiming to preserve traditional musical instruments in the form of VR.

Keywords: Tumbuk Kalang · Traditional Musical Instrument · Virtual Reality Musical Instruments · Participatory Design

1 Introduction

Tumbuk Kalang is a traditional Malay musical instrument that originated from a state in Malaysia called Negeri Sembilan, based on the pestle (*antan*) and mortar (*lesung*) used to process paddy. Traditionally, to separate the rice from the husk, several people would use pestles and coordinate their movement to pound the paddy in a single mortar. In the past, after a day of harvesting and threshing the paddy, farmers would come together at night during the full moon to pound fried unhusked rice or puffed rice called *emping* in a Tumbuk Kalang festival [1]. In the festival, a mortar is placed on cut banana trunks and several people will pound the *emping* whilst singing songs in a rhyming pattern called *pantun*, mostly about love. The audience sometimes will also join in to sing to give answers to the *pantun* expressed by the performers. The stamping of the pestles into various parts of the mortar create sounds of different timbre, and can produce several rhythms which can be played into different songs. Once the performance is finished, the pounded *emping* will be distributed among the performers and audience and eaten with grated coconut and sugar [1].

These days Tumbuk Kalang is no longer associated with the paddy harvest festival but survives as a cultural performance that has been innovated to incorporate songs and dances and is being played with other musical instruments. However, we argue that Tumbuk Kalang is a dying art form because as machines take over the process of producing rice, wooden pestles, and mortars are no longer being made. Unlike modern musical instruments that are being mass-produced, we argue that Tumbuk Kalang may be lost as pestles and mortars are no longer being made. Therefore, we propose to innovate Tumbuk Kalang as a virtual reality (VR) musical instrument to carry the tradition forward to the 21st century. A VR version of an innovative Tumbuk Kalang is beneficial for the preservation of the traditional musical instrument as it does not require the use of heavy pestles and mortars, and as VR headset becomes more accessible, more musicians can play the VR Tumbuk Kalang.

2   Related Work

Virtual Reality Musical Instruments (VRMI) is defined as a system that emulates the sound of musical instruments and provides haptic feedback with visual elements that can be viewed in VR headsets [2]. There are many examples of VRMI being developed and researched. *Carillon* is a VRMI that allows multiplayer to play a set of virtual reality rings that can be controlled by tracking the musicians' hands using Leap Motion. The audience can also see the simulated environment that the musicians see in their VR headsets through screen projection [3]. Laptop orchestra combines the use of VRMI for the conductor-performer whilst other musicians perform gestural movements which are detected by their laptop and turned into sounds [4].

VRMI has been studied from a variety of angles. One aspect of VRMI playability is the haptic feedback it provides to musicians. Since the musical instruments are built in a 3D environment, there is no physicality of the instrument other than the controllers that come with the VR headsets. AirPiano is a multi-finger virtual piano that uses a mid-air ultrasonic haptic display to allow haptic feedback like playing a real piano. The results of the study on AirPiano show that giving haptic feedback in the form of adaptive feedback can improve the experience of playing a virtual piano [5]. Haptic feedback is also done by augmenting physical musical instruments with VRMI, for example, DigiDrum which combines a real drum with VR [6]. Another aspect of VRMI being researched is affordances [7–9].

There is also research that aims to preserve traditional musical instruments using VR or Augmented Reality (AR). Syukur et al. uses virtual reality to turn gamelan into a game [10]. Meanwhile, Sundanese musical instruments are being preserved digitally using AR markerless method [11]. There is also research that developed the angklung, a traditional Indonesian musical instrument made of bamboo, using AR [12]. Meanwhile, Saffian et al. studied the requirements for creating a VR version of the Malay gamelan boning [13].

3   Methodology

In this research, we follow a research-through-design method [14] to design a new VR musical instrument based on Tumbuk Kalang. The creation of artifacts is an important aspect of research-through-design. Involving the end users throughout the process of design is crucial. Hence, we have conducted a participatory design [15] workshop with musicians to create new designs of VRMI based on Tumbuk Kalang. The participatory design workshop consists of six phases as described in the next subsections.

Fig. 1. Process used in the participatory design workshop.

3.1   Participants

There were 12 participants in this workshop. They are students of a music conservatory and play various musical instruments.

3.2   Welcome Note and Briefing

In this phase, participants were welcomed to the workshop. They were briefed about the aim of the workshop and their roles. At this stage, the participants were not introduced to Tumbuk Kalang yet.

3.3   Ice Warming Game: Pass the Bucket

To break the ice, a game called 'Pass the Bucket' was played. The participants stood in a circle and a bucket and a PVC pipe were passed around. When a participant got the bucket and the pipe, they must introduce themselves, and the musical instrument that they played, and then use the bucket and the pipe as instruments to create sounds. The next person who got the bucket and pipe cannot use the same method the other people before them used to create sounds. Each participant was given 30 s to complete the task.

3.4 Scene Setting

In this session, examples of VRMI were shown to the participants. Three videos of people playing a VRMI were shown. Then the participants were shown a video of Tumbuk Kalang performance. Before they were shown the video a question was asked if any of them were aware of Tumbuk Kalang. The participants were then briefed about VR musical instruments seen in the video and Tumbuk Kalang performance.

3.5 Innovative ins-YOU-ment

Fig. 2. The participants drawing their designs in the workshop.

The participants were then asked to design a new VR musical instrument based on Tumbuk Kalang. They were told to take inspiration from how they use the bucket and pipe in the ice-breaking session. Although the new VR musical instrument must maintain the essence of Tumbuk Kalang, they were told to innovate on the design by considering the following parameters: dimension, material, scale, sound samples, mechanics, number of players, layout, interaction, and other related info that they deemed necessary (Fig. 2).

The participants were divided into a group of six with two members for each group. They were given flip chart papers and markers to sketch their designs. This session lasted for 30 min.

3.6 Idea Presentation

After 30 min, the participants' designs on flip chart papers were collected and pasted on the walls. Each group then presented their design and demonstrated the mechanics of their instrument to everyone. Then everyone was invited to walk from one poster to the next and write comments on their sticky notes about what they thought about each of the designs, i.e., like, dislike, impractical, etc. The Post-It notes needs were stuck on the poster anonymously. Then everyone was asked to stick one dot sticker on the design that they liked the most.

3.7 Debriefing

The participants were debriefed about all the objectives of each phase of the workshop. Questions from participants were answered. Then the participants were given a chance to try a VRMI of a traditional musical instrument called Air Bonang using a VR headset.

4 Results

The workshop participants have produced six designs of VR Tumbuk Kalang. None of the participants have heard of Tumbuk Kalang before. In this section, each design is discussed. Three out of the six designs deviate very much from Tumbuk Kalang while three designs maintain the essence of Tumbuk Kalang (Fig. 3).

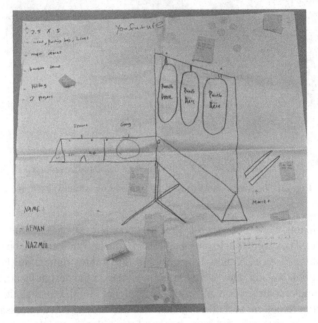

Fig. 3. YouFuture is a design that got the most votes.

YouFuture is a design that got the most votes, but it does not retain any design resemblance or playability of Tumbuk Kalang (Fig. 4).

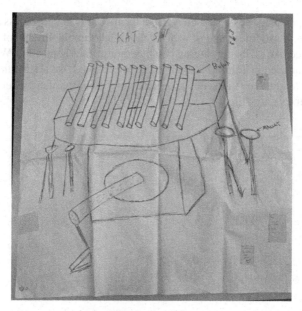

Fig. 4. Kat Sini.

Kat Sini uses bamboo that is arranged like a marimba that is played with mallets. The pestle is attached to a drum pedal and the mortar is placed on its side (Fig. 5).

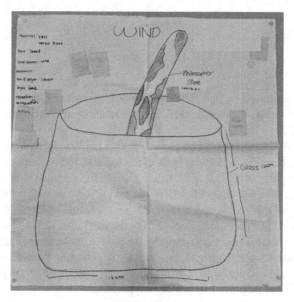

Fig. 5. Wind.

Wind is shaped like a pestle and mortar, but the mortar is made of glass and the pestle is made of stone. It uses the sound of wind as the sound sample. Instead of pounding the pestle, it is played like a Tibetan singing bowl. Although the shape of the Wind is like the pestle and mortar used in Tumbuk Kalang, since it is played like a Tibetan singing bowl it is considered to not to be in the design essence of Tumbuk Kalang where 'tumbuk' in Malay means 'to pound' (Fig. 6).

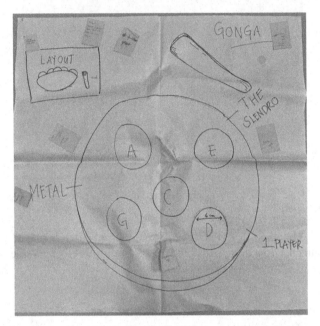

Fig. 6. Gonga.

Gonga is to be played by one player. The mortar is made of metal whilst the pestle is made of wood. Inside the mortar, there are five notes of the pentatonic scale C, D, E, G, and A (Fig. 7).

The unnamed instrument is to be played by two players. One player plays it using a pestle made of bamboo, which has bells at the top end and rubber at the bottom end. The other player plays using two mallets like playing the gamelan (Fig. 8).

Kalang Lima uses 6 notes with a C in the middle of a pentagon-shaped hole in a mortar. The notes D, E, G, A, and a high C is on each side of the pentagon, which is made of rosewood. The notes are sampled from the marimba. Kalang Lima comes with mallets made of wood and has yarn wrapping around the mallet at one end. There are two ways to create sounds with Kalang Lima. One is by pounding the side of the pentagon like Tumbuk Kalang and the other is by hitting the yarn-wrapped part to produce a more muffled sound. It can be played by one or two players.

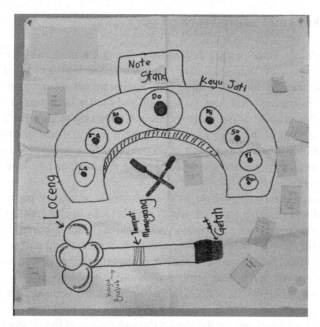

Fig. 7. Unnamed instrument.

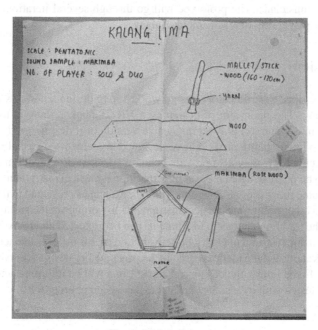

Fig. 8. Kalang Lima.

5   Discussion and Future Work

As stated previously, three designs deviate from Tumbuk Kalang, whilst three designs maintain the essence of Tumbuk Kalang. YouFuture, Kat Sini, and Wind deviate too much from the original Tumbuk Kalang with YouFuture not retaining any element of the traditional instrument. Kat Sini has a pestle and mortar but it uses a drum peddle to play them. Meanwhile, Wind does not use the pounding motion but uses swiping motion along the lip of the glass mortar to create a wind musical instrument sound. Gonga, Unnamed Instrument, and Kalang Lima maintain the essence of Tumbuk Kalang. Unnamed Instrument is the most complex among the three and Kalang Lima has a minimalist design.

All the designs received positive feedback from the workshop participants. Only Wind received one negative feedback which says it looks like an existing instrument. Perhaps, the participants did not want to give negative feedback because although the comments on the Post-It notes were anonymous, their peers could still see who pasted the notes. Therefore, we suggest that for our next participatory design workshop, the group whose design is that is being evaluated should leave the room.

From the workshop, we have decided that Kalang Lima is the design that we will continue to work on because of its simplicity and playability maintaining the essence of Tumbuk Kalang whilst extending the sounds through the use of innovative pestle. In the future, the improved design of Kalang Lima will be built as a VRMI prototype and will be tested with musicians. The prototype will go through several iterations to improve the design and playability of VR Tumbuk Kalang.

6   Conclusion

This paper described a participatory design workshop to design a new VRMI based on Tumbuk Kalang. The main aim of designing a VR Tumbuk Kalang is to preserve it so that future musicians can play an innovative version of it despite traditional pestles and mortars no longer being made. The re-designed instruments, especially when integrated with technology, may also provide become a source of motivation for younger generations to be interested and learn to play traditional musical instruments [16]. Interestingly, the same process of re-designing Tumbuk Kalang as presented in this paper can be extended to other traditional musical instruments. By doing so, the sustainability and longevity of the traditional musical instruments can be protected and transformed into a longer-term salable instrument [17]. The contribution of this paper is the new designs of VR Tumbuk Kalang and the methods used in the participatory design workshop to create a new VRMI. In the future, the design of Kalang Lima will be improved and developed as VRMI and tested with musicians to evaluate the design in order for it to be improved iteratively.

References

1. Ismail, N.: Tumbuk Kalang tarian asli masyarakat tani. Berita Harian (1988)

2. Serafin, S., Erkut, C., Kojs, J., Nilsson, N.C., Nordahl, R.: State of the art, design principles, and future directions. Comput. Music J. **40**, 22–40 (2016)
3. Hamilton, R., Platz, C.: Gesture-based collaborative virtual reality performance in carillon. In: Proceedings of the 2016 International Computer Music Conference, pp. 337–340 (2016)
4. Atherton, J., Wang, G.: Curating perspectives: incorporating virtual reality into laptop orchestra performance. In: Proceedings of the International Conference on New Interfaces for Musical Expression, pp. 154–159 (2020)
5. Hwang, I., Son, H., Kim, J.R.: AirPiano: enhancing music playing experience in virtual reality with mid-air haptic feedback. In: 2017 IEEE World Haptics Conference (WHC), pp. 213–218 (2017). https://doi.org/10.1109/WHC.2017.7989903
6. Willemsen, S., Horvath, A.-S., Nascimben, M.: DigiDrum: a haptic-based virtual reality musical instrument and a case study. In: 17th Sound and Music Computing Conference, pp. 292–299. Axea sas/SMC Network (2020)
7. Smith, L., Lyons, F., Bridges, B., Casey, R.: WithFeelVR: the spatial and textural affordances of VR as a mapping strategy for an accessible digital musical instrument. In: Proceedings of the International Computer Music Conference (2022)
8. Çamcı, A., Vilaplana, M., Wang, L.: Exploring the affordances of VR for musical interaction design with VIMEs. In: Proceedings of the International Conference on New Interfaces for Musical Expression, pp. 121–126 (2020)
9. Mills, D., Schroeder, F., D'Arcy, J.: GIVME: guided interactions in virtual musical environments. In: NIME 2021. PubPub (2021)
10. Syukur, A., Andono, P.N., Hastuti, K., Syarif, A.M.: Immersive and challenging experiences through a virtual reality musical instruments game: an approach to gamelan preservation. J. Metaverse **3**, 34–42 (2023)
11. Arifitama, B., Syahputra, A.: Cultural heritage digitalization on traditional sundanese music instrument using augmented reality markerless marker method. Jurnal Teknologi dan Sistem Komputer. **5**, 101–105 (2017)
12. Arifitama, B.: Preserving traditional instrument angklung using augmented reality technology. In: Proceedings of the 2nd International Multidisciplinary Conference 2016 (2017)
13. Saffian, K.A., Norowi, N.M., Abdullah, L.N., Sulaiman, P.S., Musib, A.F.: Playing gamelan bonang in the air: user requirements for designing a digital musical instrument for the Malay bonang. Malays. J. Music **11**, 68–83 (2022)
14. Zimmerman, J., Forlizzi, J., Evenson, S.: Research through design as a method for interaction design research in HCI. In: Proceedings of the SIGCHI Conference on Human Factors in Computing Systems, pp. 493–502. Association for Computing Machinery, New York, NY (2007). https://doi.org/10.1145/1240624.1240704
15. Bødker, S., Dindler, C., Iversen, O.S., Smith, R.C.: What Is Participatory Design? In: Bødker, S., Dindler, C., Iversen, O.S., and Smith, R.C. (eds.) Participatory Design. Synthesis Lectures on Human-Centered Informatics, pp. 5–13. Springer International Publishing, Cham (2022). https://doi.org/10.1007/978-3-031-02235-7_2
16. Julia, J., Iswara, P.D., Supriyadi, T.: Redesigning and implementing traditional musical instrument in integrated technology classroom. Int. J. Emerg. Technol. Learn. (Online) **14**(10), 75 (2019)
17. Merendino, N., Lepri, G., Rodà, A., Masu, R.: Redesigning the chowndolo: a reflection-on-action analysis to identify sustainable strategies for NIMEs design. In Proceedings of the International Conference on New Interfaces for Musical Expression (2023)

Evaluating the Effectiveness of E-Learning Website Using Electroencephalogram

Alberto Aning[1], Aslina Baharum[2(✉)], Nur Faraha Mohd Naim[1],
Nurhafizah Moziyana Mohd Yusop[3], Dian Darina Indah Darius[4],
Noorsidi Aizuddin Mat Noor[5], and Farhana Diana Deris[6]

[1] Faculty of Computing and Informatics, Universiti Malaysia Sabah, Kota Kinabalu, Sabah,
Malaysia
[2] Computing and Information System, School of Engineering and Technology, Sunway
University, 5, Jalan Universiti, Sunway City, Selangor, Malaysia
aslinab@sunway.edu.my
[3] Faculty of Defence Science and Technology, National Defence University of Malaysia, Kuala
Lumpur, Malaysia
[4] Faculty of Engineering, Universiti Pertahanan Nasional Malaysia, Kem Sungai Besi,
57000 Kuala Lumpur, Malaysia
[5] Mass Appraisal, Housing, and Planning Research Group, Centre for Real Estate Studies, Real
Estate Department, Faculty of Built Environment and Surveying, Universiti Teknologi Malaysia,
Johor Bahru, Johor, Malaysia
[6] Faculty of Social Sciences and Humanities, Universiti Teknologi Malaysia, Johor Bahru,
Johor, Malaysia

Abstract. Although e-learning technology provides numerous benefits for educators, enticing students to use e-learning services is a challenge, particularly for the e-learning websites of higher education institutions in Malaysia. E-learning websites of Malaysian higher education institutions have few guidelines for user interface design that foster emotional engagement. Due to this problem, there is a significant percentage of student disengagement on e-learning platforms. A visualization pattern as a guideline has been proposed for designing an e-learning GUI website for HEIs in Malaysia. The proposed guideline has been implemented on the prototype website's graphical user interface (GUI). The effectiveness of the GUI was evaluated using an electroencephalogram (EEG) device and resulted in 65% of the participants being in the 'Most Effective' category, with the highest average of most effectiveness standing at 32.6% . The research has demonstrated that the developed guideline increased student engagement with the GUI of the e-learning website prototype. The guideline is intended to assist higher education institutions (HEIs) and website developers and designers in creating e-learning websites that can sustain students' interest in e-learning over time.

Keywords: higher education institutions · emotional engagement · guideline · electroencephalogram

1 Introduction

In today's digital era, the significance of designing an effective website [1] has become increasingly prominent due to the multitude of tasks carried out online. The user interface (UI) serves as the sole connection between users and specific computer applications or web environments, establishing an interactive platform for both humans and machines. By enhancing various aspects of the user experience, such as information gathering, intention to revisit the site, trust, and performance, a well-crafted design can greatly enhance the success of a website [2]. At the same time, a poorly designed website may frustrate the users [3], which in turn leads the users to leave the homepage of the website without visiting the internal pages [1]. In the past, website graphical user interface (GUI) design followed a traditional approach primarily focused on designers' perspectives and ideas.

However, recent research has demonstrated the significant importance of incorporating users' opinions and viewpoints into website design, as it directly influences user satisfaction and the overall experience [1]. The role of the user interface (UI) in satisfying users and facilitating improved human-computer interaction (HCI) is crucial. The success of a website largely hinges on satisfying user needs efficiently, which, in turn, relies on the quality of communication between the user and the interface [4]. Therefore, the significance of effective web design cannot be overstated in website development. A website that elicits emotional responses from users, such as enjoyment, engagement, trust, or satisfaction, goes beyond mere usefulness and user-friendliness, as emotions play a vital role in shaping the user experience [5]. With the goal of satisfying users' emotional needs and enhancing the overall user experience, website designers are putting forth their utmost effort.

This study aims to explore how UI design elements impact emotions and how they can be strategically incorporated into website design to foster emotional engagement and positive user experiences. As stated in [6], many researchers concur that individuals' perceptions of technology significantly influence their attitudes towards e-learning environments, highlighting the importance of considering various human and social factors rather than solely relying on technical aspects. In making decisions about educational technologies, [7] emphasizes the need to take into account a wide range of contextual requirements, including social, cultural, political, and economic factors, rather than adopting a strictly technologically deterministic approach.

According to [8], the effectiveness of IT education in India is limited due to its excessively technical nature and lack of consideration for local contexts and real-world issues. Although e-learning technology offers numerous advantages, it poses challenges for educators, especially when it comes to attracting learners to their e-learning services [9]. The interface of an e-learning website serves as the initial point of contact for visiting learners, and its layout, content, information, and other attributes play a crucial role in determining the interactivity, learnability, and sustainability of the platform. Therefore, Aning and Baharum [10] have proposed new guidelines and a prototype for UID by using card sorting methods. Meanwhile, this study has been carried out to evaluate the effectiveness of the developed prototype using an electroencephalogram (EEG) device.

This present research is an extension of their earlier study. The proposed guideline is used to evaluate the emotional engagement of the user experience. An electroencephalography (EEG) device is used to measure the emotional engagement of 16 participants from UMS while using the prototype of an e-learning website developed based on the proposed guideline. The research is limited to the Malaysia region and specifically to the users of the HEIs e-learning website users, especially university members.

The paper is organized as follows. Section 2 provides an analysis of related works regarding the use of EEG in academic research. In Sect. 3, the methodology is described. Section 4 discusses the results of the EEG. Section 5 describes the discussion on the evaluation. Finally, Sect. 5 concludes the paper.

2   Related Works

Students' involvement in e-learning is determined by their skills, participation/interaction, emotions, and performance [11]. Emotional engagement is one of the characteristics used to quantify e-learning student involvement. An important research objective in the field of emotions in e-learning is to test a cognitive-affective model that explores the connections among an e-learning episode, the learner's emotional response during learning, their cognitive processing during learning, and the resulting learning outcome [12]. When students engage in academic e-learning environments, they can experience various cognitive emotions, which may be influenced by factors such as the specific activities they are involved in (e.g., video lessons or chat interactions), their life stage (e.g., younger adult or older adult), and their self-efficacy beliefs regarding e-learning technologies [13]. As stated in [14], students who express satisfaction with the online learning opportunities provided by their instructors are more likely to exhibit engagement in acquiring course-related skills, active participation, improved performance, and positive emotional experiences. Structural equation modelling determined that online course satisfaction is substantially associated with student engagement in e-learning constructs of skills engagement, emotion engagement, participation engagement, and performance engagement. [14] suggested that universities invest in Learning Management Systems (LMS) and other e-learning learning technologies that are effective, efficient, and easy to access.

Emotional engagement in e-learning has a strong relationship with student engagement. Based on the study by [15], student-instructor contact can boost emotional engagement. E-learning facilitates interaction between students and instructors and increases student participation in e-learning activities. In the meantime, [14] asserts that how educators distribute their learning materials on e-learning platforms influences student involvement. Teachers who employ e-learning platforms to their fullest capacity inspire students' interest in e-learning. There are several studies conducted concerning the emotional engagement of users toward web design based on the user experience point of view. Different approaches were performed, such as the Kansei Engineering approach and user's KPI Index engagement, wherein the data was collected and analyzed using analytical techniques to produce statistical results [16]. However, these approaches were conducted through a quantitative survey and not a direct receptive response from the brain. Electroencephalography (EEG) is a non-invasive technology that directly measures brain electrical activity through electrodes on the scalp, which is a special device called an EEG [17, 18]. EEG is commonly used in user experience research to determine the brain activity of product users during the interaction. EEG technology advancements have created headgear with enhanced usability and mobility, making them more suited for user experience research [19]. EEG is frequently utilized for empirical user experience evaluation in terms of emotion recognition for designers to comprehend users' emotions more precisely. Using an electrophysiological approach, [20] sought to investigate the emotional progression of webpages. Participants are requested to evaluate their emotional response to webpages by clicking the mouse while their EEG is recorded. The outcomes of the study establish benchmarks for evaluating the emotional impact of website design on users. Using OPENBCI technology, [21] evaluated user experience via EEG signals. OPENBCI is a low-cost solution for EEG signal collection. The investigation recorded EEG signals while participants played video games in various circumstances. Consistent EEG data analysis revealed a high level of consistency; thus, low-cost EEG (standard) signal-based technologies can produce intriguing results. [21] have shown that using EEG in user experience research can be a cost-effective choice with the correct EEG tools.

3 Materials and Methods

The methodology will be focused on achieving the objective of evaluating the effectiveness of GUI using EEG. The e-learning website is evaluated using the EEG device to detect any emotional engagement from the UID that has been implemented in the guideline. The prototype of the design interface was developed by Aning and Baharum [10] by using a Kansei-based visualization pattern. For the EEG equipment device testing, 16 university members from a local university, including students, academicians, and IT administrators, are among the participants. The wireless EEG headset is utilized to detect the participants' EEG signals. Bluetooth connectivity is used to connect the EEG headset. The EEG signals of the subjects are captured using a mobile phone application. Modifications are made to a process described in a study by [22] to accommodate the needs of this study. The wireless EEG headset is placed on the participant's head with temporary adhesives. Each participant must interact with the proposed user interface design for the e-learning website, which was developed using the Kansei engineering results-based guideline [10].

There are three tasks to be completed by the participants: Task 1. Log in, Task 2. Enroll in a new course, and Task 3. Create a new event. During interaction with the e-learning user interface, EEG signals are recorded using a mobile application that serves as an EEG recorder. After all 16 participants have tested the website, the recorded EEG data of each participant are examined to evaluate the emotional involvement that occurred while interacting with the proposed user interface design for an e-learning website.

4 Results

Based on Figs. 1, 2, 3, 4, 5, 6, 7, 8, 9, 10, 11, 12, 13, 14, 15 and 16 show the results of the EEG of the 16 participants' user experience. P01 to P16 represented Participant 1 to Participant 16.

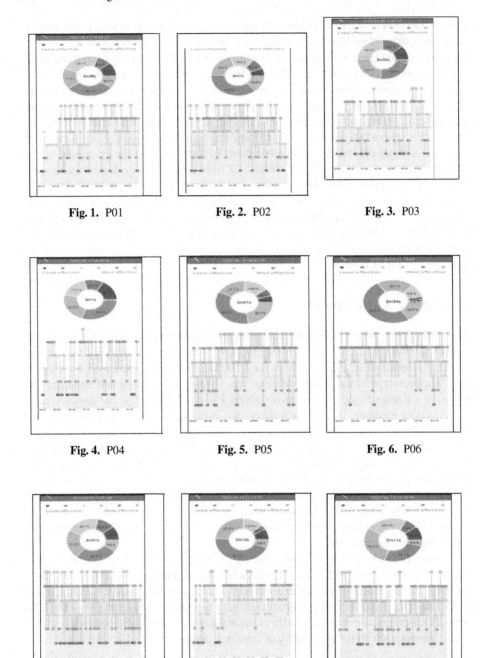

Fig. 1. P01   **Fig. 2.** P02   **Fig. 3.** P03

Fig. 4. P04   **Fig. 5.** P05   **Fig. 6.** P06

Fig. 7. P07   **Fig. 8.** P08   **Fig. 9.** P09

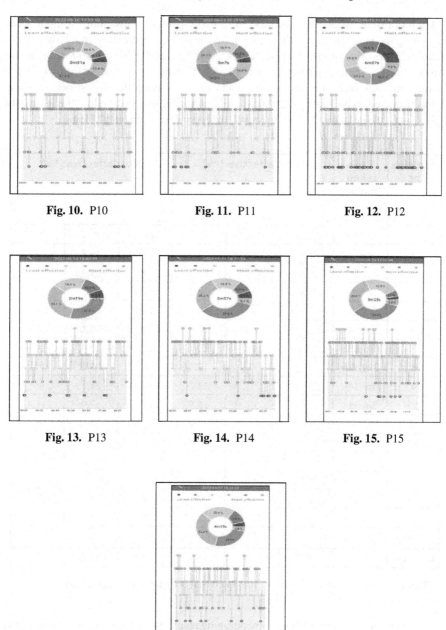

Fig. 10. P10   **Fig. 11.** P11   **Fig. 12.** P12

Fig. 13. P13   **Fig. 14.** P14   **Fig. 15.** P15

Fig. 16. P16

Based on the results shown in Fig. 17, the developed prototype is proven to provide a compelling user experience for the participants (32.6%). The average time for the participants to complete a task using the interface is 4 min 11 s. Participants 7 and 12 took a lot of time to complete the task. Still, Participant 12 shows more struggle when navigating the new interface, where they have the highest percentage in the two "Least effective" categories (Red-20.4% and Orange-14.5%) and the lowest percentage in one "Most effective" category (Neon green-18.3%). Participant 6 took 3 min and 54 s to navigate the new interface, showed excellent results, having the lowest percentage in all the "Least effective" categories (Red-1.3%, Orange-2.6%, and Yellow-9.8%) and the highest percentage in one "Most effective" category (Neon green-50.0%).

Participant	Time taken (minute and seconds)	Least effective (%)			Most effective (%)		
1	4m 38s	11.2	8.6	23.7	*17.3*	29.1	10.1
2	4m 7s	6.1	8.9	14.6	19.8	36.8	13.8
3	3m 34s	11.7	13.6	**24.3**	23.8	23.4	3.3
4	3m 1s	16.6	12.2	17.1	23.8	29.3	1.1
5	5m 21s	5.0	5.6	14.0	17.1	35.5	**22.7**
6	3m 54s	*1.3*	*2.6*	*9.8*	20.1	**50.0**	16.2
7	**6m 51s**	10.7	10.9	20.7	21.9	26.8	9.0
8	**2m 18s**	8.0	3.6	12.3	25.4	44.2	6.5
9	5m 11s	10.3	7.4	23.2	29.3	25.1	4.8
10	3m 31s	5.2	5.7	10.4	19.9	47.4	11.4
11	3m 7s	4.8	10.7	16.0	19.3	34.8	14.4
12	6m 27s	**20.4**	**14.5**	19.4	20.2	*18.3*	7.2
13	2m 19s	7.2	12.2	19.4	33.1	27.3	*0.7*
14	2m 57s	6.2	9.0	16.9	28.2	34.5	5.1
15	5m 25s	2.8	5.2	22.5	29.8	34.5	5.2
16	4m 13s	4.0	11.5	22.9	**33.2**	24.5	4.0
Average	4m 11s	*8.2*	8.9	18.0	23.9	**32.6**	8.5

Fig. 17. Time taken and effectiveness of the developed prototype. (Color figure online)

The participants mainly showed encouraging results when interacting with the newly developed prototype based on the proposed guideline. The average time taken to complete the task is four minutes and 11 s, with high effectiveness (Neon green-32.6%), which is a good start for the participants who consisted of the newly enrolled students to the university. However, some participants spent more than six minutes completing the task. The participants who spend more than six minutes to complete a task may have problems navigating the website, such as a lack of familiarity with the e-learning website and the names of the links and icons. Familiarity with icons significantly affects cognitive performance on visual search and recognition tasks [23]. The result of the evaluation shows that users have a positive experience in terms of ease and efficiency as most of the participants' brain activities effectively processed the tasks they needed to complete on the UID of the prototype.

5 Conclusions

This paper aims to evaluate the effectiveness of the developed prototype using an electroencephalogram (EEG) device. Sixteen participants of newly enrolled university students were involved in the EEG test. Participants were required to interact with the Kansei-based e-learning website prototype while wearing an EEG headgear to record their brain activity. The time taken for the participants to complete the task on the prototype website was also recorded. Based on the participants' brain activities, most of their brain signals showed that the new guideline improved their user experience. The new guideline effectively reduced the time the participant took to complete the task, with an average time of 4 minutes and 11 seconds. However, several participants took more than the average time to complete the task.

Some significant findings from this study can contribute to the e-learning situation at HEIs in Malaysia. E-learning is highly related to the Internet, where students can access an e-learning website to do tasks, assignments, and collaborative learning. A website with a good user interface can sustain students' emotional engagement during e-learning. Hence, the results obtained from the evaluation of the proposed guideline are undoubtedly helpful for the HEIs in Malaysia to improve and create standardized e-learning websites that promote emotional engagement. Besides HEIs, a company that wants to delve into the e-learning business can use the proposed guideline to create an e-learning platform or website that caters to university students in Malaysia. The proposed guideline contributes to visual patterns for emotional engagement in standard web objects for e-learning websites. The study can be improved by grouping the participants into those with zero experience in e-learning websites and those familiar with e-learning websites to evaluate the user experience of the guideline using an EEG device. In this way, more variety of results can be produced, for example, the time taken to complete a task by each of the groups.

References

1. Garett, R., Chiu, J., Zhang, L., Young, S.D.: A literature review: website design and user engagement. Online J. Commun. Media Technol. **6**(3), 1–14 (2016)
2. Lindgaard, G., Dudek, C., Sen, D., Sumegi, L., Noonan, P.: An exploration of relations between visual appeal, trustworthiness and perceived usability of homepages. ACM Trans. Comput.-Hum. Interact. **18**(1), 1–30 (2011)
3. Baharum, A., et al.: Evaluating the localization for e-learning website: case study in Universiti Malaysia Sabah. In: 2017 International Conference on Platform Technology and Service, PlatCon 2017 – Proceedings. pp. 0–4 (2017)
4. Flavian, C., Gurrea, R., Orús, C.: Web design: a key factor for the website success. J. Syst. Inf. Technol. **11**(2), 168–184 (2009). Researchgate

5. Cyr, D., Head, M., Larios, H., Pan, B.: Exploring human images in website design: a multi-method approach. MIS Q. **33**(3), 530–566 (2009)
6. Dahal, S.: Eyes don't lie: understanding users' first impressions on website design using eye tracking, Thesis (2011)
7. Kundi, G.M., Nawaz, A., Khan, S.: The predictors of success for e-learning in higher education institutions (HEIs) in N-W.F.P, PAKISTAN. JISTEM J. Inf. Syst. Technol. Manag. **7**(3), 545–578 (2010)
8. Ezer, J.: India and the USA: a comparison through the lens of model IT curricula. J. Inf. Technol. Educ. **5**, 429–440 (2006)
9. Liao, H.-L., Lu, H.-P.: The role of experience and innovation characteristics in the adoption and continued use of e-learning websites. Comput. Educ. **51**(4), 1405–1416 (2008)
10. Aning, A., Baharum, A.: Development of Kansei-based visualization pattern for e-learning website. Int. J. Adv. Comput. Sci. Appl. (2023, in press)
11. El-Sabagh, H.A.: Adaptive e-learning environment based on learning styles and its impact on development students' engagement. Int. J. Educ. Technol. High. Educ. **18**(1), 1–24 (2021)
12. Mayer, R.E.: Searching for the role of emotions in e-learning. Learn. Instr. **70**, 101213 (2019)
13. D'Errico, F., Paciello, M., De Carolis, B., Vattanid, A., Palestra, G., Anzivino, G.: Cognitive emotions in e-learning processes and their potential relationship with students' academic adjustment. Int. J. Emot. Educ. **10**(1), 89–111 (2018)
14. Baloran, E.T., Hernan, J.T., Taoy, J.S.: Course satisfaction and student engagement in online learning amid COVID-19 pandemic: a structural equation model. Turk. Online J. Distance Educ. **22**(4), 1–12 (2021)
15. Yu, J., Huang, C., Wang, X., Tu, Y.: Exploring the relationships among interaction, emotional engagement and learning persistence in online learning environments. In: 2020 International Symposium on Educational Technology (ISET) (2020)
16. Naim, N.F.M., Adzlan, S.E.M., Ismail, R., Ramli, N.A., Kian, H.C., Baharum, A.: Relationship between online shopping sites' design and user experience using a survey. J. Theor. Appl. Inf. Technol. **100**(14), 5179–5188 (2022)
17. Kumar, J.S., Bhuvaneswari, P.: Analysis of electroencephalography (EEG) signals and its categorization–a study. Procedia Eng. **38**, 2525–2536 (2012)
18. Read, G.L., Innis, I.J.: Electroencephalography (Eeg). In: Matthes, J., Davis, C.S., Potter, R.F. (eds.) The International Encyclopedia of Communication Research Methods, pp. 1–18. Wiley, Hoboken (2017)
19. Van Camp, M., De Boeck, M., Verwulgen, S., De Bruyne, G.: EEG technology for UX evaluation: a multisensory perspective. In: Ayaz, H., Mazur, L. (eds.) AHFE 2018. Advances in Intelligent Systems and Computing, vol. 775, pp. 337–343. Springer, Cham (2018). https://doi.org/10.1007/978-3-319-94866-9_34
20. Liu, W., Liang, X., Wang, X., Guo, F.: The evaluation of emotional experience on webpages: an event-related potential study. Cogn. Technol. Work **21**(2), 317–326 (2018)
21. Cano, S., Araujo, N., Guzman, C., Rusu, C., Albiol-Perez, S.: Low-cost assessment of user experience through EEG signals. IEEE Access. **8**, 158475–158487 (2020)
22. Siuly, S., Li, Y., Zhang, Y.: Electroencephalogram (EEG) and its background. In: Siuly, S., Li, Y., Zhang, Y. (eds.) EEG Signal Analysis and Classification. Health Information Science. Springer, Cham (2016). https://doi.org/10.1007/978-3-319-47653-7_1
23. Shen, Z., Zhang, L., Xiao, X., Li, R., Liang, R.: Icon familiarity affects the performance of complex cognitive tasks. I-Percept. **11**(2), 204166952091016 (2020)

Compustory: A Virtual Museum Game
for Modeling the History of Computer Evolution

Warda Azzahra[✉], Munir, and Wahyudin

Program Studi Pendidikan Ilmu Komputer, Universitas Pendidikan Indonesia, Bandung,
Indonesia
wardazzahra@upi.edu

Abstract. Museums have an educational function that can be used as a means of
education, especially in learning history at school. As we know, the COVID-19
pandemic has changed the face-to-face learning system to virtual. So, teachers
cannot invite students to study history in museums. Virtual museum games can
be an alternative solution to this problem by presenting remote facilities that can
make it easier for students to explore knowledge about history without any restrictions. This study aims to develop a virtual museum game to model the history of
computers evolution. This study uses the DDD-E model in developing this game.
The reason for using this model is that every development and addition of new
features to the game will be evaluated. Development evaluation is carried out
by conducting expert validation using the LORI instrument. The virtual museum
game "Compustory" was developed using a first-person perspective with 3D models to visualize the evolutionary history of computers. The results of the validation
show that the average percentage score obtained is 99% with the eligibility qualification of "Very Eligible" used as an educational medium to teach the history of
computer development in schools and is considered capable of making learning
more enjoyable and recreation.

Keywords: Virtual Museum Game · Computer Evolution History · 3D Models

1 Introduction

Museums have an educational function that can be used as a means of education, especially in learning history at school. Students can learn about the culture and works of past
people through museum heritage collections [1, 2]. By studying events that occurred in
the past, students can also take lessons from the events that occurred and the role models
involved [3]. Inviting students to visit museums can be used as an option for learning
history and is considered to make the learning process more enjoyable [4].

As we know, the COVID-19 Pandemic has changed most aspects of people's lives
online. In terms of learning at school, schools and teachers cannot hold study tours
such as inviting students to visit museums to learn history directly [5]. Apart from the
pandemic factor which has caused learning to be carried out from each other's homes,
visits to museums for learning purposes mean that schools need to prepare supporting
accommodations such as transportation costs and entrance tickets for visitors [6].

H. Badioze Zaman et al. (Eds.): IVIC 2023, LNCS 14322, pp. 161–174, 2024.
https://doi.org/10.1007/978-981-99-7339-2_15

Virtual museums can be an alternative solution to the above problems by presenting online facilities for users to be able to study historical relics remotely [6]. Virtual museums can function as fun educational media and allow users to explore their insights about historical heritage virtually [7]. A Google Trends data search for the keyword "Virtual Museum" shows the interest of people in parts of the world towards virtual museums in the last 12 months (see Fig. 1), where the graph shows relatively increasing numbers in several months. This can be an opportunity to interest students in learning by using virtual museums by promoting immersive experiences [8].

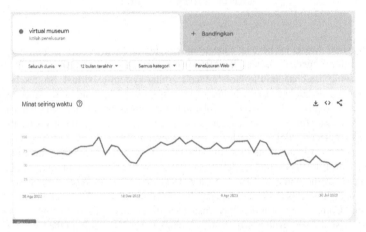

Fig. 1. Search Trends "Virtual Museum" in Google Trends

Virtual museums can be packaged in the form of games that can make it easier for students to explore knowledge about history without any restrictions [9]. The use of games is considered to have the potential to improve children's learning processes because they can present interactive visualizations to simulate real-world problems related to learning materials so as to create a fun learning atmosphere [10]. This is in line with the opinion that museums must be able to present various complex issues related to history in an informative and entertaining way [11].

Previous developments have been carried out by Pramana and Hermawan [12]. This study developed a virtual tour application for computer development using virtual reality (VR) technology. Considering that VR facilities are not widely available in several schools, it is hoped that the games developed in this study can be alternative learning media that can support student learning. Based on this, this study aims to develop a virtual museum game to model the history of computer development. Other research has also been carried out by Wulandari [13]. This research packs a virtual museum using PowerPoint media, while the current research uses the form of first-person games to package a virtual museum.

This study aims to develop a virtual museum game to model the history of computer evolution. The Virtual Museum Game developed in this research is named "COMPUS-TORY", which is a virtual museum to present material on the history of computer evolution in a fun way. The game is specially developed for the Android platform.

2   Methodology

2.1   Development Model

This research is development research that uses the DDD-E model (Decide, Design, Develop, Evaluate) in game development [14]. The reason for using this model is that in this research a virtual museum game "Compustory" will be developed where every time there is a development and addition of new features an evaluation will be carried out [15]. Schematic of the stages of the DDD-E model can be seen in Fig. 2.

Fig. 2. DDD-E Models

1. Decide, this stage determines the game goals and learning materials for the virtual game museum to be built. Game goals are objectives that must be achieved by players as well as being a benchmark for designing game designs [16].
2. Design, this stage designs the game flow system according to the predetermined game goals, use case diagrams, and the interface contained in the game.
3. Develop, this stage builds game programs and implements Unity 3D game art and 3D assets created with Blender 3D.
4. Evaluate, this stage evaluates and conducts testing to re-check the suitability of the design with the implementation results. Validation with media experts is carried out in the context of media evaluation to get input from experts regarding the game being developed.

2.2 Media Validation Instrument

The media validation instrument used to assess media feasibility refers to the media assessment instrument LORI (Learning Object Review Instrument) developed by John Nesbit, Karen Belfer, and Tracey Leacock [17], which can be seen in Table 1.

Table 1. LORI Instrument

No	Criteria	Score (1–5)
Presentation Design		
1	Design of visual and auditory information for enhanced learning	
Interaction Usability		
2	Ease of navigation	
3	Consistent interface display	
4	Quality of the interface help features	
Accessibility		
5	Ease of access	
6	Design controls and presentation formats to accommodate a variety of learners	
Standards Compliance		
7	Adherence to international standards	
Content Quality		
8	Material accuracy	
9	Balanced presentation of the material	
10	Appropriate level of material detail	
Learning Goal Alignment		
11	Alignment among learning goals	
12	Alignment among learning activities	
13	Alignment among learning assessments	
14	Alignment among learner characteristics	
Feedback and Adaptation		
15	Adaptive content or feedback is driven by differential learner input	
Reusability		
16	Learning media can be used in various variations of learning with different students	
Motivation		
17	Ability to motivate and interest identified a population of learners	

The expert who is a media validator is one of the lecturers in the computer science education department who is engaged in the design and development of learning multimedia. The expert is also a lecturer in human and computer interaction courses and design courses, and a companion lecturer in learning planning courses, so the expert's needs are needed in evaluating media on the aspects of media interactivity, design, and learning.

2.3 Data Analysis Techniques

Analysis of the results of media validation data is carried out using a rating scale with the following formula:

$$P = \frac{x}{x_i} \times 100\% \tag{1}$$

The Explanation:
P: value presentation from expert validation.
x: score obtained from each point on the instrument.
The percentage of values from the validation results that have been calculated is then analyzed for the eligibility qualifications of the media with reference to the achievement scale in Table 2 [18].

Table 2. Eligibility Qualifications

No	Achievement Scale	Qualification
1	85–100%	Very good
2	75–84%	Good
3	65–74%	Pretty good
4	55–64%	Not good
5	0–54%	Very Not Good

3 Result and Discussion

The results of this study are discussed by dividing the discussion into several points based on the stages of the DDD-E model. The decide stage discusses game goals and learning materials to be used in the virtual museum game being developed. The design stage discusses the design of the game flow and 3D asset design to create a museum model in the game. The develop stage discusses the implementation of game designs and concepts in game development. The evaluate stage discusses the results of media validation with media experts.

3.1 Deciding Game Goals and Learning Materials

This game is designed as a learning media for the history of computer development with a first-person game type, namely a game with the player's point of view as the first person so that the player feels as if he is exploring a museum virtually [20]. This game is designed for educational needs and the concept is related to learning content, so it is necessary to know the indicators of preparing learning materials to be included in game content [21]. The following are indicators for compiling learning content in the Compustory game:

Subject	:	Informatics
Learning Objectives	:	Students are expected to be able to describe and draw lessons from the history of computer development and its characters
Subject matter	:	History of Computer Evolution
Source Material	:	Informatics Teacher's Handbook for Class 10 High School [19]

Learning content is arranged based on material sources and learning goals. This game was built with educational goals so that game goals are determined referring to learning goals. So, the game concept is designed by presenting challenges in the game to achieve learning objectives [16].

3.2 Designing Game Play and Screen Flow

Game Play Design. The design of the game flow refers to the concepts that have been determined in the previous stage. To facilitate learning, the game flow is designed with reference to the stages of the discovery learning model. Discovery Learning is a learning model developed by Jerome Bruner, which guides students to discover, investigate and solve problems through observation and discussion [20, 21]. The game flow of "Compustory" is divided into three game sessions, namely an introduction session, a history exploration session, and a future planning session (see Fig. 3).

The gameplay above relates to the division of rooms in the museum. The game map in Fig. 4 explains the division of the room based on the session. The Introduction session explains the origin of the computer which was created in the Intro Room (see Fig. 4). This session is a warm-up before moving on to the next session. The History Exploration session explains the history of computer development which contains several collections of previous computers from generation to generation (see Fig. 4). Each heritage collection has an explanation of the history of its development. The Future Planning session explains today's computers that are carried out in the Future Room containing models of today's computers as we know them (see Fig. 4). This session also provides an explanation of IoT computer trends and presents some simple case examples regarding the implementation of IoT in solving problems in everyday life. Each session has a quiz that the user needs to complete. Quiz questions based on what has been learned in the session, in order to review the user's knowledge again. The questions are displayed randomly so that the challenges are not the same every time the user plays it again.

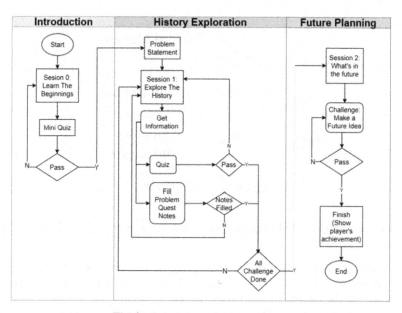

Fig. 3. Game Flow of "Compustory"

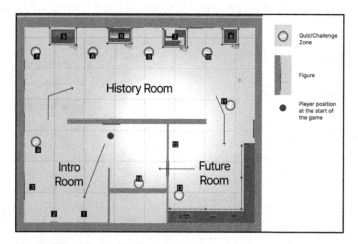

Fig. 4. Game Map and museum exploration scheme in "Compustory"

Use Case Diagram. Features that users can use in this game are exploring museums, getting historical information from selected collections, and completing challenges. The design use case diagram can be seen in Fig. 5.

Screen Design. Interface wireframe design is done as a guide to set the layout of the game display during development and to determine the required button design variations.

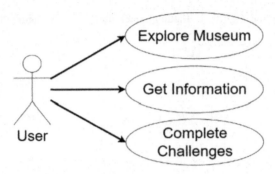

Fig. 5. Use Case Diagram

Wireframes are designed by taking into account the conditions and requirements for the appearance of screens.

For example, on the quiz start screen (see Fig. 6f), the screen will display the "Start Quiz" button if the user approaches the quiz or challenge area. If the button is pressed, the user will be directed to the quiz page according to the type of quiz or challenge. Another example of the "get info" button on the gameplay page (see Fig. 6 no. 2), the button will appear if the user approaches a collection that has an explanation. If the button is pressed, a dialog will appear providing an explanation of the collection.

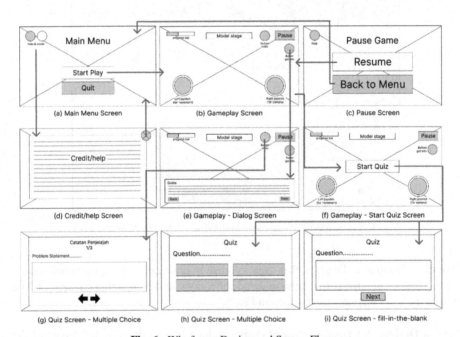

Fig. 6. Wireframe Design and Screen Flow

3.3   Game Development and Design Implementation

1st Generation   2nd Generation   3rd Generation   4th Generation

Model
References

3D Models

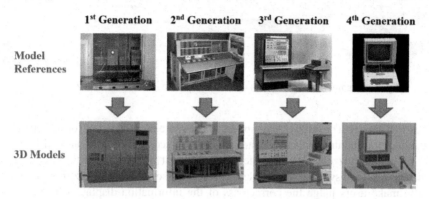

Fig. 7. Modeling museum heritage collections into 3D assets

3D Modelling. As explained in the previous gameplay system design, the museum in the game has collections that players can observe and study. Modeling of computer collections from generation 1 to generation 4 into 3D models is done by referring to model references from previous computer documentation according to their generation (see Fig. 7). Computer 3D models are made as closely as possible to give a realistic impression so that users can imagine the shape of computers in the past [22].

Design Implementation. The appearance of the game is built based on the wireframe design that was made in the previous stage, starting from the layout to the number of buttons needed. The game uses dialog boxes to convey information to players by illustrating it as if the information was explained by a tour guide (see Fig. 8). The choice of game interface color palette pays attention to the aesthetics and atmosphere of the game to be conveyed [23].

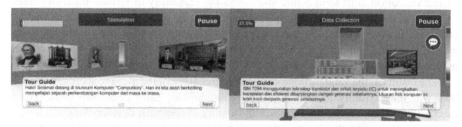

Fig. 8. In-game dialog box display. (a) Game intro. (b) Explanation of the history heritage

In-game quizzes serve to test and reinforce the knowledge the user has acquired while exploring the museum [24]. The quiz/challenge area (see Fig. 9a) appears every time the user has completed a heritage study mission and if the user approaches it a quiz

Fig. 9. In-game quiz system. (a) Quiz areas. (b) An example of a quiz in game

screen will appear. The quizzes that appear in the game have different forms depending on the question requirements. There are multiple-choice, true or false, and fill-in fields. Multiple choice quizzes contain 4 choices with different points based on the effectiveness of the choices in answering the problems presented (see Fig. 9b). Quiz true or false is used to make users judge the correctness of the information displayed based on the material that has been studied. Meanwhile, quiz fill-in fields are used to ask students' opinions regarding history or issues related to it.

Game Development. Game development uses the Unity 3D game engine with the C# programming language. Game systems are built based on game flow and user features are programmed based on use case diagrams that have been designed in the previous stage. Programming is done to manage user movement, user interaction, and some objects, and set views such as page switching and displaying messages.

Result of Game Development. The "Compustory" game was developed as a first-person game that can be played on Android devices. User control utilizes the touch screen of the smartphone. The movement of the user in the game can be controlled by using two virtual joysticks, the left joystick to control the user's movement (to go forward, backward, and turn) and the right joystick to control the camera direction.

3.4   Results of Media Validation by Experts

Media validation aims to examine and assess the feasibility of virtual museum games as learning media and test game performance. Media validation was carried out by providing an assessment questionnaire prepared based on the LORI instrument to media experts from the computer science education department. The validation results from media experts can be seen in Table 3.

The results of the validation show that the percentage of the average score obtained is 99% with the eligibility qualification "Very Eligible" (see Table 2). So, this game can be used as an educational medium to teach the history of computer development in schools. Experts also consider that this game can make learning more fun because students will feel more that they are playing games, even though they are learning.

Table 3. Results of Validation by Media Experts

No	Evaluation Aspects	Score	%
1	Presentation Design	5	100
2	Interaction Usability	4.6	9.3
3	Accessibility	5	100
4	Reusability	5	100
5	Standards Compliance	5	100
6	Content Quality	5	100
7	Learning Goal Alignment	5	100
8	Feedback and Adaptation	5	100
9	Motivation	5	100
Average Score		4.96	99%

3.5 Discussion

Game development uses the help of the Unity game maker application with its 3D assets made with Blender. The 3D model of museum exhibit objects is made as closely as possible to actual past computer objects based on the historical documentation of existing computer developments. Creation of 3D models to visualize past computer designs according to their generation. The 3D models created are useful for visualizing past computers as closely as possible. Computer modeling focuses on past computer documentation introduced in several book sources or learning modules in schools and spread on the internet. Modeling uses Blender 3D, because it has quite complete and sufficient features and the device specification requirements are not too high [25].

The UI display in the game is made from a first-person perspective. Where this game does not have a main character that describes the player in the game story (see Fig. 10). So, what the user sees on the screen seems to be his point of view directly at this virtual museum. The hope is that by using the first-person perspective concept, users can imagine actually exploring a museum virtually.

In terms of learning performance, the expert who validated this game also expressed an opinion based on the user's point of view, namely by using this game for learning the user felt more like playing a game than learning, even though the game process that the user went through was intended for learning. As for the things that need to be improvised again are aesthetic improvements to the visual game, by consistent color palette selection, and improving game graphics even better.

Limitation. The development of this virtual museum game is limited to computer modeling. The modeling is still focused on taking one example of computer design for each generation, even though in one generation there were several computer models developed by many agencies at that time. This research is still focused on the development of a virtual museum game for the history of computer development. It is hoped that in

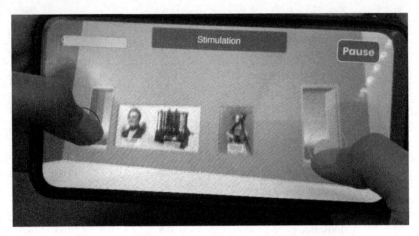

Fig. 10. In-game display when the user uses the joystick

future research the implementation of the virtual museum game design will be carried out in other historical lessons.

4   Conclusion

Based on the description and validation results that have been carried out, it can be concluded that the design of the virtual museum game "Compustory" can be used as an educational medium for students to learn about the history of computer development through virtual museum exploration. Learning history using virtual museum media can make learning more fun and recreational. Modeling the evolution of computers in the form of 3D models can visualize history more realistically and provide users with an overview of the development of computers from each generation.

Acknowledgement. We would like to thank Ms. Andini Setya Arianti, M.Ds. from Department of Computer Science Education who is willing to provide validation for the game that is being developed.

References

1. Asmara, D.: Peran Museum dalam pembelajaran sejarah. Kaganga: Jurnal Pendidikan Sejarah dan Riset Sosial Humaniora **2**, 10–20 (2019). https://doi.org/10.31539/kaganga.v2i1.707
2. Hasan, S.H.: Museum Bagi Pendidikan Sejarah Nasional. http://sejarah.upi.edu/artikel/dosen/museum-bagi-pendidikan-sejarah-nasional/. Accessed 18 Dec 2022
3. Wibowo, T.U.S.H., Maryuni, Y., Nurhasanah, A., Willdianti, D.: Pemanfaatan Virtual Tour Museum (VTM) dalam pembelajaran sejarah di masa pandemi covid-19. In: Prosiding Seminar Nasional Pendidikan FKIP, pp. 402–408 (2020)
4. Safi, J., Bau, O.B.: Pemanfaatan Museum Rempah sebagai sumber pembelajaran se-jarah. Jurnal Artefak **8** (2021)

5. Besoain, F., González-Ortega, J., Gallardo, I.: An evaluation of the effects of a virtu-al museum on users' attitudes towards cultural heritage. Appl. Sci. **12**, 1341 (2022). https://doi.org/10. 3390/app12031341
6. İlhan, G.O., Erol, M., Özdemir, F.: Virtual museum experiences of primary school teacher candidates during the COVID-19 pandemic process. Malays. Online J. Educ. Technol. **10**, 232–243 (2022). https://doi.org/10.52380/mojet.2022.10.4.259
7. Daniela, L.: Virtual museums as learning agents. Sustainability (Switzerland) **12** (2020). https://doi.org/10.3390/su12072698
8. Aiello, D., Fai, S., Santagati, C.: Virtual museums as a means for promotion and enhancement of cultural heritage. Int. Arch. Photogramm. Remote Sens. Spat. Inf. Sci. **42**, 33–40 (2019). https://doi.org/10.5194/isprs-archives-XLII-2-W15-33-2019
9. Klentien, U.: Development of virtual museum model for youth. Int. J. Inf. Educ. Technol. **12**, 313–317 (2022). https://doi.org/10.18178/ijiet.2022.12.4.1620
10. Nikolova, A., Georgiev, V.: Using serious games in e-learning for kids. In: INTED2021 Proceedings. 15th International Technology, Education and Development Conference, pp. 621–625 (2021). https://doi.org/10.21125/inted.2021.0155
11. Kersten, T.P., Tschirschwitz, F., Deggim, S.: Development of a virtual museum including a 4D presentation of building history in virtual reality. Int. Arch. Photogramm. Remote Sens. Spat. Inf. Sci. **42**, 361–367 (2017). https://doi.org/10.5194/isprs-archives-XLII-2-W3-361-2017
12. Pramana, F., Hermawan, H.D.: Aplikasi Virtual Tour Galeri Sejarah Dan Perkem-bangan Komputer Menggunakan Teknologi Virtual Reality Berbasis Android (2022)
13. Wulandari, F.: PENGARUH PEMANFAATAN MUSEUM VIRTUAL TROWULAN SEBA-GAI MEDIA PEMBELAJARAN SEJARAH TERHADAP PEMAHAMAN BELAJAR SISWA KELAS X IPS-1 SMA NEGERI LOCERET. AVATARA, e-Journal Pendidikan Sejarah **12** (2022)
14. Ivers, K.S., Barron, A.E.: Multimedia Projects in Education: Designing, Producing, and Assessing. Libraries Unlimited, Westport (2010)
15. Wahidah, N., Sari, W., Festiana, I., Nasir, N.: Game based learning: design a multi-media with DDD-E model for mathematics education. Int. J. Emerg. Technol. Learn. (iJET). **15**, 277–284 (2020)
16. Ike, T.C., Hoe, T.W.: Exploring the link between the psychological needs and the elements of game design for educational games. J. ICT Educ. **7**, 65–73 (2020). https://doi.org/10.37134/jictie.vol7.2.6.2020
17. Leacock, T.L., Nesbit, J.C.: A framework for evaluating the quality of multimedia learning resources. J. Educ. Technol. Soc. **10**, 44–59 (2007)
18. Wutun, M., Manu, G.A., Fallo, D.Y.A.: Pembuatan Game Edukasi Untuk Meninjau Efektivitas Belajar Siswa. Jurnal Pendidikan Teknologi Informasi (JUKANTI) **4**, 72–79 (2021). https://doi.org/10.37792/jukanti.v4i2.307
19. Wahyono, et al.: Buku Panduan Guru Informatika untuk SMA Kelas X. Ke-menterian Pendidikan, Kebudayaan, Riset, dan Teknologi, Jakarta (2021)
20. Bruner, J.S.: The act of discovery. Understanding Children, pp. 10–24 (1961)
21. Nurilhaq, I., Tabroni, I.: The use of the discovery learning model in improving the quality of learning of the Qur'an Hadith. In: Proceeding International Conference on Innovation in Science, Education, Health and Technology, pp. 133–142 (2022)
22. Carvajal, D.A.L., Morita, M.M., Bilmes, G.M.: Virtual museums. Captured reality and 3D modeling. J. Cult. Herit. **45**, 234–239 (2020). https://doi.org/10.1016/j.culher.2020.04.013
23. Javora, O., Hannemann, T., Stárková, T., Volná, K., Brom, C.: Children like it more but don't learn more: effects of esthetic visual design in educational games. Br. J. Educ. Technol. **50**, 1942–1960 (2019). https://doi.org/10.1111/bjet.12701

24. Sanchez, D.R., Langer, M., Kaur, R.: Gamification in the classroom: examining the impact of gamified quizzes on student learning. Comput. Educ. **144**, 103666 (2020). https://doi.org/10.1016/j.compedu.2019.103666
25. Khoirunnisa, A.N., Munir, Dewi, L.: Design and prototype development of augmented reality in reading learning for autism. Computers **12**, 55 (2023). https://doi.org/10.3390/computers12030055

The Use of Augmented Reality, Virtual Reality, and Mixed Reality in Communication Children's with ASD: Systematic Literature Review

Azizah Nurul Khoirunnisa[1]([✉]), Munir[2], Laksmi Dewi[1], Rasim[2], Nissa Nur Azizah[2], and Zsalzsa Puspa Alivia[2]

[1] Curriculum Development Study Program, Indonesia University of Education, Bandung, Indonesia
azizah@upi.edu

[2] Computer Science Education Study Program, Indonesia University of Education, Bandung, Indonesia

Abstract. Autism spectrum disorder (ASD) is a neurobiological developmental disorder that affects communication and social interaction. Autistic children often have difficulty communicating effectively, both verbally and nonverbally. Good verbal and nonverbal communication skills help children with autism participate in social interactions. In this paper, we present a systematic literature review focused on analyzing AR/VR/Mixed reality technologies used to improve communication skills in children with ASD based on research published over the last ten years and available in relevant scientific databases. We reviewed 22 studies showing target area communication, how AR/VR/Mixed reality is used in the context of communication skills in ASD children, user experience and accessibility, technology limitations, and findings. This systematic review of the literature shows that the majority of the communication areas targeted are verbal and nonverbal simultaneously. Overall, the use of AR/VR/Mixed reality can be an alternative to improve children's communication. Technologies that can facilitate the different abilities and emotions of children with ASD are considered in developing AR/VR/Mixed reality in the future.

Keywords: Systematic Literature Review · Autism Spectrum Disorder · Augmented Reality · Virtual Reality · Mixed Reality · Communication

1 Introduction

ASD (Autism Spectrum Disorder) is a brain development disorder characterized by disturbances in social interaction, verbal and non-verbal communication, and restricted, repetitive and stereotyped patterns of behavior, interests or activities [1]. The prevalence of ASD has been increasing globally, making it a significant public health problem. Intervention in the number of ASD children in various countries continues to increase, with the latest data from the Center for Disease Control and Prevention (CDC) in 2020 estimating that 1 in 36 children in the United States has an autism spectrum disorder [2].

H. Badioze Zaman et al. (Eds.): IVIC 2023, LNCS 14322, pp. 175–190, 2024.
https://doi.org/10.1007/978-981-99-7339-2_16

ASD is difficulty communicating verbally and nonverbally. Verbal communication challenges may include delayed language acquisition, echolalia (repeating words or phrases), and difficulty starting or maintaining a conversation. Whereas nonverbal communication difficulties may involve limited eye contact, unusual facial expressions, and a lack of understanding of gestures or body language [3]. As a result of this communication disorder can have a significant impact on children's ability to interact with other people, form relationships, participate in daily activities, so that they can experience difficulties in conveying the desired goals and objectives [4].

A number of studies have investigated interventions and treatments aimed at improving communication skills in children with ASD. These studies have explored a variety of approaches, including speech therapy [5], behavioral interventions [6], and technology-based interventions [7]. Speech therapy focuses on improving language skills involving hands-on interventions focused on improving the speech and language skills of children with ASD. Incorporating technology into interventions to improve communication skills in ASD is an important urgency to note. According to Roberts and Silvera, [8] through technology can help individuals with ASD to overcome the limitations of traditional approaches by offering innovative ways to help create learning environment processes, and provide the development of social skills. In addition, technology-based interventions can be easily accessed and implemented in a variety of settings, such as schools, clinics and homes, expanding the reach and availability of effective interventions. The technological interventions that have begun to be developed are the use of technology based on Augmented Reality (AR), Virtual Reality (VR), and Mixed Reality (MR).

Augmented Reality (AR), Virtual Reality (VR), and Mixed Reality are technologies used to create immersive, interactive experiences. AR is a technology that provides interactive and immersive experiences by integrating digital content into the real world [9]. Whereas VR creates a fully immersive simulation environment [10]. MR combines elements of both, namely creating real and virtual world experiences [11]. This technology has received attention in various fields, including health, education, and entertainment. They offer unique opportunities for individuals with ASD to practice and improve their communication skills in a controlled and engaging environment.

The increasing prevalence of ASD and the communication challenges faced by children with ASD require effective interventions. Technology-based interventions, including the use of AR, VR, and MR, offer exciting opportunities to improve communication skills in children with ASD. This immersive and interactive technology has the potential to create engaging learning environments, providing personalized instruction and immediate feedback. By incorporating these technologies into interventions, researchers and clinicians can contribute to improving the quality of life and social inclusion of children with ASD. Therefore, this study aims to explore the utilization of AR, VR, and MR in communication interventions for children with ASD, highlighting the urgency and potential of technology in meeting their unique needs. The aim of this paper was created by presenting a method for conducting a systematic literature review (SLR). Several literature reviews have been published on the use of augmented reality technologies in interventions with children and adolescents with ASD. Khowaja et al. (2019), have conducted SLR primary studies published in 2005 to 2018 on the use of AR to learn different skills for children and adolescents with ASD and proposed a research classification of

ASD. Berenguer et al. (2020), evaluated the effectiveness of AR technology in ASD. Lian and Sunar, (2021) have conducted SLR use of Mobile Augmented Reality for ASD-related interventions from 2010 to 2020 to identify current trends, future prospects, and possible gaps related to mobile AR technology in the field of autism spectrum disorders. Sindu et al. (2023), have conducted SLR on machine learning, VR, and AR from 2022 to 2023, from their search there are studies on machine learning and Virtual Reality for ASD Children. In addition, in the SLR research conducted by Ferreira et al. (2021), from 2007 to 2018 with VR and AR in Human Resource Management and Development, it was found that there was information related to the use that had a positive impact on VR technology for ASD children. Based on previous studies, no one has detailed SLR for interventions from AR, VR, and MR technology in ASD children's communication, therefore researchers conducted SLR using AR, VR, MR technology for interventions in ASD from 2013 to 2023 and answered five questions research (RQ). This study can have an impact on identifying current trends, the results provided, and future prospects in the field of technology for autism spectrum disorder.

Based on previous studies, no one has detailed SLR for interventions from AR, VR, and MR technology in ASD children's communication, therefore researchers conducted SLR using AR, VR, MR technology for interventions in ASD from 2013 to 2023 and answered five questions research (RQ). This study can have an impact on identifying current trends, the results provided, and future prospects in the field of technology for autism spectrum disorder.

2 Review Method

The search process followed the Preferred Reporting Items for Systematic Reviews and Meta-Analyses protocol. This type of review provides a synthesis of the state of knowledge in a field, can identify significant problems that can be corrected in further research and can produce or evaluate how and why phenomena occur.

2.1 Research Question

To cover every topic of interest in this systematic literature review, we formulated five research questions. These questions consider relevant and general aspects important for comprehending the concepts that we think are important for this study. This question can be seen in Table 1.

Table 1. Research questions for the systematic literature review

Research Question	
RQ1	What are the communication areas involved in the use of AR/VR/Mixed reality?
RQ2	How AR/VR/Mixed Reality used to enhance communication skills in children with ASD?
RQ3	What are the user experiences and accessibility considered when providing interventions using AR/VR/Mixed Reality?
RQ4	What are the technological limitations in AR/VR/Mixed Reality research in improving the communication skills of children with ASD?
RQ5	What are the findings from the AR/VR/Mixed Reality study in children with ASD?

2.2 Article Selection

Please note that the first paragraph of a section or subsection is not indented. The first paragraphs that follows a table, figure, equation etc. does not have an indent, either. Scopus was chosen because it is one of the largest databases covering various fields of knowledge. Scopus indexed journals must go through a rigorous selection process to ensure the quality of published research. Therefore, publication in the Scopus journal provides a high reputation and credibility for the author.

Table 2. Inclusion and exclusion criteria

The inclusion criteria (the article will be considered and selected with these criteria):
Articles related to the usage of AR/VR/Mixed Reality for children with ASD;
Articles related to communication skills of children with ASD;
The research articles should be published between 2013–2023;
The articles use English as its language;   Studies performed in an educative context or focused on teaching;
The exclusion criteria (the article will be eliminated if it has these following criteria):
Articles are not related to the usage of AR/VR/Mixed Reality to communicate children with ASD
The research articles are published outside of the year 2013–2023 (not in the recent ten years);
The articles do not use English as its language;

Selected articles were identified and searched using the title, keywords, and abstract of their papers with the exclusion and inclusion criteria which can be seen in Table 2. In addition, we selected articles published in 2013 to 2023. The search strategy for this research is described as follows:

Scopus:

(TITLE-ABS-KEY ("autis*") AND TITLE-ABS-
KEY ("communication" OR "social") AND TITLE-ABS-KEY ("augmented reality" OR "AR" OR "Virtual reality" OR "VR" OR "Mixed Reality")) AND PUBYEAR > 2012 AND PUBYEAR < 2024 AND (LIMIT
TO (LANGUAGE , "English")) = **707 articles**

2.3 Data Synthesis

Based on the selection criteria, we collected a total of 707 articles. The study selection process took a long time with the division of several stages of activity. The initial search yielded 707 articles on Scopus by applying several limitations such as year (2013 to 2023), type of document (article), stage of publication (final), type of source (journal), and language (English). The selection of this article uses the PRISMA flow with the following process: (1) Identification: First, perform a search on the database (Scopus) with several specific keywords to mine data; (2) Screening: After obtaining several journals from the database, researchers consider articles based on inclusion criteria; (3) Eligibility: Next, the articles that were screened were analyzed for their relevance, clarity, and quality; Lastly, (4) Included: articles selected and used in research.

The selected articles have good clarity in terms of research objectives, research questions, methods, clarity on the use of AR/VR/mixed reality, conclusions, and suggestions for further study. Eliminated studies are studies that do not meet the criteria, such as causing bias from the aspects previously described. In addition, the professor who contributed to this research, has expertise in the use of technology for children with special needs, assisted in validating the selection of articles. The articles are evaluated based on their relevance and quality. First, the relevance of the appropriate use of AR/VR/mixed reality technology to the communication skills of children with ASD. Second, the relevance of the research to the research questions on this SLR.

A search of 707 articles found on Scopus, articles that seemed relevant to the research topic were selected at this stage. The number of articles is 132 articles out of 707 articles. The next step is scanning and skimming to understand the content and relevance of the articles, and selecting the final articles to be included in the research. Selected final articles must meet the inclusion criteria. In the end, the researcher managed to collect 21 articles from journals to be used in the research. On the other hand, articles that did not meet the inclusion criteria were excluded from the list because they did not discuss several important aspects of using AR/VR/mixed reality in the communication skills of children with ASD. In addition, sometimes there are objectives, methods, results, and discussion of criteria that do not meet the unclear requirements. The stages of the article selection process can be seen in Fig. 1.

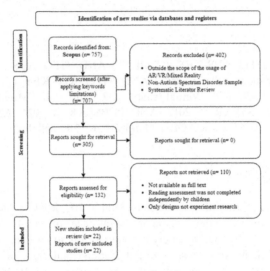

Fig. 1. PRISMA flow diagram

The articles selected are then given as a logbook to make the data synthesis process simpler. The logbook uses Google Sheets with columns containing article sources, research objectives, participants, technology used and explanations, technology limitations, areas of communication involved, and important findings. After reviewing various articles to answer research questions, researchers need to systematically describe their findings by dividing them into sections that are classified based on the research questions posed. In analyzing and synthesizing data, researchers will use literature reviews and systematic descriptions to answer each research question and reveal data through tables and figures if necessary.

3   Results

After applying the selection criteria, we gathered a total of 20 articles. These studies were analyzed under different metrics. Based on our review of these studies, we now answer our research questions, considering those studies that are relevant to the specific context of each question.

3.1   What are the Communication Areas Involved in the Use of AR/VR/Mixed Reality?

Based on the 22 collected articles, there are several types of communication involved in the use of AR/VR/Mixed reality, namely verbal, non-verbal, and a combination of verbal and non-verbal. There are 8 (36%) types of verbal communication, 4 (18%) types of non-verbal communication, and 10 (46%) types of combined verbal and non-verbal communication. Targeted non-verbal skills include facial expression [12–14], eye contact [15], gesture [7, 16–20], Emotional Expression [17, 21–24].

3.2 How AR/VR/Mixed Reality Used to Enhance Communication Skills in Children with ASD?

Several of the identified studies described the use of AR/VR/Mixed Reality, but they did not specify and/or provide details about the feature of system. However, a significant number of studies explicitly presented some feature of system that allow AR/VR/Mixed Reality to be more effective and engaging for people with ASD.

For example, Hutson (2022) analyzed the uses of VR in metaverse on improving their social interaction skills for socialization and group activities. Halabi et al. (2017), Herrerro & Lorenzo (2020) used immersive VR to presents an interactive scenario-based VR system to improve the communications skills of ASD children. The system utilizes speech recognition to provide natural interaction and role-play to evaluate the immersive environment on the social performance of autistic children. In addition, Parsons (2015), Ip (2017) designed Block Challenge as a two-player CVE game in which children had to verbally communicate and collaborate with. Additionally, Cai et al. (2013) VR with immersive visualization and movement-based interactions through the Virtual Dolphinarium allows children with ASD to act as dolphin trainers by the pool and learn communication through hand movements with virtual dolphins. Then, Yuan & Ip (2018) delivering a new collaborative virtual environment (CVE) based social interaction platform for ASD interventions. The system allows two children to play a series of interactive games in a VR environment by using simple hand movements to collaboratively move tracked virtual objects in real time through the camera. The CVE platform is Collaborative Games Design with three types of collaborative games in this paper, namely Puzzle Games (PG), Collection Games (CG), and Delivery Games (DG) (Zhao, 2018). Adaptive and socially designed VR systems respond by means of a rule-governed strategy generator (Lahiri et al. 2013). The system combines gaze information and eye physiological response to predict the participant's level of engagement, thus being able to individually adjust their response; The system is designed to deliver VR-based social tasks of varying difficulty, including two-way interaction with virtual avatars, as well as the ability to monitor behavioral views and eye physiological indicators in real-time. Also, Meins et al. (2023) using adaptive prompts in virtual reality (VR)-based driven by the emotional state of autistic children.

There are technologies enhancing engagement and facilitating realistic interactions, promoting communication skills development, namely HMD and CAVE. For example, Yuan & Ip (2018) used Immersive VRE is delivered in a four-sided Cave Automatic Virtual Environment (CAVE) that enables incredible precision and interaction with objects and avatars in virtual scenarios that include real-life situations. Children with ASD will enter CAVE individually and navigate through the VRE with the guidance and support of a coach. In addition, there is also a technology called Head-mounted displays (HMD) which provides an immersive visual and auditory experience. HMDs are relatively mobile and can be installed in any location with a power socket.

Besides technology applied in VR, there is also technology applied in AR. For examples, Mohd et al. (2019), Taryadi & Kurniawan (2018) used Picture Exchange Communication System (PECS) because of the brain performance in ASD children cannot communicate verbally and non-verbally properly so that it has an impact on cognition, behavior, and several body structures. PECS was used for this project to create a recipe book developed using AR technology as a marker based or image recognition. Also, Nubia et al. (2016) used marker-based AR with objects in the form of Animals, fruits and transport. Children are asked to describe the characteristics, sounds or movements displayed in the form of AR. The Augmented Reality (AR) technology used in Bhatt et al. (2014) studies focus on image recognition and object tracking methods in videos. Feature and edge recognition methods and other image processing methods are used in tracking to interpret images from cameras. In computer image recognition, there are two types of tracking methods, namely feature-based and model-based tracking. Horace (2016) uses applied behavioral analysis techniques, autism and related communication and training and education for children with disorders, Image Exchange Communication System (PECS), flora of time, social stories and sensor integration. Also, Bai et al. (2013) selected marker-based tracking is based on two main considerations. First, the flexibility of selecting objects to be tracked. Compared to model-based tracking which requires a pre-built 3D model, marker-based tracking allows the choice of objects to be tracked to be expanded easily. Second, avoid hiding hands (hand occlusion). In marker-based tracking, marker placement can be adjusted to reduce the impact of hiding the hand on the main object. Moreover, there were another technology named Mixed Reality. Furthermore, Lin et al. (2023) uses iAnimate Live which is a project that creates virtual environments, virtual characters (avatars), augmented reality, and animation. These people were taught to start a conversation in five steps (looking at the person and smiling, standing some distance away, using a sweet voice, asking questions, and waiting their turn to speak). All instructions are led by the avatar, while a human is present to provide the model and act as a communicative partner for the child. Sahin et al. (2018) empowered brain smart glasses which consist of a smart glasses platform combined with a series of software modules that focus on key training areas, such as increasing attention to social cues, assisting trainers' facial emotion recognition, and assisting with transitions between different environments. Then, Keshav et al. (2017) stated that Empowered Brain games correlated with the severity of ADHD symptoms in students with ASD. Liu et al. (2017) used BPS, which is a smart glasses-based behavioral aid tool designed to help children and adults with ASD improve emotional understanding, direct gaze, eye contact, and self-control. BPS is a combination of hardware and software add-ons that can be integrated into various smart glasses platforms.

3.3   What are the User Experiences and Accessibility Considered When Providing Interventions Using AR/VR/Mixed Reality?

Experience and accessibility for children with ASD are considered essential. Several reported studies have considered user experience and accessibility for children with ASD. Not many provide enough details about the use of user-friendly concepts. However, we identified all studies related to the experiences and accessibility of children with ASD regarding AutismGuide: a usability guideline to design software solutions for users with autism spectrum disorder from Aguiar et al. [25].

In terms of user experience and accessibility, the majority of studies provide adequate instruction for any given AR/VR-based intervention. One of them is the use of a

Collaborative Virtual Environment (CVE) [14, 17, 18, 23, 24], providing clear collaboration instructions so that users (children) with autism) can efficiently complete and share tasks with their peers.

Several studies using AR [19, 26–28], se visuals such as pictures, icons, photos, images, and symbols that are easy to use. Understood. The text displayed is clear, simple, precise, and familiar to children with ASD. In addition, Cai et al. [20], Herrero & Lorenzo [21], Lin et al. [29], Zhao et al. [16, 30], Taryadi & Kurniawan [7], and Hutson [22] use feedback in the form of text, motion, or sound as a form of accessibility for children with ASD.

Keshav et al. [12, 31], Liu et al. [32], Sahin et al. [13] used Empowered Brain Smartglasses, which have advantages in producing data on children's progress for Individualized Educational Program reports. In addition, smart glasses do not require a mouse, keyboard or separate screen. Another study used adaptive interventions. Lahiri et al. [15] designed a system that can present content with varying difficulty levels according to the user's ability and development level (ASD children). Meanwhile, Moon & Ke [33] present content in the form of adaptive requests according to the emotional state of ASD children.

3.4 What Are the Technological Limitations in AR/VR/Mixed Reality Research in Improving the Communication Skills of Children with ASD?

The main limitation of this study relates basically to the quality designs carried out so far. Some of the challenges in technology development for individuals on the autism spectrum (ASD). One is the use of wearable eye trackers and two-way speech modules that require the use of a mouse, which may not be suitable for individuals with a low functional level in ASD. In addition, there is no support for haptic interfaces that can provide physical feedback to the user. The flexibility of the interaction between the user and the avatar in a virtual reality (VR) environment can still be improved, as well as the adaptability. Since each individual is unique, they differ in abilities, sensory preferences, interests, and emotional situations.

In addition, there are limitations in perfectly depicting the real world, the physical interactions that can be experienced by users, and the adaptation of knowledge and skills from the virtual environment to real life. The use of the CAVE system also has limitations because it requires special space and higher costs. However, the use of Head-Mounted Display (HMD) devices can overcome some of these obstacles with their advantages in mobility and the ability to install in various locations. However, it is important to remember that using virtual reality technology without the support of a therapist or coach may not produce optimal results. Therefore, their role and presence need to be considered in the implementation of this technology. In the early stages of the prototype, there was a jitter problem in the augmentation (adding virtual elements) which could disrupt the user experience. However, this problem was minimized by applying the double exponential smoothing method in Goblin XNA.

3.5 What are the Findings from the AR/VR/Mixed Reality Study in Children with ASD?

All of the selected studies positively impacted the communication skills of children with ASD. In a study using AR, Mohd et al. [19] and Bai et al. [28] revealed that AR can be more flexible, interactive, engaging, and easy to use. While Bhatt et al. [27] found that AR games make children concentrate more, develop imagination, and receive motivating visual feedback through repetitive movements. Lin et al. [29] revealed that using AR to aid communication skills, children with ASD are more willing to engage in conversation. The results of the research conducted by Taryadi & Kurniawan [7] revealed that factors influencing the improvement of participants' communication skills were interest in the teacher, physical conditions such as hunger, satiety, sleepiness, and autism spectrum level. In addition, environmental factors also greatly influence the improvement of children's communication skills with ASD, such as supportive conditions and great motivation from the family. Meanwhile, Nubia et al. [26] found that, at the beginning of the introduction of AR media, some children with ASD were quite disturbed by the characteristics of the sounds produced by AR media; this depended on the sensitivity of the children's hearing.

In a VR study, the results of research conducted by Zhao et al. [16] showed that participants enjoyed the collaborative games presented by VR media and were getting better at collaborating in these games. In addition, it was found that participants can be positively influenced by their partners while playing this game. These spontaneous conversations can help children with ASD practice verbal behavior naturally and visually. Results of research by Halabi et al. [17], Parsons [18], and Ip et al. [14] also show that a collaborative environment can improve better performance; this is based on more motivation when working together. Likewise, research conducted by Herrero & Lorenzo [21] revealed that by using VR, the interactions provided can increase flexibility and more control over the occurrence of interactions so that VR can increase interest in communication activities for children with ASD. Similar to the research conducted by Zhao et al. [30] shows that, VR, as a real-time communication tool, guarantees a flexible and uninterrupted exchange of information.

Cai et al. [20] revealed that using VR as a visualization medium allows instructions to be delivered consistently and carried out repeatedly. VR also allows children with ASD to perform activities that are difficult to achieve or even risky if done directly in the real world. Besides that, Lahiri et al. [15], Moon & Ke [33], and Ip et al. [23] revealed that VR can be used as an adaptive intervention so that it can encourage the performance of children's communication skills with ASD. In addition, the findings of research conducted by Hutson [22] show that the use of VR has a good impact on students diagnosed with ASD in communication because it can adjust to the environmental conditions that exist in the virtual world, such as a quiet environment with low lighting, little or no music or noise, and they can adjust the sound or mute others if desired.

In Mixed Reality studies, all research results gave positive results on the communication skills of children with ASD. In addition to improving communication skills, using smart glasses as a mixed reality technology also increases the motivation and cognition of ASD children [12, 13]. Research conducted by [32] and [31] shows increased non-verbal communication, eye contact, and social engagement. It is undeniable that smart glasses are quite expensive. Meanwhile, Yuan & Ip [24] show that head-mounted displays (HMD) can overcome these cost limitations. The more mobile use of HMDs allows communication skills training to be carried out in schools to benefit the wider ASD population.

4 Discussion

In this study, we explored AR/VR/Mixed reality interventions on the communication skills of children with ASD. The communication skills that are the target of the intervention are verbal and non-verbal communication. However, 10 of the 22 studies conducted interventions targeting the development of both verbal and non-verbal communication skills simultaneously. Communication does not just involve words, it also involves body language, facial expressions, tone of voice, hand gestures, and many other nonverbal elements [34, 35]. Combining verbal and nonverbal communication learning helps in developing better social skills [36, 37]. For children with ASD who have the potential to develop verbal communication, integration of learning non-verbal communication can also help them understand the meaning of emotions, intonation and facial expressions in conversational contexts. This can enrich their use of language and help them overcome communication barriers [38].

AR/VR/MR is a solution to support communication barriers in children with ASD. This technology is able to create an interactive and immersive environment that supports the development of these skills [39–41]. Many studies present unique features in AR/VR/MR systems that enable their effective use in children with ASD. These features include speech recognition, gesture recognition, two-way interaction with virtual avatars, and social skills training through interactive scenarios. Children with ASD have a tendency to process information better through sight. Visual content, such as images, icons, and symbols, can help them better understand concepts and information than words alone [42–44].

In technology development, experience and accessibility are important factors for children with ASD. Positive experiences and good accessibility can help children with ASD participate in and benefit fully from the technology. Several studies have considered user experience and accessibility for children with ASD. This reflects an awareness of the importance of understanding and addressing the needs and preferences of children with ASD to ensure maximum benefit from these technological solutions [45]. Nonetheless, not all studies provide sufficient detail regarding user-friendly concepts. Therefore, good experience and accessibility, supported by clear instructions, appropriate feedback, appropriate visual elements, and adaptive intervention approaches, are at the heart of designing effective and beneficial technology solutions for children with ASD [20, 46]. Increased attention to these aspects can lead to more positive outcomes in technology use by children with ASD [47–50].

The literature review results highlight some of the limitations encountered in developing technologies for individuals with ASD. These limitations point to the need for further efforts to design technology solutions that are more effective, inclusive, and suited to the unique needs of those on the ASD spectrum. An adaptable system can be considered for future studies. They consider that every autistic child has different needs and ability levels [51]. Adaptable learning media allows the teacher or teacher to adjust the content, level of difficulty, and teaching methods according to the needs of each child [52, 53]. It helps ensure that autistic children get appropriate learning experiences to their level, maximizing their learning potential.

On the other hand, AR/VR/Mixed reality has shown positive results in improving the communication skills of children with ASD. However, it is important to remember that these technologies must be used with the support of a therapist or trainer, and take into account the unique and individual needs of ASD. In order to optimally support the development of communication skills, this technology must be applied carefully and adapted to the conditions and preferences of each individual.

5 Conclusion

Our systematic literature review focused on analyzing AR/VR/Mixed reality technologies used to improve communication skills in children with ASD based on research published over the past ten years and available in relevant scientific databases. Most of the use of AR/VR/MR positively impacts ASD children in improving their reading skills. Exciting features in AR/VR/MR technologies, such as voice recognition, gesture recognition, interaction with virtual avatars and training of social skills through interactive scenarios, enable their effective use for children with ASD. The needs and preferences of children with ASD are key points to consider in technology development. AR/VR/MR technologies have great potential to support children with ASD in overcoming communication barriers. The interactive environment and interesting features in the created AR/VR/MR can facilitate the development of communication skills of children with ASD. Despite the experimental results, the current study is limited in its use of AR/VR/Mixed Reality, and researchers cannot generalize to the conclusion that children with ASD can improve their communication skills. The elaboration of the limitations discussed can be a consideration for future studies.

Acknowledgment. We would like to appreciate and thank PMDSU Scholarship under Direktorat Jenderal Pendidikan Tinggi, Kementerian Pendidikan dan Kebudayaan Republik Indonesia for support throughout this research.

References

1. Kodak, T., Bergmann, S.: Autism spectrum disorder. Pediatr. Clin. North Am. **67**(3), 525–535 (2020). https://doi.org/10.1016/j.pcl.2020.02.007
2. Maenner, M.J., et al.: Prevalence and characteristics of autism spectrum disorder among children aged 8 years—autism and developmental disabilities monitoring network, 11 sites, United States, 2020. MMWR Surveill. Summ. **72**(2), 1–14 (2023). https://doi.org/10.15585/mmwr.ss7202a1
3. La Valle, C., Plesa-Skwerer, D., Tager-Flusberg, H.: Comparing the pragmatic speech profiles of minimally verbal and verbally fluent individuals with autism spectrum disorder. J. Autism Dev. Disord. **50**(10), 3699–3713 (2020). https://doi.org/10.1007/s10803-020-04421-7

4. Baixauli-Fortea, I., Miranda Casas, A., Berenguer-Forner, C., Colomer-Diago, C., Roselló-Miranda, B.: Pragmatic competence of children with autism spectrum disorder. Impact of theory of mind, verbal working memory, ADHD symptoms, and structural language. Appl. Neuropsychol. Child **8**(2), 101–112 (2019). https://doi.org/10.1080/21622965.2017.1392861
5. Kasilingam, N., Waddington, H., Van Der Meer, L.: Early intervention for children with autism spectrum disorder in New Zealand: what children get and what parents want. Int. J. Disabil. Dev. Educ. **68**(4), 521–537 (2021). https://doi.org/10.1080/1034912X.2019.1696949
6. Vietze, P., Lax, L.E.: Early intervention ABA for toddlers with ASD: effect of age and amount. Curr. Psychol. **39**(4), 1234–1244 (2020). https://doi.org/10.1007/s12144-018-9812-z
7. Taryadi, Kurniawan, I.: The improvement of autism spectrum disorders on children communication ability with PECS method multimedia augmented reality-based. J. Phys.: Conf. Ser. (2018). https://doi.org/10.1088/1742-6596/947/1/012009
8. Roberts-Yates, C., Silvera-Tawil, D.: Better education opportunities for students with autism and intellectual disabilities through digital technology. Int. J. Spec. Educ. **34**(1), 197–210 (2019)
9. Cabero-Almenara, J., Roig-Vila, R.: The motivation of technological scenarios in Augmented Reality (AR): results of different experiments. Appl. Sci. **9**(14), 2907 (2019). https://doi.org/10.3390/app9142907
10. Wohlgenannt, I., Simons, A., Stieglitz, S.: Virtual reality. Bus. Inf. Syst. Eng. **62**(5), 455–461 (2020). https://doi.org/10.1007/s12599-020-00658-9
11. Tang, Y.M., Au, K.M., Lau, H.C.W., Ho, G.T.S., Wu, C.H.: Evaluating the effectiveness of learning design with mixed reality (MR) in higher education. Virtual Real. **24**(4), 797–807 (2020). https://doi.org/10.1007/s10055-020-00427-9
12. Keshav, N.U., Vogt-Lowell, K., Vahabzadeh, A., Sahin, N.T.: Digital attention-related augmented-reality game: significant correlation between student game performance and validated clinical measures of attention-deficit/hyperactivity disorder (ADHD). Children **6**(6) (2019). https://doi.org/10.3390/children6060072
13. Sahin, N.T., Abdus-Sabur, R., Keshav, N.U., Liu, R., Salisbury, J.P., Vahabzadeh, A.: Case study of a digital augmented reality intervention for autism in school classrooms: associated with improved social communication, cognition, and motivation via educator and parent assessment. Front. Educ. (Lausanne) **3** (2018). https://doi.org/10.3389/feduc.2018.00057
14. Ip, H.H.S., et al.: Enhance emotional and social adaptation skills for children with autism spectrum disorder: a virtual reality enabled approach. Comput. Educ. **117**, 1–15 (2018). https://doi.org/10.1016/j.compedu.2017.09.010
15. Lahiri, U., Bekele, E., Dohrmann, E., Warren, Z., Sarkar, N.: Design of a virtual reality based adaptive response technology for children with autism. IEEE Trans. Neural Syst. Rehabil. Eng. **21**(1), 55–64 (2013). https://doi.org/10.1109/TNSRE.2012.2218618
16. Zhao, H., Swanson, A.R., Weitlauf, A.S., Warren, Z.E., Sarkar, N.: Hand-in-hand: a communication-enhancement collaborative virtual reality system for promoting social interaction in children with autism spectrum disorders. IEEE Trans. Hum. Mach. Syst. **48**(2), 136–148 (2018). https://doi.org/10.1109/THMS.2018.2791562
17. Halabi, O., Abou El-Seoud, S., Alja'am, J., Alpona, H., Al-Hemadi, M., Al-Hassan, D.: Design of Immersive Virtual Reality System to Improve Communication Skills in Individuals with Autism. Int. J. Emerg. Technol. Learn. (iJET) **12**(05), 50 (2017). https://doi.org/10.3991/ijet.v12i05.6766
18. Parsons, S.: Learning to work together: designing a multi-user virtual reality game for social collaboration and perspective-taking for children with autism. Int. J. Child. Comput. Interact. **6**, 28–38 (2015). https://doi.org/10.1016/j.ijcci.2015.12.002
19. Mohd, C.K.N.C.K., Shahbodin, F., Suparjoh, S., Khidir, N.A.S.M.: Application of augmented reality in learning bakery for autism spectrum disorder. Int. J. Eng. Adv. Technol. **9**(1), 2616–2620 (2019). https://doi.org/10.35940/ijeat.A9853.109119

20. Cai, Y., Chia, N.K.H., Thalmann, D., Kee, N.K.N., Zheng, J., Thalmann, N.M.: Design and development of a Virtual Dolphinarium for children with autism. IEEE Trans. Neural Syst. Rehabil. Eng. **21**(2), 208–217 (2013). https://doi.org/10.1109/TNSRE.2013.2240700

21. Herrero, J.F., Lorenzo, G.: An immersive virtual reality educational intervention on people with autism spectrum disorders (ASD) for the development of communication skills and problem solving. Educ. Inf. Technol. (Dordr.) **25**(3), 1689–1722 (2020). https://doi.org/10.1007/s10639-019-10050-0

22. Hutson, J.: Social virtual reality: neurodivergence and inclusivity in the metaverse. Societies **12**(4), 102 (2022). https://doi.org/10.3390/soc12040102

23. Ip, H.H.S., et al.: Virtual reality enabled training for social adaptation in inclusive education settings for school-aged children with Autism Spectrum Disorder (ASD). In: Cheung, S., Kwok, Lf., Shang, J., Wang, A., Kwan, R. (eds.) ICBL 2016. LNCS, vol. 9757, pp. 94–102. Springer, Cham (2016). https://doi.org/10.1007/978-3-319-41165-1_9

24. Yuan, S.N.V., Ip, H.H.S.: Using virtual reality to train emotional and social skills in children with autism spectrum disorder. Lond. J. Prim. Care (Abingdon) **10**(4), 110–112 (2018). https://doi.org/10.1080/17571472.2018.1483000

25. Aguiar, Y.P.C., Galy, E., Godde, A., Trémaud, M., Tardif, C.: AutismGuide: a usability guideline to design software solutions for users with autism spectrum disorder. Behav. Inf. Technol. **41**(6), 1132–1150 (2022). https://doi.org/10.1080/0144929X.2020.1856927

26. Nubia, R.M., Fabian, G.R., Wilson, R.A., Wilmer, P.B.: Development of a mobile application in augmented reality to improve the communication field of autistic children at a Neurorehabilitar Clinic. In: 2015 Workshop on Engineering Applications - International Congress on Engineering (WEA), pp. 1–6. IEEE (2015). https://doi.org/10.1109/WEA.2015.7370154

27. Bhatt, S.K., De Leon, N.I., Al-Jumaily, A.: Augmented reality game therapy for children with autism spectrum disorder. Int. J. Smart Sens. Intell. Syst. **7**(2), 519–536 (2022). https://doi.org/10.21307/ijssis-2017-668

28. Bai, Z., Blackwell, A.F., Coulouris, G.: Through the looking glass: pretend play for children with autism. In: 2013 IEEE International Symposium on Mixed and Augmented Reality (ISMAR), pp. 49–58. IEEE (2013). https://doi.org/10.1109/ISMAR.2013.6671763

29. Lin, L.-Y., Lin, C.-H., Chuang, T.-Y., Loh, S.C., Chu, S.Y.: Using home-based augmented reality storybook training modules for facilitating emotional functioning and socialization of children with autism spectrum disorder. Int. J. Dev. Disabil. 1–8 (2023). https://doi.org/10.1080/20473869.2023.2202454

30. Zhao, H., Swanson, A., Weitlauf, A., Warren, Z., Sarkar, N.: A novel collaborative virtual reality game for children with ASD to foster social interaction. In: Antona, M., Stephanidis, C. (eds.) UAHCI 2016. LNCS, vol. 9739, pp. 276–288. Springer, Cham (2016). https://doi.org/10.1007/978-3-319-40238-3_27

31. Keshav, N.U., Salisbury, J.P., Vahabzadeh, A., Sahin, N.T.: Social communication coaching smartglasses: well tolerated in a diverse sample of children and adults with autism. JMIR Mhealth Uhealth **5**(9) (2017). https://doi.org/10.2196/mhealth.8534

32. Liu, R., Salisbury, J.P., Vahabzadeh, A., Sahin, N.T.: Feasibility of an autism-focused augmented reality smartglasses system for social communication and behavioral coaching. Front Pediatr **5** (2017). https://doi.org/10.3389/fped.2017.00145

33. Moon, J., Ke, F.: Effects of adaptive prompts in virtual reality-based social skills training for children with autism. J. Autism Dev. Disord. (2023). https://doi.org/10.1007/s10803-023-06021-7

34. Ezeh, N.G., Anidi, O.C., Nwokolo, B.O.: Body language as a communicative aid amongst language impaired students: managing disabilities. Engl. Lang. Teach. **14**(6), 125 (2021). https://doi.org/10.5539/elt.v14n6p125

35. Purnell, L.: Cross cultural communication: verbal and non-verbal communication, interpretation and translation. In: Douglas, M., Pacquiao, D., Purnell, L. (eds.) Global Applications of Culturally Competent Health Care: Guidelines for Practice, pp. 131–142. Springer, Cham (2018). https://doi.org/10.1007/978-3-319-69332-3_14

36. Franchini, M., et al.: Variability in verbal and nonverbal communication in infants at risk for autism spectrum disorder: predictors and outcomes. J. Autism Dev. Disord. **48**(10), 3417–3431 (2018). https://doi.org/10.1007/s10803-018-3607-9

37. Watkins, L., Kuhn, M., Ledbetter-Cho, K., Gevarter, C., O'Reilly, M.: Evidence-based social communication interventions for children with autism spectrum disorder. Indian J. Pediatr. **84**(1), 68–75 (2017). https://doi.org/10.1007/s12098-015-1938-5

38. Febriantini, W.A. Fitriati, R., Oktaviani, L.: An analysis of verbal and non-verbal communication in autistic children. J. Res. Lang. Educ. (JoRLE) **2**(1), 53–56 (2021). https://doi.org/10.1111/j.1460

39. Fong, K.N.K., Ma, W.Y., Pang, H.K., Tang, P.P.K., Law, L.L.F.: Immediate effects of coloured overlays on the reading performance of preschool children with an autism spectrum disorder using eye tracking. Res. Dev. Disabil. **89**, 141–148 (2019). https://doi.org/10.1016/j.ridd.2019.03.012

40. Engel, K.S., Ehri, L.C.: Reading comprehension instruction for young students with autism: forming contextual connections. J. Autism Dev. Disord. **51**(4), 1266–1280 (2021). https://doi.org/10.1007/s10803-020-04596-z

41. Daniels, S.: Visual Learning and Teaching: An Essential Guide for Educators K–8. Free Spirit Publishing, Minneapolis (2018)

42. Solis, M., Reutebuch, C.K., Falcomata, T., Jimenez, Z., Cravalho, D.: Reading intervention for students with ASD in the middle grades: an alternating treatment study of embedded interests reading and expository text conditions. Dev. Neurorehabil. **25**(1), 45–58 (2022). https://doi.org/10.1080/17518423.2021.1942279

43. Zafiri, M., Konstantinidou, A., Pliogou, V.: The application of differentiated instruction in reading and writing to a boy with autism in early childhood education. A case study. Univ. J. Educ. Res. **7**(12), 2609–2626 (2019). https://doi.org/10.13189/ujer.2019.071208

44. Wang, X., Laffey, J., Xing, W., Galyen, K., Stichter, J.: Fostering verbal and non-verbal social interactions in a 3D collaborative virtual learning environment: a case study of youth with Autism Spectrum Disorders learning social competence in iSocial. Educ. Tech. Res. Dev. **65**(4), 1015–1039 (2017). https://doi.org/10.1007/s11423-017-9512-7

45. Chung, C.H., Chen, C.H.: Augmented reality based social stories training system for promoting the social skills of children with autism. In: Soares, M., Falcão, C., Ahram, T. (eds.) Advances in Ergonomics Modeling, Usability & Special Populations. Advances in Intelligent Systems and Computing, vol. 486, pp. 495–505. Springer, Cham (2017). https://doi.org/10.1007/978-3-319-41685-4_44

46. Light, J., McNaughton, D.: Communicative competence for individuals who require augmentative and alternative communication: a new definition for a new era of communication? Augment. Altern. Commun. **30**(1), 1–18 (2014). https://doi.org/10.3109/07434618.2014.885080

47. McKenney, E.L.W., Bristol, R.M.: Supporting intensive interventions for students with autism spectrum disorder: Performance feedback and discrete trial teaching. Sch. Psychol. Q. **30**(1), 8–22 (2015). https://doi.org/10.1037/spq0000060

48. Tay, H.Y., Kee, K.N.N.: Effective questioning and feedback for learners with autism in an inclusive classroom. Cogent Educ. **6**(1), 1634920 (2019). https://doi.org/10.1080/2331186X.2019.1634920

49. Bateman, K.J., et al.: Visual supports to increase conversation engagement for preschoolers with autism spectrum disorder during mealtimes: an initial investigation. J. Early Interv. (2022). https://doi.org/10.1177/10538151221111762

50. Meadan, H., Ostrosky, M.M., Triplett, B., Michna, A., Fettig, A.: Using visual supports with young children with autism spectrum disorder. Counc. Except. Child. (2016)
51. Munir, Kaosar, R.N., Rasim, Murtadha, I., Shahbodin, F., Riza, L.S.: Expert system using the educational game to determine children's autism levels using forward chaining. Linguist. Cult. Rev. (2021). https://doi.org/10.37028/lingcure.v5nS1.1499
52. Chen, J., Wang, G., Zhang, K.: Personalized intelligent intervention and precise evaluation for children with autism spectrum disorder. In: Proceedings of DELFI Workshops, p. 127 (2020). https://doi.org/10.18420/delfi2020-ws-114
53. Khoirunnisa, A.N., Munir, Dewi, L.: Design and prototype development of augmented reality in reading learning for autism. Computers 12(3), 55 (2023). https://doi.org/10.3390/comput ers12030055

Hybrid on a Budget: An Autoethnographic Study

Shariffah Bahyah Binti Syed Ahmad[1]([✉]) and Syed Nasir Alsagoff Bin Syed Zakaria[2]

[1] Infrastructure University Kuala Lumpur, Kajang, Selangor, Malaysia
shariffahbahyah@iukl.edu.my
[2] Universiti Pertahanan Nasional Malaysia, Kuala Lumpur, Malaysia

Abstract. This study is an autoethnography which looked at the experience of hybrid teaching of a member of the academic society. It offers insights into the thoughts and actions of a private university lecturer in identifying suitable equipment that is within the limited budget of the said lecturer. The needs, wants and constraints were the main considerations in designing an environment for hybrid teaching on a budget. The findings also highlight the physical and mental demands of conducting a hybrid class. The study produced the S2C2 Model for the setting up of a hybrid environment which in actuality can be used as a basic guide for designing hybrid classrooms for those who are on a budget as well as for those with a limitless budget.

Keywords: Hybrid Teaching · Hybrid Classroom · Autoethnography

1 Introduction

For those who have lived through the COVID-19 Pandemic experience, a certain compartmentalisation of memories has taken place where many experiences are catalogued as before COVID, during COVID and after(math) COVID. Before COVID, the majority of those involved in teaching had limited experience with online teaching. Some may recall a certain amount of resistance related to their information technology ability and capacity as well as scepticism on the effectiveness of online learning [1]. This all had to be set aside during COVID with online learning being the only way to ensure that students still had the opportunity to continue their education.

In the aftermath of COVID, a reverse exodus took place with a gradual return to campus seen throughout the world and traditional face-to-face classes resumed with an element of blended learning [2]. Blended learning, however, does not address issues related to the aftermath of COVID. In the initial after(math) COVID days, lecturers were instructed to resume physical classes though some students were not able to return to campus due to continued travel restrictions [3]. In addition, precautions against the spread of COVID continued to be undertaken on campus. Generally, students and university staff who displayed symptoms such as sore throat, fever or cough were discouraged from being present on campus [4]. Some lecturers may consider these absences as medical

H. Badioze Zaman et al. (Eds.): IVIC 2023, LNCS 14322, pp. 191–199, 2024.
https://doi.org/10.1007/978-981-99-7339-2_17

leave for the students and continue to conduct face-to-face classes while providing other asynchronous support for those who miss class.

This is a record of one lecturer's endeavours to provide, on a limited budget, continual teaching to students who were unable to attend class for various reasons, including COVID fears or travelling restrictions, via the hybrid teaching method.

2   Review of Literature

The term 'hybrid' has carried many different meanings. In 2006, Scida and Saury used the term to refer to courses offered that had three hours of class time and 2 h of web-based activities [5]. More than a decade later, Linder described a hybrid course as meeting in person for a certain number of determined hours of the week and learning through technology-mediated activities outside of the four walls of the classroom [6]. Fordham University equates hybrid courses to blended courses with face-to-face encounters interspaced with computer-based communication [7]. These uses of hybrid imply that all students are required in class at certain times and participate online at others. This is not the definition used in the paper. Instead, this paper's operational definition of hybrid teaching takes after the University of Oxford's definition of "an educational model in which some students attend a lecture or seminar in-person as normal, while others join virtually from home. Lecturers, therefore, teach remote and in-person students at the same time" [8].

Hybrid teaching models bring many organisational benefits to the institution. Even before COVID, calls for inclusivity in giving opportunities to learners who could not pursue education in the traditional setting highlighted the need for hybrid teaching [9]. For the education industry, this means enlarging the pool of potential students [10]. Hybrid allows inter-campus teaching where the same lecturer can be used to synchronously teach students from different campuses [11], saving costs and time for all involved. Another benefit is that it gives more flexibility to students to choose remote learning in the event of ill health or logistics reasons [12].

The challenges to hybrid teaching are many and varied. There is a need to adapt materials to cater to both sets of students in order to maintain equality [13, 14]. In addition, there is a mental demand on the teacher or instructor where they are required not only to multi-task but also to divide their attention and focus equally on both sets of students [15]. The teacher also needs to be technologically competent in handling different sets of teaching aids to cater to the two different types students [13]. Most of the time, teachers find that remote students are not as actively engaged as those who attend class face-to-face. This can add stress to the lecturer, especially in handling those who are present in name but not present when called upon [16].

Despite scepticism on the effectiveness of online learning specifically [1], some studies have proven that students undergoing online learning have not been negatively affected [17, 18]. Since online learning provides opportunities to remote students, this would mean that on-campus students have the opportunity to be exposed to a broader diversity in terms of views and opinions which would enrich the learning experience [13, 19]. The flexibility provided by hybrid teaching could also mean a lower drop-out rate [16] for the institution.

3   Financial Cost of Setting Up Hybrid Classrooms

In the aftermath of COVID, many institutions are now actively looking into the setting up of hybrid classrooms. Ayub et al. developed a solution to cater to on-campus and off-campus students at a private university in Malaysia [20]. Similarly, Triyason et al. designed a hybrid classroom for a Thai university to face the new normal [21]. Universiti Putra Malaysia has several recommendations for a hybrid classroom design ranging from *Set Startup* to *Set Ultimate*. Equipment recommended for the *Set Startup*, which is meant for a class of 10 students or less, includes a video camera, a wireless audio system and a Smart Board [22].

In addition to existing facilities like LCD projectors, personal or laptop computers and the internet, the new designs call for the use of equipment that has at least video-conference capabilities and high-end cameras. These would, of course, come at a cost. In UPM's *Set Startup*, the cameras and speakers alone would cost RM3,000 while those for the higher-end *Set Premium* could cost up to RM23,000 for a set. Those figures do not include other equipment [22, 23]. An estimate for *Set Premium* put the cost of RM200,000. For private institutions, these expenses are simply not viable for the moment, especially with many facing financial distress, a situation that was in existence even before COVID [24, 25, 26].

Due to the unfeasibility in terms of costs of setting up multiple numbers of costly hybrid classrooms, lecturers had to rely on their ingenuity and at times, their own resources to provide continual education to those who would otherwise miss class. This study explored the hybrid teaching experiences of a lecturer through the relatively new approach of autoethnography.

4   Research Method

Autoethnography is a compound word stemming from two terms 'auto' meaning of or by yourself [27] and 'ethnography' which is a qualitative strategy used by researchers to study cultural groups in a natural setting using mainly interviews and observation as tools [28]. In an autoethnographic study, "A researcher uses tenets of autobiography and ethnography to do and write autoethnography. Thus, as a method, autoethnography is both process and product" [29, p. 273]. In autoethnography, self-experience, especially in a natural setting, is seen as valuable data to be explored [30] for the purpose of expanding sociological understanding [31].

A review of studies using autoethnography revealed broad and wide approaches. In Malaysia, Aboo Bakar used reflective writing as the material for her autoethnographic study on her experience as an educator amidst COVID [32]. Ab Rahman et al. used "observation field notes and conversation interview" [33, p. 893] for data for their study on family cooperative sustainability. Crossley used dialogical interviews where a partner was involved in posing questions and listening to the answers [34].

This research adapted Crossley's method where a partner (the second author) worked together with the main participant (the first author) on developing interview questions and posing those questions to the main participant (the first author). It must also be highlighted that the partner in question helped in identifying and even procuring suitable equipment for the use of the main researcher. The involvement of an interviewer established a separation between the questions and the answers, helping in developing the positionality of the main researcher cum study participant. This is important as an acknowledgement of self-positions that can have an influence on the research and how these positions can influence the participants is vital to qualitative research [35].

An open-ended interview format was adopted covering six main areas: (1) Considerations; (2) Typical sequence of a hybrid class; (3) Challenges; (4) Overcoming or Coping with Challenges; (5) Final thoughts. The interviews were transcribed and thematically analysed, in which the researcher referred to herself as the participant in the third person.

This paper focuses on the data gathered from the first two areas mentioned above.

5 Data Findings and Analysis

5.1 Considerations in the Setting Up of Hybrid on a Budget

It was very obvious from the first moment when the researcher, as a lecturer, was asked to conduct a hybrid class that it would be challenging. Her response was, "...the first thing was that it won't be easy."

There was a major concern about a figurative splitting of the self into two, which was clearly expressed, "How do I divide my attention between those who are attending physically and those who are attending online?" She stated that "One of the most important things was eye contact." Without it, the sense of disconnect would be exacerbated. In an online class situation, the disconnect involved two parties i.e., the lecturer and the online students. In a hybrid classroom, it became a three-party issue with the physical student being the third party.

Another issue was the need to maintain an active and dynamic environment with movements around the classroom but to do so would mean moving herself away from the laptop's microphone and thus cutting off the sound for the remote students. She voiced it as "I would still want to walk around; then I won't be heard." This extended to the issue of the students being able to hear each other. The laptop speaker was not loud for the physical students, especially backbenchers, to hear what the remote students said. Similarly, the laptop's microphone was not powerful enough to pick up the responses of the physical students.

A similar situation occurred in terms of being able to see each other. The lecturer reflected, "How do the students see me? Again, I'm not going to be in front of the screen all the time." In terms of having sight of each other, the physical students could view the remote students on a projected screen. However, remote students would not be able to view the in-class students unless the camera was deliberately turned towards them.

Besides considerations involving sound, sight and connection, other aspects taken into account include ease of use, internet connection, software and convenience.

5.2 Equipment and Software for Hybrid on a Budget

With budgetary constraints, the equipment chosen had to be affordable to the lecturer. The first issue was the microphone. The lecturer decided on one that could easily be transferred from one person to another. A lapel microphone did not meet this ease-of-transfer requirement. Instead, a Bluetooth headphone with an attached microphone attached was chosen since it could be worn around the neck and be easily transferred from one person to another. Next was sound. Although the laptop came with a speaker, the sound was not clear enough for the physical students and thus, an external speaker was purchased.

In terms of visual equipment, two video cameras were used. The first was the laptop camera and the second was the handphone camera. Both devices were signed into the online class platform (Zoom) using two different accounts, with the latter's microphone muted. Although a gimbal was considered for the handphone camera, the cost and the weight of not only the device but also the tripod stand made it unattractive to the lecturer. Instead, the handphone camera was placed on a cheap plastic stand which provided "a macro, a wider view of the class so that the students can see some of their in-class classmates."

However, the drain on the battery life of a phone made this a short-stint endeavour. Instead, the lecturer ended up locating herself in front of the computer screen most of the time. It helped that the laptop screen could be tilted up for a view of the face of the lecturer when she was standing. This enabled her to look down for establishing eye contact with the remote students and look across the class for eye contact with the physical students. The lecturer, at times, turned the laptop camera around to provide the remote students with a view of the physical students, especially when the latter were giving longer responses to the lecturer's queries.

Other equipment used was the in-class LCD projector as well as a Bluetooth mouse and speaker, HDMI / VGA cable, and an LCD remote. The latter two were specially purchased so that the lecturer did not "have to go up and down getting all this from the IT Center."

Software used by the lecturer included Zoom Pro (prior purchase during the pandemic), WhatsApp and WeChat. Popular teaching software Padlet and Mindmeister (mind-mapping site) were initially used for the first few classes but they were found to be rather inconvenient. These sites were best accessed with a laptop which required electricity. With limited power outlets in the classroom, an alternative was identified in the form of WhatsApp which became "one of the main mediums" for students to post responses. WeChat was used when remote students had issues with Virtual Private Network (VPN) which allowed them to access Zoom or WhatsApp.

Most of the items used were already purchased for personal and online teaching use during COVID including the laptop, mouse and mobile phone. The only items purchased specifically for hybrid teaching were the headphone with attached microphone, external speaker and the plastic handphone stand. Two other items, the HDMI/VGA cable and the LCD remote, were purchased more for convenience, and their uses extended to fully face-to-face class.

5.3 Physical Preparations and Mental Awareness

The preparations for a class may seem routine and simple but the interviews revealed that a lot of thought and at times, physical effort had to be made for the hybrid class. As revealed by the lecturer, "The first thing to do is you push or pull the teacher's table into position because you need to put in such a way that you're not sitting not sitting in front of the (white) screen." Being in front of the white screen would mean that the physical students' view of the projected teaching materials would be blocked and as such, the positioning of the table was an important element for a hybrid classroom. At the same time, the table had to be near enough to the electrical outlets so that the laptop remained charging throughout the class. The lecturer also had to locate the best spot for the mobile phone (camera) to give a macro view of the classroom.

Testing out the different cables, "making sure that you get the right cable because in some classrooms, they use VGA; some classrooms they use HDMI," was one of the preparations that had to be made before a class could start. Added to this was signing onto Campus Wi-Fi for the laptop and phone. This was necessary because an automatic connection was not set up for these devices due to poor reception issues in other surrounding areas of the campus.

The lecturer then had to sign into Zoom accounts for both devices making sure that the background function was turned off because "you tend to disappear if you are too far away from the screen." Other settings include choosing the headphone's microphone and the external speaker for the audio setting on Zoom as well as for the laptop itself. Another audio-related setting was to make sure that the 'share sound' Zoom function was turned on for video sharing.

A deliberate choice was also made in not using the slideshow function for PowerPoint. The lecturer determined that it was important for the remote students to show their faces on videos to form a connection with the physical students. With the slideshow function being off, the 'faces' of these remote students were placed above the outline panes (left side) of the PowerPoint screen. This minimised the need to move the 'faces' around the screen in the event they "block your PowerPoint slides."

During in-class assignments, the lecturer relied heavily on WhatsApp. Students sometimes required constant visual access to the instruction for an activity which were put on PowerPoint slides. Displaying it on the screen would mean that the lecturer would not be able to use the laptop for other tasks. To address this, the lecturer resorted to cutting and pasting "the instructions from the PowerPoint and put(ting) it on WhatsApp." WhatsApp is also used in lieu of Padlet to post and share responses for short assignments or activities.

6   S2C2 Model for the Setting Up of Hybrid Classrooms

The basic considerations to the setting up of a budget hybrid environment are similar to that of a high-cost infrastructure. Triyason et al. listed among others communication abilities in using text messages, video conferencing capacities (sight and sound), and display of images to enable a view of all who are in a physical and virtual class. The other items listed were more complex and required the purchase of high-ticket items [21].

The physical and mental preparations saw the same aspects that had to be taken into account for a hybrid on a budget class. These aspects are Sound, Sight, Connection and Communication, represented in Fig. 1 as the S2C2 Model.

Sound is a major consideration in any hybrid class. The need for three-way communication between lecturer-physical students-remote students while at the same time

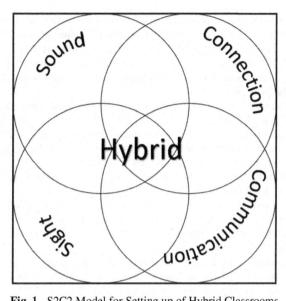

Fig. 1. S2C2 Model for Setting up of Hybrid Classrooms

allowing for a certain extent of freedom of movement led to the identification of a headphone with a microphone as the best equipment in this case.

Sight is just as important where both sets of students need not only view teaching materials but also view each other's images to establish a connection with each other as well as the lecturer. Eye contact can help to minimise the sense of disconnect.

Communication is not only helped by sound and sight but also by platforms such as WhatsApp and of course, Zoom. It is only with communication that a sense of connection could be established.

7   Conclusion

An ethnography is a study pertaining to culture and everyday occurrences of a society. This study is an autoethnography which looked at the experience of hybrid teaching of a member of the academic society. It offers insights into the thoughts and actions in identifying suitable equipment that are within the limited budget of a private university lecturer. The study also produced the S2C2 Model for the setting up of a hybrid class which in actuality can be used as a basic foundation for designing any hybrid environment, be it on a budget or on a limitless budget. This paper is the first part of a study that looked at hybrid teaching on a budget and would be followed up with another featuring the challenges that the lecturer faced.

References

1. Gratz, E., Looney, L.: Faculty resistance to change: an examination of motivators and barriers to teaching online in higher education. Int. J. Online Pedagog. Course Des. **10**(1), 1–14 (2020)

2. Wang, Z., Jiang, B., Wang, X., Niu, Y., Xue, H.: Cross-sectional investigation and correlation analysis of psychology of college students returning to campus after COVID-19 lockdown lift. Front Psychiatry (2022). https://doi.org/10.3389/fpsyt.2022.915042

3. Zhao, X., Xue, W.: From online to offline education in the post-pandemic era: Challenges encountered by international students at British universities. Front Psychol. **13** (2023). https://doi.org/10.3389/fpsyg.2022.1093475

4. Menon, S., Rajaendram, R.: Breathing life back into higher education. Star (2021)

5. Scida, E., Saury, R.: Hybrid courses and their impact on a case study at the University of Virginia. CALICO J. **23**(3), 517–531 (2006). http://www.jstor.org/stable/24156352

6. Linder, K.E.: Fundamentals of hybrid teaching and learning. New Dir. Teach. Learn. **2017**(149), 11–18 (2017). https://doi.org/10.1002/tl.20222

7. Fordham University: Types of online learning. https://www.fordham.edu/about/leadership-and-administration/administrative-offices/office-of-the-provost/provost-office-units/online-learning/types-of-online-learning/#:~:text=Hybrid%20courses%2C%20also%20known%20as,those%20face%20to%20face%20sessions. Accessed 17 Aug 2023

8. University of Oxford: What is hybrid teaching? https://www.ctl.ox.ac.uk/what-is-hybrid-teaching. Accessed 17 Aug 2023

9. Cain, W.: Technology navigators: an innovative role in pedagogy, design and instructional support. In: Redmond, P., Lock, J., Danaher, P.A. (eds.) Educational Innovations and Contemporary Technologies, pp. 21–35. Palgrave Macmillan, London (2015). https://doi.org/10.1057/9781137468611_2

10. Wang, Q., Quek, C.L., Hu, X.: Designing and improving a blended synchronous learning environment: an educational design research. Int. Rev. Res. Open Distance Learn. **18**(3), (2017). https://doi.org/10.19173/irrodl.v18i3.3034

11. Brumfield, R.G., et al.: Modifying and supplementing Annie's Project to increase impact in New Jersey and beyond. J. Ext. **55**(5), Article 8 (2017). https://doi.org/10.34068/joe.55.05.08

12. Lakhal, S., Bateman, D., Bédard, J.: Blended synchronous delivery modes in graduate programs: a literature review and how it is implemented in the master teacher program. Collect. Essays Learn. Teach. **10** (2017). https://doi.org/10.22329/celt.v10i0.4747

13. Bower, M., Dalgarno, B., Kennedy, G.E., Lee, M.J.W., Kenney, J.: Design and implementation factors in blended synchronous learning environments: outcomes from a cross-case analysis. Comput. Educ. **86**, 1–17 (2015)

14. Lightner, C. A., Lightner-Laws, C. A.: A blended model: simultaneously teaching a quantitative course traditionally, online, and remotely. Interact. Learn. Environ. **24** (2016)

15. Raes, A., Detienne, L., Windey, I., Depaepe, F.: A systematic literature review on synchronous hybrid learning: gaps identified. Learn. Environ. Res. **23** (2020). https://doi.org/10.1007/s10984-019-09303-z

16. Weitze, C.L.: Pedagogical innovation in teacher teams: an organisational learning design model for continuous competence development. In: Proceedings of the European Conference on e-Learning ECEL-2015, pp. 629–638 (2015)

17. Butz, N.T., Stupnisky, R.H.: A mixed methods study of graduate students' self-determined motivation in synchronous hybrid learning environments. Internet High. Educ. **28**(16), 85–95 (2016). https://doi.org/10.1016/j.iheduc.2015.10.003

18. Nguyen, T.: The effectiveness of online learning: beyond no significant difference and future horizons. MERLOT J. Online Learn. Teach. **11**(2), 309–319 (2015)

19. Bell, J., Sawaya, S., Cain, W.: Synchromodal classes: designing for shared learning experiences between face-to-face and online students. Int. J. Des. Learn. **5**(1) (2014). https://doi.org/10.14434/ijdl.v5i1.12657

20. Ayub, E., Lim, C.L., Yeo, D.C.H., Ismail, S.R.: Developing a solution for hybrid classroom: a pilot study from a Malaysian private university. Front Educ. (Lausanne) **7** (2022). https://doi.org/10.3389/feduc.2022.841363

21. Triyason, T., Tassanaviboon, A., Kanthamanon, P.: Hybrid classroom: designing for the new normal after COVID-19 pandemic. In: ACM International Conference Proceeding Series, pp. 1–8 (2020). https://doi.org/10.1145/3406601.3406635
22. CADe UPM: Panduan penyediaan infrastruktur pembelajaran hibrid di UPM. https://cad elead.upm.edu.my/upload/dokumen/20210719140101Infografik_Panduan_Penyediaan_Inf rastruktur_Pembelajaran_Hybrid_di_UPM.png. Accessed 17 Aug 2023
23. CADe UPM: Hybrid learning - Norma baru PdP. https://cadelead.upm.edu.my/upload/dok umen/20211118150512Hybrid_Learning_-_Norma_Baru_PdP.jpeg. Accessed 17 Aug 2023
24. Hunter, M.: The collapse of Malaysian private universities. Asia Sentinel (2020). https://www.asiasentinel.com/p/the-collapse-of-malaysian-private. Accessed 17 Aug 2023
25. Williams, G.: Private varsities struggling. New Straits Times (2018). https://www.nst.com.my/opinion/columnists/2018/12/436695/private-varsities-struggling. Accessed 17 Aug 2023
26. The Capital Post.: The collapse of Malaysian private universities – Analysis (2020). https://www.capitalpost.com.my/the-collapse-of-malaysian-private-universities-ana lysis/. Accessed 17 Aug 2023
27. Cambridge Dictionary: Auto. In: Cambridge Dictionary Preprint at https://dictionary.cambri dge.org/dictionary/english/auto. Accessed 17 Aug 2023
28. Creswell, J.W., Creswell, J.D.: Research Design: Qualitative, Quantitative, and Mixed Methods Approaches. SAGE, Newcastle upon Tyne (2022)
29. Ellis, C., Adams, T.E., Bochner, A.P.: Autoethnography: an overview. Historical Soc. Res. **36**(4(138)), 273–290 (2011). https://www.jstor.org/stable/23032294
30. Edwards, J.: Ethical autoethnography: is it possible? Int. J. Qual. Methods **20** (2021). https://doi.org/10.1177/1609406921995306
31. Wall, S.: Easier said than done: writing an autoethnography. Int J Qual Methods **7**, 38–53 (2008)
32. Aboo Bakar, R.: Tales of an educator, an administrator and a writer amidst COVID 19: an autoethnography. Int. J. Pract. Teach. Learn. **1**(2), 1–5 (2021)
33. Rahman, A.A.A., Othman, N.H., Zainol, N.R.: Challenges of family co-operative sustainabil- ity: an autoethnographic narrative. In: Alareeni, B., Hamdan, A. (eds.) ICBT 2021. Lecture Notes in Networks and Systems, vol. 487, pp. 849–856. Springer, Cham (2023). https://doi.org/10.1007/978-3-031-08084-5_61
34. Crossley, M.L.: Breastfeeding as a moral imperative: an autoethnographic study. Fem. Psychol. **19**(1), 71–87 (2009). https://doi.org/10.1177/0959353508098620
35. Holmes, A.G.D.: Researcher positionality - a consideration of its influence and place in qualitative research - a new researcher guide. Shanlax Int. J. Educ. **8**(4), 1–10 (2020). https://doi.org/10.34293/education.v8i4.3232

Adoption Barriers of Assistive Ambient Technology: A Systematic Literature Review

Nik Izyan Fatini Musri[✉], Rozianawaty Osman, Nurzeatul Hamimah Abdul Hamid, and Fariza Hanis Abdul Razak

College of Computing, Informatics and Mathematics, Universiti Teknologi MARA, 40450 Shah Alam, Selangor, Malaysia
nikizyanfatini@gmail.com

Abstract. As the global populace is aging, many countries are preparing for a better environment to age in place. Ambient assistive technology refers to devices and systems that help to improve the quality of life by promoting independence, safety, and comfort in their living environment. Despite the abundance of studies focusing on elderly technology adoption, resistance to utilizing such technology persists among this demographic. Moreover, there remains a lack of understanding regarding the barriers to technology adoption within the aging population. The elderly are more comfortable aging in place, and there is evidence that technology can play a vital role in supporting their daily life. To investigate the barriers faced by the elderly in adopting assistive ambient technology, a systematic review was conducted. This study includes articles selected from Scopus and Web of Science databases. Three groups of keywords were combined: those relating to adoption barriers, assistive technology, and the elderly. Using thematic analysis, data from 43 articles were analyzed, yielding six main themes: 1) cost; 2) environmental; 3) personal; 4) psychological; 5) social; and 6) technological. The results of this study are expected to aid in the development of technology catering to the preferences of the elderly.

Keywords: Aging · Elderly · Older adults · Adoption barriers · Assistive technology · Ambient assistive technology

1 Introduction

Assistive Technology (AT) is one of many opportunities that are necessary to reduce the disabling influence of many environments [1]. This means the technology that will assist in doing daily activities, especially with people with disabilities to do what usually people can do or even better with the help of AT. The idea of Assistive Technology (AT) refers to an innovative concept that integrates technology within residences to maintain and even enhance functional health, security, safety, and quality of life of their residents [2]. AT denotes a broad range of devices, services, strategies, and practices that are conceived and applied to ameliorate the problems faced by individuals who have disabilities [3].

With the help of AT which consists of mobility devices, hardware, software, and peripherals, this will help people with disabilities in order to perform functions that might otherwise be difficult or impossible. AT includes low vision devices, hearing aids, augmentative and alternative communication, walking frames, wheelchairs, and prostheses such as artificial legs. The field also covers information and communications technologies such as computers, screen-reading software, and customized telephones [4]. Meanwhile, in order to be principally targeted to the elderly, Ambient Assistive Technology (AAT) is an AT that focuses on the elderly [5].

The term "ambience" can be defined as 'environment or surroundings' while the related term "ambient" is defined in most dictionaries as 'encompassing, encircling' and in Spanish, ambient means surroundings, social or physical [6]. The preventive and assistance systems known as AAT enable elderly people to live independently in their homes for as long as possible. AAT is intended to reduce household potential danger risks by assisting the elderly with daily activities [7].

Despite the abundance of studies focusing on elderly technology adoption, resistance to utilizing such technology persists among this demographic. Moreover, there remains a lack of understanding regarding the barriers to technology adoption within the aging population. This paper is intended to explore the adoption barrier of assistive technology with respect to the elderly experience. Thus, the research question addressed in this paper is: what are the elderly technology adoption barriers?

2 Methods

The search strategy was conducted through the three sub-processes, known as identification, screening (which involves the inclusion and exclusion criteria), and eligibility. The sub-processes are explained as follows:

i) Step 1: Identification

The process of identification refers to the process of searching alternate terms for study's primary search terms which in this study are "adoption barrier", "assisting technology", and "elderly". As shown in Table 1, the keywords used for searching were developed by using Boolean operator, phrase searching, and field code functions on two databases, Scopus and Web of Science. The search in these two databases yielded a total of 788 articles.

Table 1. The search string.

Database	Search string
Scopus	(TITLE-ABS-KEY (barrier OR challenge OR resistance) AND TITLE-ABS-KEY ("assistive technology") AND TITLE-ABS-KEY (aging OR elderly OR "older adult" OR senior)) AND PUBYEAR > 2013
Web of Science	barrier OR challenge OR resistance (All Fields) and "assistive technology" (All Fields) and aging OR elderly OR "older adult" OR senior (All Fields)

ii) Step 2: Screening

All 788 articles were screened for this study. The selection criteria were determined using an automatic sorting function built into both databases. First, articles were selected based on the requirements listed in Table 2. Following that, only publications in the form of articles were included to ensure the quality of the reviews. Only articles originally published in English were considered for this review to reduce the possibility of translation errors. Detecting and deleting duplicate articles because some articles would be present in both databases resulting in duplication. 128 articles were removed due to duplication.

Table 2. The inclusion and exclusion criteria.

Inclusion	Exclusion
Review articles and research articles written in English	Review articles and research articles which are not written in English
Articles published between the years 2014 to 2023	Studies published before 2014
Research in which participants are elderly	Research in which participants are not elderly
Research in which place of experiment or setup be at home	Research in which place of experiment or setup other than home

iii) Step 3: Eligibility

The third process in this study is eligibility, in which the retrieved articles are manually examined by the author to ensure that the articles that passed the screening process meet the inclusion and exclusion criteria (see Table 2). To assess eligibility, the publication titles and abstracts were read and analyzed.

3 Results and Discussion

3.1 Selection

Search from both Scopus and Web of Science databases has resulted in 788 articles. Duplicates were removed (128 articles) and the remaining articles (660 articles) were screened for inclusion and exclusion criteria. In the end, only 43 articles were included for the review. This article selection process is shown using PRISMA diagram in Fig. 1.

The articles were also analyzed for its trends of publication throughout the years and also the frequency of publication by publisher. Figure 2 illustrates the publication frequency from 2014 to 2022. The graph clearly indicates a growing interest in the topic of assistive technology adoption.

Additionally, there are few publishers that have consistently published research on this particular topic. Taylor and Francis lead the way with 11 articles, followed by Springer with 7 articles (see Table 3). Other publishers, including Elsevier, Emerald Publishing, and Gerontechnology, have also contributed with single articles each.

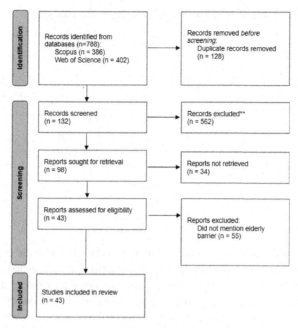

Fig. 1. Article selection.

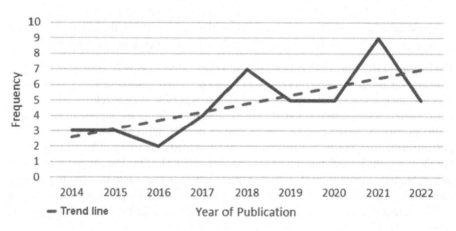

Fig. 2. Assistive technology adoption publication from year 2014 - 2022.

3.2 Elderly Technology Adoption Barrier

Based on thematic analysis, data from 43 articles were analyzed. The eligible articles were derived for the study of adoption barriers to assisting ambient technology with the aging population. Thus, the study discovered that the data from the 43 eligible articles yielded six main themes: 1) cost; 2) environmental; 3) personal; 4) psychological; 5) social; and 6) technological.

Table 3. Number of Articles based on The Publisher.

Publisher Name	Number of Articles
Taylor & Francis	11
Springer	7
MDPI	3
BMC Geriatrics	2
Frontiers	2
IEEE	2
IOS Press	2
Others*	14

Cost. This review found three sub-themes that are associated with the cost main theme which are unwillingness to pay, high cost, and unaffordable. The first theme was an unwillingness to pay. When buying things, we always consider whether the benefits are worth the price. Same as when targeting aging populations, it is necessary to evaluate the cost versus benefit of use [8–10], if not, they might be unwilling to pay when considering the cost versus benefit of use [11]. The second theme was high cost. In the study, many older adults reported that they were concerned regarding the high cost of purchase, maintenance, and service [12–14]. The third theme was unaffordable. The high cost will interrupt the elderly purchasing power. Thus, the cost of AT for the elderly should be reconsidered as some of the older adults cannot afford to purchase the devices [15, 16].

Environmental. This review found two sub-themes that are associated with the environmental main theme which are lack of awareness, and unsuitable living conditions. The first theme was a lack of awareness. There is a lack of research focusing on the elderly needs in living independently in their home [17]. More so, our community, especially the elderly shows that lack of awareness on AT that is available for the elderly [18–20]. However, the awareness should not be limited only to the elderly as the users, but also include formal and informal caretakers [16, 21, 22]. The second theme was unsuitable living conditions. Living conditions also need take into account in planning and developing aging-in place setting [23], which concerned a possible lack of access to the internet that prevents AT devices to get connected, logging data, and functioning properly [24, 25].

Personal. This review found three sub-themes that are associated with the personal main theme which are individual financial difficulties, low education level, and physical disability. The first theme was individual financial difficulties. Individual financial status and education level are mostly mentioned together in studies that had a significant effect on AT usage [23, 26], in which the more stable financial and the higher education level of the individual tend to minimize the barrier to adopting AT. The second theme was low education level. However, some studies stated not mention education but focus on education toward technology or digital literacy [27–29]. The third theme was physical disability.

Psychological. This review found two sub-themes that are associated with the psychological main theme which are privacy issues, and negative perception. The most mentioned are regarding privacy issues and negative perspectives towards AT. Privacy remains a strong barrier among the elderly [9, 14, 18, 29], due to most ATs requires personal data and information that might make them feel privacy invasions, especially ATs that use camera and microphone [10, 30–32]. The first theme was the privacy issue. The second theme was negative perception. In addition, the elderly adoption barrier is influenced by negative perception when using AT [33], which might be distorted for various reasons for example AT might make them look old or frail [34], and sensitive toward the "robot" term [10, 19, 24].

Social. This review found two sub-themes that are associated with the social main theme which are needing social influence, and the need for assistance in using. The first theme was needing social influence. Some studies mentioned that the elderly need a "support system" with the involvement of relatives, families, and caregivers [29, 35], in which to encourage and participate in using AT for example tablets. The second theme was the need for assistance in using. Introduction to AT is not enough for older adults since they will always need assistance in using the devices [21, 36].

Technological. This review found two sub-themes that are associated with the technological main theme which are unsuitable design, and unmet needs. The first theme was an unsuitable design. The most mentioned keyword in studies is "design", which refers to unsuitable or insufficient elderly-friendly design [15]. Some studies mentioned that the design needs to be aesthetically pleasing [30, 37], and more user-friendly for personalization [38–40]. The second theme was unmet needs. There are some AT designs identified as unmet needs of the elderly as a user [17, 26, 41], which leads to unfamiliarity and difficulty in use [42].

4 Conclusion

This systematic review has identified six barriers which are cost, environmental, personal, financial, social and technological, encountered by older adults in adopting assistive ambient technology. From this review, we learn that environment is as important as other factors affecting adoption of technology among the elderly. The findings of this study are anticipated to contribute to the creation of technology that aligns with the preferences of the elderly. While the review offers a comprehensive understanding of technology adoption, additional research is imperative to investigate other factors such as geographical and cultural influences.

Acknowledgment. Authors acknowledge the Ministry of Higher Education (MOHE) for funding the Fundamental Research Grant Scheme (FRGS) (FRGS/1/2021/ICT02/UITM/02/5) under the project titled, Engineering Assistive Ambient Technology for Malaysian Ageing-in-place using Experience-based Co-Design Method.

References

1. Cook, A.M., Polgar, J.M.: Assistive Technologies- E-Book: Principles and Practice. Elsevier Health Sciences (2014)
2. Yusif, S., Soar, J., Hafeez-Baig, A.: Older people, assistive technologies, and the barriers to adoption: a systematic review. Int. J. Med. Informatics **94**, 112–116 (2016)
3. Cook, A.M., Polgar, J.M., Encarnação, P.: Assistive Technologies: Principles and Practice, p. 64. Mosby (2016)
4. World Health Organization: WHO Global Disability Action Plan 2014–2021: Better Health for All People with Disability, World Health Organization (2015)
5. Cicirelli, G., Marani, R., Petitti, A., Milella, A., D'Orazio, T.: Ambient assisted living: a review of technologies, methodologies and future perspectives for healthy aging of population. Sensors **21**(10), 3549 (2021)
6. Caplow, T.: The definition and measurement of ambiences. Soc. Forces **34**(1), 28–33 (1955)
7. Schülke, A.M., Plischke, H., Kohls, N.B.: Ambient Assistive Technologies (AAT): socio-technology as a powerful tool for facing the inevitable sociodemographic challenges? Philos. Ethics Humanit. Med. **5**, 8 (2010). https://doi.org/10.1186/1747-5341-5-8
8. Hubner, S., Boron, J.B., Fruhling, A.: Use of assistive and interactive technology and relation to quality of life in aging adults. In: Proceedings of the 55th Hawaii International Conference on System Sciences, Hawaii (2022)
9. Martinez-Martin, E., Costa, A.: Assistive technology for elderly care: an overview. IEEE Access **9**, 92420–92430 (2021)
10. Sánchez, V.G., Anker-Hansen, C., Taylor, I., Eilertsen, G.: Older people's attitudes and perspectives of welfare technology in Norway. J. Multidiscip. Healthc. **12**, 841–853 (2019)
11. Nordlund, M., Stenberg, L., Intosalmi, H.: Elderly people's opinions on housing. In: The International Conference on Universal Design, Sweden (2014)
12. Albina, E.M., Hernandez, A.A.: Assessment of the elderly on perceived needs, benefits and barriers: inputs for the design of intelligent assistive technology. In: 16th International Conference on ICT and Knowledge Engineering (ICT&KE), Bangkok, Thailand (2018)
13. Pang, N., Zhang, X., Law, P.W., Foo, S.: Coping with ageing issues: adoption and appropriation of technology by older adults in Singapore. In: Zhou, J., Salvendy, G. (eds.) ITAP 2016. LNCS, vol. 9755, pp. 364–374. Springer, Cham (2016). https://doi.org/10.1007/978-3-319-39949-2_35
14. Harrington, E.E., Bishop, A.J., Do, H.M., Sheng, W.: Perceptions of socially assistive robots: a pilot study exploring older adults' concerns. Curr. Psychol. **42**, 2145–2156 (2023). https://doi.org/10.1007/s12144-021-01627-5
15. Alexandru, A., Ianculescu, M.: Enabling assistive technologies to shape the future of the intensive senior-centred care: a case study approach. Stud. Inform. Control **26**(3), 343–352 (2017)
16. Hettiarachchi, S., Subramaniam, V., Rajah, E., Gowritharan, P., Nizar, S., Saleem, S.: 'Enabling access': a pilot study on access and use of assistive products in the northern province, Sri Lanka. Disab. CBR Inclusive Dev. **30**(3), 82–112 (2020)
17. MacLachlan, M., et al.: Assistive technology policy: a position paper from the first global research, innovation, and education on assistive technology (GREAT) summit. Disabil. Rehabil. Assist. Technol. **13**, 454–466 (2018)
18. Choukou, M., Sakamoto, Y., Irani, P.: Attitude and perceptions of older and younger adults towards ambient technology for assisted living. Eur. Rev. Med. Pharmacol. Sci. **25**(10), 3709–3717 (2021)
19. Street, J., et al.: Older adults' perspectives of smart technologies to support aging at home: insights from five world café forums. Int. J. Environ. Res. Public Health **19**(13), 7817 (2022)

20. Harrington, C.N., Mitzner, T.L., Rogers, W.A.: Understanding the role of technology for meeting the support needs of older adults in the USA with functional limitations. Gerontechnology **14**(1), 21–31 (2015)
21. Kerbler, B.: An innovative built environment form for dwellings for the elderly. METU J. Fac. Archit. **31**(1), 119–137 (2014)
22. Tangcharoensathien, V., Witthayapipopsakul, W., Viriyathorn, S., Patcharanarumol, W.: Improving access to assistive technologies: challenges and solutions in low- and middle-income countries. WHO South-East Asia J. Public Health **7**(2), 84–89 (2018)
23. Löfqvist, C., Slaug, B., Ekström, H., Kylberg, M., Haak, M.: Use, non-use and perceived unmet needs of assistive technology among Swedish people in the third age. Disabil. Rehabil. Assist. Technol. **11**(3), 195–201 (2016)
24. Johansson-Pajala, R.-M., Gustafsson, C.: Significant challenges when introducing care robots in Swedish elder care. Disabil. Rehabil. Assist. Technol. **17**(2), 166–176 (2020)
25. Ravishankar, V.K., Burleson, W., Mahoney, D.: Smart home strategies for user-centered functional assessment of older adults. Int. J. Autom. Smart Technol. **5**(4), 233 (2015)
26. Vlachantoni, A.: Unmet need for social care among older people. Ageing Soc. **39**(4), 657–684 (2017)
27. Fiorini, L., et al.: Can assistive technology support social services during Covid-19 emergency? Barriers and opportunities. Int. J. Interact. Design Manuf. (IJIDeM) **16**, 359–370 (2022). https://doi.org/10.1007/s12008-021-00836-3
28. Yang, D., Moody, L.: Challenges and opportunities for use of smart materials in designing assistive technology products with, and for older adults. Fash. Pract. **14**(2), 242–265 (2021)
29. Helander, N., Weck, M., Meristö, T.: Digital assistive technologies for ageing people – learning barriers and educational approaches. In: 11th International Conference on Education and New Learning Technologies, Palma, Spain (2019)
30. Bian, C., Ye, B., Hoonakker, A., Mihailidis, A.: Attitudes and perspectives of older adults on technologies for assessing frailty in home settings: a focus group study. BMC Geriatr. **21**, 298 (2021). https://doi.org/10.1186/s12877-021-02252-4
31. Heek, J.O.-V., Schomakers, E.-M., Ziefle, M.: Bare necessities? How the need for care modulates the acceptance of ambient assisted living technologies. Int. J. Med. Informatics **127**, 147–156 (2019)
32. Schomakers, E.-M., Ziefle, M.: Privacy concerns and the acceptance of technologies for aging in place. In: Zhou, J., Salvendy, G. (eds.) HCII 2019. LNCS, vol. 11592, pp. 313–331. Springer, Cham (2019). https://doi.org/10.1007/978-3-030-22012-9_23
33. Beaudoin, M., et al.: Interviews with family caregivers of older adults: their experiences of care and the integration of assistive technology in care. Technol. Disabil. **32**(3), 199–209 (2020)
34. Peek, S.T.M., et al.: Origins and consequences of technology acquirement by independent-living seniors: towards an integrative model. BMC Geriatrics **17**, 189 (2017). https://doi.org/10.1186/s12877-017-0582-5
35. Muthu, P., Tan, Y., Latha, S., Dhanalakshmi, S., Lai, K.W., Wu, X.: Discernment on assistive technology for the care and support requirements of older adults and differently-abled individuals. Front Public Health, 10 (2023)
36. Halvorsrud, L., Holthe, T., Karterud, D., Thorstensen, E., Lund, A.: Perspectives on assistive technology among older Norwegian adults receiving community health services. Disabil. Rehabil. Assist. Technol. **18**(5), 685–692 (2023)
37. Robinson, H., MacDonald, B., Broadbent, E.: The role of healthcare robots for older people at home: a review. Int. J. Soc. Robot. **6**, 575–591 (2014). https://doi.org/10.1007/s12369-014-0242-2

38. William, J.A., Murugesh, R.: Senior citizens usage towards and perception of modern technology in India. In: Zhou, J., Salvendy, G. (eds.) ITAP 2018. LNCS, vol. 10926, pp. 179–193. Springer, Cham (2018). https://doi.org/10.1007/978-3-319-92034-4_14
39. Anghel, I., et al.: Smart environments and social robots for age-friendly integrated care services. Int. J. Environ. Res. Public Health 17(11), 3801 (2020)
40. Schiavoa, G., Mich, O., Ferron, M., Mana, N.: Trade-offs in the design of multimodal interaction for older adults. Behav. Inf. Technol. 41(5), 1035–1051 (2022)
41. Esposito, R., et al.: Supporting active and healthy aging with advanced robotics integrated in smart environment. In: Optimizing Assistive Technologies for Aging Populations. Information Resources Management Association, p. 32 (2016)
42. Ienca, M., Lipps, M., Wangmo, T., Jotterand, F., Elger, B., Kressig, R.W.: Health professionals' and researchers' views on intelligent assistive technology for psychogeriatric care. Gerontechnology 17(3), 139–150 (2018)

The Affordances and Usability Evaluation for HeartM 3.0: A Mobile Heart Monitoring Application

Muhammad Sobri[1]([✉]), Mohamad Taha Ijab[2], Norshita Mat Nayan[2,3], and Alexander Edo Tondas[3,4]

[1] Universitas Bina Darma, Palembang, South Sumatera, Indonesia
sobri@binadarma.ac.id
[2] The National University of Malaysia, Bangi, Selangor, Malaysia
[3] Charitas Roman Catholic Hospital, Palembang, South Sumatera, Indonesia
[4] Dr. Mohammad Hoesin General Hospital, Palembang, South Sumatera, Indonesia

Abstract. The use of health applications on mobile phones is gaining traction especially when the COVID-19 pandemic hit the world. Such applications enable patients to keep track of their health without the need of physically going to the hospitals to meet their doctors. In the context of mobile heart applications for heart disease patients, the need for a highly usable application is even more vital as the heart patients are considered most vulnerable if they infected by the COVID-19 virus. HeartM 3.0 is the application developed to enable the patients to carry out self-monitoring of their heart conditions. This study aims to discuss the affordances and usability evaluations of HeartM 3.0 from the perspective of the heart patients. HeartM 3.0 were evaluated based on its affordances which consist of medical, social and technological affordances, and usability elements which consist of learnability, effectiveness, memorability, error, and satisfaction. The questionnaire was adapted from the PSSUQ (Post Study System Usability Questionnaire). The study recruited thirty five heart patients in Charitas Hospital Palembang, Indonesia. From the participants' assessments, the study found that the heart patients feel satisfied with what is provided by the HeartM 3.0 application and stated that HeartM 3.0 is comfortable to use, patients are willing to use it continuously, and in overall, they are satisfied with HeartM 3.0. This paper theoretically contributes to provide recommendations to application developers and mobile health designers on the importance of meeting the affordances and usability elements desired by the users, especially for mobile health applications for chronic illnesses.

Keywords: Heart Disease · Mobile Health Application · Heartm 3.0 · Affordances · Usability

1 Introduction

Chronic disease, according to the World Health Organization (WHO), is a disease that occurs over a long period of time, is non-communicable disease (NCD) and develops slowly and occurs as a result of genetic, physiological, environmental and behavioral

H. Badioze Zaman et al. (Eds.): IVIC 2023, LNCS 14322, pp. 209–222, 2024.
https://doi.org/10.1007/978-981-99-7339-2_19

factors [1]. WHO states that heart disease is the number one cause of death world wide, taking an estimated 24.2 million, followed by death due to cancer which claimed the lives of around 10 million people, then further diabetes also claimed the lives of around 8 million people in 2020 [2]. Even so, this study will look at heart disease only and not all types of chronic diseases because heart disease is now the leading cause of death world wide. To control the heart disease that the patient suffers from, there are two ways according to [3], namely: (i) medicine, and (ii) monitoring. For medicine, it requires high costs reaching tens of millions of Rupiah, this does not only happen in Indonesia but also in America [4], according to [5] treatment costs for 30 days of care can reach up to Rp 336,240,000 (RM 96,068). This shows the expensive medical costs of heart disease.

In the era of the Fourth Industrial Revolution (IR 4.0), heart patients are able to monitor the health condition of their hearts using heart disease mobile applications anywhere and everywhere [6]. Users are able to download various heart disease mobile applications from the Google Play for Android devices and the Apple App Store for iOS-based devices. These applications are available for purchase by heart patients while some are cost-free [7]. For example, the price of the Cardio Visual application is around Rp 138,040 (RM 41,20). This application provides the affordances for heart patients to be given the use of basic features to perform self-monitoring of their heart health condition, because it is found to be more effective, the size of the device is small so it is easy to carry anywhere, and the application can be used on anytime [5]. As for advanced features that require the user to pay, for example heart patients are allowed to interact with cardiologists who have been prepared and are available in the application [8].

Based on previous research on the issues of affordances and usability of heart disease mobile applications, [9, 10] argued that many mobile health applications lack the required features needed by the patients [11, 12] and the problem of user interface design that is less than satisfactory [13]. Further, mobile heart applications also lack support for allowing communication and interaction between heart patients and their cardiologist [14]. Considering the issues of user satisfaction and usability from the previous studies and additionally considering the current issue of the highly contagious COVID-19 virus that affects the vulnerable heart patients [15], the innovative heart monitoring mobile applications have the potential to change the way heart patients and cardiologists interact remotely, there by reducing the risk of exposure to infection [16] and used in terms of (i) medical affordances [17], (ii) social affordances [18], and (iii) technological affordances [19].

Therefore, developing an effective user interface design is a big challenge. Some of researchers the involvement of user interface design in their study: [20] made design of an interactive digital nutritional education package for elderly people, [21] designing a persuasive physical activity application for older workers, [22] built of mobile application healthy diet for elderly, and [23] built of game design for cancer patients. A good user interface design should be simple, so that it is more efficient, pleasant, and works comfortably. In addition, the design principles that exist today such as [24, 25] are generic that are used to show design elements that do not focus on cultural concepts such as local language affordances that are still limited [26]

The design principles that can support the elderly as well as users who are not fluent in foreign languages such as the more pervasive English-based applications, the suggestion of a local language affordances can increase user satisfaction and the usability of the heart disease mobile application [26]. This study is a continuation and final evaluation of HeartM 3.0 [27], the objective of this study is to conduct the affordances and usability evaluation of HeartM 3.0 from the perspective of the heart patients. The following section reviews the extant literature related to the concepts of affordances and usability pertaining to mobile application design and development. The third section presents the methods used while the results and discussion are presented in the fifth section. The last section sums up the paper by concluding the research and offers pointers for future works.

2 Literature Review

This section provides an overview of the literature on the concepts of affordances and usability.

2.1 Affordances

The theory of affordance was first proposed by Gibson [28] who defines affordances as the form of user interaction with an object. The concept of affordances is then adopted by many researchers in the field of Human Computer Interaction (HCI) such as Norman [29], Kirschner et al. [30], Strong et al. [31], Anderson [32], and others. The types of affordances proposed for HeartM 3.0 application are: (i) medical affordances such as the management of medication taken, and the exercises prescribed to maintain health of the patient; (ii) technology affordances such as the personal monitoring of heart condition by personally recording the heart beat using the mobile phone, and (iii) the social affordance such as the communication between patient with their cardiologist and their sharing of vital health information with their cardiologist or family members.

2.2 Usability

Usability expert and researcher, Nielsen [24] has defined usability as a quality attribute that evaluates how easy the user interface is to use. [33] defines usability as the extent to which the user can interact with the interface in a comfortable, efficient, and effective manner. The International Organization for Standardization (ISO) [25] defines usability as the degree to which a product can be used by certain users to achieve their goals effectively, efficiently and satisfactorily, and lastly, [34] argue that usability in an application can be highlighted by, among other things, providing features or help buttons to provide information for users to use it.

3 Methods

3.1 Design Science Research Methodology

This section presents review of the methods in conducting to design of HeartM 3.0 using Design Science Research Methodology (DSRM). [35] defines DSR as a design science that is more focused on the creation of new and innovative 'artifacts' to solve problems. [35] define 'artifacts' as forms, models, methods or instantiations (prototypes or systems developed).

In this paper, the environment refers to users, namely heart patients and cardiologists and identifies real heart disease problems that were previously only known to researchers through literature review [36] and usability evaluation from existing mobile heart disease applications that have been done in [10]. The rigor cycle "bridges" the surrounding environment with DSRM which provides the need to serve as input for research activities. Meanwhile, the knowledge base consists of existing theoretical foundations, scientific methods, models, products, processes produced from previous information systems research. The meticulous cycle connects the knowledge base with DSR which provides past knowledge as reference material into DSRM. For example, the knowledge base in this study consists of heart disease, usability of heart disease health mobile applications, and user interface design concepts, data collection methods (i.e., interviews with cardiologists and the heart disease patients, PSSUQ questionnaires and observations) and data analysis methods (descriptive). The precision cycle provides constructs based on affordances theory as the material referred to in the DSRM of this research. The main component of DSRM is the design cycle which involves the process of repetition and evaluating artifacts (i.e., the iterations in the design process).

This cycle involves the production of several alternatives and design evaluation of a given need. As mentioned earlier, in DSRM, requirements are inputs from the relevance cycle, while the theories and methods used to construct and evaluate these design alternatives are inputs from the rigor cycle. According to [35] this shows the dependence of the design cycle with the two cycles in the mandatory research activities in the DSRM. Artifacts generated from the DSR process are then evaluated in the environment, which will determine whether additional iteration of the relevance cycle is required. If all the requirements have been met and satisfied, then the rigor cycle adds these newly produced artifacts to the knowledge base for reference in future research and practice. Figure 1 shows the adoption of DSRM framework in this study in order to design and develop HeartM 3.0.

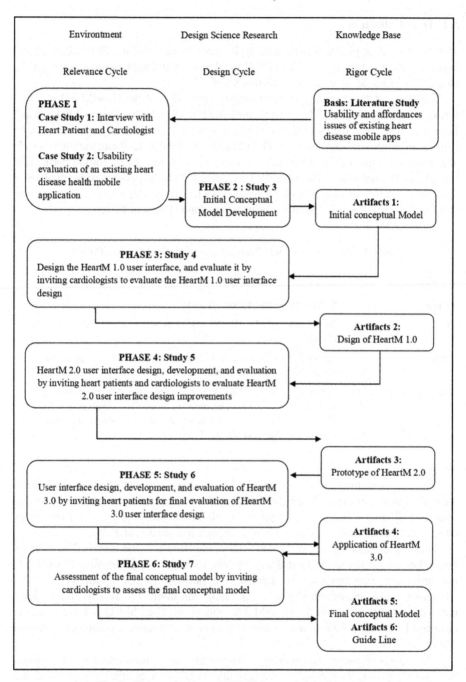

Fig. 1. Shows adoption of DSRM framework in this study

3.2   Data Collection

The HeartM 3.0 application is built using Flutter software and the Dart programming language while the database is using SQLite. The data and application storage for the HeartM 3.0 is based on a free web hosting service.

The study of the affordances and usability evaluation of the HeartM 3.0 was performed for 2 months (from March until April 2022) at the Charitas Hospital Palembang, Indonesia. The participants of this study have agreed to participate in the research by signing an informed consent letter. The Charitas Hospital Palembang authorities have also provided a special room for this study to be conducted after a formal permission was granted by the hospital's Director. Thirty-five (35) heart patients were involved in this study with the demographic characteristics such as (i) gender, (ii) age, (iii) payment, and (iv) the level of education of the heart patients are shown in Table 1.

Table 1. Demographic and Characteristics of Participants HeartM 3.0

Characteristics	Detail
Gender	51.11% male and 48.89% female
Age	40–49 years (20%), 50 - 59 years (28.88%) and 60 years over (51.12%)
Payment	Person (general) as many as 28 patient (62.22%) and pay using insurance as many as 17 patients (37.78%)
The level of education	Senior High School and Degree are the same number of 15 heart patients each (33.33%), Elementary School of 7 heart patients (15.55%), Master level of 5 heart patients (11.13%) and Diploma as many as 3 heart patients (6.66%)

The main researcher gave training on how to use the features of HeartM 3.0 to the participants. Figure 2 shows the main interface of HeartM 3.0 which has several features including measuring heart patient's using their finger, physical activity (steps taken during an exercise), medicine intake, application setting, and chat.

They were expected to use HeartM 3.0 application for one month. The primary researcher administered the Post-Study System Usability Questionnaires (PSSUQ) to the participants after they used the HeartM 3.0 application for one month (March 2022) and then for a second month (April 2022). These questionnaires were used to evaluate the usability and features of the HeartM 3.0 application. The PSSUQ is a questionnaire designed by Lewis (1990) to assess user satisfaction after using a computer system or application [37].

PSSUQ has 16 questions that include: (i) system quality, questions number 1 to number 6 which include the technical aspects of the system, such as reliability, performance and ease of understanding the system. (ii) quality of information, questions number 7 to number 12 evaluate the clarity, accuracy and completeness of the information presented by the system. (iii) quality of service, question number 13 to number 16 assess service,

Fig. 2. The main interface of HeartM 3.0

support and system response to users, and last (iv) user satisfaction of the entire question to measure the level of user satisfaction with the use of the system as a whole [37].

After that, the participants completed the questionnaires to evaluate of HeartM 3.0. A Likert-scale of 5 point from Strongly Disagree to Strongly Agree was used in the survey questionnaire. Due to space limitation, a copy of the survey questionnaire will be supplied upon request.

4   Results and Discussion

The result of data analysis to the affordances and usability evaluation of HeartM 3.0 was done by measuring its Cronbach's alpha using SPSS software. The main researcher first examines the reliability of the data. For the reliability of each item must exceed a score of 0.7, then the item used is reliable [38]. Figure 3 shows the results of reliability testing of all items of the PSSUQ. While for the validity of each item that has been stated in Table 2.

Reliability Statistics		
Cronbach's Alpha	Cronbach's Alpha Based on Standardized Items	N of Items
.812	.823	16

Fig. 3. Shows the results of reliability testing of all items of the PSSUQ

Table 2. Shows the results of validity testing of all items of the PSSUQ

Question	Score	Question	Score
1	2.91	9	2.94
2	2.77	10	3.09
3	3.23	11	2.74
4	3.14	12	2.6
5	2.29	13	2.29
6	2.97	14	2.46
7	3.71	15	2.8
8	3.2	16	2.83
System Quality			2.89
Quality of Information			3.05
Quality of Interface			2.51
Overall			2.83

Based on Table 2 on the evaluation of the HeartM 3.0 application, according to the respondents, both heart patients and cardiologists, that the design and button placement of HeartM 3.0 is consistent so that it is easy to remember (memorability). HeartM 3.0 has a small number of clicks and an interface that makes it easier for heart patients to perform activities such as heart rate recording activities (effectiveness). In addition, HeartM 3.0 has clear information to use it (learnability). Next, HeartM 3.0 provides a screen or notification when the user makes a mistake so that it is easy to fix the error to do the task again (easy to fix errors). Because of that, all respondents (cardiologists and heart patients) agreed with the quality of the system, the quality of the information, the quality of the interface, and overall felt satisfied with the affordances provided in the HeartM 3.0 application.

System Quality Variables
Based on the data to evaluate the system quality variables, it can beseen in Table 2 that the HeartM 3.0 application gets an average score of 2.89. According to the respondents, both heart patients and cardiologists from question number one to number six. This means that the level of usability is included in the "good" category, which indicates that the HeartM 3.0 application is easy to use, easy to learn, and easy to get the necessary information. For example, it is easy to find the heart rate recording feature, it is easy to find the heart rate report feature, it is easy to find the recording feature drug intake data, and easy to find physical activity recording features.

Information Quality Variables
Based on the data to evaluate the information quality variables, it can beseen in Table 2 that the HeartM 3.0 application gets an average score of 3.05. According to the respondents, both heart patients and cardiologists from question number seven to number

twelve. This means that the level of affordances is categorised in the "good" category, which indicates that the HeartM 3.0 application feels clear enough in providing information that can be understood by heart patients. Affordances of the HeartM 3.0 application provides current messages or notifications to facilitate users if the HeartM 3.0 application experiences a task failure, easy to correct in the event of task failure, there is a usage guidance screen, giving daily notifications for heart rate recording, medication nutrition notifications, and medication intake notifications.

Interface Quality Variables
Based on the data to evaluate the interface quality variables, it can be seen in Table 2 that the HeartM 3.0 application gets an average score of 2.51. According to the respondents, both heart patients and cardiologists from question number thirteen to number fifteen. This means that the level of affordances is categorised in the "good" category, which indicates that the HeartM 3.0 application has an attractive interface, both the button layout, colors and features provided make users feel satisfied.

Overall Variables
Based on the data to evaluate the overall variables, it can be seen in Table 2 that the HeartM 3.0 application gets an average score of 2.83. According to the respondents, both heart patients and cardiologists, this means that the HeartM 3.0 application as a whole is good, both in terms of system quality, information quality, and interface quality. This can be because affordances of the HeartM 3.0 application in design, and the layout of its elements such as buttons, size, color, and navigation have had consistency that has an impact on user satisfaction [39].

Affordances of HeartM 3.0
Heart patients felt satisfied with **the medical affordances** provided by the HeartM 3.0 application which is (i) works well to monitor the heartbeat, (ii) allows viewing the results of the heart beat recording on a daily, weekly and monthly that the results are easy to understand (learnability), (iii) allows the recording of medication, (iv) allows the recording of physical activity (total steps), and (v) allows viewing the results of physical activity recording on a daily, weekly and monthly basis. Besides that, HeartM 3.0 can also remind to take medication on time (morning, afternoon, and evening) and control medication intake. Figure 4 show features of measuring heart rate, and Fig. 5 show features of medication history.

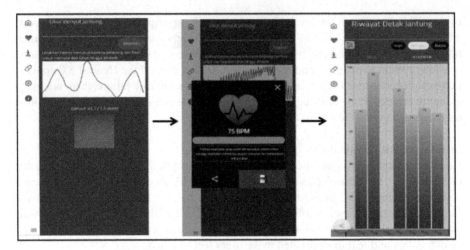

Fig. 4. Features of Medical Heart Rate Recording and Monitoring

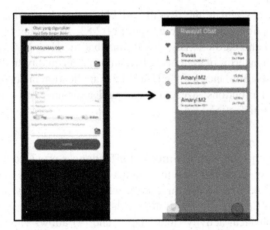

Fig. 5. Features of Medication Intake History

For the **social affordances**, heart patients felt satisfied with the social affordances provided by the HeartM 3.0 application which is (i) allows heart patients to share heart rate chart information (daily/weekly/monthly), (ii) allows heart patients share physical activity chart information (daily/weekly/monthly), (iii) allow heart patients to share the medications they take, (iv) allow heart patients to choose hospitals and cardiologists, and (v) allow heart patients to chat online with cardiologist. Figure 6 show of physical activity features.

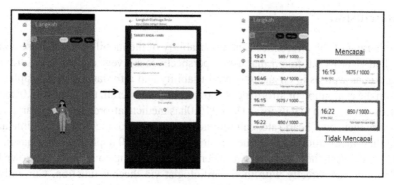

Fig. 6. Show of physical activity features

For the **technological affordances**, heart patients felt satisfied with the technological affordances provided by the HeartM 3.0 application which is (i) enabling the camera flash to work well for recording the heartbeat, (ii) displaying the duration of time in the recording of the heartbeat, (iii) display a heart rate recording chart, (iv) provide a reminder notification (memorability) of the heart rate recording, (v) provide a reminder notification (memorability) of taking medication on a daily basis both morning, afternoon, and night, (vi) provide a reminder notification of intake medicine from the hospital once a month. Beside that, HeartM 3.0 has features setting enable to heart patients (i) change to local language (i.e., English to Indonesian and vice versa), (ii) update profile, and (iii) change the password, as shown in Fig. 7.

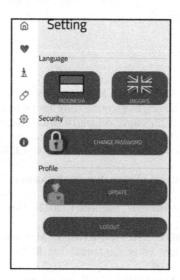

Fig. 7. Features of Setting

5 Conclusion

The evaluation of the affordances and the usability of the mobile heart disease application called HeartM 3.0 found that users' perspectives are very crucial to ensure users' satisfaction as well as in ensuring overall usability and affordances of the application. Based on the evaluation of affordances and usability, in overall, the HeartM 3.0 application gives satisfaction to it users as HeartM 3.0has medical affordances for heart patients to measure their own heart rate, can remind patients to take medication on time and to control their medication intake. The developed HeartM 3.0 applicationalso has in-built social affordancesto help and make it easier for heart patients to monitor their own heart and communicate directly with their cardiologist via thechat function. Currently, the HeartM 3.0 will launch the WhatsApp application to enable patient to communicate with their doctor.The future version aimed to include the social affordances feature such as the chatting between patient and their doctor within the system itself.

Based on the study of [19], there is still a lack of existing mobile applications that have affordances linguistic that allow users to easily change to the local language (Bahasa Indonesia). This is because not all users understand a foreign language (English) if the application is developed specifically in an international language (for example, English). Because of that, the HeartM 3.0 application has provided affordances linguistic that allow users to change the local language, which is Indonesian. Further, HeartM 3.0 has been tested on various brands of smartphones running on an Android operating system. Further research will look into porting HeartM3.0 engine such that it can also be installed and run on other mobile operating system including the iOS.

Acknowledgment. The main researcher thanked Universitas Bina Darma for providing grant funding to conduct this research.

References

1. Panah, Davoud Shariat, Hines, Andrew, McKeever, Joseph A., McKeever, Susan: An audio processing pipeline for acquiring diagnostic quality heart sounds via mobile phone. Comput. Biol. Med. **145**, 105415 (2022). https://doi.org/10.1016/j.compbiomed.2022.105415
2. Triantafyllidis, Andreas: Deep learning in mHealth for cardiovascular disease, diabetes, and cancer: systematic review. JMIR mHealth uHealth **10**(4), e32344 (2022). https://doi.org/10.2196/32344
3. Homenta, R.S.: Buku Praktis Kardiologi. Fakultas Kedokteran Universitas Indonesia, Jakarta (2014)
4. Berger, K.: Heart disease statistics. Singlecare (2022). http://www.healthline.com/health/heart-disease/statistics#2
5. Piña, I.L., Desai, N.R., Allen, L.A., Heidenreich, P.: Managing the economic challenges in the treatment of heart failure. Progr. Cardiovasc. Dis. **61**(5–6), 476–483 (2018). https://doi.org/10.1016/j.pcad.2018.10.002
6. Anshari, M., Nabil, M.: Mobile Health (mHealth) services and online health educators. Biomed. Inform. Insights, pp. 19–28 (2016). https://doi.org/10.4137/BII.S35388.TYPE
7. Sobri, M., Ijab, M.T., Mat Nayan, N.:: Systematic literature review untuk membuat model aplikasi pemantauan kesehatan cardiovascular. J. RESTI (Rekayasa Sist. dan Teknol. Informasi), **2**(2), 458–464 (2018). https://doi.org/10.29207/resti.v2i2.428

8. Lacerda, T.C., von Wangenheim, C.G.: Systematic literature review of usability capability/maturity models. Comput. Stand. Interfaces, **55**, 1339–1351 (2018)
9. Kamana, M.: Investigating usability issues of mHealth apps for elderly people. Blekinge Institute of Technology (2016)
10. Sobri, M., Ijab, M.T., Nayan, N.M.: Usability evaluation of heart disease monitoring mobile applications: a comparative study. In: Badioze Zaman, Halimah, et al. (eds.) IVIC 2019. LNCS, vol. 11870, pp. 653–662. Springer, Cham (2019). https://doi.org/10.1007/978-3-030-34032-2_58
11. Norman, D.: The Design of Everday Things, Revised AN. Basic Book, New York (1988)
12. Hartson, H.R.: Cognitive, physical, sensory, and functional affordances in interaction design. Behav. Inf. Technol. **22**(5), 315–338 (2003). https://doi.org/10.1080/01449290310001592587
13. Kraleva, R.: Designing an interface for a mobile application based on children's opinion. Int. J. Interact. Mob. Technol. **11**(1), 53–70 (2017)
14. Ribeiro, N., Moreira, L., Almeida, A.M.P., Santos-Silva, F.: Pilot study of a smartphone-based intervention to promote cancer prevention behaviours. Int. J. Med. Inform. **108**(February), 125–133 (2017). https://doi.org/10.1016/j.ijmedinf.2017.10.013
15. Edo Tondas, A., Agustian, R., Guyanto, M.: Minimal or no touch electrocardiography recording and remote heart rhythm monitoring during COVID-19 pandemic era. Indones. J. Cardiol. **41**(2), 133–141 (2020). https://doi.org/10.30701/ijc.1010
16. Ding, E.Y., et al.: Design, deployment, and usability of a mobile system for cardiovascular health monitoring within the electronic Framingham Heart Study. Cardiovasc. Digit. Heal. J. **2**(3), 171–178 (2021). https://doi.org/10.1016/j.cvdhj.2021.04.001
17. Abbaspur-Behbahani, S., Monaghesh, E., Hajizadeh, A., Fehresti, S.: Application of mobile health to support the elderly during the COVID-19 outbreak: a systematic review. Heal. Policy Technol. **11**(1), 100595 (2022). https://doi.org/10.1016/j.hlpt.2022.100595
18. Verma, J., Mishra, A.S.: COVID-19 infection: disease detection and mobile technology. PeerJ **8**, e10345 (2020). https://doi.org/10.7717/peerj.10345
19. Trzebiński, J., Cabański, M., Czarnecka, J.Z.: Reaction to the COVID-19 pandemic: the influence of meaning in life, life satisfaction, and assumptions on world orderliness and positivity. J. Loss Trauma **25**(6–7), 544–557 (2020). https://doi.org/10.1080/15325024.2020.1765098
20. Ali, N.M., Shahar, S., Kee, Y.L., Norizan, A.R., Noah, S.A.M.: Design of an interactive digital nutritional education package for elderly people. Inform. Health Soc. Care **37**(4), 217–229 (2012). https://doi.org/10.3109/17538157.2012.654843
21. Hazwani, M., Nazlena, M.A., Alan, F.S.: Designing a persuasive physical activity application for older workers: understanding end-user perceptions. Behav. Inf. Technol. **35**(12), 1102–1114 (2016). https://doi.org/10.1080/0144929X.2016.1211737
22. Mohamad Hidir, M.S., Nazlena, M.A., Shahrul Azman, M.N.: Mobile application on healthy diet for elderly based on persuasive design. Int. J. Adv. Sci. Eng. Inf. Technol. **7**(1), 222–227 (2017). https://doi.org/10.18517/ijaseit.7.1.1725
23. Irna, H., Imran, N.A., Hamidah, A., Nadhirah, R., Hanif, B.: Game design requirements through ethnography amongst pediatric cancer patients. Adv. Sci. Lett. **24**(3), 1567–1570 (2018). https://doi.org/10.1166/asl.2018.11110
24. Nielsen, J.: Usability Engineering. Morgan Kaufman, San Francisco (1993)
25. ISO: Ergonomics of human-system interaction: Usability method supporting human-centered design (2002). https://www.nen.nl/pdfpreview_83288.pdf
26. Samsuri, M.Z., Ariffin, S.A., Fathil, N.S.: Incorporating cultural design elements in mobile applications creative industries in Malaysia: a conceptual study. J. ICT Educ. **8**(2), 110–117 (2021). https://doi.org/10.37134/jictie.vol8.2.10.2021

27. Sobri, M., Ijab, M.T., Mat Nayan, N., Edo Tondas, A.: Design and evaluation of user interface design of mobile heart monitoring application. Turkish J. Comput. Math. Educ. **12**(3), 2211–2216 (2021). https://doi.org/10.17762/turcomat.v12i3.1169

28. Gibson, J.: The ecological approach to the visual perception of pictures. Leonardo **11**(3), 227–235 (1978)

29. Norman, D.: Affordance, conventions, and design. Secur. Priv. **III**, 38–42 (1999). https://doi.org/10.1145/301153.301168

30. Kirschner, P., Strijbos, J.W., Kreijns, K., Beers, P.J.: Designing electronic collaborative learning environments. Educ. Technol. Res. Dev. **52**(3), 47–66 (2004). https://doi.org/10.1007/BF02504675

31. Strong, D., et al.: A theory of clinic-EHR affordance actualization. In: Proceedings of JAIS Theory Development Workshop. Sprouts: Working Papers on Information Systems, no. 2009, pp. 9–47 (2009)

32. Anderson, C.: Health information systems affordances: how the materiality of information technology enables and constrains the work practices of clinicians. ProQuest Diss. Publ., p. 141 (2011). https://search.proquest.com/docview/916613745?pq-origsite=summon

33. Shneiderman, B.: Universal usability. Commun. ACM **43**(5), 84–91 (2000)

34. Kongjit, C., Nimmolrat, A., Khamaksorn, A.: Mobile health application for Thai women: investigation and model. BMC Med. Inform. Decis. Mak. **22**(1), 1–20 (2022). https://doi.org/10.1186/s12911-022-01944-0

35. Schwartz, D.G., Yahav, I.: Knowledge contribution diagrams for design science research: a novel graphical technique. In: Chandra Kruse, L., Seidel, S., Hausvik, G.I. (eds.) DESRIST 2021. LNCS, vol. 12807, pp. 174–187. Springer, Cham (2021). https://doi.org/10.1007/978-3-030-82405-1_19

36. Sobri, M., Ijab, M.T., Mat Nayan, N.: The usability factors of cardiovascular health monitoring mobile application : a conceptual model. In: Digital Transformation Landscape in the Fourth Industrial Revolution (4IR) Era, pp. 80–90 (2018)

37. Suwandy, R., Marpaung, S.H., Caroline, C.: Evaluasi Pengalaman Pengguna dengan Menggunakan post study system usability questionnaire (PSSUQ) Perpustakaan Digital Universitas Mikroskil. J. Pendidik. Tambusai, **6**(1), 4190–4206 (2022)

38. Garson, G.D.: Testing Statistical Assumptions. Statistical Associates Publishing (2012)

39. Pal, S., Biswas, B., Gupta, R., Kumar, A., Gupta, S.: Exploring the factors that affect user experience in mobile-health applications: a text-mining and machine-learning approach. J. Bus. Res. **156**, 113484 (2023). https://doi.org/10.1016/j.jbusres.2022.113484

Game-Based Mobile Application for Tarannum Learning

Muhammad Irfan Mohd Nadziman[1], Haslizatul Fairuz Mohamed Hanum[1](✉),
Nur Aina Khadijah Adnan[1], Norizan Mat Diah[1], and Zainab Abu Bakar[2]

[1] School of Computing Sciences, College of Computing, Informatics and Mathematics,
Universiti Teknologi MARA, 40450 Shah Alam, Selangor, Malaysia
haslizatul@uitm.edu.my

[2] School of Science and Technology, Asia eUniversity, Subang Jaya, Selangor, Malaysia

Abstract. The melodious recitation of Quran verses, known as Tarannum, impacts the reciters' and audiences' understanding and perception. Several experts on Tarannum melodies often train their apprentices in continuous lessons covering techniques on voice activation and correct recitations. The availability of an interactive application can help promote constant training and effectively complement the lessons. An interactive approach to Tarannum lessons is not widely available and is often developed for recognising the Arabic alphabet rather than practising melodies and recitations. A mobile application is one of the most widely implemented learning and training applications, as it offers interactive feedback to motivate users to continue the lessons repetitively. The lack of mobile applications to promote Tarannum learning reduces the interest in becoming competent reciters. This is because traditional melody training requires one-on-one instruction from an instructor to perfect the melody. The lack of an interactive Tarannum application affects Muslims who cannot practice the Tarannum skills and foundation through conventional learning sessions. Therefore, this project proposes a mobile learning application for Tarannum. The application can assist Muslims in learning Tarannum by improving their melodic recitation techniques and, simultaneously, can give the user an enjoyable experience by proposing a game-based learning approach. This was done in response to the need for an application to assist Muslims in learning Tarannum and evaluating their Tarannum techniques. For the extended project, the application can be enhanced by implementing an algorithm for Tarannum melody detection that will be more helpful for people who want to learn Tarannum.

Keywords: Game-Based Learning Application · Tarannum Mobile Application · Melody Training

1 Introduction

The practice of Quran recitation is known as Tarannum. One of the Quranic branches encourages the use of a melodic voice when reciting the Quran [1, 7]. Tarannum is an art of beautifying and curving the voice tone according to a specific tempo and rhythm [5].

Even though Tarannum is frequently used in educational settings, a sizable population has yet to embrace it. While relevant television programs like *Akademi Al-Quran* and *Mari* are available, Malaysians' exposure to the Tarannum melodies still needs to be improved [2]. The Qur'an is a Muslim holy book, and one of the ways to recite Quran verses is by singing them together. Singing in Quran recitations is the humming or chanting of Quranic verses, referred to as Tarannum melody [3, 4].

However, with the rapid advancement of ICT and high-end devices that have transformed us into a digital society, a new technique for learning the Tarannum is crucial [5]. Tarannum mobile applications to promote Tarannum learning led to fewer Muslims being competent in this aspect [2, 11]. This is because traditional melody training requires one-on-one instruction from an instructor to perfect the melody [2, 4]. The insufficiency of an interactive Tarannum application affects Muslims who cannot practice the Tarannum skills and foundation through conventional learning sessions [6]. In the previous Tarannum studies, Muslims or students tended to learn Tarannum by using old traditional ways. Using traditional methods, students are instructed through the face-to-face recitation of verses using talaqqi and musyafahah methods [4].

While traditional learning sessions are expensive and time-consuming, students' lessons and training would be hampered by the lack of an interactive Tarannum application [2]. Thus, the project designed and developed a mobile application to allow students to train on melodious recitations. While promoting self-learning through mobile apps, implementing game-based learning applications helps improve the users' interest and engagement in learning [8, 9]. The younger generation now mostly accepts the advantages of this game-learning method [10] and incorporates it into their daily activities.

This project focuses on creating a game-based application that trains students on Tarannum melodies, including Tarannum Bayati and Tarannum Hijaz. With a game-based learning approach, learning modules are levels of quiz sets. The first quiz set offers the Bayati Tarannum for beginners who want to start learning Tarannum. The Hijaz is set for those with basic knowledge of Tarannum (beginner level) and proceeds with a more complex quiz question. The beginner's score determines whether the user can proceed to the next intermediate level.

2 Methodology

The dataset is limited to four identified chapters from the Quran. The chapters are Al-Ikhlas, An-Nas, Al-Kafiruun and Al-Fatihah. Divided into two levels and labelled as beginner and intermediate. The development is based on Android programming for mobile apps.

All the essential requirements to develop the game are listed during the requirement analysis phase. System design analyses the feasible needs from the previous phase and focuses on the use case diagram, system flowchart, and user interface design. The system design includes system architecture, system flowcharts, and user interface designs, which analyze all requirements from the earlier stage.

2.1 Requirement Analysis

This phase is where the preliminary study and data collection is being done. The dataset will be limited to four identified chapters from the Quran. The learning modules are divided into two, in which the Bayati Tarannum is chosen for beginners who want to start learning Tarannum. At the same time, the Hijaz is set for those with basic knowledge of Tarannum [3]. The two levels are labelled beginner and intermediate, and the beginner's score determines whether the user can proceed to the intermediate level. In addition, the development will be based on Android programming for mobile apps. The list of the project requirements is in Table 1.

Table 1. List of requirements.

Requirements	Data
Content of Tarannum subject	Bayati Tarannum and Hijjaz Tarannum
Quran chapters	4 chapters: Surah Al-Ikhlas, An-Nas, Al-Kafiruun and Surah Al-Fatihah

2.2 System Development

Figure 1 is used to illustrate the development of the system. It begins when the user launches the mobile app. Users will engage with applications created with Android Studio as the primary development tool. The system contents will use the Android Game Development Kits libraries for user interaction. The local data and cache will store the user's most recent activity on the device.

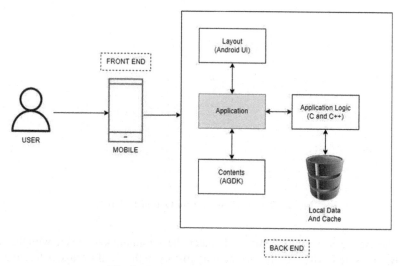

Fig. 1. System development processes.

2.3 System Modules

The system is developed with two main modules: Beginning - Option 1 and Intermediate level - Option 2. Users will first choose the sort of Tarannum they wish to learn and then select the chapters if they pick the first option. When the user completes option 2, the score will be displayed (Figs. 2 and 3).

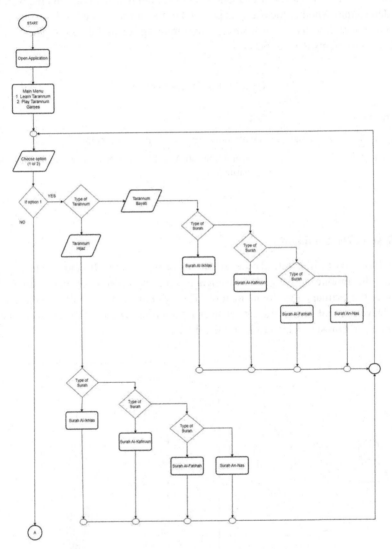

Fig. 2. System Flowchart for Option 1 Module.

If the user selects option 2, they will match the Tarannum knowledge with the song. Finally, the system will save the user activity history in the local storage before the user exits the application.

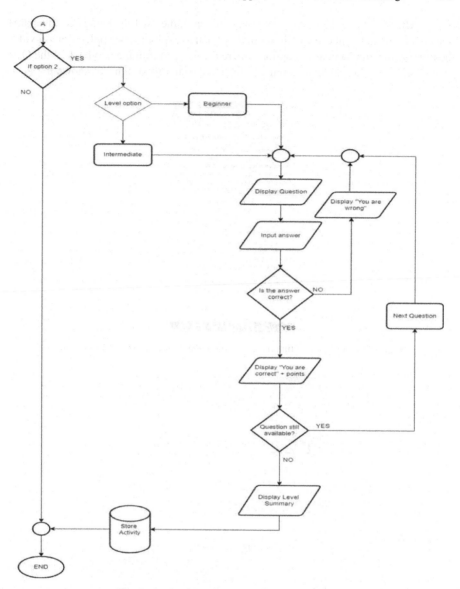

Fig. 3. System Flowchart for Option 2 Module.

3   Result and Discussion

When users first enter the application, the users will see the application's main menu that consists of the Home, Learn Tarannum, and Play buttons. If the users choose to learn Tarannum, they will be navigated to a panel that describes the general knowledge of Tarannum Bayati and Hijaz. Then, they can select which Tarannum technique they want to learn by clicking the button Tarannum Bayati or Tarannum Hijaz, as shown in

Fig. 4. After choosing the method they want to learn, they will be navigated to a panel that enables them to choose which Surah they wish to explore. The application provides the users with a media controls option, where they can control the playback of the Qari recite Surah with Tarannum technique audio and the audio's volume. as shown in Fig. 5.

Fig. 4. Learning panel that describes the general knowledge of Tarannum.

Fig. 5. Learning panel that displays and plays the sound of Qari reciting Surah al-Ikhlas with Tarannum technique

However, if the users choose to play the learning-based games in the application, the users will have to click on the play button in the main menu. The application consists of two difficulty levels: beginner level and intermediate level. In the beginning, the application only displayed the beginner-level button, as in Fig. 6.

Fig. 6. At first, only the beginner level is enabled.

Figure 7 shows that the intermediate level is enabled after the users get full marks at the beginner level.

Fig. 7. After the users get full marks at the beginner level, the intermediate level is displayed

At each level, users are given 5 questions. For each level, the users need to answer multiple-choice question types. They are required to choose the correct answer based on the questions shown in Fig. 8. The questions given are based on the topic discussed in the learning section of the application. Users need to answer all questions within a specific amount of time.

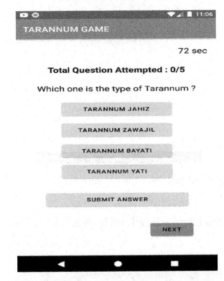

Fig. 8. Sample of question in the beginner level

For the beginner level, it is set for all questions; users are given 75 s to answer them. While the intermediate level considers the question that includes audio play, users are given a longer time, as shown in Fig. 9. The users can skip the questions by clicking on the next button and return to the question with the back button provided.

After a user finish answering all questions and clicks the submit button, the result will be displayed as shown in Fig. 10. However, if the time is finished before the submit button is clicked, the users cannot continue to answer, and the result will be displayed.

If the users get full marks, they will get a trophy, and a home button will be displayed to indicate that the level has finished. If the users fail to get full marks, they can restart the level, as shown in Fig. 11.

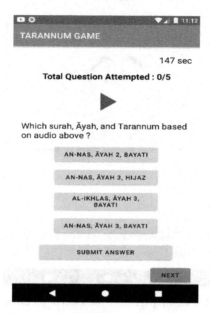

Fig. 9. Sample of questions in the intermediate level that the user needs to play an audio

Fig. 10. Result page if the users get full marks.

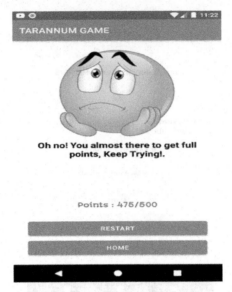

Fig. 11. Result page if the users fail to get full marks

4 Conclusion

This paper presents the development of a game-based learning application for learning Tarannum, focusing on the basic knowledge of Tarannum. Users of the Tarannum application can learn Tarannum with a more engaging approach. However, due to research time constraints, the questions' difficulty level only covers until intermediate level. For further work, the developer can implement more levels and questions so that the game will be able to test the user's knowledge better.

Acknowledgement. This paper reports on the part of the segmented works carried out by a group of final-year students. The project is conducted at and funded by the Faculty of Computing, Informatics and Mathematics, Universiti Teknologi MARA (UiTM), Shah Alam, Selangor.

References

1. Nayef, E.G., Wahab, M.N.A.: The effect of recitation Quran on the human emotions. Int. J. Acad. Res. Bus. Soc. Sci. **8**(2), 50–70 (2018). https://doi.org/10.6007/IJARBSS/v8-i2/3852
2. Awang, H., et al.: Tarannum smart learning application: embracing the beauty of tarannum through multimedia technology. Int. J. Eval. Res. Educ. **11**(2), 897–906 (2022). https://doi.org/10.11591/ijere.v11i2.22388
3. Mohamed Hanum, H., et al.: Melody training with segment-based tilt contour for Quranic Tarannum. Malaysian J. Comput. Sci. 1–14 (2021). https://doi.org/10.22452/mjcs.sp2021 no2.1
4. Hanum, H.M., Aziz, A.S., Bakar, Z.A., Diah, N.M., Ahmad, W.F.W., Ali, N.M.: Melody training for quranic tarannum, In: Proceedings - CAMP 2021: 2021 5th International Conference on Information Retrieval and Knowledge Management: Digital Technology for IR 4.0 and beyond, pp. 96–101 (2021). https://doi.org/10.1109/CAMP51653.2021.9498047

5. Zakaria, M.Z., Awang, H., Mansor, N.S., Yaakob, M.F.M., Mustapha, R., Al-Mashhadani, A.F.S.: The requirement scheme for tarannum smart learning application. J. Contemp. Soc. Sci. Educ. Stud. (JOCSSES), **2**(2), 23–29 (2023)
6. Zakaria, M.Z., Awang, H., Nur, M., Rasdi, A., Mustapha, R.: Tarannum interactive audiobook model. towards a harmonious assimilation of information and communication technology into Quranic education, **1**(2), 37–45 (2021)
7. Hasbullah N.A., Azmi, A.S., Yusoff, A.M.: View of patterns and trends in tarannum qurʾān studies from 2011–2018: a thematic review in the field of Tarannum al-Qurʾān, al-Burhān J. Qurʾān Sunnah Stud. **6**(2), 20–35 (2022)
8. Smiderle, R., Rigo, S.J., Marques, L.B., et al.: The impact of gamification on students' learning, engagement and behavior based on their personality traits. Smart Learn. Environ. **7**, 3 (2020). https://doi.org/10.1186/s40561-019-0098-x
9. Ismail, M., Diah, N.M, Ahmad, S., Abdul Rahman, A.: Eengaging learners to learn tajweed through active participation in a multimedia application (TaLA). In: Computation and Communication Technologies, In: 3rd International Conference on Advances in Computing, Control, and Telecommunication Technologies, ACT 2011, pp. 88–90 (2011)
10. Diah, N.M., Ismail, M., Ahmad, S., Mahmud, M.I.: Adaptation of environmental anticipation in educational computer game. Procedia- Soc. Behav. Sci. **42**, 74–81 (2012). https://doi.org/10.1016/j.sbspro.2012.04.168
11. Hasbullah, N.A., Fabil, N., Mohamed Yusoff, A., Azmi, A.S.: Adapting a design and development research (DDR) approach in designing the mobile application model for tarannum subject. Adv. Human. Contemp. Stud. **3**(2), 193–204 (2023)

Review of User Satisfaction Models in the Context of Digital Libraries Setting

Hend Ali Musbah Jebril[1]([✉]) and Mohammad Nazir Ahmad[2]

[1] Infrastructure University Kuala Lumpur, Kajang, Malaysia
Hendag4@gmail.com
[2] The National University of Malaysia, Bangi, Malaysia
mnazir@UKM.edu.my

Abstract. Student satisfaction is of critical importance in online education, but relatively few research has investigated the factors that contribute to it in developing nations. Libraries located in public universities have, over the course of many years, shelled out a substantial amount of money in order to subscribe to a wide variety of digital resources. These resources include online publications from respectable publishers, journals, online databases, books, monographs, and other resources for the storing of information. Previous research has shown, however, that despite online libraries' success in locating relevant material, digital library use remains low. The literature review consists largely of studies that evaluate digital libraries based on how satisfied its users are. Nevertheless, the evaluation models for user satisfaction lack the constructs, and factors that contribute to user satisfaction. The primary goals of this study are to (1) identify the most relevant models used to assess user satisfaction in digital library settings, and (2) establish the prevalence users of digital libraries. This review includes, among other things, various publications that were published between the years 2019 and 2023. It emphasized the need for study user satisfaction in the context of digital libraries since this factor could impact the useability and innovation of such education platform.

Keywords: User satisfaction · Digital library · Digital academic service · Service quality

1 Introduction

As technology has advanced, the Internet has become the primary venue for a wide range of social, commercial, and archival pursuits. Many people's daily routines now include time spent on the Internet. People are spending more time than ever before participating in online communities, hosting their own events, and making their own original material [1]. According to [2] in order for libraries to have a viable future, they need to demonstrate both rationalization of the library and innovation inside the library. With the click of a mouse, people all around the world can gain access to the vast amounts of knowledge that have been compiled on the Internet. Because of the vast amounts of data storage

H. Badioze Zaman et al. (Eds.): IVIC 2023, LNCS 14322, pp. 234–246, 2024.
https://doi.org/10.1007/978-981-99-7339-2_21

available, we now have the digital library, also known as Library 2.0. A digital library provides users with access to digital files of material that have been catalogued, indexed, and backed up by experts who are accessible to answer any questions they may have. These files could be the product of an original creation or an electronic conversion of something else, such as a book, journal article, manuscript, photograph, print, video, etc. Over time, libraries have played a crucial part in facilitating individuals' access to and interaction with a wide range of information and knowledge sources. Technology advancements have made the process of knowledge collection, storage, and management much more efficient [3]. Users are shown how digital library services can assist them get the information they need in a convenient format. Digital library services such as the OPAC systems are constantly updated and evaluated to better serve library users. This provides patrons of the library with the most recent information that is accessible. There is a need for research on the user satisfaction of digital library systems because of the ever-increasing number of users and popularity of online libraries [4]. As the information monopoly of these libraries is broken by Google, practitioners and academicians are concerned about the utilization of institutions' massive investments in the depth of their digital libraries [5]. On the other hand, there are many obstacles and problems that digital libraries must overcome, including those that are technical, economic, social, and legal in nature [6]. Thus, understanding users' level of satisfaction within digital libraries is an imperative.

A digital library is a collection of electronic materials, such as databases, that can be accessed by users from afar via communications technologies like the Internet. Recently, universities have begun to digitize academic information resources and other areas of their operations by integrating technology [7]. Despite the substantial resources put into establishing digital libraries at universities, there has been relatively little study on student satisfaction with these resources, particularly with regard to how well they complement their assignments. Consequently, the purpose of this research is to explore the models that assessed the user satisfaction of digital libraries and to identify the factors that affect students' use of digital libraries.

While a lot of time and money goes into developing DLs, it is crucial to broaden access in order to recoup those costs. Despite the substantial resources being put into the development of DLs in universities, a literature analysis reveals a lack of investigation into issues of privacy and user satisfaction. More study is required to learn about the privacy practices of these libraries and determine whether or not protecting users' personal information is warranted [8]. It is also crucial to find out if students have a firm grasp on DL services, if they are making excellent use of library resources, and if the technology is a good fit for the activities they are attempting to do. The elements, such as students' impressions of universities, that affect their use of DLs were also found. This concept is crucial for mediating the connection between the other concepts corporate image has been suggested as a topic worthy of additional study in the existing research [9].

Several scholars, for instance, have investigated what factors aid to interact with digital libraries [10]. While this is going on, other academics have tried to probe into how content of digital libraries impact users' academic achievement [11]. Another studies assessed user adoption of digital libraries [12]. As depicted by the Digital Library

Federation (DLF), digital libraries are "organizations that provide resources, including specialized staff to select, organize, enable access, interpret, distribute, protect the integrity, and ensure sustained existence of digital collections in such a way that the collections are readily and cost effectively available to be used by a defined community of users [13].

Although many studies have been conducted to evaluate digital libraries, the vast majority of them have concentrated on usability-related features, such as task achievement, with only a few making any real attempt to evaluate users' satisfaction in digital libraries and utilization. One alternate strategy for gauging digital libraries success is to examine the user continued intention to use digital library [14]. This approach has also shown promise in setting a course for the future of digital library platforms. However, there has only been a small handful of methods developed to analyze digital libraries while also analysing the user satisfaction. Researchers have also begun using generic approaches to evaluate these systems' performance. This means that it is difficult to tell whether or not these models are suitable for digital libraries objective of amassing user satisfaction data.

The primary objectives of this literature review are to (1) identify the most relevant theories and models used to evaluate digital library users' satisfaction, and (2) establish the preponderance of study participants. After outlining the steps involved in doing a review, we'll move on to a scan of relevant literature on issues like measuring user satisfaction with a digital library. The next section will consist of some final thoughts and discussion. In reality, the current research solely looks at user satisfaction in digital libraries. Not covered are qualitative investigations, prototypes, or equipment unique to the digital library environment.

2 Methodology

This section presents the steps of method that used to conduct the review process. Figure 1 shows the process as it can be seen below.

In this investigation, we use a narrative analysis of related literature. The lack of relevant literature or the author's personal attachment to a piece of literature are common motivating factors in narrative analysis. In addition to providing an in-depth analysis of previously published information, the major purpose of a narrative review is to add to the ongoing general debate on a certain topic [15]. The present study review process consists of multiple actions.

2.1 Keywords

The study utilized terms like "user satisfaction" AND "digital library" AND "academic library" and "user satisfaction model". In first round of research, we obtained 680 records." Boolean operators such as "OR" and "AND" were employed effectively during the search.

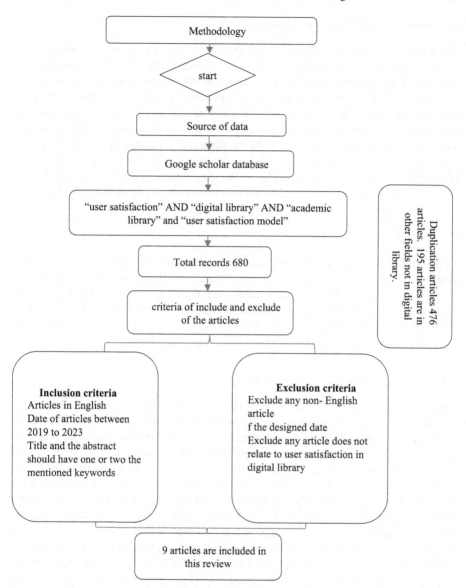

Fig. 1. Review process steps.

2.2 Database

The scholarly articles were found by using Google Scholar as the search engine. User satisfaction digital library academic library user satisfaction model were the most often used search terms. We were able to gather 680 records in our initial search.

2.3 Inclusion and Exclusion Criteria

The second phase involves filtering out irrelevant content. Therefore, we restricted ourselves to scholarly articles published in English between 2019 and 2023. The titles and abstracts of the returning papers were reviewed before the full texts were read. Articles that didn't have anything to do with student satisfaction weren't considered. Articles that did not address the topic of student and professors' satisfaction with digital libraries were disqualified. The results of this filtration process are duplication articles 476 articles and 195 articles are in other fields not in digital library. After a stricter screening process that considered both inclusion and exclusion criteria, a number of articles were found to be related to the implementation of digital libraries in the academic context. In Table 1 are compiled the articles that could have been used in this analysis as a URL [5].

3 Results

Table 1 revealed the timeline of these studies' publication. One article was published in 2019, and 2021 while three articles were published in 2020. Two articles were published in 2022, and 2023 which can be accessed through their data resources. While 2019 and 2021 was included in this review, less user satisfaction studies were conducted in 2019 and 2021 compared to 2020. The list keeps growing because numerous researches have offered different models and metrics to evaluate user satisfaction.

3.1 TAM and Digital Libraries Studies

Numerous studies have been undertaken and numerous methods and aspects for assessing the total user satisfaction have been provided by numerous researchers. Presenting prior research and extracting the components used in the models for measuring user satisfaction is the first step in the evaluation process for the current study. In related research, [16] aimed to create a framework for understanding the factors that contribute to and influence digital library users' levels of satisfaction. This research was conducted with a theoretical framework that included the Information Systems Success Model, the TAM, the Media Affinity Model, the Satisfaction-Loyalty-Engagement Model, and the Theory of Planned Behaviour was applied for this study. In developing the model, eight hypothesized linkages were made. A quantitative method was used for the research. A total of 409 Iranian college students were selected at random and given the survey to fill out for the research. The data was analyzed both descriptively and inferentially using SPSS and SmartPLS3. The findings demonstrated that a theoretical framework based on the usability of digital libraries in general and the quality of digital resources was useful for predicting and comprehending the aspects leading to user satisfaction in the field of digital libraries. Users who are more pleased with their digital library experience are more likely to share their positive opinion of it, reuse it, and actively participate in its development. The quality of a system, a service, or a piece of information can have a significant impact on how people feel about a digital library's resources and how comfortable they feel using them. This research presents a novel methodology for assessing the factors that contribute to digital library patrons feeling satisfied with their experience. The model developed for this investigation can be transferable to other studies.

Table 1. Related literature to user satisfaction in digital libraries.

No	Authors & years	Objectives	Participants	Theories/Models	Method	Results	Limitations
1	Soltani-Nejad, et al. [16]	to create a model to determine digital library user satisfaction's causes and effects	Professors, postgraduate undergraduate Iranian students and staff of the digital library	engagement theory, technology acceptance model (TAM), satisfaction-loyalty theory information system success and media affinity theory	Survey	Satisfied digital library users will reuse and suggest to other students	It is possible to look at how additional theories, such social influence and perceived involvement, affect digital library users' levels of satisfaction and loyalty
2	Khan, et al. [17]	To investigates whether useful technology and skilled user managers help users use resources, improving research productivity and academic library services	1,477-degree students	technology acceptance model (TAM)	Survey	The factor of utilization analyses how resource utilization influences user confidence, enhancing academic performance and library trust	university leaders can build modern administration, use technology to increase library resource use, and promote quality services quickly
3	Xu and Du [18]	to compare and contrast the experiences of graduate and undergraduate students using DLs	Chinese graduate and undergraduates students	Technology Acceptance Model (TAM), Affinity and Information System Success theory	Survey	To compare undergraduate and graduate students' digital library satisfaction, we can use the success theory of fine information system, TAM, and affinity theory	Our findings must be applied to additional user groups and cultures. Thus, there is a need to conduct more studies on user satisfaction in the context of DL
4	Iqbal and Rafiq [19]	Utilize structural equation modeling's confirmatory factor analysis to look at the reliability and validity of the proposed integrated digital	Pakistan users DL	Information System Success theory	Survey	The results demonstrate that the IDLUS scale has high levels of validity and reliability	The scale's psychometric study was urgently needed to assess model fit statistics on the current sample in the cultural norms
5	Omotayo and Haliru [5]	To examine the task-technology fit of digital libraries at three Nigerian universities	Nigerian users DL	Task-technology fit (TTF) model	Survey	Equally important, the study offers factual data for future research on other aspects (individual characteristics) that influence the utilization of digital learning among students	There is an empirical evidence for investigation into other variables (individual characteristics) affecting student DL use

(continued)

Table 1. (*continued*)

No	Authors & years	Objectives	Participants	Theories/Models	Method	Results	Limitations
6	Chan, et al. [9]	as part of a government-sponsored programme in Hong Kong to evaluate the utility of mobile library apps	User	S–O–R model and IS success model	Survey	The results also show that brand perception and customer satisfaction are crucial to the impact that service quality	The usability concepts can be used to evaluating the service quality of any individual app
7	Iqbal and Rafiq [20]	To define and analyze an integrated digital library user success IDLUS model	Pakistanis' users of DL	user success model	Survey	The study indicated that there is a high relationship among study latent variables	There is a recommendation to utilize IS success model
8	Sheikhshoaei, et al. [6]	To develop and validate a "digital library maturity model" (DLMM)	This study involved 4 experts	"digital library maturity model" (DLMM	Survey and Delphi method	The validity and reliability of the proposed model was confirmed	There is a need to obtain a valid and reliable proposed model to assess DL
9	Afthanorhan, et al. [21]	This research plans on modelling and researching what factors influence digital library users' satisfaction	Ordinary user of DL	Information System Success theory	Survey	The findings revealed that (System Quality and Service Quality), Information Quality had the greatest impact on customer satisfaction	Prior studies indicated that digital library utilization remains low, despite the fact that online libraries were able to locate the required data

In the same vein, research by [17] intended to investigate if, in today's technologically preoccupied environment, academic libraries are able to better serve their users by providing them with access to better technology and more knowledgeable user managers. The students at various educational institutions in the province capital filled out a paper survey that served as the study's major data source. The authors used a Likert-style scale to create the survey and consulted with experts in the field of digital libraries to ensure its usefulness before releasing it to the public. This study, grounded in the TAM, developed a conceptual model with several hypotheses to examine the validity of this approach. Structural equation modelling software was utilized for data collection, path analysis, and model building. The study's findings highlight how technology developments have improved academic achievement and services by accelerating the utilization of library resources, bolstering administration abilities, and boosting user performance. Proactive academic library services have been maintained, and the efficiency of library users has increased, thanks in large part to the skilled leadership of the institution's librarians. Future applications for the TAM-based theoretical model include facilitating the distribution of technology, enhancing management abilities, expanding library use, boosting user productivity, and furnishing cutting-edge library services. This study, which relies on survey responses from degree-seeking students in Khyber Pakhtunkhwa, is the first to offer a glimpse into the current condition of technology employed to enhance academic achievement. The report also delves into how executives may work together to reform services and increase productivity in academic libraries for both staff and students.

[18] attempts to compare and contrast the experiences of graduate and undergraduate students in regards to their satisfaction with digital libraries (DLs), drawing on the theories of Information System Success, the Technology Acceptance Model (TAM), and Affinity. The 426 valid survey responses were analyzed using descriptive statistics and One-way ANOVA. Graduate students reported higher levels of satisfaction with digital libraries across the board, including system quality, information quality, service quality, affinity, perceived ease of use, and perceived utility. Satisfaction with digital libraries varied widely among undergraduate and graduate students, and was strongly influenced by demographic factors such as age, frequency of use, and experience. Librarians and service providers at universities should take into account the similarities and differences in digital library satisfaction reported by undergraduate and graduate students, and work to enhance the usability, usefulness, and affinity of digital libraries in order to boost user satisfaction.

3.2 IS Success Model and Digital Libraries Studies

Various studies employed IS success model to assess user satisfaction in digital library. For instance, [9] combined the latest iteration of the IS success model [22] with the Stimulus-Organism-Response model S-O-R model [23] to assess the service quality of a public library app developed as part of the Hong Kong Government's mobile applications initiative and investigate how the Covid 19 pandemic has affected users' perceptions of loyalty to using library apps. We build a third-order model to illustrate the complexities of service quality and the moderating roles of customer satisfaction, attitude towards the brand, and online word of mouth. Using structural equation modelling, researchers in Hong Kong—a city where mobile services give people more agency—discovered correlations between service quality and several outcomes (including brand perception, repeat business, online recommendations, and customer satisfaction). Results also show that brand perception and customer satisfaction are crucial in influencing how loyal a customer is likely to be. Since the lockdown and social distance procedures made it difficult for individuals to search for information in public libraries in person, this study is particularly relevant during the current COVID-19 outbreak. Our research and recommendations stress the significance of including usability ideas into assessments of app services. In addition to recommending additional research into the suggested hierarchical model and other potential characteristics associated to service quality, these findings are useful to practitioners as they design the next generation of apps for smart public information services.

[13] conducted a study to (1) implement confirmatory factor analysis in structural equation modelling and (2) examine the validity and reliability of the proposed integrated digital library user success (IDLUS) scale in the context of an academic digital library computing information system. The survey included 355 complete replies (MPhil and PhD levels) from Pakistan's oldest and largest public university students. The stratified random sampling method was utilized; students from the University of Punjab's four academic divisions were selected randomly to comprise the sample. The tool was developed using the two existing paradigms for effective digital libraries and information

systems. The first is the [20] model for ensuring the success of library patrons using digital resources; it incorporates the flow model (1977), the end-user computer satisfaction model, and the overall user satisfaction model (1990) developed by [21]. The second model is a reformulation of the information system success theory 2003 by DeLone and McLean. The questions were graded on a 5-point Likert scale, and convergent validity, variance extraction, construct reliability, and discriminant validity analyses were performed. The results demonstrate high levels of validity and reliability for the IDLUS scale. As far as the authors are aware, this is the first attempt to develop a metric for measuring the success of library patrons using digital resources within the context of the Higher Education Commission-National Digital Library of Pakistan. As a result, a psychometric study of the scale was required to look at the statistics of the model fit for the current sample in the specific cultural norms. In order to create this scale, researchers in the domains of human-computer interaction, information systems, and computer-mediated communication drew on numerous theories of Web and information system success.

[20] argued that due to their complexity, digital libraries necessitate research into user success in order to develop effective user success models. The relationships between humans, machines, and businesses are modelled here. The goal of this research was to take advantage of and improve upon preexisting models for both digital library and Web success in order to specify and analyze an integrated digital library user success (IDLUS) model applicable to digital library settings, specifically the Higher Education Commission National Digital Library (HEC-NDL) of Pakistan. The sample was selected from students attending Pakistan's top public university, the University of the Punjab, using a stratified random selection method. The survey participants were requested to fill out a modified version of the original. There were 355 usable responses from the surveys that were collected. Using confirmatory factor analyses and structural equation modelling, researchers were able to assess data in a way that lent credence to the IDLUS model. The results validated the model's suppositions about the connections between the latent variables. Academics and IT professionals can benefit from the study in a number of ways, both theoretically and practically. For the first time in Pakistani library annals, the IDLUS paradigm is suggested as a blueprint for user satisfaction with digital library resources. That provided various suggestions for further study in the field of information management, especially in regards to the expansion of digital libraries on a global scale.

[21] looked into what factors influence digital library users' happiness. Delone and McLean's Information System Success Model, Version 2.0, was used as the basis for this study's methodology. The data was gathered by a method of cluster sampling. There were 353 complete questionnaires used for analysis. The findings revealed that among the quality components (System Quality and Service Quality, Information Quality had the greatest impact on customer satisfaction. Furthermore, the indirect effect was evaluated using the Preacher & Hayes method. All effects were partially mediated as a result of this strategy. In a nutshell, the quality aspects and the Information System play a significant role in shaping the intentions behind the activity.

3.3 Other Models to Assess User Satisfaction

[5] carried out a study to examine the task-technology fit of digital libraries at three Nigerian universities and to identify the factors that affect students' adoption of digital library resources. The study followed a survey design and 402 students participated by completing a questionnaire. According to the results, students make extensive use of digital libraries. There was a somewhat favorable and statistically significant association between the independent factors (task characteristics, technology characteristics, attitude, computer self-efficacy, and task-technology fit) and the dependent variable (digital library use). The research backs up the TTF model's central tenet that users are more likely to make use of an information system if it is well-suited to the activities it facilitates.

[6] carried out a study to design and test a method for gauging a digital library's level of development in accordance with the "digital library maturity model" (DLMM). The requirements for each code were determined based on a combination of literature and expert opinion. The constructed instrument's content validity was confirmed by expert opinion, and its construct validity was confirmed via confirmatory factor analysis. Cronbach's alpha was used to evaluate the design's internal consistency. At last, verification of the designed instrument's validity and dependability was achieved. Managers of digital libraries can use this assessment to determine where their libraries now stand in terms of maturity and where they want to go.

4 Discussion

While digital library evaluation has come a long way, there are still many open questions, especially in light of new developments in technology and shifting user preferences. To gauge how these tools affect digital library usability, search efficiency, and overall effectiveness, more investigation is required. Table 1 highlighted the models and significance of potential constructs that influence user satisfaction. As a result, it is suggested that future researchers may want to center their efforts on developing more comprehensive models for gathering data. Periodic evaluations of digital library platforms are necessary due to the fact that these platforms are still undergoing modifications in various elements connected to optional use, such as enhancing the user interface. Future research would benefit from putting greater emphasis on service quality because it is the most crucial factor. The study's authors express optimism that their findings would inspire them to conduct further empirical investigation with the intention of assessing and improving various methodologies and models for assessing the user satisfaction. The literature showed that most of the studies in this paper focus on undergraduate students in higher education setting and less attention has been made to the postgraduate students. Furthermore, the most employed model to assess user satisfaction is the model proposed by [24] IS success model. For instance, [9, 16, 18–21]. These studies indicted the significant of such model in the context of digital libraries and assessing the satisfaction of DL users. On the other hand, technology acceptance model (TAM) came in the second rank of model utilization in the context of user satisfaction. For example, [16–18] Although it is vital role in the digital libraries, Task characteristics and technology characteristics theory came in the third rank of usage and used only one time [5].

Furthermore, various models addressed various challenges in the context of digital libraries from user satisfaction viewpoints. For example, [16] proposed a model based on four theories, IS success, TAM and user loyalty and engagement theory, to explore the factors that lead to user satisfaction with digital libraries and the repercussions of that satisfaction. Although the model was comprehensive and included more than seven factors that impact user satisfaction, the dynamic nature of user experience and satisfaction continually needs scrutinization. The study revealed the importance of service, system, and information quality. The issues of the dynamics of technology and the abilities of management on user satisfaction and trust in library services were evaluated by a model proposed by [17]. TAM model was utilized as a theoretical base for this model. Trust as a significant factor influencing user satisfaction was also assessed. Despite the valuable results obtained by khan study, the issue of clustering technology and retrieval are other issues that need to be examined.

Differences and similarities between graduates and undergraduate students were evaluated by a model proposed by [18]. The proposed model was based on affinity theory, the success theory of fine information systems and TAM as a comprehensive theoretical instrument. Even though some steps have been made to mitigate the adverse effects of convenient sampling, it is clear that students from diverse fields of study and of varying levels are not equally represented. People, organization and technology relationship from user satisfaction was evaluated by proposing a model based on IS success model. The model obtained validity from confirmatory factor analysis and examined the factors determining the relations between technology, people and management. The challenges in task technology were investigated by the model proposed by [5]. The theoretical base of the study model was TTF model. However, the model indicated a promising result. Other individual characteristics could be included in future studies, such as self-efficacy, namely, students' competence in computers. Another model proposed by [9] investigated the mediating relationship between perceived service quality and public library app loyalty throughout COVID-19. The study recommended examining another construct, such as the effect of e-WOM further, trust, service fairness, self-efficacy and attitudinal loyalty and behavioral loyalty. Another model comes from the Pakistani environment. This model is the integrated digital library user success (IDLUS). This model was proposed to determine total user success in Pakistan digital library. However, there is still a need for improvement in the proposed scale [20]. Another significant model is "digital library maturity model" (DLMM). It is proposed by [6] to examine the development of human and financial and technological investments of a digital library in Iran. On the same regard, digital library success was also scrutinized by a model proposed by [21] based on IS model [24]. The study model showed the strength of examining service quality factor. However, the study used an observed variable that was based on an existing model, and it is possible that some of the observed variables won't be consistent with the expanded research scope. Thus, it is necessary to study other different factors from different theories. According to the evidence provided, users of digital libraries' familiarity with using technology for educational purposes differs significantly from their familiarity with using technology for other purposes.

5   Conclusion

The researchers aimed to explore the user satisfaction model in the context of digital libraries. To find answers, this study a review to the related literature was conducted. A lot of attention has already been paid to the literature regarding the effects of individuals and the spread of e-libraries, but very little research has focused on measuring user satisfaction with respect to the quality of these libraries. The findings of this study have real-world applications because they can help decision-makers enhance the quality of their services by suggesting areas in which they should concentrate their efforts to do so. This is due to the fact that the empirical evidence clearly demonstrates that Service Quality is the sole element that can influence User Satisfaction. A second consideration for the decision maker is the Intention to Use component, which was found to be significant across all model effects. The study does have some inherent flaws. To begin, this research only included institutions run by the government, so its findings are limited. Second, the current study used an observed variable based on an existing model, and it's possible that some of the observed variables won't be consistent with the expanded research scope. Third, a survey questionnaire and quantitative analysis were used to explore the interplay of the model's constituent parts in most of the studies. Another review studies can focus on user satisfaction, a hybrid method (qualitative and quantitative) approach may yield more reliable results. Research into the topic of digital library users' levels of satisfaction has been hampered by a lack of relevant literature in scholarly journals and by the neglect of reports, grey reporting, and online articles. Although this study has certain limitations, it has tried to be as conclusive as possible. Thus, it is suggested that future researchers could center their efforts on expanding the data-gathering models by include additional factors such as privacy, perceived university image would add a valuable significance for future research. Since digital libraries platforms are still undergoing improvements in various features connected to optional usage, such as enhancing the user interface, it is necessary to conduct periodic assessments of these platforms. Future research would benefit from putting greater emphasis on user service quality than on any of the other factors. The study's authors express optimism that their findings will inspire further empirical investigation into the evaluation of user satisfaction using a variety of methodologies and models. To put things in viewpoint, better assessment procedures could improve evaluations and digital library satisfaction.

References

1. Harrin, E.: Social communities of practice reflection on informal mentoring in curated online spaces. In: Social Media for Project Management, pp. 73–88. CRC Press (2022)
2. Rafi, Muhammad, Ming, Zheng Jian, Ahmad, Khurshid: Estimation of the knowledge management model for performance measurement in university libraries. Libr. Hi Tech **40**(1), 239–264 (2022). https://doi.org/10.1108/LHT-11-2019-0225
3. Manesh, M.F., Pellegrini, M.M., Marzi, G., Dabic, M.: Knowledge management in the fourth industrial revolution: mapping the literature and scoping future avenues. IEEE Trans. Eng. Manage. **68**(1), 289–300 (2020)
4. Rafi, M., JianMing, Z., Ahmad, K.: Evaluating the impact of digital library database resources on the productivity of academic research. Inf. Discov. Deliv. **47**(1), 42–52 (2019)

5. Omotayo, F.O., Haliru, A.: Perception of task-technology fit of digital library among undergraduates in selected universities in Nigeria. J. Acad. Librariansh. **46**(1), 102097 (2020)
6. Sheikhshoaei, F., Naghshineh, N., Alidousti, S., Nakhoda, M., Dehdarirad, H.: Development and validation of a measuring instrument for digital library maturity. Libr. Inf. Sci. Res. **43**(3), 101101 (2021)
7. Habibi, A., Yaakob, M.F.M., Sofwan, M.: Student use of digital libraries during COVID-19: structural equation modelling in Indonesian and Malaysian contexts. Electron. Libr. **40**(4), 472–485 (2022)
8. Ashiq, M., Rehman, S.U., Muneeb, D., Ahmad, S.: Global research on library service quality: a bibliometric analysis and knowledge mapping. Glob. Knowl. Memory Commun. **71**(4/5), 253–273 (2022). https://doi.org/10.1108/GKMC-02-2021-0026
9. Chan, V.H.Y., Chiu, D.K., Ho, K.K.: Mediating effects on the relationship between perceived service quality and public library app loyalty during the COVID-19 era. J. Retail. Consum. Serv. **67**, 102960 (2022)
10. Li, Y., Liu, C.: Information resource, interface, and tasks as user interaction components for digital library evaluation. Inf. Process. Manage. **56**(3), 704–720 (2019)
11. Rafi, M., Ahmad, K., Naeem, S.B., Khan, A.U., JianMing, Z.: Knowledge-based society and emerging disciplines: a correlation of academic performance. The Bottom Line **33**(4), 337–358 (2020)
12. Ling, E.C., Tussyadiah, I., Tuomi, A., Stienmetz, J., Ioannou, A.: Factors influencing users' adoption and use of conversational agents: a systematic review. Psychol. Mark. **38**(7), 1031–1051 (2021)
13. DigitalLibraryFederation: A working definition of digital library (1998). https://old.diglib.org/about/dldefinition.htm. Accessed 16 Mar 2014
14. Rahman, A.R.A., Mohezar, S., Habidin, N.F., Fuzi, N.M.: Critical success factors of the continued usage of digital library successful implementation in military-context: an organisational support perspective. Digit. Libr. Perspect. **36**(1), 38–54 (2020)
15. Bae, J.-M.: Narrative reviews. Epidemiol. Health, **36** (2014)
16. Soltani-Nejad, N., Taheri-Azad, F., Zarei-Maram, N., Saberi, M.K.: Developing a model to identify the antecedents and consequences of user satisfaction with digital libraries. Aslib J. Inf. Manag. **72**(6), 979–997 (2020)
17. Khan, A.U., Rafi, M., Zhang, Z., Khan, A.: Determining the impact of technological modernization and management capabilities on user satisfaction and trust in library services. Glob. Knowl. Memory Commun. (2022)
18. Xu, F., Du, J.T.: Examining differences and similarities between graduate and undergraduate students' user satisfaction with digital libraries. J. Acad. Librariansh. **45**(6), 102072 (2019)
19. Iqbal, M., Rafiq, M.: Psychometric analysis of integrated digital library user success (IDLUS) scale in academic digital library environment. Glob. Knowl. Memory Commun. (2023)
20. Iqbal, Memoona, Rafiq, Muhammad: Determinants of overall user success in an academic digital library environment: validation of the integrated digital library user success (IDLUS) model. Electron. Libr. **41**(4), 387–418 (2023)
21. Afthanorhan, A., Foziah, H., Abd Majid, N.: Investigating digital library success using the DeLone and McLean information system success 2.0: the analysis of common factor based structural equation modeling. In: Journal of Physics: Conference Series, vol. 1529, no. 4, p. 042052. IOP Publishing (2020)
22. DeLone, W.H., McLean, E.R.: Information systems success measurement. Found. Trends® Inf. Syst. **2**(1), 1–116 (2016)
23. Mehrabian, A., Russell, J.A.: An Approach to Environmental Psychology. The MIT Press, Cambridge (1974)
24. DeLone, W.H., McLean, E.R.: The DeLone and McLean model of information systems success: a ten-year update. J. Manag. Inf. Syst. **19**(4), 9–30 (2003)

Systems Integration and IoT, Cybersecurity, Energy Informatics

Design and Development of an Automated Filament Changing System for Fused Deposition Modelling (FDM) 3D Printer Using Axiomatic Design and TRIZ

Kok Weng Ng[1], Jia Wei Wong[1], JianBang Liu[2], and Mei Choo Ang[2(✉)]

[1] University of Nottingham Malaysia, Jalan Broga, 43500 Semenyih, Selangor, Malaysia
[2] Universiti Kebangsaan Malaysia, UKM Bangi, 43650 Bangi, Selangor, Malaysia
amc@ukm.edu.my

Abstract. One of the most widely used 3D printers is the Fused Deposition Modelling (FDM) printer. However, it has a very long printing process which may encounter printing failure and cause wastage of resources. Therefore, in this study, an attempt to design and develop a home-made and simple automatic filament changing system that is compatible with FDM printers using Bowden tube extrusion system. The designed system is expected to refill filaments particular for overnight 3D printing process. Axiomatic Design and TRIZ are used in this study to systematically design and solve problems faced throughout this research project. Conceptual designs were derived, and the final conceptual design consists of Central Control Sub-System, Filament Guide Sub-System, Merger Sub-System, and Spool Rollers Sub-System. The most critical sub-systems are the Filament Guide Sub-System and Merger Sub-System, which allows filament to refill without human interaction and allow two filament inputs to pass through a merging component to enable one single output. For the Central Control Sub-System, Arduino programming language was used with a MAKER UNO board, an Arduino compatible low-cost microcontroller to control the refilling process. Three limit switches which act as 2 input sensors and 1 output sensor respectively working in tandem with and 2 stepper motors were used to actuate the refilling process. The design of the automatic filament changing system was successful and the testing of the system was successful on the sub-systems level.

Keywords: Filament Changing · Fused Deposition Modelling · 3D Printing

1 Introduction

3-dimensional (3D) printing, also known as additive manufacturing (AM) developed since last decades, has now became an alternative option to the classic subtractive manufacturing. 3D printing produce parts based on the Computer Aided Design (CAD) model which is saved in.STL format unlike, the traditional subtractive manufacturing which begins with removing undesired material from an oversized raw material block

© The Author(s), under exclusive license to Springer Nature Singapore Pte Ltd. 2024
H. Badioze Zaman et al. (Eds.): IVIC 2023, LNCS 14322, pp. 249–260, 2024.
https://doi.org/10.1007/978-981-99-7339-2_22

[1]. Although 3D printing particularly Fused Deposition Modelling (FDM) type has increasingly been used to manufacture parts, the problem of running out of print materials or material filaments are well-known. Even though recent improvement has been introduced such as the feature that allows 3D printer to continue to print from where the material has run out, time wasted when the material runs out particularly in an overnight print is significant and can delay product delivery. This project explores the possibility of designing a solution to prevent stoppage of printing for FDM 3D printing with Bowden tube extrusion system.

1.1 TRIZ

TRIZ is a concept that proposed and developed by Genrich Altshuller, a Soviet engineer [2]. The first publication Altshuller made in 1956 discussed about the solution to unlimited technical contradictions with limited "Inventive Principles"[3]. In 1969, Altshuller released "The Innovation Algorithm"[4], and this is the first time that the "40 Inventive Principles" and the initial edition of "ARIZ" were conferred to the world. Observations made by Altshuller according to his notable research results [5] led to more inventive tools and forming the TRIZ toolset such as Contradiction Matrix, which is a useful tool for solving problem and inventive solutions evolution, correction and failure avoidance, and risk control [6].

1.2 Axiomatic Design

Nam P. Suh suggested Axiomatic Design principles in 1990s [7] as key principles that should be applied to all good designs. The final objective of the principles is to create a scientific theory to make improvement in design activities by giving a theoretical foundation to the designer through logical and rational thinking process and efficient tools [8]. To systemize the thinking process, and to constrain different design activities, 4 domains are proposed to symbolize the Axiomatic Design procedure's basis [9] and a design process will start from customers and progress zig zag between these 4 domains shown below (this means the design process will move from customer needs to functional requirements and then to design parameters and lastly to process variables but the movement can be going forward and backward):

1) Customer Needs (CNs).
2) Functional Requirements (FRs)
3) Design Parameters (DPs)
4) Process Variables (PVs)

The foundation of the Axiomatic Design principles defined by 2 axioms [7]:

(a) 1st Axiom (Independence Axiom): Ensure the FRs are independent to each other.
(b) 2nd Axiom (Information Axiom): Generalize the design with minimum information content of the design.

The higher the probability of success, the lower the amount of information are required for manufacturing [10]. Nonetheless, the 1st Axiom is often fulfilled, and the 2nd Axiom is not considered as a part of the evaluation procedure [11].

1.3 3D Printing

The most common and easiest AM technology or 3D printing to get accessed is the FDM technology [12]. This technology provides excellent flexibility in shaping which avoid the demand on shape-dependent tooling. However, 3D printing is also well-known for its horrible energy efficiency and time efficiency. Although 3D printing has a shorter production time compared to conventional method for low volume production, it still takes a lot of time to print a complex designed small part, excluding the design and pre and post-processing stages [13]. One of the parameters that affected the time efficiency is the printing time, where it also influenced by the print size, printing speed, and layer height [14].

Due to the parameters above, the printing can take up to 10 h to a day, even 2 days to print a part. It is very common to have a printing failure or stoppage due to the running out of filament when the part is printing overnight because it is very difficult for users to determine if the remaining filaments are enough to complete the printing. Therefore, there are products invented in the market to overcome this issue however they all have their own limitation such as long pre-processing stage [15], only able to fit on certain models of printers [16, 17].

After assessing the available products in the market, it shows that the common solution is control multiple filaments with multiple feeders where the system is installed on the printers' body. At the same time, the common cons of these products are these products required installation of parts such as hangers, etc. that are only suitable for a particular type and size of 3D printers. Therefore, there is a need for an automated filament changing system that minimise modification and installation of additional parts to an existing 3D printer.

1.4 Objectives and paper Outline

Based on the problem statement above, in this research, an automatic filament changing system is proposed to be designed to overcome the weaknesses observed from available products in the market and enable the filament to be automatically fed when the materials run out.

There are several objectives in this work. They are:

- The product has to be able to work with different type of 3D printers (Cartesian, Delta, Polar and robotic arm).
- The product should be independent from the size of the 3D printer as much as possible.
- Minimum modification should be done on the 3D printer.
- The product has to be user-friendly.
- The product has to be as compact as possible.

In Sect. 2, we describe the prototype (Hardware and Software) development that includes applications of Axiomatic Design and TRIZ, working mechanism, prototype installation, and method of testing. Then, the prototype testing result will be discussed in Sect. 3, then elaboration on obstacles encountered and possible solution is presented also. Finally, in Sect. 4 will touch on the final project outcome and judgement is made.

2 Methodology

The project starts with the listing out the FRs and DPs for the conceptual design. (Axiomatic Design). Then, the design is revised by using the Contradiction Matrix to solve the problem encountered (TRIZ). Once the design is confirmed, the prototype is then modelled and later fabricated. After the physical components are ready, then the software algorithm is generated and ready for testing.

2.1 Conceptual Design (Axiomatic Design)

Based on the printers, few functional requirements and constraints have been set up where they are:

- The system is designed for continuous long hours overnight printing instead of multi colour printing.
- The printer will only be able to print 1.75mm diameter filament due to the method of inserting filament into the extruder.
- The system is more suitable for printers which do not have built-in filament sensor or the sensor can be turned off so it will not interrupt the printing process if there is a gap between two filaments.

After referring to the available products in the market, several FRs, DPs, and references have been listed below in Table 1. From the observation on the available products, 2 out of the 3 designs only holding 2 spools of filament. An investigation made by Satterfield shows that a 1 kg of 1.75 mm diameter PLA filament is able to last 123 h and 36 min averagely [18]. Therefore, two spools of filament are sufficient for an overnight printing which also allows the user to replace the consumed spool with a new spool of filament.

The conceptual design of the product is shown in Fig. 1. Numbers labelled in the drawing is representing each DP. Label 1 is the spool rollers mentioned in DP 1; Label 2 is where the filament sensors (DP 2) will be installed; Label 3 is the PTFE tubes which act as the constrained path for filaments to pass through (DP 3); Label 4 shows that the only part will be connecting to the 3D printer which is the filament output (DP 4); DP 6 is fulfilled as the user only have to connect the filament output to the printer and the whole system can be used straightaway. However, DP 5 is not fulfilled as the PTFE tubes has maximum length of 1 m, which means that the user needs to reserve a relatively large area to set up the system.

2.2 Design Revision (TRIZ Problem Solving Tools)

The main parameters here are the main shape of the design, design complexity, versatility of the product, and ease of manufacture. The main shape of the design is affecting both versatility of product and ease of manufacture because the bigger the product is, the bigger the limitation on the space requirement. Besides that, to ease the manufacturing process, 3D printing is chosen to be fabricate the prototype. Nonetheless, the design size is relatively larger, and the design complexity of the conceptual design is also relatively higher due to the number of parts planning to use. By mapping the parameters to generic parameters on Contradiction Matrix, the relationships are shown below:

Table 1. FRs with mapped DPs and references.

Functional Requirements	Design Parameter
1. The system has to be able to locate 2 spools of filament	Spool rollers are designed for the spools. This is to fit various sizes of spool [18]
2. The infilling filament has to be continuous so it will not degrade the printing quality	Filament sensors will be attached on the filament changing system and filament will pass through them before entering the 3D printer When filament sensors detected there is shortage of filament, it will feed the backup filaments into the main path [17]
3. Filaments have to be fed at a steady speed therefore it will not exert force on the previous filament	Motors will be installed, and they will be feeding each filament respectively. Filament guide will be installed to hold the filaments firmly at the filament changing system PTFE tubes will be installed to control the movement of the filaments from the spool to the printers' extruder [17]
4. This system should be compatible to different 3D printers	The system has to attach to the 3D printer itself as less as possible so it can be transfer to another 3D printer if needed [17]
5. The system has to be as compact as possible so users with limited available spaces can still install the system	Overall dimension has to be smaller than the common 3D printer sizes [17]
6. The system has to be easy to install	Components should be as less and as simple as possible [17]

1. Ease of Manufacture vs Shape
2. Ease of Manufacture vs Design Complexity
3. Adaptability or Versatility vs Shape

Based on the contradictions above, the Contradiction Matrix is introduced here to determine the suitable Inventive Principles can be used to solve the contradictions. The respective principles are shown below in Table 2 [19].

As shown above, Principle 1, Segmentation can be found in the result of each contradiction. Therefore, segmentation will be referred to solve the contradictions above. There are several approaches suggested in Segmentation principle which are [19]:

1. Divide an object into independent parts.
2. Making an object sectional, by means easy to assemble or disassemble.
3. Increase the degree of fragmentation or segmentation.

The approaches chosen here is point 1 and point 2. Referring back to the conceptual design, the reason of the bulky design is due to the spools and the whole system is located

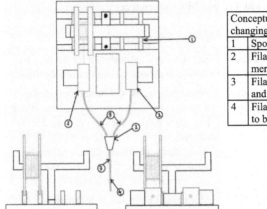

Conceptualisation of the automated filament changing system for FDM 3D printers	
1	Spool rollers sub-system concept
2	Filament guide sub-systems concept and merger sub-system concept
3	Filaments output from guide sub-systems and output from merger system
4	Filament output from merger sub-system to be fed into the FDM 3D printer

Fig. 1. Conceptual design for the proposed automated filament changing system for FDM 3D printers

Table 2. Mapped Inventive Principles for each Contradictions.

Contradictions		Inventive Principles (IP)	Solutions
Improving Feature	Worsening Feature		
Ease of Manufacture	Shape	1,13,27,28	IP 1 – Segmentation: Sub-systems are created to perform different functions
Ease of Manufacture	Design Complexity	1,26,27	IP 1 – Segmentation: Reduce design complexity by creating sub-systems for different functions
Adaptability or Versatility	Shape	1,8,15,37	IP151 – Dynamisation: Feeding the filament through filament guides to enable continuation of printing when one filament spool is used up

on the same platform, while the central control system which controlling other components are actually occupying very small spaces. By dividing the platform to separate pieces or sub-systems, the required spaces to set up the system will be relatively smaller which led to shorter production time (which also led to lower failure probability) and didn't worsen the design complexity.

3 Final Design

The final design is completed as shown Fig. 2 (A) and (B).

3.1 Central Control Sub-System

Maker Uno (Arduino Uno compatible microcontroller), two Maker Drive (Motor Driver), mini breadboard, two battery holders (4 x AA), and two stepper motors are installed on the main piece, Base. Microcontroller and motor drivers are installed by bolts and nuts, while battery holders, stepper motors, and mini breadboard are installed in the designed slot with a tight fit.

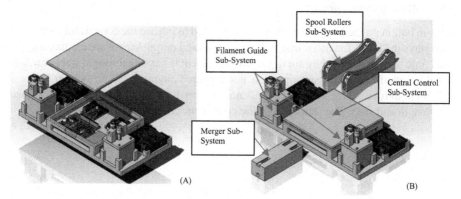

Fig. 2. Final Design (A) – Exploded view and (B) – Isometric View with labels on all 4 sub-systems

3.2 Merger Sub-system

3 limit switches, which act as input sensors and output sensor, are placed in the designated slots on the Merger piece and their horizontal and vertical motions are limited by the slot itself and Merger Keys respectively. Embedded Nuts (Copper Inserts) are inserted on the Merger piece in order to install Pneumatic Tube Connectors for the connection of pneumatic tube.

3.3 Spool Rollers Sub-system

Four identical pieces – Spool roller are assembled in pair by inserting bearings on the knobs. To minimize the space consumption, only one set of spool rollers are needed as one of the filament spools can be located on the 3D printer's designated shaft. By using bearings instead of letting the spool contact directly to the spool roller surface, the friction produced while roller can be prevented and smoothen the filament extracting process. Besides that, wide base surface of the assemblies are able to maintain the stability of the spool so it will not turn over due to any external forces.

3.4 Filament Guide Sub-system

To achieve autonomous filament changing mechanism, there should be zero human interaction with either 3D printer or filament changing system throughout the filament changing process. Filament Guide is designed referring to available filament extruder lever while there is a gap between two filaments, it will still be able to pass through the extruder without human interruption. Extruder Gears and bearings are installed on the stepper motors' shafts and designated shafts on the Filament Guide pieces. Both gears and bearings will be installed rigidly by screws so they will not have any motions except for rotation. Same as Merger Sub-stem, embedded nuts are inserted on the Filament Guide piece for the installation of Pneumatic Tube Connector.

3.5 Software Development

Built-in button on the Maker Uno board will be used to initiate the code. Initialization of code stays in "loop" function, where input sensors and output sensor are reading signals from time to time. When they are triggered as filament is passing through, stepper motor 1 will be rotating until sensor input 1 is not triggered anymore. Then, stepper motor 2 will begin to rotate once output sensor is not triggered too. It will rotate for a designed time length and stop. The flowchart of the control program is shown in Fig. 3.

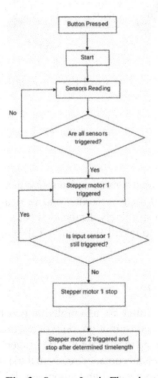

Fig. 3. System Logic Flowchart

3.6   Control on Motor Rotating Speed

Most of the initial settings of 3D printers is setting the feeding speed to be 60 mm/s, which can be modified by users based on their needs such as printing slower to get better profile or printing faster to save time. In normal condition, where prints are smaller or travelling distance of the printer bed is not much, there is not much printing time difference when the printing speed is higher than 60 mm/s [20]. Therefore, the stepper motors used will be set to rotate in a speed of 30 mm/s so that it will not exert force on the end of previous spool and cause snapping of filaments. Besides of setting the motor speed, the duration time of the motor rotating is also determined by dividing the measured length from the output sensor to output end of filament guide installed on the stepper motor that comes with 3D printer, which is approximately 1060 mm, by the proposed speed, 30 mm/s. The time needed is then evaluated to be 36 s.

3.7   Cases of Triggering the Motors

Millis function (Arduino code for running in milliseconds) begins to run once the electrical power is connected. A built-in button on the MAKER UNO is used to initiate the system. Time variables "ct", "initiate", "ptin1", and "ptin2" are introduced. "initiate" will be equal to Millis function once built-in button is pressed. When the initiate value is more than zero, the sensors will begin to start reading the values. Instead of setting cases under the situation where the sensors are triggered or not, a debounce value is introduced to eliminate the noises generated when there is vibration. Two cases are written in the code which trigger stepper motor 1 and stepper motor 2 separately.

1. If all sensors have reading values more than debounce value, "ptin1" is equal to ct, and stepper motor 1 will begin to rotate until it fulfils the condition "ct − ptin1 <36000".
2. If only input sensor 2 is reading values more than debounce value, then "ptin2" is equal to ct, and stepper motor 2 will begin to rotate until the condition "ct − ptin2 <36000.
3. Else, both the motors will not be triggered.

4   Results of the Prototype Testing and Discussions

Among the available 3D printers in workshop, Creality Ender-3 Max is chosen for testing as it meets the requirement which is:

1. It has the most common working mechanism which is Bowden system.
2. The built-in filament sensor can be turned off so the printing process will not be interrupt.

The original extruder lever is replaced by the filament guide (as shown in Fig. 4). Then, prepare a filament that is longer than 1.2 m, insert it into the left input hole of Merger, and stop when it triggered both input sensor 1 and output sensor. On the other hand, insert the new filament into the right input hole on Merger, and stop when it triggered the input sensor 2. Once the setup is ready, built-in button is pressed to initiate the system. The prototype is assembled and installed on the 3D printer as shown in Fig. 4 below. Each sub-systems are labelled and shown in Fig. 4.

During the prototype testing, it is critical for the sensors to have good contacts as the sensors are very sensitive to ensure the system works consistently.

For the Filament Guide Subassembly, during setup, the filament can be inserted and pass through the filament guide subassembly and fed by the stepper motors. However, it is vital for the bearing shaft to have sufficient stiffness and able withstand the high pressure exerted by the filament when the filament squeezes through the small gap (about 1.65 mm in diameter) between the extruder gear and the bearing shaft.

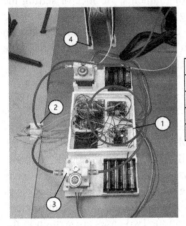

Number	Sub-system
1	Central Control Sub-System
2	Merger Sub-System
3	Filament Guide Sub-System
4	Spool Rollers Sub-System

Fig. 4. General assembly of the automated filament changing system for FDM 3D printers.

(i)   (ii)

Fig. 5. Replaced filament guide sub-systems (i) and spool rollers subassembly (ii) for the automated filament changing system for FDM 3D printers

For Merger Subassembly, all the electronic components can be inserted into designated slot accurately and can be triggered while filaments passing through in the pathway. Filaments are able to enter the merger from different inputs and exit from the same output. However, if the filament breaks inside the pathway, the merger piece will not be functioning properly in the current design. Therefore, for future work, a merger sub-system that can facilitate the removal of the broken filament from the piece when the filament breaks inside the path would be crucial to solve this problem.

For Spool Rollers Subassembly, the bearings can fit into the knob tightly and allow smooth rotation for filament spool as shown in Fig. 5 (ii). There is a small possibility of the filament spool to fall off from the spool rollers subassembly due to a small back force exerted on the spool filament and the changes of the centre of mass for the spool during printing. This problem occurred due to the small contact area between spool rollers subassembly and the table/flat surface and can be mitigated by increasing the base area and sufficient support design. With reference to the Central Control System, all the components are required to be installed rigidly to ensure the system work as expected. Due to restriction of space of the system, all electrical connections need to be well soldered and properly insulated to avoid any occurrence possibility of short circuit and to ensure electrical stable connection.

The initial testing on the sub-systems and the complete system have been successful with manual triggering and the releases of the filament guide sub-system as shown in Fig. 5 (i) before progressing into automated triggering. The filament manages to move smoothly and followed the run-out filament until it reaches the feeder motor at the 3D printer which successfully pull the replacement filament following the run-out filament into the print nozzle with the motors of the filament guide sub-system released or not clamping onto the replacement filament.

5   Conclusion

As conclusion, with the aid of Axiomatic Design and TRIZ principles, a home-made simple, and compatible with different kind of 3D printers, as well as an user-friendly automatic filament changing system is proposed, designed and fabricated. Further improvements are needed to increase its reliability from the perspectives of

 i. Utilisation of stiffer bearing shaft and with higher dimensional accuracy
 ii. Improvisation of secure and more robust electrical connection within a restricted space
iii. Exploring other sensors than limit switches
 iv. Enhancing the program to include artificial intelligence to upgrade the system to become more adaptive or flexible.

By implementing the suggested improvements, the filament changing system should be able to automatically allow filament to be changed in a variety of conditions and scenarios without human intervention.

References

1. Ding, D., Pan, Z., Cuiuri, D., Li, H., Larkin, N., van Duin, S.: Automatic multi-direction slicing algorithms for wire based additive manufacturing. Robot. Comput. Integr. Manuf. **37**, 139–150 (2016)
2. Terninko, J., Zusman, A., Zlotin, B.: Systematic Innovation: An Introduction to TRIZ (Theory of Inventive Problem Solving). Taylor & Francis (1998)

3. Orloff, M.A.: Inventive Thinking Through TRIZ: A Practical Guide. Springer, Heidelberg (2013)
4. Al'tshuller, G.S., Shulyak, L., Rodman, S.: The innovation algorithm: TRIZ, systematic innovation and technical creativity. Technical Innovation Center (1999)
5. Souchkov, V.: Accelerate Innovation with TRIZ (2017)
6. Souchkov, V.: Breakthrough thinking with TRIZ for business and management: an overview (2007)
7. Suh, N.P., Suh, P.N.: The Principles of Design. Oxford University Press, Oxford (1990)
8. Suh, N.P.: Axiomatic Design: Advances and Applications. Oxford University Press, Oxford (2001)
9. Rauch, E., Matt, D., Dallasega, P.: Application of axiomatic design in manufacturing system design: a literature review. Procedia CIRP **53**, 1–7 (2016)
10. El-Haik, B.: Axiomatic Quality: Integrating Axiomatic Design with Six-Sigma, Reliability, and Quality Engineering. Axiomatic Quality: Integrating Axiomatic Design with Six-Sigma, Reliability, and Quality Engineering (2005)
11. Kulak, O., Cebi, S., Kahraman, C.: Applications of axiomatic design principles: a literature review. Expert Syst. Appl. **37**, 6705–6717 (2010)
12. Dizon, J.R.C., Espera, A.H., Chen, Q., Advincula, R.C.: Mechanical characterization of 3D-printed polymers. Addit. Manuf. **20**, 44–67 (2018)
13. Ćwikła, G., Grabowik, C., Kalinowski, K., Paprocka, I., Ociepka, P.: The influence of printing parameters on selected mechanical properties of FDM/FFF 3D-printed parts. In: IOP Conference Series: Materials Science and Engineering, vol. 227, p. 012033 (2017)
14. Pires, F.Q., et al.: Predictive models of FDM 3D printing using experimental design based on pharmaceutical requirements for tablet production. Int. J. Pharm. **588**, 119728 (2020)
15. Kim, H.S., Kong, I.B.: Automatic filament exchanging method of 3D printers. In: USPTO (ed.) Han Sung Kim SangMyung University Industry-Academy Cooperation Foundation, Korea (2019)
16. Průša, J.: Multi material upgrade 2.0 is here! https://blog.prusa3d.com/multi-material-upgrade-2-0-is-here_8700/
17. Dvorak, C.R., Rubens, J., Blythe, D.J.: Automatic mechanical spool changer for 3-D printers. In: WIPO (ed.) Germany (2018)
18. Satterfield, C.: How long will 3D printer filament last? A quick look. https://3dprintknowledge.com/how-long-will-a-roll-of-3d-printer-filament-last/
19. Gadd, K., Goddard, C.: TRIZ for Engineers: Enabling Inventive Problem Solving. Wiley, Hoboken (2011)
20. Dwamena, M.: Speed vs quality: do lower speeds make prints better? https://3dprinterly.com/speed-vs-quality-do-lower-speeds-make-prints-better/

Blockchain-Based Traceability Method - A Review

David Wong You King[1,2], Muhammad Arif Riza[1], Liew Kok Leong[1,2(✉)],
Ummul Hanan Mohamad[1], Rabiah Abdul Kadir[1], Mohammad Fairus Zulkifli[1],
and Mohammad Nazir Ahmad[1]

[1] Institute of Visual Informatics, Universiti Kebangsaan Malaysia, 43600 Bangi, Selangor,
Malaysia
p119039@siswa.ukm.edu.my
[2] 22-08, Level 22, Lingkaran TRX, Tun Razak Exchange, Menara Exchange106,
55188 Kuala Lumpur, Malaysia

Abstract. Effective output optimization in various industries requires precise monitoring of all processes and data involved. To facilitate further optimization, information must be easily accessible and traceable. While data traceability can be achieved using various technologies, some methods may have limitations, such as a lack of real-time monitoring or difficulty integrating with existing systems. In recent years, the emergence of blockchain technology has enabled new possibilities for data traceability. Blockchains are composed of blocks of hashed data that are linked to earlier blocks, providing a reliable means of tracing data. This paper explores the fundamental concepts of blockchain technology and its features, highlighting the limitations of traditional traceability systems and the advantages offered by blockchain. Then, this paper reviews existing literatures to provides a comprehensive overview of blockchain-based traceability methods, offering insights into their applications, benefits, challenges, and future prospects.

Keywords: Consortium · Decentralized · Ethereum · Industrial Process · Smart Contracts

1 Introduction

Data traceability is crucial for optimizing the quality of a product or a service. For example, in food industries, product traceability is important to help identify the processes that each product undergo. Meanwhile, agricultural industries require crop traceability to ensure optimized quality in large batches of crops. To add, service or tourism industries need data traceability to ensure proper transactions and the security of customers' data (Nyaletey, et al. 2019). However, with the existence of many layers of the whole process, traceability of data can be very difficult to manage. Due to this, many large industries with large production capabilities experience difficulties in tracing each of their products for quality checks.

Traditional traceability methods, such as barcodes and quick response codes (QR), are cost-effective and easy to implement (Qian et al. 2012; Tarjan, et al. 2014). However,

H. Badioze Zaman et al. (Eds.): IVIC 2023, LNCS 14322, pp. 261–275, 2024.
https://doi.org/10.1007/978-981-99-7339-2_23

they lacked real-time monitoring capabilities and do not provide enough information to conduct detailed analysis and optimize the traceability process.

Artificial intelligence (AI) technology has emerged as a potential solution to enhance data traceability. AI can provide early warnings of potential errors in the traceability process, allowing organizations to proactively address any issues beforehand. For example, AI algorithms can analyze data from multiple sources, including sensors and tracking systems, to identify anomalies and deviations from expected patterns. However, AI technology is complex, therefore it requires highly skilled workers to operate and maintain it (Zhang and Lu 2021).

The Internet of Things (IoT) is another technology that has the potential to enhance data traceability. IoT involves connecting devices and sensors to the internet, allowing for remote monitoring and real-time data collection. When integrated with traceability systems, IoT can provide valuable insights into the journey of a product or service, helping organizations to optimize their processes and improve the quality of their offerings. However, implementing IoT can be costly and the devices can be vulnerable to hacking, which could compromise the traceability of the product (Cui, Chen, et al. 2019).

Differing from IoT, blockchain (BC) technology is based on its implementation. It is a method that is less susceptible to external attacks due to its decentralized nature. In general, blockchains are a chain of information that are stored in the form of hashes within a block. Information blocks will be created, and a newer block will be generated following the previous block for new information. This creates a link of information blocks that can easily be accessed and traced. As more blocks are created in the chain, the system is considered more stable and less susceptible to data attacks (Jiang et al. 2022).

Since blockchain technology has emerged as a promising solution to address the data traceability challenges, this review paper analyzes existing methods and frameworks for establishing traceability, covering industries such as food, pharmaceuticals, luxury goods, and electronics. It evaluates the benefits and challenges associated with implementing blockchain-based traceability systems, addressing scalability, interoperability, and regulatory considerations. Additionally, the paper identifies emerging trends and future research directions in the field, emphasizing the need for interdisciplinary collaboration, standardization efforts, and advanced analytics. Overall, this review serves as a valuable resource for researchers, practitioners, and policymakers interested in harnessing blockchain technology for transparent and accountable traceability.

2 Blockchain Traceability Methods

Applications of BC in traceability are still at infancy stage and under continuous improvement. There are several methods discussed from other studies as shown in Table 1. Each of the methods was used in conjunction with data traceability for products and industries.

Data traceability in IoT involves the tracing of data from various devices that are connected to the internet. All kinds of data are continuously generated from different fields and industries. A large amount of data will require sufficient security measures and handling. However, due to the enormous amount of data that stems from various devices, data traceability can be a challenge if conventional methods are used. Hence, Qiao

Table 1. Various methods for blockchain traceability methods.

Blockchain Traceability Technique	Application Domain	Mechanism	Advantages	Disadvantages	Design/run time	Data standardization	References
Consortium blockchain	Dynamic data tracing in IoT	- Verification nodes list - Authorizing some of the trusted nodes based on the boundary conditions	-Consortium blockchain can set the openness to the public according to the application scenario -Auditing of dynamic data by multiple agencies in a specific background	-Only approved nodes to join in is more suitable for the management of dynamic data	High run time	Possible but requires extensive mechanism modification	Qiao et al. 2018
Custom mathematical model based on Food Quality Index (FQI) algorithm	Food quality traceability	-Mathematical modeling is devised for the calculation of the food quality index considering the storage time as the selected quality parameter	-Suitable for traceability in the food industry due to its nature of implementation	-Model is tailored to food quality traceability only. Substantial mathematical model modification is necessary for other applications	High design time for building the modeling	Not possible	George et al. 2019

(continued)

Table 1. (*continued*)

Blockchain Traceability Technique	Application Domain	Mechanism	Advantages	Disadvantages	Design/run time	Data standardization	References
Hyperledger Fabric (consortium blockchain)	Food safety risk traceability	Multiple components at each part of the system: Orderer, Client, Endorser, Committer	- Visualization methods to intuitively show risks and help the traceability analysis of food – Good tamper security	- Slow processing speed and scalability of generating blocks - The visual analysis data quality may be affected by sampling errors	High run time due to slow processing speeds	Possible but difficult to achieve	Hao et al. 2020
Control policy model based on smart contract	Medication Traceability	- Byzantine fault tolerance (PBFT) modeling for score-keeping mechanism, allow the consensus algorithm to optimize upon facing dishonest nodes	- Eliminates the need for centralized institutions and third-party organizations - Provides a full record of the medication circulation process - High level of security and privacy protection	- The study was only reported on a small scale on a single PC rather than clustering deployment - All information is stored on the blockchain as proposed leading to poor memory utilization	Low run time	Not possible	Zhu et al., 2020

(*continued*)

Table 1. (*continued*)

Blockchain Traceability Technique	Application Domain	Mechanism	Advantages	Disadvantages	Design/run time	Data standardization	References
Ethereum smart contracts	COVID-19 tracking from external sources	-The system connects decentralized applications (DApps), dashboards, smart contracts, oracles, and web feed sources within the same decentralized Ethereum network	- Receives data from various web feed sources - On one of the well-known blockchains – Ethereum	- Uncertainty of implementation and operations costs due to the fluctuation of Ethereum gas fees for transactions - The blockchain network traffic becomes bulky as the number of transactions increases every day - Restriction on the block size and time interval used to create a new block	-Low design time -Low run time	Not possible	Marbouh et al. 2020
Raft consensus algorithm	Personal Information Registration	-Each same nodes have multiple states. Can switch states/roles	The entities involved in the transaction can obtain sufficient transaction-related evidence to resolve possible future disputes after the execution of the transaction	- Susceptible to info leaks	High design time	Possible but difficult to achieve	Jiang et al. 2020

(*continued*)

Table 1. (*continued*)

Blockchain Traceability Technique	Application Domain	Mechanism	Advantages	Disadvantages	Design/run time	Data standardization	References
Stochastic batch dispersion model and Negative binomial distribution	Food supply chain traceability	- Reduction of mixing of data in batches - After attaining traceability, 'batch dispersion problem' data is integrated with Blockchain to achieve transparency. The second part of the problem is to ensure the safety of this data inside the 'distributed ledger'	- The stochastic model and the optimum batch size give an insight into the composition of each product which proves more the amount of data is fed into the Blockchain, the safer it becomes	- Susceptible to attack at early implementation - 5-level model dispersion was created specifically for food production. Extensive modification of the model may be required and tested for other use	High design time	Not possible due to modeling is tailored only specifically to the use case	Maity et al., 2021
Traceability system based on Ethereum SHA-3 algorithm	Smart farming	-Entry information, Information inquiry, and verification with the algorithms	-Distributed ledger using blockchain technology -Complete Decentralization	The system is implemented together with QR code technology. Thus share the disadvantages of QR code technology for traceability -Data standardization can be a challenge	Low design time	Possible but difficult to achieve	Liao et al. 2019

et al. (2018) proposed the traceability of data using consortium blockchain. Consortium blockchains are accessible to the appointed members of an organization. These members can set the read-write access permission and assign additional rules to the blockchain. In the study, the blockchain mechanism follows a verification nodes list which is formulated based on a set of boundary conditions. Each node possesses its own credibility based on its behavior. The credibility of the nodes was maintained based on how well they served other nodes in data verification. A node's credibility will be negatively impacted if it is inactive or denied service for a period of time. The node with low credibility will be removed from the list specified by the governing agency.

The proposed method by Qiao et al. (2018) allowed the formation of a high-quality data chain in terms of a node of trustfulness and security. The formation of a data blockchain is achievable due to the boundary conditions applied to the consensus nodes. The boundary conditions are formulated to allow nodes with high credibility to the main data chain. Any foreign, dishonest, or attacking nodes will have lower credibility scores and will most unlikely to be accepted in the main chain. However, the boundary conditions for the consensus nodes do not eliminate the possibility of attacking nodes gaining acceptance into the main chain. Hence, the proposed data traceability method is still risky due to dishonest nodes having a chance to infiltrate the main chain. The node verification could lead to a high run time of the system and data standardization from mixed parameters can also be difficult.

In the food industry, data traceability with blockchain technology has been proposed (George, et al. 2019) with the aid of the Food Quality Index (FQI). Data traceability in the food industry has been implemented with different technologies throughout the years. The tracking of various information in food production such as product tracking, raw material information, and logistics allows continuous improvement of the overall operations. Barcodes and QR codes have been implemented to allow data traceability for products and materials. However, this technology can be difficult to implement, especially for large production-scale industries. It requires a carefully structured algorithm build that leads to high design time especially if data standardization is required. Therefore, with blockchain, it is possible to implement within an industry for data traceability due to its long-term effectiveness and scaling. When information is stored in a blockchain, its accessibility is more efficient compared to centralized storage.

The study proposed by Hao et al. (2020) was similar to Qiao et al. (2018) in terms of the boundary condition implemented. It was a model centered around parameters such as the shelf life, nutritional value, and storage time of the product. These data are collected via sensors and manually keyed in by farmers. The data is recorded and processed within the blockchain to determine its food safety. The determination of food safety is based on a food index constructed from prescribed standards made by the regulatory authority. A curve estimation based on shelf life versus weightage was made. Extremum points are derived based on the curve estimation and serve as the range of values determining whether the food is safe for consumption.

The proposed blockchain traceability method (George et al., 2019) based on the food index has potential use in the food and beverage (F&B) industries. The boundary conditions prepared based on the shelf life of food allow the construction of the food index. Since the food index can be different for each type of food, the method allows for additional food indexes to be updated within the blockchain boundary conditions. However, this method can only be used for food products. Its workability is not explained for other kinds of production such as crops, electrical components, data services, etc. A different boundary condition with different algorithms will be required for other industries.

Blockchain technology is constantly being improved and combined with other technology for data traceability. A combination of blockchain technology and visualization technology has also been proposed. This blockchain traceability method was built around Hyperledger Fabric technology. This technology enables flexibility in terms of the number of parties involved in the development of a blockchain platform. The main component of Hyperledger Fabric is (Hao et al. 2020):

a) Orderer – Receives all transactions throughout the main designated network before packing the data into blocks.
b) Client – The user that is utilizing a software development kit (SDK) to access and request transactions from the Hyperledger network.
c) Endorser – These nodes endorse clients that requested a transaction initiation. A client must obtain enough endorsements from the endorser node to fully initiate a transaction.
d) Committer – Receives the packaged blocks from Orderers. These nodes verify the block's transaction validity before updating the ledger.

The proposed method in the mentioned study utilized several layers in its framework. A business layer serves as a contact point between a human user and a computer. The operation of uploading data and visualizing them through the display is the primary purpose of this layer. Users can write or update their smart contracts through the Application Programming Interface (API) that can be accessed through this layer. The communications layer of the framework houses the main protocols of the P2P network and network structures. Synchronization data between all nodes occur in the communications layer via the Gossip data communication protocol. The communications layer is a bridge between the business layer and the database layer. The stored data ledgers are kept within the database layer in the form of data blocks. The sophisticated framework with hyper ledger technology allows visualization mapping of data. The visualization is useful for mapping out data in terms of food quality to assist in the prediction of shelf life or identification of defects. However, the framework suffers from the speed of data processing, high program run time and block generation scaling. The added visualization of data suffers from extended delays as the number of data blocks increases.

The utilization of blockchain in the pharmaceutical and medical industry can be potentially beneficial. For medicinal supplies, it is required by the Global traceability standards that all items are assigned a unique identification number. The identification number aids in tracing the movement of pharmaceutical products throughout the supply chain. Zhu et al. (2020) proposed a traceability method with the aid of blockchain infrastructure. The pharmaceutical products will be assigned their ID number after manufacturing and this number will be recorded into the blockchain. Wholesalers and retailers serve as an intermediate node that can update the status of the medication on the blockchain (its location within the supply chain) via a peer-to-peer (P2P) network.

The system proposed by Zhu et al. (2020) consisted of a smart contract, a blockchain network, and a web client for the user. Smart contract coded using Python contains a mechanism of practical Byzantine Fault Tolerance (PBFT) for establishing a consensus among participating nodes. In the PBFT mechanism, the amount of network traffic can increase quickly due to nodes attempting to reach a consensus. This can lead to a slower time for information processing and transfer. This is remedied with the introduction of a score-keeping system. This system aids the nodes to reach consensus quickly before the network traffic is congested. Each node can receive a form of reward or punishment depending on the process of reaching a consensus. A dishonest node (carrying modified/tampered/forged information) from a set of nodes would cause the set to be deducted of score points. A set of nodes with low score points will have a lower probability to be selected for the consensus operation process. This ensures that the set of nodes with higher scores are nodes that can be trusted the most.

Network traffic will then be reduced since the low-scored nodes that can hinder the consensus process have less probability to participate. The system does show its potential as an organized BC-based data traceability system, however, the overall system is good for one form of data at a time. In the mentioned study, only the medication ID forms the hash before being participated throughout the system of nodes for validation. The scoring system would collapse if different forms or data parameters were to be validated. The system would suffer from a data standardization issue due to the nodes' inability to be given proper scoring or the potential in receiving penalties (Zhu, et al. 2020).

Besides the creation of an organization's own smart contracts and blockchain systems, it is also possible for data traceability to utilize public commercial blockchain networks for data traceability. It can be desirable to utilize an established and well-known blockchain network for data traceability for stability purposes. Marbouh et al. (2020) proposed a data traceability method during the COVID outbreak in 2019. Resource deployments are a challenge, especially in the mass mobilization of vaccines and medical equipment. The proposed data traceability method involves the use of Ethereum blockchain network. The public blockchain network eliminates the need for internal, intermediary nodes for validation. Therefore, data traceability and validation can be achieved at less cost. In addition, the Ethereum blockchain also allows multiple smart contracts to be implemented for certain desired purposes.

There were three Ethereum smart contracts created by Marbouh et al. (2020) for tracking of COVID-19-related data; a registration contract that handles the web information of participating stakeholders and web sources, a reputation contract that assigns scores based on the quality and trustfulness of web sources and an aggregator smart contract tasked with the retrieval of the latest information updates from nodes. The system allows for multiple information and parameters to be tracked within the blockchain network. Unlike privately developed blockchain networks, public network like Ethereum requires gas fees for each successful data transaction and smart contract code execution. More complex smart contracts with additional codes may lead to an increase in costs. Furthermore, with the price movement of Ethereum coins, its gas fee will be greatly impacted leading to difficulties in operational costing calculation.

For sensitive information traceability, a method was proposed by Jiang et al. (2020). The system was centered on a service provider, certification center and the user whose information is to be transacted. For added security purposes, the system does not involve users to immediately upload their personal information to the certification center (can be government bodies, employers, etc.). The user is required to register and generate an identity in the system before the certification provides the new user with a unique identification number. The user then needs to encrypt his personal information with the provided identification number before sending the data to the service provider. The service provider then generates a random symmetric record key and encrypts the information package (that includes all the sensitive personal information).

The certification center (original information requestor) will decrypt the record key with the information package and sends the user the same record key for safekeeping. The certification center will check the record key and identification number. If both number matches and no tempering on all the backups of the package transactions, the certification center will release the data key to the service provider. This technique demonstrated a secure method for tracing sensitive data. However, it can be challenging in terms of scalability due to the numerous amounts of encryption involved. It also does not allow ease of data access for each node which can be difficult for organizations with multiple intermediary bodies serving as nodes in between.

A batch of information can be traced within the blockchain network with the proper mathematical modeling. Within the overall production process, various items and raw materials need to be tracked at once (within one transaction) and this can be challenging to achieve with minimal use of smart contracts and basic mathematical models of data traceability. One needs to tailor specific mathematical modeling depending on how many steps or phases are involved in the processing of several different raw materials into their respective end products. Most products nowadays average on undergoing 4–6 major processes before a raw material reaches its commercial form. A stochastic batch dispersion model was proposed by Maity et al. (2021) to achieve data traceability for food processing optimization. The batch processing of products makes it suitable for use with mathematical models that minimize the sum of links between the packaged product and its respective raw materials. This way, the inconsistency of data due to completed products from external sources can be minimized. The stochastic batch dispersion model considers 5 levels of process within the production supply chain. The individual levels represent the state of the product; therefore level 1 is the raw material, and level 5 is the finished product. There are two stages of the mathematical model with the first being the determination of fixed proportions of the finished raw materials of the product. The second stage of the model assist in which raw materials are required to be outsourced to fulfill any remaining customer demand. Secondary stage acts are the corrective measure for the mathematical model to ensure product traceability and the correct proportion of raw material used.

Blockchain systems can be integrated with sensors for quality inspection and data traceability, and this has been proposed (Liao and Xu 2019). The Ethereum blockchain is used as the underlying architecture for the system and is the data entry point. The information regarding the product is stored within the public blockchain and can be retrieved via a QR code. This system architecture shares a similarity with other studies (Marbouh et al. 2020) that involve separate layers of traceability system via the business layer, data layer, and user interfacing layer. Although the system can have data standardization due to having the QR code as the form of information retrieval technique, the efficiency of the QR code falls behind newer tracking technologies such as VR/AR, IoT, Big Data, and AI.

3   Category of Blockchain Traceability

Based on the literature, there are at least three different categories of BC traceability methods. These methods vary greatly in terms of implementation, algorithm, and system structures.

3.1   Consortium Centric Blockchains

A consortium blockchain is one of the methods in BC-based traceability used. This technique has been utilized by Qiao et al. (2018). This technique involves several specialized nodes or trusted nodes for the verification of data chains. These networks of nodes are governed by personnel who is the member of an organization (alliance). The personnel can access the nodes through the agency gateway. The read and write access permissions can be granted based on the preferences of the alliance. The data in the blockchain can be made to be either private or public to all alliances. The system can be reliable and flexible due to the full control of alliance members and their transparency, but consortium-based blockchains can lead to slow processes due to the nodes waiting for the approval of other nodes. The distrustful nodes can still be chosen by other nodes to be accepted into the main chain. It is possible that consortium-centric blockchains on their own can suffer from reliability issues.

3.2   Smart Contracts

Blockchain networks such as Ethereum rely on proof of stake for node verification. Ethereum possesses smart contracts that can be utilized in data traceability. Smart contracts are software agents that are inserted in blockchain networks. Figure 1 is an example of a smart contract-based blockchain system operation. These agents enable the automatic verification of transactions with no interference from third-party entities. This increases the transaction approval efficiency and transaction processing time. In a work proposed by Marbouh et al. (2020), an Ethereum smart contract was utilized for data traceability of COVID-19 cases. The study aims to solve the data traceability issues regarding medical supply chains and cases of COVID-19. These data can be overwhelming and lack security for a standard centralized data storage to handle. Therefore, the proposed work considered using three smart contracts within an Ethereum blockchain ecosystem to aid in data traceability. Smart contracts can be beneficial since it is open to flexibility for the user to add additional parameters to suit the industry traceability needs. It is easy to apply smart contracts to existing public domain networks such as Ethereum. However, the gas prices (fee) for transaction processing are inconsistent as the value of Ethereum fluctuates depending on the cryptocurrency market. Estimation of cost can be challenging due to the ups and downs of the gas fee pricing.

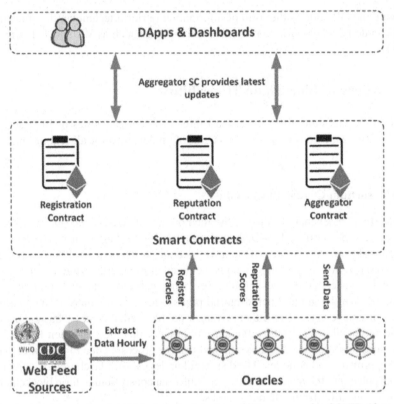

Fig. 1. A smart contract assisted blockchain data traceability process for COVID-19 tracking (Dounia, et al. 2020).

3.3 Custom Algorithms and Mathematical Modeling

Another method with data traceability with BC is the modification of custom algorithms. This requires detailed programming with a strong emphasis on the mathematical model built around the data traceability process and its elements. For instance, the Byzantine fault tolerance algorithm can enhance the blockchain process for nodes to achieve consensus (Zhu et al. 2020). This means that the algorithm can enhance other blockchain methods if well-coded. However, a strict and complex rule must be specified for each item or type of information. As more types of different information exist in the blockchain, the algorithm can suffer from errors. Hence, multiple different types of items, transactions, and information lead to a data standardization issue and limit the true potential of the blockchain traceability method based on the algorithm.

4   Discussion

Several different methods in blockchain traceability methods involve the modification of different parts of a system. The consensus-centric method focuses on the roles of different nodes within the system. Therefore, it is implemented within the blockchain network itself. This technique can be suitable for traceability methods where a transaction of information is uniform, and trustfulness is required. An example of such potential use can be the traceability of sensitive data of employees or financial information. It is compatible to be integrated within various systems, however, it may not be able to 'plug and play' from one system to another. It is possible that this method must work with another blockchain method to enhance its usability options.

The use of the public blockchain domain with the support of smart contracts is another viable method for agricultural traceability. Since more additional conditions can be set to nodes, the system can be made to be more accessible for use with traceability of various products and raw materials movement within a supply chain. Furthermore, since the public domain is used, the system is more stable than a custom-made blockchain due to more nodes can participate in the proof of stake/works. Some potential examples of public blockchains include Ethereum, Polygon Matic, and Tron. The system would require a transacting fee that usually costs a particular cryptocurrency acting as the 'gas fee'(Marchesi, Marchesi, Destefanis, Barabino, & Tigano, 2020). Since cryptocurrency fluctuates greatly over time, estimation of system operational costs can be proven challenging.

Another modification can be made to the algorithm of a blockchain itself. For this type of blockchain traceability method, proper mathematical modeling must be constructed from scratch for most use cases. It requires highly trained personnel to develop but offers a high degree of customization for its use case in data traceability. It can be extremely complex for data integration due to the modeling becoming increasingly convoluted. For instance, for growing only one type of crop, not only the seeds and fertilizers need to be considered. A specific type of fertilizer must also be considered for maintaining the crops. Furthermore, other parameters such as humidity-adjusting water sprinklers, soil pH maintenance, and crop movement via harvesting and logistics can add up to form an extremely complex system. Bugs and errors can be very difficult to remedy for a sophisticated system. Therefore, it can be unfavorable for the system to be easily marketed for industries to be used in their data traceability needs.

A potential gap can be identified based on the literature on data traceability of various usage scenarios. The implementation of blockchain technology for data traceability is still seldom compared to other more understood data traceability methods such as RFIDs, IoTs, and AI. Within the context of blockchain itself, several methods have been proposed for various usage scenarios, but they possess weaknesses. The most commonly found weakness in blockchain technology data traceability is the scalability, implementation, and data standardization issues. These weaknesses show a potential gap for the development of a more refined blockchain data traceability method.

5   Conclusions

This review paper presents an overview of the use of blockchain technology for data traceability in various industries. Through a thorough analysis of traditional traceability methods, the limitations of existing approaches are identified, emphasizing the need for more robust and efficient solutions. The review highlights the potential of artificial intelligence and the Internet of Things as complementary technologies to enhance data traceability. However, challenges such as the complexity of AI and the vulnerabilities of IoT devices are acknowledged. In this context, blockchain technology emerges as a promising solution due to its decentralized and transparent nature. By exploring different traceability methods, a holistic understanding of the benefits and challenges associated with blockchain-based traceability systems is revealed. The evaluation of research studies showcases the diverse approaches taken, emphasizing the importance of factors such as data standardization, processing speed, and cost. The paper also underscores the significance of interdisciplinary collaboration, standardization efforts, and advanced analytics in further advancing blockchain-based traceability systems. By leveraging blockchain-based traceability, organizations can drive positive transformations in achieving transparency, accountability, and efficiency.

Acknowledgements. This research is supported by the Industrial Grants from ARB Cloud Sdn Bhd (No: ZG-2022–003), ARB Big Data Sdn. Bhd, (No: ZG-2022–006) and Universiti Kebangsaan Malaysia (UKM). High appreciation goes to the above sponsors.

References

Cui, H., Chen, Z., Xi, Y., Chen, H., Hao, J.: IoT Data Management and Lineage Traceability: A Blockchain-based Solution. Paper presented at the 2019 IEEE/CIC International Conference on Communications Workshops in China (ICCC Workshops) (2019)

George, R.V., Harsh, H.O., Ray, P., Babu, A.K.: Food quality traceability prototype for restaurants using blockchain and food quality data index. J. Clean. Prod. **240**, 118021 (2019). https://doi.org/10.1016/j.jclepro.2019.118021

Hao, Z., Mao, D., Zhang, B., Zuo, M., Zhao, Z.: A novel visual analysis method of food safety risk traceability based on blockchain. Int. J. Environ. Res. Public Health **17**(7) (2020). https://doi.org/10.3390/ijerph17072300

Jiang, N., Wang, W., Wu, J., Wang, J.: Traceable method for personal information registration based on blockchain. IEEE Access **8**, 52700–52712 (2020). https://doi.org/10.1109/ACCESS.2020.2981175

Jiang, S., Li, Y., Wang, S., Zhao, L.: Blockchain competition: the tradeoff between platform stability and efficiency. Eur. J. Oper. Res. **296**(3), 1084–1097 (2022). https://doi.org/10.1016/j.ejor.2021.05.031

Liao, Y., Xu, K.: Traceability system of agricultural product based on block-chain and application in tea quality safety management. J. Phys: Conf. Ser. **1288**(1), 012062 (2019). https://doi.org/10.1088/1742-6596/1288/1/012062

Maity, M., Tolooie, A., Sinha, A.K., Tiwari, M.K.: Stochastic batch dispersion model to optimize traceability and enhance transparency using Blockchain. Comput. Ind. Eng. **154**, 107134 (2021). https://doi.org/10.1016/j.cie.2021.107134

Marbouh, D., et al.: Blockchain for COVID-19: Review, Opportunities and a Trusted Tracking System (2020)

Marchesi, L., Marchesi, M., Destefanis, G., Barabino, G., Tigano, D.: Design patterns for gas optimization in ethereum. Paper presented at the 2020 IEEE International Workshop on Blockchain Oriented Software Engineering (IWBOSE) (2020)

Nyaletey, E., Parizi, R. M., Zhang, Q., Choo, K.K.R.: BlockIPFS - blockchain-enabled interplanetary file system for forensic and trusted data traceability. Paper presented at the 2019 IEEE International Conference on Blockchain (Blockchain) (2019)

Qian, J.-P., Yang, X.-T., Wu, X.-M., Zhao, L., Fan, B.-L., Xing, B.: A traceability system incorporating 2D barcode and RFID technology for wheat flour mills. Comput. Electron. Agric. **89**, 76–85 (2012). https://doi.org/10.1016/j.compag.2012.08.004

Qiao, R., Zhu, S., Wang, Q., Qin, J.: Optimization of dynamic data traceability mechanism in Internet of Things based on consortium blockchain. Int. J. Distrib. Sens. Netw. **14**(12), 1550147718819072 (2018). https://doi.org/10.1177/1550147718819072

Tarjan, L., Šenk, I., Tegeltija, S., Stankovski, S., Ostojic, G.: A readability analysis for QR code application in a traceability system. Comput. Electron. Agric. **109**, 1–11 (2014). https://doi.org/10.1016/j.compag.2014.08.015

Zhang, C., Lu, Y.: Study on artificial intelligence: The state of the art and future prospects. J. Ind. Inf. Integr. **23**, 100224 (2021). https://doi.org/10.1016/j.jii.2021.100224

Zhu, P., Hu, J., Zhang, Y., Li, X.: A blockchain based solution for medication anti-counterfeiting and traceability. IEEE Access **8**, 184256–184272 (2020). https://doi.org/10.1109/ACCESS.2020.3029196

Responding to Regional Revitalisation and Socio-economic Challenges in Japan: Government Approaches and Use of Advanced Technologies

Yasuki Shima[1]([⊠]) and Ali Fathelalem Hija[2]([⊠])

[1] Meio University, Okinawa, Japan
y.shima@meio-u.ac.jp
[2] Joaan Bin Jassim Academy for Defence Studies, Al Khor, Qatar
ali@meio-u.ac.jp

Abstract. Japan has one of the world's fastest ageing populations, leading to a shrinking workforce and labour shortages in various industries, with consequent impacts on various aspects of Japanese life and society. Economic stagnation and deflation, energy security and environmental concerns, agricultural decline and its socio-economic effects, advances in technology and innovation are now key issues facing Japan, and government policies and initiatives have been designed to address these challenges and concerns. The objective of this paper is to explore the approaches and policies of the Japanese government and the status of the promotion and adoption of advanced technologies to address the socio-economic challenges facing Japan. The research paper examines the policies and approaches of the government, companies and farmers, and the status of the use of advanced technologies in agriculture to address socio-economic challenges, in line with the achievement of globally promoted goals. This research paper highlighted the policies and approaches applied by the government, companies and farmers, and the current status of the use of advanced technologies in agriculture to address socio-economic challenges and global strategic goals. The study shows that the Ministry of Agriculture, Forestry and Fisheries is leading the Japanese government's efforts to promote the use of advanced technologies to increase agricultural production and address socio-economic issues such as an ageing population, rural depopulation and economic stagnation in rural areas, as young people migrate to cities. Meanwhile, the Japanese government continues its initiatives and commitment to the global goals of developing sustainable energy and food supplies.

Keywords: Socio-Economic Challenges · Smart Agriculture · Government Initiatives

1 Introduction

Formulated by Japan's Ministry of Agriculture, Forestry and Fisheries (MAFF) in accordance with the Basic Act on Food, Agriculture and Rural Areas, the Basic Plan for Food, Agriculture and Rural Areas is a medium-to-long-term vision for agricultural policy that

H. Badioze Zaman et al. (Eds.): IVIC 2023, LNCS 14322, pp. 276–287, 2024.
https://doi.org/10.1007/978-981-99-7339-2_24

sets out the direction of action for the next decade. Consists of a programme for the implementation of specific measures to realise the basic principles of the law, which are to ensure a stable food supply, to enable a multifunctional role for agriculture, to achieve sustainable agricultural development, and to develop rural areas. The Act was first approved in 1999, and the basic plan is revised approximately every five years, with the latest update being in 2020. Five-yearly periodic reviews are carried out to respond to changes in the various circumstances surrounding food, agriculture and rural development [1].

With one of the world's fastest ageing populations, Japan is facing specific socio-economic challenges. The shrinking labour force and personnel shortages in various industries are having an impact on various aspects of Japanese people's lives and society as a whole. Economic stagnation and deflation, energy and food security, environmental concerns, the decline of agriculture and its socio-economic consequences, and international competition in terms of technology and innovation are serious issues facing Japan, and government strategies and initiatives are required to address these effectively.

Under the Basic Act for Food, Agriculture and Rural Areas, various strategies and initiatives are being developed and promoted to address and tackle these socio-economic and global issues. The basic plan affects farmers, farmland, management and the stability of supplies, in addition to promoting innovation, the use of digital technology, and measures to address environmental concerns and issues.

The aim of this paper is to explore the approaches and policies of the Japanese government and the status of the promotion and adoption of advanced technologies to address the socio-economic challenges facing Japan. The research paper examines the policies and approaches of the government, companies and farmers, and the status of the use of advanced technologies in agriculture to address socio-economic challenges, in line with the achievement of globally promoted goals.

The paper highlights the key socio-economic challenges and concerns facing Japan at the domestic level, as well as some more global issues and concerns for the country. We examine the measures and approaches applied by the government, businesses and farmers, and the current usage of advanced technology in agriculture to address these socio-economic challenges and goals. Figure 1 provides a conceptual framework for the scope and focus of our research.

The remainder of this paper is organised as follows. Section 2 provides a brief overview of Japan's socio-economic challenges and current global issues. Section 3 reports on the main strategies and initiatives that have been introduced in Japan to address these challenges. The use of digital technology and innovative applications in agriculture in Japan, and some use cases and expectations, are discussed in Sect. 4. Section 5 summarises our findings. Section 6 concludes our manuscript and suggests some directions for future research.

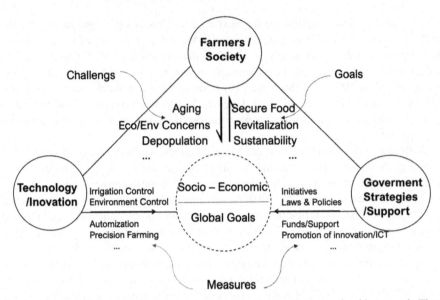

Fig. 1. A conceptual framework showing the scope and issues of concern for this research. Three main themes are the government, farmers and technological impacts, with measures and expected links to the theme of socio-economic challenges and globally promoted issues.

2   Socio-economic Challenges in Japan and Global Issues

2.1   Ageing and Population Decline

In 2022, Japan's population was around 124.95 million, of which 30% were aged 65 or over [2]. Japan's population grew at an annual rate of less than 1% between about 1951 and 2022, resulting in a declining and ageing population (see Fig. 2).

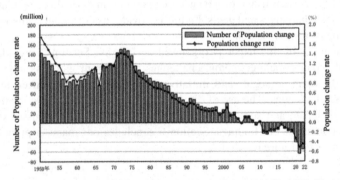

Fig. 2. Increases/decreases in population and percentage changes 1950–2022 (Source: Ministry of Internal Affairs and Communications, press release 1st October 2022 [2]).

In terms of Japan's industrial structure, we note that the number of workers in industry in the primary sector was about 2.05 million in FY2023, compared with 16.68 million in

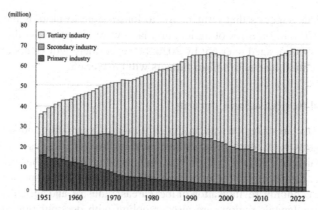

Fig. 3. Changes in employment by sector (primary-tertiary), 1951–2022 annual averages (Source: Statistics Bureau of the Ministry of Internal Affairs and Communications: Labour Force Survey 2023 [3])

the 1950s [3] (see Fig. 3). The annual population growth rate has been below 1% since about 1970–1980, and is currently –0.6%.

2.2 Labour Shortages

The MAFF of Japan updates and publishes statistical data on agriculture, forestry and fishery products each year. According to the results of the current Survey of Agricultural Structure, Japan had about 2.2 million farming households in FY2003 [4]. This number has been decreasing every year, and by FY2022 the total had been reduced to about 980,000 [5]. The results for FY2022 show a decrease of 5.4% from the previous year (Table 1), meaning that about 55% of agricultural holdings have been lost in the 20 years since 2003.

Table 1. Number of agricultural corporations (Source: Ministry of Agriculture, Forestry and Fisheries: Agricultural Structure Survey, pp. 2 (2022) [5])

Number of agricultural corporations	Business units	Personal business	Groups business	
	1 + 2	1	2	Corporations
2021	1,030.9	991.4	39.5	31.6
2022	975.1	935.0	40.1	32.2
Percentage change (%)	−5.4	−5.7	1.5	1.9

An industrial structure map produced by the Regional Economy Society Analysing System (RESAS) shows that the number of farmers aged 65 and over has continued to increase since 2005, while the total area of agricultural land in use has declined rapidly since 2015. This suggests that farmers are no longer able to farm as they age [6]. In 2005, about 370 million acres of agricultural land were in use across the country, and 57% of farmers were aged over 65; by 2020, however, there will be about 324 million acres of agricultural land and 70% of farmers will be over 65.

2.3 Regional Revitalisation Concerns

Japan's economy has struggled with prolonged periods of stagnation and deflation, which have limited growth, discouraged investment, and imposed challenges in multiple fields. Japan's Revitalisation Strategy, which was announced in 2012 and has been revised on a yearly basis, has promoted the use of advanced technology to respond to challenges relating to the economy, revitalisation of local areas, industry, and agriculture [7]. Local governments in Japan's regions are also grappling with depopulation and economic stagnation in rural areas as the ageing of the population continues and young people migrate to urban areas. The government has implemented a regional revitalisation policy through which incentives and support are offered to businesses, farmers and individuals willing to relocate to and invest in rural areas. Infrastructure improvements and various financial and other incentives are also offered [8].

2.4 Food Security and Environment and Global Issues

To remain competitive on the global stage, Japan must continue to promote innovation and technological progress. In 2016, the Japanese government launched its vision of a 'super-smart society' or 'Society 5.0'. This vision is based on the recognition of current global trends: the pace of technological, economic and social change has accelerated, and businesses and communities are struggling to keep up. In Vision 2016, Japan looks beyond Industry 4.0, which involves the use of digital and communication technologies from a global perspective, to address the country's social challenges through the idea of Society 5.0 [9].

The Sustainable Development Goals (SDGs) of the United Nations Agenda 2030 provide a remarkable shared global vision for a safe and sustainable world that will allow all people on the planet to thrive. The SDGs are designed to be universal, in that they apply to all countries of the world. In particular, high-income countries such as Japan are required to contribute to issues such as reducing waste, greenhouse gas emissions and overall resource use, while ensuring sustainable energy and food supplies [10].

2.5 Investment and Promotion of Technological Advancements and Innovation

To remain competitive on the global stage, Japan needs to continue to encourage innovation and technological advancement. The government has therefore invested in research and development across a range of industries and provides funding and support for technology start-ups and research institutions. Japan is also focusing on emerging technologies such as AI, robotics, biotechnology and quantum computing [10–12].

Over the past few decades, Japan has developed and implemented a variety of strategies with the aim of commercialising scientific discoveries and technological innovations [12]. The emergent, all-hazard approach to smart cities and communities is marked by collaborative, multilevel governance and is increasingly being coordinated under the rubric of the industrial policy of Society 5.0. Japanese technology and innovation policies are integrated with the global SDGs [13].

3 Japan's Strategies and Measurements for Agricultural Issues

3.1 Insights into the Japanese Government's Approaches: Acts, Strategies and Initiatives

In this section, we look at the approaches applied by the Japanese government at various levels to address challenges and issues of concern. With a focus on initiatives and practices in smart agriculture, we review the different actions that have been taken. Figure 4 illustrates the levels at which these actions have been applied, from the highest level of acts and laws to the lower levels of the use cases and practices that deliver the expected and desired results. In the following subsections, we highlight three plans and initiatives for the use of smart agriculture.

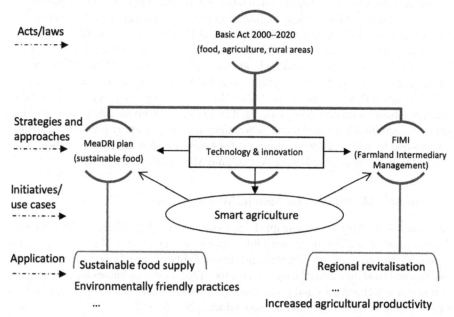

Fig. 4. Diagram showing the Basic Act and strategies and initiatives for smart agriculture practices.

3.2 Basic Plan for Food, Agriculture and Rural Areas

According to a survey by Tabayashi et al., the number of people in Japan who own land but do not farm it has been increasing since the late 1980s, due to the ageing of the agricultural labour force; this trend in Japanese agriculture became particularly pronounced in the 1990s [14]. In response to this issue, the Japanese government enacted the Basic Law on Food, Agriculture and Rural Areas in 1999, which aimed to achieve stable food distribution and sustainable development of agriculture. In addition, the Basic Plan for Food, Agriculture and Rural Areas was formulated in 2000, and later structural improvements were made to the agricultural aspects of the law [15, 16].

The Basic Plan for Food, Agriculture and Rural Areas is a medium-to-long-term vision for agricultural policy, and sets out the basis for measures to be taken over the next decade. It is a programme for the implementation of specific measures to realise four basic principles: securing a stable food supply, enabling a multifunctional role for agriculture, sustainable agricultural development, and the development of rural areas. Although the Act was first approved in 1999, the basic plan is revised approximately every five years, with the most recent update having taken place in 2020. These five-year periodic reviews are carried out to respond to changes in various circumstances relating to food, agriculture and rural development [1].

These strategies have enabled effective and stable agricultural management; however, despite improvements for vegetable and fruit tree farmers, structural improvements in rice paddies and fields have lagged behind. In 2005, the Japanese government introduced the Cross-Category Management Stabilisation Measures for Paddy and Field Crops to support farmers, as reported in the MAFF Annual Report published in May 2021 [17].

Support for farmers includes the establishment and operation of the Agricultural Land Management Organisation (commonly known as 'agricultural land banks') in each of Japan's prefectures in 2014. This scheme consolidates a certain amount of idle farmland owned by small farmers who are no longer able to farm due to old age, and leases it to younger farmers who do not own any land or to farmers who already own established farms. Agricultural land banks are corporations that are set up by prefectures, munic-ipalities and agricultural organisations on the basis of a plan legally established in the Revised Law for Strengthening the Agricultural Management Infrastructure [18].

3.3 The MeaDRI Strategy for Sustainable Food Systems

The Japanese Strategy for Sustainable Food Systems (MeaDRI: Measures for Achieving Decarbonisation and Resilience with Innovation) was launched in May 2021, and aims to enhance the productivity potential and sustainability of Japan's agriculture, forestry, fisheries and food industries through innovation. The strategy promotes the development of innovative technologies and production systems and their social implementation, as well as changes in the behaviour of stakeholders [19].

The elements of this strategy include zero CO_2 emissions from agricultural practices, the introduction of technologies for electrification and hydrogenation of agricultural machinery, and reductions in the use of chemical pesticides, in addition to increasing the production of organic food. Innovative, smart uses of relevant advanced technologies are key approaches to achieve the objectives of the strategy. Some of the socio-economic challenges related to agriculture and farming in Japan include an ageing population of farmers, rural depopulation, a broad tendency towards decline in agricultural production, land degradation, impacts on the local economy, and impacts on the traditions and cultures of local society. Strong emphasis is also placed on the use of advanced technology to address the socio-economic challenges facing Japan.

Tackling these challenges and other long-term strategic goals and global commitments requires a comprehensive approach, with well-coordinated initiatives and actions. The government and local authorities have implemented various strategies and measures, including promoting and supporting the use of innovative applications and effective use of advanced technologies, and providing several forms of support and incentives. Initiatives include offering financial incentives, supporting agricultural education and training, investing in rural infrastructure, and promoting agricultural tourism [14].

3.4 Establishment of Farmland Intermediary Management Institutions

To accelerate the transfer of farmland to business farmers in 2014, regional government-supported institutions were established in each prefecture as reliable intermediary farmland managers. This scheme was known as *Nochi Bank*, or Farmland Bank [20].

The Japanese government introduced the Farmland Bank programme to prevent further abandonment of farmland and to revitalise the agricultural industry [18]. The objectives of Farmland Bank institutions are to help lease farmland, to improve infrastructure if necessary, and to lease land to business farmers. In essence, the program gave more power to prefectural authorities to accommodate new actors and resources in lease arrangements, with the aim of accelerating farmland aggregation and achieving better economies of scale. In many areas of Japan, agriculture has become difficult to maintain, and labour shortages cannot be filled due to a lack of agricultural successors and the ageing and migration of the population, among other factors [21]. The amount of abandoned farmland in Japan has been increasing in recent decades; this threatens food security and the natural environment, as the land may be transformed into new ecosystems and damage existing ones [22]. It also has a negative impact on the government's long-standing efforts to increase food self-sufficiency in Japan [23]. This leads to a decrease in domestic agricultural production and a decline in food self-sufficiency, as the amount of agricultural land that can be effectively used decreases and the amount of abandoned land increases. According to a report published by the Ministry of Agriculture and Fisheries in 2022, the total area of abandoned farmland was 423,000 hectares, almost doubling from 21.7% in 1990, and the abandonment of farmland continues [4].

According to the MAFF in Japan, there are many farmers or agriculture-related companies willing to lease farmland, most of which are scattered across the countryside far from regularly accessed areas [19]. Recent statistics and reports show an increasing number of abandoned farms. In such cases, renting the land would be a viable option in order to maintain the area under cultivation.

In this study, we explore the use of smart agriculture as one way to address the challenges of rural areas in Japan, and as an approach to revitalising these regions.

3.5 Promotion of Technological Advancements and Innovation in Agriculture

To remain competitive in the global context, Japan needs to continue to encourage innovation and technological advancement. The government has invested in research and development across a range of industries, providing funding and support for technology start-ups and research institutions, and is currently focusing on emerging technologies such as AI, robotics, biotechnology and quantum computing [24].

The Japanese government has recognised the fact that in the domain of agriculture, there are still a wide range of labour-intensive tasks and processes that require skilled farmers. In the face of a considerable decline in the working power of the ageing population of experienced, skilled farmers, the government is making great efforts to promote the use of advances in science and technology to save labour and reduce the burden. The MAFF is launching several initiatives in conjunction with private companies, universities, research institutes and other organisations to realise 'smart agriculture', which uses robotic technology and ICT to achieve ultra-labour-saving and high-quality production [25].

4 Current Smart Agriculture and Other Government Initiatives

4.1 Investment and Promotion of Technological Advancements and Innovation

To maintain its competitiveness, Japan continues to encourage innovation and technological advancements. The country has a long history of using technology to improve agricultural practices, and embraced agricultural mechanisation and advanced irrigation systems as early as the 1960s and 1970s, which significantly increased productivity and crop yields [26]. Japan's MAFF has defined smart agriculture as a mode of agricultural production that uses robotic technology and ICT to achieve significant labour savings and high-quality production [23].

To take advantage of these technological advances, smart agriculture has been promoted and supported by the Japanese government with a view to increasing production and enabling efficient management at all stages of farming, including cultivation, marketing and the supply chain, as well as to cope with the decline in labour and the dwindling number of experienced farmers [27].

Modern farms and agricultural businesses operate very differently from those of a few decades ago, largely due to advances in technology, including sensors, equipment, machinery and information technology. Today, sophisticated technologies such as robots, temperature and moisture sensors, aerial imagery and GPS technology are actively used. These advanced devices and precision farming and robotic systems allow farms to be more profitable, more efficient, safer and more environmentally friendly. Many other benefits are expected from the use of technology in agriculture, such as increased crop productivity, and reductions in the use of water, fertiliser and pesticides. As the Internet of Things is gaining in importance in applications related to smart farming, almost all of the top technology firms are investing in and supporting this technology in their own way to develop innovation in agriculture [28].

4.2 Use Cases in Smart Agriculture

The MAFF created a report on smart agriculture use cases, based on a survey of 148 such cases, in 2019–2020 [29]. These included applications such as controlled water management and intelligent irrigation systems, plant growth monitoring, pesticide spraying systems using drones, semi-automated harvesting, environmental control (temperature, humidity, etc.), farm yields, transport automation, and decision-making data platforms. Since 2019, the MAFF has implemented a smart agriculture demonstration project to introduce advanced technology to production sites and clarify the effects in terms of farm management. Thus far, the project has been launched in 217 districts nationwide. The government is also considering support for the introduction of smart agriculture services, as well as human resources development programs to address the current lack of workers who are familiar with smart agricultural technology and data utilisation in farming [30].

4.3 Challenges and Expectations

With high expectations for a remarkable contribution to the revitalisation of rural areas, the Japanese government and other organisations have promoted the use of smart agriculture. As per a recent 2023 MAFF report on smart agriculture, although the effects of smart agriculture have been felt, such as labour savings, burden reduction, and the ability of even non-skilled workers to operate advanced farms, several important issues have become apparent [30]. The high cost of smart technology products and services, a lack of sufficient ICT literacy, and difficulties in integrity are some of challenges preventing the wider use and diffusion of smart agriculture in Japan. The initial investment required for technology adoption is still significant. It has also been reported that a lack of compatibility is a major factor hindering the adoption of technology by farmers [31]; even though the novelty of intelligent agricultural technologies may be recognised, a farmer may not adopt these due to a belief that such technology is incompatible with the current state of the farm. It has been reported that various equipment and services are being offered in areas such as rice farming, greenhouse horticulture and livestock farming, but it is still difficult to choose, and many of these systems are still at the demonstration stage.

With regard to the expectations for these approaches, we note that the introduction of technology and the transfer of abandoned farmland to farm management schemes have proved to be effective and worthwhile (Table 1 [5]).

In summary, socio-economic issues have been addressed through a multi-pronged approach of policies and measures. In Vision 2016 of Society 5.0, Japan looks beyond Industry 4.0, which uses digital and communication technologies in a broad and general perspective, to address the country's social challenges [9, 12]. On the economic side of the challenges, in addition to promoting the use of advanced technology and smart agriculture, the strategy for agricultural sustainability and development includes developing agricultural management and labour, ensuring stable and high income sources through a variety of practices, and establishing robust distribution networks [14, 32].

5 Conclusion

Japan is facing multiple socio-economic difficulties and concerns, and there are also several global issues that are indirectly influenced by international competition and commitment to global issues, for example via the SDGs. The government has placed food security, agricultural development and regional and rural revitalisation at the centre of its national strategies.

The concentration, securing and reuse of abandoned farmland through the adoption of intermediary management institutions and smart agriculture and digital technology have been promoted. Improvements to agricultural management and infrastructure for agricultural production are being promoted, together with innovation in agricultural production and distribution bases (the acceleration of smart agriculture, and promotion of the use of digital technology and environmental policies).

The government has been active in supporting laws, introducing policies and providing initiatives and support to enterprises, people and local governments. This study has examined some of the approaches applied by the government, enterprises and farmers, and has reviewed the status of the use of advanced technologies in agriculture to address socio-economic challenges and global strategic goals.

This study has shown that the MAFF is leading the Japanese government's efforts to promote the use of advanced technologies to increase agricultural production and tackle issues such as an ageing population, rural depopulation and economic stagnation in rural areas as young people migrate to cities. The Japanese government is continuing its initiatives and commitment to the global goals of developing sustainable energy and food supplies.

In future work, we intend to study the use of advanced technology and data-sharing platforms to address farming related challenges, with a focus on use and case studies.

Acknowledgements. This work was supported in part by the Meio University Research Grant: 2021 Interdisciplinary Joint Projects (corresponding author: F. Ali Hija, Joaan Bin Jassim Academy for Defence Studies, Qatar, fali@jbjjcsc.mil.qa).

References

1. MAFF, Basic Plan for Food, Agriculture and Rural Areas. https://www.maff.go.jp/e/policies/law_plan/attach/pdf/index-13.pdf. Accessed 24 July 2023
2. Ministry of Internal Affairs and Communications: Population projection information press release (1 October 2022), pp. 1–6 (2023)
3. Statistics Bureau of the Ministry of Internal Affairs and Communications: Labor force survey (2023)
4. Ministry of Agriculture, Forestry and Fisheries: Current situation and countermeasures for dilapidated farmland (2022)
5. Ministry of Agriculture: Forestry and Fisheries: Agricultural structure survey, p. 2 (2022)
6. Regional Economic Analysis System RESAS: Industrial structure map, https://resas.go.jp/. Accessed 23 July 2023
7. Dae-yeob, Y.: The Abe administration's growth strategy: policy idea, institutional change, and state-driven policy governance. Seoul J. Jpn. Stud. 4(1), 65–101 (2018)
8. Cao, C.: Analysis of the development path and model for Japanese characteristic agriculture. Geograph. Res. Bull. 1, 85–92 (2022)
9. Fukuda, K.: Science, technology and innovation ecosystem transformation toward society 5.0. Int. J. Prod. Econ. 220, 107460 (2020)
10. Smith, M.S., et al.: Advancing sustainability science for the SDGs. Sustain. Sci. 13, 1483–1487 (2018)

11. Yamamoto, Y., Masahide S., Hiroki T.: Quantum information science and technology in Japan. Quant. Sci. Technol. **4**(2) (2019)
12. Holroyd, C.: Technological innovation and building a 'super smart' society: Japan's vision of society 5.0. J. Asian Pub. Policy **15**(1), 18–31 (2022)
13. Barrett, B, FD., Andrew D,. Masaru Y.: Japanese smart cities and communities: Integrating technological and institutional innovation for Society 5.0. In: Smart Cities for Technological and Social Innovation, pp. 73–94. Academic Press (2021)
14. Tabayashi, A., Kikuchi, T., Nishino, T.: Strategies for sustaining and developing agriculture and regional conditions in Japan. J. Geography (Chigaku Zasshi) **128**(2), 337–358 (2019)
15. Ministry of Agriculture, Forestry and Fisheries: Basic Plan for Food, Agriculture and Rural Areas (2000)
16. Ministry of Agriculture, Forestry and Fisheries: Basic Plan for Food, Agriculture and Rural Areas (2020)
17. MAFF Summary of the Annual Report on Food, Agriculture and Rural Areas in Japan (2021)
18. Tsubaki, S.: Effects and issues of establishment of the farmland re-distribution institutions. Rural Econ. Res. **35**(2) (2018)
19. Ministry of Agriculture, Forestry, and Fisheries of Japan: Strategy for Sustainable Food Systems, MeaDRI (2021)
20. Ministry of Agriculture, Forestry, and Fisheries of Japan: About Farmland (Nouchi) Bank, 2023, https://www.maff.go.jp/j/keiei/koukai/kikou/shitumon.html#Q1. Accessed 24 July 2023
21. Ministry of Agriculture, Forestry, and Fisheries of Japan: Survey on Occurrence and Dissolution of Dilapidated Farmland (2017)
22. Kobayashi, Y., Motoki H., Kan H., Futoshi, N.: Drivers of land-use changes in societies with decreasing populations: a comparison of the factors affecting farmland abandonment in a food production area in Japan. PLoS One **15**(7), e0235846 (2020)
23. Kitano, S.: Estimation of determinants of farmland abandonment and its data problems. Land **10**(6), 596 (2021)
24. Barrett, B. F. D., DeWit, A., Yarime, M.: Japanese smart cities and communities: Integrating technological and institutional innovation for Society 5.0. In: Smart Cities for Technological and Social Innovation, pp. 73–94. Academic Press (2021)
25. Li, D., Teruaki, N., Yosuke, C., Kuang, J.: A review of smart agriculture and production practices in Japanese large-scale rice farming. J. Sci. Food Agric. **103**(4), 1609–1620 (2023)
26. Toshiyuki, K.: Development of the farm machinery industry in Japan: a case study of the walking type tractor. Hitotsubashi J. Econ. **28**(2), 155–171 (1987)
27. Shiokawa, S.: Principles and policy development of the basic law on food, agriculture and rural areas: achievement and future. Agric. Econ. Soc. Jpn. **22**, 36–40 (2020)
28. Farooq, M.S., Shamyla, R., Adnan, A., Tariq, U., Yousaf, B.Z.: Role of IoT technology in agriculture: a systematic literature review. Electronics **9**(2), 319s (2020)
29. Matsumoto, M.: Japan's initiative on smart agriculture. In: 1st Knowledge Sharing ERIA Workshop on 'Enhancing Food Supply Chain Resilience and Food Security in ASEAN with Utilization of Digital Technologies' (2021)
30. Ministry of Agriculture, Food and Fishing: On smart agriculture (2023). https://www.maff.go.jp/j/kanbo/smart/attach/pdf/index-93.pdf (in Japanese)
31. Ayu, W., Nakano, S.: Exploring the characteristics of smart agricultural development in Japan: Analysis using a smart agricultural kaizen level technology map. Comput. Electron. Agric. **198** (2022)
32. Yamamoto, M.: Overview of the special issue: "a regional analysis of strategies for sustaining and developing agriculture in Japan. J. Geography (Chigaku Zasshi) **128**(2), 155–162 (2019)

Evaluation of Smart Community Engagement in Riyadh, Saudi Arabia

Norshuhani Zamin[1]([✉]), Mervin Esckalin Mary[2], Abdul Wahab Muzaffar[2],
Ku Ruhana Ku-Mahamud[3], and Mohd Azhar Ibrahim Residi[4]

[1] College of Computer Studies, De La Salle University, Manila, Philippines
norshuhani.zamin@dlsu.edu.ph
[2] College of Computing and Informatics, Saudi Electronic University, Riyadh, Saudi Arabia
[3] School of Computing, Universiti Utara Malaysia, Kedah, Malaysia
[4] Faculty of Leadership and Management, Universiti Sains Islam Malaysia,
Nilai, Negeri Sembilan, Malaysia

Abstract. COVID19 has created a global effect on economies, people and governments around the world. This includes the Kingdom of Saudi Arabia (KSA). Although the KSA's peak of reported COVID cases was from March to July 2020 the pattern shows significant reduction from August 2020 onwards. Nonetheless, many people are still losing their jobs and businesses are shutting down. Due to the prolonged lockdown period announced by the KSA government from 9 March 2020, there has been an increased, 70%, demand for digital services during the lockdown, as compared to the previous year (according to the government figures). This is due to the high restriction of movements for everyone. People started to use online services to purchase items and food; meanwhile, lessons in schools and universities remained online to the date this proposal was written. Many people are also working from home. Online systems such as Tabaud, Mawid, Tawakkalna and Tetamman Many apps were developed for use during the pandemic. For example, the Tabaud, Mawid, Tawakkalna and Tetamman apps for smartphones are among the latest by KSA government efforts to combat and contain the virus. The KSA introduced Vision 2030 to empower their people to diversify the economy of the country. In Vision 2030, the KSA has prioritized the rapid growth of ICT as a building foundation of digital development. This study focuses on evaluating the smart community engagement in Riyadh focusing on the level of acceptance and execution from the perspective of the public and relevant agencies. This research seeks to understand the level of community engagement in Riyadh towards the use of ICT in improving quality of life. This could help move forward the development of the smart community concept involving the engagement of relevant authorities.

Keywords: Community Engagement · E-Services · Online Systems · Smart City

1 Introduction

The vision of smart community engagement is fast becoming a reality with the convergence of information and communication technology (ICT). Advances in ICT provide communities with improved living environments and quality of life. Social stability and economic growth have been achieved by governments in many countries through ICT. It is predicted by the United Nations that, in 2050, 66% of the global population will be well connected by ICT [1]. Consequently, it is essential for local authorities to communicate critical information with their community effectively using ICT in order to improve the quality daily life in the community. The need for a diversified communication strategy is significant and includes the use of the Internet of Things (IOT) as a touch point to reach people in a timely manner. For this reason, the government should start to redefine citizen engagement by including all possible methods by which to receive information, search for content, manipulate data and share with each other as well connect with other parties. It is important for the community and local government to understand the smart community concept in order to enable successful smart engagement. The awareness, trust and confidence of the society need to be established when developing smart community engagement.

The KSA has launched Vision 2030 which comprises three main pillars: Vibrant Society, Thriving Economy, and Ambitious Nation. In the Vibrant Society pillar, the practice of sustainable living, community care, and an efficient healthcare system are characterized by the Saudi heritage, national pride, and religious culture of Islam. In achieving sustainable and official social living, several initiatives have been introduced to support Vision 2030 which include G20 (a collective responsibility with other countries to forge mutually beneficial solutions for some pressing global challenges and create opportunities for humanity), Tam Hub (Tam is a leading expert in public engagement and crowd sourcing to support the idea from the community and assist in the design and execution as public initiatives), Think20 or T20 (a Saudi Arabia think tank group) to support the G20 process by facilitating interaction between G20 communities and research communities, and Civil 20 or C20 (there are many working groups under C20 from around the world, one is the Digital Economy Working Group. This committee emphasizes a human-centered and fully inclusive digital economy with the aim that half of the world's population should gain access to the digital economy either as content creators or users). We have found numerous initiatives by the KSA government in supporting Vision 2030 [2]; however, most are still at the nascent phase. No study appears to measure the engagement level of the community in the KSA on using smart technology and applications.

Careful planning of programs and usage of technology is crucial for the implementation of smart community engagement. The technology and program must be designed to frame its purpose and should link back to specific goals of implementing smart community engagement. Although some initiatives have been developed for the community using technology such as mobile applications, Riyadh is yet to have its own blueprint in developing and implementing the smart community engagement concept. Since no single blueprint can fit all communities due to the uniqueness of each community, this study aims to evaluate and understand the level of smart community engagement in Riyadh as our pilot community in the KSA focusing on its local context. To achieve this, online survey has been employed involving several stakeholders of public and private organizations which link to support Vision 2030. Results from the survey show the level of engagement between the community and organizations in Riyadh in terms of awareness, trust and confidence of using online services and engagement between the community and local authorities, which will be used in the blueprint development of future research.

2 Related Work

2.1 Community Engagement

A research study in [3] examines community engagement which has been promoted through the use of technology to bridge rural digital divides. The respondents were rural librarians, investigated on their community engagement initiatives through the use of technology. The results showed that social media is the most used technology between librarians and the community. A study by Corbett and Le Dantec [4] investigates the practices of community engagement at different municipal councils across different departments and agencies in selected United States cities. Data on how the practices made by the engaging residents towards their local government were gathered through a series of interviews. The findings showed that more productive participation from residents can be produced through digital intervention. Furthermore, better community engagement can be obtained if the community is aware of the existence of certain departments. Additionally, Corbett and Le Dantec [5] studied trust in digital civics where investigation on how technology can build interesting relationships and services between government agencies and citizens in governance was performed. The focus was on the utilization of trust to support the work of community engagement. Crowdsourcing has been suggested by Haltofova [6] to foster community engagement. The findings showed that crowdsourcing can be used to facilitate participative processes where community engagement can be fostered. Crowdsourcing has been shown to significantly contribute towards the openness and accountability of decision making, in which case information obtained through crowdsourcing is useful to public officers and the community.

Marisa and Simon [7] highlight the importance of leadership in the success of smart community engagement. The leader must collaborate with a different leadership development program to nurture engaged communities. This creates the opportunity for leaders in the community to collaborate in a coherent environment by giving them the opportunity to meet different leaders from diverse industries of the smart community. Poor community engagement leads to high poverty, a low level of education, and a high crime rate. The prominent leader always focuses on providing a quality life for the people in their community. In addition, a successful, engaged, community is also dependent on how they are connected in the ecosystem, as raised by Joel et al. [8] who propose a smart engagement ecosystem that can connect more people through physical, digital, online, and hybrid engagement approaches. This conceptual model suggests that people may communicate through non-linear and reactive approaches. Community engagement can collect public feedback and opinions through top-down and bottom-up participants, which helps the infrastructure development of the smart community.

2.2 ICT and Community Engagement

Nowadays, the Smart Community is the new development concept that helps to interconnect different communities, cities, regions, businesses, and citizens, for the betterment of economic growth and environmental development. These concepts must be incorporated with technology such as ICT, social media, cloud computing, artificial intelligence (AI), and the IoT. With the rapid development of information technology, there is a necessity to develop new applications and connect the people of different places. Different countries focused on renewing their cities and started building smart communities which have gradually become an important countermeasure. The required countermeasures have been analyzed for upgrading the intelligent application in the era of a smart community by Shuyang Yang et al. [9] who discuss the different issues in the development of a smart community and propose a solution to build a smart community through AI. The residents' data are collected and processed through data quantification.

The contribution of new technology in the promotion of community engagement has been studied by Delitheou et al. [10]. Their findings suggest that the use of social media will allow better public information and recommendations for improving the method of community communication. A study by Gobin et al. [11] shows that computerized, intuitive, and efficient services are essential for smart community engagement. Thus, local councils should provide efficient online services. Wood and Fowlie [12] highlight that better trust and positive perceptions towards local government can be obtained through community communicators. Further, policy makers and those involved in the delivery of public services are encouraged to consider methods of social marketing that can benefit their community. Lindskog [13] states that ICT infrastructure and its applications are core in order to assist involvement of all stakeholders in the development and management of the smart community concept in Australia. However, the smart community will not exist unless all parties are willing to collaborate. The findings also highlight that one of the main enablers is the broadband infrastructure which can promote a much more sophisticated generation of smart community initiatives. Recently, Mitchell and Steven [14], exploring the connection between the smart community and smart cities, discovered the different challenges associated with smart cities, identified the need for modern leadership, and talked about the opportunities related to smart cities from the perspective of improving the smart community. The public and community leaders find many challenges in terms of managing revenue, expenses, services, and technology. Every year many people move to other cities or countries and, consequently, the leaders of these communities should be the responsible persons for such people's safety, security, and accommodation.

Chai [15] discusses the different security measures such as authentication, encryption, and access control in the development of smart cities. There is a lot of possibility of malicious attacks when we involve technology. These attacks have been identified and solutions given to resolve such attacks in the field of water supply, electricity supply, and other services which purely depend on ICT. The ICT in smart cities uses sensors, gateways, data, and applications. Consequently, it becomes mandatory to think about the importance of smart city security. The research analyzed different types of attackers and the goal of the attackers. The research outcome has introduced a new security framework for smart cities that consists of five main core functions as follows:

- Identify – To identify the different hardware assets, software assets, and people associated with the organization.

- Protect – To define the security measures and policy defined by the organization. Training must be given to the people in the organization and the chief security officer must ensure that everyone is following the policy for data protection.
- Detect – To detect the malware and vulnerability affecting the security measure.
- Respond – To respond to any attacks or incidents based on the level of impact.
- Recovery – To recover the system by following the security guidelines. Every action must be recorded for further verification.

As the smart city concept is related to the Internet of Things (IoT), Badis et al. [16] integrate IoT into the development of smart cities using the LoRa Ultra-NarrowBand (UNB) technology. LoRa is a wireless technology devised to afford the Low-Power within Wide-Area Networks (LPWANs) which is mandatory for IoT services and provides interoperability services without undertaking any complex installation. It also uses SigFox devices for this purpose which work very effectively and use power only at the time of transmission.

2.3 Smart Community Studies in other Countries

Investigation of the studies indicates that public engagement plays a fundamental role for achieving the right level of commitment to deliver successful smart city projects. Mazhar et al. [17] suggest that community engagement acts as a tool for delivering smart city innovation. A case study based on Nottingham was adopted as a research strategy, where the major focus was on implementing sustainable energy and carbon management initiatives. For this purpose, data were collected with the help of semi-structured interviews from Nottingham City Council, leaders from three local community groups and other stakeholder organizations between April and August 2016. Analysis of these data were carried out with the help of NVivo 11, a software package.

Recently, De Hoop et al. [18], investigating four case studies as research strategies in three types of urban environment (the natural and build environment and the ambient), analyzed the kind of knowledge about the urban environment that can be generated with the help of smart urbanism. For this purpose, data collection was performed by semi-structured interviews from key stakeholders and analysis of primary documents about the project. Moreover, Macke et al. [19] evaluated smart sustainable cities and the community sense based on three factors: environmental well-being, material well-being, and public services and facilities. This evaluation was performed on data collected from southern Brazil with the help of onsite survey in October 2017. Furthermore, Ferraris et al. [20] examined the role of universities in smart city project stakeholders' engagement and management processes. The research strategy consisted of a multiple case study approach to show an effective illustration of multi-actor management in an innovation city's ecosystem. Data gathering was performed in two steps: first a questionnaire was used to collect data from students of Russia and Italy between November 2017 and February 2018; and second, interviews with key informants and document analysis was performed.

Leite [21] examined the factors that drive the formation of innovation networks consisting of government, companies, and societies, and the methods in which these actors collaborate in a network for the development of technologies which have high social impact. For this purpose, two smart city projects in Europe were selected; data gathering was performed by conducting interviews with key informants during two periods (2013–2014), (2015–2018) and by analyzing secondary sources (company reports, international and local media coverage). Subsequently, analysis of these data was performed by utilizing NVivo. Meanwhile, in China, Dapeng et al. [22], working on a pilot project examining China's smart city standardization and assessment practice, started their study from the national policy evolvement, its standardization system, assessment policy, and methods. The pilot study started in 2012 and covered 24 different domains. Based on the results, they developed China's National Strategy for Urbanization, called top-level design, in 2014. The top-level design gives the overall planning and design procedure of a city and focuses on the objective of smart city construction, construction methods, and framework. Based on this study, they [22] developed the standardized approach during the years 2015 to 2017. Today, they are working on a new type of smart city in which the government involves different kinds of assessment methods to evaluate the performance of the cities focusing on citizen-oriented services and friendlier environment. They used different indicators to assess the fields like transportation, education, healthcare, etc. The pilot study has been completed in over 300 cities in which 280 cities submitted their valid assessment results.

Jang et al. [23] describe the smart city development of Taiwan which uses a dual development model called the top-down and bottom-up approach. The bottom-up approach is also called the theme-based approach whereas the top-down approach is called the needs-based approach. These approaches support transforming smarter urban governance and help to improve the business model and the livelihood of the residents in various sectors like government, agriculture, healthcare, mobility, retail, and energy. ICT helps to solve many issues in urbanization and aging societies. This project, directed by the Industrial Development Bureau (IDB) of the Ministry of Economic Affairs, Taiwan, uses a Public-Private Partnership (PPP) model to allocate the tasks between public and private sectors in an ideal way. AI and IoT play a major role in their project to develop such smart communities in various sectors.

Muhammad et al. [24] developed a smart city project called REMOURBAN (REgeneration MOdel for accelerating smart URBAN transformation) based in Nottingham. They tried to identify the important barriers to smart community engagement through qualitative research methods. The data were collected from senior managers and stakeholders of Nottingham City Council through 13 semi-structured interviews. This extended to a group of five community leaders from three local community groups. All the results and feedback were documented and a new strategy was developed from this qualitative research approach. They identified barriers like lack of interest, lack of knowledge, lack of understanding, lack of resources, lack of funds, lack of time, and lack of partnership.

2.4 Smart Community Studies in the KSA

To date, there appear to be no studies related to smart community or digital community engagement between citizens and local authorities to improve the quality of lives. A few studies on community engagement are found but in different contexts, among which is the study of community engagement in higher education conducted at Princess Noura

University [25] which aimed at addressing how female students respond to diverse engagements provided at the university, often linked to teaching, research, outreach and service-learning activities. Similarly, a study in the US [26] on how international Saudi students build the relationship with the community around Ohio University reported that the students felt a low level of engagement with the local community, as they had difficulty embracing the local culture due to the difference in religious beliefs.

Recently, a study by four schools in Saudi Arabia was conducted to measure the engagement of students to perform community-based research projects within the community where the schools are located [27] instead of in the laboratory. The study concluded that the process is not easy, with less support obtained from the community due to lack of community engagement awareness, sustainability of relationships with the community, lack of funding, and policy changes. However, an interesting project called NEOM [28] was launched in 2017 by the Royal Highness Crown Prince Mohammed Bin Salman as a centerpiece of Vision 2030 in the KSA. The NEOM project, initially funded by the KSA government, is an on-going international project introducing a new concept for urban sustainability by setting a high standard for community health, environmental protection and the effective and productive use of technology. As NEOM is only at its initial phase of development it is working on vital processes of community engagement largely by trial and error. Hence, a blueprint for community engagement using technology is significant in order to support NEOM's initiative.

3 Methodology

The instrument/questionnaire in the current study was designed and developed to address the current practice and expectation of communities in Riyadh, KSA. Items in the questionnaire were adopted and adapted from Mehra, Sikes, and Singh [3], Corbett and Le Dantec [4, 5], and Cabitza and Locoro [29].

The questionnaire contained 19 items arranged in four sections:

A. Demographic data of the respondents (6 questions)
B. Current status of community engagement for Riyadh city (7 questions)
C. Communication and feedback status (4 questions)
D. Suggestions of respondents towards the smart community concept (2 questions)

The questionnaire was designed in both English and Arabic language. Most of the questions were designed as close-ended and only Section D contained open-ended questions to give respondents flexibility to express their views and recommendations about the smart community concept in Riyadh.

4 Results and Findings

Results were obtained based on descriptive and inferential statistics analysis on the data. This section contains discussion on the demographic data of the respondents, the current status of the engagement between the community and the authority, communication and feedback status between the community and the authority, and finally the results of several hypotheses tests.

4.1 Demographic Data

The number of people who voluntarily participated in this study is 81 (i.e., 32% male and 68% female). Approximately 67% were between the ages of 21 and 49 while the remaining respondents were either less than 20 years old or 50 years old or older. About 25% of the respondents were from Al-'Olayya and Al-Rawdhah districts while 10% were from Al-Shemal and 9% from Al-Malaz. Other respondents (56%) were from other districts in Riyadh municipality. Half of the participants (41) work in the public sector and about half (40) held a Bachelor degree as their highest education level (refer to Fig. 1).

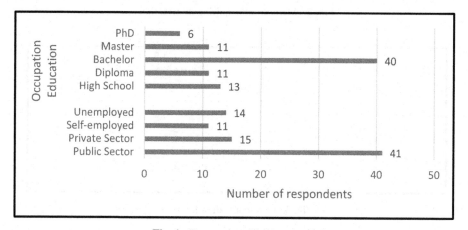

Fig. 1. Respondents' backgrounds

Understanding the meaning of the smart community concept is important and the results indicated that approximately 64% (52) of the participants understood the concept. However, only 8% (4) truly understood the real concept.

4.2 Community Engagement Current Status

Figure 2 depicts the various ways adopted by the community in acquiring information from organizations and service providers. From a multi-answer question, social media is shown by approximately 83% (67 out of 81) of the respondents to be the most popular way in acquiring information from organizations in Riyadh.

It seems that communication methods between the community and organizations have a similar trend regarding the method of acquiring information. Answers from a multi-answer question also reveal that social media is, again, the best option and out-numbers email and mobile apps, as depicted in Fig. 3. Telephones remained a popular method but writing letters and over-the-counter are the least popular communication methods.

The results effectiveness of the present communication method indicate that the present communication method is rated as moderately effective by half of the respondents. The results also indicate that about 81% of the community were aware of the online

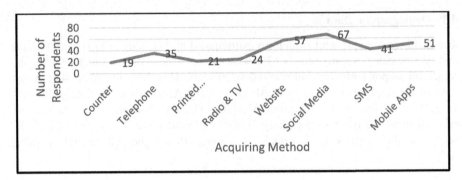

Fig. 2. Methods of acquiring information

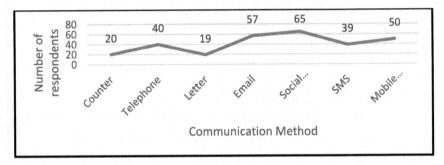

Fig. 3. Communication methods

services. High-level usage (about two-thirds) is also observed among respondents who use several online services provided by Riyadh municipality through its official website. However, the customer service and e-library are not popular with the respondents, as depicted in Fig. 4. The 'e-services' in the figure refers to all government-related electronic services such as renewal of driving license, house rental contract, hajj and umrah application, traffic violation management and passport related tasks.

4.3 Communication and Feedback Status

The satisfaction level of communication between the community and officers at organizations and service providers in Riyadh is shown in Fig. 5. Only five organizations, i.e., public transportations, hospital, National Water Company, Saudi Electricity company, and mobile data providers, received high satisfaction ratings among the respondents for their services.

Figure 6 displays the number of respondents with the opportunity to meet face-to-face with public figures, state legislators, and organization heads. Overall, there are very few meetings between the community and head of departments or the mayor. The results indicate that the heads of the public relation department and administrative development are the most reachable individuals.

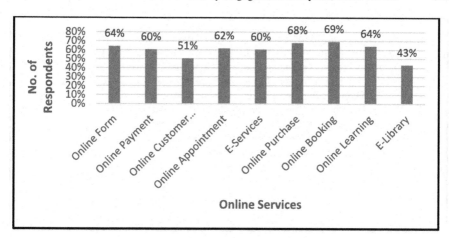

Fig. 4. Usage of online services

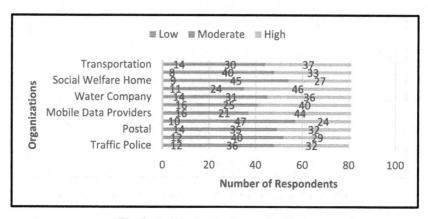

Fig. 5. Satisfaction level towards officers

The engagement level between the community and the authority is moderate for 41% of the community as shown in Fig. 7. High level of engagement was achieved as indicated by 35% of the respondents. Thus, authorities should engage more with the community to increase the level of engagement. Different levels of education and exposure to technology could be the reasons for the low engagement.

4.4 Hypothesis Testing

Independent Pearson Chi-Square tests with $\alpha = 0.05$ were conducted to evaluate hypotheses on the association between variables.

The relation between the respondents' trust and confidence is related to effectiveness of the systems as well as frequency of use is supported since $p < 0.05$, as shown in Table 1. Further analysis showed that the respondents' trust and confidence is related to effectiveness of the systems as well as frequency of use, as displayed in Table 2.

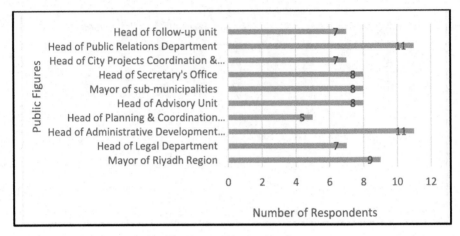

Fig. 6. Meeting opportunity

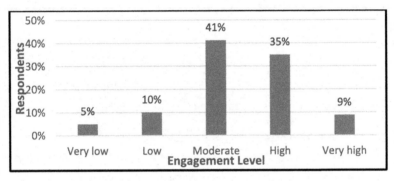

Fig. 7. Engagement level of community with authorities

Thus, usage of the online systems will be frequent if the community has the trust and confidence of effective systems. Furthermore, as shown in Table 2, the occupation type and respondents' level of education play an important role in the usage frequency.

Table 1. Hypotheses on usage frequency

H1	Trust and confident is related to effectiveness of systems ($\chi^2_{(4)} = 16.764$ p-value: 0.002)
H2	Trust and confident is related to frequency of system use ($\chi^2_{(2)} = 7.738$, p-value: 0.021)

Table 2. Hypotheses trust and confidence while using the systems

H3	Frequency of system used is related to respondent's age ($\chi^2_{(10)}$ = 9.437 p-value: 0.491)
H4	Frequency of system used is related to respondent's gender ($\chi^2_{(2)}$ = 2.437, p-value: 0.296)
H5	Frequency of system used is related to occupational type ($\chi^2_{(6)}$ = 58.734, p-value: 0.000)
H6	Frequency of system used is related to education level ($\chi^2_{(8)}$ = 36.369, p-value: 0.000)

5 Conclusion

The smart community concept is understood by a very small number of respondents. The findings clearly indicate that the type of jobs, solely and independently from all other socio-economic and demographic variables, could explain the positive effect on knowledge about the smart community concept. The data also illustrate that many online services have been made available by organizations and they are well picked up and frequently used by the community who have good educational backgrounds and professional jobs. Additionally, many service providers are competing to give the best communication access service in the city of Riyadh. It is believed that good communication access with various online services has become a successful digital framework to support the awareness and, hence, will improve the acceptance of the smart community concept in Riyadh.

Acknowledgement. The authors extend their appreciation to the Deputyship for Research and Innovation, Ministry of Education in Saudi Arabia for funding this research work through the project number 7915-CAI-2020–1-2020-I.

References

1. Bosek, L.: Information Sharing, Transparency, and E-Governance Among County Government Office in Southeastern Michigan. Master of Public Administration, Department of Educatiion, Leadearship and Public Service, Northern Michigan University, USA (2017)
2. Vision 2030: National Transformation Program 2020. "Vision2030" (2018). http://vision 2030.gov.sa/sites/default/files/NTP_En.pdf. Accessed 12 May 2022
3. Mehra, B., Sikes, E.S., Singh, V.: Scenarios of technology use to promote community engagement: overcoming marginalization and bridging digital divides in the southern and central Appalachian Rural libraries. Inf. Process. Manage. 57(3), 1–15 (2020)
4. Corbett, E., Le Dantec, C.A.: The problem of community engagement: disentangling the practices of municipal government. In: Proceedings of the 2018 CHI Conference on Human Factors in Computing Systems, pp. 1–13. ACM, New York (2018a)
5. Corbett, E., Le Dantec, C.A.: Exploring trust in digital civics. In: Proceedings of the 2018 Designing Interactive Systems Conference (Dis 2018), pp. 9–2. ACM, New York (2018b). https://doi.org/10.1145/3196709.3196715

6. Haltofova, B.: Fostering community engagement through crowdsourcing: case study on participatory budgeting. Theor. Emp. Res. Urban Manage. **13**(1), 5–12 (2018)
7. Marisa, C., Simon, C.: Building engaged communities - a collaborative leadership approach. MDPI Smart Cities **1**, 155–162 (2018). https://doi.org/10.3390/smartcities1010009
8. Joel, F., Martin, T., Hank Haeusler, M.: Redefining community engagement in smart cities: design patterns for a smart engagement ecosystem. IGI Global, pp. 13–53 (2020). https://doi.org/10.4018/978-1-7998-4018-3.ch002
9. Shuyang, Y., Hongqing, G., Chongbao, R., Rijia, D.: Measures and suggestions for smart community development based on urban renewal. Hindawi. Wirel. Commun. Mobile Comput. **2022**, Article ID 9566640,1–8 (2022). https://doi.org/10.1155/2022/9566640
10. Delitheou, V., Bakogiannis, E., Krriakidis, C.: Urban planning: integrating smart applications to promote community engagement. Heliyon, Celpress **5**(5), e0167 (2019)
11. Gobin-Rahimbux, B., et al.: Smart communities initiatives. In: Proceedings of the 3rd ISOneWorld Conference, vol. 16, pp. 14–16. Las Vegas, NV, USA (2004)
12. Wood, M., Fowlie, J.: Using community communicators to build trust and understanding between local councils and residents in United Kingdom. Local Econ. **28**(6), 527–538 (2013)
13. Lindskog, H.: Smart communities initiatives. In: Proceedings of the 3rd ISOneWorld Conference, vol. 16, pp. 14–16, Las Vegas, NV, USA (2004)
14. Mitchell, G., Steven, F.: Organization and community intelligence in Smart City F. and Beyond. Wiley, Pepperdine University, Los Angeles, California, USA, pp. 47–55 (2022). https://doi.org/10.1049/smc2.12022
15. Chai, K.T.: Security for smart cities. IET Smart Cities **2**, 95–104 (2020). https://doi.org/10.1049/iet-smc.2020.0001
16. Badis, H., Rida, K., Sherali, Z., Achraf, F., Lyes, K.: IoT technologiesfor smart cities. IET Netw. **7**, 1–13 (2018). https://doi.org/10.1049/iet-net.2017.0163
17. Mazhar, M., Kaveh, B., Sarshar, M., Bull, R., Fayez, R.: Community engagement as a tool to help deliver smart city innovation: a case study of Nottingham, United Kingdom. In: ECEEE (European Council for an Energy Efficient Economy) Summer Study Proceedings: Consumption, Efficiency & Limits, France, Stockholm: ECEEE, pp. 807–820 (2017)
18. de Hoop, E., Moss, T., Smith, A., Löffler, E.: Knowing and governing smart cities: four cases of citizen engagement with digital urbanism. Urban Govern. **1**(2), 61–71 (2021). ISSN 2664-3286
19. Macke, J., Sarate, J.A.R., de Atayde Moschen rate, S.: Smart sustainable cities evaluation and sense of community. J. Clean. Prod. **239**, 103–118. https://doi.org/10.1016/j.jclepro.2019.118103, ISSN 0959-6526,2019
20. Ferraris, A., Belyaeva, Z. Bresciani, S.: The role of universities in the Smart City innovation: multistakeholder integration and engagement perspectives. J. Bus. Res. **119**, 163–171 (2020). https://doi.org/10.1016/j.jbusres.2018.12.010, ISSN 0148–2963
21. Leite, E.: Innovation networks for social impact: an empirical study on multi-actor collaboration in projects for smart cities. J. Bus. Res. **139**, 325–337 (2022). https://doi.org/10.1016/j.jbusres.2021.09.072, ISSN 0148-2963
22. Dapeng, Z., Xi, W., Wenge, R., Yu, Y., China's practice of smart city standardization and assessment. IET Smart Cities **3**(4), 211–218 (2021)
23. Jang, H., Leu, B.C., Lin, Y.Y., Yi, L., Dai, Y.G.: Smart city development in Taiwan. Wiley IET Smart Cities **3**, 125–141 (2021). https://doi.org/10.1049/smc2.12008
24. Mazhar, U.M., Kaveh, B., Sarshar, M., Bull, R., Fayez, R.: Community engagement as a tool to help deliver smart city innovation: a case study of Nottingham, United Kingdom. In: ECEEE Summer Study Proceedings Mobility, Transport, Smart and Sustainable Cities, pp 807–820 (2017)

25. Jacob, W.J., Sutin, S.E., Weidman, J.C., Yeager, J.L. (eds.): Community Engagement in Higher Education: Policy Reforms and Practice. Springer, Heidelberg (2015). https://doi.org/10.1007/978-94-6300-007-9

26. Kusek, W.A.: Evaluating the struggles with international students and local community participation. J. Int. Stud. **5**(2), 121–131 (2015)

27. Gaffar, A.M., Magzoub, M.E.M., Mahmoud, I.: Do community-based medical schools produce more community-based research? A review of four medical schools in Sudan and Saudi Arabia. Health Prof. Educ. **6**(1), 19–30 (2020)

28. Farag, A.A.: The story of NEOM city: opportunities and challenges. In: Attia, S., Shafik, Z., Ibrahim, A. (eds.) New Cities and Community Extensions in Egypt and the Middle East, pp. 35–49. Springer, Cham (2019). https://doi.org/10.1007/978-3-319-77875-4_3

29. Cabitza, F., Locoro, A.: Questionnaires in the design and evaluation of community-oriented technologies. Int. J. Web Based Commun. **13**(1), 4–31 (2017)

Cloud Service Provider Cost for Online University: Amazon Web Services versus Oracle Cloud Infrastructure

Yazeed Al Moaiad[1($\boxtimes$)], Zainab Abu Bakar[2], Ahamd Mhd Emad Diab[1],
Norshuhani Zamin[3], and Yazrina Yahya[4]

[1] Faculty of Computer and Information Technology, Al-Madinah International University,
57100 Kuala Lumpur, Malaysia
yazeed.alsayed@mediu.edu.my
[2] School of Science and Technology, Asia e University, 47500 Subang Jaya, Malaysia
[3] College of Computer Studies, De La Salle University, Manila 1004, Philippines
[4] Faculty Information Science and Technology, Universiti Kebangsaan Malaysia, 43600 Bangi,
Malaysia

Abstract. The number of Cloud Service Providers (CSPs) that provide their services differs from each other in terms of cost. This has made it difficult for companies and organizations to choose the best and least expensive cloud service providers. In light of the current crises that the world is going through and with the many financial problems faced by many companies, including Al-Madinah International University, it was necessary to take some measures that would mitigate the impact of financial problems, and therefore this study came to present a comparative study between each of cloud service providers Amazon Web Services (AWS) and Oracle Cloud Infrastructure (OCI) which provide Virtual Private Server (VPS) services in terms of cost to help Al-Madinah International University in making the appropriate decision in choosing the cloud service provider that suits its financial requirements.

Keywords: Cloud Service Providers · Amazon Web Services · Oracle Cloud Infrastructure · Virtual Private Server

1 Introduction

Cloud computing is an on-demand computing power, database, storage, applications and other IT resources delivery via the medium of the internet, and the cost of this type of computing follows the 'pay-as-you-go' method. The platform of a cloud services provides user with fast access to flexible and low-cost IT resources, allowing user to perform many tasks like sharing files or executing their business operations [1].

In their study, Rashid and Chaturvedi [2] discussed cloud computing model, and according to the authors, the model comprises five major features namely, broad network access, rapid elasticity, resource pooling, on-demand self-service, and measured service. Furthermore, there are three available service models associated with cloud computing namely software as a service (SaaS), platform as a service (PaaS), and infrastructure as a service (IaaS). The four deployment models of Cloud computing are as follows: public cloud, private cloud, hybrid cloud and community cloud. These allows cloud computing to offer the following benefits to users: easy management, low cost, seamless services, disaster management and green computing [3].

Despite the prominence of Cloud computing, it can be challenging to find the most appropriate cloud service providers (CSPs) because user wants to find the one with the best performance at low cost, while allowing the risks to be dispensed across various vendors. Providers of computing service are various, and the five best ones as listed in Aljamal, El-Mousa, and Jubair [4] are: Amazon Web Services (introduced in 2006), Microsoft Azure (introduced in 2010), Google Cloud Platform (introduced in 2008), Oracle Cloud (introduced in 2012), and IBM Cloud (introduced in 2011).

Amazon Web Service (AWS) and Oracle cloud are the most popular cloud providers. In particular, AWS provides user with Amazon Elastic Compute Cloud (EC2) comprising various resizable offerings and solutions (Amazon, 2019). As reported by Amazon (2017), approximately a million people from over 190 countries were users of EC2 cloud, which is accessible within 52 availability zones in 18 geographical constituencies. Amazon offers user virtual machine instances with various configurations to resolve complex problems, and these machine instances can be purchased [5].

Meanwhile, Oracle Cloud Infrastructure was built by Oracle, and it encompasses a virtual cloud data center with well-regulated resources, offering user with maximum security. Oracle software is employed by Oracle servers in operating within their data center – it has been known as database solutions. Oracle offers user with various instances of cloud computing including the standard virtual machines and the bare metal compute instances. Oracle also offers other services including managed load balancing services, access and identity management, software-defined virtual cloud networks (VCNs), remote block storage, and high-performance managed databases [6].

2   Research Question

Based on the challenges and considerations within the realm of VPS services and cloud computing found in the literature regarding the complex and evolving nature of VPS services and cloud computing gives rise to these research questions:

1. What are the VPS's (virtual private server) features?
2. How the comparison works through the analysis of the VPSs service?
3. What is the preferred decision based on the result of the comparison?

3   Importance of the Research

Cloud computing provides various services to user including storage, applications and processing power, via the Internet, utilizing the pay-as-you-go method. This on-demand hosted service brings various benefits to user. Selby (2018) relevantly stated that the services provided by cloud service providers are reliable. For companies, the use of cloud services saves them from having to purchase an infrastructure, which means that the company does not need to dispose any servers, hardware, software, OS, and applications once they become outdated. Also, having no requirement to purchase the infrastructure means significant cost saving.

The importance of the study is that it shows cost difference between Amazon Web Services and Oracle Cloud Infrastructure, which will help Al-Madinah International University in comparing the operating cost of its servers on both Amazon Web Services and Oracle Cloud Infrastructure. Hence, the university could make the best decision in terms of its cost, so that it could maintain the quality and continuity of the services it provides, in light of the current circumstances facing the university especially with the persistent Corona pandemic, which has negatively affected the educational life globally.

4 Literature Review

Cloud computing essentially comprises computing power, memory, and storage, accessible via the Internet and its pricing is based on pay-as-you-go mechanism [7]. This form of computing is cost effective as user does not need to purchase specific infrastructure, and neither does user need to incur the cost associated with management and maintenance [8]. Software-defined virtual networks link cloud resources, and through advanced routing techniques, these networks [9] forward traffic between these resources. In addition, there is an official web portal provided by cloud that allows access and management of resources, and so, administrators could create, control, monitor, delete and purchase resources as needed [8].

4.1 Cloud Computing Service Models

Cloud computing essentially provides user with a vast gamut of infrastructure-based services via platform as an instrument of production, and through certain software, customer is provided by application licenses for an on-demand service. In this regard, the National Institute of Standards and Technology (NIST) has listed three kinds of service models commonly employed by cloud computing as follows: IaaS (Infrastructure as Service), PaaS (Platform as a Service), and SaaS (Software as a Service) [10]. The details of each are provided in the ensuing subsection.

Infrastructure as a Service (IaaS): Cloud computing that employs the IaaS model involves the use of a group of virtualized computing resources such as CPU, OS, network bandwidth, Memory, monitoring service and Application Software, and as described [11], this model as service provider, allows user to install and manage virtual machines, operating systems and applications included. As stated by Miyachi [12], IaaS may allow user to control the operating systems, storage, and apps, but not cloud infrastructure. Additionally, user may have (but only little) control over some networking components.

Platform as a Service (PaaS): PaaS is more advanced than IaaS. This type of cloud computing involves the execution and maintenance of system software (i.e., the operating system) and other computing resources [13]. The services provided by PaaS type cloud computing include web service integration, collaboration, scaling, DB integration, security [2], and also application design, development and hosting.

Software as a service (SaaS): Cloud service providers utilizing the software as a service (SaaS) model would provide the operation and maintenance of application software, operating system and other resources, and the main aim of SaaS, as described by

Miyachi [12] is to provide user with interface that allows user to use and manage the cloud-built software. SaaS is essentially a web-based application interface with the use of the internet for service delivery, and the services are accessed through a web-browser. Gmail, Google Sheet, and Google Docs are among the services provided by Google, which are accessible via various devices such as laptops and smartphones. SaaS differs from the other two models in a sense that it does not require licensing, installation, upgrade, maintenance or specific software on the user's device [2].

4.2 Cloud Computing Deployment Models

Deployment models illustrate the cloud environment access type. Cloud services provide customers with various types of deployments including public clouds, private clouds, hybrid clouds, and community clouds. All of these models are hosted and organized by providers of cloud computing to meet the specific demands of users as customers. The different types of Cloud Computing Deployment Models as the following in the next subsections.

Public Cloud: Public cloud offers an open cloud environment, and so, all can access it. According to Birje [14], public cloud is off-premise, and so, various enterprises can employ its service delivery to users by obtaining it from the third party. In public cloud, client and resource provider have service level agreement, and among the commonly known providers of cloud service include Google, Amazon, Oracle Cloud Infrastructure, Rackspace and Microsoft [15].

Private Cloud: Unlike public cloud, private is on-premise and its services and infrastructure are highly controlled by an organization; it is also owned by a specific organization. In essence, private cloud provides services within an organization with the purpose of preserving privacy and security, and examples of such type of cloud include RedHat and Seagate [16].

Community Cloud: Community cloud encompasses a cloud infrastructure that the owner organization shares with its customers of identical interests like in terms of policy, security requirements, mission, and so forth [17]. The infrastructure of this type of cloud is supervised, and used by various institutions that share similar core business, projects or shareable demands infrastructures, like hardware and software, for the purpose of decreasing the IT costs. Community cloud can be jointly managed several institutions or managed by the cloud service providers [18].

Hybrid Cloud: Hybrid cloud combines two or more cloud deployment models, and these models can be of public, private or community clouds type. Each type of cloud retains their feature, while functioning in combination with other types of cloud. Hybrid cloud is managed internally, or hosted by an internal or external third party. For some clients, the cost of utilizing this type of cloud is rather high [19].

4.3 Cloud Computing Pricing Model

Google, Oracle, Amazon, and IBM as leaders in cloud service provision, are consistently expanding their computing infrastructures and platforms, to assure the provision of excellent computing, data storage, database, and network applications services. Also, new features and capabilities have been added to their application services like audio, video, finance, email, office applications, in addition to data processing services.

Relevantly, the pricing models of service provider can significantly affect the selection and use of cloud resources by clients. In general, service providers offer clients various options of services, and usually, the offered services are in accordance to the service types, for instance, email, web services, infrastructure, data storage, database, data processing, data sharing, accounting, and many more. Accordingly, the common pricing models of cloud computing services are as presented in the following subsections [20].

Static Pricing Model: Static pricing model provides rather stable price charging, that is, the price remains the same for a long time. Here, cloud provider will first determine the prices of the resources. In the model, fixed pricing comprises the pay-per-use pricing and the subscription pricing. This type of pricing is simple and clear but it may not sufficiently serve all users because users may have different needs. Another problem with this type of pricing is that even though it gives providers profit when the demand increases, but loss may incur if the price remains the same over time [21].

Dynamic pricing model: Dynamic pricing model or variable pricing involves the use of target service price by service provider, based on the supply and demand of the service. Hence, price will be increased with high demand, and vice versa. Higher pricing causes the non-affording tenants (consumers or clients) to withdraw, leading to demand drop, which will lead to price drop, which will encourage some tenants to increase their usage (increased demand), and the cycle continues. As can be observed, price changes are a dynamic process, influenced by demand and supply. Auctions or price negotiations exemplify the use of dynamic pricing model [22].

4.4 Amazon Web Services (AWS) Pricing

The purpose of Amazon web services (AWS) is to simplify people's usage of the internet related facilities by charging them like other service/facility companies would (e.g., electricity companies), and so, user of AWS only pays for the used services. Comparatively, owning an infrastructure means that owner will have to pay whether it is being used or not, but with AWS, the concept embraced is that of pay-as-you-go, whereby user only pays for what is being used [23].

AWS EC2 Instance Pricing: Amazon Elastic Compute Cloud (Amazon EC2) presents user with countless of virtual machine environment as instances, for application development and deployment with no requirement to pay for hardware frontal cost. In fact, the resources can be expanded or reduced, in accordance to the needs of user. In its resource's allocation, there are three kinds of pricing models offered by Amazon for three kinds of instances namely Reserved Instance, On-demand Instance and spot instance [19].

Those purchasing the on-demand instances can pay off their selected rented computing environment. Here, no upfront payments or long-term commitments are required. The prices are based on the type of instances, for instance, OS specifications, Memory, CPU aggregate, and so forth. Meanwhile, those choosing reserved instances would pay about 50% less, on one-time payment for a long-term instance reservation, and the duration of subscription would vary from one to three years [24].

AWS database services pricing: There are two types of database services offered by Amazon Web Services. The first one provides subscribers with a compute environment in which they could configure it in order that it fits the conventional database services like SQL Server, Oracle, or MySQL. In addition, Amazon Machine Images (AMI) can be bought from the AWS marketplace, and in order to ease user, this AMI is already preconfigured with the install images.

In terms of pricing, it employs the pricing models employed for EC2 instances, and the database licenses cost may also be included in the pricing. Another service provided by AWS is Relational Database Service (RDS), which is a wholly managed version of the database services. RDS is easy to set up, scale, and operate, and it is also cost-effective. Also, it executes data system patching, duplication, backups, and other operational activities of management, automatically [25]. Subscriber does not need to worry about maintenance.

AWS storage system pricing: There are two types of storage services offered by AWS, namely Simple Storage Service (S3) which concerns object storage, and Elastic Block Store (EBS) which is a block-based service. S3 is to store objects of various types like media files, flat files, and other forms of data files. In S3. These files are stored in buckets (folders) and are accessible via a web interface or API calls. Meanwhile, EBS volumes provide consistent block storage for usage with EC2 instances. These consistently available storage volumes are very reliable, and can be attached to instances in region similar to that of EBS volume [23]. However, S3 storage cannot be directly mounted as drives for an EC2 instance, and APIs are required to allow S3 buckets access by those instances.

4.5 Oracle Cloud Infrastructure (OCI) Pricing

Oracle Cloud Infrastructure employs the pay-as-you-go pricing, and in fact, this type of pricing is the default pricing option for a new cloud client (tenant). OCI, the measurement of use is according to various types of metrics, based on certain type of cloud resource. Tenant will be charged on their credit card, and an invoice will be issued. Such pricing option is appropriate when the services used are for purposes like evaluation, prototyping, or when tenant wants to avoid estimating the regular service consumption in the coming months. The use is commitment-free and fully flexible, with no requirement for unused credit payment [26].

Oracle Cloud Compute Service: Oracle Cloud Infrastructure offers user with quick, flexible, and inexpensive compute competency, for all types of computing tasks; it provides user with exceptionally flexible VM and bare metal instances for optimal price-performance [32]. OCI allows user to provision and handle instances, and user can generate instances as required, in order to fulfil their computing and application requirements. User can securely access their created instances from their computer; they can restart them, attach and detach volumes to them, and then terminate them when they no longer need them. Upon termination of the instances, all changes made to the local drives of the instances will be gone, while the saved changes to volumes attached to the instance will be kept.

Oracle Cloud Capacity Types: In the launch of compute instances, user of OCI could select the specific type of host capacity to use, while the default is the on-demand capacity. Hence, instead of using the on-demand capacity, user could choose to employ preemptible capacity, capacity reservations, or dedicated capacity [32], as briefly explained below:

- On-demand capacity: This type of capacity requires user to pay only for the used compute capacity, and the rate of pay is by the second, and in accordance to the shape, user pays only for the duration of the running of their instances, in seconds. However, this type of capacity does not guarantee capacity availability, in the launch of large workloads [32].
- Preemptible capacity: This type of capacity is cost saving as it allows user to employ preemptible instances in running workloads that only need to run for only short periods, or that can be interjected upon the reclaim of the capacity. Preemptible instances are comparable to the regular compute instances in terms of functioning. However, the capacity of preemptible instances will be reclaimed when there is a need for it elsewhere, resulting in the termination of the instances [32].
- Reserved capacity: This capacity is for future usage, and so, it is available whenever user needs it for creating compute instances. Reserved capacity is used when user launch instances on the reservation, and upon the termination of these instances, the capacity is returned to the reservation, causing increase in the unused capacity within the reservation. Unused reserved capacity is metered in different manner, unlike the reserved capacity [32].
- Dedicated capacity: Dedicated capacity is used in running VM instances for a single tenant, and this capacity is exclusively owned by one tenant. In other words, this type of capacity is not shared. It allows user/tenant to fulfil the regulatory requirements for isolation, preventing infrastructure sharing. Equally, such capacity allows user to fulfil the node-based or host-based licensing requirements, which needs the licensing of the whole server [32].

Oracle Cloud Object Storage The service Oracle Cloud Infrastructure Object Storage is a storage platform that provides user with dependable, cost-efficient, and durable storage over the internet. This service allows storage of indefinite amount of unstructured data of any type, such as analytic data and rich content data like videos and images. Object Storage assures user safe and secure storage and retrieval of data directly from the internet or from the platform of cloud. It also provides user with various management interfaces so that user could manage the storage easily. The platform is flexible, and so, user could start small and scale seamlessly, with no performance or reliability problem [32].

5 Methodology

The research methodology of this comparative study comprises three phases, and the purpose of this study is to compare cloud service providers in terms of cost factors that affect the decision of technology managers regarding the adoption of cloud computing, as well as the choice of the cloud service provider that suits the financial requirements of the institutions. Notably, this study is a valuable addition to the knowledge reservoir through its empirical evidence on the cost factor and the impact of IT compliance on cloud adoption – the evidence will be of value to researchers in cloud technology evaluation. The methodology of this research consists of three phases as the following:

- Phase 1: Data Collection
- Phase 2: Analysis comparison of selected Cloud Service Providers based on Cost criteria
- Phase 3: Evaluation and validation of the comparison result of the Selected Cloud Service Providers

5.1 Phase One: Data Collection

During phase one, data and information related to cloud computing and cloud service providers and related services are collected, mainly from practical papers from international conferences, accredited journals, and relevant websites, as preparation for the next phase.

The prime focus of this study's data collection phase is the gathering of primary and secondary data. There are four steps to this phase as follows:

- Step 1: Identify Cloud Service Providers
- Step 2: Identify IAAS Model Users
- Step 3: Cloud Computing Cost Service
- Step4: Price Calculator

Step 1: Cloud Computing Service Providers
In this step, two of the most important and best Cloud Service Providers (CSPs) are identified, and they are Amazon Web Services and Oracle Cloud Infrastructure. Both are studied to understand their physical capabilities, characteristics and the services that they provide. These two providers are selected on the grounds that Al-Madinah International University obtains the services of these two providers for managing systems and databases within the work system of this institution.

Step 2: Price Calculator
In this step, the researcher finds the tools, which will be used to calculate the cost of VPSs. These tools are provided by Amazon Web Services and Oracle Cloud Infrastructure; each cloud service provider has its own tool to calculate the estimated cost of the services to be subscribed. The Pricing Calculators are web-based planning tools that can be used to create estimated prices for AWS and OCI use cases. It can also be used to model the solutions before building them, explore the AWS and OCI service price points, and review the calculations behind the estimations. In addition, it can be used in to manage the expenditure of the organization, find cost saving opportunities, and make informed decisions when using Amazon Web Services and Oracle Cloud Infrastructure.

In our research, these tools will be used to find out the prices of the services provided by both OCI and AWS, especially Virtual Private Servers (VPSs) services. These tools allow the entering of data about the specifications of VPSs, including RAM, CPU, SSD storage and network bandwidth, and then, the tools will process these data and give an estimated cost based on current prices in the global market. After obtaining the estimated cost of these virtual servers in both OCI and AWS, a price comparison between the selected VPSs will be made later in the next phase of this study, which is the comparison phase.

5.2 Phase Two: Analysis and Comparison of Selected Cloud Service Providers

The actual analysis and comparison between AWS and OCI will be done based on the cost factor of VPS services, and Al-Madinah International University will be a case study for this comparison. Al-Madinah International University has a set of servers on both AWS and OCI, and these virtual private servers have different specifications and run many different systems that are important to the work environment in this university.

5.3 Phase Three: Evaluate and Validate the Comparison Result

At this stage, the results of the analysis and comparison from the previous stage will be evaluated and validated. This will determine which of the cloud service providers, namely OCI and AWS, provides VPS services at the lowest possible cost. This will help Al-Madinah International University in making the most appropriate decision in choosing the most suitable cloud service provider based on their preferences and requirements in terms of cost.

6 Result and Discussion

In this research, the researcher conducted an analysis and comparison study between Two cloud service providers which are Amazon Web Services (AWS) and Oracle Cloud Infrastructure (OCI) in terms of cost. Upon completion of the work in this research, this research will help Al-Madinah International University in choosing the most suitable cloud service provider in terms of cost and that suits the requirements of this university. Where the researcher began with the analysis phase of the VPS service of this university in both AWS and OCI, then defining the cost-calculating tool and finally the stage of making a comparison and validating the cost differences between AWS and OCI for the VPS service.

In this research, the researcher, through the analysis phase of the virtual private service, presented the operational specifications of some servers that Al-Madinah International University operates in both AWS and OCI. These specifications include storage capacity, RAM Memory and the number of cores processor used in Servers and network Bandwidth. These specifications were also clarified and presented in the following Table 1:

After presenting the specifications of the Virtual Private Servers, the researcher applied these specifications for each VPS on the cost-calculating tool for both AWS and OCI in order to clarify and showing the cost of these VPSs in the mentioned cloud service providers. Therefore, after Validating and knowing the cost of these VPSs in AWS and OCI, the researcher presents in the following table the final comparison of Amazon Web Services (AWS) and Oracle Cloud Infrastructure (OCI) in terms of cost.

Table 1. Specifications of virtual private service

VPS Name	RAM Memory	CPUs	Storage	Network Bandwidth
VPS1	17 GB	2 cores	700 GB HDD	up to 1 Gb/s
VPS2	17 GB	2 cores	500 GB HDD	up to 1 Gb/s
VPS3	16 GB	2 cores	350 GB SSD	up to 1.4 Gb/s
VPS4	30 GB	2 cores	1 TB SSD	up to 2 Gb/s

Table 2. Comparison of Amazon Web Services (AWS) and Oracle Cloud Infrastructure (OCI) in terms of cost

VPS Name	RAM	CPUs	Storage	Network Bandwidth	AWS	OCI
VPS1	17 GB	2 cores	700 GB HDD	up to 1 Gb/s	253.88 USD/month	244.02 USD/month
VPS2	17 GB	2 cores	500 GB HDD	up to 1 Gb/s	243.08 USD/month	235.52 USD/month
VPS3	16 GB	2 cores	350 GB SSD	up to 1.4 Gb/s	312.83 USD/month	228.03 USD/month
VPS4	30 GB	2 cores	1 TB SSD	up to 2 Gb/s	464.17 USD/month	429.38 USD/month

Finally, the results of the comparison in Table 2 show that all VPS servers are more expensive when hosted in Amazon Web Services (AWS) cloud service provider, and this indicates that it is the most expensive VPS service in term of cost, and that Oracle Cloud Infrastructure (OCI) is the least expensive in terms of cost. Therefore, the Oracle Cloud Infrastructure is the most preferred and most suitable for the needs of Al-Madinah International University.

At this time, the world is going through economic difficulties today and educational institutions are surly affected by them, and in terms of reducing operational costs while maintaining the quality of education, it is clear that Oracle Cloud Infrastructure cloud service provider is the preferred and most appropriate choice for Al-Madinah International University to operate and host its servers as a VPS service.

7 Conclusion

It has become difficult for cloud users to choose the best cloud service provider that suits the basic requirements of the organizations with the expansion of many cloud service providers in the technology world. The new user is unable to understand the quality of the basic features that are most important to his organization and thinks more about which company can best fit his organization's requirements among the broad and diverse service providers. This analysis and comparison study helps organizations in general and Al-Madinah International University in particular to choose the best and most appropriate cloud service provider in terms of cost of the VPS service while maintaining the quality of this service.

The future business will be more comprehensive and takes into consideration the reputation of cloud service providers, which contributes to high efficiency and trust. The purpose of this comparative study is to help companies used Virtual Private Servers service, especially Al-Madinah International University, in reducing the costs of this service by choosing the least expensive service provider for this service, in an attempt to meet the economic challenges that come with increasing obstacles and conditions that the world is going through in current time. Therefore, knowing more about the requirements of Al-Madinah International University to serve virtual servers to achieve the main objective of this thesis, which is to choose the least expensive cloud service provider while maintaining the same quality of this service.

8 Future Works

Choosing the best cloud service provider in terms of cost while maintaining the quality of the services provided enables companies and educational organization to reduce costs and save expenses. Moreover, the saved expenses and costs can be used to find other cloud services that benefit companies and organizations and raise their quality of the services which they provide. Therefore, the future work looks at developing an integrated plan to relocate all the VPSs of Al-Madinah International University which located in AWS from AWS to OCI, with adding the most important university systems such as human resources management system and the financial system to VPS service with OCI cloud service provider.

References

1. Al Moaiad, Y., Abu Bakar, Z., Al-Sammarraie, N.A.: Prioritization tool of Cloud Computing service provider based on user requirement. In: 2016 IEEE Conference on Open Systems (ICOS), Langkawi, Malaysia, pp. 36–412016. https://doi.org/10.1109/ICOS.2016.7881985
2. Rashid, A., Chaturvedi, A.: Cloud computing characteristics and services: a brief review. Int. J. Comput. Sci. Eng. 7(2), 421–426 (2019)
3. Malik, M.I., Wani, S.H., Rashid, A.: Cloud computing-technologies. Int. J. Adv. Res. Comput. Sci. 9(2) (2018)
4. Aljamal, R., El-Mousa, A., Jubair, F.: A comparative review of high-performance computing major cloud service providers, April 2018
5. Amazon Web Services: An Introduction to High Performance Computing on AWS. An Introduction to High Performance Computing on AWS, August 2015
6. Oracle. Oracle Cloud Infrastructure. https://cloud.oracle.com/. Accessed Mar 2019
7. Amazon Web Services: Amazon Aurora pricing (2017a). https://aws.amazon.com/rds/aurora/pricing/. Accessed Mar 2022
8. Amazon: "High-Performance Computing Lens, AWS Well-Architected Framework (2017)
9. Marathe, A., et al.: A comparative study of high-performance computing on the cloud. Presented at the Proceedings of the 22nd International Symposium on High performance Parallel and Distributed Computing, New York, New York, USA (2013)

10. Haji, L.M., Ahmad, O.M., Zeebaree, S.R., Dino, H.I., Zebari, R.R., Shukur, H.M.: Impact of cloud computing and internet of things on the future internet. Tech. Rep. Kansai Univ. **62**(5), 2179–2190 (2020)
11. Jader, O.H., Zeebaree, S.R., Zebari, R.R.: A state of art survey for web server performance measurement and load balancing mechanisms. Int. J. Sci. Technol. Res. **8**(12), 535–543 (2019)
12. Miyachi, C.: What is "Cloud"? It is time to update the NIST definition? IEEE Cloud Comput. **3**, 6–11 (2018)
13. Moaiad, Y.A., Bakar, Z.A., Al-Sammarraie, N.A.: Constructing dynamic infrastructure as a service model (diaas) according to user preferences. In: Yacob, N., Mohd Noor, N., Mohd Yunus, N., Lob Yussof, R., Zakaria, S. (eds.) Regional Conference on Science, Technology and Social Sciences (RCSTSS 2016). Springer, Singapore, pp. 185–194 (2018). https://doi.org/10.1007/978-981-13-0074-5_17
14. Privacy and security, and examples of such type of cloud include RedHat and Seagate (Birje, Challagidad, Goudar, & Tapale, 2017)
15. Modi, C., Patel, D., Borisaniya, B., Patel, A., Rajarajan, M.: A survey on security issues and solutions at different layers of Cloud computing. J. Supercomput. **63**(2), 561–592 (2013)
16. Ali, M., Khan, S.U., Vasilakos, A.V.: Security in cloud computing: opportunities and challenges. Inf. Sci. **305**, 357–383 (2015)
17. Thakur, N., Bisen, D., Rohit, V., Gupta, N.: Review on cloud computing: issues, services and models. Int. J. Comput. Appl. **91**(9), 34–39 (2014)
18. Diaby, T., Rad, B.B.: Cloud computing: a review of the concepts and deployment models. Int. J. Inf. Technol. Comput. Sci. **9**(6), 50–58 (2017)
19. Sackey, F.N.A.: Strategies to Manage Cloud Computing Operational Costs (Doctoral dissertation, Walden University) (2018)
20. Soni, A., Hasan, M.: Pricing schemes in cloud computing: a review. Int. J. Adv. Comput. Res. **7**(29), 60 (2017)
21. Hummaida, A.R., Paton, N.W., Sakellariou, R.: Adaptation in cloud resource configuration: a survey. J. Cloud Comput. **5**(7), 1–16 (2016). https://doi.org/10.1186/s13677-016-0057-9
22. Singh, H.: Using CloudWatch with SageMaker. In Practical Machine Learning with AWS, pp. 155–165. Apress, Berkeley, CA (2021)
23. Kumar, D., Baranwal, G., Raza, Z., Vidyarthi, D.P.: A survey on spot pricing in cloud computing. J. Netw. Syst. Manage. **26**(4), 809–856 (2018)
24. AWS: (2019a). Overview of amazon web services. https://d1.awsstatic.com/whitepapers/aws-overview.pdf
25. Jakóbczyk, M.T.: Practical Oracle Cloud infrastructure. J. Syst. Softw. **103**(2015), 167–181 (2020)
26. Oracle Cloud Infrastructure: Overview of Object Storage (2022c). Accessed 21 Mar 2022

Elevating Database Performance: Current Caching and Prefetching Strategies for Online Databases in Nigeria

Olatunji Austine Kehinde[1], Zahidah Zulkifli[2]([⊠]), Ely Salwana Mat Surin[3], Nur Leyni Nilam Putri Junurham[1], and Murni Mahmud[2]

[1] Department of Library and Information Science, Kulliyyah of Information and Communication Technology, International Islamic University Malaysia, Kuala Lumpur, Malaysia
[2] Department of Information Systems, Kulliyyah of Information and Communication Technology, International Islamic University Malaysia, Kuala Lumpur, Malaysia
zahidahz@iium.edu.my
[3] Institute of Visual Informatics, Universiti Kebangsaan Malaysia, Bangi, Malaysia

Abstract. This study investigated caching and prefetching techniques to improve data access performance in online databases, considering factors like data popularity, access patterns, and cache coherence. The research design adopted for this study was the descriptive survey. The population comprised of 1387 undergraduates computer science students in public tertiary institutions in Ekiti State. Simple random sampling technique was adopted to select 150 computer science students from three public tertiary institutions in the study area. The instrument used for data collection was a structured 4 Likert type questionnaire. The questionnaire was distributed to the respondents to find out the effectiveness of caching and prefetching techniques on online database. The instrument was both face and content validated by two experts from department of computer science in Bamidele Olumilua University of Education Science and Technology, Ikere-Ekiti, Ekiti State. The reliability of the instrument was ensured using Pearson Product Moment Correlation formula which yielded a coefficient of 0.97. The data collected were analyzed using descriptive statistics such as mean and standard deviation. The result showed that the current caching and prefetching techniques employed in online databases are highly effective; the different access patterns have effect on the effectiveness of caching and prefetching techniques in online databases and there are impacts of cache coherence mechanisms on the efficiency of caching and prefetching techniques in online databases. It was therefore recommended that the inclusion of caching and prefetching in curriculum is important across all educational level in Nigeria. In addition, caching and perfecting has come under fire for focusing mostly on computer science.

Keywords: Caching · Prefetching · Online Database · Online Database Performance

H. Badioze Zaman et al. (Eds.): IVIC 2023, LNCS 14322, pp. 314–327, 2024.
https://doi.org/10.1007/978-981-99-7339-2_27

1 Introduction

Information communication technology (ICT) has revolutionized the dissemination and flow of information, making it unrestricted by any boundaries Dar, Sharma, Srivastava, and Sakalle [6]. Therefore, with the advent of technology, the use of online databases has become increasingly important in academic research across the globe. Hence, it is important for universities in Nigeria and southwest in particular, to provide access to online databases to enhance teaching, learning, and research activities. Online databases have gained popularity among librarians and users due to their speed, flexibility, wide range, and currency. These databases are accessible worldwide and crucial for tertiary students, providing access to information resources and engaging in learning processes without physical constraints. Digital libraries have transformed the internet into an essential platform for academic research Akinola, et al., [2]; Hourcade, et al., [20]; Lesk, [24]. Therefore, with the increasing availability of online databases, students can conveniently access a wide range of information remotely, enabling them to solve academic tasks, conduct research, and enhance their knowledge Kumar [39].

As a result, university libraries have made significant investments in online database subscriptions, aiming to provide students with unrestricted access to these invaluable resources, regardless of their geographical location Nwokedi, Nwokedi, Chollom, and Adah, [29]. However, the exponential growth of data and the escalating demand for real-time access to information have presented significant challenges for online databases. One of the critical challenges is ensuring efficient data access performance, as it directly influences the overall efficiency and user experience of online applications. To effectively optimize data access performance in online databases, it is necessary to consider several factors including data popularity, access patterns, and cache coherence.

Data popularity, which refers to the frequency of data items being accessed, plays a significant role in determining which data should be cached or prefetched. Though, distributed systems offer a valuable approach to address the challenges posed by large-scale applications that generate massive volumes of data, if data reliability, availability, accessibility, and fault tolerance together with reduced data access time and network traffic will be achieve, the replication of data across diverse locations within the system should be overlook Hamdeni, Hamrouni and Charrada, [18]. Therefore, by prioritizing popular data, the system can better anticipate and meet user demands, leading to improved overall performance.

Access patterns also play a crucial role in understanding how data is accessed in online databases. Analyzing the patterns of user queries and transactions can help identify recurring sequences and dependencies in data access. This knowledge can be leveraged to design efficient caching and prefetching strategies that align with these access patterns, further enhancing the performance of the database.

Another crucial consideration is cache coherence, which ensures that multiple cache copies of the same data item remain consistent. In online databases, where multiple users may concurrently access and modify shared data, maintaining cache coherence becomes vital. By implementing appropriate mechanisms, such as cache invalidation or data synchronization protocols, conflicts and inconsistencies can be minimized, leading to a more reliable and efficient data access environment.

2 Background of Problems

Online databases are crucial in academic research environments, with high-performing databases significantly impacting application performance. Challenges like query processing speed, scalability costs, and data accessibility complicate achieving an optimized balance. Similarly, the speed gap between processors and memories has led to the use of cache memories to meet data demands. Multiple levels of cache are implemented to mitigate long memory latencies, benefiting programmes that efficiently utilize the cache. However, programmes accessing large data sets or inefficiently using the cache suffer performance losses. Memory prefetching, a technique to enhance performance, involves fetching data into the cache before it is needed to avoid cache misses. Efficient prefetching techniques are crucial for modern computer architectures, ensuring improved performance in high-performance and power-constrained systems. It is against this backdrop that this study is set to investigate caching and prefetching techniques to improve data access performance in online databases, considering factors like data popularity, access patterns, and cache coherence.

A database is an organized set of data stored on a computer for easy accessibility and search ability. It is a computer-based record-keeping system that records and retains information in a timely manner, enabling individuals to access quick information. Databases consist of serviceable raw data, such as physical properties, statistical or numerical data, bibliographical information, and non-bibliographical information. Each field contains words and numbers, allowing for easy searches in specific fields. Databases are set up with a single software programme that provides access to all data for all users Upadhyay and Deepmala [9].

Prefetching is a proactive strategy that involves moving data to higher cache levels, anticipating its future use Payami [34]. Data and instruction prefetching are crucial techniques for optimizing computer system performance. Data prefetching involves diverse techniques, while instruction prefetching often relies on branch prediction. Both techniques can be achieved through software, hardware, or a combination of both, each offering its own advantages and disadvantages Payami [34]; Nyholm [31].

Delagi, Glasco and Flynn [10] in a study titled 'update-based cache coherence protocols for scalable shared-memory multiprocessors' two hardware-controlled update-based cache coherence protocols were presented. The study discussed the two major disadvantages of the update protocols: inefficiency of updates and the mismatch between the granularity of synchronization and the data transfer. The study also presented two enhancements to the update-based protocols, a write combining scheme and a finer grain synchronization, to overcome these disadvantages. The results demonstrate the effectiveness of these enhancements that, when used together, allow the update-based protocols to significantly improve the execution time of a set of scientific applications when compared to three invalidate-based protocol. Similarly, Hakan and Per [17] agreed in the study titled an adaptive update-based cache coherence protocol for reduction of miss rate and traffic that coherence misses limit the processor usage even though directory-based write-invalidate cache coherence methods have the ability to enhance the performance of large-scale multiprocessors.

As a result, so-called competitive-update protocols, which are hybrid write-invalidate/write-update protocols, have been investigated as a way to lower the coherence miss rate and have been proven to be a better coherence policy for a variety of applications. Sadly, these approaches may result in substantial traffic spikes for applications that frequently use migratory items. If the network bandwidth is insufficient, these traffic peaks may cancel out the performance benefit of a decreased miss rate. In this paper, they suggested extending a competitive-update protocol with an adaptive technique that has been previously published and may dynamically identify migrating items and lessen the coherence traffic they generate. The miss rate and bandwidth need of this adaptive protocol can be reduced by as much as 71% and 26%, respectively, compared to a write-invalidate approach, according to thorough architecture simulations based on five scientific and engineering applications.

3 Related Work

Prefetching technology is divided into heuristic prefetching and reasoning prefetching. Heuristic prefetching technology is inspiring by analyzing the history of file access, in which to find the data access patterns, and establish a file access sequence model as a basis for data prefetching. Reasoning prefetching technology is inferencing based on relevant information and rules provided by the upper application. It detects the data it needs in advance and read it into the buffer. For the cloud storage system, the upper application is transparent to it, so the heuristic prefetching technology has been widely studied and used (Hamdeni, Hamrouni and Charrada, [18]; Payami, [34]). Heuristic prefetching algorithms are roughly divided into methods based on timing analysis and data mining based methods. Timing analysis method is the most widely used based on Markov chain model, which basic idea is to use the file as a state, the file access process is abstracted as a probability matrix, and to predict the next file access in turn.

Block-level prefetching is relatively simple and easy to implement. It does not require sophisticated prediction models and is often used in underlying storage systems. File-level prefetching requires strong dependencies between files access, or it will exacerbate I/O stress and pollute caches. The upper layer of cloud storage system is often a public user, user's access often has behavioral regularity, and Kroeger et al.'s research proves that access rule between files exists. Access patterns can be found out by analyzing and mining the access sequence. For small files, the random read on disk can be transferred into sequential read through the file relevance prefetching. It can greatly improve the efficiency of file reading. The disadvantages of these methods lie in inefficiency of updates and the mismatch between the granularity of synchronization and the data transfer.

The caching and prefetching strategies for online database is to discover the potential rules from a large number of access records and generate a pattern library, which can be used as a prediction of future file access. For cache strategy, the throughput of sequential access is much higher than random access. If the files that are relevant to the access can be centralized in one file (cache), disk pressure can be effectively alleviated by prefetching data since random accesses are changed to sequential accesses. Efficient prefetching techniques are crucial for modern computer architectures, ensuring improved performance in high-performance and power-constrained systems through high popularity, access pattern and data coherence.

4 Methodology

This section deals with the application of survey design of the descriptive type. A descriptive survey seeks to find out certain facts concerning an existing phenomenon. The details of survey design of the descriptive type are also discussed below:

Survey design can be described as an outline, a general arrangement or plan from which something is observe and may be made. According to Nworgu [30] a research survey design is a plan or blue print which specifies how data relating to a given problem should be collected and analysed. To this regard, this method of inquiring has become a popular research methodology since the 1990s and it was widely used in educational research and within that field, there are several well documented standards to support its use.

The population comprised of 1387 undergraduates computer science students in public tertiary institutions in Ekiti State. Simple random sampling technique was adopted to select 150 students from three public tertiary institutions in the study area. The instrument used for data collection was a structured 4 Likert type questionnaire. The questionnaire was titled "Database Performance: Current Caching and Prefetching Strategies for Online Databases in Nigeria" (DPCCPSODN) and divided into two sections. Section A contains item designed to obtain personal data about respondents while section B was designed to answer research questions for the study. The respondents were guided to respond to each item thus: SA-Strongly Agree (4); A - Agree (3); D - Disagree (2) and SD - Strongly Disagree (1). Also, HE - Highly Effective (4), ME - Moderately Effective (3), LE – Low Effect (2) and NE - Not Effective (1).

The questionnaire provided five (5) different items on question 1 to question 4 that require the respondents to tick one out of four options on how effective are the current caching and prefetching techniques employed in online databases; how different access patterns affect the effectiveness of caching and prefetching techniques in online databases; the impacts of cache coherence mechanisms on the efficiency of caching and prefetching techniques in online databases and how novel caching and prefetching techniques be designed to optimize data access performance in online databases, considering factors such as data popularity, access patterns, and cache coherence.

The questionnaire was distributed to the respondents to find out the effectiveness of caching and prefetching techniques on online database. The instrument was both face and content validated by two experts from department of computer science in Bamidele Olumilua University of Education Science and Technology, Ikere-Ekiti, Ekiti State, Nigeria. The reliability of the instrument was ensured using Pearson Product Moment Correlation formula which yielded a coefficient of 0.97.

The data collected were analyzed using descriptive statistics such as mean and standard deviation. The mean decision value was calculated thus: ($\frac{4+3+2+1}{4} = \frac{10}{4} = 2.5$). The mean values greater than or equal to 2.50 indicated "Agreed" by the respondents to the statement in question, otherwise "Disagree".

5   Results and Discussion

5.1   Results

There are 4 Questions has been asked during the survey. The details of the questions and results are as follows:

Question1: How effective are the current caching and prefetching techniques employed in online databases?

Table 1. Effectiveness of caching and prefetching techniques on online database

No	Items	Mean	Standard Deviation	Decision
1	Caching and prefetching techniques are effective as they increase performance by decreasing access time for obtaining data	3.05	1.19	Effective
2	Caching and prefetching techniques are effective as they help in retaining frequently accessed data within memory	3.03	0.89	Effective
3	Caching and prefetching techniques are effective as they help to cut down the number of times that a hard drive must be accessed or a network connection utilized	3.43	0.80	Effective
4	Caching and prefetching techniques are effective as they help in storing data retrieved from queries that may be needed again	3.32	0.78	Effective
5	Data is retained from across multiple HTTP request and can be reused without incurring additional access time	3.27	0.89	Effective
	Grand Mean	3.25	0.87	Agreed

Note: Mean greater than 2.50 'Effective' otherwise 'Not Effective'

Question 2: How do different access patterns affect the effectiveness of caching and prefetching techniques in online databases?

Table 2. Effect of different access patterns on effectiveness of caching and prefetching in online database

No	Items	Mean	Standard Deviation	Decision
1	Access pattern improves object layout and increase the effectiveness of caching and prefetching in online database	3.22	0.82	Agreed
2	Access pattern reduces the number of cache misses by prefetching future memory references based on the similarity of access pattern among memory page	3.21	0.83	Agreed
3	Access pattern keeps track of previous accesses to line in hot pages	3.27	0.83	Agreed
4	Access pattern increases the amount of memory level parallelism	2.97	0.92	Agreed
5	Access pattern increases availability by storing data in a faster and more accessible location	3.33	0.97	Agreed
	Grand Mean	3.09	0.93	Agreed

Note: Mean greater than 2.50 'Agreed' otherwise 'Disagreed'

Question 3: What are the impacts of cache coherence mechanisms on the efficiency of caching and prefetching techniques in online databases?

Table 3. Impact of cache coherence mechanisms on the efficiency of caching and prefetching techniques in online databases

No	Items	Mean	Standard Deviation	Decision
1	Cache coherence mechanism keeps track of where each copy of each shared data block is located and stores it in a directory	3.84	0.99	Agreed
2	Cache coherence is as a result of each CPU has its own private data cache, a similar duplicate of the shared memory location which help to present simultaneously in multiple caches	3.88	1.12	Agreed
3	Cache coherence mechanism enables recently used local variables to enter the proper cache and remain there through numerous reads and writes while using the protocol to maintain consistency of shared variables that may be present in multiple caches concurrently	3.31	0.86	Agreed
4	Cache coherence mechanism enables all processors to update to the new value updated by the new processor	3.21	0.82	Agreed
5	Cache coherence mechanism guarantee that any new value is broadcast to all processors	3.17	0.98	Agreed
	Grand Mean	3.48	0.95	Agreed

Note: Mean greater than or equal to 2.50 'Agreed' otherwise 'Disagreed'

Question 4: How can novel caching and prefetching techniques be designed to optimize data access performance in online databases, considering factors such as data popularity, access patterns, and cache coherence?

Table 4. Design of novel caching and prefetching techniques to optimize data access performance in online databases

No	Items	Mean	Standard Deviation	Decision
1	Propose a cost-based caching model where different costs will be incurred depending on whether a missed data item is prefetched or fetched	3.35	0.86	Agreed
2	Formulate or reformulate the optimal caching and prefetching problem in as a mini-cost flow problem	3.44	0.80	Agreed
3	Analytically characterised the optimal policy by providing sufficient condition under which prefetching the missed data is the optimal choice	3.99	0.77	Agreed
4	Propose a lightweight "look-ahead" approximation policy based on the insights revealed by the characteristics of the optimal policy	3.04	1.16	Agreed
5	Conduct extensive experiment using CND traces and synthetic data requests that are generated from both heavy and light-tailed popularity distribution	3.94	0.78	Agreed
	Grand Mean	3.64	0.98	Agreed

Note: Mean greater than or equal to 2.50 'Agreed' otherwise 'Disagreed'

5.2 Discussion

The result of analysis presented in Table 1 revealed how effective the current caching and prefetching techniques employed in online databases are. The mean values in the table ranges from 3.03 to 3.43 and they are greater than 2.50 which indicated that majority of the respondents agreed that the current caching and prefetching techniques employed in online databases are highly effective. This implies that caching and prefetching techniques increase performance by decreasing access time for obtaining data (3.05), caching and prefetching techniques help in retaining frequently accessed data within memory (3.03), caching and prefetching techniques help to cut down the number of times that a hard drive must be accessed or a network connection utilized (3.43), caching and prefetching techniques help in storing data retrieved from queries that may be needed again (3.32) and data is retained from across multiple HTTP request and can be reused without incurring additional access time (3.27). The grand mean (3.25) in the table is greater than 2.50 which confirmed the fact that the current caching and prefetching techniques employed in online databases are highly effective. This finding is similar to the finding of Waleed, Siti & Abdul [41] that caching and prefetching are two effective solutions to lessen Web service bottleneck, reduce traffic over the internet and improve scalability of the Web system.

The result of analysis presented in Table 2 revealed how different access patterns affect the effectiveness of caching and prefetching techniques in online databases. The mean values in the table ranges from 2.97 to 3.33 and they are greater than 2.50 which indicated that majority of the respondents agreed with the statement in item 1–5 of table two. This implies that access pattern improves object layout and increase the effectiveness of caching and prefetching in online database (3.22), access pattern reduces the number of cache misses by prefetching future memory references based on the similarity of access pattern among memory page (3.21), Access pattern keeps track of previous accesses to line in hot pages (3.27), Access pattern increases the amount of memory level parallelism (2.97) and access pattern increases availability by storing data in a faster and more accessible location (3.33).The grand mean (3.09) in the table is greater than 2.50 which implies that the different access patterns has effect on the effectiveness of caching and prefetching techniques in online databases. This result correlate with Waleed, Siti & Abdul [41] that access patterns affect the effectiveness of caching and prefetching techniques since the Web proxy caching exploits the temporal locality and the web prefetching utilizes the spatial locality of the Web objects, Web proxy caching and prefetching can complement each other. Thus, combination of the caching and the prefetching helps on improving hit ratio and reducing the user-perceived latency.

The result of analysis presented in Table 3 revealed impacts of cache coherence mechanisms on the efficiency of caching and prefetching techniques in online databases. The mean values in the table ranges from 3.17 to 3.88 and they are greater than 2.50 which indicated that majority of the respondents agreed with the statement in item 1–5 of table three. This implies that cache coherence mechanism keeps track of where each copy of each shared data block is located and stores it in a directory (3.84), cache coherence is as a result of each CPU has its own private data cache, a similar duplicate of the shared memory location which help to present simultaneously in multiple caches (3.88), cache coherence mechanism enables recently used local variables to enter the proper cache and remain there through numerous reads and writes while using the protocol to maintain consistency of shared variables that may be present in multiple caches concurrently (3.31), cache coherence mechanism enables all processors to update to the new value updated by the new processor (3.21) and Cache coherence mechanism guarantee that any new value is broadcast to all processors (3.17). The grand mean value (3.48) in the table is also greater than 2.50 which indicated that there are impacts of cache coherence mechanisms on the efficiency of caching and prefetching techniques in online databases. This implies that the coherence of caching and prefetching strategies can potentially improve latency up to 60%, whereas caching strategy alone improves the latency up to 26%. Keycdn [22] suggested an application of web log mining to obtain web-document access patterns and used these patterns to extend the well-known GDSF caching policies and prefetching policies.

The result of analysis presented in Table 4 revealed how novel caching and prefetching techniques be designed to optimize data access performance in online databases. The mean values in the table ranges from 3.04 to 3.99 and they are greater than 2.50 which indicated that majority of the respondents agreed with the statement in item 1–5 of table four. This implies that novel caching and prefetching techniques can be designed by proposing a cost-based caching model where different costs will be incurred depending on whether a missed data item is prefetched or fetched (3.35), formulating or reformulating the optimal caching and prefetching problem in as a mini-cost flow problem (3.44), analytically characterised the optimal policy by providing sufficient condition under which prefetching the missed data is the optimal choice (3.99), proposing a lightweight "look-ahead" approximation policy based on the insights revealed by the characteristics of the optimal policy (3.04) and conducting extensive experiment using CND traces and synthetic data requests that are generated from both heavy and light-tailed popularity distribution (3.94). The grand mean value (3.64) in the table is greater than 2.50 which justified the claims. This implies that the combination of the web caching and the web prefetching doubles the performance compared to single caching which enhance data access performance in online databases.

Even though there has been development in the field of data caching and fetching, the inclusion of data popularity, access pattern and cache coherence mechanisms on caching and prefetching in curriculum is important across all educational level in Nigeria. In addition, caching and perfecting has come under fire for focusing mostly on computer science.

6 Contribution to Body of Knowledge

The study contribute to the body of knowledge by introducing a novel relevancy-based replacement policy to replace the caches of data nodes and global cache node whenever there is a need to create space for storing the incoming patterns. This will improve the effectiveness of data popularity, data access pattern and cache coherence mechanism in the field of research work.

7 Conclusion

Based on the finding of the study, it was concluded that the current caching and prefetching techniques employed in online databases are highly effective. This is because they increase performance by decreasing access time for obtaining data, they help in retaining frequently accessed data within memory, they help to cut down the number of times that a hard drive must be accessed or a network connection utilized, they help in storing data retrieved from queries that may be needed again and data is retained from across multiple HTTP request and can be reused without incurring additional access time.

The study also concluded that the different access patterns have effect on the effectiveness of caching and prefetching techniques in online databases. There are impacts of cache coherence mechanisms on the efficiency of caching and prefetching techniques in online databases.

Even though there has been development in the field of data caching and fetching, the inclusion of caching and prefetching in curriculum is important across all educational level in Nigeria. In addition, caching and perfecting has come under fire for focusing mostly on computer science.

References

1. Ajala, O.: Design and implementation of an improved electronic document management system being a submitted dessertation in partial fulfillment of higher degree (2015). https://www.academia.edu/34539436/

2. Akinola, A., Shorunke, O., Ajayi, S. A.: Awareness and use of electronic database by postgraduates in University of Ibadan (2018). https://www.researchgate.net/publication/329556980

3. Baba, M.A., Yusuf, A., Maijama'a, L., Ahmad, A.: Performance analysis of the encryption algorithms as solution to cloud database security. Int. J. Comput. Appl. **99**(14), 21–31 (2014)

4. Cucchiara, et al.: Temporal analysis of cache prefetching strategies for multimedia applications (2001). https://www.researchgate.net/publication/3895113

5. Daniel, G., Sunyé, G., Cabot, J.: PrefetchML: a framework for prefetching and caching models (2017). https://hal.science/hal-01362149/document

6. Dar, S.A., Sharma, R., Srivastava, V., Sakalle, U.K.: Investigation on the electronic structure, optical, elastic, mechanical, thermodynamic and thermoelectric properties of wide band gap semiconductor double perovskite Ba_2InTaO_6. RSC Adv. **9**(17), 9522–9532 (2019)

7. Lilja, D.J.: Cache coherence in large-scale shared memory multiprocessors: issues and comparisons. ACM Comput. Surv. **25**(3), 303–338 (1993)

8. Lilja, D.J., Marcovitz, D.M., Yew, P.-C.: Memory Referencing Behavior and a Cache Performance Metric in a Shared Memory Multiprocessor, Center for Supercomputing Research and Development Report No. 836, University of Illinois, Urbana (1989)

9. Deepmala, A.K.U., Sharma, P.K.: Online data bases: a review of literature. Ilkogretim Online **19**(4), 7111–7123 (2020)

10. Delagi, B.A., Glasco, D.B., Flynn, M.J.: Update-based cache coherence protocols for scalable shared-memory multiprocessors (1993). https://www.researchgate.net/publication/2575854

11. Diao, Y., et al.: Comparative studies of load balancing with control and optimization techniques (2005)

12. Gustafsson, E., Nilbert, B.: Cache coherence in parallel Multiprocessors, Uppsala 24th February 1997, Department of Computer Science, Uppsala University (1997)

13. Enteriscloud: Cloud database vs Traditional Database (2023). https://enteriscloud.com/cloud-database-vs-traditional-database/

14. Fang, J., Xu, Y., Kong, H., Cai, M.: A prefetch control strategy based on improved hill-climbing method in asymmetric multi-core architecture. J. Supercomput. **79**(10), 10570–10588 (2023). https://doi.org/10.1007/s11227-023-05078-6

15. Fortinet: What is Catching Data? (2023). https://www.fortinet.com/resources/cyberglossary/caching#:~:text=Caching%20Data%20is%20a%20process,they%20can%20be%20accessed%20faster

16. Pfister, F., et al.: The IBM research parallel processor prototype (RP3): introduction and architecture. In: International Conference on Parallel Processing, pp. 764–771 (1985)

17. Hakan, G., Per. S.: An adaptive update-based cache coherence protocol for reduction of miss rate and traffic (2005). https://www.researchgate.net/publication/220759002

18. Hamdeni, C., Hamrouni, T., Charrada, F.B.: Adaptive measurement method for data popularity in distributive systems (2016). https://www.researchgate.net/publication/308278613

19. Hasslinger, G., Okhovatzadeh, M., Ntougias, K., Hasslinger, F., Hohlfeld, O.: An overview of analysis methods and evaluation results for caching strategies. Comput. Netw. **228**, 109583 (2023)

20. Hourcade, J.P., Bederson, B.B., Druin, A., Rose, A., Farber, A., Takayama, Y.: The international children's digital library: viewing digital books online. Interact. Comput. **15**(2), 151–167 (2003)

21. Hennessy, J., Patterson, D.: Computer Architecture: A Quantitative Approach, 5th edn. Morgan Kaufmann (2011)
22. Keycdn, N.D.: What is Prefetching and Why Use It (2023). https://www.keycdn.com/support/prefetching
23. Khan, M.: Optimizing performance in highly utilized multicores with intelligent prefetching. In: Digital Comprehensive Summaries of Uppsala Dissertations from the Faculty of Science and Technology 1335, 54 p. Acta Universitatis Upsaliensis, Uppsala (2016). ISBN 978-91-554-9450-6
24. Lesk, M.: Understanding Digital Libraries. Elsevier (2005)
25. Marcelo, F.: Data access patterns: the features of the main data access patterns applied in software industry (2019). https://medium.com/mastering-software-engineering/data-access-patterns-the-features-of-the-main-data-access-patterns-applied-in-software-industry-6eff86906b4e
26. Marty, M.R.: Cache Coherence Techniques For Multicore Processors being a dissertation submitted in partial fulfilment of the requirements for the degree of Doctor of Philosophy (Computer Sciences) (2008). https://research.cs.wisc.edu/multifacet/theses
27. Dubois, M., Scheurich, C., Briggs, F.A.: Synchronization, coherence, and event ordering in multiprocessors. Computer 21(2), 9–21 (1988)
28. Naeem, M.A., Rehmat, M.A., Kim, B.: A comparative performance analysis of popularity-based caching strategies in named data networking (2020). https://ieeexplore.ieee.org/stamp/stamp.jsp?arnumber=9034036
29. Nwokedi, V.C., Nwokedi, G.I., Chollom, K.M., Adah, J.E.: Assessment of online usage patterns of Elsevier database amongst academics of Environmental Sciences, University of Jos (2017)
30. Nworgu, B.G.: Research design, population sampling and data collection (1991). https://www.cram.com/essay/Research-Design-Population-Sampling-And-Data-Collection/FJPCYAK46R
31. Nyholm, G.: Evaluation of memory prefetching techniques for modem applications. Master of Science Thesis, Electrical Engineering Department, Linköping University (2022)
32. Oliver, R.L., Teller, P.J.: Dynamic and adaptive cache prefetch policies (2000)
33. Patterson, R.H, Gibson, G.A., Ginting, E., Stodolsky, D., Zelenka, J.: Informed prefetching and caching. In: Advanced Prefetching and Caching of Models with PrefetchML, vol. 35 (1995)
34. Payami, M.: Instruction prefetching techniques for ultra low-power multicore architectures. Master Thesis, Alma Mater Studiorum - Università Di Bologna (2016)
35. PhoenixNAP: What is distributed database? (2021). https://phoenixnap.com/kb/distributed-database
36. Biswas, P.: What is the cache coherence problem in distributed systems? How can it be overcome? (2023). https://www.quora.com/What-is-the-cache-coherence-problem-in-distributed-systems-How-can-it-be-overcome
37. Ramadan, E., Babaie, P., Zhang, Z.-L.: Performance estimation and evaluation framework for caching policies in hierarchical caches. J. Comput. Commun. 144, 44–56 (2019). https://www.sciencedirect.com/science/article/abs/pii/S0140366419303524
38. Roland, L.L.: The effectiveness of caches and data prefetch buffers in large-scale shared memory multiprocessors (1987). Abstract retrieved from https://dl.acm.org/doi/10.5555/913856
39. Roy, P., Kumar, S., Satija, M.P.: Problems in searching online databases: a case study of select central university libraries in India. DESIDOC J. Libr. Inf. Technol. 32(1), 59–63 (2012)
40. Podlipnig, S., Böszörmenyi, L.: A survey of web cache replacement strategies. ACM Comput. Surv. 35(4), 374–398 (2003)

41. Waleed, A., Siti, M.S., Abudul, S.I.: A survey of web caching and prefetching a survey of web caching and prefetching (2011). https://www.researchgate.net/publication/265986051
42. The web largest resources for definitions and translations (2023): Definitions retrieved from https://www.definitions.net/definition/online+database

Exploring Data Wiping Practices in the Royal Malaysian Air Force (RMAF) HQ

Syed Nasir Alsagoff Bin Syed Zakaria$^{(\boxtimes)}$, Kuan Fook Chao$^{(\boxtimes)}$, and Zuraini Zainol$^{(\boxtimes)}$

Department of Computer Science, Faculty of Defense Science and Technology,
Universiti Pertahanan Nasional Malaysia, Kem Sungai Besi, 57000 Kuala Lumpur, Malaysia
{syednasir,3221735,zuraini}@upnm.edu.my

Abstract. Data wiping is a very important part of cybersecurity. It is the act of deleting data so that it cannot be recovered. The Royal Malaysian Air Force (RMAF) as part of the Malaysian Armed Forces (MAF) has also recognized the importance of data wiping in safeguarding national security. Senior staff officers at the RMAF headquarters, Ministry of Defence (MINDEF), are given laptops for work-related purposes. As such, the laptops might contain secret and top-secret work-related documents. When the officer is posted out from MINDEF, laptops will have to be returned. Malaysia is experiencing rapid economic growth and digital transformation, but it faces cybersecurity challenges that threaten its stability. Cyber threats come from various sources, leading to data breaches and other incidents. Data wiping, the secure erasure of data from storage devices, is crucial for protecting sensitive information. The Personal Data Protection Act (PDPA) requires organizations to implement data erasure measures. This paper aims to explore the current data wiping practices in the RMAF.

Keywords: Data Wiping · Secret · Military · Cybers threats

1 Introduction

Cyber threats in Malaysia come from various sources, including hackers, cybercriminals, state-sponsored actors, and insiders. These threats can lead to data breaches, identity theft, financial fraud, espionage, and other cyber incidents that can have severe consequences for individuals, organizations, and the nation as a whole [1].

Data wiping is a critical security measure that can help to protect the data of the Malaysian Armed Forces (MAF) from cyber-attacks. Data wiping, also known as data sanitization, is a technique used to securely erase data from storage devices to ensure that it cannot be accessed or recovered by unauthorized individuals. The primary goal of data wiping is to overwrite the existing data with random or predefined patterns, making it irretrievable using standard data recovery methods [2].

The Personal Data Protection Act (PDPA) is one of the main data protection laws in Malaysia that governs the collection, processing, and handling of personal data. The PDPA requires organizations to implement appropriate measures to protect personal data, including ensuring that data is securely erased when it is no longer needed. Failure to comply with the PDPA can result in legal and financial consequences, including fines and imprisonment [3].

The MAF is also aware of how crucial data erasure is to maintaining national security. The MAF has implemented various policies and procedures for data wiping, including the use of advanced data wiping technologies and periodic audits of data wiping practices. However, despite the legal and institutional framework for data wiping in Malaysia, there are still challenges and gaps. Many organizations, including government agencies, private entities, and individuals, lack awareness, knowledge, and skills related to data wiping, resulting in inadequate or ineffective data wiping practices.

Therefore, there is a need for research on data wiping practices in Malaysia to identify gaps, challenges, and best practices, and propose recommendations to improve the effectiveness and compliance of data wiping practices. Such research can help mitigate cybersecurity risks, protect national security, comply with data protection regulations, maintain organizational reputation and trust, and advance knowledge and best practices in the field of cybersecurity.

In the Defence White Paper 2020, the Ministry of Defence emphasizes the need for a holistic approach to cybersecurity that encompasses various areas such as personnel, processes, and technology [4]. This includes adequately training personnel in cybersecurity best practices, as well as the development of robust policies and procedures for data protection, including the secure wiping of data. Proper data wiping is critical to preventing sensitive information from falling into the wrong hands, whether through malicious intent or accidental data breaches [5]. This is particularly important in the defence sector, where the loss of sensitive information could compromise national security and put lives at risk [6].

These measures include the use of specialized software and tools for data wiping, as well as the implementation of policies and procedures for the secure storage and disposal of sensitive information. The Ministry of Defence also conducts regular audits and assessments of its cybersecurity measures to ensure that they remain effective and up-to-date. In addition to these measures, the Ministry of Defence also emphasizes the need for ongoing cybersecurity education and training for all personnel, from senior leadership to frontline employees. This includes not only technical training on cybersecurity tools and procedures but also developing a culture of cybersecurity awareness and vigilance. Cybersecurity Malaysia is a government agency entrusted with the responsibility of protecting Malaysia's cyberspace and ensuring the safety and security of its digital infrastructure [7].

In August 2020, a report revealed that 70 sensitive Royal Malaysian Navy (RMN) documents were sold on the dark web, posing a significant risk to national security. The documents, which contained classified information such as ship logs and technical specifications of the naval vessels, were reportedly stolen by hackers or insiders who gained unauthorized access to RMN's computer systems [8].

The incident highlights the importance of effective cybersecurity measures, including data wiping, to prevent data breaches and cyber threats in the MAF. Data wiping is the secure deletion of data from storage devices to prevent unauthorized access and data recovery. In the case of the RMN, it is unclear if the data on the compromised systems was wiped, which could have potentially prevented the stolen data from being sold on the dark web [8].

This research aims to improve RMAF cybersecurity by ensuring that sensitive and confidential data is properly erased from storage devices, rendering it inaccessible to unauthorized individuals or entities. Enhancing data wiping practices can significantly reduce the risk of data breaches, identity theft, data leaks, and other cybersecurity incidents, which can have severe consequences for individuals, organizations, and the nation as a whole. To achieve this goal, the research will employ an appropriate approach to assess the awareness, knowledge, and practices of data wiping within the RMAF.

The rest of this paper is organized into several sections. Section 2 explores the concept of data wiping and prevalent techniques, as well as how the military handles data. Section 3 discusses the importance of Data Wiping in Cybersecurity. Section 4 discusses the current data wiping practices of the Royal Malaysian Air Force (RMAF). Finally, we conclude this paper with future work in Sect. 5.

2 Background and Related Work

In this section, some background information on data wiping practices is discussed.

2.1 Data Wiping

Data wiping is considered as one of the anti-forensic techniques. On the other hand, data sanitization, also known as data wiping, is a method used to ensure that unauthorised individuals do not have access to the deleted data [2]. This process overwrites the existing data with random or meaningless information, making it unrecoverable even with advanced forensic techniques [9]. This is crucial to prevent unauthorized access to sensitive information and to ensure data privacy and security [10]. Proper deletion of data wiping is crucial for compliance with data protection regulations. There are two main approaches of data wiping: (i) partition wiping and (ii) file wiping.

- Partition Wiping: This approach focuses on wiping an entire partition on a storage device. It involves the following aspects:

  a. NTFS Volume Boot Record (VBR): The first case of partition wiping relates to the VBR, which is a structure in the header of the NTFS file system. Some partition wiping tools create the VBR structure after the wiping process. If the wiping tool does not generate the VBR, the partition is considered unusable and requires formatting to be used again.

  b. Overwritten Data Type: The second case of partition wiping is related to the type of data overwritten during the process. Different data sanitization standards may be implemented in various ways. Some methods use a random pattern, while others utilize a random specific hex value. The choice of approach can affect the entropy values of the overwritten data. Random patterns yield higher entropy values closer to one, whereas a focus on specific random values yields entropy values closer to zero.

- File wiping is considered one of the basic and fundamental techniques for preserving privacy and ensuring data security. It involves overwriting the data within individual files to make them unrecoverable [11]. It includes the following considerations:

  a. File Types: File wiping encompasses three types of files. The first type is the file itself, which contains both file system metadata and actual data. These files can be checked by both the Windows Operating System and file wiping tools.
  b. Deleted File Metadata: The second type consists of files that appear as deleted in the Master File Table (MFT) entry but still retain recoverable data. Although these files are not visible in the Windows OS, file wiping tools or digital forensic tools can identify them. By applying data sanitization standards, the actual data of these files can be changed to a non-recoverable state.
  c. Deleted File Metadata: The second type consists of files that appear as deleted in the Master File Table (MFT) entry but still retain recoverable data. Although these files are not visible in the Windows OS, file wiping tools or digital forensic tools can identify them. By applying data sanitization standards, the actual data of these files can be changed to a non-recoverable state.
  d. Overwritten Metadata and Data: The last type includes areas where both the metadata and actual data of a file are overwritten, including slack areas. Even in these areas, fragments of data may be recoverable. However, a file wiping tool can use data sanitization standards to overwrite the remaining data in the slack area, making it non-recoverable [12].

There are several methods available to ensure the secure disposal of information. Three common methods are discussed in this section: Clear, Purge and Destroy [19]. To determine the appropriate method, users should consider the type of information, the storage medium, the risk to confidentiality, and future plans for the media. Factors such as cost and environmental impact should also be considered when assessing the selected method. The goal is to choose a sanitization method that effectively mitigates the risk of unauthorized disclosure of information [13]. NIST provides guidelines and standards for secure data destruction, including recommendations for the clear/purge process on different types of media, such as flash memory. Media sanitization consists of three processes: clear, purge and destroy.

- Clear. This process involves replacing the target data with non-sensitive information, including both the logical storage location of files and all user-accessible areas. However, it is important to note that overwriting may not be suitable for damaged or non-rewriteable media, and it may not address all areas where sensitive data can be retained. Factors such as media type, size, and technology (such as flash memory-based devices with wear leveling) can affect the feasibility of overwriting. In cases where dedicated storage devices are not involved, such as basic cell phones or office equipment, the "Clear" operation may refer to returning the device to its factory state or deleting file pointers, as these devices may not support direct rewriting or media-specific techniques. In such cases, manufacturer resets or procedures that do not involve rewriting may be the only option for clearing the device and associated media, as long as the user interface does not allow retrieval of the cleared data [13].

- Purge. The process of purging data from media involves various methods that must be applied with consideration for the specific media type. These methods include overwrite, block erase, and cryptographic erase, using dedicated device sanitize commands that employ media-specific techniques. Destructive techniques such as incineration, shredding, disintegrating, degaussing, and pulverizing can also effectively purge the data by rendering the media unusable and making data recovery infeasible. However, certain methods like bending, cutting, and some emergency procedures may only damage the media partially, allowing for potential data recovery through advanced laboratory techniques. Degaussing, when properly matched to the media's coercivity, can purge legacy magnetic devices, but it should not be solely relied upon for flash memory-based or magnetic devices containing non-volatile non-magnetic storage. It is important to consult the device manufacturer for coercivity details. Degaussing may render many types of devices unusable, effectively acting as a destruction technique as well [13].
- Destroy. Media destruction is an important aspect of data sanitization, and various techniques and procedures are available for this purpose. Complete destruction of media can be achieved through methods like disintegration, pulverization, melting, and incineration. These methods are usually carried out by specialized facilities with the necessary capabilities. Shredding is another effective technique, particularly for flexible media like diskettes, where the media is physically removed from its container and shredded into small pieces to prevent data reconstruction. To further enhance security, the shredded material can be mixed with non-sensitive material of the same type. Destructive techniques become necessary when other clear or purge methods are not applicable or fail to effectively sanitize the media. These techniques ensure that the target data becomes infeasible to retrieve both through device interfaces and state-of-the-art laboratory techniques, providing a robust level of data protection [13].

2.2 Common Technique Used in Data Wiping

Scholars [14, 15] have listed several data wiping techniques/standards are most commonly used in various data wiping methods. The DoD 5220.22-M method offers two main variants: 3-phase and 7-phase. This method is developed and supported by the US National Industrial Security Program. The algorithm consists of several steps: writing zeros and verifying; writing ones and verifying; and writing random characters and verifying. By following this sequence, the method is intended to ensure the effective erasure of data from the storage device.

The NCSC-TG-025 method is a standard developed and supported by the US National Security Agency (NSA). It builds on the DoD 5220.22-M wiping techniques but provides additional options, particularly with respect to the number of overwriting processes. This standard offers more flexibility in selecting the number of overwrites performed during the data wiping process. It is developed to improve security and data erasure capabilities, aligning with the requirements of national security organizations.

The AFSSI-5020 method is a standard developed and supported by the United States Air Force. It is similar to the DoD 5220.22-M method, but it differs in the verification process during the last step. The AFSSI-5020 process involves writing 0 to the storage device, followed by writing 1, and then a random character. However, the specific difference lies in the verification step during the final phase. This method is designed to meet the data wiping requirements of the United States Air Force, ensuring secure and reliable erasure of sensitive information.

The AR 380-19 method is a standard developed and supported by the United States Army. It has a distinct process for data wiping, consisting of several phases. In this method, the process involves writing a random character to the storage device, followed by writing a typical character. Next, a specified character complement is written, and the verification of the written data is performed. This standard is designed specifically to meet the data wiping requirements of the US Army, ensuring the secure and effective erasure of sensitive information from storage devices.

The NAVSO P-5239-26 method is a standard developed and supported by the United States Navy. It provides guidelines for secure data wiping from storage devices. The process involves several steps, including writing a specified character to the storage device, followed by writing the typical character complement. Then, a random character is written, and the verification process is performed to ensure the integrity of the data wiping. This method is specifically designed to meet the data sanitization requirements of the US Navy, ensuring the proper removal of sensitive information from storage devices.

The Gutmann 35-passes method, developed by Peter Gutmann, was once considered a highly secure data wiping method. This method involves performing 35 passes, during which a random character is repeatedly written to the storage device. While this method was designed with the intention of ensuring data erasure, its effectiveness on modern storage devices is questionable. Newer data wiping methods, such as those mentioned earlier, have been developed to address the challenges and complexities associated with modern storage technologies.

The Schneier method, developed and supported by Bruce Schneier, is a data wiping technique that involves 7 passes to securely erase information from a storage device. The process includes the following steps: (i) Writing 1 to the storage device, (ii) Writing 0 to the storage device, and (iii) Writing a pattern of random characters in the next 5 passes. By performing these 7 passes, the Schneier method aims to make it difficult for any data recovery attempts, enhancing the security of data erasure on the storage device.

2.3 Data Handling in Military

According to the Malaysian Armed Forces Staff Manual (Service Writing) [16], the security classification system used by the MAF is standard across the various services under the MAF. The security classification is assigned to documents based on the level of security information they contain and indicates the potential risk to national or international security if the information is disclosed without authorization. The purpose of the security classification is to ensure appropriate protection and control of sensitive information. The security classifications used within the MAF are as follows:

- TOP SECRET (RAHSIA BESAR). Information and material, the unauthorized disclosure of which would cause exceptionally grave damage to the nation. This could include information about the location of weapons, the identity of undercover agents, or the details of a pending military operation.
- SECRET (RAHSIA). Information and material, the unauthorized disclosure of which would damage the interests of the nation. This could include information about troop movements, weapons systems, or intelligence gathering.

- CONFIDENTIAL (SULIT). Information and material, the unauthorized disclosure of which would be prejudicial to the nation's interests. This could include information about personnel records, financial information, or operational plans.
- RESTRICTED (TERHAD). Information and material, the unauthorized disclosure of which would be undesirable to the interests of the nation. This could include general information about the military, training materials, or administrative procedures.

The primary objective of this manual is to offer comprehensive guidelines for the effective management of security within the MAF. A key aspect of security management involves understanding and leveraging military intelligence derived from various textual sources. These sources include smartphone texts, email communications, social media posts, and documents. RMAF personnel are therefore required to exercise careful analysis and comprehension of the data and information shared through these textual sources. The ease of data sharing facilitated by modern devices emphasizes the importance of a thorough understanding of the content being shared. By ensuring a meticulous grasp of this information, RMAF personnel can enhance their ability to extract valuable intelligence while upholding security measures within the organization.

Proper device disposal is paramount for organizations to mitigate risks and uphold data confidentiality. Inadequate disposal practices can result in legal and ethical implications due to potential data confidentiality breaches. To address this, implementing a policy that outlines appropriate procedures for cleaning or destroying devices containing sensitive and confidential data, as well as licensed software, is crucial [17]. Mitigating these risks requires robust security measures, employee training, and proper data management protocols.

3   The Importance of Data Wiping in Cybersecurity

3.1   Data Wiping Guidelines in the Military

The guidelines or manuals within the MAF serve as documented references for each headquarters and unit. These documents outline the policies and guidelines specifically related to cybersecurity in the MAF. Some of the key policies and guidelines that pertain to cybersecurity within the MAF are as follows:

- *Defence White Paper.* This paper is a strategic document that outlines the requirements, goals, and priorities for the defence sector of a country. It serves as a guiding document for the military and defence organizations in safeguarding the nation's interests, sovereignty, and security. In the context mentioned, the Defence White Paper highlights the need for the MAF to address emerging challenges, including cyber warfare, in order to protect the country's interests in the modern warfare environment.
- *Polisi Keselamatan Siber MAMPU.* This policy is a comprehensive policy framework utilized by government agencies to effectively manage cybersecurity and information and communication technology (ICT) within their organizations. This policy aims to provide guidelines and best practices for ensuring the confidentiality, integrity, and availability of digital assets, as well as protecting against cyber threats and risks.

- *Information and Communication Technology Security Policy v5.0.* This policy sets out the framework and requirements for ensuring the security of information and communication technology systems within MINDEF. It applies to all civilian and armed forces personnel who have access to or are responsible for MINDEF's ICT infrastructure and resources.
- *General Order of the Armed Forces (PAAT 1/13).* This directive serves as a comprehensive guideline for all armed forces personnel regarding the usage of the internet and intranet. The directive outlines specific prohibitions and restrictions in order to ensure the secure and appropriate use of these communication platforms within the armed forces.
- *General Order of the Armed Forces 3/13 (PAAT 3/13).* This directive specifically addresses the usage of social media platforms by armed forces personnel. This directive serves as a comprehensive guideline to ensure responsible and appropriate behaviour in the online social media environment, while upholding the reputation and integrity of the armed forces.
- *Malaysian Armed Forces Security Order 2019.* This recent publication consolidates various Acts and orders within the MAF. Serving as a comprehensive guide, this security order is intended to be followed by all MAF leadership and personnel. It is essential for every individual within the MAF to have a thorough understanding of this document. By encompassing relevant legislation and directives, the Malaysian Armed Forces Security Order 2019 provides a unified framework to ensure adherence to security protocols and procedures throughout the organization.
- *Manual Pengurusan ICT Bahagian Komunikasi Dan Elektronik 2021.* This manual provides guidance and procedures for managing information and communication technology (ICT) in the Communication and Electronics Division. The manual covers various aspects, including ICT infrastructure management, network administration, data management, and security protocols. It serves as a reference for personnel involved in ICT operations, emphasizing the importance of efficient and secure ICT practices to ensure smooth operations within the division. The manual aims to establish standardized procedures and guidelines for the effective management of ICT resources and to promote a secure and reliable ICT environment within the division.

3.2 Data Sanitization in Organization

NIST had different procedures and guidelines. The guidelines mentioned in this section emphasize the importance of media reuse within the Department of Defence (DoD) while ensuring the complete removal of data and information from operable media. Here is a more detailed summary:

- *Media Reuse.* The objective is to sanitize media to ensure that no data or information remains on media that are to be reused within the DoD.
- *Clearing and purging.* For unclassified media, it is necessary to clear the data before reuse. This involves removing all data from the media, ensuring that no sensitive information remains. Media containing sensitive data, excluding Controlled Unclassified Information (CUI) or Personally Identifiable Information (PII), should be purged before reuse. Purging ensures that any residual data is thoroughly removed from the

media, rendering it unrecoverable. The National Institute of Standards and Technology Special Publication 800-88 provides detailed guidelines and references for implementing these sanitization practices.

- *Complete Data Removal.* To ensure the removal of data from information systems, storage devices, and peripheral devices with storage capacity, various methods can be employed. These methods include degaussing (erasing magnetic fields), smelting, incinerating, disintegrating, or pulverizing the media. The goal is to render the stored information completely unrecoverable, preventing any potential reconstruction.
- *Classified Media Reuse.* For classified media, it is essential to clear the data before reuse and limit the reuse to classified environments. Chairman of the Joint Chiefs of Staff Instruction 6510.01F provides specific instructions and guidelines for clearing and reusing classified media. It is crucial to ensure that classified storage media is not sanitized and declassified for reuse in an unclassified environment to maintain the integrity and security of classified information.
- *Spillage Events.* In the case of spillage events, where classified or sensitive information may have been inadvertently disclosed or compromised, the current 624 Operations Centre Tasking Order should be consulted for appropriate procedures and actions to be taken.

4 Current Data Wiping Practices of the RMAF

The *Manual Pengurusan ICT Bahagian Komunikasi Dan Elektronik 2021* identifies two categories of risks associated with personal mobile devices: (a) device-related risks and (b) application-related risks [18]. Device-related risks stem from the storage of data internally or in the cloud, information transmission outside the organization, and device loss. The RMAF has less control over personal mobile devices compared to provided personal computers or laptops. Application-related risks arise from the downloading and installation of third-party mobile applications that interact with official organizational data stored on the devices. To address these risks, the manual suggests four steps for ensuring the security of personal mobile device usage:

- *Step 1: Risk Reduction through Mobile Device Management (MDM).* Organizations should identify and register authorized personal mobile devices accessing official data. Official information should be classified, and allowed devices and applications should be determined based on the classification. MDM tools can assist with device configuration, software and application distribution, encryption, password administration, remote wipe, and lock
- *Step 2: Risk Reduction in App Downloads through Guidelines and Awareness Campaigns.* Downloaded applications from unknown sources pose significant security threats. Establishing control over application downloads and promoting awareness among RMAF personnel can mitigate these risks. Trusted app stores should be used for application downloads.
- *Step 3: Internal Application Development.* Developing internal mobile applications with authentication mechanisms before accessing organizational data is recommended as the third step. This approach reduces reliance on downloading apps from untrusted sources.

- *Step 4: Conducting Security Audits on Devices, Infrastructure, and Mobile Applications.* Comprehensive security audits should be performed to assess mobile device infrastructure, conduct penetration tests on devices and servers, evaluate application security for potential information leaks, and assess the alignment of instructions and procedures with best practices.

However, the current practice of laptop policy in RMAF involves passing on laptops without performing any data wiping. This means that when laptops are transferred or reused within RMAF, the data stored on them is not properly erased or sanitized. This practice poses a significant risk in terms of data security and confidentiality.

5   Conclusion

In conclusion, data wiping is a critical aspect of cybersecurity to protect sensitive information from unauthorized access and data breaches. RMAF recognizes the importance of data wiping in safeguarding national security and has implemented various guidelines and policies to ensure secure data disposal. However, there are challenges that need to be addressed, including awareness and knowledge gaps among personnel, limited resources and infrastructure, compliance with regulations, integration with existing systems, and keeping up with evolving threats. By addressing these challenges and enhancing data wiping practices, the RMAF can strengthen its cybersecurity posture, mitigate risks, and ensure compliance with data protection regulations. This research aims to explore the current data wiping practices in the RMAF, propose guidelines for improvement, and verify the effectiveness and compliance of data wiping guidelines. By doing so, it will contribute to the overall enhancement of data security within the RMAF and the protection of sensitive information.

References

1. Malaysia Cyber Security Strategy 2020–2024. https://asset.mkn.gov.my/wp-content/uploads/2020/10/MalaysiaCyberSecurityStrategy2020-2024.pdf. Accessed 25 May 2023
2. Yusof, N.A.B., Abdullah, S.N.H.B.S., bin Md Senan, M.F.E., Sahri, M.B.: Data sanitization framework for computer hard disk drive: a case study in Malaysia. Int. J. Adv. Comput. Sci. Appl. **10**(11), 398–406 (2019)
3. Laws of Malaysia - Personal Data Protection Act 2010. https://www.pdp.gov.my/jpdpv2/assets/2019/09/Personal-Data-Protection-Act-2010.pdf. Accessed 27 May 2023
4. Defence White Paper. https://www.mod.gov.my/images/mindef/article/kpp/DWP-3rd-Edition-02112020.pdf. Accessed 20 June 2023
5. Shivashankar, M., Mary, S.A.: Privacy preservation of data using modified rider optimization algorithm: optimal data sanitization and restoration model. Expert. Syst. **38**(3), e12663 (2021)
6. Mat, B., Pero, S.D.M., Wahid, R., Shuib, M.S.: Cyber security threats to Malaysia: a small state security discourse. Sustain. Glob. Strateg. Partnership Age Uncertainties **5**(6), 31 (2020)
7. CyberSecurity Malaysia. https://www.cybersecurity.my/data/content_files/46/880.pdf. Accessed 20 June 2023
8. Malaysian Navy RMN papers put up on Dark Web - MY Military Times, 29 July 2023. https://mymilitarytimes.com/index.php/2020/08/17/malaysian-navy-rmn-papers-put-up-on-dark-web/. Accessed 20 June 2023

9. Borham, N.A.M., Mohamad, K.M.: DocWIPE: data wiping tool using randomized 512-gram. Appl. Inf. Technol. Comput. Sci. **2**(2), 155–164 (2021)
10. Reardon, J., Basin, D., Capkun, S.: SoK: secure data deletion. In: Symposium on Security and Privacy, pp. 301–315 (2013)
11. Wani, M.A., AlZahrani, A., Bhat, W.A.: File system anti-forensics–types, techniques and tools. Comput. Fraud Secur. **2020**(3), 14–19 (2020)
12. Oh, D.B., Park, K.H., Kim, H.K.: De-Wipimization: detection of data wiping traces for investigating NTFS file system. Comput. Secur. **99**, 102034 (2020)
13. Kissel, R., Regenscheid, A., Scholl, M., Stine, K.: Guidelines for media sanitization, pp. 800–888. US Department of Commerce, National Institute of Standards and Technology (2014)
14. Wei, M., Grupp, L., Spada, F.E., Swanson, S.: Reliably erasing data from {flash-based} solid state drives. In: 9th USENIX Conference on File and Storage Technologies (FAST 11) (2011)
15. Ölvecký, M., Gabriška, D.: Wiping techniques and anti-forensics methods. In: 16th International Symposium on Intelligent Systems and Informatics (SISY), pp. 000127–000132 (2018)
16. E-Doktrin. https://www.airforce.mil.my/index.php/en/informasi/penerbitan/e-doktrin. Accessed 29 July 2023
17. Hughes-Lartey, K., Li, M., Botchey, F.E., Qin, Z.: Human factor, a critical weak point in the information security of an organization's Internet of things. Heliyon **7**(3) (2021)
18. Manual Pengurusan ICT Bahagian Komunikasi Dan Elektronik. In Portal Rasmi TUDM. https://www.airforce.mil.my/index.php/bm/allcategories-ms-my/informasi/penerbitan/manual-pengurusan-ict-bahagian-komunikasi-dan-elektronik. Accessed 29 July 2023
19. Ahn, N.Y., Lee, D.H.: Schemes for privacy data destruction in a NAND flash memory. IEEE Access **7**, 181305–181313 (2019)

Affordances-Based Behavior Change for Energy Efficiency Among Malaysians: A Conceptual Model

Mohamad Taha Ijab[1]([✉]), Hamizah Mohamad Hariri[1], Norshita Mat Nayan[1], Mohd Azul Mohamad Salleh[1], and Suraya Hamid[2]

[1] The National University of Malaysia, Bangi, Selangor, Malaysia
taha@ukm.edu.my
[2] The University of Malaya, Kuala Lumpur, Malaysia

Abstract. Climate change is a pressing global issue that affects countries worldwide. To mitigate its impacts, reducing carbon emissions is crucial. One approach is minimizing energy consumption, including among domestic consumers. Understanding the driving factors influencing consumer behavior change is essential, and Information Systems (IS) have been proposed as intervention tools. However, research on how IS's functional affordances influence behavior changes in residential energy consumers is lacking, along with comprehensive models for explaining behavior change. The need to address climate change has prompted the search for strategies to reduce carbon emissions. Energy consumption reduction, particularly in households, is pivotal. This demands an understanding of factors driving consumer behavior change, wherein Information Systems (IS) can play a role. However, research gaps exist concerning the influence of IS functional affordances on residential energy consumers' behavior change. The research aims to achieve several objectives. First, it seeks to study the factors that shape behavior change in energy efficiency, specifically those enabled by IS. Second, the goal is to formulate an affordance-based model that elucidates behavior change towards energy efficiency. Lastly, the research aims to evaluate and validate this proposed model. To address the objectives, a multi-faceted approach leveraging key theories is adopted. The Affordance Theory, Sensemaking Theory, Belief-Action-Outcome Framework, and Energy Informatics Framework will provide valuable insights. By integrating these theories, a preliminary Affordance-based Behavior Change Model for Energy Efficiency is conceptualized. This research holds significant potential outcomes. It can shed light on the factors influencing behavior change in the context of energy efficiency, facilitated by IS. The development of an affordance-based model could offer a comprehensive framework for understanding and predicting consumer behavior changes.

Keywords: Climate Change · Energy Informatics · Behavior Change · Affordance Theory · Energy Efficiency · Intervention Tool

1 Introduction

Behavior change is about altering habits and behaviors for the long term [1, 2]. Accord-ing to [3], behavior change is complex, and research and practice in this field still struggle to consolidate agreed and successful methods and interventions for behavior change. Theories and literature on behavior change are also vast [3–5]. The Theory of Planned Behavior (TPB), Theory of Reasoned Action (TRA), Social Cognitive The-ory, Value-Belief-Norm Theory (VBN), Norm Activation Theory, Self-Efficacy Theory, Utility Theory, Rational Choice Theory, and Belief-Action-Outcome with Sense making are some examples of theories used for understanding the causal relationships among people's beliefs, norms, attitudes, and behaviors.

Therefore, due to the multiple theories, various constructs, various levels of analysis (i.e., individual, organizational, community, and societal) and it is studied in various inter-disciplinary domains from health psychology to education to computer science, behavior change is a complicated and difficult phenomenon to synthesize and problematic in terms of developing agreed, functional interventions for change [3, 5].

Current behaviour change researches are often too theoretical using constructs of various behavior change theories, rarely measure the aspect of interventions [2, 6, 7], some research are discounting on the time element where behavior change is indeed a process unfolds over time [8], and the limited consideration on the aspect of affordance for the interventions being used [9]. Hence, research in behavior change can be consid-ered lacking parsimony [10]. Today's technological advances in the field of ICT provide new opportunities to the behaviour change research to progress process-based theory driven research [2].

Such Information System (IS)-based interventions can promote a more nuanced understanding of intervention processes not previously studied. According to [11], behavior change has been identified as an important determinant to curb energy con-sumption. However, studies in the field of Information Systems (IS) on behavioral change for energy efficiency are still lacking, especially in the context of Malaysia. [5] claim that behavior change studies must include the aspects of interventions responsible for, and likely to facilitate behavior change. Further, IS are increasingly used as an intervention tool to enable and to promote environmentally sustainable behaviors [7, 12–14].

IS for environmental sustainability is commonly called "Green IS", and they can enable practices and processes with improved environmental performance [15, 16]. One the research topics within Green IS is Energy Informatics (EI). EI recognises the role that IS can play in reducing energy consumption and CO_2 emissions [13]. EI is concerned with analysing, designing and implementing various energy systems to increase the efficiency of the demand and supply of energy. However, within the context of EI, knowledge about how IS can exactly be designed with ample functional affordance to carry out this role is still nascent, emergent, and incomplete [7, 14]. There are also limited studies investigating on the factors driving residential energy users to practice energy efficiency and ask how their actual behaviors and decisions of IS users can actually be changed through IS.

In addition, [14] claimed that there is lack of awareness on the existence of energy efficiency functions offered by certain IS among residential users even though such IS are already provided by the energy providers. Hence, users need further learning while the IS used as intervention for energy efficiency should be prominent in demonstrating its functional affordances from the promotion, caption and placement of the feature within the IS [7, 14, 17, 18]. Thus, there exist a research gap in studying the affordance-based behavior change model for energy efficiency that is enabled by IS as the intervention tool.

2 Literature Review

2.1 Climate Change and the Trend of Rising Energy Consumption in Malaysia

The National Energy Balance report published by the Malaysian Energy Commission in 2017 stated that energy consumption in Malaysia has seen a 20.7% contribution from the residential sector [19]. The average electricity consumption for residential was 345 kWh per month based on the survey of 348 samples in Malaysia. The electricity consumption for residential in Malaysia is expected to rise due to increasing appliance ownership, economic improvement and changing lifestyle as mentioned in the Green Technology Master Plan Malaysia 2017–2030. During the recently concluded COP26 in Glasgow, Scotland, Malaysia has echoed the language of developed countries with the goal to be "carbon neutral" or to achieve "net zero" emissions by 2050 [20].

2.2 Behavior Change on Energy Efficiency Using IS

To support the country's aspiration to become a net zero nation, consumers need to be educated and be given awareness as well as technological intervention IS tool to change their energy hungry behaviors such that they are able to monitor, analyse, and reduce their electricity consumption. Studies have consistently showed that changes in behavior aided by IS could contribute to efficient energy use leading to conclusions of energy consumption reduction ranging from 7% up to 20% [14]. However, reduction in energy consumption did not come just from curtailment of excessive energy use, but also the modification of lifestyle factors contributing to more efficient energy use. This is the premise of the Energy Informatics Framework by [13] who state that IS can be used to change social norms to increase energy efficiency. Further, environmental awareness could be a contributor to changes in behavior towards activities and decisions that affect energy use [14].

2.3 Theoretical Limitations and Lack of Parsimony in Current Behavior Change Research

The concept of parsimony often plays a role in scientific research, where more parsimonious explanations are generally preferred. Parsimony is a guiding principle that suggests that all things being equal, one should prefer the simplest possible explanation for a phenomenon or the simplest possible solution to a problem [10]. Current behaviour change researches are often too theoretical using constructs of various behavior change theories, rarely measure the aspect of interventions [2, 6, 7], some research are discounting on the time element where behaviour change is indeed a process unfolds over time

[8], and the limited consideration on the aspect of affordance for the interventions being used [9].

As shown in Table 1 below, research on behavior change in the context of environmental studies are employing a variety of theories and no consensus over what constitute behavior change. Some researchers are explaining behavior change solely from the constructs of attitude, habits, or intentions, or are just studying the actual behavior (post-change). Some researchers are not considering behavior change as a process [21–23], not viewing behavior change relate to time factor [17, 22, 24, 25], and most are not considering the role of affordances and how intervention tool can be designed with affordances in mind [4, 25–27].

Table 1. Literature Analysis of Existing Works on Behavior Change Studies (Source: Own Analysis)

References	Environmental Context Studied	Theories and Constructs Used	Process Element	Time Element	Affordance-Based Element
[28]	Relationship between environmental concern and specific environmentally related behaviors (Green electricity products purchase)	Theory of Planned Behavior (TPB) with Situated Cognition: Green Attitude → Intention → Purchase	✓	✓	X
[21]	Attitude-behavior inconsistency in environmental consumerism (purchase of green products)	Social Dilemma Theory and Reference Group Theory: Trust → Behavior	X	X	X
[22]	Green electricity (renewable energy purchase behavior)	Institutional Theory Habit → Behavior	✓	✓	X
[27]	Reason both for and against adopting solar panels mediate the relationship between consumers' attitudes, values and adoption intentions	Behavior Reasoning Theory Attitude → Intention	X	X	X
[24]	Study about the association between behavior intention and actual behavior in the consumption of green products	Theory of Planned Behavior with Social Dilemma Theory Product Attributes → Behavior	✓	X	X
[4]	Explore the relationship between energy use, behavioral determinants, and effective strategies to promote more efficient behaviors	Review different types of behavior change theories and models but conduct that practical implementation of these theoretical approaches has proven to be inefficient	✓	✓	X

(continued)

Table 1. (*continued*)

References	Environmental Context Studied	Theories and Constructs Used	Process Element	Time Element	Affordance-Based Element
[7]	How information systems can enable sensemaking of environmental information by users, and how this support for sensemaking affect beliefs, actions, and outcomes of work practices (i.e.paper printing)	Belief-Action-Outcomes and Sensemaking Theory	√	√	X
[9]	Adopting a theory of affordances as a guiding heuristic, environmental policy-makers are better equipped to promote policies that translate sustainable thinking into sustainable behavior	Theory of Affordances	√	√	√ Lack of affordances create gaps between sustainable thinking and sustainable behavior
[17]	Develops design principles for information systems (IS) that support organisational sensemaking in environmental sustainable transformations using the concept of affordances	Sensemaking Theory and Affordances Theory (Triggering disruptive ambiguity and surprise; Noticing an bracketing; Labeling and categorizing; Open and inclusive communication; Presumptive disclosure and action planning)	√	X	√ Describe the action possibilities required in sensemaking in environmental sustainability transformations, identify material properties of IS that afford these possibilities to study the design of IT artefacts
[25]	Attitudes, affect, cognition, and their relationship will the corresponding behaviors on four ethical consumption issues; purchasing energy-saving products	Theory of Attitude Cognitive Predictor → Attitude	√	X	X
[23]	Developing strategic design interventions for triggering collective sustainable behavior change, particularly within urban contexts	Affordances Theory	X	X	X When designing an intervention, the affordances of the intervention must be able to remove constraints for sustainable behaviors

Based on Table 1 above, it can be argued that the realm of environmental studies has seen a surge in research endeavors aimed at unraveling the intricacies of behavior change. However, this surge has brought forth a complex landscape characterized by a lack of consensus on the fundamental nature of behavior change itself. The multifaceted nature of this phenomenon has led researchers down diverse theoretical paths, resulting in varying interpretations and approaches. At the core of this divergence lies the question of what precisely constitutes behavior change. Some scholars adopt a focused perspective, concentrating solely on individual constructs like attitude, habits, or intentions as explanatory factors for behavior change. This reductionist approach, while offering insights into specific aspects, may overlook the holistic process of behavior change and its intricacies. Moreover, a significant portion of research seems to prioritize the observation of post-change behavior, disregarding the temporal aspect and trajectory of change. This static outlook hinders a comprehensive understanding of the dynamics that accompany behavior change over time.

Interestingly, a subset of researchers appears to detach behavior change from its temporal context, emphasizing the current state without delving into the transformative journey that underlies it. This neglect of the temporal dimension may limit the ability to capture the nuanced evolution of behaviors and the influences that shape them. Additionally, while the literature acknowledges the role of intervention tools in facilitating behavior change, a notable gap persists in terms of considering the design of these tools with respect to affordances—the inherent capabilities of a tool to influence users' actions. The concept of affordances remains largely unexplored in the context of behavior change interventions, despite its potential to shape the effectiveness of such tools. Considering this landscape, it becomes evident that a comprehensive and unified understanding of behavior change in the context of environmental studies is still a work in progress. Integrating diverse theories and accounting for the temporal dimension and affordances could provide a more holistic framework. This analytical discussion underscores the need for scholars to embrace a more encompassing view, aligning theoretical perspectives and acknowledging the multifaceted nature of behavior change. Such a synthesis could not only advance the field but also yield more effective strategies for fostering sustainable behavioral transformations.

2.4 Behavior Change and Affordance Theories for Energy Efficiency Using IS

According to [29], human behavior is determined by multiple factors and changing well-established behavioural patterns is difficult to do. However, successful behavior change for energy efficiency can contribute to (i) the reduction of energy costs, and (ii) promote more efficient use of energy. Based on [30]'s theory of affordances, affordance is described as opportunities for action that are directly offered by the intrinsic perceptual properties of objects that allow us to use the tools. Functional affordance is a form of affordance, and [31] defined functional affordances as a design feature that helps users accomplishes work. It is also commonly seen as the usefulness of a system's function.

In the context of this research, the work to be accomplished is how individual consumers' way of managing their energy consumption. One of the IS for monitoring energy consumption is MyTNB portal (including its mobile application counterpart) provided by the national energy supplier, Tenaga Nasional Berhad. However, there is currently no research has been conducted to investigate the impacts of outcomes from implementing the functional affordances of MyTNB with regards to energy efficient behavior change. Thus, as of now, there is limited strategic design interventions can be suggested for MyTNB based on empirical studies guided by theories and data collections such as proposed in this study.

3   The Proposed Conceptual Model and Discussion

[29] posit that their Theory of Planned Behavior (TPB) can be used as a framework for behavior change interventions. According to the TPB, human behavior is guided by three kinds of considerations: (i) beliefs about the likely consequences of the behavior performed, (ii) beliefs about what important others think the user should do, and (iii) beliefs about the user's ability to carry out the behavior. These beliefs provide the basis for the formation of an intention to engage in the behavior.

However, the actual performance of the behavior depends very much on behavioral control. Interventions are effective to the extent that they produce changes in the beliefs that underpin intentions and when they ensure that people have the skills and resources needed to enact their intentions. The control variables to be used in investigating the behavioral intentions are perceived usefulness of the studied IS, perceived ease of use, perceived compatibility, social norms (of social circles who are also using MyTNB for energy consumption monitoring), IT experience in general, and energy efficiency experience. These control variables will be used as they may influence the energy users' move from beliefs to actions and outcomes as framed with the BAO Framework discussed below.

The time dimension will be added as according to [3], implementing and maintaining behaviour change have a temporal element as behavior change takes time. This is because behavior change need to be learnt and absorbed into routine. Due to this, the "before" and "after" situation will be studied. Hence, this study needs to be conducted using experiments and/or observations held over a period of time (i.e., longitudinal study) to observe and measure the actual outcomes derived from the behavior change before and after using the IS.

TPB will be integrated with the Belief-Action-Outcomes (BAO) with Sensemaking Theory in order to provide a more holistic and whole some view of how affordance-based behavior change model can be conceptualized. The BAO framework suggests that environmental outcomes can be improved through IS that act on either belief or action formation. Combining BAO with Sensemaking Theory [32], it allows for an understanding of the ambiguity that surrounds energy efficiency practices. This is because Sensemaking structures cognitive processes involved in sensing, weighing, and synthesizing external stimuli into the formation of beliefs [33].

The Sensemaking theory states that through sensemaking, circumstances are turned into a situation that is comprehended explicitly and that enables to translate beliefs into actions. Environmental sensemaking there for involves the sensing, weighing, and synthesizing of external stimuli in a way that lead to pro-environmental beliefs. The Sensemaking will be operationalized using the identified functional affordances of MyTNB, which are: (i) monitoring electricity consumption through energy analytics visualisation; (ii) analysing electricity use by processing data on household activity inconjunction with energy consumption data in order to establish a dynamic model of energy behavior; (iii) comparing electricity consumption especially when consumers have multiple premises on the same energy subscription accounts, and (iv) learning of better ways to use electricity more efficiently through the feedback channelled via the IS (i.e., MyTNB).

Synthesizing on the constructs and insights from the reviewed literature and theories above, a conceptual model for affordance-based behavior change for energy efficiency is proposed (refer Fig. 1). Empirical data collection needs to be conducted in order to evaluate and validate the model.

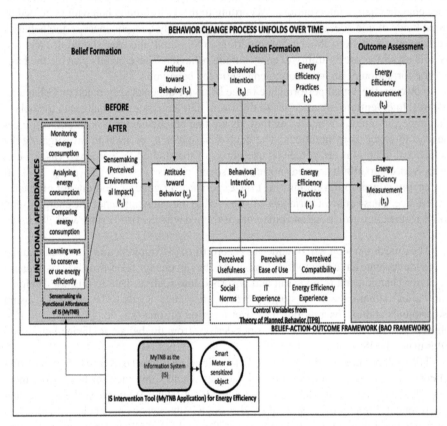

Fig. 1. Proposed Affordance-Based Behavior Change Model for Energy Efficiency

4   Conclusion

Research on Energy Informatics is gaining momentum and efforts are being geared towards enhancing people's awareness on how they can play their part and contribute to the "net zero" emissions goal as per aspiration of the country during COP26. Using constructs from several behavior change theories and insights from literature added with empirical data, an affordance-based behavior change model for energy efficiency can be conceptualized and formulated. Hence, future works will aim to empirically test the proposed conceptual model.

As the literature suggested, affordances theory can be used to explain how energy management applications such as myTNB can be designed to better support energy savings behavior. According to this theory, the design of a tool or environment provides cues that suggest possible actions to the user. Affordances refer to the possibilities for action that are suggested by the design of the tool or environment. By designing an energy management application with appropriate affordances, users can be encouraged to take actions that lead to energy savings.

Acknowledgment. Authors acknowledge the Ministry of Higher Education (MOHE) for funding under the Fundamental Research Grant Scheme (FRGS) (FRGS/1/2022/ICT03/UKM/02/8).

References

1. Verplanken, B., Orbell, S.: Changing behavior using habit theory. In: Hagger, M., et al. (eds.) The Handbook of Behavior Change, Cambridge Handbooks in Psychology, pp. 178–192 (2020). https://doi.org/10.1017/9781108677318
2. Duckworth, A.L., Gross, J.J.: Behavior change. Organ. Behav. Hum. Decis. Process. **161**, 39–49 (2020)
3. Chamberlain, K., Lyons, A.: Critical and qualitative approaches to behavior change. In: Hagger, M., et al. (eds.) The Handbook of Behavior Change, Cambridge Handbooks in Psychology, pp. 430–442 (2020). https://doi.org/10.1017/9781108677318
4. Karatasou, S., Marina, L., Santamouris, M.: Models of behavior change and residential energy use: a review of research directions and findings for behavior-based energy efficiency. Adv. Build. Energy Res. **8**, 137–147 (2014). https://doi.org/10.1080/17512549.2013.809275
5. Hagger, M.S., Cameron, L.D., Hamilton, K., Hankonen, N., Lintunen, T.: Changing behavior: a theory and evidence-based approach. In: Hagger, M., et al. (eds.) The Handbook of Behavior Change, Cambridge Handbooks in Psychology, pp. 1–14 (2020). https://doi.org/10.1017/9781108677318
6. Steg, L., Vlek, C.: Special issue energy efficiency and behavioral change through ICT. J. Energy (2022)
7. Degirmenci, K., Recker, J.: Boosting green behaviors through information systems that enable environmental sensemaking. In: International Conference on Information Systems, Dublin, Ireland (2016)
8. Sheeran, P., Klein, W.M.P., Rothman, A.J.: Health behavior change: moving from observation to intervention. Annu. Rev. Psychol. **68**, 573–600 (2017). https://doi.org/10.1146/annurev-psych-010416-044007
9. Kaaronen, R.O.: Affording sustainability: adopting a theory of affordances as a guiding heuristic for environmental policy. Front. Psychol. **8**, 1–13 (2017). https://doi.org/10.3389/fpsyg.2017.01974
10. Hagger, M.S., Hamilton, K.: Changing behavior using integrated theories. In: Hagger, M., et al. (eds.) The Handbook of Behavior Change, Cambridge Handbooks in Psychology, pp. 208–224 (2020). https://doi.org/10.1017/9781108677318
11. Lossin, F., Loder, A., Staake, T.: Energy informatics for behavioral change. Comput. Sci. Res. Dev. **31**, 149–155 (2014). https://doi.org/10.1007/s00450-014-0295-3
12. Elliot, S.: Transdisciplinary perspectives on environmental sustainability: a resource base and framework for IT-enabled business transformation. MIS Q. Manag. Inf. Syst. **35**, 197–236 (2011)

13. Watson, R.T., Boudreau, M.-C., Chen, A.J.W.: Information systems and environmentally sustainable development: energy informatics and new directions for the IS community. MIS Q. Manag. Inf. Syst. **34**, 23–38 (2010)
14. Yew, M.H.: Modelling the factors that influence the adoption intention of a residential energy management information system (REMIS). Ph.D. thesis, RMIT University, Australia (2019)
15. Ijab, M.T.: A process model for green information system innovation. In: 6th International Conference on Research and Innovation in Information Systems (ICRIIS), pp. 1–6 (2019)
16. Butler, T., Hackney, R.: The role of information mechanisms in the adoption of Green IS to achieve eco-sustainability in municipalities. Inf. Manag. **58**, 1–70 (2021). https://doi.org/10.1016/j.im.2020.103320
17. Seidel, S., Kruse, L.C., Szekely, N., Gau, M., Stieger, D.: Design principles for sensemaking support systems in environmental sustainability transformations. Eur. J. Inf. Syst. **27**, 221–247 (2017). https://doi.org/10.1057/s41303-017-0039-0
18. Kavanagh, D.J.: Changing behavior in the digital age. In: Hagger, M., et al. (eds.) The Handbook of Behavior Change, Cambridge Handbooks in Psychology, pp. 416–429 (2020). https://doi.org/10.1017/9781108677318
19. Sena, B., et al.: Determinant factors of electricity consumption for a Malaysian household based on a field survey. Sustainability **13**, 818 (2021). https://doi.org/10.3390/su13020818
20. Loong, Y.S.: After COP26 glasgow, what next for Malaysia's climate policy? Malaysiakini (2021)
21. Gupta, S., Ogden, D.T.: To buy or not to buy? A social dilemma perspective on green buying. J. Consum. Mark. **26**, 378–393 (2009). https://doi.org/10.1108/07363760910988201
22. Litvine, D., Wüstenhagen, R.: Helping "light green" consumers walk the talk: results of a behavioural intervention survey in the Swiss electricity market. Ecol. Econ. **70**, 462–474 (2011). https://doi.org/10.1016/j.ecolecon.2010.10.005
23. Kaaronen, R.O., Rietveld, E.: Practical lessons for creating affordance-based interventions for sustainable behavior change. One Earth **4**, 1412–1424 (2021). https://doi.org/10.1016/j.oneear.2021.09.013
24. Chowdhury, P., Samuel, M.S.: Artificial neural networks: a tool for understanding green consumer behavior. Mark. Intell. Plan. **32**, 552–566 (2014). https://doi.org/10.1108/MIP-06-2013-0099
25. Lee, H., Cheon, H.: Exploring Korean consumers' attitudes toward ethical consumption behavior in the light of affect and cognition. J. Int. Consum. Mark., 98–114 (2018). https://doi.org/10.1080/08961530.2017.1376241
26. Marechal, K.: Not irrational but habitual: the importance of "behavioural lockin" in energy consumption. Ecol. Econ. **69**, 1104–1114 (2010)
27. Claudy, M.C., Peterson, M., O'Driscoll, A.: Understanding the attitude-behavior gap for renewable energy systems using behavioral reasoning theory. J. Macromarketing **33**, 73–287 (2013). https://doi.org/10.1177/027614671348
28. Bamberg, S.: How does environmental concern influence specific environmentally related behaviors? A new answer to an old question. J. Environ. Psychol. **23**, 21–32 (2003). https://doi.org/10.1016/S0272-4944(02)00078-6
29. Ajzen, I., Schmidt, P.: Changing behavior using the theory of planned behavior. In: Hagger, M., et al. (eds.) The Handbook of Behavior Change, Cambridge Handbooks in Psychology, pp. 17–31 (2020). https://doi.org/10.1017/9781108677318
30. Gibson, J.J.: The Ecological Approach to Visual Perception. Houghton-Mifflin Co., Boston, MA (1979)
31. Hartson, R.: Cognitive, physical, sensory, and functional affordances in interaction design. Behav. Inf. Technol. **22**, 315–338 (2003). https://doi.org/10.1080/01449290310001592587

32. Weick, K.E.: Sensemaking in Organizations. Sage Publications, Thousand Oaks, CA (1995)
33. Tallon, P.P., Kraemer, K.L.: Fact or fiction? A sensemaking perspective on the reality behind executives' perceptions of IT business value. J. Manag. Inf. Sys **24**, 13–54 (2007). https://doi.org/10.2753/MIS0742-1222240101

Intelligent Data Analytics

The Role of Mass Media as a Communications Distributor for Tourism Villages in Indonesia

Prasiwi Citra Resmi[1], John J. O. I. Ihalauw[1], Dwiyono Rudi Susanto[1], Damiasih Damiasih[1], Suhendroyono Suhendroyono[1], and Tutut Herawan[1,2(✉)]

[1] Sekolah Tinggi Pariwisata Ambarrukmo Yogyakarta, Jalan Ringroad Timur No. 52, Bantul, Daerah Istimewa Yogyakarta 55198, Indonesia
{prasiwicitra,tutut}@stipram.ac.id
[2] AMCS Research Center, Jalan Griya Taman Asri, Yogyakarta 55512, Indonesia

Abstract. The management of tourist villages is not far from the touch of stakeholders in a tourism area regarding the pentahelix component i.e.: academia, business, community, government, and media. Developments that continue to increase in today's modern era make tourism very close to the mass media. The mass media has undergone many changes, which have a high potential to support the information dissemination system as a tourist communicator closest to tourists. This paper presents the role of mass media as a communications distributor for tourism villages in Indonesia. We use library research approach aimed to explore the role of the mass media as a communicator for tourism villages in general and in a concentrated manner. We collect data from 100 scientific articles relevant to the topic of in-depth discussion to find a portrait of the situation or an in-depth exploration of the mass media as a communicator in a tourist village as a whole, general and focused so that a specific role can be found as a core communicator in a tourist village. The results found the form of mass media which is divided into three forms: print media, electronic media, and online media; where it was found that mass media has a principal core role as a communication distributor in disseminating information on tourism villages, with the main role of developing theories regarding the processes and effects of mass communication. In developing the theory in the form of: Composing the message; Presenting the message; and Channeling the message. Our study contributes to a better understanding of the current research landscape and identifies areas for future research development related to the role that the mass media in the tourism industry.

Keywords: Mass media · Communicators · Tourism village · Indonesia · Pentahelix · Review

1 Introduction

The Covid-19 Pandemic is an extraordinary challenge, especially for the people of Indonesia. Almost all sectors have felt the impact in the last three years, starting from the health, agriculture, service trade and investment, and property sectors, not to mention the infrastructure, utilities, transportation, and tourism sectors, which have experienced an extraordinary impact during the Covid-19 Pandemic. In 2023, the government will start implementing the *"Gas* and Brakes" policy in the parallel stage of efforts to balance the national economy. Ideas in a press release [1], Indonesia government carries out many *"Gas"* policies through the support of priority programs for the people of Indonesia, the implementation of social protection programs for the community and also business incentive programs for the community. In the concept of the "Brake" policy, the government also carries out several programs such as the 3M implementation campaign, Equal distribution of public vaccinations, and restrictions on the scope of movement or mobility so that it is expected to be able to control the rate of spread of Covid-19. With the emergence of the government's *"Gas* and Brakes" program, the term "New Normal" has emerged, which was explained by [2] an effort or effort to return residents' lives to normal with new adaptation procedures, which are expected to save residents' lives with the full awareness that the Covid-19 outbreak is still around us and protecting the Indonesian nation. Considering these adaptations, it is realized that all post-pandemic Management cannot be separated from the full support and cooperation of Stakeholders or Pentahelix comprising Academic, Business, Community, Government, and Media [3–7].

The development of the Tourism Village in the current era is not far from the positive impact of the use of mass media. The number of publications from the mass media can help spread information about tourism potential in a tourism village and its objects. In [8] stated that the lack of published data in recent years led to a lack of in-depth information about travel to tourists. Even though it is realized by the community and stakeholders stated in [9] that the condition of the tourist village has many strengths and many opportunities that are still not fully utilized so that a superior strategy is found in the field of strengths and opportunities in the form of developing sustainable tourism products following the trends and interests of visiting tourists through collaboration between role models as a means promotion through renewable social media as well as increasing the quality and quantity of facilities at tourist sites within the tourist village area.

With modern developments, media use is very important in daily use. The mass media became an important intermediary or communicator in delivering information. The mass media itself is divided into three classifications: print media, electronic media, and online media. Print media is divided into several types, such as newspapers, magazines, books, and so on, and electronic media is divided into two types, namely radio, and television. In contrast, online media includes internet media such as websites, social media, and others. These three media are important in the Pentahelix collaborative relationship in developing tourism villages [10–15]. Thus, the role of the media is of great concern to the tourism village development program both in terms of the observation aspect and the functions and benefits of the mass media itself [16].

From the background above, it is realized that the mass media is an important basis that must be used to strengthen the message to be conveyed; through the mass media, the delivery of information related to tourism can continue to grow rapidly. This delivery of information to the recipient as the communicant requires means through various channels or channels for conveying messages called the mass media. In the tourism industry, disseminating information on tourist villages is very important when referring to the attractiveness aspects of tourist villages. Without using the role of the mass media in providing information related to tourist objects, it will be difficult to seek tourist visits and regional development [17]. The current development of tourism can help economic growth in terms of employment opportunities, individual income levels, improving living standards, and other sector in-country visits.

Through the bibliometric method, it was found that the most dominant theme studied was in the form of communication synergy from stakeholders into activities in the form of synergy between community groups, government, academic groups, business people, and the media sector [18–20].

Therefore, this paper presents the role of mass media as a communications distributor for tourism villages in Indonesia. The library research approach is employed which aims to explore the role of the mass media as a communicator for tourism villages in general and in a concentrated manner.

2 Proposed Method

The initial consideration for choosing a theme is carried out by observing research opportunities and conducting field observations related to the existence of social media in a tourist village. This research is the result of research library Research conducted by collecting 100 articles from journals, books, and articles related to research topics through Google Scholar. The research protocol was carried out only in 3 limited scopes in the form of Mass Media, Communicators, and Tourism Villages. After that, review activities were carried out to search for data, input data, and measure data in depth so that they could answer the results of the existing descriptive hypothesis in the form of "the role of the mass media as the main communicator of tourist villages?". Data analysis was done in Sum, Median, and Average from the review results. This study aims to analyze and present data findings in the form of the Special role of the mass media as a communicator in a tourist village as a whole, general and focused. This role model can be redeveloped and become the basic concept that can be implemented in many tourist village locations closely related to mass media communication. It was considered that the media is included in the five stakeholder concepts in regulating the minister of tourism of the Republic of Indonesia. Pentahelix can foster harmonious, sustainable values and collaborate in every activity, good facilities, and services to foster experiential values and travel values useful for all perspectives of related parties. Hence, we use the literature review method, it is expected to find the core role of mass media as one of the stakeholders without reducing the essence of its duties and responsibilities in supporting tourism village development programs.

3 Results and Discussion

3.1 Mass Media as a Message Channel

Discussing more deeply developments related to mass media today it is explained in [21] that the media plays an important role in bridging information on the core elements of tourism villages to the world and the wider community. Within the limits of being transparent to the wider community, but if examined more deeply, the media must also have ethical principles in disseminating the information. Some should be known by the wider community, some are not. When media awareness as a stakeholder has been integrated with the local population, the media will know which ones should be disseminated to the wider community and the world, and which ones should not.

It is clearly stated in [22] the Media as one of the stakeholders, as stated in the Global Code of Tourism Ethics Article 6 paragraph 1 where "Tourism professionals have an obligation to provide objective and honest information to tourists about their destination and on the conditions of travel, hospitality and stay". So the media is expected to be able to explore and know the characteristics of the environment, daily life forms unique habits that become the culture of society, so the media must know which information should be disseminated to audiences and the world, and which should not.

The mass media is a medium often used by the public to convey social heritage through values or ideas from a unique idea to others. Sometimes this mass media can become a track record of social stories or old ideas for the next generation. This mass media is often used as a means of communication carried out close and far from each other or delivery with many people. In his book [23] argues that the media is a tool or means that can be used to convey messages from communicators to the general public. So, the notion of the mass media itself is a tool often used in conveying information or messages from informant sources to the public. Based on the scientific field, mass media comes from the basis of communication science. Where the dissemination of information begins with communicators who convey messages or ideas to other parties, In addition, in the current industrial era 5.0, the use of new media as a marketing tool for the potential of tourist areas has become very rapidly developed and runs effectively, efficiently. In his book [24] an organization or business, communication has a very important role as a form of coordination between members in the organization to convey ideas and ideas. There are six conditions for communication to occur, namely:

a. Source: Information delivery centers aim to strengthen the contents of the message.
b. Communicator: Individuals or groups are intermediaries for the delivery of information to other parties.
c. Communicate: Relevant parties receive the information conveyed by the communicator.
d. Message: The entire information conveyed by the communicator to the communicant with various purposes such as influencing, changing the attitudes and behavior of a group or organization, etc.
e. Channel: It is a media facility that communicators use to convey information to other parties.
f. Effects: The impact or result of a delivery of information conveyed by the communicator. Impact changes can be appropriate or not follow the expectations of the communicator.

The types of mass media that are widely used in the lives of the general public are generally in the form of "The Big Five of Mass Media" (Five Big Mass Media) in the form of newspapers, magazines, radio, television, as well as films. These types of mass media operate in the fields of information and education as well as in the field of recreation. Types of mass media are divided into three groups, according to [25] Print Media, Electronic Media, and Online Media. Significant shows that social media reshapes the social identity, social structure, and social relations of tourism village communities both in terms of social relations, representation of tourist space and community lifestyle participation. So that stakeholders get social coercion to adapt to the impact of this social media.

According to [26] Mass media comes from communicators who provide information to the communicant. In the science of communication described in his findings, The results of this study found that there is an emerging role of social media influencer communication as a third party liaison from each stakeholder through content production, content distribution interaction and personal appearance on the social web [27] argued that the elements of mass communication consist of:

a. The source as a communicator (the source),
b. Message as communiqué (the message),
c. Channels as messengers (the channel),
d. The receiver is the communicant (the receiver).

Understood from the findings of the elements of communication, it is concluded that the communicator is a source of messages and the media as an extension as well as a channel for messages from the communicator to form information into a series of communication messages to inform, provide input, disseminating, entertaining, and serving readers as information counselors in the form of delivery. Who has character? As stated in his research [25] namely publicity (Distribute), Periodicity (fixed/scale), Universality (general), Actualization (Renewable), Continuity (Continuous), and Documentation.

Stakeholder communication itself is very important and it is also explained in [28] that the urgency of synergy between the government and the community in tourism development. The government acts as a tourism facilitator while the community acts as a tourism promoter. By making it accessible to tourists, the number of tourists will increase. Meanwhile, the community is developing tourism so that tourists can sell a lot of money for tourist attractions. In this way, local people's income can increase.

Clearly explained by [29] "As social scientists and other researchers turned their attention to the mass media, it also became an important principle that would play a key part in developing theories concerning the processes and effects of mass communication." which means As social scientists and other researchers turn their attention to the mass media, it is also an important principle that will play a key role because it has the potential to offer insights in developing theories regarding the processes and effects of mass communication. In Table 1, the mass media contains operational definitions of variables related to composing, presenting, and distributing messages.

Table 1. Operational Process Role of Mass Media

Character	Special Features	References
Message Builder	Any specific mass-communicated message will only have limited effects on an audience	[30, 31]
	Exposure to mass communication content is assumed to provide needed gratification	[32–34]
	mass media content depicting the nature and worth of members of various categories	[29, 35–37]
	In citizen journalism, this is one of its advantages in the packaging and disseminating of information to the wider community. 'Proximity' or "proximity" is closely attached to information produced by citizen journalism, carried by netizens as ordinary people in conveying information in citizen journalism reports	[3, 38–41]
	The public, in consumed information and mass media coverage, has the main indicator, namely the credibility of the news. The credibility of the mass media is the main aspect that mass media agencies must possess. (credibility) The credibility of the mass media involved greatly influences public trust in a report	[42–46]
Message Presenter	The content of that new mass media had to be consistent with the tastes and interests of these new kinds of readers. Today, in the increasingly competitive world of mass communication, that combination is still one that can spell	[30, 32, 35, 47, 48]
	Social Expectations Theory identifies the significant part played by mass communications in the socialization process in societies where young people widely attend to media-provided entertainment content	[19, 25, 49, 50, 51]

(continued)

Table 1. (*continued*)

Character	Special Features	References
	A message conveyed by the mass media will reach every eye and ear; it will have an immediate and powerful effect, shaping the thoughts and conduct of all who receive it	[13, 16, 18, 23–25, 52–54]
	The study results also show that with two different mass media, there is the same style when presenting women in the mass media and to the public, namely by using the word "Beautiful" as a reader attraction. (Attractiveness)	[19, 24, 55–59]
	Researchers found (Similarity) similarities in the topic of disinformation clarified by TV2 News Online and DR News Online. Disinformation clarification reports on News Online	[23–25, 39, 49, 60–63]
Message Relay	Mass communication begins with senders, "professional communicators whose principal objective is to make a profit. They decide on the meanings and goals of a message to be presented to an audience via their particular medium	[16, 29, 64–66]
	The Mass Media as Cultural Superstructure But how do the mass media fit into this complex picture of a priority	[29, 67, 68, 56, 69]
	The media are teachers providing unintended instruction on being, knowing, and doing as they seek to entertain and present news. The Media as Teachers of Incidental Lessons When our modern mass media provide us	[25, 16, 18, 23, 29, 47, 70–74]

(*continued*)

Table 1. (*continued*)

Character	Special Features	References
	Without adequate information channels through interpersonal sources, the mass media has some beginning to supply information	[75–79]
	Violations are committed by publishing news that is not following YouTube content and does not ask for permission in advance or do not have resource access rights (Authorization) to the content owner to make news where the mass media makes a profit	[80–84]

From the operational findings of the mass media above, it was found that it only has two main roles in developing theories regarding the processes and effects of mass communication. The process of delivering effects is inseparable from the type of characteristics of the mass media as Message Compilers, Message Presenters, and Message Channels. In detail, each character has five special characteristics, which are presented in the Fig. 1 below.

Message Builder (People)	Message Presenter (Method)	Message Relay (Tool)
•1. Limited effect on the audience •2. provide satisfaction needs •3. describe the nature and value of members •4. 'Proximity' or "proximity" •5. Public credibility or trust	•1. Consistent Content •2. Entertaining •3. Has an impact on shaping thinking and behavior •4. reader appeal. (Attractiveness) •5. Similarity or similarity of topics	•1. Make a Profit •2. Cultural Superstructure •3. Indirect Instruction Giver •4. As an Information Supplier •5. Resource access rights (Authorization)

Fig. 1. Research Methods Scheme

From the findings of the literature review, three main roles of mass media were found:

1) Message Compiler with five main factors: limited effect on the audience, messages that provide satisfaction to the audience's information needs, messages that are able to describe the value of members, closeness of message delivery and the value of public trust in message delivery.
2) Message Presenter with 5 supporting factors in the form of: consistent delivery, Opinion herding, Can form reactions to the nature of public thinking, has a presentation of attractiveness and uniqueness and valid topics or similarities with field areas.
3) Message Distributor with 5 influence impact factors in the form of: generating profits, being a disseminator of cultural information, generating indirect real instructions, as a supplier of information and having the right to authorize wide distribution.

3.2 Mass Media in Tourism Villages

In [85] there is a difference in the meaning of village tourism and tourism village. Village tourism is an activity to invite tourists to visit a village, where tourists can see and learn the value of the authenticity of certain villages following the uniqueness and potential of the village they have. In comparison, Tourism Village is said to be a tourism asset based on rural potential with all its uniqueness and attractiveness. It can be empowered and developed as a tourism product to attract visitors to the village location. As expressed by [86] Something to See, Something to Do, and Something to Pay. A tourist village has its characteristics as written by [87] Tourism villages have criteria in the form of four basic things, namely:

a. The unique potential of a unique tourist attraction is in the form of the physical character of the environment or the culture in the community. (Nature, Physical Environment, Culture)
b. The tourist village has supporting infrastructure facilities and tourism activities such as accommodation, interaction rooms, and other facilities. (Infra-structure, Accessibility)
c. The tourist village must implement a form of interaction with visitors or tourists in the form of tourist visits coming to the location of the tourist village. (Attitude and order of community life)
d. Tourism villages have support for participation and initiatives from the community to develop their environmental tourism villages. So that it can form a distinctive culture from the tourist village naturally. (Institutional, HR)

The villagers themselves usually have the characteristics of having a culture of knowing each other, knowing each other between thousands of souls or between other communities, and having the same feeling of attachment to a preference for a rural habit and economic perspective or what is usually understood as a way of doing business influenced by nature. Such as the climate, and the state of nature, not a non-agricultural or part-time job. The village itself, according to his book [88] divided based on the level of development, namely:

a. Underdevelopment Village or Pioneering Village (Swadaya Village) This village lacks human or labor resources and management funds. So that the potential owned in the tourist village is not maximized, this village is usually located in a remote area or far from the city, so there are minimal supporting facilities and infrastructure.
b. Developing Village (Swakarsa Village) in this village, the physical and non-physical potentials that are owned have begun to be used or exploited. However, utilizing financial resources or owning natural products is still lacking. Usually, this village is located in a specific border area or transitions from remote to urban areas.
c. Maju Village (Self-sufficient Village) This village is a village that is said to be well-off both in terms of human resources, physical and non-physical potential, as well as in terms of development capital so that the community can utilize and maximize all the potential that exists to the fullest. The life of the self-sufficient village community is often said to have been similar to or following the development model of a modern city. In terms of diverse livelihoods, this community has been supported by complete infrastructure to support the life of this progressive rural community.

Many emerging concepts of tourism village development are currently the main tasks in preparing and presenting aspects of products and services, traditional architecture, spatial planning of tourist villages, and other components of tourism village infrastructure. The importance of stakeholder management and community involvement in creating a good and sustainable tourism village can become a brand in increasing the number of visitors. Smart Tourism has been widely implemented in tourist village locations through digital-based offers and marketing (Branding). This digitalization transformation in the 4.0 and 5.0 eras has given rise to many benefits and orientations of views in today's society to meet the travel needs of tourists.

So that there is a lot of research that describes mass media as a communicator or source of information, even though it is known that the notion of mass media itself is a means of connecting communication from communicators or centralized sources of data that will be conveyed to the communicant to produce a certain effect for the recipient of the message. According to [89] the type of mass media is known: Print, Electronic, and Online. The three media become communication channels for communicators to provide information and news to meet the public's information needs. In other words, the role of the mass media here acts as a Communication Distributor. Known to [90] Distributors themselves are Entities or intermediary parties between consumers; distributors are also the first party to obtain products/services from first parties to help distribute products/services, obtain target customers, monitor price stability as well as help consumers to obtain the products/services needed more easily. When viewed from the basic understanding and level of function and responsibility, the mass media has the same role as a Distributor but in the Dissemination of Communication Information, or a "Communication Distributor." The mass media here has a role that focuses on only two things, namely:

a. Information Dissemination Process

The information obtained by Mass Media Management from the source Communicator will go through the stages of information processing, such as: Composing Messages, Presenting Messages, and Channeling Messages.

b. The Mass Communication Effect.

His book has widely discussed some of the many effects of disseminating this information [25] hat there are three main effect classifications in the form:

a. Cognitive Effects (relating to thought or understanding reasoning)
b. Affective Effects (related to the feelings of the recipient of the message/communicant)
c. Behavioral Effects (related to intention, determination, effort, and action after getting a communication connection from the mass media).

Hence, from the results Library research conducted, then describe the results of the conclusion that the mass media has a role as a "Communication Distributor" with the Flowchart Model is given in Fig. 2 as follow.

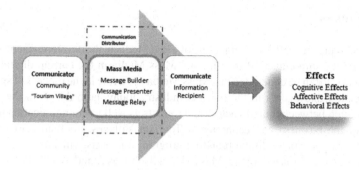

Fig. 2. Communication distributor flowchart

In the findings of Fig. 2 above, there are three main actors of disseminating a communication based on [91], the first is the Communicator. This first perpetrator is the source of information or messages that want to be disseminated, this is taken by the community or all levels of society of a tourist village. Second, mass media, found mass media is a tool for disseminating information so that mass media has a role like a communication distributor. These mass media actors will automatically compile, present and distribute messages to the general public. The third is Communicant which is the recipient of the message conveyed by the mass media in detail so that it can produce 3 main effects, namely those also discussed in [92] in the form of Cognitive effect, Affective effect, and Behavioral effect. So it is very important that the mass media not only receive but also understand deeply the news that will be presented so that the value of the information presented will be much more relevant to the communicants who receive. It is concluded in its role that this media stakeholder factor is the last tool after the availability of all content that will be presented by the community/communiqué, academics, business and government to be presented more widely.

It is hoped that the awareness of the role of mass media can help tourism villages be much more optimal in developing tourism villages in their areas.as done by [93] about the management of distribution by social media has a high potential in reaching a large audience and various models. Social media can be optimized to empower a tourism village to gain new influences. Some development activities such as creating social media accounts, taking interesting photo spots and profile videos from a tourist village are then uploaded on the social media. So it is expected that tourists become aware, interested and finally persuaded to visit. In [94], they said that the management of tourism villages through the digitalization system has a very positive impact both in terms of the number of visit traffic, the value of community welfare and the value of purchasing power of visitors which can continue to increase every year.

So it's good that the main role of this communication is the provision of maximum communicators in providing the best content for the mass media, so that when the tourism village is ready, the mass media will immediately take pictures and create content as well as possible and help the welfare level of the tourism village which is even more developed through the number of visits and income obtained by the community.

4 Conclusion

This paper has presented the important role of Mass Media in the development of Tourism Villages and the importance of maximizing Mass Media in the current digital era for tourism actors. It can be concluded that Mass Media has a role in the process of spreading communication that occurs in the tourism industry today, both that is in the form of communication between tourism actors and tourists as well as communication methods in terms of the business and economy of Tourism Villages. Tourism actors and the mass media can become a digital branding program for tourist villages to increase the number of visits to a tourist village. Mass Media itself was found as a "Communication Distributor" for tourism villages.

Acknowledgments. This work is supported by Ambarrukmo Tourism Institute, Yogyakarta, Indonesia.

References

1. Head of Communication Bureau, LI and PKKBPHL: Preparing to Face the Challenges of 2023, the government Focuses on Increasing Employment and Quality of Human Resources (2023). www.ekon.go.id
2. Saleha, T.Y., Sanjaya, B., Hanapi, A., Februanti, S.: Relationship level of community knowledge about Covid-19 with health protocol implementation in the new normal era: a literature review. COVID-19 Int. J. Covid-19 Res. **2**(3) (2022)
3. Pugra, I.W., Oka, I.M.D., Suparta, I.K.: Kolaborasi pentahelix untuk pengembangan desa timpag menuju desa wisata berbasis green tourism. Bhakti Persada Jurnal Aplikasi IPTEKS **7**(2), 111–120 (2021)
4. Resmi, P.C., et al.: A bibliometric analysis on pentahelix tourism researches. Int. J. Adv. Manag. Bus. Intell. **3**(3) (2022)
5. Sumarto, R.H., Sumartono, S., Muluk, M.R., Nuh, M.: Penta-Helix and Quintuple-Helix in the management of tourism villages in Yogyakarta City. Australas. Acc. Bus. Finan. J. **14**(1), 46–57 (2020)
6. Halibas, A.S., Sibayan, R.O., Maata, R.L.R.: The Penta Helix model of innovation in Oman: an Hei Perspective. Interdisc. J. Inf. Knowl. Manag. **12** (2017)
7. Idzham, N.A.S.K., Ismail, Z.: Development of primary school history course using augmented reality. Indonesian J. Adv. Comput. Sci. Inf. Technol. **4**(1) (2023)
8. Sulasmi, S.: E-marketing strategy for culinary food SMEs during the Covid-19 pandemic in 2020. Int. J. Adv. Technol. Manag. Entrepreneurship **3**(1) (2022)
9. Calzada, I.: Critical social innovation in the smart city era for a city-regional European horizon 2020. P3T J. Public Policies Territories Soc. Innov. Territory **6**, 1–20 (2013)
10. Tonkovic, A.M., Veckie, E., Veckie, V.W.: Applications of Penta Helix model in economic development. Econ. Eastern Croatia Yesterday Today Tommorow **4**, 385–393 (2015)
11. Purnomo, E.P., Fathani, A.T., Setiawan, D., Fadhlurrohman, M.I., Nugroho, D.H.: Penta-Helix Model in sustaining Indonesia's tourism industry. In: Antipova, T. (ed.) Advances in Digital Science, pp. 477–486. Springer, Cham (2021). https://doi.org/10.1007/978-3-030-71782-7_42
12. Putra, T.: A review on Penta Helix actors in village tourism development and management. J. Bus. Hospitality Tourism **5**(1), 63 (2019)

13. Budhi, M.K.S., Lestari, N.P.N.E., Suasih, N.N.R.: The recovery of the tourism industry in Bali province through the Penta-Helix collaboration strategy in the new normal era. Geo J. Tourism Geosites **40**(1), 167–174 (2022)
14. Palestho, A.B., Octanisa, D.S.: Reconstructing penta-helix: a study of a literature review. Jurnal Ilmiah Mahasiswa Manajemen, Bisnis dan Akuntansi (JIMMBA) **5**(1), 1–16 (2023)
15. Chamidah, N., Putra, A.H.P.K., Mansur, D.M., Guntoro, B.: Penta Helix element synergy as an effort to develop villages tourism in Indonesia. Jurnal Manajemen Bisnis **8**(1), 01–22 (2021)
16. Jannah, S.N., Kuswardani, R.: Social media-based digital marketing for Pujon Kidul Malang tourism village. Int. J. Adv. Manag. Finan. **3**(3) (2022)
17. Tajuddin, N.I.A., Burkhardt, J.M., Tajuddin, S.N.A.A.: German language acquisition through social media: tiktok influence on young learners. Int. J. Adv. Lang. Educ. Linguist. **4**(1) (2023)
18. Resmi, P.C., Widodo, W.I., Ermawan, K.C., Anggraini, F.D., Ihalauw, J.J., Susanto, D.R.: A decade analysis communication model in tourism: a bibliometric approach. Int. J. Adv. Digit. Libr. Inf. Sci. **3**(1) (2023)
19. Setyanto, T.J., Purnama, Y., Kherenhapukh, W.: A bibliometric analysis on quality tourism in Indonesia from 2012–2022. Int. J. Adv. Sports Tourism Recreation **3**(1) (2023)
20. Ajie, A.P., Kurniawati, D., Devylia, D.: A bibliometric analysis on alternative tourism in Indonesia from 2012 to 2022. Int. J. Adv. Tourism Hospitality **3**(2)
21. Zaini, M.I.H.A., Zakuan, A.H.A., Elsani, V., Fidantyo, M.N., Wahab, A.Y.A.: Media coverage during covid-19 pandemic: the death of the two journalists in Ukraine and Palestine. Int. J. Adv. Commun. Media J. **2**(1) (2023)
22. UNWTO: Kode Etik Global Untuk Pariwisata. Dalam *buletin* Kependudukan/dikeluarkan oleh Divisi Kependudukan Departemen Urusan Ekonomi dan Sosial, Perserikatan Bangsa-Bangsa (2001)
23. Cangara, H.: Utilization of new media in tourism marketing communication: marketing strategy conducted by government tourism office of west Sulawesi. In: International Conference on Communication, Policy and Social Science (InCCluSi 2022), pp. 246–254. Atlantis Press, November 2022
24. Koesomowidjojo, S.R.M.I.: Dasar-Dasar Komunikasi. Bhuana Ilmu Populer (2020)
25. Senyao, S., Ha, S.: How social media influences resident participation in rural tourism development: a case study of Tunda in Tibet. J. Tour. Cult. Chang. **20**(3), 386–405 (2022)
26. Enke, N., Borchers, N.S.: Social media influencers in strategic communication: a conceptual framework for strategic social media influencer communication. In: Social Media Influencers in Strategic Communication, pp. 7–23. Routledge (2021)
27. Berlo, D.K.: Communication as process: review and commentary. Ann. Int. Commun. Assoc. **1**(1), 11–27 (1977)
28. Susanti, R., Purwandari, S., Prilosadoso, B.H.: Penta Helix as strategy of tourism village development in Karangasem Village, Bulu District, Sukoharjo Regency. Int. J. Soc. Sci. **2**(4), 1979–1984 (2022)
29. DeFleur, M.L., DeFleur, M.H.: Mass Communication Theories: Explaining Origins, Processes, and Effects. Routledge (2016)
30. Ball-Rokeach, S.J., DeFleur, M.L.: A dependency model of mass-media effects. Commun. Res. **3**(1), 3–21 (1976)
31. Batinic, B., Appel, M.: Mass communication, social influence, and consumer behavior: two field experiments. J. Appl. Soc. Psychol. **43**(7), 1353–1368 (2013)
32. Wimmer, R.D., Dominick, J.R.: Mass Media Research. Cengage Learning (2013)
33. Samani, M.C., Guri, C.J.: Revisiting uses and gratification theory: a study on visitors to annah rais homestay. Jurnal Komunikasi: Malays. J. Commun. **35**(1), 206–221 (2019)
34. Tubbs, S.L., Carter, R..: Mass communication. In: Shared Experiences in Human Communication, pp. 259–283. Routledge (2020)

35. Liechty, M.: Media, markets and modernization: youth identities and the experience of modernity in Kathmandu, Nepal. In: Youth Cultures, pp. 166–201. Routledge (2022)
36. Xie, C., Yu, J., Huang, S.S., Zhang, J.: Tourism e-commerce live streaming: identifying and testing a value-based marketing framework from the live streamer perspective. Tour. Manage. **91**, 104513 (2022)
37. Hamidi, F., Shams Gharneh, N., Khajeheian, D.: A conceptual framework for value co-creation in service enterprises (case of tourism agencies). Sustainability **12**(1), 213 (2019)
38. Ningsih, I.N.D.K.: Proximity: Kedekatan yang diusung citizen jounalism. Ultimacomm: Jurnal Ilmu Komunikasi **7**(1), 83–95 (2015)
39. Muslich, M.: Kekuasaan media massa mengonstruksi realitas. Jurnal Bahasa dan Seni **36**(2), 150–159 (2008)
40. Huertas, A.: How live videos and stories in social media influence tourist opinions and behaviour. Inf. Technol. Tourism **19**(1–4), 1–28 (2018). https://doi.org/10.1007/s40558-018-0112-0
41. Liberato, P., Liberato, D., Abreu, A., Alén-González, E., Rocha, Á.: Generation Y: the competitiveness of the tourism sector based on digital technology. In: Antipova, T., Rocha, Á. (eds.) Information Technology Science, vol. 724, pp. 227–240. Springer, Cham (2018). https://doi.org/10.1007/978-3-319-74980-8_21
42. Djati, L.H.U.S.G., Gunung, B.K.M.U.S., Bandung, D.: Kredibilitas media online dalam pandangan mahasiswa
43. Metzger, M.J., Flanagin, A.J.: Digital Media, Youth, and Credibility, p. 212. The MIT Press (2007)
44. Weingart, P., Engels, A., Pansegrau, P.: Risks of communication: discourses on climate change in science, politics, and the mass media. Public Underst. Sci. **9**(3), 261 (2000)
45. Biagi, S.: Media/Impact: An Introduction to Mass Media. Cengage Learning (2014)
46. Sana, C.: Participatory communication as a mechanism for activating sustainable tourism development (2022)
47. Gujbawu, M., Ekhareafo, D.O.: Research methods and procedures in mass communication (2012)
48. Monaco, S.: Tourism and the new generations: emerging trends and social implications in Italy. J. Tourism Futures **4**(1), 7–15 (2018)
49. Pangaribuan, O.C., Irwansyah, I.: Media cetak Indonesia di era revolusi industri 4.0. Jurnal Pewarta Indonesia **1**(2), 119–130 (2019)
50. Ong, Y.X., Sun, T., Ito, N.: Beyond influencer credibility: the power of content and parasocial relationship on processing social media influencer destination marketing campaigns. In: Stienmetz, J.L., Ferrer-Rosell, B., Massimo, D. (eds.) ENTER 2022, pp. 110–122. Springer, Cham (2022). https://doi.org/10.1007/978-3-030-94751-4_11
51. Hysa, B., Zdonek, I., Karasek, A.: Social media in sustainable tourism recovery. Sustainability **14**(2), 760 (2022)
52. Farmaki, A.: Animosity and tourism: resident perspectives. J. Travel Res., 00472875221146784 (2023)
53. Fang, H., Zhang, T., Zhang, Y.: Reflection on the communication of urban image of chaoshan area in the era of new media. In: SHS Web of Conferences, vol. 155, p. 02003. EDP Sciences (2023)
54. Hartanto, Y., Firmansyah, M.A., Adhrianti, L.: Implementation digital marketing pesona 88 curup in to build image for the decision of visit tourist attraction. In: 4th Social and Humanities Research Symposium (SoRes 2021), pp. 589–594. Atlantis Press, April 2022
55. Miranti, A.: Narasi "Cantik" sebagai bentuk eksploitasi perempuan pada pemberitaan pedagang perempuan viral di media massa. SEMIOTIKA: Jurnal Komunikasi **14**(2) (2020)

56. Puspitasari, I., Sari, E.D.P., Purwandari, G.A., Setiawan, K.: Meso-structure analysis of banyumas tourism promotion media. In: International Conference on Academia-Based Tourism Revival 2022 (ABTR 2022), pp. 177–191. Atlantis Press, March 2023
57. Yono, S., Sudarmanto, B.A., Murdowo, D.A.: Cultural attractions development based on Putri Boki Dehegila Legend at the tourist attractions fea of Morotai Island District. In: International Conference on Academia-Based Tourism Revival 2022 (ABTR 2022), pp. 120–130. Atlantis Press, March 2023
58. Zhou, Q., Zhu, K., Kang, L., Dávid, L.D.: Tea culture tourism perception: a study on the harmony of importance and performance. Sustainability **15**(3), 2838 (2023)
59. Marine-Roig, E.: Content analysis of online travel reviews. In: Handbook of e-Tourism, pp. 1–26. Springer International Publishing, Cham (2022)
60. Yonas, A.R., Nugrahani, H.S.D.: Media Massa Eropa Utara dan Konter terhadap disinformasi pemberitaan pandemi Covid-19. Perspektif Pengkajian Eropa dan Best Practice Denmark-Finlandia bagi Media Massa Indonesia. Jurnal Kajian Wilayah **12**(1), 45–60 (2022)
61. Khadka, B.B.: Impact of social media, Dipayal Silgadhi Municipality, Doti, Nepal. DMC Res. J. **5**(01), 55–72 (2023)
62. Madzík, P., Falát, L., Copuš, L., Valeri, M.: Digital transformation in tourism: bibliometric literature review based on machine learning approach. Eur. J. Innov. Manag. **26**(7), 177–205 (2023)
63. Jadhav, G.G., Gaikwad, S.V., Bapat, D.: A systematic literature review: digital marketing and its impact on SMEs. J. Indian Bus. Res. **15**(1), 76–91 (2023)
64. Rathore, B.: Digital transformation 4.0: a case study of LK Bennett from marketing perspectives. Int. J. Enhanced Res. Manag. Comput. Appl. **10**(11), 45–54 (2023)
65. Jansson, A.: The transmedia tourist: a theory of how digitalization reinforces the de-differentiation of tourism and social life. Tour. Stud. **20**(4), 391–408 (2020)
66. Kayumovich, K.O.: Particular qualities use of social media in digital tourism. Gwalior Manag. Acad. **28**(1), 21–28 (2020)
67. Parra, J.F.E., Erazo, C.P.M., Castelo, E.M.S., Polo, S.M.Z., Reyes, K.P.C.: Augmented reality for the development of sustainable tourism in the chimborazo wildlife production reserve. Russian Law J. **11**(3s) (2023)
68. Nurhayati, B.R.: Cultural objects and traditions of Negeri Soya of Ambon as a tourist attraction. In: 3rd International Conference on Business Law and Local Wisdom in Tourism (ICBLT 2022), pp. 136–146. Atlantis Press, January 2023
69. Ba, C.: Invisible Superstructure of the Visible. On_Culture (13) (2022)
70. Abbas, F., Pasallo, S.: Peran Media Massa Cetak (Koran) Dalam Meningkatkan Pariwisata Danau Dua Rasa (Labuan Cermin). Berau **1**, 91–105 (2013)
71. Sanborn, F.W.: A Cognitive Psychology of Mass Communication. Taylor & Francis (2022)
72. Jiang, M., Lam, A.H., Chiu, D.K., Ho, K.K.: Social media aids for business learning: a quantitative evaluation with the 5E instructional model. Educ. Inf. Technol., 1–23 (2023)
73. Zizka, L., Chen, M.M.: "Sanitary measures, social distancing, safety": the evolution of Swiss hoteliers' Covid-19 communication through three snapshots. Tourism Hospitality Res., 14673584231162279 (2023)
74. Wright, D.W.: 'Edutainment' in Dark tourism: toward a child's perspective. In: Children, Young People and Dark Tourism, pp. 155–171. Routledge (2022)
75. Lee, U.K.: Tourism using virtual reality: media richness and information system successes. Sustainability **14**(7), 3975 (2022)
76. Angus, I.H.: Media beyond representation. In: Cultural Politics in Contemporary America, pp. 333–346. Routledge (2022)
77. Schiller, H.I.: The privatization and transnationalization of culture. In: Cultural Politics in Contemporary America, pp. 317–332. Routledge (2022)

78. Fitriana, K., et al.: Collaborative governance in developing tourism potential through tourism villages. In: Unima International Conference on Social Sciences and Humanities (UNICSSH 2022), pp. 156–171. Atlantis Press, January 2023

79. Andayana, M.N., Primus, L.A.K.E., Oktavianto, A.B.: The effectiveness of whatsapp social media use as a public communication means in Tune Village, Tobu District, Tts District. J. Tourism Econ. Policy **2**(3), 213–225 (2023)

80. Ginting, A.R.: Perlindungan Hak Moral dan Hak Ekonomi terhadap Konten Youtube yang Dijadikan Sumber Berita. Jurnal Ilmiah Kebijakan Hukum **14**(3), 579–596 (2020)

81. Shen, H., Wall, G.: Social media, space and leisure in small cities. Asia Pacific J. Tourism Res. **26**(2), 73–80 (2021)

82. Gonçalves, T.C., Gaio, C.: Corporate sustainability disclosure and media visibility: mixed method evidence from the tourism sector. J. Bus. Res. **155**, 113447 (2023)

83. Chin, W.L., Noorashid, N.: Communication, leadership, and community-based tourism empowerment in Brunei Darussalam. Adv. Southeast Asian Stud. **15**(2) (2022)

84. Jang, H., Park, M.: Social media, media and urban transformation in the context of overtourism. Int. J. Tourism Cities (2020)

85. Sudibya, B.: Wisata Desa dan Desa Wisata. Jurnal Bali Membangun Bali **1**(1), 22–26 (2018)

86. Yoeti, O.A.: Dasar-dasar Pengertian Hospitality dan Pariwisata. Bandung: PT. Alumni (2010)

87. Rahayuningsih, T., Haryanta, D., Wedowati, E.R., Rejeki, F.S., Puspitasari, D.: Tourism village development: a case study in Cepokolimo Village, Pacet District, Mojokerto Regency. Asian J. Arts Hum. Soc. Stud., 32–41 (2022)

88. Hayat, R.A.N.Z.: Pencanangan Desa Wisata Berbasis Pemberdayaan. Malang: Inteligensia Media (2018)

89. Resmi, P.C., Widodo, W.I., Ermawati, K.C., Anggraini, F.D., Ihalauw, J.J., Susanto, D.R.: Communication in tourism: a review and open problems. Int. J. Adv. Commun. Media J. **3**(1)

90. Rheny, S.: The difference between distributors and suppliers, agents and resellers. Expert's Corner, 30 September 2022

91. Thadi, R.: Proses Komunikasi Instruksional dalam Pembelajaran Vokasional. JOEAI (J. Educ. Instr.) **2**(1), 49–55 (2019)

92. Fitriansyah, F.: Efek komunikasi massa pada khalayak (studi deskriptif pengguna media sosial dalam membentuk perilaku remaja. Cakrawala: Jurnal Humaniora Bina Sarana Informatika **18**(2), 171–178 (2018)

93. Astuti, P.A.A., Athallariq, M.I., Febbyani, A.W., Islamiyah, J.S., Nurfiansyah, D., Putra, T.S.O.: Optimization of social media as media promotion of historial tourist destination in Surabaya. Prospect: Jurnal Pemberdayaan Masyarakat **2**(1), 23–35 (2023)

94. Sukmadi, S., Goeltom, A.D.L., Darmawan, H., Simatupang, V., Tarunajaya, W.B.: Strategi pengembangan digital tourism dalam meningkatkan kunjungan wisatawan ke desa wisata alam endah kecamatan rancabali, kabupaten bandung. Media Bina Ilmiah **17**(6), 1141–1148 (2023)

Creating Values for Big Data Analytics through Business and Technology Alignment

Luen Mun Chong[✉], Suraya Yaacob, Wan Farahwani Wan Fakhruddin,
and Nur Azaliah Abu Bakar

Faculty Technology and Informatics Razak, Universiti Teknologi Malaysia, Kuala Lumpur,
Malaysia
munchong.luen@utm.graduate.my

Abstract. Meaningful insights are the most important outcome of a big data analytics project (BDA). As the BDA project has been widely used to facilitate business decisions, many organizations focus on gaining valuable insights into their business performance, especially as one of the determining factors for organizations to outrun their competitors in the industry. The research from the current literature found that there needs to be more technical consideration for the valuable measure of business performance based only on the business perspective rather than considering the advanced technological perspective: big data analytics. On the other hand, the technical point of view is focused more on data than realizing real business needs. Hence, this research aims to introduce, identify, or develop know-how mapping between business and technical points of view for valuable insights. So then, the BDA can work on understanding what the business would want and aligning it with what the data could provide. With that, the first step is to identify elements and define the definitions of the valuable insights. Second, this research will serve as a how-knowledge guideline for business analytics in achieving valuable insights. This research is intended to shed light and clarify valuable insights from business and technical points of view while developing any BDA project in the business organization.

Keywords: Business Analytics · Business Analysis · Value · Business Understanding · Data Understanding

1 Introduction

Nowadays, data plays an essential role in everyone's life. However, data itself could not best represent the information flowing around us. The term big data has been used since then. It is an important element and a topic that has been introduced differently based on different perspectives. Big data generally refers to datasets that exceed the capacities of conventional database software that can capture, store, manage, and analyze them [1]. Such representation provides an excellent perspective that big data is not just about the amount of data but can be perceived from various perspectives.

Big data is defined as high-volume, high-velocity, and high-variety information assets that demand cost-effective, innovative forms of information processing for enhanced insight and decision-making. It is a term used to describe a large amount of information that is generated and delivered at high speed, including both structured and unstructured sources, with the possible presence of uncertainty and incongruences, non-reliable information, and untruthful information [3]. Other introduced angles of big data can be simplified with varieties of Vs, namely velocity, volume, variety, and veracity. The data needs to be analyzed to extract useful insights from such a high volume of data that could be non-reliable, leading to what is referred to as Big Data Analytics (BDA). Essentially, BDA is a way to process and analyze large amounts of data to uncover useful insights and make informed decisions.

BDA, regarded as the next frontier of innovation, competition, and productivity [4], has piqued the interest of academics and practitioners ranging from large corporations to small and medium-sized businesses. Many people believe that the art of BDA can help organizations meet their specific business goals [5] or create new business values. According to International Data Corporation (IDC), big-data and big-data analytics-related services marketing in Asia Pacific (excluding Japan) will grow at a 16.3% CAGR from 2016 to 2019 [6]. Many market leaders, including Google, Apple, Amazon, Facebook, and Alibaba, have begun reshaping business competition and consolidating large markets in the age of big data and analytics [7]. As can be seen, corporations from various industries are attempting to adapt to the trend of big data, and multiple perspectives of analysis have been conducted to extract value from big data.

Many academic studies [8, 10] concentrate on analyzing business value from a data or system perspective or even from a strategic management perspective, while others are primarily from industries. According to [9], the values of big data can be reflected from the cost effectiveness, people empowerment, research and development utilization, and process improvement. Furthermore, BDA considers IT business value from three perspectives: transactional, strategic, and transformational [11]. With the three perspectives, it elaborates that BDA could assist in decision-making that could reduce operating costs, create more competitive advantages, align IT with business strategies, and improve employee skill levels. However, little research investigates the perspective of bridging the business understanding with the data understanding, where valuable data is ensured to be used to achieve the business objectives. As a result, this research emphasizes the importance of using a model to bridge the gap between the data obtained, the business objectives, and the insights obtained from the data to achieve the business objectives.

2   Working Background

Big Data is a term that has spread widely and is used by various businesses. Not only within enterprises, but it has also been a topic on which many researchers have focused to support how businesses could leverage big data to gain business values and be proactive in making business decisions rather than reacting to situations. Big data has been widely associated with a few terminologies, including many datasets, exploration, collection or capture, storage, or analysis. McKinsey defined big data as datasets that are so large that traditional database software tools cannot handle, capture, store, manage, or even analyze them. Furthermore, big data is defined as the extraction of value from large amounts of diverse data via high-speed data exploration, collection, or even analysis [12]. With such an understanding of a large number of data, followed by various collection and analysis, business is attempting to extract values from the large amount of data that has been collected or captured. Profit maximization, customer retention, and business fulfillment are some examples of values identified by researchers that can be extracted from big data. Previously, enterprises tended to overlook extremely detailed data when it came to big data. However, with the recent emergence of big data technologies, such details are now being noticed, and such data are contributing a lot of value creation to enterprises. As a result, organizations place a high value on understanding big data and the techniques for processing large datasets to create value effectively.

A process is a series of actions or steps taken to achieve a particular objective or goal. With the need to achieve a certain objective or goal, business dwells on the process in multiple aspects. A process typically involves steps, objective and human, which match what a business has. As a result, when a business requires analysis or has an analytical requirement, it is defined as a business analysis process or a business analytics process. These processes have their own unique steps, involve various stakeholders, and have specific objectives, but ultimately share the same fundamental understanding of what a process is.

The business analysis process is an organizational method that identifies current operations that could be improved for better efficiency. As always, this is an ongoing process with organizations expanding or reaching new levels of maturity as well as technological advancement, which has been hard to be caught up with by organizational operations. Therefore, regular analysis of the current process in organizations is unavoidable and could even support be reducing inefficiencies due to fast-moving technologies and methodologies introduced. That research focuses on defining the most efficient business analysis process from time to time to accommodate the fast-moving trend of technologies and supporting organizations to have a generalized formula that could be followed. It is important to have a business analysis process formulated and followed by an organization because an inefficient business process can lead to significant financial losses for the company and missed deadlines. It is always a fatal blow to a company that needs more efficient business processes, but at the same time, identifying inefficient processes is challenging. On the other hand, a different struggle has been proposed in the business analysis process [13]. Rather than identifying inefficient business processes, Brandenburg proposed that helping stakeholders understand the value of business analysis would be a bigger challenge, as stakeholders tend not to understand the value of business analysis. Despite the challenges shared by different researchers, there are some other challenges born due to the business analysis process, and one of the most discussed topics is data generated due to changes in the business process. Many business processes neglect this factor; however, the steps of the business analysis and business analytics processes have many similarities, with both processes having the main goal of supporting the business.

The business analytics process is an iterative chain of processing steps that use collected data to turn them into decisions or information [14]. The business analytics process serves a similar definition but adds the point that it could help resolve business problems using relevant data and give added value to enterprises in gaining a competitive advantage in the marketplace. The information from multiple researchers shares that the business analytics process is a step-in business that could support the advancement of enterprises to the next level of business because, in the business analytics process, there are possibilities to include predictive modeling into the business analytics process. Such modeling could provide organizations with trends by analyzing big data collected. According to [15], predictive modeling requires an algorithm that works with historical data. For big data, with a high velocity of data generated, organizations could easily see trends in real-time. Such trends are the values that could be obtained and disregarded financially or internally for business strategies.

Focusing on the perspective of values from data, the perspective of value takes on the business value derived from data initiatives [16]. However, such focus is always assumed and not applied. Such assumptions always stand from the perspective of how data is an organizational asset as well as an improvement of the organization, for example, cost reduction, revenue generation, or risk mitigation. Regardless of the assumptions made, the value generated by big data analytics is a realization of information technology [11]. Supporting that, Byeonghwa Park et al. found in their proposal information that IT business value consists of transactional, strategic, transformational, and informational value [17]. Each of the values still serves the perspective of cost-effectiveness, innovation formation, expansion, or improvement of business capabilities, as well as improving organizational productivity. It could be seen that all the values focus on looking at the value obtained from big data analytics from the business perspective while using IT knowledge of big data. Therefore, it could be seen that in terms of value, it refers to benefits that businesses could gain in terms of behavior studies, problem-solving, enhancement, or predictability through the big data collected.

On the other hand, a different perspective of value lies from the perspective of IT, in which data accessibility, data precision, and data usability work as well as part of the value that could be obtained from big data analytics. The mentioned value is known as the informational value, which serves as the part to measure the values that data could contribute [11]. In terms of informational value, the consideration is how fast multiple or different users could access the data, how easily the data could be accessed, or even how accurate the collected data is to be used for analysis. Hence, it could be understood that the value consists of two perspectives, business, and IT, where they correspond with one another in gaining the best out of big data analytics, according to Fig. 1. As extension, it could be observed that values are not just considered from a business perspective but also from a technical perspective. In Fig. 1, the business value observed from the Kaplan Norton Balanced Scorecard is used as the basis of business value, where it pinpoints the business values based on the parties involved. Adding to the research of Byeonghwa Park et al., business values are categorized as transactional, strategic, transformational, and informational value, but the core of the categorization works with the Kaplan Norton Balance Scorecard, which is customer, financial, and internal business processes, and learning and growth. For instance, transactional value could be obtained from a customer or financial perspective, while strategic value could be mapped to financial and internal business processes. Therefore, the business values in Fig. 1 are used as part of the alignment definition.

For technical values, the focus is on four elements: data, data source, data analysis and stakeholders. The elements are identified according to different frameworks, and one of the main contributions of the identification was from Data Value Map [18]. In Data Value Map, different perspectives of technical values have been shared. However, with studies with different business analysis frameworks, only common attributes have been retained where the technical values are essential in alignment. Data and data sources technically represent what data should be used, where it is located and what the current data looks like. Such information is important for an alignment as it allows stakeholders from different perspectives to be on the same view for the same business value. Furthermore, a stakeholder is considered technical values, where the correct stakeholders make much difference when understanding and generating the needed business value. Lastly, data analysis is the technical value; proper data analysis modeling would improve overall innovation of solutions and capability improvement. In most cases, especially big data analytics, a good and effective data analysis modeling could help perform a data prediction model, which benefits an organization from a business values perspective.

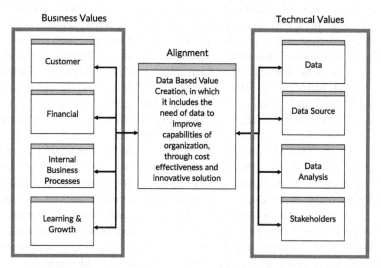

Fig. 1. Business-Technical Value Alignment

3   Business-Data Requirement Framework

The research extends to a business-data requirement framework based on multiple frameworks developed, for instance, Resource Based View, Dynamic capabilities, Kaplan-Norton, Data Value Map, Business Analysis and Business Analytics framework. The framework structure aims to support business value derivation while business requirements are being requested and raised. The framework embeds business analysis or analytics frameworks into business requirements specification (BRS) templates to obtain different values from available data, such as transactional, strategic, transformational, and informational value. As BRS provides clarity in ensuring effective alignment and works as a comprehensive standard or methodology to reduce failure in BDA projects, it should also be data-centric instead of user-centric [19]. Furthermore, a new process has been introduced in the study: data acquisition, data analysis and value discovery, and use case consolidation. However, the model has not been able to be validated. Extending from the study, the research proposed blending different process frameworks into the BRS to make a complete user- and data-centric framework that could generate the required values. With the intention for data blend, the framework could be broken down step by step targeting a more precise business value and followed with the analysis of the current database to ensure precise business values are realistic with the data on hand. Figure 2 shares the framework representation, and the section will be explained in the following paragraph.

3.1 Business Value Alignment

Values are the focus of a BDA project being requested and executed. In the business-data requirement framework, the business alignment is split into two main categories of values, which aim to allow business users to define the business requirements accordingly. In the value understanding, four value perspectives are transactional, strategic, transformational, and informational value [11]. While focusing on Balance Scorecard, four values have been focused on: customer, financial, internal business process, and learning and growth [20]. Based on the values defined and definition from Balanced Scorecard, values could be specified within strategic management and business management value, where financial and internal business process values are answered towards shareholders. At the same time, customer and learning and growth focus externally. Serving values as the base, the design workflow structure of BRS would have to be split according to values definition from Balanced Scorecard and perspective analysis, as values answer to different stakeholders. In the business value alignment, the framework is well proposed to consider and understand the different levels of business understanding (e.g., aims and objectives) to increase the capability of technical data understanding. The initial step of identifying the business background and process background, as such, allows users to understand the initial needs, which leads to the current development of the project. Process background also connects and conveys a message to understand possible business scenarios for the business background. Finding relevant business scenarios through business background or process allows users to backtrack possible impediments before leading to the aims and objectives.

The stakeholder engagement matrix (Responsible-Accountable-Consulted-Informed (RACI) matrix) is one of the main features to govern stakeholder engagement as well as functionality [21]. To ensure the person responsible is accountable or should be consulted or informed during business value as well as data technicality definition, the RACI matrix helps to keep track and defines clear responsibilities for each team role and responsibilities in BDA project deliverables.

In accordance with the business aim and business objectives, the business aim is to ensure users have clearer long-term targets, while business objectives which are short-term goals used to build towards the business aim [22]. In the proposal of flow, the business aim comes before the business objectives because a business aim could be built up by many business objectives, and it is always easier and clearer to work in detail about a business objective if the long-term is achievable. Getting one step deeper than business objectives, business cases aim to allow users to clarify the relation of the case to business values or insights. In terms of a business case with financial or internal business process impact, it is required to be differentiated between strategic or business definition; as shared, the business case with strategic impact would require answering questions targeted to shareholders of organizations compared to business which requires understanding the behavior of customers or learning and growth on the current business scenario.

Finally, having the possibility to bifurcate between the categories of business values, a listing of the definitions should be considered by the unit to make sure the defined business case is workable and worth investing on the business case. In the listing of definition, it consists of target, impact, impediments, success criteria and expected outcome as the main elements aimed to support users justify business case, or business objectives raised as the more detail explanation could be provided, the lesser elements of surprise where could help in raising the success rate of BDA project. Data coverage is one element that differs in the pathway between strategy and business. In relation to business definition, data coverage should be considered instead of strategic definition; for example, data on hand does not work best to understand customer's needs or even in customer learning behavior that organizations require to continue improving and creating values. While in the strategic definition, data coverage is not considered where shareholders for an organization or how the organization should excel are towards a group of defined stakeholders.

3.2 Data Technical Alignment

Data technical alignment is the details of data technical consideration. The framework proposed as facilitation allows business users and technical developers to map and get a common understanding between business and data technical understanding. The concept of common understanding is most important between business and data understanding because it allows less contradiction and failure for BDA projects, as common understanding could reduce the possibility of unretrievable data [22, 24]. Hence, to clearly understand and have a workable business case or business objectives, additional steps are required compared to different analytics or analysis framework.

Current database analysis suggests collecting information from existing data storage, disregarding manual, or automatic data. Such collection plays an important role, allowing the developer to understand possible data currently used for analysis or value generation. Such values could be reused or re-defined, allowing a more up-to-date or precise value generated for strategic or business purposes. Data assessment could also be performed with database analysis, whereby a data dictionary is generated. As a data dictionary works as a collection of attributes, names, and definitions, it is useful throughout the stage, allowing business users to understand data conventions along the project and the definition of current values defined, finding out the required changes. In addition, with a data dictionary as an assessment, one of the cons is allowing the data to be analyzed easier where a consistent collection could be used between developer and business users. Extension to having data assessment process, data collection, and data exploration are generic processes allowing specific data sets collected and being explored for easier navigation as well as the discovery of incomplete data.

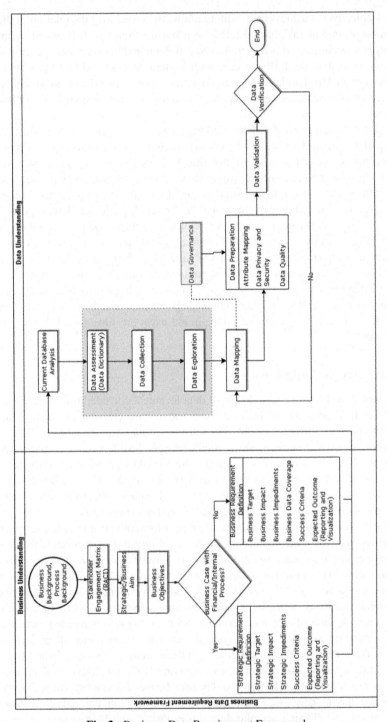

Fig. 2. Business-Data Requirement Framework

However, in terms of data exploration, it indeed offers what each field represents; with a proper data mapping process, it is easier to have a data analyst point out possible missing fields or complete data. On top of that, a data mapping activity allows the business stakeholder to identify the required data before the data analyst or data scientist works on the data, reducing the failure rate of BDA projects.

For the steps as follow, data preparation is required where the selected data through data mapping could be performed, in other words, retrieved from the current system or planned system, classifying whether the information is mandatory or optional, as well as getting the location of where the data is being stored. Data preparation is a phase consisting of data selection, data cleaning, data transformation and data integration [25], however in the perspective of big data analytics, data cleaning, transformation and integration should logically be considered after data validation and verification by the business instead of along the data preparation, the reason being cleaning, and transforming high volume of data would be a wastage of time if the data is not validated or verified to be required.

As a result, in the process of data preparation, instead of cleaning, transformation or data integration, attribute mapping, data privacy and security, and data governance is inserted. As data preparation allows data analysts or data miners to work on the data as preparation, attribute mapping allows the definition of data to be identified as early as possible, avoiding unnecessary data issues during transformation or cleaning. On top of that, data privacy, security, and governance are in place as part of data preparation because, without a definition of data privacy and security, extracted data may not be accessible to the person who defines the field to be extracted. As a result, it will violate data security which could be a point for big data analytics project failure. Nevertheless, data governance is a topic that should be worked on during the initial data preparation as it requires a vast amount of knowledge and definition for data consistency, as well as a definition for the analytics system to ensure the data maintained are up to standard.

Finally, data validation and verification serve a role in allowing business users to get a chance to confirm the required data and validate that the extracted data follows the current sets of formats or uniqueness or type. As the research investigates getting an alignment between business and technical understanding, each component serves a level of importance progressively; the framework should support clarification for business users and data analysts at the same time, support guide steps that should be taken to ensure data obtained could be used to generate business values.

Lastly, to ensure the alignment would match or unmatched between business and data, success criteria which has been defined in the early stage together with stakeholders would work best whereby it could reflect the readiness of both business and data.

3.3 The Implementation in Real Organizational Settings

In real life organizations, business-data requirement framework could be implemented in a way that it covers alignment between technology and business values.

According to Zain [10] framework in relation to big data could be used to support business in making quality, efficient, strategic thinking and planning, transparency, accountability, and data driven decision as well support business perspective for financial, people, process and research and innovation. Addition to that such values are critical obstacles for organizations in identifying strategic values from big data analytics, as a result with proposed framework, such values should be taken into consideration at the beginning before any data project being initiated.

Furthermore, through interviews conducted with the organizations, reviewing business process of an organization could work as a continual breakthrough of new insights validating the business-data requirement framework would be workable in real life organizations expediating and smoothing the while working process as well as assist in future easier decision making.

One of the critical element is to measure how valuable is the In the research, three elements mentioned, data analytics insights, decisional paradigm, and impact to business are shown in the proposed framework.

Extension to measure the values of the proposed framework, the component of values mentioned in [10] would be the best measurement for organization as it covers all aspects mentioned by Kaplan-Norton Balance Scorecard which is known for measuring organization performance.

4   Conclusion

The business-data framework was discussed throughout this study, and a substantial review was performed, ensuring business and technical-related understanding was explained and unveiled. On top of that, an improvement on the process framework definition has been proposed to facilitate business and technical data understanding as the current issues faced by organizations focused on the relation mapping between business and technical data mapping to obtain useful values. While focusing on values, there are limited publications in defining values in data but focusing more on the categorization of values instead of the definition of value (e.g., Kaplan Norton Balanced Scorecard). On the other hand, multiple publications dating from the year 2000 onwards focus on the framework of enhancing business framework or technical data framework separately instead of enhancing both frameworks as one. Therefore, finding publications directly related to the research intent or interest is challenging. As a result, to ensure the proposed framework could work as intended, demonstration and evaluation methodology is used to get various improvements, such as improving the meaning of value and the possible technical data understanding from different perspectives, either data analysts or project stakeholders. Hence, we wish organizations could use the framework to define, clarify, and refine further between business and data understanding. As future for validating further on the framework, demonstration to and evaluation from experts from industries would be conducted to ensure the framework workability with respect to Design Science Research Methodology (DSRM) as based on evaluation, it would be a method that could be used for extensive adaptation to daily use [26].

References

1. Borne, K.: Top 10 Big Data Challenges – A Serious Look at 10 Big Data V's. (2014). https://www.mapr.com/blog/top-10-big-data-challenges-serious-look-10-big-data-v's
2. Gartner. Big data (2016). http://www.gartner.com/it-glossary/big-data/

3. Fosso Wamba, S., Akter, S., Edwards, A., Chopin, G., Gnanzou, D.: How "big data" can make big impact: findings from a systematic review and a longitudinal case study. Int. J. Prod. Econ. **165**, 234–246 (2015). https://doi.org/10.1016/j.ijpe.2014.12.031

4. Manyika, J., Chui, M., Brown, B., Bughin, J., Dobbs, R., Roxburgh, C., Byers, A.H.: Big data: the next frontier for innovation, competition, and productivity (2011). http://consultancy.nl/media/McKinsey-BigDataTheNextFrontierforInnovation-1998.pdf. Accessed 17 Mar 2017

5. Mikalef, P., Boura, M., Lekakos, G., Krogstie, J.: Big data analytics and firm performance: findings from a mixed-method approach. J. Bus. Res. **98** (2019). https://doi.org/10.1016/j.jbusres.2019.01.044

6. Roche, S.: IDC Reveals 53% of Organizations in the APEJ Region Consider Big Data and Analytics Important for Business. http://www.idc.com/getdoc.jsp?containerId=prAP41208316. Accessed 21 Apr 2016

7. Sun, Z., Huo, Y.: A managerial framework for intelligent big data analytics. In: Pervasive Health: Pervasive Computing Technologies for Healthcare, pp. 152–156 (2019). https://doi.org/10.1145/3305160.3305211

8. LaValle, S., et al.: Big data, analytics and the path from insights to value. MIT Sloan Manag. Rev. **52**(2), 21–31 (2011)

9. Kwon, O., Lee, N., Shin, B.: Data quality management, data usage experience and acquisition intention of big data analytics. Int. J. Inf. Manag. **34**(3), 387–394 (2014)

10. Zain, M.Y., et al.: Valuable insights framework for big data and analytics in the Malaysian public sector organization. In: 2023 International Congress on Human-Computer Interaction, Optimization and Robotic Applications (HORA). IEEE (2023)

11. Park, B., Noh, M., Lee, C.K.: The relationships between capabilities and values of big data analytics. ACM Int. Conf. Proc. Ser. 132–134 (2020). https://doi.org/10.1145/3426020.3426052

12. Sharda, R., Delen, D., Turba, E.: Business Intelligence and Analytics: Systems for Decision Support (10th Edn). Pearson, Boston (2018)

13. An Introduction to Business Analysis and the Business Analyst Process Framework (bridging-the-gap.com) (2021). https://www.bridging-the-gap.com/business-analysis-process/

14. Big Data in Business Analytics: Talking About the Analytics Process Model - SAS Users (2019). https://blogs.sas.com/content/sgf/2019/05/14/big-data-in-business-analytics-talking-about-the-analytics-process-model/

15. The Business Analytics Process | LinkedIn (2021). https://www.linkedin.com/pulse/business-analytics-process-leonardo-anello-1e/

16. Sammon, A.: The Data Value Map: A Framework for Developing Shared Understanding on Data Initiatives (2017)

17. Ren, S.J., Wamba, S.F., Akter, S., Dubey, R., Childe, S.J.: Modelling quality dynamics, business value and firm performance in a big data analytics environment. Int. J. Prod. Res. **55**(17), 5011–5026 (2017). https://doi.org/10.1080/00207543.2016.1154209

18. Sammon, A.: The Data Value Map: A Framework for Developing Shared Understanding of Data Initiatives (2017)

19. Altarturi, H.H., Ng, K.-Y., Ninggal, M.I.H., Nazri, A.S.A., Ghani, A.A.A.: A requirement engineering model for big data software. In: 2017 IEEE Conference on Big Data and Analytics (ICBDA), Kuching, pp. 111–117 (2017). https://doi.org/10.1109/ICBDAA.2017.8284116

20. Kaplan, R.S., Norton, D.P.: Alignment: Using the Balanced Scorecard to Create Corporate Synergies. Harvard Business Press (2006)

21. What Is a RACI Matrix? https://project-management.com/understanding-responsibility-assignment-matrix-raci-matrix/#raci-matrix-definitions

22. Setting Business Aims and Objectives. https://www.bbc.co.uk/bitesize/guides/z4b2qp3/revision/1#:~:text=A%20business%20aim%20is%20the,it%20to%20meet%20its%20aim

23. Reasons Why Big Data Projects Fail. https://datafloq.com/read/reasons-behind-the-failure-most-big-data-projects/
24. Simple Reasons Why Data Projects Fail. https://towardsdatascience.com/5-simple-reasons-why-data-projects-fail-98fd04c41738
25. Ahmad, Z., Yaacob, S., Ibrahim, R., Wan Fakhruddin, W.F.:The review for visual analytics methodology. In: 2022 International Congress on Human-Computer Interaction, Optimization and Robotic Applications (HORA), Ankara, pp. 1–10 (2022). https://doi.org/10.1109/HORA55278.2022.9800100
26. Venable, J.R., Pries-Heje, J., Baskerville, R.L.: Choosing a design science research methodology. In: ACIS 2017 Proceedings, vol. 112 (2017). https://aisel.aisnet.org/acis2017/11

Web-Based Mental Health Predicting System Using K-Nearest Neighbors and XGBoost Algorithms

Nurul Farhanaa Zulkefli[1], Norizan Mat Diah[1(✉)], Azlan Ismail[1],
Haslizatul Fairuz Mohamed Hanum[1], Zaidah Ibrahim[1], and Yunifa Miftachul Arif[2]

[1] School of Computing Sciences, College of Computing, Informatics and Mathematics,
Universiti Teknologi MARA, Shah Alam, Malaysia
norizan289@uitm.edu.my
[2] Informatics Engineering, Faculty of Science and Technology, Universitas Islam Negeri
Maulana Malik Ibrahim, Malang, Indonesia

Abstract. Problems with mental health are common presently and have been a worry for a long time. Mental health problems, like anxiety, depression, and panic attacks, can be caused by numerous things. Therefore, recognising the start of mental disease is becoming increasingly crucial to maintaining a good life balance. This study uses machine learning to identify any possible mental health disorders in an individual to attain this goal. The investigation employed supervised machine learning to predict mental health status, namely K-Nearest Neighbors (KNN) and XGBoost, with performance evaluation criteria including accuracy, precision, recall, and F1 score. When these two algorithms were compared, it was discovered that XGBoost produced a more effective prediction model, which was then employed to develop a web-based mental health prediction system. The web-based method creates a questionnaire for mental health issues. Based on the user's responses to the questions, the system will predict his or her mental health status as normal, depression, anxiety, stress, loneliness, or regularity. Every component of the system, including buttons and forms, has been successfully tested using functionality tests. Moreover, the system's advantages, weaknesses, and future study directions are identified.

Keywords: K-Nearest Neighbors · Mental Health · Predicting · XGBoost

1 Introduction

A person's mental health needs to be looked after correctly because their mental state provides a general picture of who they are. Today's fast-paced lifestyle changes are raising concerns about mental health. Many people are experiencing various kinds of psychological health issues because of this. According to a 2011 World Health Organisation (WHO) executive board assessment, depression will contribute to the worldwide disease burden by 2030. As a result, today in Malaysia, the National Health and Morbidity Survey conducted by the Ministry of Health Malaysia (MOH) revealed that mental health

© The Author(s), under exclusive license to Springer Nature Singapore Pte Ltd. 2024
H. Badioze Zaman et al. (Eds.): IVIC 2023, LNCS 14322, pp. 381–396, 2024.
https://doi.org/10.1007/978-981-99-7339-2_32

problems occur not only among adults but also among people aged 16 and above, where the rate of depression was 29.2% among approximately 4.2 million people, meaning one in three Malaysians has experienced mental health problems [1].

In 2019, a new coronavirus (COVID-19) epidemic had a more significant impact on the cause of mental disease. Since COVID-19 has radically changed how people live, work, and study while simultaneously creating a health risk [2]. For example, during a lockdown, some people may lose their employment, while others may need to work numerous occupations to supplement their income. A person infected with COVID-19 may suffer issues with their mental health since they must be quarantined, leading them to worry about their employer, family, and themselves. During the COVID-19 epidemic, the WHO predicted an increase in instances of depression, self-harm, and suicide. Stress may lead to mental illness, and everyone has the potential to experience it. Stress is a physiological imbalance resulting from a mismatch between a person's ability and drives to satisfy a given situation's demands. It is an emotional tension or strain from a challenging or unfavourable situation. If the stress is too extreme, it can result in anxiety and depression [3]. It is essential to identify individuals who are at risk, to avoid mental health problems and enhance care quality, as mentioned in Kumar et al. [4]. Anxiety, sadness, and stress are the three most common psychological problems. People experiencing this type of health crisis tend to keep their thoughts and feelings to themselves, making them depressed and lonely.

People suffering from this are frequently reluctant to express their emotions to their doctors, family members, or friends. It has been discovered that the signs and symptoms of mental health conditions are not always obvious, and many patients are unaware of their illnesses until they are admitted to hospitals for treatment [5]. As a result, these patients recover more slowly and require significantly more expensive care to achieve the desired health outcome. Once a mental disorder has been found, it needs to be treated so it does not worsen. An early mental health diagnosis is related to a person's level of mental health. Anyone exhibiting abnormal behaviour should get immediate treatment from a psychologist to be correctly diagnosed with the type of mental illness they are experiencing [3]. One-on-one interactions and therapy sessions can be used to accomplish this. The WHO highlighted that improper diagnosis and treatment, mainly if it occurs late, can result in various illnesses. There are various categories of mental disorders. Therefore, it is impossible to assume that everyone has the same type of mental disorder because each person has a different problem. Sometimes, one person may have more than one type of mental disorder. Furthermore, each type of mental disorder also has several degrees, including mild, moderate, and severe; therefore, as technology evolves, it can assist psychiatrists in adequately diagnosing patients with mental disorders.

2 Background Study

The prevention and treatment of mental disorders have become a top goal in public health as mental disease is rising and has become a global burden. For example, during the third wave of the COVID-19 pandemic in Malaysia, 390 (25.1%) of the 1554 respondents had severe depressive disorders, while 530 (34.1%) had mild anxiety symptoms [6]. Therefore, the importance of implementing digital technology to enhance access, engagement, and treatment outcomes is increasing, which has led to the emergence of a wide variety of health technologies and applications in response to the need for more effective mental health care that is more customised and effective [7].

Health technologies like mobile apps and wearable tech are often used to help with and keep track of the symptoms of mental health risk assessments. For instance, research has led to the development of mobile apps allowing pregnant mothers to self-report their mental health, such as their prenatal depression and mood, on their own devices. It helps those needing it while reducing the administrative burden that paper questionnaires place on respondents [8]. The heart rate variability (HRV) data from wearables on the wrist can also be used to predict general health indicators. For example, research by [9] used HRV data to predict how stress or anxiety, unrelated to the heart, could affect how well the heart works. The different ways that health technology can be used to predict or find mental illness depend on machine learning to predict the data.

Supervised machine learning is one of the subclasses of machine learning. This approach is used to do detection or prediction tasks because the goal of it is to forecast or categorise a specific outcome of interest [10], such as determining if a patient has a mental disease or not; therefore, it is an appropriate method to apply since the study's results must be classified. Mental health issues can range from severe to mild and regular [4]. Supervised machine learning is also suitable for large data structures, such as clinical, social, and demographic predictors [11].

The support vector machine (SVM) is an algorithm for supervised machine learning, frequently used for prediction purposes because SVM has the unique capacity to deal with linear and non-linear data. It also supports kernel functions, including the linear, polynomial, and radial basis functions, for fine-tuning performance. SVM can be applied to classification and regression issues. However, one of its main applications is binary classification, where it examines the training examples and chooses a hyperplane to divide them into two classes [12, 13]. SVM is not appropriate for this study because the result will involve more than two classifications, not a binary classification but a categorised one. Nevertheless, some researchers also employ the SVM methodology, as seen in a study [14] that uses the method to classify data related to schizophrenia. The study's findings showed that data on schizophrenia had been appropriately identified, with an overall accuracy rate of 90.1%.

K-Nearest Neighbor (KNN) is an instance-based learning classifier using Euclidean distance, and this approach determines how similar the predefined classes and the classes to be classified are. The new data point will be compared to the k nearest sample data points, and the class with the most significant number of those neighbours will be considered the data point's class [3]. However, because only storing the training samples is done during the training phase, this classification strategy is also known as a lazy classification technique. Although this method performs well with fewer dimensions, it also consumes much memory. Islam et al. [15] used KNN to identify depression, and they employed various KNN techniques, including Fine, Medium, Coarse, Cosine, Cubic, and Weighted KNN; 71% of the results were accurate. Furthermore, KNN can produce a definite result suitable for this study.

Boosting is an ensemble learning method using numerous algorithms rather than one main algorithm to improve prediction performance. Feature importance and selection are determined using weaker models, and boosting will repeatedly generate weak learners that may not be correct models and utilise them to build more vital models, which are helpful in supervised learning. Gradient boosting is one of the many boosting types used to solve classification problems by linearly combining essential variables. This method operates similarly to a decision tree by comparing attributes and applying decision rules. It evaluates the decision path depending on the node's attribute and then uses the result to provide a class label.

The other boosting variant is AdaBoost, which only predicts using a single feature and uses a weak learner known as Decision Stump. All the observations will initially be given the same weights, and then the misclassified observations will be given more weight in the second Decision Stump. The process is repeated until the bias and variance are as low as possible and the best classification model is created. The study conducted by [16] found that the predicting performance of the seven SML models is based on accuracy, specificity, and sensitivity, and the results show that Adaboost is one of the two best predictive models for predicting early symptoms in patients infected with COVID-19. Another study used AdaBoost to detect depression and achieved a final accuracy of 91.62%. The study also used the XGBoost method, achieving the highest final accuracy score, 97.80% [17].

These are the two best algorithms that can be employed by health technology to predict or detect mental illness, depending on machine learning to forecast the data.

3   Methodology

The methodology workflow, once the primary activity, is illustrated in Fig. 1 below.

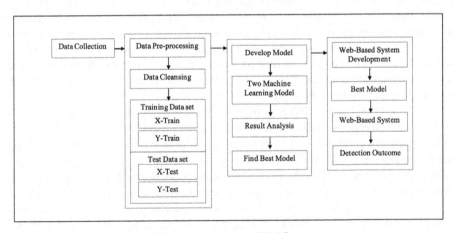

Fig. 1. Methodology Workflow

Based on the methodology workflow in Fig. 1, data will be collected after identifying the issue and using a similar system, and the dataset will undergo pre-processing. After processing, the dataset will be split into a train set and a test set, with 80% and

20%, respectively. The machine learning techniques chosen for this research, KNN and XGBoost, will be applied to the training data after pre-processing. Model validation will then be performed to determine the best model. The web-based system will employ the selected best model to produce the detection results.

3.1 Data Collection

The dataset was obtained from the Kaggle created by Zaman [18], and it also utilised research by [19] and [20]. The dataset comprises 25 columns corresponding to a set of questions and 40 thousand rows representing yes or no answers to those questions. For instance, if the column name is "suicidal thought", the question will be "Have you ever considered harming yourself?" and the answer will be yes or no. Figure 2 below illustrates the first mental illness dataset used in this study.

suicidal.thought	feeling.tired	close.frien	social.mec	weight.gain	material.p	introvert	popping.u	having.nig	avoids.pe	feeling.ne	trouble.co	blamming	Disorder
no	no	no	no	no	no	no	no	no	no	no	no		Anxiety
yes	no	no	no	no	no	no	no	no	no	no	no		Depression
no	yes	yes	yes	yes	yes	yes	no	no	no	no	no		Loneliness
no	no	no	no	no	no	no	yes	yes	yes	yes	yes	yes	Stress
no	no	no	no	no	no	no	no	no	no	no	no		Normal
no	no	no	no	no	no	no	no	no	no	no	no		Anxiety
yes	no	no	no	no	no	no	no	no	no	no	no		Depression
no	yes	yes	yes	yes	yes	yes	no	no	no	no	no		Loneliness
no	no	no	no	no	no	no	yes	yes	yes	yes	yes	yes	Stress
no	no	no	no	no	no	no	no	no	no	no	no		Normal
no	no	no	no	no	no	no	no	no	no	no	no		Anxiety
yes	no	no	no	no	no	no	no	no	no	no	no		Depression
no	yes	yes	yes	yes	yes	yes	no	no	no	no	no		Loneliness
no	no	no	no	no	no	no	yes	yes	yes	yes	yes	yes	Stress
no	no	no	no	no	no	no	no	no	no	no	no		Normal
no	no	no	no	no	no	no	no	no	no	no	no		Anxiety
yes	no	no	no	no	no	no	no	no	no	no	no		Depression
no	yes	yes	yes	yes	yes	yes	no	no	no	no	no		Loneliness
no	no	no	no	no	no	no	yes	yes	yes	yes	yes	yes	Stress

Fig. 2. Mental Illness Dataset

Based on Fig. 2, the 'disorder' column, which has five classes (anxiety, depression, stress, loneliness, and normal), indicates the target class for the dataset. The second dataset is also from the Kaggle website, "Student Mental Health Analysis" by Lambino [21]. This dataset contains 101 rows and ten columns. The student mental health analysis dataset is shown in Fig. 3.

Timestamp	Choose yc	Age	What is your course?	Your cur	What is yc	Marital st:	Do you have Depression?	Do you have Anxiety?	Do you have Panic attack?	Did you seek any specialist for a treatment
8/7/2020 12:02	Female	18	Engineering	year 1	3.00 - 3.49	No	Yes	No	Yes	No
8/7/2020 12:04	Male	21	Islamic education	year 2	3.00 - 3.49	No	No	Yes	No	No
8/7/2020 12:05	Male	19	BIT	Year 1	3.00 - 3.49	No	Yes	Yes	Yes	No
8/7/2020 12:06	Female	22	Laws	year 3	3.00 - 3.49	Yes	Yes	No	No	No
8/7/2020 12:13	Male	23	Mathemathics	year 4	3.00 - 3.49	No	No	No	No	No
8/7/2020 12:31	Female	19	Engineering	Year 2	3.50 - 4.00	No	No	No	Yes	No
8/7/2020 12:32	Male	23	Pendidikan islam	year 2	3.50 - 4.00	Yes	No	Yes	Yes	No
8/7/2020 12:33	Female	18	BCS	year 1	3.50 - 4.00	No	Yes	Yes	No	No
8/7/2020 12:35	Female	19	Human Resources	Year 2	2.50 - 2.99	No	No	No	No	No
8/7/2020 12:39	Male	18	Irkhs	year 1	3.50 - 4.00	No	Yes	Yes	Yes	No
8/7/2020 12:39	Female	20	Psychology	year 1	3.50 - 4.00	No	No	No	No	No
8/7/2020 12:39	Female	24	Engineering	Year 3	3.50 - 4.00	Yes	Yes	No	No	No
8/7/2020 12:40	Female	18	BCS	year 1	3.00 - 3.49	No	No	No	No	No
8/7/2020 12:41	Male	19	Engineering	year 1	3.00 - 3.49	No	No	No	No	No
8/7/2020 12:43	Female	18	KENMS	Year 2	3.50 - 4.00	No	Yes	No	No	No
8/7/2020 12:43	Male	24	BCS	Year 3	3.50 - 4.00	No	No	No	No	No
8/7/2020 12:46	Female	24	Accounting	year 3	3.00 - 3.49	No	No	No	No	No
8/7/2020 12:52	Female	24	ENM	year 4	3.00 - 3.49	Yes	Yes	Yes	Yes	No
8/7/2020 13:05	Female	20	BIT	Year 2	3.50 - 4.00	No	No	Yes	No	No

Fig. 3. Student Mental Health Analysis Dataset

Based on Fig. 3, it can be observed that the dataset does not have the target class. It indicates that the dataset needs to undergo data pre-processing to include the target class.

3.2 Data Pre-processing

The dataset for this study needs to undergo data pre-processing and cleaning before code implementation. These steps must ensure that the data produces accurate results and is simple to use and understand. This study uses two datasets, both of which require data pre-processing. For the first dataset, checking for any missing values is the first stage in the data cleaning process, and a missing value will be removed from the dataset if it exists. To find the missing value in the dataset, we will utilise the isnull () method. The method will return a Boolean value. If the values are NA (i.e., "not available"), the method will return "True", indicating the presence of missing values. Otherwise, the values will return "False", indicating no missing values. The total missing values for each column are depicted in Table 1 below.

Table 1. Number of missing values for each column (first dataset)

No	Feature	Mutual Information
1	feeling.negative	0.507611
2	Introvert	0.506302
3	weight.gain	0.503632
4	over.react	0.503621
5	having.trouble.with.work	0.503527
6	sweating	0.503190
7	change.in.eating	0.502702
8	feeling.tired	0.501224
9	blaming.yourself	0.501009
10	anger	0.500718
11	close.friend	0.500604
12	having.nightmares	0.498475
13	having.trouble.in.sleeping	0.498436
14	avoids.people.or.activities	0.498253
15	trouble.in.concentration	0.498054
16	popping.up.Stressful.memory	0.497267
17	panic	0.497048
18	hopelessness	0.496930

(continued)

Table 1. (*continued*)

No	Feature	Mutual Information
19	breathing.rapidly	0.496256
20	social.media.addiction	0.495580
21	suicidal.thought	0.495196
22	feeling.nervous	0.491316

Table 1 shows a relatively small difference in the value of mutual information between the features, with the range of values falling between 0.4 and 0.5. Based on the result, all the features have at least one non-zero mutual information score with every other feature. It is helpful because mutual information scores of zero indicate that a feature and every other feature are entirely independent. However, the higher values could be more beneficial as features with significant mutual information might be unnecessary and should be removed [22]. After determining the shared information values, we will select the top 10 features for this project. To achieve this, we will utilise the "SelectKBest" library and a mutual information classifier to identify the K-Best features and find the most suitable ones. Choosing the most essential features is crucial as it can shorten training time, reduce noise, and improve the model's accuracy. The selected features are displayed in Table 2 below.

Table 2. Top 10 best features

No	Feature
1	feeling.nervous
2	panic
3	trouble.in.concentration
4	hopelessness
5	anger
6	social.media.addiction
7	weight.gain
8	having.nightmares
9	feeling.negative
10	blaming.yourself

Based on Table 2, only these ten features, including the target class, will be used for this study, and any additional features that were not selected as the best features will be removed from the dataset. Finally, the dataset will be saved as a cleaned dataset and used for training, testing, and developing the web-based model. The first step in data pre-processing for the second dataset is renaming the columns, as the original dataset had excessively long column names. Next, we used the same method, the isnull() method, to check for any missing values. The results of the missing value are shown in Table 3 below.

Table 3. Number of missing values for each column (second dataset)

No	Column name	Number of missing values
1	Gender	0
2	Age	1
3	Course	0
4	Year	0
5	CGPA	0
6	Married	0
7	Depression	0
8	Anxiety	0
9	Panic Attack	0
10	Seeking Treatment	0

Since there is one missing value in the column "Age", as shown in Table 3, the row with the missing value will be removed. Next, we created a new column called "Mental Health Issues" and assigned a "Yes" or "No" value next to each student's name to indicate if they had mental health problems. This new column will serve as the target class for this second dataset. To determine the value for the new column, we will use the values from the "Depression", "Anxiety", and "Panic Attack" columns. After this process, the dataset will be used for training and testing.

3.3 Model Development

The development of web-based mental health detection involves two steps. The first step entails training and testing the model using the KNN and XGBoost algorithms and selecting the best model. To classify a new data point, KNN looks at its K nearest neighbours and determines how closely it fits with the current data. The new data point is then assigned a class label based on the class labels of its K Nearest Neighbors, with all the K-neighbors selected from the training set [23]. The nearest distance is calculated using the Manhattan distance. The hyperparameter utilised for KNeighborsClassifier is depicted in Fig. 4 below.

```
classifier= KNeighborsClassifier(n_neighbors=5, metric='manhattan', p=1 )
trained_model = classifier.fit(X_train, y_train)
```

Fig. 4. Hyperparameter for KNN Classifier

The value of K has been set to a default of five since we began utilising the Scikit-Learn library. Therefore, the hyperparameter 'p' is set to 1 with the selected Manhattan distance, and the classifier starts training.

On the other hand, the XGBoost technique addresses the trade-off between the complexity of the model, which is influenced by factors like depth, number of trees, and others. It learns the data using a boosted tree ensemble [17]. Figure 5 illustrates the hyperparameters that were used.

```
XGBClassifier(base_score=0.5, booster='gbtree', colsample_bylevel=1,
              colsample_bynode=1, colsample_bytree=1, eval_metric='mlogloss',
              gamma=0, gpu_id=-1, importance_type='gain',
              interaction_constraints='', learning_rate=0.300000012,
              max_delta_step=0, max_depth=6, min_child_weight=1,
              monotone_constraints='()', n_estimators=100, n_jobs=16,
              num_parallel_tree=1, objective='multi:softmax', num_class=5, random_state=0,
              reg_alpha=0, reg_lambda=1, scale_pos_weight=None, subsample=1,
              tree_method='exact', use_label_encoder=False,
              validate_parameters=1, verbosity=None)
```

Fig. 5. Hyperparameters for XGBoost Classifier

The hyperparameter 'objective' is set to 'multi:softmax' because the classification involves more than one class, and the softmax objective is used. This setting returns the predicted class instead of probability. Since the 'objective' hyperparameter is set to 'multi:softmax', it is also necessary to set the 'num_class' hyperparameter, representing the number of unique classes.

Next, downloading and installing the essential Python libraries, such as KNeighborsClassifier, XGBClassifier, pandas, train_test_split, classification_report, and confusion matrix, is also required to implement the KNN and XGBoost algorithms. The code used to import the library is shown in Figs. 6 and 7 below.

```
from xgboost import XGBClassifier
from sklearn.model_selection import train_test_split
from sklearn.metrics import classification_report, confusion_matrix
import pandas as pd
```

Fig. 6. Import Libraries for XGBoost

```
import pandas as pd
from sklearn.neighbors import KNeighborsClassifier
from sklearn.metrics import classification_report, confusion_matrix
from sklearn.model_selection import train_test_split
```

Fig. 7. Import Libraries for KNN

The code for importing the cleaned dataset, training, and testing the model, and displaying the model's accuracy will be used to create a web-based application.

3.4 Testing Model

In the fourth phase, all models are tested to evaluate their accuracy, which is the ultimate goal of the study. After implementing each model, the process begins with calculating accuracy, precision, recall, and F1 score. The evaluation will utilise a confusion matrix comprising true positive (TP), true negative (TN), false positive (FP), and false negative (FN) values to measure accuracy, precision, recall, and F1-score. The formulas for accuracy, precision, recall, and F1-score are illustrated in Fig. 8.

$$Accuracy = \frac{TP + TN}{TP + TN + FP + FN} \tag{1}$$

$$Precision = \frac{TP}{TP + FP} \tag{2}$$

$$Recall = \frac{TP}{TP + FN} \tag{3}$$

$$F1 - score = \frac{2 \times Precision \times Recall}{Precision + Recall} \tag{4}$$

In the confusion matrix, "true positive (TP)" refers to accurately diagnosing a patient with a mental disorder. In contrast, "true negative (TN)" refers to correctly diagnosing a patient without a mental disorder. "False positive (FP)" occurs when the model incorrectly predicts that a patient without a mental disorder has one. "False negative (FN)" happens when the model incorrectly identifies a mentally disordered individual as healthy. The accuracy result is deemed excellent only if the F1 score closely matches the accuracy. The ratio of correctly predicted positive observations signifies the number of individuals with mental disorders that were predicted as positive out of all correctly predicted positive observations. On the other hand, the recall result is the ratio of correctly predicted positive observations to all actual observations in a class. It demonstrates how effectively the model identifies patients with mental disorders. The F1 score represents a weighted average of precision and recall values, providing a balanced measure of the model's overall performance.

4 Model Testing Results and Analysis

After data pre-processing, the cleaned dataset will be utilised to create training and testing sets. The dataset is divided into training and testing sets with 80% and 20% split, respectively. The performance of both models using the first dataset is displayed in Table 4.

Table 5 indicates that both models have achieved good accuracy, precision, recall, and F1-score results. Since both models performed well, it is difficult to determine which one is better. Therefore, we proceeded to train the models using different datasets. The dataset underwent data pre-processing before being used for training and consists of two target classes: "yes" or "no". We utilised the value "yes" as the output to indicate that the student has a mental health issue. Table 5 below presents the results of the model using the second dataset.

Table 4. Performance results for the first dataset between KNN and XGBoost

Model	KNN	XGBoost
Accuracy (%)	100	100
Precision	1	1
Recall	1	1
F1-Score	1	1

Table 5. Performance results for the second dataset between KNN and XGBoost

Model	KNN	XGBoost
Accuracy (%)	80	100
Precision	1	1
Recall	0.71	1
F1-Score	0.83	1

Based on Table 5, KNN has an accuracy of 0.8, which results in a model accuracy of almost 80%. Concerning precision, we obtained a score of 1, signifying a very high accuracy with a low false-positive rate. Recall represents the number of positive instances correctly identified for the target class, and we achieved a recall score of 0.71, which is considered good and indicates a high-class label of "yes." Moving on to the F1-score, we attained a value of 0.83, which is commendable as it demonstrates a minor difference from the accuracy metric. However, XGBoost has shown significantly improved results, as it achieved 100% accuracy, precision, recall, and F1 scores, indicating outstanding performance. Therefore, XGBoost emerges as the superior model and will be utilised for a web-based mental health detection system.

4.1 Web-Based System Development Results

The web-based system was developed using Flask, a Python web framework. The system takes input data related to the XGBoost model, which has been utilised as the best model in this research, and incorporates it into Flask. The system accurately displays the result of a mental disorder based on the user's input from a list of questionnaires. The trained XGBoost model is employed to process the user's input, and Flask utilises this model to determine the detection value. Figure 8 below depicts the system's home page.

The home page will display two main buttons. Pressing the first button, "Take the test now", will direct the user to the questionnaire form, as illustrated in Fig. 9. On the other hand, clicking the second button, "Mental Health Information", will provide users with details about mental health, including the definitions of mental illness for the four types that will be used as the system's results.

Figure 9 displays the form that users must complete to receive the result of the mental health detection. The form consists of ten questions, and for each question, there

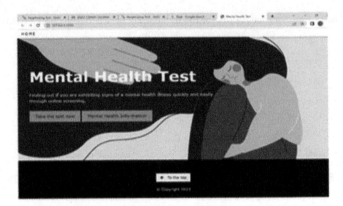

Fig. 8. Home Page

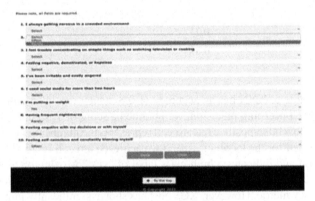

Fig. 9. Questionnaire Form

are four different answer options; "Often", "Rarely", "Yes", and "No". "Rarely" and "No" indicate that the user has not experienced the mentioned aspect, while "Often" and "Yes" imply that the user has. The user is allowed to select only one answer for each question. Once the user has finished selecting his or her answers, they need to click the "Done" button to submit the form to the system. After submitting the form, the system will process the data using the XGBoost model and then display the result, as shown in Fig. 10 below.

Figure 10 shows an example of a result that the user may receive. The system can generate results such as "You might have an anxiety symptom", "You experience loneliness", "You experience stress", or "You are normal", based on the user's input and the analysis performed by the XGBoost model. The system will retain the information the user entered during the screening test. However, once the user returns to the home page or decides to retake the online screening test, the input data will be cleared. Both the input data and the result are represented in Fig. 11 below.

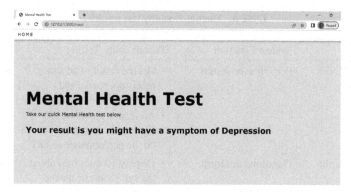

Fig. 10. Mental Disorder Detection Result

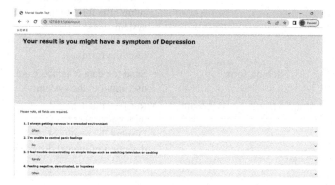

Fig. 11. Input Data

4.2 Functionality Test and Results

Each module in the web-based system has been tested for functionality to ensure proper operation, including the buttons, submission form, and results. Table 6 below presents the results of each module's functionality test.

Table 6 demonstrates that each module's results have been successfully tested, indicating that the best model among the two suggested algorithms, KNN and XGBoost, has been chosen. Furthermore, all buttons in the web-based system are in good working order, and the button on the questionnaire form will only be activated after the user has answered all questions. The user has successfully obtained the testing results displayed using the XGBoost model. In conclusion, the functionality test of the system is completed, and any errors discovered during testing have been addressed and corrected. Any necessary system improvements can now be implemented during the implementation phase.

Table 6. The functionality test results

Module	System Function	Functionality Testing	Result
Module 1: Model Evaluation	Performance results	• Get the result of accuracy, precision, recall, and F1-score from training • All results are above 0.5 • Choose the best model based on the performance results	Success
Module 2: Button functionality	Questionnaire form	• Display 10 questions about the symptoms of mental disorders • Insert data for each question • Click the "Done" button to submit the form to the system • Click the "Clear" button to reset the form	Success
	Submit form	• Send the data obtained from user input to the system	Success
Module 3: Detection outcome	Mental disorder result	• Retrieve the data and test it with the selected model • Display the results of the detection of mental disorders	Success

5   Conclusion

Both models have yielded intriguing results. Despite achieving 100% accuracy, we further tested them using other datasets and discovered that XGBoost outperformed KNN. Hence, the selected model is well-suited for constructing a web-based system that delivers the desired outcome. The web-based version of the system offers a diverse range of questions pertaining to mental health symptoms. Consequently, users will better understand any potential mental health issues they may be experiencing. The community in Malaysia stands to benefit significantly from this project as it raises awareness about the importance of seeking expert medical care among those who utilise the system and obtain results related to mental disorders. Many individuals may be unaware of their mental health conditions, so the system encourages them to seek assistance promptly before their situation exacerbates.

Acknowledgements. The College of Computing, Informatics and Mathematics, Universiti Teknologi MARA, Shah Alam, Selangor, Malaysia is acknowledged for supporting this work.

References

1. Hassan, M.F., Mohd, H.N., Kassim, E.S., Hamzah, M.I.: Issues and challenges of mental health in Malaysia. Int. J. Acad. Res. Bus. Soc. Sci. **8**(12), 1685–1696 (2018). https://doi.org/10.6007/IJARBSS/v8-i12/5288

2. Beckstein, A., Rathakrishnan, B., Hutchings, P.B., Mohamed, N.H.: The covid-19 pandemic and mental health in Malaysia: current treatment and future recommendations. Malaysian J. Publ. Health Med. **21**(1), 260–267 (2021). https://doi.org/10.37268/mjphm/vol.21/no.1/art.826

3. Srividya, M., Mohanavalli, S., Bhalaji, N.: Behavioral modeling for mental health using machine learning algorithms. J. Med. Syst. **42**, 88 (2018). https://doi.org/10.1007/s10916-018-0934-5

4. Kumar, P., Garg, S., Garg, A.: Assessment of anxiety, depression and stress using machine learning models. Procedia Comput. Sci. **171**, 1989–1998 (2020). https://doi.org/10.1016/j.procs.2020.04.213

5. Lu, H., Uddin, S., Hajati, F., Khushi, M., Moni, M.A.: Predictive risk modelling in mental health issues using machine learning on graphs. In: Proceedings of the 2022 Australasian Computer Science, pp. 168–175 (2022). https://doi.org/10.1145/3511616.3513112

6. Marzo, R.R., et al.: Depression and anxiety in Malaysian population during third wave of the COVID-19 pandemic. Clin. Epidemiol. Global Health **12**, 100868 (2021). https://doi.org/10.1016/j.cegh.2021.100868

7. Thieme, A., Belgrave, D., Doherty, G.: Machine learning in mental health: a systematic review of the HCI literature to support the development of effective and implementable ML systems. ACM Trans. Comput. Hum. Interact. **27**(5), 1–53 (2020). https://doi.org/10.1145/3398069

8. Doherty, K., et al.: Engagement with mental health screening on mobile devices: results from an antenatal feasibility study. In: Proceedings of the 2019 CHI Conference on Human Factors in Computing Systems, pp. 1–15 (2019). https://doi.org/10.1145/3290605.3300416

9. Coutts, L.V., Plans, D., Brown, A.W., Collomosse, J.: Deep learning with wearable based heart rate variability for prediction of mental and general health. J. Biomed. Inform. **112**, 103610 (2020). https://doi.org/10.1016/j.jbi.2020.103610

10. Isa, A.M., Ahmad, S., Diah, N.M.: Detecting offensive Malay language comments on YouTube using support vector machine (SVM) and Naive Bayes (NB) model. J. Positive School Psychol. **16**(3), 8548–8560 (2022)

11. Jiang, T., Gradus, J.L., Rosellini, A.J.: Supervised machine learning: a brief primer. Behav. Ther. **51**(5), 675–687 (2020). https://doi.org/10.1016/j.beth.2020.05.002

12. Albagmi, F.M., Alansari, A., Saad, D., Shawan, A., Alnujaidi, H.Y., Olatunji, S.O.: NC-ND license prediction of generalized anxiety levels during the covid-19 pandemic: a machine learning-based modeling approach. Inf. Med. Unlock. **28**, 100854 (2022). https://doi.org/10.1016/j.imu.2022.100854

13. Aiman Awangku Bolkiah, A.H., Hamzah, H.H., Ibrahim, Z., Diah, N.M., Mohd Sapawi, A., Hanum, H.M.: Crime scene prediction using the integration of K-means clustering and support vector machine. In: IEEE 10th Conference on Systems, Process and Control (ICSPC), pp. 242–246 (2022). https://doi.org/10.1109/ICSPC55597.2022.10001768

14. Rampisela, T.V., Rustam, Z.: Classification of schizophrenia data using support vector machine (SVM). J. Phys.: Conf. Ser. **1108**, 012044 (2018). https://doi.org/10.1088/1742-6596/1108/1/012044

15. Islam, M.R., Kamal, A.R.M., Sultana, N., Islam, R., Moni, M.A., Ulhaq, A.: Detecting depression using K-nearest neighbors (KNN) classification technique. In: International Conference on Computer, Communication, Chemical, Material and Electronic Engineering, IC4ME2, pp. 1–4 (2018). https://doi.org/10.1109/IC4ME2.2018.8465641

16. Ibrahim, Z., Diah, N.M., Rizal, N.A., Yuri, M.N.: Prediction of early symptoms of COVID-19 infected patients using supervised machine learning models. Int. J. Acad. Res. Bus. Soc. Sci. **11**(12), 2633–2643 (2021). https://doi.org/10.6007/IJARBSS/v11-i12/11991

17. Arun. V., Prajwal, V., Krishna, M., Arunkumar, B.V., Padma, S.K., Shyam, V.: A boosted machine learning approach for detection of depression. In: Proceedings of the 2018 IEEE Symposium Series on Computational Intelligence (SSCI), pp. 41–47 (2019). https://doi.org/10.1109/SSCI.2018.8628945

18. Zaman, R.: Mental Disorder Symptoms Datasets. In: Kaggle (2020). https://www.kaggle.com/datasets/rohitzaman/mental-health-symptoms-datasets. Accessed 30 Oct 2020

19. Kumar, P., Chauhan, R., Stephan, T., Shankar, A., Thakur, S.: A machine learning implementation for mental health care. Application: smart watch for depression detection. In: 11th International Conference on Cloud Computing, Data Science & Engineering (Confluence), pp. 568–574 (2021). https://doi.org/10.1109/Confluence51648.2021.9377199

20. Ogunseye, E.O., Adenusi, C.A., Nwanakwaugwu, A.C., Ajagbe, S.A., Akinola S.O.: Predictive analysis of mental health conditions using AdaBoost algorithm. Paradigmplus. **3**(2), 11–26 (2022). https://doi.org/10.55969/paradigmplus.v3n2a2

21. Lambino, P.: Student Mental Health Analysis. In: Kaggle (2022). https://www.kaggle.com/datasets/rohitzaman/mental-health-symptoms-datasets. Accessed 19 Oct 2022

22. Chattopadhyay, S.: MIME: mutual information minimizer for selection of categorical features. In: EEE International Conference on Electronics, Computing and Communication Technologies (CONECCT), pp. 1–3 (2021). https://doi.org/10.1109/CONECCT52877.2021.9622559

23. Katarya, R., Maan. S.: Predicting mental health disorders using machine learning for employees in technical and non-technical companies. In: Proceedings of 2020 IEEE International Conference on Advances and Developments in Electrical and Electronics Engineering (ICADEE), pp. 1–5 (2020). https://doi.org/10.1109/ICADEE51157.2020.9368923

Genre Classification in Music using Convolutional Neural Networks

Andrew Bawitlung and Sandeep Kumar Dash(✉)

National Institute of Technology, Mizoram, India
andrew_bawitlung@nitmz.ac.in

Abstract. With the advancement of technology and computational power, crafting a chart-topping song has become more effortless than before, achievable from the convenience of our residences with just a computer at hand. This has led to the emergence of vast arrays of catalogs of music, containing a variety of genres and styles from different music makers with different ethnicities and backgrounds, resulting in a large database that clogs most music streaming platforms with little automated categorization. Based on the GTZAN audio dataset, this paper revisits the use of Convolution Neural Networks (CNN) for classifying different types of music genres. Using Mel-frequency cepstral coefficients (MFCC) features, the CNN model achieved an accuracy of 85%. As a result of the careful design of the CNN model, it is on par with many latest and greatest CNN frameworks.

Keywords: Genre · Audio · Music · Classification · Neural Networks · Cnn · Mfcc

1 Introduction

In recent years, we saw a rise in the release of music and songs from different artists worldwide. This is largely due to the shift in the Music Industry, internet, and technology where artists are no longer required to be signed by a major record label for creating physical records. These records or songs were mainly recorded in multi-million dollar recording studios. Nowadays, any artist can record their songs on their laptops with budget recording gear and can be uploaded to top streaming websites almost free of charge where most music is played. In many ways, an individual can be their own record label if they know the proper marketing strategy on social media. Over the years, we have seen many social media artists like Tyler Ward, Bella Poarch, and Jacob Collier who started their music careers from scratch and continue to have very successful careers and social media influencing power as independent artists. Some even made successful performances at the Grammy's or to even won multiple Grammy Awards starting with no more than a laptop to create music which was not remotely possible a few years ago. This resulted in an exponential increase in the catalog of music where many artists build their fan base and platform from different social media and started their independent music careers without needing to sign with a major record label. Thousands of music and songs are released on streaming platforms like Spotify, iTunes, and YouTube every day and

H. Badioze Zaman et al. (Eds.): IVIC 2023, LNCS 14322, pp. 397–409, 2024.
https://doi.org/10.1007/978-981-99-7339-2_33

there is an increase in music catalogs all over the world as a result of this. Due to the increase in music catalog, genres that were never heard before emerged over time. Some genres like blues and jazz show a decrease in their variation and diversity while other genres like pop keep on evolving making hybrid genres like country-pop, etc. [1]. This demonstrates the necessity for regularly updating our database to accurately recognize emerging trends in music genres. The continuous emergence of new sounds is a result of the convenient access to Digital Audio Workstations (DAWs) on personal computers. This accessibility has also contributed to the rise of unconventional genres like Dubstep, characterized by the absence of traditional instruments. Such genres would have been extremely challenging, if not impossible, to produce using the conventional method of live recording in a studio. With all these advancements, it is practically impossible for humans to create a catalog for the different types of music genres and hence needed a modern approach to solving the issue. Major streaming websites, although not perfect have a lot of tools implemented for the better experience of their users. These features include the classification of music based on its mood, genre, region, and much more. This type of classification does a lot for the users as the algorithm finds songs that are best suited for studying our listening habits, music taste, and favorite genre of our music. It is due to one of these reasons that a good and reliable music genre classification algorithm is needed which will classify the music whenever new music is added to the catalog. We should also be aware of the connection between music and culture since most types of genres are heavily related to the culture where they originated and keeps on evolving. There are certain musical scales like the Blues scale, Chinese scale, Arabic scale, etc. which originated from a particular part of the world. Even though these genres are loved by people all over the world, they have a certain cultural background from where they originate. Due to the roots that these different music genres have, it is difficult to have a concrete idea of what genre a certain type of music is since it can be quite subjective. That being said, the majority will agree upon the traditional music genre classification although it might also have its sub-genre category.

As the volume of data continues to surge exponentially across various media formats such as text, images, videos, and audios, the inherent challenge of extracting meaningful insights from these vast datasets becomes increasingly complex. In this era of data deluge, the task of systematically classifying and categorizing such diverse forms of information has emerged as a formidable endeavor, necessitating the application of advanced machine learning methodologies. Within the realm of audio content, specifically music, the need for precise and efficient genre classification has become paramount. The multifaceted nature of music, encompassing its intricate interplay of melodies, rhythms, harmonies, and lyrics, renders manual categorization an arduous and often subjective undertaking. In response to this, the integration of machine learning techniques presents a pragmatic solution to address the intricacies inherent in music genre classification.

This paper uses Convolution Neural Network (CNN) model to classify the GTZAN Genre Collection [2] using a Convolution Neural Network model. In Sect. 2, the paper discussed the recent works done on music classification as well as the past literature on how this topic was addressed using machine learning techniques. Section 3 discussed the GTZAN data set where the detailed audio metadata is mentioned. Section 4 describes the Mel-frequency cepstral coefficients (MFCC) extracted features of the audio and the

CNN model. MFCC is the most commonly used feature that can be selected for audio processing [3] and the details about this feature are discussed along the CNN model. Section 5 shows the methodology used for the classification and Sects. 6 and 7 have the result analysis and future work.

2 Related Work

Classification of music based on its genre is a fundamental task in music information retrieval that involves categorizing songs into different genres or types based on their audio features. Various machine learning algorithms have been employed to tackle this task, and one popular approach is the use of convolutional neural networks. CNNs have been proven to be effective in identifying music genres by classifying songs into their respective genre based on spectrograms extracted from the audio signals [4]. In this study, Convolutional Neural Networks were also used for spectrogram classification. Over the past few years, quite a few works have been done in this field. A literature review was written by Busola *et al.* in 2022 [5] in which they reviewed and analyzed the performance of various methods based on different extracted features to compare their performance. Several different types of features were extracted from a variety of databases, where the features were extracted from. It is common to use tools such as the spectrogram, mel spectrum, and MFCC for analyzing data. As a result, the paper also discusses the use of traditional classification methods such as CNN, Support vector machines (SVM), and combinations of different models which give varying results depending on the types of features that were extracted and also on the method they used. They mentioned that the features extracted played a vital role in its classification and amongst all the models, Convolutions Neural Network (CNN) seems to contribute the highest accuracy as compared to others. In 2023 Persian music classification using PMG-Net deep neural network was done where it obtained 86% accuracy [6]. Using Cross-Modal Neural Model Reprogramming, Hung *et al.* [7] used IDS-NMR method with jointly ImageNet and AudioSet pre-training and got an accuracy of 85.1%. Pelchat *et al.* [8] also acquired 72% on the accuracy using their CNN model. Tang *et al.* [9] used MFCC features extracted on the GTZAN data set and used Long Short-Term Memory (LSTM) model and got a classification accuracy of 50% to 60% and this is still pretty low to be usable at a practical level. Vishnupriya and Meenakshi [10] also used MFCC extracted features on Million Song Dataset (MSD) and the accuracy obtained for MFCC features was 47% using the CNN model. Just like previously mentioned, it is also not impressive in accuracy and needs a better adjustment on its CNN model. Chillara *et al.* [11] when using spectrogram-based models, got 88.54% accuracy on their CNN model and 64.0625% on their ANN model. The Spectrogram-based models used here show how spectrogram extraction is promising since it is a very simple feature and is also used on other applications. Chathuranga *et al.* [12] used two feature sets that represent the frequency domain and used SVM model and reported a 78% accuracy in their model. This goes to show that even when combining two features we still get a lower accuracy as compared to the previously mentioned and thus thereby concluding how important it is to have good ways of extracting features. Y. Yi *et al.* (2021) [13] tested many models like RNN-LSTM, KNN, NB, CNN, and SVM in which MFCC features and got

70.21% on the CNN model which yields the highest amongst the other model shows the contribution of CNN model and its reliability amongst others. Dhall *et al.* in 2021 [14] shows that using Fourier transform, Q transform, and MFCC transform spectrograms, they acquired almost 100% in training accuracy using CNN-based AlexNet and LeNet-5 but shows quite less testing accuracy when compared with the training accuracy. This is by far one of the best accuracy results where different types of CNN models are used. This goes to show that more improvement can be made regarding feature extraction and the types of models used. A new way of extracting features was also proposed by Tao Li *et al.* in 2003 [15] in which, the authors proposed a method called DWCH that can be used to extract both local and global information from music signals. This is done by computing histograms on the Daubechies wavelet coefficients of the music signals. This shows a promising result when compared to other traditional feature extraction. In 2007, Meng *et al.* proposed a temporal feature integration method that produces two different feature sets: diagonal autoregressive (DAR) and multivariate autoregressive (MAR). They found that the MAR features performed better than the DAR features but at the cost of increased computational complexity [16]. Tao *et al.* 2005 [17] classified taxonomy for music genre classification by automatically generating genre taxonomies based on the confusion matrix via linear discriminant projection. Costa *et al.* in 2012 [18] used texture features which is one of the popular ways of extracting features from images. The texture features were based on Local Binary Pattern and resulted in outperforming the audio content-based features where they got 82.33% and 80.65% performance on the different data-set they used. This finding shows that we can also use image-based feature extraction and since there is a lot of literature already on image classification, it might also be wise to implement and use the methods of image classification and their processes to get more accurate and usable models.

3   Data Description

This paper used the popular GTZAN dataset from MARYSAS which was released in 2001 [2]. The data set contains most of the traditional music genres which were popularly listened to at the time. The music is comparatively different when compared to its modern equivalent in terms of its loudness, clarity, and other properties. For example, genres like Jazz are relatively quieter when compared to the Metal genre but, Jazz in 2023 tends to be louder than the 2000s metal genres. Although similarities will be there in how we feel or perceive the genre from different times, it is important to mention the shifts and evolution of the music genre throughout the years. The GTZAN dataset from MARYSAS consists of 10 genres from Blues to Metal and the full information is given in Table 1. Each audio files are processed in 30 s long and they are at a sample rate of 22050 Hz, 16-bit depth, and mono audio files and these pre-processed properties were used for the experimentation. The standard sample rate of CDs and the majority of audio streaming platforms plays at 44100Hz and has a bit-depth of 16 bits and are of stereo files where the original features. The audio files are distributed very equally in all the categories, and each category has around 1000 audio files.

Table 1. Distribution of data-set

Genre	No. of audio files
Pop	1000
Rock	998
Jazz	1000
Metal	1000
Classical	998
Disco	999
Blues	1000
Reggae	1000
Country	997
Hip-Hop	998
Total	9,990

4 Methodology

4.1 Mel-Frequency Cepstral Coefficients Feature Extraction

Amongst the different ways of representing audio files, the paper focuses on Mel-frequency cepstral coefficients (MFCC) which are a small set of features, usually about 10–20 that concisely describe the overall shape of a spectral envelope of each audio file. Unlike traditional methods which are used to process data, the MFCCs have the time, amplitude, and timbre of the sound in their properties. This paper extracted 13 coefficients from each audio file. The visual representation of MFCC features for one audio file is shown in Fig. 1 where it represents the MFCC in a time scale where the x-axis is the time domain and the y-axis is the coefficients, the color of the coefficients represents the magnitude. One of the unique features of MFCC is that it took into consideration the timbre of the sound, which means that even if the sound might be of the same pitch and amplitude it takes into consideration the properties of the sound. An example would be a C-key note in a piano and a guitar, even though it might be of the same pitch and amplitude, we can distinguish that both are of different instruments.

The Mel scale is a logarithmic scale that is more aligned with how humans perceive sound frequencies. This makes the MFCC features more discriminative for speech recognition tasks. MFCC feature extraction is a process of transforming a speech signal into a set of features that are more suitable for speech recognition. An expression for the inverse Discrete Cosine Transform (DCT) can be obtained by windowing the signal, applying the Discrete Fourier transform (DFT), taking the log of the magnitude, shifting the frequencies to a Mel scale, and applying the inverse Discrete Fourier transform (DFT) [19].

The steps in obtaining MFCC are:

1. Spectral envelopes in decibels are derived from logarithmic filter bank out- puts, which are then multiplied by 20.
2. Perform the Discrete Cosine Transform (DCT) on the spectral envelope to obtain the MFCCs.
3. Take the MFCCs and extract the cepstrum coefficients.

$$cc = \sum_{n=1}^{TF} Sncos\left[a(n-0.5)\left(\frac{\pi}{TF}\right)\right]i = 1, 2, \ldots.L$$

The MFCC coefficient, denoted as cc, represents the ath coefficient in the MFCC sequence. TF refers to the total number of triangular filters present in the filter bank. Sn represents the log energy output of the nth filter coefficient. L represents the desired number of MFCC coefficients to be calculated.

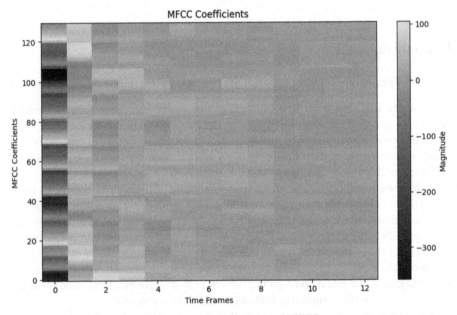

Fig. 1. Visual representation of MFCC.

4.2 Convolution Neural Network Model

Convolution Neural Networks (CNN) are made of neurons but unlike other neural networks, their weights are dynamic as well as their biases. The main architecture of a Convolution Neural Network (CNN) consists of a list of layers that transforms 3-dimensional, i.e., width, height, and depth of the image volume into a 3-dimensional output volume where every neuron in the current layer is connected to a small patch of output from the previous layer which is basically layering multiple neural networks. It uses M filters, which are feature extractors that extract features like edges, corners, and so on. CNN is one of the most widely used neural networks in classifying images, it has also been used quite a lot of time on other types of classifications such as music, speech, and many more. For these reasons, the paper tested the traditional CNN model on the MFCC extracted features and see how much better or worst it will perform when compared to the other recent CNN models discussed previously.

The model uses multiple convolutional layers with increasing depth (64, 128, 256). This ensures the exaction of the abstract and hierarchical input of the MFCCs. The batch normalization after each Convo2D stabilizes the network. The model has a dropout regularization after each max pooling layer and this reduces the overfitting and in turn, also minimizes the model from relying on specific features or neurons. The Max pooling layers (2, 2) are used for the normalization of the layers which helps in reducing the spatial dimensions of the feature maps while retaining the important features. The model architecture combines the advantages of batch normalization, dropout, regularization, max pooling, and ReLU and Softmax activation to create a powerful and effective CNN model which can still compete with other advanced neural networks.

The CNN the input layer has Conv2D type input with 64 Filters and a kernel size of (3,3). The activation uses ReLU, A BatchNormalization is used and MaxPooling2D type in pooling layer. The Convolutional Block 1 and 2 both uses Conv2D with 128 and 256 filters respectively with a kernel size of (3,3) and ReLU activation function. The output layer has the Softmax activation. During training the Adam Optimizer is used using a batch size of 32 with the Sparse Categorical Cross-Entropy based loss function with a total number of 70 epochs.

The full summary of the model is shown in Table 2.

Table 2. Convolution Neural Network Model Summary

Layer (type)	Output Shape	Parameters
Conv2D	(None, 130, 13, 64)	640
batch normalization	(None, 130, 13, 64)	256
max pooling2d	(None, 65, 6, 64)	0
dropout	(None, 65, 6, 64)	0
conv2d_1	(None, 65, 6, 128)	73856
batch_normalization_1	(None, 65, 6, 128)	512
max_pooling2d_1	(None, 32, 3, 128)	0
dropout_1	(None, 32, 3, 128)	0
conv2d_2	(None, 32, 3, 256)	295168
batch_normalization_2	(None, 32, 3, 256)	1024
max_pooling2d_2	(None, 16, 1, 256)	0
dropout_2	(None, 16, 1, 256)	0
flatten	(None, 4096)	0
dense	(None, 512)	2097664
batch_normalization_3	(None, 512)	2048
dropout_3	(None, 512)	0
dense_1	(None, 10)	5130
Total Parameters:	2,476,298	
Trainable Parameters:	2,474,378	
Non-trainable Parameters:	1,920	

5 System Architecture

From the GTZAN audio dataset, the audio files are taken in with their existing proper-ties i.e., using 22050 Hz sample rate and 16-bit depth into libROSA which is a library used for manipulating audio files and examination. Here the MFCC features are extracted from the audio files where we take a total of 13 coefficients. 25% was used for testing and the others were used for training. From there the same MFCC which was saved in.*json* file is trained using our CNN model. The training data set, which is 75% of the dataset is fed into the CNN classifier where the model is trained and the testing was done with the test dataset and thereafter the results were obtained. The overview of the system architecture is shown in Fig. 2.

6 Results and Analysis

The test accuracy and the overall accuracy obtained from the model is 85%. Not surprisingly as shown by other literature, the F1 score in the CNN is mostly high. Amongst the different genres, the Classical genre got the highest F1 score of 95%, and Blues and

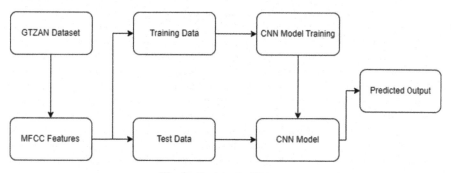

Fig. 2. System Architecture

Metal both got an F1 score of 90%. The lowest F1 score were Rock and Country which get an F1 score of 69% and 78% respectively. The confusion matrix shown in Fig. 3 shows us the performance of our CNN model and it shows that the majority of the predicted outputs are quite accurate in their predictions when looking at the color palette. Figure 4 shows the accuracy and error evaluation graph with a 70-epoch timeline. When compared with other classification techniques like PMG-Net [6] which get an accuracy of 86% or Pelchat *et al.* (2020) [8] where their improvement in accuracy is from 69% to 72%. Our CNN model still performs better or on par when compared to other methods. This goes to show that the CNN model along with the MFCC features works seamlessly

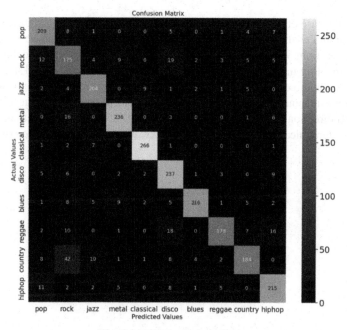

Fig. 3. CNN Confusion Matrix

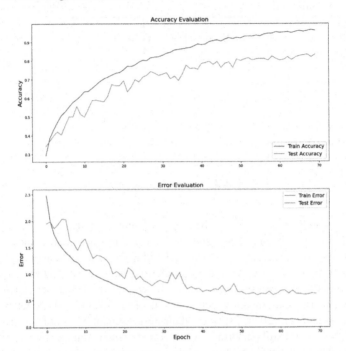

Fig. 4. CNN accuracy and error evaluation.

together in the case of music genre classification. However, Wen *et al.*(2023) [20] introduce the parallel channel attention (PCA) concept to establish extensive temporal and
spectral connections within the music composition. They also investigate the effects of
different weighting methodologies on PCA, achieving an accuracy of 91.4% using the
same GTZAN audio dataset. Prabhakar *et al.* (2023) [21] achieved a significant breakthrough in music genre classification, attaining an exceptional 93.51% accuracy. They
combined Bidirectional Long Short-Term Memory (BiLSTM) with an Attention mechanism and a Graphical Convolution Network (GCN), outperforming the conventional
CNN model.

Despite our CNN model's slightly inferior performance compared to more intricate advanced techniques, it demonstrates competitive capability relative to state-of-the-art methods. Furthermore, it remains comparatively superior to other CNN models. Detailed evaluation metrics for our CNN model can be found in Table 3.

Table 3. CNN Classification Report

Genre	Precision	Recall	F1-score	Support
Pop	0.83	0.89	0.86	235
Rock	0.64	0.75	0.69	234
Jazz	0.88	0.89	0.89	228
Metal	0.90	0.90	0.90	262
Classical	0.95	0.96	0.95	278
Disco	0.78	0.89	0.83	265
Blues	0.96	0.85	0.90	254
Reggae	0.92	0.77	0.84	232
Country	0.87	0.71	0.78	260
Hip-Hop	0.82	0.86	0.84	249
Accuracy			0.85	2497
Maro Avg			0.85	2497
Weighted Avg	0.86	0.85	0.85	2497

7 Conclusion and Future Works

Utilizing the MFCC features within the GTZAN audio dataset reveals a discernible trend within the outcomes. Specifically, in the context of feature extraction, the CNN architecture demonstrates superior performance relative to alternative extracted features. The CNN model employed in this study exhibits a notably elevated accuracy rate in contrast to preceding iterations of CNN models. Furthermore, it exhibits competitiveness alongside more contemporary and pretrained CNN models. When juxtaposing the accuracy attained through our model, employing MFCC feature extraction, our findings consistently achieve higher scores when contrasted with models employing diverse audio feature extraction techniques. This indicates that the MFCC feature, in most instances, tends to be the preferred choice as the better feature.

While our approach also validates the efficacy of utilizing MFCC for feature extraction and employing a Convolutional Neural Network for classification, similar to previous studies, it is crucial to acknowledge that the realm of music genres is constantly changing. Previously unfamiliar music genres have now risen to the top of global charts, a phenomenon unimaginable two decades ago. Given the swift evolution within the music industry, it is imperative to stay attuned to the present-day music landscape. Furthermore, among all the literature we have examined, there has been an absence of classification techniques that account for the music's association with its corresponding subgenre. This particular feature is important because there are many pieces of music today which can be classified into multiple genres. This is also clear when releasing music to these different streaming platforms. There are a lot of times when one can enter a secondary genre or subgenre when cataloging our music into a popular streaming platform. Since these secondary tags are already in use in the real world, implementing these will also help a lot in classifying music genres and help in a more accurate accuracy. Since classifying music genres seems to be subjective in quite a lot of scenarios, tagging certain music genres with its sub-genre seems will give a more accurate representation of how humans classify genres and better improve the usability of the methods and machines.

References

1. Negro, G., Kovács, B., Carroll, G.R.: Bustin' out: the evolution of novelty and diversity in recorded music. In: Cattani, G., Deichmann, D., Ferriani, S. (ed.) The Generation, Recognition and Legitimation of Novelty (Research in the Sociology of Organizations, vol. 77, Emerald Publishing Limited, Bingley, pp. 51–87 (2022)
2. Sturm, B.L.: The GTZAN dataset: Its contents, its faults, their effects on evaluation, and its future use. arXiv preprint arXiv:1306.1461 (1999)
3. Retta, Ephrem A., et al.: Kinit classification in ethiopian chants, Azmaris and modern music: a new dataset and CNN benchmark. arXiv preprint arXiv:2201.08448 (2022)
4. Bora, K., Barman, M.P., Patowary, A.N., Bora, T.: Classification of assamese folk songs' melody using supervised learning techniques. Indian J. Sci. Technol. 16(2), 89–96 (2023)
5. Falola, B., Alabi, E., Ogunajo, F., Fasae, O.: Music genre classification using machine and deep learning techniques: a review 03, 35–50 (2022). https://doi.org/10.17605/OSF.IO/FZQXW
6. Farajzadeh, N., Sadeghzadeh, N., Hashemzadeh, M.: PMG-Net: Persian music genre classification using deep neural networks. Entert. Comput. 44, 100518 (2023)
7. Hung, Y.N., Yang, C.H.H., Chen, P.Y., Lerch, A.: Low-resource music genre classification with cross-modal neural model reprogramming. In: ICASSP 2023–2023 IEEE International Conference on Acoustics, Speech and Signal Processing (ICASSP), pp. 1–5. IEEE (2023)
8. Pelchat, N., Gelowitz, C.M.: Neural network music genre classification. Can. J. Electr. Comput. Eng. 43(3), 170–173 (2020)
9. Tang, C.P., Chui, K.L., Yu, Y.K., Zeng, Z., Wong, K.H.:Music genre classification using a hierarchical long short term memory (LSTM) model. In: Proceedings of SPIE 10828, Third International Workshop on Pattern Recognition, 108281B, 26 July 2018
10. Vishnupriya, S., Meenakshi, K.:Automatic music genre classification using convolution neural network. In: 2018 International Conference on Computer Communication and Informatics (ICCCI), pp. 1–4 (2018). https://doi.org/10.1109/ICCCI.2018.8441340
11. Chillara, S., et al.: Music genre classification using machine learning algorithms: a comparison. Int. Res. J. Eng. Technol. (IRJET) 6(05), 851–858 (2019)
12. Chathuranga, D., Jayaratne, L.: Automatic music genre classification of audio signals with machine learning approaches. GSTF J Comput 3, 14 (2013)
13. Yi, Y., Zhu, X., Yue, Y., Wang, W.: Music genre classification with LSTM based on time and frequency domain features. In: 2021 IEEE 6th International Conference on Computer and Communication Systems (ICCCS), pp. 678–682 (2021)
14. Dhall, A., Srinivasa Murthy, Y.V., Koolagudi, S.G.: Music genre classification with convolutional neural networks and comparison with f, q, and mel spectrogram-based images. In:

Biswas, A., Wennekes, E., Hong, TP., Wieczorkowska, A. (eds.) Advances in Speech and Music Technology. Advances in Intelligent Systems and Computing, vol. 1320, pp. 235–248. Springer, Singapore (2021). https://doi.org/10.1007/978-981-33-6881-1_20

15. Li, T., Ogihara, M., Qi, L.: A comparative study on content-based music genre classification. In: Proceedings of the 26th annual international ACM SIGIR conference on Research and development in information retrieval (SIGIR '03). Association for Computing Machinery, New York, NY, USA, pp. 282–289 (2003)

16. Meng, A., Ahrendt, P., Larsen, J., Hansen, L.K.: Temporal feature integration for music genre classification. IEEE Trans. Audio Speech Lang. Process. **15**(5), 1654–1664 (2007)

17. Li, T., Ogihara, M.: Music genre classification with taxonomy. In: Proceedings. (ICASSP '05). IEEE International Conference on Acoustics, Speech, and Signal Processing (2005)

18. Costa, Y.M.G., Oliveira, L.S., Koerich, A.L., Gouyon, F., Martins, J.G.: Music genre classification using LBP textural features. Sig. Process. **92**(11) 2723–2737 (2012)

19. Rao, K.S., Manjunath, K.E.: Speech Recognition using Articulatory and Excitation Source Features, SpringerBriefs in Speech Technology (2017)

20. Wen, Z., et al.: Parallel attention of representation global time–frequency correlation for music genre classification. Multimedia Tools Appl. 1–21 (2023)

21. Prabhakar, S.K., Lee, S.-W.: Holistic approaches to music genre classification using efficient transfer and deep learning techniques. Expert Syst. Appl. **211**, 118636 (2023)

Harnessing Technology for Efficient Coagulation Profile E-Reporting: A Design Thinking Approach

Puteri N. E. Nohuddin[1,2(✉)], Prasis Ja Singh[3], Kelvin Ch'ng[3], Phan Nop So Phon[3], Nora Azima Noordin[2], Zahidah Abd Kadir[2], and Zuraini Zainol[4]

[1] Institut Visual Informatik, Universiti Kebangsaan Malaysia, Bangi, Malaysia
puteri.ivi@ukm.edu.my
[2] Higher Colleges of Technology, Sharjah, UAE
[3] International Medical University, Bukit Jalil, Kuala Lumpur, Malaysia
[4] Universiti Pertahanan Nasional Malaysia, Kuala Lumpur, Malaysia

Abstract. The coagulation profile report contains international normalized ratio (INR) blood test, activated partial thromboplastin clotting time (APTT), platelets, and fibrinogen. The report is for identifying abnormal blood clotting tendencies by examining key factors associated with bleeding issues. Traditional paper-based reporting methods frequently encounter difficulties such as manual data entry errors, delayed result dissemination, and restricted accessibility. The incorporation of technology in coagulation profile e-reporting offers a promising solution for addressing these deficiencies and revolutionizing the documentation and communication of laboratory results. This exploratory study seeks to evaluate the practicability and prospective advantages of integrating technology into coagulation profile reporting processes. Utilizing a design-thinking methodology, this study investigates the stakeholder and users using persona, empathy, journey mapping, ideation and prototyping processes in order to determine the requirements for a proposed mobile application. The paper presents a solution to enhance existing operations by describing its components, prototype design, and validation procedure. The solution is driven by the imperative to provide timely notifications to healthcare providers regarding the availability of laboratory results in the electronic medical record (EMR) system.

Keywords: Coagulation · Mobile application · Prototyping · Design Thinking

1 Introduction

In the era of digital transformation, healthcare systems are perpetually investigating novel ways to optimize the delivery of patient care [1]. Coagulation profile reporting is essential for the diagnosis and treatment of a variety of bleeding disorders, coagulation abnormalities, and thrombotic events [2]. Nevertheless, traditional paper-based reporting methods frequently present significant obstacles, such as manual data entry errors, delayed result dissemination, and limited accessibility. Utilizing technology for efficient coagulation profile e-reporting has the potential to resolve these deficiencies and revolutionize the documentation and communication of laboratory results [3]. This exploratory study seeks to examine the viability and potential benefits of integrating technology into coagulation profile reporting processes. By investigating electronic platforms, data interoperability, and streamlined workflows, this study provides the groundwork for future research to uncover the full benefits of technology in optimizing coagulation profile reporting and thereby enhancing patient outcomes.

The innovation team applied the Design Thinking approach to address the problem of delayed communication of coagulation profile results for children who are receiving therapeutic intravenous (IV) Heparin after cardiac surgeries in the critical care unit (PSICU). The team wanted to understand the needs and challenges of the primary users who were affected by the communication gaps between two hospital-wide system, namely the laboratory information system (LIS) and Electronic Medical Record (EMR). The primary users included a critical care nurse, a main responsible physician and a laboratory representative. The team used various tools such as Persona Canvas, Empathy Map, and User Journey Map to empathize with each user and document their characteristics and experiences for analysis.

The team identified the main difficult points from the interviews and observation of the workflow. They found that there was no integrated system that alerted the healthcare providers when the test results were available in EMR. This caused delays and inefficiencies in delivering quality care and ensuring patient safety. The team defined this problem as the core issue that needed a solution.

This report proposes a solution to improve the current operation by describing its components, prototype design and validation process. The solution was inspired by the need to provide timely notifications to the healthcare providers about the availability of the laboratory results in EMR.

The paper is organized as follows: Sect. 2 discusses background and related topics on technology for coagulation profiling and design thinking for healthcare. Section 3 elaborates the design thinking methodology of collecting data, analysis and design. Followed by Sect. 4 presents the proposal of Coagulation Profile E-Reporting prototype design. Finally, Sect. 5 concludes with a summary of the research.

2 Literature Review

Coagulation profile e-reporting plays a crucial role in the diagnosis and management of various hematological disorders. With the advancements in technology, there is a growing need to explore innovative approaches to enhance the efficiency of coagulation profile reporting. This literature review aims to examine the existing research on harnessing technology and applying a design thinking approach to improve the process of coagulation profile e-reporting.

2.1 Technology-Enabled Coagulation Profile Reporting

In recent years, there has been a significant rise in the adoption of technology for healthcare applications. Digital platforms and electronic health records (EHRs) have been utilized to facilitate the reporting of coagulation profiles efficiently. Studies have shown that electronic reporting systems improve accessibility, reduce errors, and enhance communication between healthcare professionals [4, 5]. Technology-enabled coagulation profile reporting has become crucial to diagnosing causes of hemorrhages, developing anticoagulant drugs, assessing bleeding risk in extensive surgery procedures and dialysis, and investigating the efficacy of hemostatic therapies. In this regard, advanced technologies such as microfluidics, fluorescent microscopy, electrochemical sensing, photoacoustic detection, and micro or nano electromechanical systems (MEMS/NEMS) have been employed to develop highly accurate, robust, and cost-effective point of care (POC) devices. These devices measure electrochemical, optical, and mechanical parameters of clotting blood which can be correlated to light transmission or scattering, electrical impedance, and viscoelastic properties [6]. Real-time point-of-care (POC) measurement of coagulation parameters can improve patient outcomes in clinical settings such as surgical and minimally invasive cardiac procedures, critical care units, and emergency departments [7].

2.2 Design Thinking In Healthcare

Design thinking is an iterative problem-solving approach that prioritizes user needs and experiences. Its application in healthcare has shown promising results in enhancing patient-centered care and improving workflow efficiencies. Several studies have highlighted the benefits of design thinking in the development of innovative healthcare solutions [8]. [9] mentions that compared to conventional expert-driven procedures, design thinking may provide treatments that are useable, acceptable, and effective. Recent research reports the use of design thinking in a range of innovation projects across medical disciplines, including pediatrics, psychiatry, radiology, gastroenterology, cancer, orthopedics, and surgery, as well as in hospital operations and healthcare management [10]. Design thinking has proved to be such a catalyst by involving patient-centric providers and IT specialists in solution development and creating a very specific future preview and, thus, clear requirements [11].

2.3 Application of Design Thinking in Coagulation Profile E-Reporting

Limited research has explored the integration of design thinking principles into coagulation profile e-reporting. However, studies in other healthcare domains have demonstrated the potential of design thinking in improving the usability and efficiency of digital healthcare systems. [9, 12, 13]. Applying design thinking principles to the design and implementation of coagulation profile reporting systems can enhance user satisfaction and improve clinical outcomes. [9] defines applied design thinking studies as those that include user or need assessment, iterative prototyping or testing with user feedback, and testing the intervention with target users. A review by [14] showcased a design thinking approach that prioritized user needs, efficiency, and streamlining processes. The coagulation reports were developed using an intuitive and user-friendly online interactive template, allowing easy access and utilization. JavaScript was utilized to facilitate easy editing and updating of the website's content. The web system also enabled users to copy and paste directly from the website into their reporting software, reducing turnaround time and cost. [15] demonstrated that employing a design thinking approach improved perceived information about antibiotics and enhanced understanding between nurses and providers. Their study showed that a mobile app contributed to nurses' overall information situation, including perceived persuasiveness, usability, user satisfaction, and relevance. The app centralized existing information, improving nurses' access to information and speeding up scenario-based tests. To mitigate medical errors, [16] employed a user-centered design (UCD) approach to enhance the alert system's user interface design. Usability designers conducted initial interviews and incorporated user feedback to develop low-fidelity prototypes. The prototypes were refined to meet user preferences for concise, clear alerts and improved access to relevant drug interaction information.

2.4 User-Centered Design and Coagulation Profile E-Reporting

User-centered design approaches emphasize involving end-users in the development process to ensure that technology solutions meet their needs effectively. In the context of coagulation profile e-reporting, user-centered design can enhance the accessibility and usability of the reporting systems. Research has shown that involving healthcare professionals and patients in the design process leads to more effective and efficient systems [17–19]. The integration of technology and design thinking in coagulation profile e-reporting holds great potential for improving the efficiency and effectiveness of reporting systems. By adopting user-centered design approaches and leveraging the power of digital platforms, healthcare organizations can enhance the accessibility, accuracy, and usability of coagulation profile reporting. Further research is needed to explore the specific design principles and technological solutions that can be applied to optimize coagulation profile e-reporting.

The incorporation of intended users and stakeholders at an early stage of development can provide an understanding of medical needs, technology perception, and interface preferences. [17] conducted a user-centered design (UCD) approach through focus groups that involved asthmatic patients and clinical care providers during the application's development. The study reveals that both groups provide different attributes, where patients prioritize low cost and emergency contacts, while care providers prioritize patient monitoring, EHR integration, peak flow measurements, and pharmacy connectivity. Using these requested and discovered features, the study incorporated them into the prototype application. [18] redesigned the user interface to target a cohort of elders and middle-aged persons, which involved them through eye activities using Kinect motion sensing equipment. The study proposes a systematic usability testing method using physiological and psychological data to improve the usability of products for the elderly. It suggests specific suggestions for motion exercise system designers and encourages the use of the proposed method by other researchers. The method can be customized for evaluating other healthcare devices or systems. Meanwhile, [19] involved participants through semi-structured telephone interviews, which were then summarized into matrices for the analysis and identified key themes for the application intervention and its implementation characteristics. The study found that eliciting provider feedback at an early stage of development and incorporating the findings into interventions improves their effectiveness.

3   Design Thinking Process

Design Thinking promotes user-centric innovation by encouraging empathy, collaboration, and iteration, resulting in effective solutions that are tailored to user needs. In this study, a five-step process is adopted for solving the issues: empathize (understand consumers), define (identify requirements), ideate (generate ideas), prototype (develop solutions), and test (obtain feedback).

3.1   Persona, Empathy Mapping and Journey Mapping Analysis

Persona, Empathy Mapping & Journey Mapping Analysis are three techniques that are used in the requirement gathering process. Persona is a technique that is used to understand the user group and investigate users' needs and requirements [20]. Empathy Mapping is a technique that is used to understand the user's emotions and feelings [21]. This technique helps the team to understand the user's perspective and design the product accordingly. Journey Mapping Analysis is a technique that is used to understand the user's journey from start to finish [22]. This technique helps the team to identify the pain points and design the product accordingly. The initial step involves gathering feedback from direct end users of the existing system through the use of Personal Canvas, which includes interviews and observations in the PSICU care processes.

Three (3) key personas directly involved in the problematic process are identified, and each persona is provided with their own persona map, empathy map, and journey map. The personas are informed about their selection and willingly participate by completing the Personal Canvas. Subsequently, face-to-face interviews are conducted to gather information for the empathy map. The journey map template is employed, and discussions are held among personas, users, and customers to gather all necessary information for completing the journey map. The findings from all the persona maps, empathy maps, and journey maps are analyzed to derive insights.

Table 1 summarizes the insights gathered from the persona, empathy and journey mappings. This information supports the application requirements and design.

In short, findings from Table 1, challenges included nurses manually tracing lab results from the lab system, delayed communication of coagulation test results to the pediatric cardiothoracic surgeon, and difficulties encountered by lab technicians in notifying nurses about rejected samples for coagulation profile tests.

3.2   Idea Generation

Based on the analysis of the empathy map and journey map for three key stakeholders, namely the pediatric cardiothoracic surgeon, critical care nurse, and lab manager, the primary users' issues have been identified and consolidated. The issues comprised of the manual process of tracing lab results from the lab system by nurses, delayed communication of coagulation test results to the pediatric cardiothoracic surgeon, and challenges faced by lab technicians in contacting nurses to notify them about rejected coagulation profile test samples.

[26] incorporated SCAMPER as part of their design strategies for microfluidic design. Similarly, to address these issues, this study utilized the SCAMPER technique

Table 1. Requirement gathering using persona, empathy and journey maps.

Critical Care Nurse:	Prasis Singh
Mr. Prasis encountered technical obstacles that hindered the optimal delivery of healthcare in the Pediatric Intensive Care Unit (PICU). One such obstacle was that doctors provided verbal orders for blood tests, which could easily be overlooked in the fast-paced environment. To enhance accuracy and efficiency, it is recommended to utilize the electronic medical record (EMR) system for test orders. In addition, the process of drawing blood from critically ill pediatric patients presents challenges, often resulting in inadequate samples, lysed samples, or repeated pricking that causes discomfort to the patient. The Accuvein Finder, a device that visualizes veins, can greatly assist in this process. However, due to budget constraints, its acquisition is often considered a luxury rather than a necessity. The responsibility for maintaining the pneumatic tube system used for blood sample transport lies with facility management. Frequent breakdowns cause delays in sample delivery, thereby prolonging turnaround times. Ensuring prioritized maintenance of the tube system is crucial to ensuring efficient and timely delivery of samples to the laboratory	
Pediatric Cardiothoracic Surgeon	Dr Hala
Dr. Hala, an experienced pediatric cardiothoracic surgeon at Prince Sultan Cardiac Center, is known for his maturity and positive demeanor. His primary goals involve performing complication-free cardiac surgeries and closely collaborating with the nursing team to provide optimal postoperative care. Dr. Hala is well aware of the challenges faced by ICU nurses, such as heavy workloads, staffing shortages, and budget constraints. He expresses hope that the hospital management will promptly address these issues Upon reviewing the journey map, Dr. Hala expresses concern regarding the possibility of ICU nurses forgetting to inform him about coagulation test results. He suggests that the hospital management implement a result notification system to ensure timely communication of test results to him. Such a system would also alleviate the burden on nurses, who currently have to manually track and trace the results in the system. Dr. Hala emphasizes the importance of receiving prompt notifications to facilitate efficient decision-making and enhance patient care	
Lab Manager	Ms. Elkady
Ms. Elkady, an experienced lab manager with 8 years of service at Prince Sultan Hospital, expresses her frustration regarding the absence of equipment upgrades during her tenure. Despite an increase in patient load, the laboratory unit has witnessed minimal improvements since the hospital's establishment in 1978. Inadequate turnaround times are attributed to insufficient senior lab technicians and outdated machines that struggle to handle the volume of blood tests. Rather than utilizing an automated system, the manual loading of blood samples into analyzers is still required. Furthermore, the current coagulation profile analyzer can process only a limited number of samples at a time, whereas the state-of-the-art analyzer shown in Fig. 5 boasts a significantly higher throughput of 390 tests per hour. Due to budget constraints, requests for new equipment often go unnoticed. One major technical challenge faced by Ms. Elkady is the absence of an automated workflow where analyzer results can be directly inputted into the electronic medical record (EMR) system via a connection module. As a result, lab technicians must manually enter results into the EMR, leading to time consumption and the potential for errors. Ms. Elkady hopes for the integration of an automated notification system, along with an acknowledgment of receipt, into the existing EMR system to streamline processes and enhance efficiency	

(see Fig. 1) to generate ideas and decided to replace the manual tracing process with a mobile application. This solution aims to alleviate the identified issues of the stakeholders and offer additional value-added features. The hospital's head of information technology was involved in designing a prototype of the desired phone application.

The proposed mobile application, named Lab Live Tracing System, will serve as a pilot project initially implemented in the intensive care unit. If it is successful in addressing the initial stakeholder concerns, the application can be extended to other clinical areas. The application will be available for download on both IOS and Android operating systems, allowing users to access it on their mobile devices.

For the pilot project, approved users, including nurses, doctors, and clinical laboratory technicians working in the intensive care unit, will be issued unique user IDs and passwords to log into the system. This ensures user identification and authentication. The mobile application will be linked to the hospital's lab information system (LIS), enabling automatic display of completed blood test results within the application.

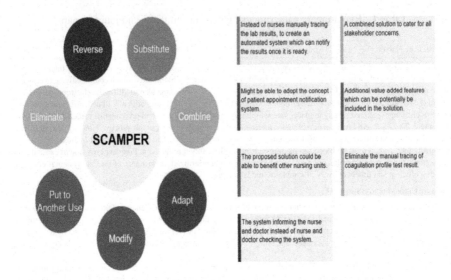

Fig. 1. Scamper

One distinctive feature of the application is its ability to recognize the nurse and doctor who ordered the test and send them notifications when the results are ready. This resolves the issue of manual tracing faced by critical care nurses. Additionally, the application allows lab technicians to promptly notify the nurse if a blood sample is rejected, triggering the need for a new sample.

Furthermore, the application includes a built-in chat system, enabling attending nurses and doctors to discuss and update the patient's management plan based on the latest blood results. It also incorporates a reminder function to facilitate task execution and coordination among nurses and doctors related to patient management.

The application features an intensive care unit bed board, providing users with patient-specific information such as name, age, diagnosis, attending consultant, and details of lab test results. Lastly, the lab technician can directly contact the nurse or doctor on duty through the application to communicate critical test result values or inform them about rejected blood samples.

Overall, the Lab Live Tracing System mobile application presents a comprehensive solution to streamline coagulation profile e-reporting, enhance communication between stakeholders, and improve patient care in the intensive care unit.

3.3 Prototype Design

The core method in design practices is prototyping [23, 24]. The objective of prototyping is to materialize an idea [25]. The prototypes are intended to represent a design created prior to the existence of the ultimate product. Figure 2 depicts an ideal prototype should undergo a few iterations prior to being finalized in order to identify any flaws. The input and feedback of end consumers are essential to the development of a product that is both useful and productive. In this study, the researchers propose a development of a

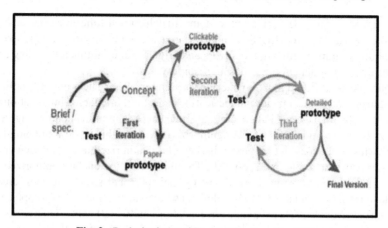

Fig. 2. Redesigning and Prototyping Iteration [23]

mobile application, Lab Live Tracing System (LLTS), that facilitates communication between users (surgeons, critical care nurses, and lab technicians). This mobile platform will provide real-time access to blood test results and alert users to critical values and sample errors.

4 Proposed Solution

The motivation for the proposed solution stemmed from a persistent challenge faced by healthcare providers in the PSICU. They lack awareness of laboratory results availability after processing and entering blood investigations into the LIS. Through the empathy journey, the team gained insights into the demanding and fast-paced environment of the PSICU, where post-operative patients require continuous observation and intensive care. Physicians and nurses in the unit face significant workloads, impacting their cognitive functions regarding coagulation profile results. To address this, a user-friendly alerting system called Lab Live Tracing System (LLTS) is introduced. It offers real-time access to critical values in the Coagulation Profile, enabling timely adjustments to patient care, such as modifying IV Heparin dosages, ultimately enhancing workflow and improving the quality of care in the PSICU.

The users who will benefit from LLTS include critical care nurses, surgeons, and lab technicians. Currently, there is no existing notification system for critical values, requiring critical care nurses to regularly log into the Electronic Medical Record system to track Coagulation Profile results. However, the demanding work environment in the PICU can hinder this process and consume valuable time.

LLTS will offer a distinct solution by providing users with access to patient results anytime and anywhere through their own mobile devices. Lab technicians will be able to alert PICU staff about critical values or sample errors, while staff nurses will receive real-time updates on test results. Surgeons will also have direct communication with staff nurses, allowing them to modify patient management plans accordingly.

This integrated mobile application system will deliver real-time updates to all health-care professionals involved. LLTS facilitates seamless communication among stakehold-ers, enabling prompt rectification of errors and critical values, ultimately saving crucial time and enhancing patient outcomes after surgery.

Figure 3 depicts the application interface design for LLTS. The proposed application has 6 main interfaces that include authentication page, Staff in-charged information page, Patient-Ward board page and Patient Critical Value Pages. The authentication page allows authorized users to login to LLTS. The authorized users are able to view and monitor the patients who in the coagulation profile listing. Only authorized users can view and act on the critical value alerts. As a result, LLTS implementation enables authorized users to conveniently access patients' results using their personal mobile devices, ensuring anytime, anywhere availability. Lab technicians have the capability to promptly notify PICU staff of critical values or sample errors. Additionally, staff nurses receive real-time updates on test results, while surgeons can directly communicate with staff nurses and make necessary adjustments to patient management plans.

Nevertheless, the proposed LLTS application could be limited by its reliance on personal mobile devices for access, which could introduce compatibility and security issues. In environments with diverse device types and operating systems, it may be dif-ficult to ensure seamless functionality. Furthermore, an excessive reliance on mobile devices may hinder the effectiveness of LLTS for staff who are unfamiliar with technol-ogy. In addition, network connectivity issues may disrupt real-time updates, delaying the transmission of vital information during monitor the patients.

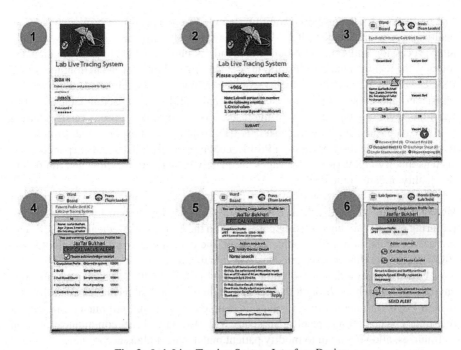

Fig. 3. Lab Live Tracing System Interface Design

5   Conclusion

In critical patient care settings, the fragmented nature of the workflow increases the risk of human errors in following up on abnormal laboratory test results. Failure to recognize or timely act upon these results can lead to diagnostic errors, potential adverse events, and liability claims. In this study, a mobile application called LLTS is proposed using a design-thinking approach. The processes of persona, empathy, and journal mapping assisted the researchers in gathering requirements. Thus, an automated notification system for abnormal results can partially improve follow-up for patients in the Pediatric Intensive Care Unit (PICU). Additionally, requiring healthcare providers to acknowledge receipt of test results has the potential to promote timely management for PICU patients. To address these safety concerns, a multidisciplinary intervention incorporating human-computer interaction and a reliable tracking system for test result notifications is necessary. However, it is important to note that while health information technology (HIT) innovation plays a significant role, the attitude, perception, and knowledge of end users are ultimately crucial in maximizing the potential benefits of HIT and improving healthcare quality.

References

1. Stoumpos, A.I., Kitsios, F., Talias, M.A.: Digital transformation in healthcare: technology acceptance and its applications. Int. J. Environ. Res. Public Health. **20**(4), 3407 (2023). https://doi.org/10.3390/ijerph20043407
2. Mumford, A.D., et al.: Guideline for the diagnosis and management of the rare coagulation disorders. Br. J. Haematol. **167**, 304–326 (2014). https://doi.org/10.1111/bjh.13058
3. Alexis, B.C., et al.: Electronic health records and genomics: perspectives from the association for molecular pathology electronic health record (EHR) interoperability for clinical genomics data working group. J. Mol. Diagnost. **24**(1), 1–17 (2022)
4. Hermes, S., Riasanow, T., Clemons, E.K., et al.: The digital transformation of the healthcare industry: exploring the rise of emerging platform ecosystems and their influence on the role of patients. Bus. Res. **13**, 1033–1069 (2020). https://doi.org/10.1007/s40685-020-00125-x
5. Evans R.S.: Electronic Health Records: Then, Now, and in the Future. Yearb Med Inform. (Suppl 1):S48-S61, (2016). https://doi.org/10.15265/IYS-2016-s006
6. Mohammadi, A.M., Erten A., Yalcin O.: Technology advancements in blood coagulation measurements for point-of-care diagnostic testing. Front. Bioeng. Biotechnol. 7(395) (2019). https://doi.org/10.3389/fbioe.2019.00395
7. Toben, B., Martin, M.: Rapid assessment of coagulation at the point of care with the hemochron signature elite system. Point Care: J. Near-PatientTesting Technol 19(4), 116–121 (2020). https://doi.org/10.1097/POC.0000000000000216
8. Health Care Providers Can Use Design Thinking to Improve Patient Experiences, Harvard Business Review, 31 August 2017. https://hbr.org/2017/08/health-care-providers-can-use-design-thinking-to-improve-patient-experiences
9. Altman, M., Huang, T.T.K., Breland, J.Y.: Design thinking in health care. Prev. Chronic Dis. **15**, 180128 (2018). https://doi.org/10.5888/pcd15.180128
10. Oliveira, M., Zancul, E., Fleury, A.L.: Design thinking as an approach for innovation in healthcare: systematic review and research avenues. BMJ Innov. **7**(2), 491–503 (2021). https://doi.org/10.1136/bmjinnov-2020-000428

11. Vetterli, C.: Design thinking in healthcare—enabler for digitalization in complex environments: why healthcare is adequate to proof the potential of design thinking for software-intensive ecosystems. In: Hehn, J., Mendez, D., Brenner, W., Broy, M. (eds.) Design Thinking for Software Engineering. Progress in IS, pp. 191–200. Springer, Cham (2022). https://doi.org/10.1007/978-3-030-90594-1_13

12. Novak, L.L., Harris, J.W., Koonce, T.Y., Johnson, K.B.: Design thinking in applied informatics: what can we learn from project HealthDesign? J. Am. Med. Inf. Assoc. **28**(9), 1858–1865 (2021). https://doi.org/10.1093/jamia/ocab081

13. Crosby, L.E., Joffe, N.E., Dunseath, L.A., Lee, R.: Design joins the battle against sickle-cell disease. Des. Manag. Rev. **24**(2), 48–53 (2013). https://doi.org/10.1111/drev.10241

14. Quesada, A.E., Jabcuga, C.E., Nguyen, A., Wahed, A., Nedelcu, E., Nuyen, A.N.D.: Interpretation of coagulation test results using a web-based reporting system. Lab. Med. **45**(4), 347–360 (2014). https://doi.org/10.1309/LMAI721FKQMGFEFZ

15. Wentzel, J., Van Drie-Pierik, R., Nijdam, L., Geesing, J., Sanderman, R., Van Gemert-Pijnen, J.E.W.C.: Antibiotic information application offers nurses quick support. Am. J. Infect. Control **44**(6), 677–684 (2016). https://doi.org/10.1016/j.ajic.2015.12.038

16. Luna, D.R., Rizzato Lede, D.A., Otero, C.M., Risk, M.R., González Bernaldo de Quirós, F.: "User-centered design improves the usability of drug-drug interaction alerts: experimental comparison of interfaces. J. Biomed. Inform. **66**, 204–213 (2017). https://doi.org/10.1016/j.jbi.2017.01.009

17. Gaynor, M., et al.: A user-centered, learning asthma smartphone application for patients and providers. Learn. Heal. Syst. **4**(3), 1–13 (2020). https://doi.org/10.1002/lrh2.10217

18. Chiu, M.C., Huang, P.H., Tsao, S.H.: Redesigning the user interface of a healthcare management system for the elderly with a systematic usability testing method. J. Ind. Prod. Eng. **36**(5), 324–334 (2019). https://doi.org/10.1080/21681015.2019.1647883

19. Danitz, S.B., et al.: When user-centered design meets implementation science: integrating provider perspectives in the development of an intimate partner violence intervention for women treated in the United States' largest integrated healthcare system. BMC Womens Health **19**(1), 1–12 (2019). https://doi.org/10.1186/s12905-019-0837-8

20. Ferreira, B., Silva, W., Barbosa, S.D.J., Conte, T.: Technique for representing requirements using personas: a controlled experiment. IET Softw. **12**, 280–290 (2018). https://doi.org/10.1049/iet-sen.2017.0313

21. Punyalikhit, R.: Empathy and emotional customer journey map methods: for designing creative learning space. Int. Hum. Soc. Sci. Art **8**(5), 35–58 (2015)

22. Elizarova, O., Kahn, P.: Align and combine, customer journey mapping and COM-B analysis to aid decision-making during the design process. In: Storni, C., Leahy, K., McMahon, M., Lloyd, P., Bohemia, E. (eds.), Design as a catalyst for change - DRS International Conference, Limerick, Ireland. (2018) https://doi.org/10.21606/drs.20188.208

23. Camburn, B., et al.: Design prototyping methods: state of the art in strategies, techniques, and guidelines. Des. Sci. (2017). https://doi.org/10.1017/dsj.2017.10

24. Brian, L.: Prototyping: the dual actions. Cubic J. 54–73 (2020). https://doi.org/10.31182/cubic.2020.3.024

25. Ansell, C., Sørensen, E., Torfing, J.: Cocreating SDGs through experimentation and prototyping, Co-Creation for Sustainability, Emerald Publishing Limited, Bingley, pp. 105–119 (2022). https://doi.org/10.1108/978-1-80043-798-220220008

26. Lee, J.W., Daly, S.R., Huang-Saad, A.Y., et al.: Using design strategies from microfluidic device patents to support idea generation. Microfluid. Nanofluid.Nanofluid. **22**, 70 (2018). https://doi.org/10.1007/s10404-018-2089-6

The Impact of Preprocessing Techniques Towards Word Embedding

Mustazzihim Suhaidi[✉], Rabiah Abdul Kadir, and Sabrina Tiun

Universiti Kebangsaan Malaysia, UKM, IIR4.0 Kuala Lumpur, Malaysia
p100520@siswa.ukm.edu.my

Abstract. In this study, we analyze the performance of various pre-processing methods and classification algorithms on health-related tweet data on Twitter. The data set consists of a number of different pre-processing methods, such as Z-score Scaling, Min-max Scaling, Decimal Scaling, Log Transformation, Percentage Scaling, and Log2 Scaling, as well as two main classification algorithms: Naive Bayes and Logistic Regression. The results of the analysis show that the pre-processing method has a significant effect on the performance of the classification algorithm. Z-score Scaling emerges as a stable option and provides good accuracy for both algorithms. However, Min-max Scaling is more suitable for Logistic Regression than Naive Bayes. In addition, Logistic Regression tends to provide higher accuracy in some pre-processing methods. We also suggest further exploration to understand how this pre-processing method might apply to different types of data and its impact on other classification algorithms. In addition, the selection of alternative models, hyperparameter optimization, and data enrichment are areas that can be improved to obtain better classification results. This study underscores the importance of careful pre-processing and selection of appropriate pre-processing methods in applying classification algorithms to text data. The results and recommendations in this study can be a guide for researchers and practitioners in making better decisions in the classification analysis of Twitter data about health.

Keywords: Preprocessing · NLP · Word embedding · Classification

1 Introduction

Data are not always "clean"; the presence of redundant, inconsistent, noisy, and/or missing data in a dataset indicates that data are not clean and need to be handled before applying any machine learning algorithm. Data preprocessing is concerned with solving such issues. In addition, data normalization, discretization, and transformation are data preprocessing tasks [1]. To get the quality of data, machine learning (ML) provides one of the most meaningful steps called data preprocessing.

The data preprocessing task includes certain steps like data preparation, integration, cleaning, normalization, scaling, and data reduction techniques to reduce the complexity, of noisy and irrelevant elements using feature selection and discretization, etc. After this, the outcome expected a final dataset for further analysis using ML algorithms [3].

© The Author(s), under exclusive license to Springer Nature Singapore Pte Ltd. 2024
H. Badioze Zaman et al. (Eds.): IVIC 2023, LNCS 14322, pp. 421–429, 2024.
https://doi.org/10.1007/978-981-99-7339-2_35

Many researchers have worked on different approaches using machine learning algorithms or a combination of algorithms as ensemble methods to improve the performance of the document classifier [2]. Recently, the focus of enhancing document classification is not only on the classification model or algorithm but also on the improvement of document representation [4]. Document representation is one important step in the document classification process under the preprocessing stage which is primarily used to transform documents from the full-text version into a document vector. Word embeddings have gained popularity in most NLP tasks because of their ability to generate low-dimensional and dense vector representations of words [5]. More significantly, their unique feature is the capturing of the syntactic and semantic relationship between words.

2 Related Work

In this section, we present an overview of related work on text preprocessing and word embeddings, and how our work aims to bridge the gap between those efforts.

2.1 Text Preprocessing

Preprocessing refers to transforming the redundant, missing, unnecessary, and inconsistent data into an appropriate format that is suitable for the models' training. Various steps are performed during the preprocessing phase to improve the suitability of the raw data and elevate the performance and efficiency of the models [6]. Preprocessing steps of stop word removal, conversion to lowercase, and tokenization have been performed with the help of a natural language tool kit (NLTK) and Keras libraries in Python [7–9].

This section describes the preprocessing factors applied to the training corpus that is then used to generate word representations and the order of the pre-processing factors which we need to follow when applying to the corpus. Preprocessing factors (Basic, spellcheck, negation, part-of-speech, stop words, stemming [10].

Basic: A group of common text preprocessing applied at the very beginning, such as removing HTML tags, removing numbers, and lowercasing. This step removes all common punctuation from text, such as "@%* = ()/ +" using the NLTK regexp tokenizer.

Spellcheck: A case can be made for either correcting misspellings and typos or leaving them as is assuming they represent natural language text and its associated complexities [10]. In this step, we identify words that may have been misspelled and correct them.

Negation: Negation is a mechanism that transforms a positive argument into its inverse rejection. Specifically, in the task of affective analysis, negation plays a critical role as negation words can affect the word or sentence polarity causing the polarity to invert in many cases [11].

2.2 Document Classification

Document classification refers to the process of categorizing or assigning labels to documents based on their content, characteristics, or other relevant features. It is a fundamental task in natural language processing (NLP) and information retrieval [12]. The goal of document classification is to automatically organize large collections of textual documents into predefined categories or classes [13].

In document classification, a machine learning model is typically trained on a labeled dataset, where each document is associated with a known category or class [14]. The model learns to identify patterns and relationships in the textual data, allowing it to make predictions or assign labels to unseen or new documents [15].

Document classification has various applications in different domains, such as spam detection, sentiment analysis, topic modeling, news categorization, customer feedback analysis, and document organization for information retrieval systems [16]. By automatically assigning categories to documents, document classification enables efficient information organization, retrieval, and analysis, saving time and effort for users [17].

The process of document classification involves several steps, including data preprocessing (such as tokenization, stemming, and removing stop words), feature extraction (converting text into numerical representations), model training (using machine learning algorithms), and evaluation (assessing the performance of the model on test data) [10]. The choice of features, algorithms, and evaluation metrics may vary depending on the specific task and dataset [18].

Overall, document classification plays a crucial role in managing and making sense of large volumes of textual data, enabling effective organization, retrieval, and analysis of documents for various applications and domains.

2.3 Word Embedding

Preprocessing techniques refer to the steps taken before generating word embeddings, such as tokenization, stemming, removing stop words, normalizing text, or applying other text cleaning methods [19]. These techniques can help in reducing noise, standardizing the input, and improving the quality of the resulting word embeddings.

The impact of preprocessing techniques on word embedding can be explored in terms of various aspects [4], including:

Semantic and syntactic information: Different preprocessing techniques can affect the preservation of semantic and syntactic relationships between words in the resulting word embeddings [14]. The paper may analyze how certain preprocessing methods enhance or diminish the semantic similarity or syntactic regularities captured by word embeddings.

Dimensionality and sparsity: Preprocessing techniques can influence the dimensionality and sparsity of word embeddings. The paper may investigate how different preprocessing methods affect the number of dimensions in the vector space representation and whether they lead to denser or sparser embeddings [20].

Performance in downstream tasks: The authors may evaluate the impact of preprocessing techniques on the performance of word embeddings in various downstream natural languages processing tasks, such as text classification, named entity recognition, sentiment analysis, or machine translation [15]. The study may high light how specific preprocessing techniques contribute to better or worse performance in these tasks.

Computational efficiency: Preprocessing techniques can also have an impact on the computational efficiency of generating word embeddings. Certain preprocessing methods may increase or decrease the computational complexity or resource requirements of the embedding process, and the paper may discuss these aspects [8].

By investigating the impact of preprocessing techniques on word embedding, the paper aims to provide insights into the importance of data preparation steps and guide researchers and practitioners in choosing appropriate preprocessing methods to enhance the quality and effectiveness of word embeddings in different NLP applications [21].

3 Methodology

The process of converting letters into numbers before text classification is carried out, and is continued at the feature extraction stage. Before the data set is used, it is necessary to process text preprocessing. Preprocessing techniques can have a significant impact on the word embedding results [14]. Following are some of the impacts that may arise as a result of applying preprocessing techniques to word embedding [22]:

1. Noise reduction: Preprocessing techniques such as removing punctuation, special characters, or numbers, and selecting relevant characters can reduce noise in text data. This can help prevent irrelevant influences or distractions on word embedding formation, thereby improving the quality of word representation [10].
2. Standardization of text: Preprocessing can assist in producing a more consistent representation of words by converting letters to lowercase, removing trailing spaces, or normalizing word form [23]. With consistent standardization, word embedding can better capture similarities in meaning and relationships between words that are similar but appear in different forms.
3. Improved semantic cohesion: By applying appropriate preprocessing techniques, such as stemming or lemmatization, the various tenses can be reduced to more general base forms or roots [24]. This helps in increasing semantic cohesion so that words with similar meanings are closer together in the word embedding vector representation.
4. Reduction of irrelevant dimensions: Preprocessing can help in reducing irrelevant dimensions in the vector representation of word embedding. For example, eliminating stop words (words that are common and contribute little in meaning) can reduce representational complexity and increase the focus on more informative important words [6].
5. Computational efficiency: Efficient preprocessing techniques can help reduce data size and increase processing speed. By reducing the complexity of text data through preprocessing, the training process and the use of word embedding can be more efficient in terms of time and computational resources required [24] (Fig. 1).

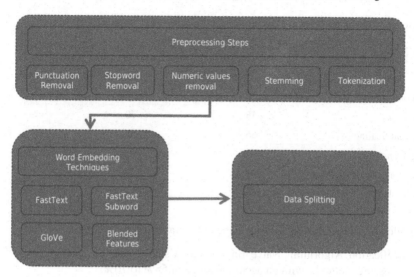

Fig. 1. Framework of Research Evaluation

4   Results and Discussions

Our experiment aims to check the effectiveness of several available pre-processing methods (Z-score, Min-max, Decimal Scaling, Log Transformation, Percentage Scaling scaling log2) on classification accuracy. By using two classification models namely; Naive Bayes and logistic regression.

The following steps can be taken in the context of the scaling method on text vectors:

1. Text Feature Extraction:
    Use techniques like TF-IDF or word embedding to turn text into feature vectors.
2. Numerical Feature Extraction (Optional):
    If have numeric features other than text vectors, arrange them in matrix or separate vector form.
3. Normalization or Adjustment of Numerical Features:
    If have numeric features of a different scale, you can normalize or scale them. The commonly used method is Min-Max normalization or Z-score standardization.
4. Merger Features:
    After the numeric features are normalized or adjusted, you can combine these numeric feature vectors with the text feature vectors created earlier.
5. Data Sharing, Model Selection, Training, and Evaluation:
    Continue with the data sharing, model selection, training, and evaluation steps as previously described.

So, the results are obtained as shown in the table and graph below.

| Pre- Processing Method | Classification Model accuracy (%) | |
	Naive Bayes	Logistic Regression
Z-score	70	70
Min-max	55	70
Decimal Scaling	66	67
Log Transformation	62	62
Percentage Scaling	61	69
Scaling log2	66	69

Following are some conclusions that can be drawn from the table:

1. Classification Algorithm: Naive Bayes: Has a stable level of accuracy in various pre-processing methods, with an accuracy range of 55% to 70%.
2. Logistic Regression: Shows a more consistent level of accuracy on several pre-processing methods, with an accuracy range between 62% to 70%.
3. Pre-Processing Method: Z-score Scaling: Provides good performance on both classification algorithms, with 70% accuracy on both.
4. Min-max Scaling: Shows lower accuracy on Naive Bayes (55%), but good performance on Logistic Regression (70%).
5. Decimal Scaling: Provides similar results between the two classification algorithms, with accuracy ranging from 66% to 67%.
6. Log Transformation: Has a similar accuracy in both classification algorithms, which is 62%.
7. Percentage Scaling: Shows lower accuracy on Naive Bayes (61%), but good performance on Logistic Regression (69%).
8. Scaling log2: Shows similar results between the two classification algorithms, with accuracy ranging from 66% to 69%.

Furthermore, based on the data in the table the graphical form can be displayed as follows (Fig. 2);

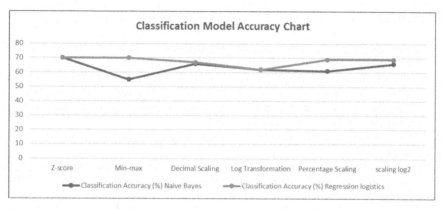

Fig. 2. Classification Model Accuracy Chart.

Based on the graph above, it can be explained that the Naive Bayes and Logistic Regression Algorithms have different performances depending on the pre-processing method used. The most stable pre-processing method that gives good performance for both algorithms is Z-score Scaling. Min-max Scaling is better suited for Logistic Regression than Naive Bayes. Decimal Scaling gives consistent results on both algorithms. Log Transformation tends to give lower accuracy in general. Percentage Scaling is better suited for Logistic Regression than Naive Bayes. Scaling log2 gives balanced results on both algorithms.

5   Conclusion

In order to analyze the performance of various pre-processing methods and classification algorithms on Twitter's health data, the following conclusions can be drawn: Pre-Processing Methods Effect: Pre-processing methods have a significant impact on the performance of the classification algorithms. Z-score Scaling stands out as a stable option providing good accuracy for both algorithms, while Min-max Scaling is more effective on Logistic Regression. Naïve Bayes vs. Logistic Regression: Naive Bayes Algorithm shows stable performance, but Logistic Regression tends to provide higher accuracy in certain pre-processing methods. Numerical Feature Adjustment: Normalization or scaling of numeric features plays an important role in improving model performance. Mainly, Z-score Scaling provides consistent results. Determination of the Best Method: The choice of pre-processing method and classification algorithm must be adjusted to the purpose of analysis and data characteristics. Z-score Scaling may be an initial choice due to its consistency, but further adjustments need to be made based on specific needs.

References

1. Performance, A., Alshdaifat, E., Alshdaifat, D., Alsarhan, A., Hussein, F., Moh, S.: The effect of preprocessing techniques, applied to numeric. Data. **6**, 11 (2021)
2. Iturra-bocaz, G., Bravo-marquez, F.: RiverText: A Python Library for Training and Evaluating Incremental Word Embeddings from Text Data Streams RiverText : A Python Library for Training and Evaluating Incremental Word Embeddings from Text Data Streams, vol. 1, no. 1. Association for Computing Machinery (2023)
3. Misra, P., Yadav, A.S.: Impact of preprocessing methods on healthcare predictions. SSRN Electron. J. (2019)
4. Rabut, B.A. Fajardo, A.C., Medina, R.P.: Multi-class document classification using improved word embeddings. In: ACM International Conference Proceeding Series, pp. 42–46 (2019)
5. Hadiprakoso, R.B., Setiawan, H., Yasa, R.N.: Text Preprocessing for Optimal Accuracy in Indonesian Sentiment Analysis Text Preprocessing for Optimal Accuracy in Indonesian Sentiment Analysis Using a Deep Learning Model with Word Embedding. August (2021)
6. Obaid, H.S., Dheyab, S.A., Sabry, S.S.: The impact of data pre-processing techniques and dimensionality reduction on the accuracy of machine learning. In: IEMECON 2019 - 9th Annual Information Technology, Electromechanical Engineering and Microelectronics Conference, vol. 4, pp. 279–283 (2019)
7. Mafunda, M.C., Schuld, M., Durrheim, K., Mazibuko, S.: A word embedding trained on South African news data. African J. Inf. Commun. **30**, 1–24 (2022)
8. Karim, M., Missen, M.M.S., Umer, M., Sadiq, S., Mohamed, A., Ashraf, I.: Citation context analysis using combined feature embedding and deep convolutional neural network model. Appl. Sci. **12**(6), 3203 (2022). https://doi.org/10.3390/app12063203
9. Nurhadi, N., Abdul Kadir, R., Mat Surin, E.S.: Classification complex query SQL for data lake management using machine learning. J. Inf. Syst. Technol. Manag. **6**(22), 15–24 (2021)
10. Babanejad, N., Davoudi, H., Agrawal, A., An, A., Papagelis, M.: The role of preprocessing for word representation learning in affective tasks. IEEE Trans. Affect. Comput. **5**(7), 5799–5810 (2023)
11. Yohannes, D., Assabie, Y.: Amharic text clustering using encyclopedic knowledge with neural word embedding. arXiv Prepr. arXiv:2105.00809 (2021)
12. Joseph, P., Yerima, S.Y.: A comparative study of word embedding techniques for SMS spam detection. In: Proceedings of 2022 14th IEEE International Conference on Computational Intelligence Communication Networks, CICN 2022, December, pp. 149–155 (2022)
13. Nazir, S., Asif, M., Sahi, S.A., Ahmad, S., Ghadi, Y.Y., Aziz, M.H.: Toward the development of large-scale word embedding for low-resourced language. IEEE Access **10**(June), 54091–54097 (2022)
14. Li, S., Gong, B.: Word embedding and text classification based on deep learning methods. MATEC Web Conf. **336**, 06022 (2021)
15. Lassner, D., Brandl, S., Baillot, A., Nakajima, S.: Domain-specific word embeddings with structure prediction. Trans. Assoc. Comput. Linguist. **11**, 320–335 (2023)
16. Faisal, M.R., Budiman, I., Abadi, F., Nugrahadi, D.T., Haekal, M., Sutedja, I.: Applying features based on word embedding techniques to 1D CNN for natural disaster messages classification. In: 2022 5th International Conference on Computer and Informatics Engineering. IC2IE 2022, December, pp. 192–197 (2022)
17. Albalawi, Y., Buckley, J., Nikolov, N.S.: Investigating the impact of pre-processing techniques and pre-trained word embeddings in detecting Arabic health information on social media. J. Big Data **8**(1), 1–29 (2021). https://doi.org/10.1186/s40537-021-00488-w
18. Alam, S., Yao, N.: The impact of preprocessing steps on the accuracy of machine learning algorithms in sentiment analysis. Comput. Math. Organ. Theory **25**(3), 319–335 (2019)

19. Rahimi, Z., Homayounpour, M.M.: TensSent: a tensor based sentimental word embedding method. Appl. Intell. **51**(8), 6056–6071 (2021)
20. Ahn, Y., Rhee, E., Lee, J.: Dual embedding with input embedding and output embedding for better word representation. Indones. J. Electr. Eng. Comput. Sci. **27**(2), 1091–1099 (2022)
21. Beldar, P.R., Rakhade, R., Khond, V., Kavale, P., Bhadak, M.: Effect of word embedding techniques on clustering of Netflix movies and TV shows dataset. Int. J. Innov. Res. Technol. **9**, 7 (2022)
22. Bouaine, C., Benabbou, F., Sadgali, I.: Word embedding for high performance cross-language plagiarism detection techniques. Int. J. Interact. Mob. Technol. **17**(10), 69–91 (2023)
23. Shi, S., Xu, Y., Xu, X., Mo, X., Ding, J.: A preprocessing manifold learning strategy based on T-distributed stochastic neighbor embedding. Entropy **25**(7), 1–12 (2023)
24. Firoozi, T., Bulut, O., Epp, C.D., Naeimabadi, A., Barbosa, D.: The effect of fine-tuned word embedding techniques on the accuracy of automated essay scoring systems using neural networks. J. Appl. Test. Technol. **23**(February), 21–29 (2023)

Predict Traffic State Based on PCA-KMeans Clustering of neighbouring roads

Bagus Priambodo[1(✉)], Bambang Jokonowo[1], Samidi[2], Azlina Ahmad[3], and Rabiah Abdul Kadir[3]

[1] Universitas Mercu Buana, Meruya Selatan Jakarta, Jakarta 11650, Indonesia
bagus.priambodo@mercubuana.ac.id
[2] Universitas Budi Luhur, Ciledug 12260, Indonesia
[3] Universiti Kebangsaan Malaysia, 43600 Bangi, Selangor, Malaysia

Abstract. During the past few years, time series models and neural network models have been widely used to predict traffic conditions based on historical data, speeds, weather, accidents, and special holidays. However, in previous studies, these models were commonly used for predicting traffic flow, rather than predicting traffic flow propagation. Research in traffic flow propagation is relevant because it may guide people in avoiding neighbouring roads which are affected by congestion. We proposed the similarity of Principal Component Analysis (PCA) to investigate the relationship between roads by clustering similarity values between target roads and neighbouring roads. The results were then visualized on a map for further observation. Furthermore, the high relationship roads obtained from the cluster were then used for predicting traffic state using a naïve Bayes method. Based on the visualization of results on maps, and by observing the prediction results using naïve Bayes, obtained that utilizing PCA with K-Means improves the outcomes in obtaining high relationship roads compared with k-means only.

Keywords: Traffic state prediction · Naïve Bayes · PCA · Spatial Relationship · K-Means

1 Introduction

Traffic congestion is a condition where number of vehicles surpass maximum road capacity. The main characteristics of road congestion are slow average speed, long travel duration, and length of the vehicle queueing on the road. An effective method or model is needed to identify traffic congestion. One way to find the distribution of congestion in a road network is to evaluate the relationship between congestion and increasing traffic flow. Several factors may affect traffic congestion. Among the factors used in previous studies [1] to predict traffic state or traffic congestion are vehicle speed, weather, accidents, and special holidays. One of the many complexities of traffic congestion is that it fluctuates and related to each other. Traffic congestion can spread from one road to other roads in a surrounding area [2]. Understanding the relationship of roads around a congested location can provide useful information to assist drivers in avoiding congestion. Results of this study can be used to increase performance of clustering road segment using k-means.

In this paper, we will report the findings of our study that is to find relationship between roads in a neighbouring area based on similarity of traffic using two factors namely speed and number of vehicles. We use congestion index in interval of 20 min to obtain high similarity traffic between roads as indicator for high relationship roads. For evaluation purposes, we compare the results of traffic state prediction using naïve bayes based on the correlation method.

Previous studies have shown that adjacent roads demonstrated a similar traffic pattern on the same interval day and time [3, 4]. Studying the relationship between roads in adjacent areas will provide information to guide the driver to avoid traffic jams and the surrounding impact. Furthermore, the results of this finding may consider to increase the performance of prediction of traffic condition. Previous studies used Bayesian network [5–7] to predict traffic congestion. However, these studies considered only connected roads as factors that influence traffic flow. We know that traffic congestion is a ripple effect from a congested road to neighboring roads. In other words, if there is a congestion, it will propagate through neighbouring roads due to increasing traffic flow.

In general road segment road will be have correlation with other road segment they are connected in upstream, downstream or both [8, 9], they are connected in upstream, downstream or both. Other research determine the congestion correlation between two roads segments [10], from road X to road Y with distance d. If congestion state occurs in road X at time t and at time t + T, congestion state occurs at road Y. Many studies use dynamic relationship road to predict traffic flow. A study by [11] use multiple linear regression to find high relationship road between roads. Other study use tensor PCA to extract the relationship by reducing the features [12–14].

Based on Fig. 1, we can expect that the traffic condition on road III and road IV will also impact the traffic condition on neighbouring roads like road I and road II. In other words, traffic condition on road III would be affected by the traffic condition of neighbouring roads.

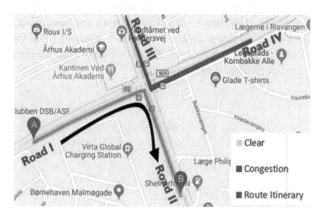

Fig. 1. Road III and its neighbouring roads.

In this paper, we report the findings of our study that is to find relationship between roads in a neighbouring area based on similarity of two traffic flow factors namely average speed and volume of vehicle. Principal component analysis (PCA) is one of the standard algorithm used for data representation [15, 16]. The main idea of the PCA method is feature extraction of main data [17], and transformation of primary data into small set of characteristic feature [18]. In this study, we investigate the relationship between roads by clustering PCA value between a target road and neighbouring roads using k-means. The results are then used for prediction of traffic state using naïve Bayes method. For evaluation purposes, we compare the results of traffic state prediction using naïve Bayes method based on k-means without PCA.

2   Related Work

Instead using connected road some studies use dynamic relationship roads approached for predicting traffic flow. Dynamic relationship roads mean, the relationship between roads segment in neighbouring area is determined by roads that have similar traffic condition [19]. A study by [10] determine the correlation between road segments by observed the traffic condition between two roads at same time in a given distance. Clustering approach is used also as another way to find similar traffic condition between road segments. Clustering method set the road segment into clusters based on historical data. This approach grouping the road segments with same traffic condition in the same cluster. Previous study clustering similar road segment using k-means based on density and speed [20], based on GPS data[21] shown in Fig. 2. A study by [22] used spectral clustering to group road segment based traffic condition in neighboring area.

K-Means Clustering has been used widely for clustering in intelligent transportation system. Previous study clustering similar road segment using k-means based on density and speed [20], other study using k-means to segment traffic condition based on driving feature [23], other study clustering road segment using k-means based on GPS trajectory data [21]. Another study clustering road safety on road segment using k-means [24]. Some study used canopy k-means to clustering road segment [25]. Sum of squares, silhouette graph [23, 26], and elbow curve [20, 27] is used to evaluate the result obtained within cluster to find optimal numbers of k.

3   Methodology

There are several stages of the method in this research, as shown in Fig. 2

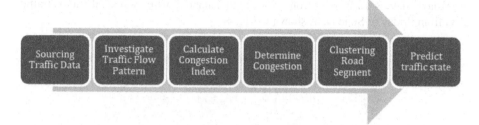

Fig. 2. Diagram of methodology.

3.1   Sourcing and Pre-processing

In this study, we used the dataset obtained from the IoT sensors located in Aarhus, Denmark [28–30]. The approximate number of sensors at this place is 449 as displayed in Fig. 3.

Fig. 3. Map of IoT traffic sensors location in the city of Aarhus, Denmark.

3.2 Investigate Traffic Flow Pattern

Some studies discovered that there is a difference in traffic flow pattern on weekends and on weekdays [3, 22]. We considered road 158324 to studying the traffic flow pattern and we discovered that there exists a similar pattern of traffic flow on weekdays. The weekdays' data is traffic data from Monday to Thursday while weekend data is traffic data from Friday to Sunday, as shown in Fig. 4.

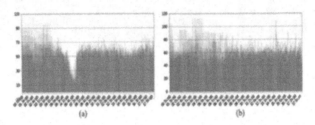

Fig. 4. (a) Traffic pattern on weekdays, (b) Traffic pattern on weekends.

3.3 Calculate Congestion Index

To determine the level of road congestion, various definitions and variables of traffic congestion were formed. Traffic congestion rank was defined by Rothenberg [31] as the condition in which number of vehicles on the road surpasses the carrying capacity of standard road service level. Some study used congestion index by considering the saturation degree, travelling speed and a combination of both [32]. A different study accounted for the speed performance index by segmenting congestion level as four, three or two as needed [33]. In this study, the congestion index was determined for a given time interval to calculate the similarity between roads to obtain the congestion level. Congestion index was calculated based on the travelling speed [32], with some adjustments. Instead of hourly calculation, the congestion index was calculated every 20 min using the formula given in (1).

$$CI = \frac{NDT - Vavg_{intervaltime}}{NDT - Vmin_{intervaltime}} \times \frac{Volume_{intervaltime}}{Volume_{day}} \times 100 \tag{1}$$

NDT: normal driving time in kilometre per hour or speed limit, as shown in Table 1..
$Vavg_{interval\ hours}$: average speed in interval hours.
$Vmin_{interval\ hours}$: minimum speed in interval hours.
$Volume_{interval\ hours}$: number of vehicles in interval hours.
$Volume_{day}$: number of vehicles in a day.

Table 1. Example of traffic data taken from sensor 173225.

Duration From	Duration To	Start Point	End Point	Cross Observation Data
2014-11-13 10:40:00	2014-11-13 10:40:00	City: Aarhus Street: Nørre-port 93, Postal Code: 8000, Coordinates (lat,long): 56.161, 10.211	City: Aarhus Street: Spanien 63 Postal Code: 8000 Coordi-nates (lat,long): 56.148, 10.209	Distance be-tween two points in me-ters: 1490 Du-ration of meas-urements in seconds: 202 NDT in KMH: 27 EXT ID: 359 Road type: MA-JOR_ROAD

3.4 Determining Congestion

To determine the level of road congestion, various definitions and variables of traffic congestion were formed. Traffic congestion rank was defined by Rothenberg [31] as the condition in which number of vehicles on the road surpasses the carrying capacity of standard road service level. Another study used congestion index by considering the saturation degree, travelling speed and a combination of both [32]. A different study accounted for the speed performance index by segmenting congestion level as four, three or two as needed [33, 34]. In this study, the congestion index was determined for a given time interval (20 min) to calculate the similarity between roads to obtain the congestion level.

As observed in Fig. 5, the road congestion occurred between 06:10 AM until 08:10 AM. From Table 2. show that, the congestion index was found between three (3.03) to five (5.41). In Denmark, the average speed of regular traffic in town is 50 km/hour [35]. Based on this information, we defined traffic congestion as the situation when average speed is below 50 km/h. As we can observed from Table 3., when the average speed is 50 km/hour, the congestion index value is around 3. Thus, for this study, we consider that a road is congested when the congestion index is above or equals 3.

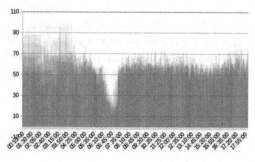

Fig. 5. The average speed on road 158324 every five minutes.

Table 2. Congestion on road 158324 from 05.40 – 09.20 am.

Time	Congestion index			Avg Speed			Volume		
5:40–6:00	2.73	63	62	57	57	4	6	14	17
6:00–6:20	3.03	57	55	50	50	12	12	15	13
6:20–6:40	3.83	41	41	47	45	16	20	11	11
6:40–7:00	4.52	45	47	39	28	12	12	20	23
7:00–7:20	4.25	23	25	25	14	24	21	15	17
7:20–7:40	5.41	13	13	14	15	22	20	17	15
7:40–8:00	3.98	21	23	26	48	18	30	22	16
8:00–8:20	3.71	53	56	56	57	11	20	18	13
8:20–8:40	2.6	58	57	52	59	13	8	14	10
8:40–9:00	2.69	68	58	51	52	7	10	12	9
9:00–9:20	2.81	57	60	61	58	5	5	9	12

3.5 Clustering Road Segment

Principal Component Analysis (PCA) is a common method for dimensionality reduction. PCA method reduce linear projection that maximises the scatter of all projected samples. The principal idea is, that a high-dimensional dataset is often explained by correlated variables and therefore they only keep the meaningful dimensions for most of the information, further detail about the equation in [36, 15]. In this study, we used PCA similarity between roads as well as neighbouring roads, to obtained the similarity features between roads in neighbouring roads/ PCA is used as a method for extracting features [15]. To evaluate the successful of our similarity clustering result, we defined neighbouring roads as all roads within a distance of 5 km from a target road. PCA value of each road then clustered using k-Means method. In this study we observed the majority of the variance in each road as shown in Fig. 6. Figure 6 show the average majority of variance on each road is below the first five components. However, in our study we considered the first ten of component to be clustered using k-Means. Generally elbow curve [27, 20] is used to evaluate the result obtained within cluster to find optimal numbers of k. Instead using these methods, we use the percentage of similarity of traffic state to find optimal numbers of k cluster, we expressed the similarity following (2), and the cluster similarity expressed following (3) [37]. The line chart of similarity of traffic state is shown in Fig. 7. Coefficient is given by Eq. (2) [5, 6].

$$Similarity = \frac{1}{n}\sum\nolimits_{j=2}^{n}\left(Road_1 == Road_j\right) \qquad (2)$$

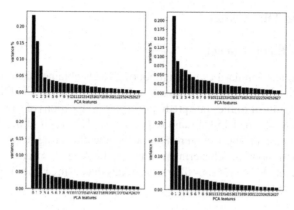

Fig. 6. The variance of principal component from four roads segments.

Figure 7 shows that k cluster PCA k-Means is lower than k-Means only when achieving high similarity between roads.

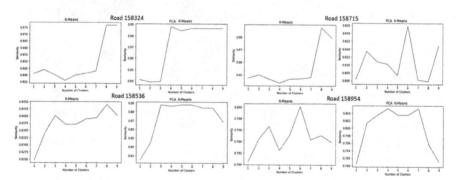

Fig. 7. Line chart of optimal k based on similarity of traffic state using K-Means and PCA-Means.

3.6 Predict Traffic State

The best four highest similarity The neighbouring roads obtained from PCA similarity with target road is used for prediction using naïve bayes method. We can define the problem using formula (2). The probability of traffic state in target road, given the evidence provided by features Road 1 through Road n, is equal to the product of the probabilities of each conditioned on the traffic state in target road, the prior probability of traffic state in target road, with a scaling factor 1/Z as follows.

$$P(R_{state}|R_i, \ldots, R_n) = \frac{1}{Z} p(R_{state}) \prod_{i=2}^{n} p(R_i|R_{state}) \qquad (3)$$

R_{state}: Traffic state in target road.

$R_i, \ldots, R_n$: traffic state in neighbouring roads.

4 Result and Discussion

4.1 Clustering Road Segment

The best four highest similarities of neighbouring roads obtained from PCA similarity with target road are used for prediction using the naïve Bayes method. For evaluation, we present the results of traffic state prediction at six (6) locations of roads, namely road 158324, road 158536, road 158715 and road 158954. The result of the clustering road segment is presented in Fig. 8. Figure 8(a) shows the clustering result using k-means only, and Fig. 8(b) shows the clustering result using PCA and k-means. Based on Fig. 8, the result shows that PCA k-Means filter more roads than using k-means only (see roads 158715 and 158954).

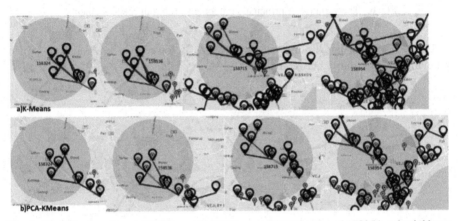

Fig. 8. Visualisation of road 158324, road 158536, road 158715 and road 158954 and neighbouring roads, (a) using K-Means (b) PCA and K-Means.

4.2 Prediction of traffic state

The results of average prediction in neighbouring roads 158324 and neighbouring roads 158536 is given in Table 3., while the average accuracy of prediction result of all neighbouring roads is given in Table 4.. From Table 3. and Table 4., we observed that the average accuracy of prediction utilizing PCA with k-means has better accuracy than K-Means only.

Table 3. The results of prediction accuracy using naïve bayes based on neighbouring roads.

On Roads	k-Means	k-Means with PCA
158324	0.86	0.91
158536	0.9	0.93
158715	0.85	0.92
158954	0.89	0.89

Table 4. The average results of prediction accuracy using naïve bayes based on neighbouring roads.

Neighbouring Area	k-Means	k-Means with PCA
158324	0.81	0.89
158536	0.82	0.86
158715	0.77	0.84
158954	0.75	0.78

4.3 Discussion

Based on In this study, our main interest is to find high relationship roads in a neighbouring area for prediction of traffic state. The results show that utilized PCA with K-Means produced better results in investigating relationship between roads. From visual analysis using maps, results show that utilizing PCA with K-Means filtered more roads which have relationship with target roads. Figure 9 shows comparison of the two methods. Prediction based on k-Means with PCA performed better when compared with prediction based on k-Means only.

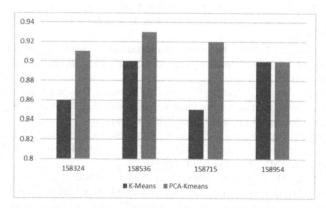

Fig. 9. Comparison of prediction accuracy of road 158324, road 158536, road 158715, and 158954 based on high relationship roads in neighbouring area.

5   Conclusion

Our interest is to improve clustering road segment using k-means algorithm to investigate the relationship betweeen road segments. Traffic flow on a road will affect the traffic flow on roads surrounding it. However, not all roads affect traffic flow of neighbouring roads. Only roads with high relationship with target road may affect the traffic flow in a neighbouring area. We used the Principal Component Analysist to extract the feature of traffic flow in a day and time. PCA is a method that has been widely used for feature extraction. By combining PCA with k-Means, it improves the results in obtaining high relationship roads using k-Means clustering. Thus, the prediction of traffic state based on combining PCA with k-Means produce better results when compared with the predictions based on K-Means only. Our experiments show that implements PCA improved performance of clustering road segment using k-means method.

Acknowledgement. The authors would like to thank the Ministry of Education, Culture, Research, and Technology of Indonesia for funding this research work through the KDN Research Grant Scheme. The authors would also like to extend the acknowledgement for the use of the service and facilities of the Intelligent Big Data Analytics Lab at Universitas Mercu Buana.

References

1. Smith, B.L., Demetsky, M.J., Smith, B.L.: Short-Term Traffic Flow Prediction: Neural Network Approach. Transp. Res. Rec. 98–104 (1994)
2. Wang, Z., Lu, M., Yuan, X., Zhang, J., Wetering, H.V., De,: Visual traffic jam analysis based on trajectory data. IEEE Trans. Vis. Comput. Graph. **19**, 2159–2168 (2013). https://doi.org/10.1109/TVCG.2013.228
3. Lee, K., Hong, B., Jeong, D., Lee, J.: Congestion pattern model for predicting short-term traffic decongestion times. In: 2014 17th IEEE International Conference on Intelligent Transportation Systems, ITSC 2014, pp. 2828–2833 (2014). https://doi.org/10.1109/ITSC.2014.6958143
4. Ko, E., Ahn, J., Kim, E.: 3D Markov process for traffic flow prediction in real-time. Sensors **16**(2), 147 (2016). https://doi.org/10.3390/s16020147
5. Kim, J., Wang, G.: Diagnosis and prediction of traffic congestion on urban road networks using Bayesian networks. Australas. Transp. Res. Forum **2016**, 1–21 (2016). https://doi.org/10.3141/2595-12
6. Aung, S.S., Naing, T.T.: Naïve bayes classifier based traffic detection system on cloud infrastructure. 2015 6th Int. Conf. Intell. Syst. Model. Simul. 193–198 (2015). https://doi.org/10.1109/ISMS.2015.45
7. Priambodo, B., Ahmad, A., Kadir, R.A.: Predicting traffic flow propagation based on congestion at neighbouring roads using hidden Markov model. IEEE Access. **9**, 85933–85946 (2021). https://doi.org/10.1109/ACCESS.2021.3075911
8. Yu, B., Song, X., Guan, F., Yang, Z., Yao, B.: K-nearest neighbour model for multiple-time-step prediction of short-term traffic condition. J. Transp. Eng. **142**, 04016018 (2016). https://doi.org/10.1061/(ASCE)TE.1943-5436.0000816
9. Lee, E.M., Kim, J.H., Yoon, W.S.: Traffic Speed Prediction Under Weekday, Time, and Neighboring Links' Speed: Back Propagation Neural Network Approach. In: Huang, D.S., Heutte, L., Loog, M. (eds.) Advanced Intelligent Computing Theories and Applications. With Aspects of Theoretical and Methodological Issues, pp. 626–635. Springer, Heidelberg (2007). https://doi.org/10.1007/978-3-540-74171-8_62

10. Wang, Y., Cao, J., Li, W., Gu, T.: Mining traffic congestion correlation between road segments on GPS trajectories. In: 2016 IEEE Int. Conf. Smart Comput. SMARTCOMP 2016. (2016). https://doi.org/10.1109/SMARTCOMP.2016.7501704
11. Liu, Z., Li, Z., Li, M., Xing, W., Lu, D.: Mining road network correlation for traffic estimation via compressive sensing. IEEE Trans. Intell. Transp. Syst. **17**, 1880–1893 (2016). https://doi.org/10.1109/TITS.2016.2514519
12. Han, Y., Moutarde, F.: Analysis of Large-scale Traffic Dynamics using Non-negative Tensor Factorization. arXiv Prepr, 1–12 (2012)
13. Han, Y., Moutarde, F.: Analysis of large-scale traffic dynamics in an urban transportation network using non-negative tensor factorization. Int. J. Intell. Transp. Syst. Res. **14**(1), 36–49 (2014). https://doi.org/10.1007/s13177-014-0099-7
14. Xing, X., Zhou, X., Hong, H., Huang, W., Bian, K., Xie, K.: Traffic flow decomposition and prediction based on robust principal component analysis. In: 2015 IEEE 18th International Conference on Intelligent Transportation Systems, pp. 2219–2224 (2015). https://doi.org/10.1109/ITSC.2015.358
15. Lionnie, R., Alaydrus, M.: Biometric identification system based on principal component analysis. In: Proceedings of 2016 12th International Conference Mathematics Statistics Their Applications ICMSA 2016 Conjunction with 6th Annual International Conference Syiah Kuala University, pp. 59–63 (2017). https://doi.org/10.1109/ICMSA.2016.7954309
16. Thakur, S., Sing, J.K., Basu, D.K., Nasipuri, M., Kundu, M.: Face recognition using principal component analysis and RBF neural networks. In: Proceedings of 1st International Conference Emergency Trends Engineering Technology ICETET 2008, pp. 695–700 (2008). https://doi.org/10.1109/ICETET.2008.104
17. Nugroho, A., Warnars, H.L.H.S., Isa, S.M., Budiharto, W.: Comparison of binary particle swarm optimization and binary dragonfly algorithm for choosing the feature selection. In: 2021 5th International Conference on Informatics and Computational Sciences (ICICoS), pp. 24–28 (2021). https://doi.org/10.1109/ICICoS53627.2021.9651779
18. Eleyan, A., Demirel, H.: PCA and LDA based face recognition using feedforward neural network classifier. In: Gunsel, B., Jain, A.K., Murat Tekalp, A., Sankur, B. (eds.) Multimedia Content Representation, Classification and Security, pp. 199–206. Springer, Heidelberg (2006). https://doi.org/10.1007/11848035_28
19. Hu, C., Xie, K., Song, G., Wu, T.: Hybrid process neural network based on spatio-temporal similarities for short-term traffic flow prediction. In: Proceedings of the 11th International IEEE Conference on Intelligent Transportation Systems Beijing, China, 12–15 October 2008. pp. 253–258 (2008)
20. Mondal, M.A., Rehena, Z.: Identifying traffic congestion pattern using k-means clustering technique. In: Proceedings - 2019 4th International Conference on Internet of Things: Smart Innovation and Usages, IoT-SIU 2019, pp. 1–5. IEEE (2019). https://doi.org/10.1109/IoT-SIU.2019.8777729
21. Necula, E.: Analyzing traffic patterns on street segments based on GPS data using R. Transp. Res. Procedia. **10**, 276–285 (2015). https://doi.org/10.1016/j.trpro.2015.09.077
22. Wang, X., Peng, L., Chi, T., Li, M., Yao, X., Shao, J.: A hidden markov model for urban-scale traffic estimation using floating car data. PLoS ONE **10**, 1–20 (2015). https://doi.org/10.1371/journal.pone.0145348
23. Montazeri-Gh, M., Fotouhi, A.: Traffic condition recognition using the k-means clustering method. Sci. Iran. **18**, 930–937 (2011). https://doi.org/10.1016/j.scient.2011.07.004
24. Ghadi, M.Q., Török, Á.: Comparison of different road segmentation methods. Promet - Traffic - Traffico. **31**, 163–172 (2019). https://doi.org/10.7307/ptt.v31i2.2937
25. Lin, X., Xu, J.: Road network partitioning method based on Canopy-Kmeans clustering algorithm. Arch. Transp. **54**, 95–106 (2020). https://doi.org/10.5604/01.3001.0014.2970

26. Zaki, J.F., Ali-Eldin, A., Hussein, S.E., Saraya, S.F., Areed, F.F.: Traffic congestion prediction based on Hidden Markov models and contrast measure. Ain Shams Eng. J. (2019). https://doi.org/10.1016/j.asej.2019.10.006

27. Laña, I., Del Ser, J., Olabarrieta, I.: Understanding daily mobility patterns in urban road networks using traffic flow analytics. In: International Workshop on Urban Mobility & Intelligent Transportation Systems (UMITS), pp. 1157–1162 (2016). https://doi.org/10.1109/NOMS.2016.7502980

28. Bischof, S., Karapantelakis, Athanasios Nechifor, C.-S., Sheth, A., Mileo, A., Barnaghi, P.: Real time IoT stream processing and large-scale data analytics for smart city applications. In: Real Time IoT Stream Processing and Large-scale Data Analytics for Smart City Applications (2014)

29. Kolozali, S., Bermudez-Edo, M., Puschmann, D., Ganz, F., Barnaghi, P.: A knowledge-based approach for real-time IoT data stream annotation and processing. In: Proceedings - 2014 IEEE International Conference on Internet of Things, iThings 2014, 2014 IEEE International Conference on Green Computing and Communications, GreenCom 2014 and 2014 IEEE International Conference on Cyber-Physical-Social Computing, CPS 20. pp. 215–222 (2014). https://doi.org/10.1109/iThings.2014.39

30. Bischof, S., Karapantelakis, A., Sheth, A., Mileo, A.: Semantic Modelling of Smart City Data Description of Smart City Data. In: W3C Workshop on the Web of Things Enablers and services for an open Web of Devices. pp. 1–5 (2014)

31. Zhang, Y., Ye, N., Wang, R., Malekian, R.: A method for traffic congestion clustering judgment based on grey relational analysis. ISPRS Int. J. Geo-Inf. 5, 71 (2016). https://doi.org/10.3390/ijgi5050071

32. Wang, W.X., Guo, R.J., Yu, J.: Research on road traffic congestion index based on comprehensive parameters: taking Dalian city as an example. Adv. Mech. Eng. 10, 1–8 (2018). https://doi.org/10.1177/1687814018781482

33. He, F., Yan, X., Liu, X., Ma, L.: A traffic congestion assessment method for urban road networks based on speed performance index. Proc. Eng. 137, 425–433 (2016). https://doi.org/10.1016/j.proeng.2016.01.277

34. Priambodo, B., Ahmad, A., Kadir, R.A.: Investigating relationships between roads based on speed performance index of road on weekdays. In: Zaman, H.B. (ed.) Advances in Visual Informatics: 6th International Visual Informatics Conference, IVIC 2019, Bangi, Malaysia, November 19–21, 2019, Proceedings, pp. 582–591. Springer International Publishing, Cham (2019). https://doi.org/10.1007/978-3-030-34032-2_51

35. Hels, T., Lyckegaard, A., Pilegaard, N.: Evaluering af trafiksikkerhedstiltag - en vejledning (2011)

36. Belhumeur, P.N., Hespanha, J.P., Kriegman, D.J.: Eigenfaces vs. fisherfaces: recognition using class specific linear projection. IEEE Trans. Pattern Anal. Mach. Intell. 19(7), 711–720 (1997). https://doi.org/10.1109/34.598228

37. Priambodo, B., Ahmad, A., Kadir, R.A.: Prediction of average speed based on relationships between neighbouring roads using K-NN and neural network. Int. J. online Biomed. Eng. 16, 18–33 (2020). https://doi.org/10.3991/ijoe.v16i01.11671

Unleashing Trustworthy Cloud Storage: Harnessing Blockchain for Cloud Data Integrity Verification

Zhenxiang Li[1,2(✉)], Mohammad Nazir Ahmad[1], Yuanrong Jin[1,2], Wang Haipei[1,2], and Liang Zhantu[1]

[1] Infrastructure University Kuala Lumpur, Kuala Lumpur, Malaysia
`222923380@s.iukl.edu.my`
[2] Sichuan Vocational College of Information Technology, Guangyuan, China

Abstract. This position paper explores the transformative potential of blockchain technology in ensuring data integrity within cloud storage systems. The increasing adoption of cloud storage services has raised concerns about the security and integrity of stored data. In this paper, we argue that integrating blockchain technology into cloud data integrity verification schemes offers a robust and decentralized solution. Through a comprehensive review of relevant literature, we examine the benefits and challenges associated with this approach. Our analysis reveals that blockchain-based data integrity verification schemes provide tamper-proof and transparent mechanisms, enhancing trust and security in cloud storage environments. We further discuss the potential impact of this integration on data privacy, scalability, and performance. While acknowledging the current limitations and ongoing research efforts, we propose that embracing blockchain for cloud data integrity verification can foster a new era of trustworthy and reliable cloud storage systems. This position paper aims to stimulate further discussion and research on the transformative role of blockchain in ensuring data integrity within the cloud.

Keywords: Cloud Storage · Integrity Verification · Blockchain

1 Introduction

The proliferation of cloud storage services has revolutionized the way we store and access data, offering convenience, scalability, and cost-efficiency [1]. However, this rapid growth has also brought forth concerns regarding the security and integrity of stored data [2, 3]. As organizations increasingly rely on cloud storage for critical and sensitive information, the need for robust data integrity verification mechanisms becomes paramount [4].

Traditional approaches to data integrity verification in cloud storage rely heavily on centralized systems and cryptographic techniques [5]. While these methods have provided a level of security, they are not without their limitations. Centralized systems introduce single points of failure and vulnerabilities to cyber-attacks, raising doubts about the trustworthiness of data stored in the cloud [6]. Furthermore, cryptographic techniques,

H. Badioze Zaman et al. (Eds.): IVIC 2023, LNCS 14322, pp. 443–452, 2024.
https://doi.org/10.1007/978-981-99-7339-2_37

while effective in ensuring data confidentiality and integrity during transmission, often fall short in verifying the integrity of data once it is stored in the cloud.

In recent years, blockchain technology has emerged as a disruptive force with its decentralized and transparent nature [7]. Initially developed to support cryptocurrencies like Bitcoin, blockchain has evolved beyond its financial applications and found relevance in various domains, including cloud storage. By leveraging blockchain's core features, such as immutability, transparency, and distributed consensus, it is possible to establish a novel paradigm for data integrity verification in cloud storage systems [8].

This position paper aims to explore the potential of blockchain-based cloud data integrity verification schemes and advocate for their adoption in the industry. We will critically analyze the advantages and challenges associated with integrating blockchain technology into existing cloud storage architectures. Through a comprehensive literature review, we will examine the state of the art, identifying notable research contributions and areas of improvement.

Furthermore, we will discuss the potential impact of blockchain on key aspects of cloud storage, such as data privacy, scalability, and performance. By presenting a well-rounded assessment of the current landscape and future possibilities, this paper intends to stimulate further discussion, research, and development in this vital area of cloud security.

In conclusion, this paper sets the stage for a comprehensive examination of blockchain-based cloud data integrity verification schemes. By highlighting their potential benefits and addressing existing challenges, we aim to establish a persuasive case for embracing blockchain technology as a transformative solution for ensuring trustworthy and secure cloud storage systems.

2   Research Motivation

In recent years, with the popularization and development of the Internet, the number of Internet users has increased and the types of user data have become more diverse, from simple text to pictures and videos. With the development of the Internet of Things technology, more and more terminal devices such as cars and smart wearable devices are connected to the Internet of Things. All these have led to an explosive growth in computer data.

IDC (International Data Corporation) predicts that by 2025, the total amount of data generated globally will reach 163ZB [9]. More and more data has become a burden on users' limited storage resources. However, cloud computing, with its high efficiency, high scalability and low cost advantages, is widely used in the field of information technology and has completely changed the way data is stored, accessed and shared. Therefore, more and more users choose to store data on cloud storage servers that provide cloud storage services to save local resources [10].

With the increasing popularity of cloud services and the rapid growth of cloud data volume, cloud storage systems usually deploy deduplication technology to reduce cloud data redundancy and improve storage utilization. In order to ensure storage security, users will also store data in ciphertext form on the cloud through encryption algorithms.

The randomization characteristics of traditional encryption algorithms will cause different ciphertexts to be generated from the same plaintext data, which will cause conventional data redundancy detection mechanisms to fail. In order to achieve secure deduplication of encrypted data, most existing schemes will use deterministic convergent encryption algorithms to ensure the uniqueness of ciphertexts and at the same time rely on trusted third parties to ensure the security and integrity of cloud data.

However, the introduction of third parties will cause cloud storage systems to face the threat of collusion attacks. In addition, the existing centralized cloud storage model requires users to fully trust cloud storage service providers and entrust them with data management rights. At this time, the ownership and management rights of cloud data are separated and directly separated from users' physical control, so they will face security issues such as brute force cracking, unauthorized access and loss or damage.

In order to protect the integrity of cloud storage data, [11] proposed a scheme for verifying the integrity of cloud storage data. Based on homomorphic verification tags and sampling strategies, it achieves verification of the integrity of cloud storage data with constant communication overhead without downloading data blocks to the local. However, in the above scheme, the verification of integrity verification evidence is performed by the Data Owner (DO), which brings a large computational overhead to the DO. [12] proposed the introduction of a trusted Third Party Auditor (TPA) to accept DO's entrustment to challenge and verify the integrity verification evidence of the Cloud Service Provider (CSP), freeing DO from the computational overhead of the verification phase.

Although the introduction of TPA reduces DO's computational overhead, it also brings additional security issues. First, in TPA-based schemes, there is a security assumption that TPA is completely trustworthy. However, in the real world, there is no completely trustworthy entity and TPA may also violate the cloud storage data integrity verification protocol. On the one hand, dishonest TPA may always return a verification pass result to save computational resources. On the other hand, TPA may accept bribes from CSP and collude with CSP to deceive users and cover up data damage. In TPA-based schemes, there is often also a security assumption that DO is honest. In reality, DO may falsely accuse CSP in order to seek compensation when data is intact.Secondly, in TPA-based schemes, there is a lack of arbitration mechanisms. When one party determines that the protocol is running abnormally, it cannot determine which party has violated the protocol through protocol operation information.Finally, TPA-based schemes have centralized limitations. The entire protocol operation depends on the normal operation of TPA. When TPA crashes or is maliciously invaded, the entire verification protocol will fail or even endanger user data security.

Blockchain is the underlying core technology of Bitcoin [13] and has advantages such as decentralization, non-tampering, openness and transparency, traceability and auditability [14]. Blockchain is essentially a decentralized distributed database that can achieve data consensus among nodes in large-scale distributed networks without trusted central nodes and can be combined with smart contracts to achieve trusted distributed computing.

Combining blockchain technology with cloud storage data integrity verification can reduce the centralization risk of protocols by using the decentralized characteristics of blockchain; the immutability and traceability of blockchain can realize audit of verification results and solve trust issues among three parties; using the public transparency of blockchain, Bitcoin, Ethereum and other public blockchains such as Bitcoin can also be used as external trusted data sources to replace some parameters in the protocol to improve the fairness and credibility of the protocol, combining blockchain technology with cloud data integrity verification has become a research trend.

However, most existing blockchain-based cloud data storage integrity verification schemes use blockchain as a distributed log database to build secure file directories. Due to the lack of privacy protection for outsourced data and dispute arbitration between DO and CSP to ensure truly fair transactions in most schemes, it is also unable to effectively improve the security of outsourced data.

Therefore, the research motivation of this paper is to develop a blockchain-based cloud data security verification scheme specifically designed for cloud data. By organically combining blockchain technology with cloud storage systems and achieving related technical goals through relevant technical solutions, it ensures that user data privacy information is not leaked during the verification process and that relatively fair transactions can be conducted between DO and CSP.

This research interested in (a) Blockchain, (b) Integrity Verification, and (c) Cloud Data. A diagram of the key research areas that intersect in this paper is shown in Fig. 1.

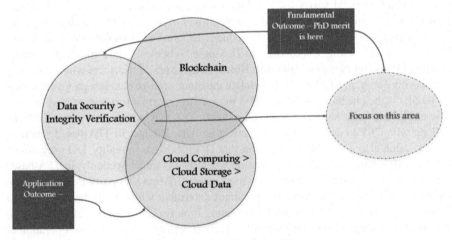

Fig. 1. Intersection Key Areas Diagram

3 Statement of the Problem

Cloud storage technology provides users with convenient data storage services and ample computing resources, greatly reducing the burden of software and hardware management [15]. As a result, an increasing number of enterprises and users choose to outsource their data to remote cloud storage service providers. Despite the numerous advantages of cloud storage technology mentioned above, ensuring the security and reliability of data on cloud platforms has always been a significant concern, severely hindering the development of cloud storage technology.

In the cloud computing environment, outsourced data may be subjected to malicious activities such as tampering, deletion, or substitution due to various factors such as hardware and software vulnerabilities, network transmission failures, and hacker attacks [16]. For users, their data needs to be uploaded to cloud storage service providers and stored in remote cloud platforms allocated by these providers. At this point, the ownership and management rights of the data become separated for the users. Due to the lack of complete data copies, it becomes challenging for users to directly verify the integrity of data on the cloud platform.

Traditional integrity verification methods require users to download the complete file directly from the server and perform local verification. However, this approach incurs significant computational and storage costs, making it a daunting task for users with limited computing resources [17]. This poses several difficulties for ordinary users, including:

- Time and bandwidth constraints: The amount of data in cloud storage can be substantial, requiring a considerable amount of time to complete the download. Additionally, if the user has limited network bandwidth, the download speed may be slow, resulting in an extended download process.
- Cost considerations: Some cloud storage service providers may charge fees for data downloads. Frequent downloads of large amounts of data can increase the cost burden for users.
- Network instability: Unstable network connections can lead to intermittent or interrupted downloads, further complicating the data integrity verification process.
- Storage device space limitations: Users with limited local storage device space may not be able to download all the data at once. They may need to free up space after downloading a portion of the data and then proceed with the remaining download operations.
- Data security and privacy protection: Data security and privacy protection should be taken into account during the data download process. Users may need to adopt appropriate security measures to ensure that data is not leaked or subjected to malicious attacks during the download and storage processes.

As for cloud storage service providers, on one hand, they provide honest data storage services to users for the remuneration they receive [18]. On the other hand, they may feel curious about the uploaded data and engage in unauthorized access. Malicious cloud storage service providers might even disclose cloud data directly to attackers for profit or delete outsourced data with less access frequency to reduce storage costs while concealing the deletion from users. Disputes often arise when it comes to compensation for cloud storage data loss. The reasons for disputes can sometimes be attributed to unequal contract terms, as cloud service providers typically include disclaimers and liability limitation clauses in their service contracts, which may restrict the users' rights. The compensation terms and conditions in the contract may favor the cloud service provider, making it challenging for users to receive adequate compensation. Alternatively, difficulties may arise in proving liability and causation: Investigating and proving the responsibility and causes of cloud storage data loss often require technical and legal support. Users may need to provide substantial evidence to prove that the data loss was a result of the cloud service provider's negligence or intentional actions.

In existing cloud data integrity verification schemes, most of them introduce a Third Party Auditor (TPA) to assist users in interacting with cloud storage services and jointly execute the cloud data integrity verification protocol. However, the third-party auditor is not entirely trustworthy and may engage in malicious behavior. They could collude with malicious cloud storage service providers for their own commercial interests, thereby compromising the privacy of user data. Therefore, combating collusion attacks and ensuring the integrity of cloud data is a significant challenge in cloud security storage systems.

On the other hand, although blockchain technology can provide decentralized and tamper-resistant security services for transaction information, it currently lacks the capability to directly meet the requirements of large-scale and diverse outsourced data due to its lightweight storage capacity. In other words, the current blockchain systems cannot directly replace cloud storage systems for storing and managing outsourced user data.

[19–23] proposed a cloud data integrity verification scheme based on blockchain, which supports public verification and blockless verification, but the verification information and process are not traceable, nor do they support anti-communist Conspiracy attacks and arbitration of disputes between DOs and CSPs.

[23–25] support dispute arbitration but cannot achieve dynamic update of stored data, nor support public verification and distributed verification. [26, 27] support public verification and distributed verification, unfortunately, there is no research on implementing dispute arbitration to ensure transaction fairness. [28, 29] mentioned dispute arbitration, but none of them supported distributed verification; [30, 31] proposed more comprehensive solutions, dynamic update, privacy protection, Security goals such as public verification can be achieved, but consideration of distributed verification and dispute arbitration is still lacking. The Table 1 presents the comparison of the above different schemes.

√: It is considered in this work; ×: It is not considered in this work; -: Its model is a private verification model without TPA, and there is no problem of collusion attacks; DU: Dynamic Update; PP: Privacy Protection; BV: Blockless Verification; Tr: Traceability; PV: Public Verification; DV: Distributed Verification; DA: Dispute Arbitration; CAR: Collusion Attack Resistance.

A total of 13 literatures were counted in the above table. Figure 2 shows the severity of missing studies of these evaluation indicators. For example, in the DA indicator, 10 literatures did not meet or did not mention this part of the content, while for the DV and CAR indicators 9 and 8 respectively did not meet or did not mention this part of the content.

Table 1. Comparison of different schemes

Literature	DU	PP	BV	Tr	PV	DV	CAR	DA
[19]	✗	✓	✓	✗	✓	✗	✗	✗
[20]	✓	✗	✓	✓	✓	✓	✗	✗
[21]	✗	✗	✓	✗	✓	✗	✗	✗
[22]	✓	✓	✗	✗	✓	✗	✗	✗
[23]	✗	✗	✓	✓	✗	✗	-	✓
[24]	✗	✗	✓	✓	✗	✗	-	✓
[25]	✗	✓	✓	✓	✓	✓	✓	✗
[26]	✓	✓	✓	✓	✗	✓	✓	✗
[27]	✓	✓	✓	✓	✓	✓	✓	✗
[28]	✓	✓	✓	✗	✓	✗	✗	✗
[29]	✗	✓	✓	✓	✓	✗	-	✓
[30]	✓	✓	✓	✓	✓	✗	✓	✗
[31]	✓	✓	✓	✓	✗	✗	✓	✗

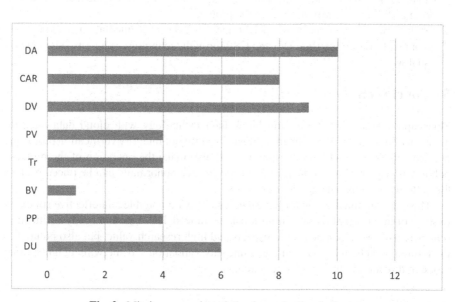

Fig. 2. Missing research statistics for evaluation indicators

In summary, most of the existing blockchain-based cloud data storage integrity verification schemes use the blockchain as a distributed log database to build a secure file directory, lack the distributed verification and dispute arbitration between DO and CSP to ensure the real fairness of the transaction. Therefore, the existing schemes are not comprehensive enough to protect the DO's outsourced data storage security. At the same time, most schemes still need to be enhanced and improved in terms of collusion attack resistance, distributed verification, and dynamic update operations. Obviously, it is a significant challenge to organically integrate blockchain technology into traditional cloud storage systems to address the security risks associated with outsourced data in the centralized architecture of traditional cloud storage.

4 Proposal

Based on a comparative analysis of the above literature, this paper suggests that research into future blockchain-based cloud data integrity verification schemes should focus on:

1. Support for data dynamics.Existing schemes tend to use the Merkel hash tree as a dynamic data structure to support data dynamic operations, but the data-based support dynamic schemes often have greater communications and computing costs.
2. Attack and Defense of the Agreement.Combining blockchain technology with cloud data integrity authentication can give the blockchain the characteristics of decentralization, traceability, etc. to the cloud dataintegrity verification protocol, but some of the security issues that affect the blockchain, such as double-expense attacks, distributed rejection attack, selfish mining attack, block retention attack, etc., will also bring additional security hazards to the protocol.
3. Ensure fair transactions between DO and CSP.The implementation of automated dispute arbitration between DO and CSP through technology is a more efficient and equal way.

5 Conclusion

This paper reveals that combining blockchain technology with cloud data integrity authentication can increase the reliability and stability of integrity verification protocols, eliminate the risk of single point failure, and also make the operation of the protocol publicly transparent, when the protocol is performed abnormally can be traced back to the party who violates the agreement.

This paper pointed out that blockchain can provide tangible and effective solutions to some of the inherent flaws of traditional centralized TPA-based integrity verification schemes, with broad application prospects and high research value, but also pointed to the future blockchain-based cloud data integrity validation scheme with a higher value research direction in this field of research.

References

1. Atieh, A.T.: The next generation cloud technologies: a review on distributed cloud, fog and edge computing and their opportunities and challenges. Res. Berg Rev. Sci. Technol. 1, 1–15 (2021)
2. Haque, A.K.M.B., Bhushan, B., Dhiman, G.: Conceptualizing smart city applications: requirements, architecture, security issues, and emerging trends. Expert. Syst. 39, e12753 (2022). https://doi.org/10.1111/EXSY.12753

3. Saxena, S., Bhushan, B., Ahad, M.A.: Blockchain based solutions to secure IoT: background, integration trends and a way forward. J. Netw. Comput. Appl. **181**, 103050 (2021). https://doi.org/10.1016/J.JNCA.2021.103050

4. Mughal, A.A.: Well-architected wireless network security. J. Human. Appl. Sci. Res. **5**, 32–42 (2022)

5. Gong, J., Navimipour, N.J.: An in-depth and systematic literature review on the blockchain-based approaches for cloud computing. Cluster Comput. **25**, 383–400 (2022). https://doi.org/10.1007/S10586-021-03412-2/METRICS

6. Gupta, R., Kumari, A., Tanwar, S.: A taxonomy of blockchain envisioned edge-as-a-connected autonomous vehicles. Trans. Emerg. Telecommun. Technol. **32**, e4009 (2021). https://doi.org/10.1002/ETT.4009

7. Bagloee, S.A., Heshmati, M., Dia, H., Ghaderi, H., Pettit, C., Asadi, M.: Blockchain: the operating system of smart cities. Cities **112**, 103104 (2021). https://doi.org/10.1016/J.CITIES.2021.103104

8. Yaqoob, I., Salah, K., Jayaraman, R., Al-Hammadi, Y.: Blockchain for healthcare data management: opportunities, challenges, and future recommendations. Neural Comput. Appl. **34**, 11475–11490 (2022). https://doi.org/10.1007/S00521-020-05519-W/METRICS

9. Xia, W., et al.: A comprehensive study of the past, present, and future of data deduplication. Proc. IEEE **104**, 1681–1710 (2016). https://doi.org/10.1109/JPROC.2016.2571298

10. Tabrizchi, H., Kuchaki, R.M.: A survey on security challenges in cloud computing: issues, threats, and solutions. J. Supercomput. **76**, 9493–9532 (2020). https://doi.org/10.1007/S11227-020-03213-1/METRICS

11. Ateniese, G., Kamara, S., Katz, J.: Proofs of storage from homomorphic identification protocols. In: Matsui, M. (ed.) Advances in Cryptology – ASIACRYPT 2009. LNCS, vol. 5912, pp. 319–333. Springer, Heidelberg (2009). https://doi.org/10.1007/978-3-642-10366-7_19

12. Wang, C., Chow, S.S.M., Wang, Q., Ren, K., Lou, W.: Privacy-preserving public auditing for secure cloud storage. IEEE Trans. Comput. **62**, 362–375 (2013). https://doi.org/10.1109/TC.2011.245

13. Nakamoto, S.: Bitcoin: A peer-to-peer electronic cash system. Decentralized business review (2008)

14. Guo, H., Yu, X.: A survey on blockchain technology and its security. Blockchain Res. App. **3**(2), 100067 (2022). https://doi.org/10.1016/j.bcra.2022.100067

15. Zhu, J., Chen, H., Pan, P.: A novel rate control algorithm for low latency video coding base on mobile edge cloud computing. Comput. Commun. **187**, 134–143 (2022). https://doi.org/10.1016/J.COMCOM.2022.02.009

16. Ometov, A., Molua, O.L., Komarov, M., Nurmi, J.: A survey of security in cloud, edge, and fog computing. Sensors **22**(3), 927 (2022). https://doi.org/10.3390/s22030927

17. Boobalan, P., et al.: Fusion of federated learning and industrial internet of things: a survey. Comput. Netw. **212**, 109048 (2022). https://doi.org/10.1016/J.COMNET.2022.109048

18. Xie, M., Yu, Y., Chen, R., Li, H., Wei, J., Sun, Q.: Accountable outsourcing data storage atop blockchain. Comput. Stand Interfaces **82**, 103628 (2022). https://doi.org/10.1016/J.CSI.2022.103628

19. Huang, H., Chen, X., Wang, J.: Blockchain-based multiple groups data sharing with anonymity and traceability. Sci. China Inf. Sci. **63**, 1–13 (2020). https://doi.org/10.1007/S11432-018-9781-0/METRICS

20. Lu, N., Zhang, Y., Shi, W., Kumari, S.: Security KC-C. A secure and scalable data integrity auditing scheme based on hyperledger fabric. Elsevier **92**, 101741 (2020). https://doi.org/10.1016/j.cose.2020.101741

21. Yu, H., Yang, Z., Tu, S., Waqas, M., Liu, H.: Blockchain-based offline auditing for the cloud in vehicular networks. IEEE Trans. Netw. Serv. Manage. **19**, 2944–2956 (2022). https://doi.org/10.1109/TNSM.2022.3164549

22. Zhao, Q., Chen, S., Liu, Z., Baker, T.: YZ-IP: blockchain-based privacy-preserving remote data integrity checking scheme for IoT information systems. Inf. Process. Manage. **57**, 102355 (2020)

23. Huang, P., Fan, K., Yang, H., Zhang, K., Li, H., Yang, Y.: A collaborative auditing blockchain for trustworthy data integrity in cloud storage system. IEEE Access **8**, 94780–94794 (2020). https://doi.org/10.1109/ACCESS.2020.2993606

24. Zhang, C., Xu, Y., Hu, Y., Wu, J., Ren, J., Zhang, Y.: A Blockchain-based multi-cloud storage data auditing scheme to locate faults. IEEE Trans. Cloud Comput. **10**, 2252–2263 (2022). https://doi.org/10.1109/TCC.2021.3057771

25. Zhang, Y., Geng, H., Su, L., Lu, L.: A blockchain-based efficient data integrity verification scheme in multi-cloud storage. IEEE Access **10**, 105920–105929 (2022). https://doi.org/10.1109/ACCESS.2022.3211391

26. Xie, G., Liu, Y., Xin, G., Yang, Q.: Blockchain-based cloud data integrity verification scheme with high efficiency. Secur. Commun. Netw. **10**, 105920–105929 (2021). https://doi.org/10.1155/2021/9921209

27. Zhou, Z.: A scalable blockchain-based integrity verification scheme. Wirel. Commun. Mob. Comput. **2022**, 1–13 (2022). https://doi.org/10.1155/2022/7830508

28. Li, J., Wu, J., Jiang, G., Srikanthan, T.: Blockchain-based public auditing for big data in cloud storage. Inf. Process. Manage. **57**, 102382 (2020). https://doi.org/10.1016/j.ipm.2020.102382

29. Liu, Z., Ren, L., Feng, Y., Wang, S., Wei, J.: Data integrity audit scheme based on quad Merkle tree and blockchain. IEEE Access (2023).https://doi.org/10.1109/ACCESS.2023.3240066

30. Li, X., Yi, Z., Li, R., Wang, X.-A., Li, H., Yang, X.: SM2-based offline/online efficient data integrity verification scheme for multiple application scenarios. Sensors **23**(9), 4307 (2023). https://doi.org/10.3390/s23094307

31. He, K., Huang, C., Shi, J., Hu, X., Fan, X.: Enabling decentralized and dynamic data integrity verification for secure cloud storage via T-Merkle hash tree based blockchain. Mob. Inf. Syst. **2021**, 1–17 (2021). https://doi.org/10.1155/2021/9977744

A Novel Approach of Adpative Window 2 Technique and Kalman Filter- "KalADWIN2" for Detection of Concept Drift

Anagha Chaudhari[1]([✉]), Hitham Seddig A.A.[1], Roshani Raut[2], and Aliza Sarlan[1]

[1] Universiti Teknologi PETRONAS (UTP), Bandar Seri Iskandar, 31750 Tronoh, Perak, Malaysia
anagha_21002260@utp.edu.my
[2] Pimpri Chinchwad College of Engineering, Pune, Maharashtra 411044, India

Abstract. A recommendation engine (RE) is a machine learning technique that provides personalized recommendations and anticipates a user's future preference for a collection of goods or services. In Online Supervised Learning (OSL) settings like various REs, where data vary over time, Concept Drift (CD) issue usually occurs. There are many CD Detectors in the literature work but the most preferred choice for the non-stationary, dynamic and streaming data is the supervised technique- Adaptive Window (ADWIN) approach. The paper aims towards the limitations of the ADWIN approach, where ADWIN2 approach is more time &memory efficient than ADWIN. The paper also focusses on novel proposed technique of the combination of Kalman Filter and ADWIN2 approach, named-"KalADWIN2", as it's the best estimator for detection even in noisy environment. It ultimately helps in fast CD detection in REs.

Keywords: Concept Drift · ADWIN · ADWIN2 · Kalman Filter · KalADWIN2

1 Introduction

The accuracy of classification results in Machine Learning (ML) Models decreases, because of the Concept Drift (CD) problem, which may render ML-Models inapplicable. Thus, to keep the findings' accuracy level high, ML-Models must be able to adjust swiftly to changes [1].

Several circumstances account for the features' evolution over time. It can be because of the complexity of the sources, distribution, or data formats, which vary over time. The categorization boundary or clustering centers that vary continually over time are referred to as Concept Drift [1].

Problem of Concept Drift: Concept drift has become more significant in both data mining and machine learning activities [9]. Instead of static databases, data is now arranged as data streams. Moreover, concepts and data distributions should evolve throughout time [2].

© The Author(s), under exclusive license to Springer Nature Singapore Pte Ltd. 2024
H. Badioze Zaman et al. (Eds.): IVIC 2023, LNCS 14322, pp. 453–467, 2024.
https://doi.org/10.1007/978-981-99-7339-2_38

Need for Concept Drift Adaptation: Idea drift is a phenomenon that happens in non-stationary or dynamic environments where the distribution of the data may change with time [2]. By saving concept descriptions, which can then be later reviewed and utilized, the concept drifts can be promptly adjusted. Hence, to handle data in non-stationary situations, adaptive learning is necessary. The present model must be changed to preserve accuracy when concept drift is found [2].

Over the past ten years, concept drift has gained popularity as a research area, and numerous algorithms have been created [2, 3]. Window-based techniques, weight-based approaches, and ensemble classifiers are the three primary classes of methodology proposed for addressing concept drifts [4, 5]. There are three stages to the Concept Drift process: CD detection, drift interpretation (where and how does it occur in the data), and drift analysis & CD adaptability (drift response) [6, 7].

The sliding window is the most popular continuous rebuild strategy for managing concept drift. The classifier is trained or updated using new training data from a window that contains a labelled set of recent examples. Sliding window techniques disregard prior training examples that might be indicative of an earlier notion [8–10]. A sensitive system that reacts quickly to changes can be produced using small windows. This comes at a high price, especially when it comes to stable data delivery. A broad window, on the other hand, might produce a trained classifier that gradually adapts when the notion changes [8–10].

Hence, the major focus for the Concept Drift Detection is on **ADWIN-A Daptive WIN dowing (ADWIN)** to handle concept drift in data streams [11].

Section 2 of the remaining paper provides an overview of ADWIN algorithm, followed by the limitations of ADWIN. The details of ADWIN2 algorithm are discussed in Section 3. Kalman filter elaboration is presented in Part 4, along with applications of Kalman Filter. Section 5 talks about the advantages of the combination of ADWIN2 and Kalman Filter. The conclusion is mentioned in Section 6.

2   Adaptive Windowing (ADWIN)

2.1   Window Based Methods

This technique collects the incoming data objects and turns them into a batch of data (or window). Two windows are commonly used in window-based techniques [12]. The initial window is used to keep older instances of the data stream, while fresh instances are introduced afterwards. These two window instances were compared, and the results showed the drift and explained why the data distribution had changed. Both fixed and adaptive window sizes are available [12]. A fixed window is one that maintains the same size throughout the course of the analysis. The adaptive window, however, alters its size in response to drift conditions. When drift is detected, the data window is shrunk; when there is no drift condition, it is widened [12].

An adaptive sliding window-based approach is called ADWIN. The window is constantly updated in accordance with the rate of change depicted in the data from Bifet, 2009, [12, 13]. The window size is dynamically increased and decreased in accordance with whether the context has changed or not. Furthermore, ADWIN functions well since it lowers the frequencies of false positives and false negatives [12].

For streaming data like E-Commerce platforms, a popular choice for Concept Drift detection is **ADWIN (ADaptive WINdowing)** [14].

Adwin is an algorithm that instantly recognizes concept drifts and modifies ML models to account for them. The ML model is computed using an adjustable window that is maintained by the algorithm [13]. If no concept drift is found, Adwin expands the window (adds the most recent tuples). The model can therefore rely on expanding training data. When Adwin notices a concept drift, it reduces the window by deleting outdated tuples. The method, displayed in Fig. 7 [13], recognizes idea drifts on a per-tuple basis, thus users are not required to define minimum or maximum periods between concept drifts beforehand. This eliminates a significant disadvantage of methods that recompute models on a regular basis using fixed-size windows (i.e., batches) of data [15].

ADWIN's drawback is that it can only handle one-dimensional data [12]. It keeps distinct windows. In the case of n-dimensional raw data, each one belongs to each dimension. It therefore maintains multiple windows, which takes up more time and memory. The improved version of ADWIN, called ADWIN2, uses less time and memory [12]. When the average distribution difference between two successive windows is greater than a threshold-defined threshold, drift detection occurs. By identifying the slow, progressive drift, ADWIN2 gets over the drawback of ADWIN. When the window size is WS, memory and time requirements are O (log WS) [12].

3   Adaptive Windowing 2 (ADWIN2)

As it thoroughly examines every "large enough" sub window of the current window for potential cuts, the ADWIN algorithm is computationally expensive. Additionally, the window's explicit contents are maintained, incurring a growing memory cost. We offer an updated version of ADWIN2 that uses data stream algorithmics to lower these expenses [13, 16–18] and [19].

The ADWIN2 algorithm maintains a data structure with the following properties:

- It uses O (M ·log(W/M)) memory words (assuming a memory word can contain numbers up to W) [13].
- It can process the arrival of a new element in O (1) amortized time and O (log W) worst-case time [13].
- It can provide the exact counts of 1's for all the sub windows whose lengths are of the form $\lfloor (1 + 1/M)i \rfloor$, in O(1) time per query [13].

Since ADWIN2 tries O (log W) cut points, the total processing time per example is O (log W) (amortized) and O (log2 W) (worst-case).

Let's look at an example shown in Fig. 1-Sliding Window Example: a sliding window with 14 elements. We register it as:

If a new element is "1," we establish a new bucket of content with a capacity equal to the number of elements that have been added since the last "1" whenever a new element is added. The remaining buckets are then compressed after that: We combine the two earliest buckets, adding their combined capacity, producing a bucket of size 2i + 1 when there are M + 1 buckets of size 2i. Therefore, if we believe that a word may contain a

1010101	101	11	1	1

Content: 4   2   2   1   1

Capacity: 7   3   2   1   1

Fig. 1. Sliding Window Example

number up to W [13], we utilize O (M log W/M) memory words. The window in [18] is maintained at a constant W size. The approximation mistake is caused by the absence of data for the final bucket. Instead of (conceptually) removing a single element like in a conventional sliding window structure, in this case, each time we detect change, we shorten the window by eliminating the last bucket. This enables us to maintain an accurate count because we know that we are dumping precisely 2i "1"s when we empty a whole bucket [13].

In our example, suppose M = 2, if a new element"1″ arrives then, as shown in Fig. 2-

1010101	101	11	1	1	1

Content: 4   2   2   1   1   1

Capacity: 7   3   2   1   1   1

Fig. 2. Sliding Window Example with M = 2 & new element "1"

There are 3 buckets of 1, so we compress it:

1010101	101	11	11	1

Content: 4   2   2   2   1

Capacity: 7   3   2   2   1

Fig. 3. Sliding Window Example with Compression (3 buckets of size 1)

And now as we have 3 buckets of size 2 as shown in Fig. 3, we compress it again, as shown in Fig. 4,

1010101	10111	11	1

Content: 4   4   2   1

Capacity: 7   5   2   1

Fig. 4. Sliding Window Example with Compression (3 buckets of size 2)

And finally, if we detect change, we reduce the size of our sliding window deleting the last bucket [13], as shown in Fig. 5:

$$\boxed{10111}\ \boxed{11}\ \boxed{1}$$

Content: 4   2   1
Capacity: 5   2   1

Fig. 5. Sliding Window Example with deletion of last bucket

We additionally keep buckets of the two elements capacity and content in the case of real values. We save the total of the real values we want to sum in content [13]. We only allow for capacity that is a power of two. We employ O (log W) buckets and examine O (log W) potential cuts, same as in the boolean case. Each bucket requires log W + R + log log log W bits in memory, where R is the number of bits required to hold a real integer [16–18] and [19].

With or without flushing, ADWIN2 outperforms practically all fixed-size window estimators. This demonstrates that ADWIN2's flexibility to change the size of its window can be a very helpful tool for precisely measuring the likelihood of uncommon events [16–18] and [19].

4 Kalman Filters

The Kalman Filter is named after Rudolf E. Kálmán (May 19, 1930—July 2, 2016). The Kalman Filters are used for both stationary and non-stationary environments. The Kalman filtering is a relatively simple state space algorithm to produce estimates of the hidden variables based on uncertain and inaccurate measurements. It predicts the system's future state based on past estimations [20].

Kalman Filter is applied to model systems with multiple noisy inputs and outputs hopefully less noisy and more accurately estimated output data. It is applicable to stationary and non-stationary situations.

The Kalman Filter is a filter that removes noise from input data to determine the best estimate. The state estimate is projected by the Kalman filter onto the data measurements [20].

In Machine Learning [ML] and Image Processing applications, Kalman Filter plays a very important role in data capturing process & removing the noise from the input data. The most challenging part in any application is to provide accurate and precise data—many external hidden factors create problems in accuracy and precision. The Kalman filter estimates the hidden variables based on inaccurate and uncertain measurements, as it also provides a future state prediction based on the previous estimation.

Usage of Kalman Filter: The Kalman filter is used to-

- Track objects like missiles or people based on their current measured position to estimate their position and velocity more accurately in the future [20].
- In order to determine the vehicle's state, position, and velocity, navigation systems use sensor data from an inertial measurement unit (IMU) and a GNSS receiver as input [20].

- Computer vision applications for feature tracking or cluster tracking [20].

  Explanation of Kalman Filter, Fig. 6 [20]:

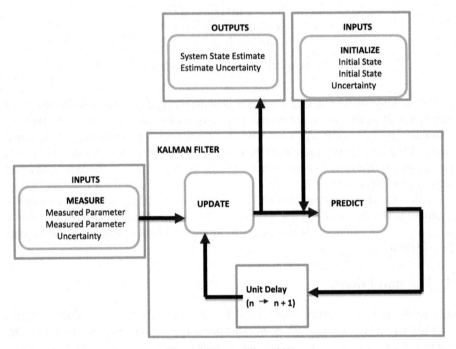

Fig. 6. Kalman Filter [20]

The Kalman Filter has two inputs:

1. Initialization is performed only once and has parameters [25].
- Initial state [25]
- Initial state uncertainty [25]

Even if the initialization parameters are not exact, the Kalman Filter will close the gap between the predicted value and the actual value [20].

2. Every filter cycle includes measurements, each of which has specific parameters.
- Measured System State
- Measurement Uncertainty

The Kalman Filter also needs a measurement uncertainty parameter, which is supplied by the equipment vendor, in addition to the measurement [20].

There are two steps in the Kalman Filter process:

1. **Prediction step**: Based on the prior observations, the Kalman Filter forecasts the system's upcoming state.
2. **Update step**: Given the measurement at that time step, the Kalman Filter assesses the system's present state.

The Kalman Filter only needs to keep the previous estimate data since it changes the prediction of state variables depending on the observation in the previous step. As a result, the Kalman Filter requires small computational power [20].

The Kalman Filter may keep all previously observed data without using any additional storage capacity.

- As it does not need to use all the prior estimated or measured data in each phase of the prediction process, it is computationally efficient.

The Kalman Filter outputs are:

- System State Estimate
- Estimate Uncertainty

The Kalman Filter flowchart is described in detail in Fig. 7 [26]:

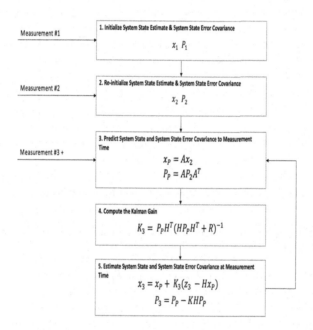

Fig. 7. Kalman Filter Flowchart [26]

Working of Kalman Filter: The Kalman algorithm predicts the system state for the next time step. The Kalman Filter operates in a "predict-correct" loop, as shown in Fig. 8:

Start with initialization, and this step is performed only once for the first measurement. The Kalman Filter predicts the system state at the following time step once it has been initialized and provides the prediction's uncertainty [20]. After receiving the measurement, the Kalman Filter updates (or corrects) the prediction and uncertainty of the present state [20].

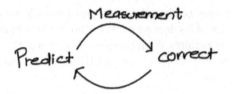

Fig. 8. Predict-Update Loop in Kalman Filter

Based on the system's dynamic model, the Predict process extrapolates the current system state and the estimation of its uncertainty to the subsequent system state [20].

Kalman Filter can be explained and elaborated further through mathematical equations/formulas, as shown in Fig. 9 [20].

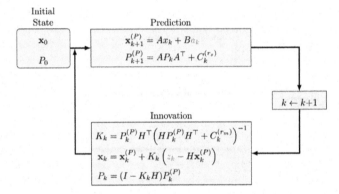

Fig. 9. Mathematical Representation of Kalman Filter [20]

The **prediction equation** predicts the next system state based on the knowledge of the current state [20].

$$x_{t|t-1} = F_t x_{t-1|t-1} + B_t U_t$$

where,

x = Estimated State
F = Matrix for transition between states
U = Control Variable
B = Control Matrix
t = Current time frame
t-1 = Previous time frame

The State Update equation is used by the **Update process** to estimate the system's current state [20].

$$x_{t|t} = x_{t|t-1} + K_t(y_t - H_t x_{t|t-1})$$

where,

x = Estimated State
K = Kalman Gain
y = Measurement Variable
H = Measurement Matrix
t = Current time frame
t-1 = Previous time frame

The **Kalman Gain** is computed throughout the **state update process**, and outputs **Estimate of the current system state** and the **level of uncertainty in that estimate**, which will input the predicted process [20, 25].

Example: Figure 10, is a simple state having only position and velocity:

$$\vec{x} = \begin{bmatrix} p \\ v \end{bmatrix}$$

Fig. 10. Kalman Filter Example

There are many other conceivable combinations of location and velocity that could be true, but some of them are more likely than others-Fig. 11. We don't know what the real position and velocity are: [21].

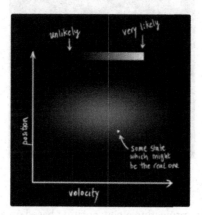

Fig. 11. Velocity Vs Position Case 1

The term "filter" refers to the act of "filtering out" the noise to obtain the "best estimate" from noisy data [21].

However, in addition to cleaning up the raw measurements, a Kalman filter also projects these measurements onto the state estimate [21].

The Kalman Filter makes the supposition that both the variables—in this case, position, and velocity—are random and Gaussian distributed. Each variable has a mean value μ, which is the random distribution's midpoint (and represents its most likely state), and a variance σ^2, which represents its level of uncertainty [21].

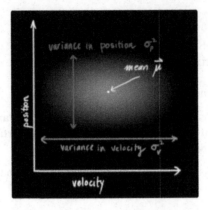

Fig. 12. Velocity Vs Position Case 2

Position and velocity in the Fig. 12, are uncorrelated, which implies that you cannot infer anything about the potential value of one variable from the state of the other [21]. The following example demonstrates something more intriguing: Velocity and position are connected. The velocity you have affects your chances of seeing a specific position:

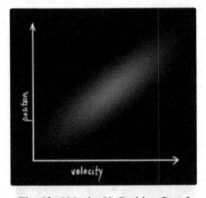

Fig. 13. Velocity Vs Position Case 3

If, for instance, we are projecting a new position based on an old one, then this kind of circumstance might occur-Fig. 13. Our position will be further away if our velocity was high because we most likely travelled farther [21]. We didn't travel as far if we're travelling slowly.

It's crucial to keep track of this kind of relationship because it provides us with additional knowledge: one measurement provides some insight into what the others might be. To extract as much information as we can from our unsure measurements, we use the Kalman Filter [21].

A covariance matrix is used to represent this correlation-Fig. 14, [21]. The degree of correlation between the ith state variable and the jth state variable is, in essence, represented by each element of the matrix Σ_{ij}. It doesn't matter if you switch i and j because the covariance matrix is symmetric, as you would have guessed. Since covariance matrices are frequently referred to as " Σ " we refer to their elements as " Σij " [21].

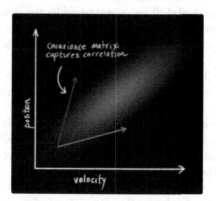

Fig. 14. Velocity Vs Position Case 4

Applications of Kalman Filter: The uses of the Kalman filter in the real world are varied. Giving precise, on-going updates on an object's position and velocity based simply on a series of observations, each of which contains some mistake, would be one possible application [22]. For a related, more specific example, consider the tracking of a target using radar, which involves measuring the target's location, speed, and acceleration at each time instant with significant noise deterioration [22]. The Kalman filter uses the target's dynamics, which control how it changes over time, to reduce the effects of noise and.

provide a reliable estimate of the target's location now (filtering), in the future (prediction), or in the past (interpolation or smoothing). Other uses include tracking targets using RADAR, robot localization and map development from range sensors/beacons, weather forecasting, voice augmentation, economics, autopilot [22], and determination of planet orbit parameters from limited earth observations [23].

5   Proposed Novel Approach- KalADWIN2 (Kalman Filter + ADWIN2)

The Kalman filter, which creates estimates of variables of the system being controlled by processing available sensor measurements, is one of the most popular estimating methods. In a wide range of contexts, Kalman filtering and related estimating techniques have shown to be incredibly helpful [24].

Even though the Kalman filter has no memory, it can nonetheless benefit from having one. The state covariance and measurement covariance, two system characteristics that should be determined beforehand in order to run a Kalman filter, must be known [24]. In the context of learning from a data stream, these are typically challenging to quantify, and they can also change over time. The Kalman filter can estimate the current value of these covariances from the window that ADWIN maintains adaptively, and it is guaranteed to contain recent examples [24].

On the other hand, **ADWIN, which we will refer to as a linear estimator, is slightly slow in identifying a gradual shift because it provides the same weight to every case in the window. The most recent examples should be given more weight if there is a slow, gradual change. The Kalman filter does this same action while estimating** [24].

Because it thoroughly examines every "large enough" sub window of the current window for potential cuts, the initial iteration of ADWIN is computationally expensive [24].

Additionally, the window's explicit contents are maintained, incurring a growing memory cost. We introduced a new version, ADWIN2, in [13] **that utilises concepts created in data stream algorithmics to swiftly discover a good cut point in order to minimise these costs** [16–19] **and** [24].

Nearly all fixed-size window estimators are beaten by ADWIN2. This demonstrates that **ADWIN2's flexibility to change the size of its window** can be a very helpful tool for correctly tracking the likelihood of uncommon events [13].

Hence, the novel combination of **Kalman Filters and ADWIN2, named as** "KalADWIN2" algorithm as shown in the proposed architecture-Fig. 15, provides the advantages of **quality Estimator** and **good Change Detector**, respectively. This novel hybrid combination of **KalADWIN2** delivers the best estimation/prediction of any object in the online real time processing, including random noise/uncertainties.

The "KalADWIN2" approach will eventually help to find/detect the concept drifts/uncertainties in huge dynamic, non-stationary Machine Learning (ML) frameworks. The novel proposed approach will overcome the issue of concept drift (CD) detection which further solves the CD adaptation process through federated learning algorithms in ML environments (E-Commerce based Recommendation Engines).

Optimization in Kalman Filters:

A Kalman filter is an ideal estimator, or one that extrapolates parameters of interest from inaccurate, insufficient, and unreliable observations [23]. Processing fresh measurements as they are received is recursive.

Optimality of Kalman filtering assumes that errors have a **normal (Gaussian) distribution** [23]. A continuous probability distribution for a real-valued random variable in statistics is known as a **normal distribution or Gaussian distribution**. It is a common misconception (perpetuated in the literature) that the Kalman filter cannot be rigorously applied unless all noise processes are assumed to be Gaussian.

When only the mean and standard deviation of the noise are known, the Kalman filter is the best linear estimator. Perhaps non-linear estimators should be used instead [23].

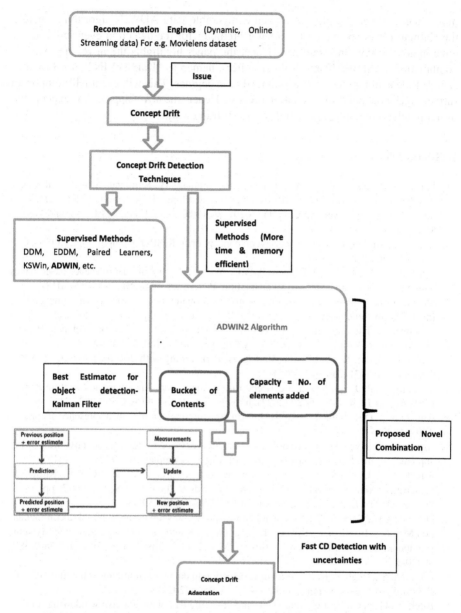

Fig. 15. Proposed Novel Architecture **KalADWIN2** (ADWIN2 + Kalman Filter)

6   Conclusion

The paper focussed on the idea of the concept drift, which requires detection and adaptation in recommendation engines. For the detection of concept drift in online streaming, dynamic data/platforms, the ADWIN2 algorithm will help in fast detection, which is more time and memory efficient, when comparable with ADWIN algorithm, whereas the Kalman filters are the best estimator/predictor for the detection even in the noisy environment or few uncertainties. Hence, the paper highlights the novel approach of combination of ADWIN2 and Kalman Filters, named as "KalADWIN2", for fast concept drift detection process in recommendation engines. This will eventually support in further quick concept drift adaptation process. Hence, the novel approach is expected to overcome the problem of concept drift in ML frameworks.

References

1. Jameel, S.M., Hashmani, M.A., Alhussain, H., Rehman, M., Budiman, A.: A critical review on adverse effects of concept drift over machine learning classification models. (IJACSA) Int. J. Adv. Comput. Sci. Appl. 11(1) (2020). www.thesai.org [Scopus, Elsevier and Web of Science]
2. Kadve, Y., Suryawanshi, V.: A Review on concept drift. IOSR-J. Comput. Eng. (IOSR-JCE) 17(1), 20–26 (2015). Ver.11
3. Nguyen, T.T.T., Nguyen, T.T., Liew, A.W.C., Wang, S.L.: Variational inference based bayes online classifiers with concept drift adaptation. Pattern Recognit. **81**, 280–293 (2018)
4. Sun, Y., et al.: Online ensemble using adaptive windowing for data streams with concept drift. Int. J. Distrib. Sens. Netw. **12**(5), 4218973 (2016). https://doi.org/10.1155/2016/4218973
5. Tsymbal, A.: The problem of concept drift: definitions and related work, Technical Report, Department of Computer Science, Trinity College, Dublin, Ireland (2004)
6. Gama, J., Medas, P., Castillo, G., Rodrigues, P.: Learning with drift detection. Lect. Notes Comput. Sci. **3171**, 286–295 (2004)
7. Lima, M., et al.: Learning under concept drift for regression—a systematic literature review. IEEE Access **10**, 45410–45429 (2022). https://doi.org/10.1109/ACCESS.2022.316978
8. Klinkenberg, D.R., Renz, I.: Adaptive information filtering: learning in the presence of concept drifts (1999)
9. Khamassi, I., Sayed-Mouchaweh, M., Hammami, M., Ghédira, K.: Self-adaptive windowing approach for handling complex concept drift. Cognit. Comput. **7**(6), 772–790 (2015)
10. Kuncheva, L.I.: Classifier ensembles for changing environments. In: Roli, F., Kittler, J., Windeatt, T. (eds) Multiple Classifier Systems. MCS 2004. LNCS, vol. 3077, pp. 1–15. Springer, Berlin (2004). https://doi.org/10.1007/978-3-540-25966-4_1
11. Desrosiers, C., Karypis, G.: A Comprehensive Survey of Neighborhood-based Recommendation Methods. In: Ricci, F., Rokach, L., Shapira, B., Kantor, P. (eds.) Recommender Systems Handbook, pp. 107–144. Springer, Boston, MA (2011). https://doi.org/10.1007/978-0-387-85820-3_4
12. Agrahari, S., Singh, A.K.: Concept drift detection in data stream mining: a literature review. J. King Saud Univ. Comput. Inf. Sci. **34**, 9523–9540 (2022)
13. Bifet, A.; Gavaldà, R.: Learning from time-changing data with adaptive windowing. In Proceedings of the 2007 SIAM International Conference on Data Mining, Minneapolis, MN, USA, pp. 443–448, 26–28 April 2007
14. https://deepchecks.com/how-to-detect-concept-drift-with-machine-learning-monitoring/
15. Philipp, M.G., et al.: Scalable detection of concept drifts on data streams with parallel adaptive windowing. In: Technische Universität Berlin, 21st International Conference on Extending Database Technology (EDBT), 26–29 March 2018, ISBN 978-3-89318-078-3 on OpenProceedings.org
16. Babcock, B., Babu, S., Datar, M., Motwani, R., Widom, J.: Models and issues in data stream systems. In: Proceedings of 21st ACM Symposium on Principles of Database Systems (2002)

17. Babcock, B., Datar, M., Motwani, R.: Sampling from a moving window over streaming data. In: Proceedings of 13th Annual ACM SIAM Symposium on Discrete Algorithms (2002)
18. Datar, M., Gionis, A., Indyk, P., Motwani, R.: Maintaining stream statistics over sliding windows. SIAM J. Comput. **14**(1), 27–45 (2002)
19. Muthukrishnan, S.: Data streams: algorithms and applications. In: Proceedings of 14th Annual ACM-SIAM Symposium on Discrete Algorithms (2003)
20. Khandelwal, R.: An easy explanation of Kalman filter, March 2022. https://arshren.medium.com/an-easy-explanation-of-kalman-Filter
21. How a Kalman fflter works, in pictures. https://www.bzarg.com/p/how-a-kalman-filter-works-in-pictures/
22. Laaraiedh, M.: Implementation of Kalman Filter with Python Language, IETR Labs, University of Rennes (2012)
23. Kleeman, L.: Understanding and applying kalman filtering. In: Department of Electrical and Computer Systems Engineering, Monash University, Clayton (1996)
24. Bifet, A., Gavaldà, R.: Kalman filters and adaptive windows for learning in data streams. In: Todorovski, L., Lavrač, N., Jantke, K.P. (eds.) Discovery Science. DS 2006. LNCS, vol. 4265, pp. 29–40. Springer, Berlin (2006). https://doi.org/10.1007/11893318_7
25. Sivaraman, D., Ongwattanakul, S., Suthakorn, J., Pillai, B.M.: Nonlinear dynamic states' estimation and prediction using polynomial predictive modeling estimation. IEEE Can. J. Electr. Comput. Eng. **46**(3), 185–195 (2023)
26. https://thekalmanfilter.com/kalman-filter-explained-simply/

Unleashing the Power of Visuals: A Captivating Exploration of Scientific Data Visualization Methods and Techniques

Aslina Baharum[1](✉), Rozita Ismail[2], Ismassabah Ismail[3],
Noorsidi Aizuddin Mat Noor[4], Farhana Diana Deris[5], and Suhaida Halamy[6]

[1] Computing and Information System, School of Engineering and Technology, Sunway University, Jalan Universiti, Bandar Sunway, Selangor, Malaysia
aslinab@sunway.edu.my

[2] College of Computing and Informatics, Universiti Tenaga Nasional, Putrajaya Campus, Kajang, Malaysia

[3] Centre of Foundation Studies, Universiti Teknologi MARA Cawangan Selangor, Kampus Dengkil, Dengkil, Selangor, Malaysia

[4] Mass Appraisal, Housing, and Planning Research Group, Centre for Real Estate Studies, Real Estate Department, Faculty of Built Environment and Surveying, Universiti Teknologi Malaysia, Johor Bahru, Johor, Malaysia

[5] Faculty of Social Sciences and Humanities, Universiti Teknologi Malaysia, Johor Bahru, Johor, Malaysia

[6] School of Information Science, College of Computing, Informatics and Mathematics, Universiti Teknologi MARA Cawangan Sarawak, Kota Samarahan, Malaysia

Abstract. Scientific visualizations are the building blocks for conveying results and ideas to a wide range of audiences. It is one of the steps in the data science process, and it should be done before the data presentation phase. Because some data is not easy to read for humans, visualization can help transform the data into visual content such as graphs or plots, as the requirement for scientific visualization techniques and methods is increasing greatly. Reviewing various visualization methods is necessary to increase knowledge about it. In this paper, an overview of scientific data visualization methods and techniques has been reviewed. To conduct the experiment, a total of five peer-reviewed articles relating to scientific visualization techniques were chosen. The problem with this study is that people still do not have a clear idea of how to use or what is the importance of scientific visualization. The findings of this paper show that the occurrence of visualization techniques improves the effectiveness of reading data and helps people to understand data in a more vivid way. A systematic literature review has been adopted in this study to assist the author in doing a study without bias. Finally, this paper can help readers increase their knowledge of the scientific visualization technique.

Keywords: Scientific Visualization · Systematic Literature Review · Visualization techniques

H. Badioze Zaman et al. (Eds.): IVIC 2023, LNCS 14322, pp. 468–477, 2024.
https://doi.org/10.1007/978-981-99-7339-2_39

1   Introduction

Visualization is the most essential technique for communicating science. It helps people to convert complex problems into valuable information [1]. Because images are easier for the brain to understand than words or figures, excellent visuals are an extremely significant aspect of academic literature [2]. With the rising accessibility and amount of data, effective methods for analyzing and communicating the information contained in datasets in simple, easy-to-understand formats are required [3]. Scientific visualization is a word that addresses the display of physical and scientific data. Data visualization refers to any graphic that investigates or conveys data in any field. Scientific visualization is a branch of study that investigates the efficiency of various forms of visuals in displaying data [4]. Despite recent advances in multidisciplinary research, basic problems in scientific visualizations persist and can hinder effective communication through graphics. The scientific visualization discussion can be either discipline-specific, generic, or addressed from a theoretical or psychological standpoint in a variety of books and journal articles [5].

Science visualization was initially known as "scientific computational visualization", and its roots may be traced back to the vacuum tube computer, which featured computer graphics [6]. Scientific visualization, on the other hand, was given a relatively accurate positioning, which is defined as the use of research results obtained through computer graphics and image processing to create visual images to replace those typically large and complex digital representations and aid people in better understanding scientific and technological concepts and scientific data results [7].

Scientific visualization is important because it focuses on new ways of displaying data so that important aspects may be highlighted and hidden patterns can be examined easily. When compared to going through the raw statistics and language in the data, a successful visualization method speeds up information understanding by orders of magnitude. Visualization plays a crucial role in scientific discovery, security, and competitiveness, according to the NIH/NSF Visualization Research Challenges Report, and the insights it gives will assist in "finding new ideas, techniques, and methodologies, and enhance the daily life of the general public [8]." Today, visualization is being used to facilitate knowledge development beyond conventional academic boundaries in a variety of science areas [9].

However, even though many studies have reported the importance of scientific visualization, there is still not enough research to give an overview of scientific visualization techniques. The problem with this study is that people still do not understand scientific visualization's usage or importance. Thus, the purpose of this study is to provide an overview of Scientific Data Visualization Methods and Techniques by reviewing several scientific visualization techniques. The following research questions were addressed in this study to guide our work:

RQ1: What is the currently existing scientific data visualization technique?
RQ2: What is the objective of the existing scientific data visualization technique?

This paper presents an overview of Scientific Data Visualization Methods and Techniques. Then, the rest of the paper is organized as follows: i) Related Studies. In this section, this paper discussed several researchers with similar interests and scientific visualization to show how important this research is; ii) Methodology. In this section, this paper discussed the systematic literature review that was used in this paper; iii) Result and Discussion. In this section, this paper showcases and reviews the data visualization technique collected from other research articles. The author has discussed the findings from the review of the data visualization techniques; iv) Conclusion. In this section, the major findings and limitations of this research have been summarised. Then, some recommendations for practical applications and future research are provided.

2 Related Studies

This section presents some previous works focused on data visualizations in different areas.

Bayoumi et al. [10] have proposed an article that seeks to increase knowledge of the data being provided as well as interest in using visuals to deliver data to users. This study also stated that the benefit of medical visualization is for people to understand the relationships between attributes better. Therefore, the authors of this study try to understand the attributes better so that they can detect breast cancer in earlier stages, which also means the patient can have a better treatment. This study uses Tableau Public 10.4 to visualize their chosen dataset because this visualization tool is easy to use and contains many beneficial and efficient features. This study also uses 2D visualizations to visualize their numeric data. This study uses their visualization result to help the diagnosis of a tumour by determining whether it is malignant or benign. They use the CART tree to transform the parameters on the CART into an interactive visualization that benefits all people who are interested in breast cancer diagnosis results. The authors also stated that this visualization process is quick and effective; those interested have to do some required measurements, and then the result can be produced immediately. The limitation of this study is that the authors have less knowledge regarding the parameters that affect the determination of whether that tumour is malignant or benign [10].

Opgenhaffen [11] attempted to address the gap by describing a chaine opératoire archaeological study of an antique using scientific visualization and shape analysis tools on 3D digital and physical reproductions of the artifact. This study analyzes a small stone object found in the PylaKokkinokremos site with scientific visualization and 3D shape analysis. They did a 3D documentation of the overall shape of that object; this visualization allows for a more quantitative analysis of the item and a more accurate assessment of its orientation in three dimensions. The article also proposed several pipelines for analyzing such artifacts in the future:

- Capture colour information in accordance with professional photographic standards.
- Shadow mapping and screen space ambient occlusion can help with visual analysis when an object's skin has intrinsic patterns and uneven geometries.
- Change light directions and use shaders like radiance scaling and Xray to improve the visual perception of the item.
- Colour curvature approaches are useful for describing an object's skin, especially when attempting to distinguish smooth sections from imperfections.

The limitation of this study is that there is a limited amount of usage of scientific visualization for artifact analysis [11].

Kelleher and Braswell's [12] article covers the fundamentals of scientific visualization and concerns for the visualization of enormous datasets. This introductory overview gives some advice on visualization, such as plot type, encoding attributes, and groupings. The author stated that iteration is the main concern when making plots of big datasets. This article also points out some challenges when visualizing a big dataset. First, a big dataset often causes the synthesis and elimination of essential pieces of information through aggregation. Second, a large dataset contains different types of data or variables. How to illustrate broad correlations across numerous variables or descriptors using multi-dimensional data becomes the challenging part. This article also stated some considerations for picking plot type, encoding attribute, and overall visualization. First, match the plot type and encoding attribute to the main message because visualization is based on the choice of encoding attributes. Second, as you finetune your visualization, keep in mind the overall composition. Third, consider how you may simplify and clarify your main point [12].

3 Methodology

In this study, a systematic literature review process has been conducted to reduce and minimize potential biases [13]. This technique is the process of finding, assessing, and synthesizing all available information regarding an impact or a topic area in a methodical manner. A Systematic Literature Review, unlike a conventional or narrative literature review, follows a set of quality-enhancing standards, including stringent output inclusion rules, with the goal of limiting potential biases in the sample of studies.

3.1 Article Collection

In this section, a comprehensive search of peer-reviewed articles was carried out. The search statement yielded keywords, which were organized into sets relevant to the research kind, sources, and repositories. Combinations of terms for "scientific data visualization techniques" were utilized as search queries. For example, "scientific visualization", "data visualization", "scientific visualization technique", "data visualization", "overview of scientific visualization", "literature review of scientific visualization". The duration of publication was set between the years 2018 to 2022. The following databases were utilized: Science Direct, IEEE Xplore, NCBI, ACM Digital Library, SpringerLink, and Scopus.

3.2 Inclusion and Exclusion Criteria

The selection phase determines the overall validity of the literature review. Hence it is critical to specify specific inclusion and exclusion criteria. The paper is maintained if and only if it meets at least one of the criteria for inclusion. Otherwise, it is discarded if it does not fit into either category.

Inclusion criteria:

- Related to the reviewing visualization technique
- Related to the application of visualization technique
- Related to comparing visualization technique

Exclusion criteria:

- Is not a full paper
- Is from the website
- It does not relate to visualization

4 Results and Discussion

The following Table 1 gives an overview of scientific visualization techniques.

Table 1. An Overview of Scientific Visualization Techniques.

	Visualization Technique	Aims	Source
1	HPC network models	Visualize Parallel Network Simulations	[14]
2	Streamline visualization	To facilitate the observation and visual inspection of changes in the climate in real-time	[15]
3	Feature enhancement volume visualization	To provide a better understanding of different features within volume data.	[16]
4	Vis integrate with OSPRay	To visualize the output of the largest simulation to date of astrophysical turbulence	[17]
5	Fusion technique	To map distinct variable domains to different visual channels	[18]

Based on Table 1, five techniques of scientific visualization that selected from five peer-reviewed articles have been identified. The next section will discuss the technique mentioned in Table 1.

4.1 HPC Network Models

Ross et al. [14] use HPC network models from the CODES simulation framework to develop 3D visualizations for parallel discrete event simulations. The authors use the

Visualization Toolkit (VTK) to develop the visualization, and the author stated that the visualization can be presented by using visualization software such as ParaView. The authors stated that by displaying congestion statistics in the context of the network's physical topology, the visualization could give insight into the behaviour of the models across simulated time. The authors also stated that this visualization tool could assist non-experts in more effectively using optimistic PDES in their work. An example of visualization using HPC network models as Fig. 1.

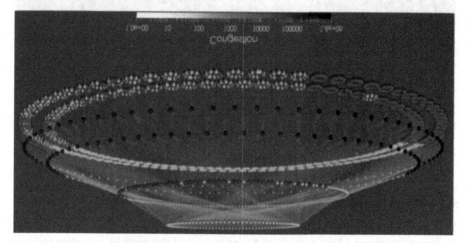

Fig. 1. Visualizing Network Congestion by [14]

4.2 Streamline Visualization

Wang et al. [15] presented a scientific visualization technique called the streamline technique. This technique allows visualization for the multi-dimensional, time-series climate data that appears on the online virtual globe to be happened in real-time. It also allows the visualization to become interactive and dynamic. The authors use a scientific visualization tool which is the PolarGlobe. It can provide real-time online access to large numerical simulation data on the climate and ocean. PolarGlobe can provide a clearer view of the interactions between the local terrain and atmospheric changes. The authors also stated that PolarGlobe is a tool for determining the causes of catastrophic weather and climate catastrophes. The authors report that this technique can be applied smoothly to visualize data in other Earth science domains, such as oceanography and polar sciences. An example of a streamlined visualization technique is as Fig. 2.

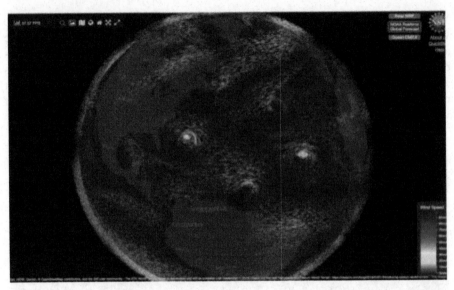

Fig. 2. Real-time Visualization of Global Wind in North Atlantic Hurricane Season by [15]

4.3 Feature Enhancement Volume Visualization

Xu et al. [16] present a visualization method based on the feature enhancement volume rendering technique. Many research domains have used this method, including medical imaging visualization, geological investigation, and scientific computing. This technique is basically representing a three-dimensional (3D) dataset as a two-dimensional (2D) dataset to help experts understand data. It allows complicated data to be parsed and elaborate 3D relationships to be revealed. The authors focus on four features of visual enhancement in this technique. First, the external feature which is used to strengthen the visual perception of datasets, such as physical surface, feature surface, and iso-surface. Second internal feature; the goal is to increase awareness of the linkage of core volume data features. Third is the structure feature; its purpose is to improve the spatial correlation between various groups within a volume. Fourth is the Ideographic feature. It adds a wide range of expression styles to improve the readability of large amounts of data. An example of feature enhancement volume visualization is as Fig. 3.

4.4 Vis Integrate with OSPRay

The integration between VisIt and OSPRay enable better prediction of required parameters and is able to detect possible bottleneck. This integrated rendering toolkit is able to develop highly flexible scientific visualizations of the biggest astrophysical turbulence simulations to date. The advantage of this visualization is it has a tremendous visual effect, which is critical for navigating enormous datasets and guiding additional quantitative analysis [17]. The example of Vis integrated with the OSPRay technique is as Fig. 4.

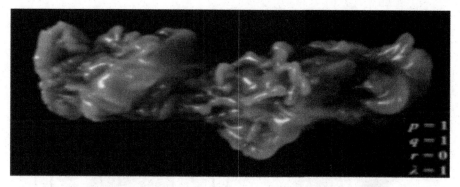

Fig. 3. Visualization of The Shockwave Data Rendering by [16]

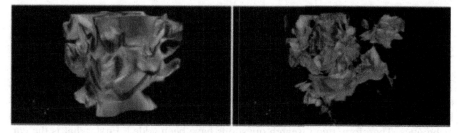

Fig. 4. Visualization of Density (left) and Magnetic Field (right) Evolution by [17]

4.5 Fusion Technique

Fusion visualization is a common rendering technique that maps distinct variable domains to different visual channels, such as colours, textures, opacity, and icons, and then combines these channels in a logical fashion. The authors stated that fusion visualization contains three categories: data fusion, feature fusion, and image fusion. First, data fusion generates a new field by fusing multiple variables to investigate the linkage among variables; this makes the multivariate variable easier to understand. Second, feature fusion may provide full play to fused features of separate variables or those across variables, as well as prevent new colours and retain depth information among features, allowing for a more intelligible visualization of numerous features. Third, Image fusion is straightforward and intuitive, making it simple to investigate multivariate data's inherent linkages [18]. An example of a fusion technique is as Fig. 5.

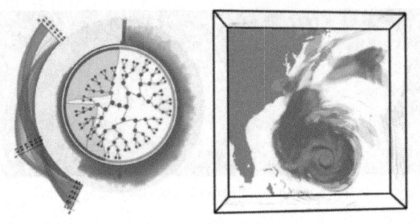

Fig. 5. The Visualization Exploration of Uncertain Data Sets Using Data Fusion by [18]

5 Conclusion

The increase in the requirement for scientific visualization techniques has led to the purpose of this literature review. This paper aims to provide an overview of Scientific Data Visualization Methods and Techniques by reviewing several scientific visualization techniques. Therefore, two research questions have been added. First, what is the currently existing scientific data visualization technique? Second, what does the objective of the existing scientific data visualization technique? This paper's findings show that using visualization techniques helps people understand data more vividly and improves the effectiveness of reading data. This result and discussed section have showcased five techniques of scientific visualization that were selected from five peer-reviewed articles. This literature review can increase knowledge regarding the scientific visualization technique of readers. Moreover, researchers can use this literature review's results in future studies related to scientific visualization techniques. Finally, it is advised for future research about the overview of scientific visualization techniques to have a larger amount of techniques to review.

References

1. Kraska, T.: Northstar: an interactive data science system (2021)
2. Kietzmann, T.C., McClure, P., Kriegeskorte, N.: Deep neural networks in computational neuroscience. In: Oxford Research Encyclopedia of Neuroscience (2019)
3. Fatih, M.: A comparative analysis of breast cancer detection and diagnosis using data visualization and machine learning applications. In: Healthcare, vol. 8, no. 2, p. 111. Multidisciplinary Digital Publishing Institute (2020)
4. Eivas, L.F., Zenkovych, I.O., Uchitel, A.D.: The students' brainwork intensification via the computer visualization of study materials (2020)
5. Fırat, E.E., Laramee, R.S.: Towards a survey of interactive visualization for education. In: Proceedings of the Computer Graphics and Visual Computing, pp. 91–101 (2018)

6. Sun, E., Chen, Z., Li, S., Li, X.: Real-time Data Visualization of Intelligent Networked - Vehicles. In: Proceedings of the 2020 International Conference on Computing, Networks and Internet of Things, pp. 180–184 (2020)

7. Kanke, V., Vinogradova, N., Polozhentseva, I., Korotenko, V.: The philosophical foundations of scientific visualization. In: Revista Inclusiones, pp. 251–259 (2020)

8. Goodman, A.A., Borkin, M.A., Robitaille, T.P.: New Thinking on, and with, Data Visualization. arXiv preprint arXiv:1805.11300 (2018)

9. Zou, X., Yue, W.L., LeVu, H.: Visualization and analysis of mapping knowledge domain of road safety studies. Accid. Anal. Prevent. **118**, 131–145 (2018)

10. Bayoumi, S., Alghamlas, M., Alshehri, A., Alruthae, M.: A review on scientific visualization. case study: breast cancer. In: 2018 21st Saudi Computer Society National Computer Conference (NCC), pp. 1–5. IEEE (2018)

11. Opgenhaffen, L.: Tradition in transition: technology and change in archaeological visualisation practice. Open Archaeol. **7**(1), 1685–1708 (2021)

12. Kelleher, C., Braswell, A.: Introductory overview: recommendations for approaching scientific visualization with large environmental datasets. Environ. Modelling Softw. 105113 (2021)

13. Korakakis, V., Whiteley, R., Tzavara, A., Malliaropoulos, N.: The effectiveness of extracorporeal shockwave therapy in common lower limb conditions: a systematic review including quantification of patient-rated pain reduction. Br. J. Sports Med. **52**(6), 387–407 (2018)

14. Ross, C.J., Wolfe, N., Plagge, M., Carothers, C. D., Mubarak, M., Ross, R.B.: Using scientific visualization techniques to visualize parallel network simulations. In: Proceedings of the 2019 ACM SIGSIM Conference on Principles of Advanced Discrete Simulation, pp. 197–200 (2019)

15. Wang, S., Li, W.: Capturing the dance of the earth: PolarGlobe: real-time scientific visualization of vector field data to support climate science. Comput. Environ. Urban Syst. **77**, 101352 (2019)

16. Xu, C., Sun, G., Liang, R.: A survey of volume visualization techniques for feature enhancement. Visual Inf. **5**(3), 70–81 (2021)

17. Cielo, S., Iapichino, L., Günther, J., Federrath, C., Mayer, E., Wiedemann, M.: Visualizing the world's largest turbulence simulation. Parallel Comput. **102**, 102758 (2021)

18. He, X., Tao, Y., Wang, Q., Lin, H.: Multivariate spatial data visualization: a survey. J. Vis. **22**(5), 897–912 (2019)

Blockchain Technology for Traceability Monitoring in Food Supply Chain

Mohammad Fairus Zulkifli[1]($\boxtimes$), Rabiah Abdul Kadir[1], Mohammad Nazir Ahmad[1], David Wong You King[2], and Muhammad Badrun Al-Muhaimin Baharon[2]

[1] Institute Visual Informatics, Universiti Kebangsaan Malaysia, Bangi, Malaysia
p121866@siswa.ukm.edu.my
[2] ARB Berhad, 22-08, Level 22, Menara Exchange106, Lingkaran TRX, Tun Razak Exchange, 55188 Kuala Lumpur, Malaysia

Abstract. Food supply is the network of companies, individual activities and resources involved in the creation and delivery of food product to customers. The food supply include all the stages of the food process, from raw material acquisition to final delivery of the finished food product. In Malaysia, food supply in a critical issue because the country is heavily reliant on food imports to meet its domestic demand. The factors influence the food supply in Malaysia are dependency on imports food, climate change, infrastructure and logistics, food safety and security and consumer demand. Based on this issues, fluctuate prices of poultry product are happened in Malaysia. In this study, blockchain technology is propose to solve the situation. Blockchain technology has the potential to change the food supply by providing a transparent, traceability, and security to the system for tracking and verifying the information and detail of the poultry product from the farm to the consumer table. Feature like traceability and transparent in blockchain can provide end-to-end traceability of poultry product, allowing consumers to track the entire journey information of the product from the farm to the retail store. Based on this feature, it can help prevent fraudulent document and manipulation price by identifying the original price state by government each stages in food supply.

Keywords: Food Chain · Blockchain · Traceability · Transparent · Manipulation price · Fraudulent documents

1 Introduction

1.1 Food Supply

In agricultural practice, food supply are important part in agriculture. Food supply plays a crucial role to meet the food demand of a growing global population food supply [1]. In general, food supply are refers to the entire process that food goes through, from production to consumer, involving various stages and actors. The food supply includes the following key component is Agricultural production stage involves activities such as farming, rearing, and crop cultivation. Farmers and producers grow, harvest, and raise food products.

H. Badioze Zaman et al. (Eds.): IVIC 2023, LNCS 14322, pp. 478–492, 2024.
https://doi.org/10.1007/978-981-99-7339-2_40

Processing and manufacturing stage, where the food undergoes processing and manufacturing to transform raw ingredients into processed or packaged food products. Food processing companies and manufacturing facilities play a crucial role in this stage. The Distribution and logistics, once the food is processed and packaged, it needs to be transport from production facilities to various points of sale or distribution centers. This stage involves logistics, including transportation, warehousing, and inventory management. Distributors, wholesalers, and logistics companies are responsible for moving the food products efficiently and safely.

Retail and food service stage involves the sale of food products to consumers. Retailers, such as supermarkets, grocery stores and specialty food shops, sell food directly to consumers. Food service establishments, including restaurants, cafeterias, and food trucks, prepare and serve meals to customers. Consumption is the final stage of the food supply is the consumption of food by individuals or households. Consumers purchase and consume food products for nourishment and enjoyment.

Efficient coordination, collaboration, and information sharing to between in the food supply are essential to ensure a smooth flow of food products, minimize food waste, maintain food safety, and meet consumer demands. Implementing latest technology in food supply are need to enhance transparency, traceability and security in this environment.

1.2 Situation Food Supply in Malaysia

Malaysia has a relatively stable food supply. The country has a diverse agricultural sector that produces a wide range of food products. Malaysia also imports a significant amount of food to meet the demand for specific products to supplement domestic supply. These imports include items such as dairy products, and meat.

In some period, the poultry products number are very tight and the price are not reasonable. Even the government of Malaysia are not aware and not inform their citizen. The food supply for poultry product are sometimes uncontrolled by enforcement. The price are fluctuate unconditionally make people mad to government and retailer. This possible issue for poultry product resources are not enough, bird flu and demand on festival ceremony. One of the challenges related to the food supply in Malaysia is the issue of price fluctuations and fraud. This challenge can have negative consequences on both producers and consumers. Here are some key aspects of this challenge:

Fluctuating prices can occur due to various factors, including changes in supply and demand dynamics, weather conditions, transportation disruptions, and global market trends. Price volatility can affect the affordability and accessibility of food for consumers and profitability of producers. Sudden spikes in prices can lead to food insecurity for vulnerable populations. Price manipulation and fraudulent practices can occur at different stages of the food supply.

In some cases, the lack of transparency and traceability within the food supply makes it difficult to track and identify the source of price fluctuations and fraudulent activities. Limited visibility into pricing mechanisms and inadequate traceability systems can hinder efforts to address price fraud effectively. Insufficient resources, capacity, and coordination among regulatory agencies may result in difficulties in detecting and addressing fraudulent practices effectively.

Lack of access to accurate and timely market information can lead to imbalances in bargaining power and unfair practices. This is unethical and irresponsible action do by producer, processing, distributor or retailer. The exploitation behavior can cause of taking advantages by price manipulation and fraudulent practices.

1.3 Problem Raise in Food Supply in Malaysia

Issues with food supply can affect the economy of consumers because they have to spend more to buy chicken products. To determine the issue, an investigation into price fluctuations been done. Issues occur due to lack of transparency, traceability and data security can change in documents on products. In this researched, food supply in Malaysia facing challenges in maintain and controlling information product of food supply from producer phase until consumer. The one of the challenges is to control the price in food supply in each stages (Table 1).

Table 1. Research Question and Objective.

Research Question	Research Objective
1. How to control and maintain price poultry product in food supply?	1. To controlling price from sudden increase poultry product in food supply
2. How to allow consumer review range price poultry product to avoid fraud?	2. To allow consumer review range price of poultry product to avoid fraud

1.4 Research Scope

This paper study is how to implement blockchain technology into food supply system. Implement blockchain technology can control issue price fluctuate and fraud documentation. The research is for poultry product. The issues of this poultry industry is problem to monitoring and trace price form produce until consumer for price range and in poultry industry are easy manipulate by distributer or third party. In this paper, we propose traceability system using blockchain as a based decentralized system for the Malaysia poultry industry.

1.5 Research Motivation

In this research paper, study show the challenges contribute to this fraudulent and manipulation price issues are lack of transparent, traceability and mutable information in the food supply. In this research paper, technology can encounter this challenges is by using blockchain technology. Blockchain technology are come with features transparency, traceability and immutable.

Price fluctuate in under issue from fraud documentation. If the documentation of the product can be manipulated. The issue of price manipulation can happen because of this issue are relate each other. The solution to these problems lies in improving transparency, traceability, and security of food supply activities.

Blockchain are helps in developing a decentralized environment with an immutable, secure and transparent ledger can be a potential solution. In blockchain, transactions are record in chronological order with the aim of creating permanent. In this paper, we focus particularly on using blockchain for food supply processes to check price of the product. This innovative technology will ease the management of poultry product in food supply, thereby enabling farmers to participate without intervention. It will also enable various stakeholders including customers to track and trace agricultural goods as they move forward in the chain.

2 Literature Review

2.1 Food Supply

Food supply have grown and complicated from result of increased globalization and intense market rivalry. However, due to the current state of the food supply chain, it is difficult for food manufacturers and retailers to confirm the source of their products. In food supply, the component includes production, processing, transporting, retailing, and consumption. Throughout this, food is move from a farmer producing the crop to the consumer buying it from stores. Every step requires raw materials and labor to take it to the next step. There is a list of steps: [2].

1. Production - The food supply begins at this level. It is where all food is source. Farmers here are responsible for growing crops and livestock.
2. Processing and packaging - This stage transforms the raw material and primary food into products suitable for consumption. Once it is complete, food deliver for packaging so that it can be deliver to next stage.
3. Distributing - Once the food is ready to be consume, it is deliver to the right store or provider. Distributors distributed commodities, manage inventory, minimize costs, and do other things to increase the value of a food item.
4. Retailer - This step directly connects with the consumer. It takes care of delivering the products. Everything from receiving the allotted products to selling them is cover.
5. Consumer - The consumer is the one who purchases food from a shop and consumes it.

In Fig. 1. Show traditional way food supply environment to process poultry product until bought by consumer. To this day, the existing method is inefficient and unstable. As transactions are prone to fraud, intermediaries are commonly utilize to reduce the total cost of transfers. Finally, when people shop locally, they are not aware of the products origins or the production's impact on the environment. The present food supply has some additional disadvantages. There are huge costs and very little honesty and transparency in recent food supply. Poor communication between the participants in the chain is also a big problem that leads to a lot of issues like wastage of food and many more [3]. A strong food supply is essential for addressing customer demand for good communication that is traceability, transparent and security.

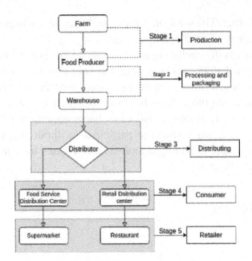

Fig. 1. Traditional Food Supply

2.2 Food Supply Technology and Solution

Food supply technology have various technologies are to address price fluctuations in the food supply and mitigate the risks associated with them. Here are some technologies that can help like:

Internet of Things (IoT) by using IoT devices can collect real-time data on various factors that influence pricing, such as weather conditions, inventory levels, transportation conditions, and consumer demand. This data can integrated with analytics platforms to provide insights into food supply dynamics and enable accurate pricing decision.

RFID (Radio Frequency Identification) and barcode technologies provide accurate and efficient tracking of products throughout the food supply. These technologies enable real-time visibility into inventory levels, product movement, and pricing information, facilitating better inventory management and pricing decision-making.

Blockchain technology offers a decentralized and immutable ledger that can enhance transparency and traceability in the food supply. By recording transactions and product information on a blockchain, stakeholders can have a transparent view of pricing details and ensure that there are no unauthorized changes or manipulations to prices.

Implementing these technologies can enhance food supply visibility, improve data accuracy, and enable effective pricing strategies. The successful implementation of these technologies requires transparent, traceability and security data within the food supply ecosystem.

2.3 Food Supply in Malaysia

In Malaysia, price of poultry product are control by government under ministry of Ministry of Domestic Trade and Costs of Living (Malaysia). Price of poultry will different in festive season and others situation that is allow by this ministry, where the price low as usual situation. Regarding this permission, price fluctuate still happen even this law enforcement be done. Retailer or distributor in food supply, who not responsible will increasing the price without permission and break a rule of the price by making hoax and rumors like shortages of product in this situation. To relate the information and product, information of the product easily manipulate and change because of lack control from this publish information side from government.

There lot of initiative done by government and non-government organization to handle this fluctuate issues by In Malaysia, various technologies use to address and manage price fluctuations in the food supply. While specific technologies can vary across industries and companies, here are some commonly employed technologies in Malaysia:

Enterprise Resource Planning (ERP) systems integrate and manage various aspects of the food supply, including inventory, procurement, production, and sales. By providing real-time data and streamlining processes, ERP systems enable better demand forecasting, inventory management, and pricing decisions. Electronic Data Interchange (EDI) facilitates the electronic exchange of business documents and transactions between trading partners.

Food supply management software platform offer end-to-end visibility and collaboration capabilities, allowing stakeholders to monitor and manage the food supply in real-time. These platforms enable better coordination, communication, and decision-making, helping to mitigate price fluctuations and optimize food supply performance.

Payment systems and financial technology (Fintech): Digital payment systems and financial technology solutions facilitate secure and efficient transactions between food supply partners. These technologies streamline financial processes, reduce payment delays, and enhance transparency, contributing to stable pricing and smoother transactions.

It is important to note that the adoption and utilization of these technologies can vary among different companies and industries in Malaysia. Factors such as the size of the organization, industry sector, and digital readiness influence the extent to which these technologies are implement. Based on this usage of the technologies, the feature transparent, traceability and security that in immutable in lack and may allow fraudulent of documentation and manipulation price.

2.4 Blockchain

Satoshi Nakamoto [4] introduces the concept of Bitcoin and blockchain in the peer to peer version of electronic cash transactions. The concept of decentralization described to explain an electronic cash system. The work elaborates on a decentralized consensus protocol in a distributed network environment to establish trust among unknown entities. A number of alternative applications have conceptualized and implemented on top of this consensus protocol. However, the lack of tuning perfection, lack of state, value and blockchain blindness introduce severe limitations to the scope of such decentralized applications.

Vitalik Buterin [6] introduces Ethereum and its design rationale throwing light on how it is different from Bitcoin. It is equipped with Turing completeness that enables the creation of smart contracts and customized decentralized applications. Szabo in 1994 [7], Introduce Smart contracts allow self-executing contracts. The related code and the agreements they contain exist across a decentralized blockchain network. The contracts are invoking when the system state's meets a set of predefined conditions and then they publish irreversible and tamper-proof transactions on the underlying blockchain.

A smart contract can have various case [8] in Food supply like to achieve intermediary free and automated contract execution. Smart contract is the feature to execute script in the blockchain network. Important features of blockchain technology is highly secure system, it use of cryptography which is a method of protecting information and communications through the use of codes so only the intended recipient can read and process it. Shared source of truth make everyone in the food supply network is referring to the same data rather than each party using their own database that can be manipulate without other parties knowing. Blockchain is a system of digitally recording information on a database that are sharing among computers in the blockchain network in a way that is very difficult for someone to manipulate information or cheat the system.

The blockchain efficiently records what entity issued a credential or certificate in a verifiable and permanent way. Everyone in the network has a copy of the ledger every time it is update for complete transparency. Then immutable make data is record on the blockchain, it is permanent and very difficult to change. If someone tries to tamper with the data, everyone in the network will know about it. That allow blockchain technology to provide security in effectively.

2.5 Relationship Between Food Supply and Blockchain

By analyze the technology and solution been done in food supply in Malaysia for poultry product, There are lack of one component that is immutable. This component are curial when consumer compare price with range recommended. Then, price is overprice than range. Consumer may assume manipulation price happen. If the price can be change without permission this fluctuate issue still happen.

Based on research, relationship between food supply and blockchain is traceability feature. By using food supply application, the traceability component allow to check detail for comparing product price. Traceability are only can be check information in limited access. As consumer, feature transparent available to know implicit information should be share by retailer. Price is not restrict information on the poultry product history. For the security feature, the information should be immutable. Immutable allow the information can be trusted. For this study, blockchain technology is the best technology for these features.

According to Bushra [9] highlights the potential of blockchain technology in making food supply management more secure, resilient and transparent while also discussing the limitations of traditional food supply like information delay, limited visibility, etc. It concludes by mentioning the various services blockchain is capable of providing in this food supply.

Dabbene [10] analyze how the concept of traceability, technologies and industry requirements impact modern food supply management processes and discuss different aspects of food supply management that are relevant to traceability like food crisis management, bulk product tracking, fraud prevention, anti-counterfeit concerns, quality and identity-preservation concerns.

Kamilaris [11, 12] discuss the role blockchain plays in food supply management systems and its impact, enumerates initiatives and developments in this sector, and elaborates on probable barriers and challenges which prevent its widespread adoption in the domain. Potential benefits of blockchain like traceability, fairer pricing of produce, reduce dependence on intermediaries and transparent financial transactions have listed are good to avoid manipulation from retailer. The changes are only when government give instruction. Relationship between food supply and blockchain technology show have transparent feature make product information is allow to be checked and traceability feature allow consumer to review prices [13].

By check this component traceability, transparent and immutable are need in food supply, the blockchain technology are the best solution to fulfill this component for food supply. By using food supply powered with blockchain. Consumer can be easily tracing information of poultry product. Relationship between food supply and blockchain is blockchain can provide traceability and immutable. Figure 2 blockchain based food supply by Patel in 2022 [2].

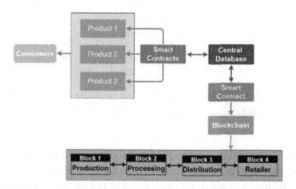

Fig. 2. Blockchain based Food Supply

Blockchains enhance security compared to traditional food supply. Blockchain ledgers protect privacy in addition to preserving unchangeable data. Public blockchains have pseudonymity, which enables individuals to interact with the ledger using a fresh address without disclosing their real identities. Permissioned and private blockchains can offer complete network anonymity in the ways listed below. Parties may sign up for a private blockchain or consortium anonymously after receiving advance certification through an off-chain food supply technique. Blockchain technology and food supply able to collaborate to support immutable feature, improve transparency and improve traceability information [14].

3   Methodology

3.1   Model of Blockchain for Food Supply

To propose model, we are following the existing flow diagram from food supply chain in Malaysia and suit it with model we choose to create model. According to Tan [4] food supply in Malaysia was structure like in the Fig. 3 below, the structure how from produce to consumer. Based on the image growers is produce and final consumer.

After study the structure, we can conclude the main entities involve in the flow diagram are growers as produce, middleman, fresh market, centralized planning system as processing and manufacturing, and distribution can be food manufacturing industry and retail store as retails and consumer as final consumer.

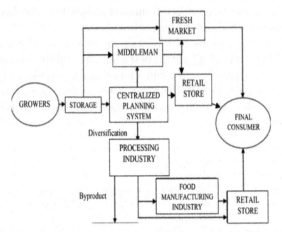

Fig. 3. Flow diagram of the agricultural food supply in Malaysia that involved huge range of activities from grower, wholesaler and manufacturer before reaching to the final consumer.

After the flow diagram are assigned the main component are playing important rule where there will be checkpoint or track history for consumer to comparing price for each product consumer bought it. In order to solve the problem with food supply issue of price, we suggest using a blockchain base solution. To illustrate this, we consider the Hub and Spoke model it is a model that has centralize. To suit the Flow diagram of the agricultural food supply in Malaysia with the hub and spoke model. Figure 4 show Hub and Spoke model.

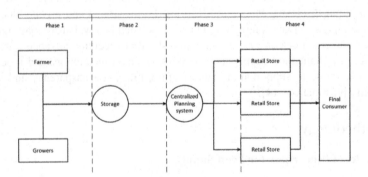

Fig. 4. Hub and Spoke Model

Work step:

Phase 1: The farmer and growers produce is collect by storage where the produce is accumulate and arrange to be sell further.

Phase 2: Storage centers transport the produce to Centralized Planning System.

Phase 3: The sorted and graded goods are collect from Centralized Planning System.

Phase 4: Final consumer buy and pick up poultry product from the retail stores. They can trace their origins using the product tag, which is available as a barcode on the product.

In order to solve the problems with traditional food supply management, we suggest using a blockchain based solution. To illustrate this, we consider the Hub-And-Spoke model. It is a model that has a centralized warehousing and shipment processing system that resembles the structure of a bicycle wheel. The center of the wheel is the hub or a distribution center and each spoke represents the direction of a delivery. Distribution centers or warehouses are strategically place within the city from where reaching out to multiple delivery locations within an area is possible with the most optimal travel distance and time.

3.2   Implementation of Blockchain for Food Supply

To implement blockchain technology into food supply system, In this paper create one conceptual framework model to allow consumer to tracing product information that provide feature traceability, transparent and security.

This model would apply in food supply system, For this implementation, the food supply system is apply blockchain distributed ledger for all stage in supply chain,Second phase create feature of traceability feature to allow the feature of blockchain to used supply chain. All four phases, namely farmers to organized buying centers, buying centers to hubs, hubs to retail stores and retail outlets to the consumer. The various entities along with their functionalities and propose workflow are and shown in Fig. 5 Proposed Conceptual Framework Model for Blockchain in Food Supply:

Production. The farmer first registers himself on the blockchain. After registering, he adds the crop information that he is going to produce on the blockchain. After this process, the farmer sells these crop batches to the buying centers. He adds the transport information like the source, destination, dated to the blockchain.

Processing and Manufacture. The buying center registers on the blockchain. It receives the produce sold by the farmer. These batches are serialize and information pertaining to each batch is add to the blockchain thus connecting the initial information of the farmer related to the crops batch-wise. This helps the buying center track the farmer's side of the information. Further, the logistics information for the batches sold to the hub is add by this entity.

Distribution and Logistic. The Hub registers itself on the blockchain. It can track the delivery of his serialized batches from the buying center for delivery. Once the batch is receive, the hub grades, sorts and packs the batches as per quality, quantity and price. After this processing, tag numbers are gave to the packaged products and this data is upload onto the blockchain. The packages are thus connect to the batch number information. After this, the hub arranges for the selling of the packages of the crops to the retail store managers.

Retails and Food Service. The store manager registers itself onto the system and buys the products from the nearest hub. Transport information for the movement of goods from the hub to the store is add by this entity. With the help of tag numbers, retail stores can track the origin of the produce until the farmer. The products, then sold to consumers.

Consumption. The customers, on purchasing the products from the store, can trace the origin of the product they bought with the help of product information on the products. The customer will merely scan this product information using a barcode scanner and will be show the entire history of the purchased product.

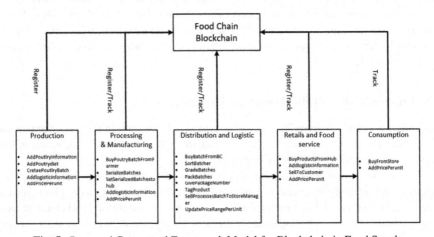

Fig. 5. Proposed Conceptual Framework Model for Blockchain in Food Supply

To understanding the proposed conceptual framework model. Figure 6 architecture blockchain based food supply with proposed model. Architecture show how to implement blockchain in supply chain by develop Traceability system. Proposed model are insert in treacebility system. System are develop for food supply by web application has a Web interface which various entities in the food supply can use to publish relevant information on the blockchain. This information is accessible to all intermediaries as well as the end consumer via the tracking feature of the platform. User accesses the User Interface for this feature and enters a product information. Features of blockchain technology apply in food supply for poultry industry:

- **Transparency**: Show documenting a product's journey across the food supply reveals its true origin and touchpoints, which increases trust and helps eliminate the bias found in today's opaque food supply due to centralization, which is eradicated by introduction of smart contracts.
- **Traceability**: Blockchain provides the ability to track the progression of assets, record the information, and show previous price range records. Anyone can view the provenance and journey of an asset in real-time, whether the asset is physical or digital hence enabling transparency,

- **Security**: Shared an indelible ledger with codified rules could potentially eliminate the possibility of being con- trolled by any single entity. It also disallows any form of unauthorized change and ensures that authenticity is maintain.

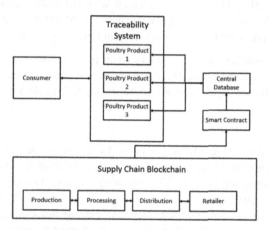

Fig. 6. Architecture Blockchain in Food Supply with Proposed Model

3.3 Challenges Implementation

The challenges in implementing blockchain technology in supply chain can bring several benefits, including increased transparency, traceability, and security. There are guide on how to apply blockchain to a supply chain:

- **Identify the Supply Chain Use Case**, determine which aspect of your supply chain can benefit from blockchain.
- **Define the Network Participants**, identify the participants in your supply chain network, including suppliers, manufacturers, distributors, retailers, and other relevant stakeholders. Each participant will have a node on the blockchain network.
- **Design the Smart Contracts**, develop smart contracts that govern the interactions and transactions between participants. Smart contracts are self-executing agreements that automate processes and ensure compliance with predefined rules.
- **Establish Consensus Mechanism**, determine the consensus mechanism that will validate transactions on the blockchain.
- **Create Immutable Records,** Store relevant information about each transaction or event on the blockchain as immutable records. This information may include product details, timestamps, location data, quality certifications, and ownership transfers.
- **Enable Traceability and Transparency**, Provide a user interface or application layer for stakeholders to access and track the supply chain data. This interface should allow participants to view the entire history of a product, from raw materials to the end consumer, ensuring transparency and traceability.

- **Implement Security Measures,** Utilize cryptographic techniques to secure data integrity and ensure that only authorized participants can access sensitive information. Consider implementing private and public key infrastructure (PKI) to authenticate and encrypt transactions.
- **Deploy and Scale,** Once you are satisfied with the testing results, deploy your blockchain solution to the live supply chain network. Monitor its performance, collect feedback from participants, and continue optimizing the system as needed.

Implementing blockchain in the supply chain is a complex endeavor that requires collaboration and cooperation among all stakeholders. It's essential to consider the costs, technical feasibility, and legal implications before embarking on a blockchain project.

4 Discussion

Blockchain provide multiple advantages in the food supply. Blockchain can increases security, transparency, and traceability of data. In this section, we discuss the benefits of using blockchain in food supply. The following are advantages of using blockchain technology in food supply are:

Improved quality control and food safety. We can use blockchain to make the food supply more transparent, remove of inefficient procedures and ensuring that the quality control conditions are optimal. Monitoring the product by tracing in food chain, check update of the product and condition. Recheck product of the raw chicken is spoil for example, is a common problem for farmers all around the world.

Besides that, enable farmers to monitor components that might harm their product. Monitoring the quality product including of the seal, condition of the product allocate, checking inappropriate temperature these devices would be connected to the blockchain ledger, the farmers will have a more clear idea and a far better outlook of the situation as these devices will give results in real-time which would lead to the prevention of monetary.

Lastly, increased traceability in the food supply, Consumer are demand movements of the products, customers demand to know every stage of food production. Businesses want management software to improve safety, quality, and traceability. Using blockchain technology, clients may get exact information on food's origin, producer, freshness, and growing circumstances. Scan the product at each step to update the database.

Food supply and blockchain technology are suitable to use it together because of blockchain feature. According to discussion, blockchain give lot of impact for food chain, monitoring, traceability and Immutable. From this research, we found many aspect of food supply are be covered by using blockchain technology.

5 Conclusion and Future Research

Blockchain technology has great value and strong potential in resolving data integrity concerns, boosting transparency, enhancing security, avoiding fraud, and other issues creating a sense of trust and secrecy. Implement with food chain, making the system robust and more trusted. Blockchain technology possible to replace traditional systems or applications. Blockchain also may be a useful supplement to legacy systems and may even lead to the construction of new ones shortly.

This paper we suggest a method based on conceptual model. Our conceptual framework provides all the components and technologies that are required to enhance the informed consent process. By using blokchain, system are decentralized. Information and data are depend on distributed ledger that come with transparent, traceability and immutable information feature. Blockchain technology can complete our research objective to maintaining price and checking previous price. This feature avoid data from tempered that contributed to produce documentation or information unchanged and prevent fraudulent. The model purpose for allow consumer to check and trace information of the price of the poultry product they want buying.

As future work, we plan on introduce a report mechanism in the system itself, along with information of poultry product are immutable. If the retailer or distributor rise the price by using this system, consumer can make a report to enforcement to take legal action to retailer or distributor that manipulate price and raise the price at will. Furthermore, it can work with enforcement application to lodge a report to them. In a more extensive study in the food supply is need to advance the maturity of the field for blockchain technology, as it is still in the exploratory stage and many legal and technological challenges remain to be resolved.

References

1. Djekic, I., Batlle-Bayer, L., Bala, A., Fullana-I-palmer, P., Jambrak, A.R.: Role of the food supply chain stakeholders in achieving UN SDGS. Sustain. **13**(16), 1–16 (2021). https://doi.org/10.3390/su13169095
2. Patel, D., Sinha, A., Bhansali, T., Usha, G., Velliangiri, S.: Blockchain in food supply chain. Procedia Comput. Sci. **215**(January), 321–330 (2022). https://doi.org/10.1016/j.procs.2022.12.034
3. Luzzani, G., Grandis, E., Frey, M., Capri, E.: Blockchain technology in wine chain for collecting and addressing sustainable performance: an exploratory study. Sustain. **13**(22), 1–17 (2021). https://doi.org/10.3390/su132212898
4. Tan, S.P. et al.: A review on post-COVID-19 impacts and opportunities of agri-food supply chain in Malaysia, no. May (2023). https://doi.org/10.7717/peerj.15228
5. Nakamoto,S.: bitcoin: a peer-to-peer electronic cash system. SSRN Electron. J. (2008). https://doi.org/10.2139/ssrn.3977007
6. Buterin, V.: A next-generation smart contract and decentralized application platform. Etherum, no. January, pp. 1–36 (2014). [7]. http://buyxpr.com/build/pdfs/EthereumWhitePaper.pdf
7. Szabo, N.: Formalizing and securing relationships on public networks. First Monday **2**(9) (1997)
8. Mohanta,B.K., Panda, S.S., Jena, D.: An overview of smart contract and use cases in blockchain technology. In: 2018 9th International Conference on Computing, Communication and Networking Technologies. ICCCNT 2018, pp. 1–4, 2018. https://doi.org/10.1109/ICCCNT.2018.8494045
9. Rambhia, V., Mehta, R., Shah, R., Mehta, V., Patel, D.: Agrichain: a blockchain-based food supply chain management system. In: Lee, K., Zhang, L.J. (eds.) Blockchain – ICBC 2021. ICBC 2021. Lecture Notes in Computer Science(), vol. 12991, pp. 3–15. Springer, Cham (2022). https://doi.org/10.1007/978-3-030-96527-3_1
10. Dabbene, F., Gay, P., Tortia, C.: Traceability issues in food supply chain management: a review. Biosyst. Eng. **120**, 65–80 (2014). https://doi.org/10.1016/j.biosystemseng.2013.09.006

11. Kamilaris, A., Fonts, A., Prenafeta-Boldú, F.X.: The rise of blockchain technology in agriculture and food supply chains. Trends Food Sci. Technol. **91**(May 2018), 640–652 (2019). https://doi.org/10.1016/j.tifs.2019.07.034.1

12. Shahid, A., et al: Blockchain-based agri-food supply chain: a complete solution. IEEE Access **8**, 69230–69243 (2020). https://doi.org/10.1109/ACCESS.2020.2986257

13. Xu, J., Guo, S., Xie, D., Yan, Y.: Artificial intelligence in agriculture blockchain: a new safeguard for agri-foods. Artif. Intell. Agric. **4**, 153–161 (2020). https://doi.org/10.1016/j.aiia.2020.08.002

14. Sunny, J., et al.: Blockchain: A Makeover to Supply Chain Management. In: Sachdeva, A., Kumar, P., Yadav, O.P., Tyagi, M. (eds.) Recent Advances in Operations Management Applications. LNME, pp. 351–363. Springer, Singapore (2022). https://doi.org/10.1007/978-981-16-7059-6_26

Data Mining in Establishing the Indirect Reference Intervals of Biochemical and Haematological Assays in the Paediatric Population: A Review

Dian N. Nasuruddin[1]($\boxtimes$), Ely Salwana[1], Mahidur R. Sarker[1], Adli Ali[2],
and Tze Ping Loh[3]

[1] Institute of Visual Informatics, Universiti Kebangsaan Malaysia, Bangi, Malaysia
p112770@siswa.ukm.edu.my
[2] Paediatrics Department, Pusat Perubatan Universiti Kebangsaan Malaysia, Kuala Lumpur, Malaysia
[3] Department of Laboratory Medicine, National University Hospital, Lower Kent Ridge Road, Singapore

Abstract. Reference intervals (RIs) are fundamental values accompanying medical laboratory results that allow interpretation by medical practitioners, thus influencing patient management. Traditionally, RIs are established by recruiting 120 healthy reference individuals and applying statistical analysis to the results. This method is challenging due to the technical and ethical issues involved. Therefore, many laboratories either adapt RIs provided by the manufacturers of their analytical platforms or the results of RI studies done in other countries. The advent of data mining technology has allowed an alternative method, the indirect RIs (IRIs) approach, which applies appropriate statistical techniques to patient data stored in the laboratory electronic medical records to establish the IRIs. This review briefly highlights the historical aspect of IRI determination, provides a general outline of the steps involved and reviews publications that have used data mining to establish the paediatric IRI over the past ten years.

Keywords: Data mining · Reference intervals · Indirect approach · Continuous centile curves · Paediatrics

1 Introduction

The application of data mining in the medical domain, including the diagnostic medical laboratory, has recently seen an increasing trend. Data mining can be broadly defined as 'a set of mechanisms and techniques, realised in software, to extract hidden information from data' [1]. It is a subprocess of knowledge discovery in data (KDD) which is the 'non-trivial process of identifying valid, novel, potentially useful and ultimately understandable patterns in data' [2]. The technical approaches of applying data mining in the medical world include data clustering and classification, making predictions, finding

H. Badioze Zaman et al. (Eds.): IVIC 2023, LNCS 14322, pp. 493–507, 2024.
https://doi.org/10.1007/978-981-99-7339-2_41

frequent patterns, analysing changes, and detecting anomalies. Clinical laboratory test results are paramount to evidence-based medicine, with nearly 80% of medical decisions made on the information provided by laboratory reports [3]. Without an accompanying set of reference intervals (RIs), a test result on its own is of little value [4]. A reference interval (RI), as defined by Ceriotti [5], "is an interval that, when applied to the population serviced by the laboratory, correctly includes most of the subjects with characteristics similar to the reference group and excludes the others."

The RI serves as a health-associated benchmark with which to compare an individual test result and is vital in the implementation of mobile health monitoring system (mHealth) as we usher in the 4.0 industrial revolution. This system would enable clinicians and empower patients by illustrating the trace of critical physiological parameters, generating early warnings/alerts, and indicating the need for any significant changes to the results, consultation, medication, and treatments [6]. However, establishing accurate and reliable RI is considerably complex [7]. The paediatric RIs (PRIs) should reflect the dynamic biological and biochemical changes throughout the developmental growth to ensure correct diagnosis and treatment [8].

While the concept of RIs and their values appears simple, defining paediatric reference intervals (PRIs) using the direct method involving 120 presumed healthy reference individuals per partition is daunting and taxing. The cost of conducting a direct reference interval study based on the activity-based-costing (ABC) method described is also high [9]. Due to the obstacles accompanying the establishment of PRIs using the direct method, an alternative which is the indirect method, has started to garner a lot of attention. The indirect reference interval (IRI) method involves data mining of routine paediatric laboratory results collected for other purposes, including routine clinical care and screening from the laboratory information system (LIS). By using appropriate statistical techniques, PRIs are subsequently established [10]. The primary clinical data mining method used in IRI is descriptive cluster analysis, which is finding similar groups of objects to form clusters. It is an unsupervised machine-learning-based algorithm that acts on unlabeled data. A group of data points would comprise a cluster in which all the objects would belong to the same group, i.e., the partitioning of similar data points. The clustering methods commonly used include partitioning and density-based methods.

The IRI is based on identifying a distribution amid the data and does not require assessment of all individual results in the dataset as belonging to the reference population [10]. The IRI method assumes that the examined dataset consists of a mixture of parametrically distributed samples from healthy individuals and pathological samples not described by that distribution. In a sufficiently large dataset with a dominant fraction of physiological test results for the examined analyte, the distribution of non-pathological values can be estimated using advanced statistical methods and the pathological test results are assumed to have no substantial impact on the RIs [11].

This paper aims to highlight the historical aspect of IRI determination and the assessment of publications that have used data mining to establish the IRI in the pediatric population over the past ten years. This paper is arranged into five sections. Section two briefly explains the data mining in indirect PRIs establishment. This is followed by a summary of selected articles that utilised data mining to establish PRIs in Sect. 3, a discussion of the results in Sect. 4 and ending with the conclusion in Sect. 5.

2   Data Mining in IRI Establishment

This section describes the historical aspect of data mining in IRIs and the general steps involved in its establishment.

2.1   The Indirect Methods for RIs Establishment

The foundation of establishing IRIs using patients' results stored in the LIS was laid as early as the 1960s by Robert G Hoffman, who proposed the application of statistics in medicine in the Journal of the American Medical Association [12] and was documented initially by John Glick in 1972. However, it was not until the personal computer arrived in the 1980s that enough computing power was available to apply it generally [13]. Subsequently, C. G. Bhattacharya explored a graphical method to identify Gaussian distribution components in 1967 [14]. This has paved the way for other scholars to apply the method in their research.

T Kouri and his team developed RIs for haematological blood indices partitioned for gender by combining data mined from the LIS and diagnostic data. They surmised that data mined from hospitalised patients based on diagnostic information may apply to other analytes. Horn and Pesce 1998 developed a robust approach for establishing RIs for small datasets. [15]. Later in 2019, a modified version was presented by Horn et al. to accommodate larger distributions of reference intervals [16]. The REALAB project by Grossi et al. in 2005 established RIs for 23 basic tests using approximately 15 million records using a multivariate algorithm. [17]. A novel approach of using a kernel-smoothed density function based on a bimodal method to estimate the distribution of the combined data for both non-diseased and diseased populations was developed by Arzideh et al. in 2007. This is a more advanced procedure to determine RIs from data mined in laboratory databases without considering any diseased population distribution. [18]. The Clinical Laboratory Standard Institute (CLSI), in its 2010 guidelines issue, has guided the establishment of RIs for quantitative clinical laboratory tests. The indirect method was briefly mentioned as an alternative, not a primary one, to replace direct RIs. With the explosion of big data technology, the challenges in recruiting reference individuals and the exorbitant cost involved in developing RIs using the direct method, especially in the paediatric population, many researchers from around the globe have taken an interest in exploring and conducting studies focusing on developing PRIs from data mining of patient data from diagnostic laboratories using the indirect method. This has led to the improvement of the methodology and statistical techniques in leaps and bounds [18–22].

2.2   The Indirect Methods for Paediatric RIs (PRIs) Establishment

A long-standing gap exists in the PRIs, especially in the neonates and young infant subgroups. This is because of the difficulty and ethical issues in obtaining blood from the healthy paediatric population. With the growth of technology and the availability of large laboratory databases, the indirect reference interval method is seen to have the full potential to fill in this gap. The challenge is determining the physiological samples amidst the pathological samples in the mixed laboratory dataset using either the metadata-driven or primary statistical strategy. The availability of many data set points has also contributed to the development of continuous percentile charts or dynamic reference intervals of biochemical and haematological analytes, which better represent the dynamic physiological development in the paediatric population, especially during the neonatal/infantile period and throughout puberty [23, 24]. The indirect method has mainly been used to establish paediatrics IRIs (PIRIs) for biochemical analytes such as calcium and bone markers, alkaline phosphatase, creatinine, lipids, arterial blood gases, creatinine and trace minerals [22, 25–33]. Apart from that, the indirect method has also been successfully used to establish haematological reference intervals for full blood count indices and coagulation profiles in many countries [21, 34–39].

2.3   The Steps Involved in IRI Establishment

The general steps involved in the IRI establishment, whether metadata driven or statistically-driven, include data collection, cleaning, data analysis and result verification. Data analysis comprises three main processes: partitioning of the input dataset according to desired groups, statistical analysis, which includes outlier removal, calculation of cumulative frequency (cdf) of each result, calculation of the inverse cdf of a standard Gaussian distribution and graphing the inverse cdf versus each of the measured analyte value and performing piece-wise linear regression in R software to identify the linear portion of the distribution. This is followed by graphing the linear part of the distribution and using linear regression to determine the equation that represents the linear portion of the distribution. Next, by using the linear equation, the 2.5th and 97.5th centiles may be extrapolated and taken as the lower and upper reference intervals [40]. In metadata-driven studies, additional steps are taken in the data cleaning process to remove results associated with abnormality of other analytes from any patients with known diseases, or the opinion of subject matter experts.

In calculating continuous reference intervals, additional steps would need to be taken. This involves dividing the datasets into overlapping timeframes, excluding pathological values using statistical methods, and calculating the 2.5th, 50th and 97.5th percentiles of the remaining values of each parameter using statistical and graphical software such as R and R Studio. Special consideration in the IRI is the verification of the various indirect approaches. To verify the newly established IRIs, many researchers may directly compare the results with previously published articles in the literature to assess the agreement or may perform an in-house verification using the standard verification procedure described by CLSI EP28-A3c, which emphasises that three approaches that can be used to verify RIs, i.e. subjective assessment, using a small number (n = 20) of reference individuals or using a large number or reference individual (n = 60 but fewer than 120). In the second and third approaches, if no more than 2 of the 20 samples (i.e., 10% of the test results) fall outside the RI, at least provisionally, it may be received for use. However, if 3 or 4 of the 20 samples fall outside the RI, a second set of 20 reference specimens should be obtained, and if again three or more of the new specimens (i.e., $\geq$ 10% of the test results) OR 5 or more of the original 20 falls outside the RI, the user should re-examine the analytical procedures used and consider possible differences in the biological characteristics of the two populations sampled.

At the time of writing this article, there are many published algorithms for derivation of IRI. Among them include the Hoffman and the modified Hoffman methods, the Bhattacharya method, the Arzideh method, and the Wosniok method [41]. Simulation studies are highly recommended in comparing the various indirect methods' diagnostic efficiency and allow appropriate statistical confidence analysis [42].

3 Summary of Published Studies on RI Establishment Using Indirect Method in the Paediatric Population

Tables 1, 2 and 3 summarise the studies that employed the indirect method to establish paediatric reference intervals. Three databases (Scopus, EBSCO Medline and WOS) were searched using the terms' data mining', 'data analytics', 'big data', 'calculating', 'constructing', 'developing', 'establishing', 'reference interval', 'normal range', 'reference limit', 'reference curves', 'paediatrics', 'child', 'adolescent', 'newborn', and 'neonate' from 2012 through July 2022.

Table 1 presents a detailed summary of published papers reporting the establishment of PRIs of biochemical assays by indirect methods. This study will compare selected studies based on a few criteria, including the year, the country in which the study was conducted, the analytes included in the study, the methods used, discrete vs continuous PRIs and the type of partitioning established. Ten studies were included from 2012 through 2022.

In 2012, Eduardo et al. from Argentina established discrete age-specific thyroid hormones IRIs using laboratory results over a period of 5 years involving 7581 children [43, 44]. This study was meta-data driven as rigorous exclusion criteria were applied to the data prior to the final analysis. This study established higher TSH and T4 values than a previous direct RI study done in German [44], highlighting the importance of population-specific RIs. In the same year, a group of researchers from Israel established their discrete IRI partitioned by age for TSH and free T3 using results from over 11,000 children and adolescent and found that the then RI used were too low and suggested the transference of their results to other laboratories [45]. There was no partitioning based on gender done for both studies. Another study in the UK published in 2013 successfully established age and gender-specific IRIs for serum prolactin to aid in diagnosing neurometabolic conditions affecting dopamine metabolism [46]. This study extracted over ten years of data from 2369 hospital patients. The established IRI was comparable with previously published IRIs [47] and has filled the knowledge gap by providing the prolactin RI for infants under one year. In the same year, a group of researchers in America established the discrete age-specific IRIs for calcium using 4629 datasets. This meta-data-driven study found that the calcium IRIs were broader than the currently used and suggested that the differences may reflect seasonal or ethnic heterogeneity [48].

The Canadian group in 2014 published a paper studying the validity of establishing PRIs based on hospital patient data by comparing the age and gender-specific discrete PRIs results of 13 biochemical analytes established using the indirect method (modified Hoffmann) to results obtained in the CALIPER study [40]. This statistically-driven study analysed over 200,000 data points per analyte and found that the indirect PRIs established were generally wider than the CALIPER study. Another single-centre, metadata-driven study in Turkey published in 2015 analysed 1709 data points and developed gestational age-specific TSH and free T4 continuous IRIs. They found that free T4 correlated with gestational whilst TSH remained unchanged irrespective of gestational age [49]. In the same year, a team of researchers from Denmark published the results of their multicentre, statistically-driven study that analysed the creatinine results of over 11,000 data sets. The continuous age and gender-specific IRIs showed that age dependency was seen in both boys and girls from birth to adulthood [50].

A large multicentre, statistically-driven study in the Netherlands published in 2019 [51] analysed 7,574,327 results of children visiting their general practitioners and established discrete age and gender-specific IRIs of 18 biochemical analytes with the aim to adapt them as standardised national RIs. They found that there were significant age effects for liver enzymes and creatinine. One single-centre, statistically-driven study done in Pakistan was published in 2021. The group analysed 96104 data points and established discrete IRI for creatinine and found that the serum creatinine dynamics differ across gender and age groups. Compared to CALIPER, their creatinine IRIs were lower. This is thought to be due to the different genetic structures and, again, highlights the importance of developing population-specific RIs. Another large statistically-driven multicentre study in Germany established high-resolution age and gender-specific continuous IRIs for 15 biochemical analytes using an analysis of 217, 883 - 982,548 samples per analyte which showed high concordance to the continuous RIs of other large direct studies (CALIPER and HAPPi Kids) [52].

Table 2 presents a detailed summary of published papers reporting the establishment of PRIs of haematological and coagulation assays by indirect methods. Six studies are included. The first study was done in Romania and published in 2013. This group of researchers conducted a single-centre, meta-data-driven study of 845 patient data sets to establish discrete IRIs for erythrocyte parameters specific for one-day-old neonates [34]. They found that the results were comparable to previously published direct RIs [53]. The same team later in the following year published an article on the discrete IRIs for platelet parameters in the first day of life, neonates, using 1124 patient datasets and partitioning the results according to gender [54]. The obtained values for some parameters agreed with the literature, while some differed [55]. This supports the need for establishing population-specific haematology reference intervals.

Zierk et al. in 2013 published the results of a statistically-driven German single-centre study of age-specific continuous IRIs using analysis of 56,253 – 60,394 data points for various haematology indices [35]. In this study, the results were comparable to the previously published KiGGS study and managed to capture biological events. Then in 2018, Weidhofer et al. from Australia established continuous age and gender-specific IRIs for coagulation parameters [36]. This study extracted data from two centres and analysed 19,684–55,101 data sets. The resulting IRIs highlighted the coagulation parameters' age-dependent dynamics, and some of the parameters showed concordance with previous literature [56]. In 2019, Zierk and his team of researchers published the results of a large German metadata-driven multicentre study that analysed 9,576,910 samples from 358,292 patients that established continuous percentile charts of various haematology parameters partitioned according to age and gender [37]. They observed complex age and sex-related dynamics in haematology analytes during all periods of

Table 1. Published papers reporting the establishment of PRIs of biochemical assays by indirect methods

No	Author(s), year, country	Title	Discrete/Continuous, Partitioning
1	E. A. Chaler et al. (2012), Argentina [43]	Age-specific thyroid hormone and thyrotropin reference intervals for a pediatric and adolescent population	Discrete, Age
2	Strich, D. et al. (2012), Israel [45]	Current normal values for TSH and FT3 in children are too low: evidence from over 11,000 samples	Discrete, Age
3	Aitkenhead, H. et al. (2013), United Kingdom [46]	Establishment of paediatric age-related reference intervals for serum prolactin to aid in the diagnosis of neurometabolic conditions affecting dopamine metabolism	Discrete, age and gender
4	Roizen, J. et al. (2013), USA [48]	Determination of reference intervals for serum total calcium in the vitamin D-Replete pediatric population	Discrete, Age
5	Shaw, J. et al. (2014), Canada [40]	Validity of establishing pediatric reference intervals based on hospital patient data: A comparison of the modified Hoffmann approach to CALIPER reference intervals obtained in healthy children	Discrete, age and gender
6	Imamoglu, E. et al. (2015), Turkey [49]	Nomogram-based evaluation of thyroid function in appropriate-for-gestational-age neonates in intensive care unit	Continuous, Gestational age specific
7	Søeby, K. et al. (2015), Denmark [50]	Mining of hospital laboratory information systems: a model study defining age- and gender-specific reference intervals and trajectories for plasma creatinine in a pediatric population	Continuous, age and sex

(continued)

Table 1. (*continued*)

No	Author(s), year, country	Title	Discrete/Continuous, Partitioning
8	Den Elzen, W. P. J et al. (2019), The Netherlands [51]	NUMBER: Standardised reference intervals in the Netherlands using a 'big data' approach	Discrete, age and sex
9	Ahmed, S. et al. (2021), Pakistan [30]	Indirect determination of serum creatinine reference intervals in a Pakistani pediatric population using big data analytics	Discrete, Age
10	Zierk, J. et al. (2021), Germany [52]	High-resolution pediatric reference intervals for 15 biochemical analytes described using fractional polynomials	Continuous, age and gender

childhood and adolescence. Compared to their previous work in 2013, the current IRIs was narrower and showed high concordance with the KiGGS study. Another group of researchers from Germany published another article in 2022 [21]. This metadata-driven study was done in Berlin and Brandenburg to establish discrete IRIs for various haematology parameters. A total of 27,554 patient datasets were analysed, and age, as well as sex-specific IRIs, were established. The IRIs from this study showed differences from previously published articles which might be explained by the different population distribution due to high foreign influx [57, 58]. This further reiterates the need for the establishment of population-specific reference intervals.

Table 3 summarises three published papers reporting the establishment of PRIs of various biochemical, haematological, coagulation and other multi-discipline assays by indirect methods. Six studies are included. The first study was done in Germany by Zierk and his team of researchers [22]. This single-centre statistically driven study established the age and sex-dependent continuous reference intervals for 13 biochemical analytes and haematological parameters. In their research, electrolytes and total protein showed age-specific changes but not sex-specific. One of the analytes studied, alkaline phosphatase, showed complex dynamic patterns, and most of the analytes' IRIs were comparable to CALIPER and KiGGS studies.

Table 2. Published papers reporting the establishment of PRIs of haematological assays by indirect methods

No	Author(s), year, country	Title	Discrete/Continuous, Partitioning
1	Grecu, D. S., et al. (2013), Romania [34]	Quality in post-analytical phase: indirect reference intervals for erythrocyte parameters of neonates	Discrete, Age-specific for one-day-old neonates
2	Zierk, J. et al. (2013), Germany [35]	Indirect determination of pediatric blood count reference intervals	Continuous, Age
3	Grecu, D. S., et al. (2014), Romania [54]	Quality assurance in the laboratory testing process: indirect estimation of the reference intervals for platelet parameters in neonates	Discrete, Age (First day of life) and sex
4	Weidhofer, C. et al. (2018), Austria [36]	Dynamic reference intervals for coagulation parameters from infancy to adolescence	Continuous, age and gender
5	Zierk, J. et al. (2019), Germany [37]	Next-generation reference intervals for pediatric hematology	Continuous – percentile charts, age and gender
6	Mrosewski, I. et al. (2022), Germany [21]	Indirectly determined hematology reference intervals for pediatric patients in Berlin and Brandenbur	Discrete, age and sex-specific

A team from Korea presented the results of their large multicentre study in 2021. This metadata-driven study established the discrete age and gender-specific IRIs for haematology, biochemical and coagulation parameters. The PRIs determined from this study differed from existing results and PRIs from other ethnicities. Subsequently, a team of researchers from America also published their age and gender-specific discrete reference intervals for 266 individual analytes across multiple clinical disciplines [59]. Patient results from 13 laboratories amounting to a total of 71,594,330 total patients test results were analysed in this statistically-driven study, and the team has successfully established IRIs with very powerful sample sizes for each age bracket.

Table 3. Published papers reporting the establishment of PRIs of biochemical, haematological and coagulation assays by indirect methods

No	Author(s), year, country	Title	Discrete/Continuous, Partitioning
1	Zierk, J., et al. (2015), Germany [22]	Age- and sex-specific dynamics in 22 hematologic and biochemical analytes from birth to adolescence	Continuous, age and sex-dependent change during development
2	Sung, J. Y. et al. (2021), Korea [60]	Establishment of Pediatric Reference Intervals for Routine Laboratory Tests in Korean Population: A Retrospective Multicenter Analysis	Discrete, age and sex
3	Fleming, J. et al. (2022), USA [59]	Development of nationwide reference intervals using an indirect method and harmonised assays	Discrete, age and gender (neonatal, paediatric, adults, geriatric)

4 Summary of Published Studies on RI Establishment Using Indirect Method in the Paediatric Population

This narrative review provides a historical review of data mining in the paediatric IRI determination and an assessment of the published articles within the past years that have utilised data mining in establishing the paediatric indirect reference intervals over the past ten years. There are many advantages of using the indirect method compared to the direct method. Indirect methods harness the power of big data that increases statistical power, are representative of the true population and allow easy application of complex statistical analysis to be applied to thousands and even millions of deidentified data points pulled from the laboratory database of a single or many centres for fast outlier removal, transformation and partitioning to establish robust IRIs. Applying further statistical analysis would allow for the creation of continuous or dynamic percentile charts that better represent the fluid physiological changes seen in children. The indirect method also provides analysis of retrospective data of difficult-to-obtain samples such as body fluids, CSF, and amniotic fluid, as the steps involved are identical to the analysis of data for serum, plasma, or whole blood samples.

On the contrary, the direct method is tedious as it involves recruiting healthy reference individuals, which is hard to come by, especially in healthy paediatric populations. The limited sample size reduces the statistical power, and application to a larger population is debatable. The typically small number of results hinders the ability to partition the data; hence, only discrete RIs could be established for certain arbitrarily set age brackets. Samples from reference samples would need to be collected, processed, and stored for batch analysis which may take longer. This cycle may also introduce bias in the result. Ethical issues involved are among the more challenging hurdles, as researchers would need to obtain informed consent from the parents of the paediatric reference individuals to allow the collection of data and venepuncture to be conducted. It is also more expensive to conduct the direct method as it involves the cost of reference individuals' reimbursement, labour of testing and the cost of reagents and consumables.

Recently, there has been a significant increase in the number of publications on the indirect method, especially over the past five years. This signifies an interest in IRI establishment as an alternative to the laborious direct method. The boost of interest, especially of the laboratorians, to embark and report results of indirect reference interval studies is most likely contributed by the advantages of the indirect method discussed previously, coupled with the advanced database available in the laboratory, readily available volume of patient data stored for analysis plus easy access to statistical analysis tools developed by the previous group of researchers. Initially, it was noted that many of the earlier publications reviewed did not include a thorough description of the data mining and the statistical methods used in the IRI establishment. However, subsequent publications have included detailed step-by-step descriptions of that IRI establishment entails.

Jones et al. [10] have proposed a checklist of the minimum requirements for publication of IRI studies which include details of study design, a description of the population and the data source, a description of available records of preanalytical and analytical processes, the data set selection and filtering criteria, the description of the data set inclusive of number of samples, median, kurtosis and initial analysis of partitioning. The description of the statistical process inclusive of outlier detection, method and transformation, results of statistical analysis, comparison with other statistically reliable peer-reviewed published studies and final recommendations and discussion of the study would also need to be included. This would allow future researchers to understand the overall steps involved and critique the study to find any weaknesses, strengths, and opportunities for improvements before conducting their own population-specific indirect reference studies.

4.1 Comparison of Indirect PRIs Between Countries

Most of the reviewed articles were done in the European population. Only two studies were done in the Asian population (Pakistan and Korea). Data mining and indirect sampling have allowed multiple laboratories in a country or a region to conduct IRI studies using the same methodology and analytical platforms to establish common reference intervals. However, caution needs to be exercised. This is exemplified by the results of two studies in different regions in Germany that have shown variability in their IRI results. The difference might be due to the difference in the population, as one region is known to have a high foreign influx [21, 37]. Many other studies done in Europe have reported good agreement with previously reported RIs established by both the direct and indirect methods [35, 37]. However, variability is still seen especially wider values of certain analytes [40, 48]. The two studies done in the Asian continent [30, 60] have also come up with different IRIs than the ones currently used in their population and previously published PRIs from other countries. This serves as a reminder to laboratories from other countries, especially those with diverse multi-ethnic heterogeneous populations, to be cautious in the transference of IRI results from different countries and further highlights the necessity of establishing own population-specific reference intervals preferably partitioned according to age, gender, and ethnicity.

4.2 Discrete vs. Continuous IRIs

The centile charts are familiar among most health care providers and parents as they are used to assess their children's developmental growth. The application of centile charts in biochemical and haematological paediatrics RI has led to the transformation of discrete RIs to dynamic continuous percentile charts [61, 62]. Percentile RI charts enable the removal of the arbitrarily set age group partitions that may confuse the interpretation of results, especially in children between age group brackets [63]. The intuitive percentile charts allow the physiological patterns and dynamics of paediatrics analytes to be visually represented. Seven articles described in this review have developed continuous reference intervals for various biochemical, haematological and coagulation assays [22, 35–37, 49, 50, 52]. The majority were multicentre studies and were statistically driven. Most of the studies applied the Arzideh method [64, 65, 22, 35–37, 52] and the kosmic software [52] in the calculation of continuous RIs. Even though there is a move towards developing continuous percentile charts, one major hurdle remains. Currently, many laboratories' information systems are unable to incorporate advanced mathematical functions or graphical representations of patient results [3]. Hopefully, this obstacle will soon be overcome, and continuous reference percentiles can be integrated fully into clinical practice.

5 Conclusion

This paper observed that data mining techniques have been employed successfully in establishing PIRIs. Caution must be exercised during data cleansing as this process must be done thoroughly to ensure the voracity of the established PRIs. There is still a paucity of data regarding the PRIs based on different ethnicities. Many of the published PRIs were based on the Caucasian population and might not be suitable for the transference of PRIs to other medical diagnostic laboratories elsewhere. Therefore, many authors have highlighted the importance of establishing the age, sex and ethnicity-specific to the population. Many researchers are moving towards the establishment of dynamic continuous PRIs using a few recently published algorithms and programs that help to understand the physiological dynamic changes in paediatric biochemistry and complement age-specific RIs in the tracking, interpretation and application of the results in clinical patient management.

References

1. Coenen, F.: Data mining: past, present and future. Knowl. Eng. Rev. **26**(1), 25–29 (2011)

2. Fayyad, U., Piatetsky-Shapiro, G., Smyth, P.: From data mining to knowledge discovery: an overview. In: Advances in Knowledge Discovery and Data Mining, Editor. AAAI Press/The MIT Press, Menlo Park (1996)
3. Hoq, M., et al.: Paediatric reference intervals: current status, gaps, challenges and future considerations. Clin. Biochem. Rev. **41**(2), 43–52 (2020)
4. Katayev, A., Balciza, C., Seccombe, D.W.: Establishing reference intervals for clinical laboratory test results: is there a better way? Am. J. Clin. Pathol. **133**(2), 180–186 (2010)
5. Ceriotti, F.: Establishing pediatric reference intervals: a challenging task. Clin. Chem. **58**(5), 808–810 (2012)
6. Mat Nayan, N.: Model for monitoring chronic disease in MHealth applications: a case of Asian country. IRAJ (2020)
7. Tahmasebi, H., et al.: Pediatric reference intervals for biochemical markers: gaps and challenges, recent national initiatives and future perspectives. EJIFCC **28**(1), 43–63 (2017)
8. Lyle, A.N., et al.: Current state of pediatric reference intervals and the importance of correctly describing the biochemistry of child development: a review. JAMA Pediatr. **176**(7), 699–714 (2022)
9. Ibrahim, R., et al.: Estimation of cost of diagnostic laboratory services using activity based costing (ABC) for implementation of Malaysia diagnosis related group (MY-DRG®) in a teaching hospital. Malays. J. Publ. Health Med. **17**, 1–8 (2017)
10. Jones, G.R.D., et al.: Indirect methods for reference interval determination – review and recommendations. Clin. Chem. Lab. Med. (CCLM) **57**(1), 20–29 (2019)
11. Zierk, J., et al.: Indirect determination of hematology reference intervals in adult patients on Beckman Coulter UniCell DxH 800 and Abbott CELL-DYN Sapphire devices. Clin. Chem. Lab. Med. **57**(5), 730–739 (2019)
12. Yang, D., Su, Z., Zhao, M.: Big data and reference intervals. Clin. Chim. Acta **527**, 23–32 (2022)
13. Hoffmann, G., Lichtinghagen, R., Wosniok, W.: Simple estimation of reference intervals from routine laboratory data. Lab. Medizin **39**(6) (2016)
14. Bhattacharya, C.G.: A simple method of resolution of a distribution into gaussian components. Biometrics **23**(1), 115–135 (1967)
15. Horn, P.S., Pesce, A.J., Copeland, B.E.: A robust approach to reference interval estimation and evaluation. Clin. Chem. **44**(3), 622–631 (1998)
16. Beasley, C.M., Jr., et al.: Adaptation of the robust method to large distributions of reference values: program modifications and comparison of alternative computational methods. J. Biopharm. Stat. **29**(3), 516–528 (2019)
17. Grossi, E., et al.: The REALAB project: a new method for the formulation of reference intervals based on current data. Clin. Chem. **51**(7), 1232–1240 (2005)
18. Arzideh, F., et al.: A plea for intra-laboratory reference limits. part 2. a bimodal retrospective concept for determining reference limits from intra-laboratory databases demonstrated by catalytic activity concentrations of enzymes. Clin. Chem. Lab. Med. **45**(8), 1043–1057 (2007)
19. Farrell, C.L., Nguyen, L., Carter, A.C.: Data mining for age-related TSH reference intervals in adulthood. Clin. Chem. Lab. Med. **55**(10), e213–e215 (2017)
20. Lo Sasso, B., et al.: Reference interval by the indirect approach of serum thyrotropin (TSH) in a Mediterranean adult population and the association with age and gender. Clin. Chem. Lab. Med. **57**(10), 1587–1594 (2019)
21. Mrosewski, I., et al.: Indirectly determined hematology reference intervals for pediatric patients in Berlin and Brandenburg. Clin. Chem. Lab. Med. **60**(3), 408–432 (2021)
22. Zierk, J., et al.: Age- and sex-specific dynamics in 22 hematologic and biochemical analytes from birth to adolescence. Clin. Chem. **61**(7), 964–973 (2015)
23. Zierk, J., Metzler, M., Rauh, M.: Data mining of pediatric reference intervals. J. Lab. Med. **45**(6), 311–317 (2021)

24. Higgins, V., Adeli, K.: Advances in pediatric reference intervals: from discrete to continuous. J. Lab. Prec. Med. **3**(1), 77–82 (2018)
25. Omosule, C.L., et al.: Pediatric ionised calcium reference intervals from archived radiometer data. Clin. Biochem. **104**, 13–18 (2022)
26. Gallo, S., et al.: Redefining normal bone and mineral biochemistry reference intervals for healthy infants in Canada. Clin. Biochem. **47**(15), 27–32 (2014)
27. Gennai, I., et al.: Age- and sex-matched reference curves for serum collagen type I C-telopeptides and bone ALP in children and adolescents: an alternative multivariate statistical analysis approach. Clin. Biochem. **49**(10–11), 802–807 (2016)
28. Monneret, D., et al.: Reference percentiles for paired arterial and venous umbilical cord blood gases: An indirect nonparametric approach. Clin. Biochem. **67**, 40–47 (2019)
29. Ahmed, S., Zierk, J., Khan, A.H.: Establishment of reference intervals for Alkaline phosphatase in Pakistani children using a data mining approach. Lab. Med. **51**(5), 484–490 (2020)
30. Ahmed, S., et al.: Indirect determination of serum creatinine reference intervals in a Pakistani pediatric population using big data analytics. World J. Clin. Pediatr. **10**(4), 72–78 (2021)
31. Ammer, T., et al.: RefineR: a novel algorithm for reference interval estimation from real-world data. Sci. Rep. **11**(1), 16023 (2021)
32. Ha, F., et al.: The reference intervals of whole blood copper, zinc, calcium, magnesium, and iron in infants under 1 year old. Biol. Trace Elem. Res. **200**(1), 1–12 (2022)
33. Dathan-Stumpf, A., et al.: Pediatric reference data of serum lipids and prevalence of dyslipidemia: results from a population-based cohort in Germany. Clin. Biochem. **49**(10–11), 740–749 (2016)
34. Grecu, D.S., et al.: Quality in post-analytical phase: indirect reference intervals for neonates erythrocyte parameters. Clin. Biochem. **46**(7–8), 617–621 (2013)
35. Zierk, J., et al.: Indirect determination of pediatric blood count reference intervals. Clin. Chem. Lab. Med. **51**(4), 863–872 (2013)
36. Weidhofer, C., et al.: Dynamic reference intervals for coagulation parameters from infancy to adolescence. Clin. Chim. Acta **482**, 124–135 (2018)
37. Zierk, J., et al.: Next-generation reference intervals for pediatric hematology. Clin. Chem. Lab. Med. **57**(10), 1595–1607 (2019)
38. Zeljkovic, A., et al.: Indirect reference intervals for haematological parameters in capillary blood of pre-school children. Biochemia Medica **31**(1), 134–142 (2021)
39. Bracho, F.J.: Reference intervals of automated reticulocyte count and immature reticulocyte fraction in a pediatric population. Int. J. Lab. Hematol. **44**(3), 461–467 (2022)
40. Shaw, J.L.V., et al.: Validity of establishing pediatric reference intervals based on hospital patient data: a comparison of the modified Hoffmann approach to CALIPER reference intervals obtained in healthy children. J. Clin. Biochem. **47**(3), 166–172 (2014)
41. Ozarda, Y., et al.: Comparison of reference intervals derived by direct and indirect methods based on compatible datasets obtained in Turkey. Clinica Chimica Acta: Int. J. Clin. Chem. **520**, 186–195 (2021)
42. Haeckel, R.: Indirect approaches to estimate reference intervals. J. Lab. Med. **45**(2), 31–33 (2021)
43. Chaler, E.A., et al.: Age-specific thyroid hormone and thyrotropin reference intervals for a pediatric and adolescent population. Clin. Chem. Lab. Med. **50**(5), 885–890 (2012)
44. Elmlinger, M.W., et al.: Reference intervals from birth to adulthood for serum thyroxine (T4), triiodothyronine (T3), free T3, free T4, thyroxine binding globulin (TBG) and thyrotropin (TSH). Clin. Chem. Lab. Med. **39**(10), 973–979 (2001)
45. Strich, D., Edri, S., Gillis, D.: Current normal values for TSH and FT3 in children are too low: evidence from over 11,000 samples. J. Pediatr. Endocrinol. Metab. **25**(3–4), 245–248 (2012)

46. Aitkenhead, H., Heales, S.J.: Establishment of paediatric age-related reference intervals for serum prolactin to aid in the diagnosis of neurometabolic conditions affecting dopamine metabolism. Ann. Clin. Biochem. **50**(2), 156–158 (2013)
47. Cook, J., et al.: Pediatric reference ranges for prolactin. Clin. Chem. **38**(6), 959 (1992)
48. Roizen, J.D., et al.: Determination of reference intervals for serum total calcium in the vitamin d-Replete pediatric population. J. Clin. Endocrinol. Metab. **98**(12), E1946–E1950 (2013)
49. Imamoglu, E.Y., et al.: Nomogram-based evaluation of thyroid function in appropriate-for-gestational-age neonates in intensive care unit. J. Perinatol. **35**(3), 204–207 (2015)
50. Søeby, K., et al.: Mining of hospital laboratory information systems: a model study defining age- and gender-specific reference intervals and trajectories for plasma creatinine in a pediatric population. Clin. Chem. Lab. Med. **53**(10), 1621–1630 (2015)
51. Den Elzen, W.P.J., et al.: NUMBER: Standardised reference intervals in the Netherlands using a 'big data' approach. Clin. Chem. Lab. Med. **57**(1), 42–56 (2018)
52. Zierk, J., et al.: High-resolution pediatric reference intervals for 15 biochemical analytes described using fractional polynomials. Clin. Chem. Lab. Med. **59**(7), 1267–1278 (2021)
53. ÖZYÜREK, E., et al.: Complete blood parameters for healthy, SGA, full-term newborns. Clin. Lab. Haematol. **28**(2), 97–104 (2006)
54. Grecu, D.S., Paulescu, E.: Quality assurance in the laboratory testing process: indirect estimation of the reference intervals for platelet parameters in neonates. Clin. Biochem. **47**(15), 33–37 (2014)
55. Wasiluk, A., et al.: Platelet indices in SGA newborns. Adv. Med. Sci. **56**(2), 361–365 (2011)
56. Toulon, P., et al.: Age dependency for coagulation parameters in paediatric populations. Results of a multicentre study aimed at defining the age-specific reference ranges. Thromb. Haemost. **116**(1), 9–16 (2016)
57. Zierk, J., et al.: Indirect determination of hematology reference intervals in adult patients on Beckman Coulter UniCell DxH 800 and Abbott CELL-DYN Sapphire devices. Clin. Chem. Lab. Med. (CCLM) **57**(5), 730–739 (2019)
58. Herklotz, R., et al.: Metaanalysis of reference values in hematology. Ther. Umsch. **63**(1), 5–24 (2006)
59. Fleming, J.K., et al.: Development of nation-wide reference intervals using an indirect method and harmonised assays. Clin. Biochem. **99**, 20–59 (2022)
60. Sung, J.Y., et al.: Establishment of pediatric reference intervals for routine laboratory tests in korean population: a retrospective multicenter analysis. Ann. Lab. Med. **41**(2), 155 (2021)
61. Griffiths, J.K., et al.: Centile charts II: alternative nonparametric approach for establishing time-specific reference centiles and assessment of the sample size required. Clin. Chem. **50**(5), 907–914 (2004)
62. Koduah, M., Iles, T.C., Nix, B.J.: Centile charts I: new method of assessment for univariate reference intervals. Clin. Chem. **50**(5), 901–906 (2004)
63. Loh, T.P., et al.: Development of paediatric biochemistry centile charts as a complement to laboratory reference intervals. Pathology **46**(4), 336–343 (2014)
64. Arzideh, F., et al.: An improved indirect approach for determining reference limits from intra-laboratory data bases exemplified by concentrations of electrolytes/Ein verbesserter indirekter Ansatz zur Bestimmung von Referenzgrenzen mittels intra-laboratorieller Datensätze am Beispiel von Elektrolyt-Konzentrationen. J. Lab. Med. **33**(2), 52–66 (2009)
65. Arzideh, F., Wosniok, W., Haeckel, R.: Reference limits of plasma and serum creatinine concentrations from intra-laboratory data bases of several German and Italian medical centres: comparison between direct and indirect procedures. Clin. Chim. Acta **411**(3–4), 215–221 (2010)

A Visual-Based Energy Efficient Digital Agro (EE i-Agro) Project for Design & Technology Subject, Based on Computational Thinking Skills Across STEM

Halimah Badioze Zaman[1,3]($\boxtimes$), Rahimah Ismail[2], Nazrita Ibrahim[1,3], and Ummul Hanan Mohamad[2,3]

[1] Institute of Informatics and Computing in Energy (IICE), Universiti Tenaga Nasional, (UNITEN) Jalan Ikram, 43000 Kajang, Selangor, Malaysia
hbzivi@gmail.com
[2] Institute of Visual Informatics (IVI), Universiti Kebangsaan Malaysia, 43600 Bangi, Selangor, Malaysia
[3] Malaysian Information Technology Society (MITS), Bangi, Malaysia

Abstract. Computational Thinking (CT) is a concept used as a systemtic way of thinking and in problem-solving process, not just for computer science but other domains of knowledge. Various research conducted at high school and tertiary levels of education has shown that CT integrated into lessons across STEM have shown positive results. This study conducted at elementary school integrates CT with the Design and Technology (RBT) subject particularly in the Visual-Based Project Production Package Model (VB-P3) across STEM, using computational thinking skills, in the Energy Efficient i-Agro Reservoir Crop System (EE i-Agro) project production process for the Design and Technology (RBT) subject in primary schools. This package is aimed at improving students' problem-solving and thinking skills by making them more creative and innovative. The VB-P3 also includes the development of RBT Energy Efficient i-Agro learning model and modules (EEi-Agro LMM). The VB-P3 model was based on the 'prototyping' iterative model comprising of five (5) main phases; namely analysis, design, development, implementation, and evaluation with appropriate iteration. This model is also based on the COMEL learning model with attributes such as interactivity, fun learning, engaging and motivating, which helps students' learning, with additional components and elements. Hence, this paper highlights the evaluation of the Visual-Based Project Production Package Development (VB-P3) model to develop the Energy Efficient i-Agro Reservoir Crop System (EE i-Agro) Project which can improve thinking and problem-solving skills, to prepare students for the new learning environment and instill sustainability practices in students facing energy transition, climate change and global warming experienced globally.

Keywords: Computational Thinking · Design and Technology · Learning Model · Visual-based Energy Efficient Project · Sustainability

© The Author(s), under exclusive license to Springer Nature Singapore Pte Ltd. 2024
H. Badioze Zaman et al. (Eds.): IVIC 2023, LNCS 14322, pp. 508–525, 2024.
https://doi.org/10.1007/978-981-99-7339-2_42

1 Introduction

Energy Transition, climate change and global warming are challenges faced globally and Malaysia like the rest of the nations in the world have the aspiration to keep the promise made at the Paris Agreement in 2015 and reiterated at the Glasgow Convention in 2021 to be zero carbon emission nation by 2050. In order to do this, governments need to advocate and draw awareness to the whole population so that everyone contributes to making the country a neutral carbon nation. Advocacy and awareness must start from young and the best way to instill this awareness is through students in elementary schools. It was with this in mind, that the approach of integrating digital technology with computational thinking (CT) through an effective problem solving teaching and learning strategy, to teach the subject Design and Technology, specifically on the topic of modern Reservoir Crop System was raised. It was thought very apt and timely to design and develop a Visual-Based Project Production Package (VB-P3) model to develop the Energy Efficient i-Agro Reservoir Crop System (EE i-Agro) Project which includes both digital and computational thinking (CT) attributes as well as sustainability.

Computational thinking (CT) is important because it is stipulated in the Malaysian Education Development Plan (PPPM) 2015–2025, that the education system must be able to produce students who can communicate confidently, work effectively as a team, use critical, creative and innovative thinking, practice positive values in solving problems. Above all, they must be compettitive and aware of what is happening in the world. Thus, the education approaches and strategies undertaken are expected to produce students that are not only excellent in producing knowledge learned during examinations, but have acquired scientific, critical, creative and systematic thinking skills which gives them the skills needed to solve problems that is put forth to them. More often most studies in Malaysia [1, 2] have found that students that despite many efforts undertaken by the government to address this critical issue, data shows that students are still weak in thinking and problem solving. Although many students score excellent results in memory recollection questions in examinations, they fail to excel in problem solving type questions, due to the fact they are unable to solve the given problem systematically and effectively [1]. It has also shown in many studies that students generally are less capable to solve open-ended problems because they lack the practice, as well as the creativity and innovative thinking skills which CT can provide.

Imagination or reimagining is a concept that is important in a subject like Design and Technology (RBT). As one would imagine, creative and innovative thinking requires imagination and reimagining of things, concepts, ideas and surroundings. Thus, creativity and innovation encompasses reimagining or imaginative thinking [2, 3]. The Design and Technology (RBT) subject in Malaysia has undergone through many evolutions [4] and today its curriculum place imoortance on knowledge, problem solving skills, thinking skills and the process or working steps in realising the product expected from the project. The curriculum is created such that the students need to generate ideas through reimagining the porduct they want to create through ideation, and ensure that the end product design is solving a 'real' problem and can be applied meaningfully. This means that the ability to be creative and innovative – simply explained would be to have the ability to use one's imagination- to collect, recollect, digest and generate new or original ideas [3, 4] to produce a practical product to solve 'real' problem. Through this new curriculum, the teachers have a significant role in ensuring that the students that undergoe this subject will be able to generate new or original and practical ideas to solve 'real' problems imaginatively using various creative and innovative approaches.

2   Importance of Computational Thinking and Composition of its Elements

It is not a doubt that computational thinking is important for not only school children but everyone. Hence, it is important to be taught to students and it should be taught not as a 'stand alone' subject but integrated into the different domains of knowledge be it science or non science fields [5, 6, 8]. This is apparant in most studies conducted [7, 9, 10], that when CT is integrated well, it is promising in helping students to solve problems practically, critically, creatively and systematically. The CT skills also help them to think scientifically and analytically to solve complex 'real' problems [11, 12, 13]. Researchers on CT have not come to a real concensus on what is the composition of the elements that constitute the concept of CT. Table 1 shows the composition of the elements of CT by the respective researchers. Based on the table it can be observed that only three (3) elements: Decomposition, Abstraction and Algorithm are almost unanimously agreed as crucial to be included in the CT concept. However, all the other twelve (12) elements despite not unanimously agreed by the researchers do contribute to CT in one way or another. Thus, they are elements that can be considered when planning programmes to be integrated with CT.

Elements in CT contribute to creating thinking skills that can help students think analytically and systematically to solve complex 'real' problems and create products that are practical and useful [11, 13]. The Malaysian Education System has adopted the integration of CT in various subjects in schools since 2017 [14, 15]. However, since that time, not all teachers have mastered the skills in integrating CT in the subjects they are teaching. The same challenge is faced with teachers teaching Design and Technology (RBT). Teachers of Design and Technology (RBT) are still working hard in trying to integrate CT skills in their teaching especially on production projects. How do they ensure that CT elements that helps develop CT skills are incorporated in the process of imagining and reimagining of ideas when designing the Energy Efficient i-Agro Reservoir Crop System (EE i-Agro) production project. It was found that integrating CT effectively in this ideation process can help students' creativity in building innovative tools to design practical and useful product; in this project creating an energy efficient Reservoir Crop System that can have a significant impact to modern urban sustainable crop farming. When the system is perfected, it can even have an impact to society [16–19].

Elements:
D-Decomposition. Abs-Abstraction. Al-Algorithm. V-Visualisation. E-Evaluation. L-logic. PR-Pattern Recognition. P-Parallelism. G-Generalisation.Dg-Debugging. RD-Representation Data. S-Simulation. F-Formulation. C-Communication. I-Interactive. M-Modeling. MR-Mathematical Reasoning. Cn-Conception. CPS-Computational Problem Solution. DS-Designing Systems. Re - Reimagining.

Table 1. Elements of Computational Thinking (CT) Concept based on Researchers

Elements of CT Concept

	D	Abs	Al	V	E	L	PR	P	G	Dg	RD	S	F	C	I	M	MR	Cn	CPS	DS	Re
R1		/						/						/	/	/		/	/		
R2	/	/	/	/													/		/		
R3	/	/	/					/			/	/	/								
R4		/	/		/																
R5	/	/	/			/	/														
R6	/	/	/			/	/			/											
R7		/	/																		
R8	/	/	/	/	/		/		/												
R9	/	/	/	/	/	/	/														/
R10	/	/	/	/	/	/															
R11	/	/	/		/																
R12	/	/	/			/															
R13	/	/	/						/	/											
R14				/			/													/	
R15	/	/	/		/				/												
TOTAL	11	14	13	5	6	5	5	2	3	2	1	1	1	1	1	1	1	1	2	1	

* *Legend:*

Researchers

1. Wong [6]. 2. Shanmugam [11]. 3. ISTE & CSTA [38]. 4. Lee [32]. 5. Asarani & Yassin [13]. 6. Selby & Woodland [39]. 7. Yuliana [40]. 8. Angeli [17]. 9. Halimah [10, [45]. 10. Azlin [41]. 11. Fagerlund [18]. 12. Brackman [42]. 13. Chalmers [43]. 14. Voogt [8]. 15. Yadav [9].

3 Material and Development Methodology of EE i-Agro

The methodology applied in this study involved the development and the observational approach. The development approach was applied to the development of the Visual-based Production Project Package (VB-P3) model and the development of the Energy Efficient i-Agro Reservoir Crop System (EE i-Agro) production project. This paper shall highlight the development methodology of the VB-P3 model and the observational approach on the ideation process of designing the Energy Efficient i-Agro Crop System (EE i-Agro). This is to observe in detail how CT skills (mainly through the elements of CT) are integrated in the process of imagining and reimagining when creating the EE i-Agro production project.

3.1 Prototyping Iterative Life Cycle Development Model of VB-P3

The Prototyping Iterative Life Cycle Development Model of VB-P3 was developed to create a systematic methodology to design and develop the Energy Efficient Reservoir Crop System (EE i-Agro) project. Figure 1 shows the Prototyping Iterative Life Cycle Development model of the Visual-Based Project Production Package (VB-P3).

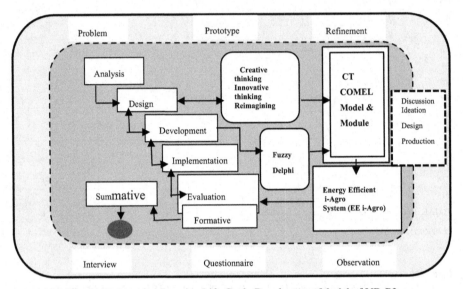

Fig. 1. Prototyping Iterative Life Cycle Development Model of VB-P3

For this paper, the Prototyping Iterative Life Cycle Development model of the Visual-based Project Production Package (VB-P3) will focus on the development Module of EE i-Agro (MEE i-Agro)) and the summative evaluation of the Design and Technology Learning Module integrating CT Skills Across STEM (LM-CTSTEM-EE i-Agro), which was created based on the Design and Technology Learning Model for primary schools adopted from the CTCOMEL learning model [12, 20] (the CTCOMEL learning model will not be discussed here, as it has been discussed in other published works) [12, 20] and digital EE i-Agro worksheets or e-EE i-Agro Sheets.

3.2 Learning Modules: MEE i-AGRO and *e-EE i-Agro Sheets*

The MEE i-AGRO module and e-EE i-Agro Sheets were designed and developed for the teaching and learning of the RBT subject, in ensuring the effectiveness of conducting the Visual-Based Project Production Package (VB-P3)activities effectively. The Development of MEE i-Agro module was developed based on the fundamental components and elements of the CTCOMEL Learning Model, comprising basic learning theories, teaching and learning strategies, planned learning, computational thinking approach, inquiry and imaginative thinking and learning assessment. This production package topic is depicted in the MEE i-Agro module as indicted in Fig. 2. This learning module is used throughout the project production activities that were conducted either physical or online approach. The e-EE i-Agro Sheets was uploaded into the Google Classroom of Elementary Class 5.

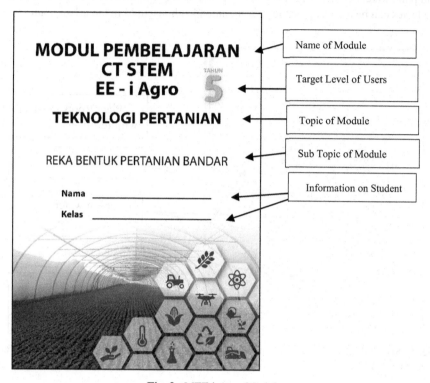

Fig. 2. MEE i-Agro Module

The MEE i-Agro will be the guide to the students on how they can start their Project Production on Energy Efficient crop farming. The module will give examples graphically on how farming of fruits and vegetables are done to give them the initial ideas. They have to think in their respective groups (four in a group) how they can grow fruits or vegetables in the modern urban lifestyle (in high rise homes such as flats, apartments or condominiums). During their discussions, they will integrate the CT elements of creativity, visualisation with reimagining, the latest element introduced by [25–27] then sketch the ideas in the MEE-i-Agro module that has blank notes for students their related ideas to the topic taught. Figure 3 shows one of the sketches done by one of the groups in Kelas 5.

Based on the diagram, the sketch done by the members of Group 4, from Kelas 5 Pintar is interesting. As observed during the Ideation stage, their discussions were dynamic, with all four (4) giving their ideas and one (1) member (amongst this four) was sketching it out to make sense of the ideas. They had tried many ideas and this was the final version of their expected product, to design and develop a water reservoir crop planting system that would help save energy. The idea to use a water pump and connect it to a controller that will time the water flow that is need to ensure that the roots of the plants will get the balance nutrients from the water and the electric pump will be stopped at certain time of the day so that the use of energy is efficient and the electricity used to pump the water necessary for the plants and the living organisms in the water, including the fishes can be an energy saving for the intended household in the urban homes.

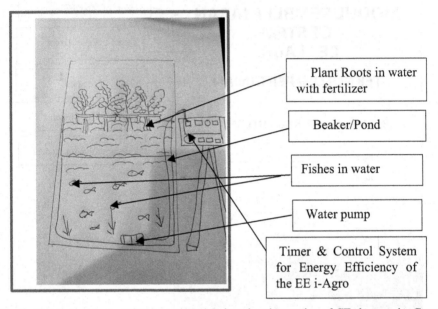

Fig. 3. Sketch done in the MEE i-Agro Module based on integration of CT elements by Group 4, Kelas 5 Pintar

Thus, through the observation made using the VB-P3 Observational Checklist (VB-P3OC), it had clearly shown the importance of CT integration in the ideation process. The observational findings showed the outcome which is indicated as the sketch shown in Fig. 3, the obvious use of generation of ideas, decomposition, abstraction, logic, reimagining and visualisation, which all represent CT elements. Thus, the process of ideation in the design of project production in Design & Technology (RBT) subject for elementary 5, requires the integration of CT elements.

The other learning module in the VB-P3 Package is the *e-EE i-Agro Sheets* that is indictaed in. Figure 4. Based on this module, each student can access the *e-EE i-Agro Sheet* using the Ministry of Education (MOE) email given to each student. This module was created in both Malay and English version and had undergone the required validity testing conducted by module development experts and RBT Teachers.

The *e-EE i-Agro Sheets* module allow teachers and students to conduct the analysis and design stage of the Project Production both physically and online. This *e-EE i-Agro Sheets* were generated using the.

LiveWorkSheet (LWS) application. Figure 4 shows the digital *e-EE i-Agro Sheets* used by the students during the implementation of the *Reservoir Crop* EE i-Agro system based on the Visual-Based Project Production Package (VB-P3).

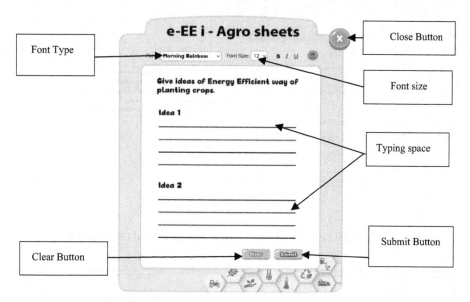

Fig. 4. The digital Learning Module: *e-EE i-Agro Sheets of the VB-P3*

The *e-EE i-Agro Sheets* were designed as as an interactive and fun learning resource for students. They can access it wherever they are.

Figure 5 shows the section of the *e-EE i-Agro Sheets* of the LWS apps which provides a variety of attractive colour options that allow the students to use the colours to highlight the questions and answers they give in the diagrams available in the e-EE-i-Agro sheets based on the colours provided. This makes the question and answering process of the lesson conducted more engaging and motivating for the students.

Figure 6 shows the finish button in the Digital Learning Module of *e-EE i-Agro Sheets* allows the students to press the 'finish button' as soon as they are confident with their answers. This increases their self efficacy and confidence in conductiong their activities. They all will have almost 'personalised questions' as the questions are generalised enough that will fit any design done by the groups on the reservoir crop system solution that each group had produced, and uploaded the sketch of their team's 'reservoir crop system' that they did in the MEE i-Agro Module, into the digital module *e-EE i-Agro Sheets*.

e-EE i-Agro Sheets of the VB-PP3

They then move on to the digital learning module to answer the questions in the LWS apps. As soon as they have completed the tasks of answering the questions and had pressed the finish button, the marks they achieved will be displayed. This immediate response encourages students to use the system because they did not have to wait to see to see their achievements.

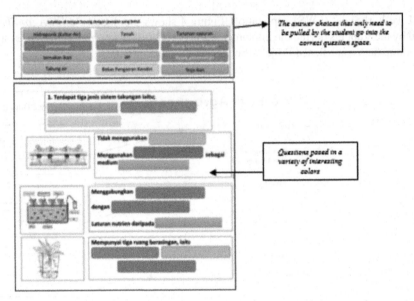

Fig. 5. Digital Learning Module: Section on Personalized Color section

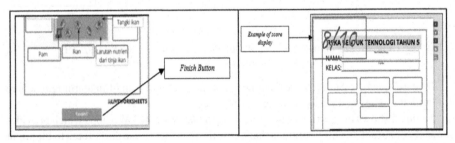

Fig. 6. Digital Learning Module of e-EE i-Agro Sheets of the VB-P3: Finish Button & Score Display Section

This also helps students to gain their confidence and efficacy levels in problem-solving related to the subject of design and technology generally, and the design of 'reservoir crop system' specifically.

4 Results and Discussions

The results of the study were obtained from the following: i. Observation conducted on the classroom interaction between teacher and students as teacher runs the induction process before introducing the lesson on the topic of 'reservoir crop system'; ii. Observation conducted on the students as they were undergoing their ideation process and implementing their ideas into production; iii. Observation of integration of CT skills in teaching & learning by students; iv. Observation on practice through exercises conducted by students on their project; v. Questionnaire administered on students on the e- modules; vi. Interviews conducted with teachers on strengths and weaknesses of the modules.

4.1 Findings on Study Conducted on Classroom Interaction During the Design and Technology (RBT) Class for Year 5

Observational Evaluation at Induction of Lesson.
This observational evaluation was conducted during the induction stege of the lesson of RBT, on the topic, Reservoir Crop System. Observations were administered by RBT teachers, appointed as study informants and by the researchers themselves using an observation checklist. Based on the instrument used, that is the observational checklist, the findings can be summarised as indicated in Table 2.

During the induction, the teacher showed to class a video on modern farming using many techniques such as hydrophonics, aquaphonics, fertigation, rooftop and vertical farming. The idea was to excite and motivate students to be engaged in the lesson that was going to be taught by the teacher. The objective was also to engage students in discussions and test on their existing experience and knowledge on agriculture and urban farming.

Teacher probe students during the discussion so as to encourage them to use their CT skills in making critical observations and thinking creatively and systematically when giving their suggestions. Teachers want the students to think of all the experience that they have on farming generally, then decompose the ideas, make abstraction, pattern recognise some of the previous farminig techniques that they know and answer the questions by the teacher with best answer that is logical, scientific, but creative as well as innovative.

As can be observed from Table 2, teacher scaffolds students to be involved in recall, recollection, decomposition and abstraction on their previous experience and knowledge, in order to make logical and scientific decision on which technique they like best and why. This has helped the students make critical and constructive conclusion when arriving at the solution they provide.

Observational Evaluation on Application of CT Skills in Learning Process of RBT.
Based on the in-depth observation made using the observational checklist, findings indicated that the students constantly applied CT skills throughout the RBT classroom [28–30] session, especially during the visual-based EE iAgro system develoment project. This was clearly observed during the ideation and design sequence stage when the actual skteches were done and the system implemented. The findings in this observation was based on the activity conducted to produce the visual sketches for the EE i-Agro project using the CT-Imagining-Pattern Recognition-Decomposition-Abstraction-Algorithm (CT-IPDAA) approach. Each group will try to produce a design based on the members' ideas. They adopted the imagining concept and pattern recognise what they know, experience and research. When they have gathererd all the information they needed, they decompose, make abstraction and apply the correct steps to finally sktech the design based on the concept and attributes of the design that the group have agreed upon. It was observed that the groups has adopted the CT skills systematically [21, 28] by

Table 2. Observational Evaluation of Students at Induction of Lesson

Source	Statement
Teacher	Tell me what you saw on the video?
Student 1 (S1)	Farming…Hyro farming, teacher
Student 2 (S2)	At my house, we have vertical plants…. You can buy from the nursery…
Student 3 (3)	I see before…. Strawberries grown using hydrophonics.
Teacher	Okay… Lets go step by step… What did you see first in the video – tell me which technique did you first saw and subsequently?
Student 3 (3)	First… I think… They showed hydrophonics technique growing melons in Selangor; then teacher,….. They showed aquaphonics technique growing spinash in Sabah; and lastly, they showed vertical farming growing strawberries in Fraser's Hill….right teacher?…
Teacher	Yes, good S3, Anyone wants to tell me which technique you have seen in real life before? Which technique you like best and why?
Student 1 (S1)	I have seen hydrophonics…. in growing tomatoes…. I follwed my father to a tomato farm. The process I saw quite complicated….. But I like aquaphonics best of all ----- Because I can breed fish and grow plants at the same time…….. Yes that is why teacher
Student 2 (S2)	I too like aquaphonics teacher… You can have two living things at the same time ---
Student 3 (3)	Teacher… Actually, all interesting… But… They all are not easy to do… But in urban houses--- maybe best is aquaphonics… Can have 'artificial pond' and grow plants at the same time
Teacher	Class you are all corret…. Now I want you to break in your groups and discuss on the best technique and how can you create an energy efficient agriculture technique for urban farming that can be sold as a product for others to buy

implementing the CT-IPDAA approach in creating the sktech design for the EE i-Agro production project.

Based on Table 3, it is clear that *Group 2, Kelas 5 Pintar* were successful in integrating CT skills in the Ideation/Imagining stage of the Design process of their EE i-Agro production project using the CT-IPDAA approach. It was interesting to observe that throughout the session, there was talking and laughing noise amongst the students. They all were having fun.

Questionnaire Evaluation on Students' Statement on the Activities of Project Production: Open Ended Question.

Table 4, shows results of the statements made by the students through the open ended questions of the questionnaire administered during the learning activities related to the Energy Efficient i-Agro system for the topic *Agricultural Technology*, of the Design & Technology (RBT) subject for Year 5. Results of the open-ended question, eight (8) students demonstrated that they all enjoyed the activities conducted during the project

Table 3. Observation on use of CT in Ideation/Imagining Stgae (CT-IPDAA)

Source	Statement/Mannerism/Gesture	
Group 2 (Kelas 5 Pintar)		CT-IPDAA
Student 3 (S3)	*"Okay lets all think what we know about reservoir crop system atau sistem tanaman takungan untuk rumah di bandar,.........macam rumah pangsa...kondo....Imagine what sistem is suitable....."* *[Everyone was silent...thinking and imagining.Then after 10 min S1 broke the silence]*	**Imagining (I)**
Student 1 (S1)	*"We know about hydophonics, aquaphonics and aquaphonics....I think it is sesuai for kondo....Let's do aqua hydrophonics..."*	**Pattern Recognition (P)**
Student 4 (4)	*[S4 looks in deep thoughts...then he answered]* *Ya setuju...*	*[Response to I and P above]*
Student 3(S3)	*S2.....*"what do you think?"	
Student 2 (S2)	*"Ya, aqua hydrophonics is doable..... Hydrophonics sukar....vertical farming too is difficult... ya saya setuju "[all agree and smile]*	**Decomposition (D)**
Student3 (3)	*"Okay so out of the three methods, we choose aqua hydrophonics.... What do we know about this method?.... if we want to sketch need to know this method well.... Many ways to do... What do we do?"*	**Abstraction (A)**
Student 4 (S4)	*"We can use a fish pond...indoor fish pond...in a big glass bekas...trough...let's check buku MM-EE i-Agro"*	*[Response to D and A above]*
Student 1 (S1)	*"Yes we could have pump to make sure the nutrients from the fish get to the roots of the plant... Kita boleh tanam spinach...bayam..."*	*[Response to D and A above]*
Student 3 (S3)	*"Haaaa....Idea bagus tu... Cikgu kata sistem mesti jimat dan cekap tenaga atau apa? enery efficient.?., maybe kita boleh guna timer "*	*[Response to D and A above*

(continued)

Table 3. (*continued*)

Source	Statement/Mannerism/Gesture	
Student 2 (S2)	*"Kena tambah pengawal – sistem kawal supaya boleh kawal bila switch on atau off dari jauh....rumah saya ada sistem kawal----boleh dapat senang..."*	*[Response to D and A above]*
Student 3 (S3)	*"Let now go step by step so senang nak sketch nanti....."* *[They then went through step by step on how they will design the EE i-Agro sistem – the Spinach reservoir crop system]* *[They successfully conducted the design process applying the CT-IPDAA]*	***Algorithm (A)***

Table 4. Students' Statement on the Activities of Modules VB-P3

Source (Students)	Statement
S1	*"I have never done a project on growing vegetables this way before..."*
S2	*"This is my first time planting spinach this way..... Having a fish pond at the same time..."*
S3	*"I think it's the best activity I have done so far. The reason is that I have never planted any plants in myy life... it's hard...to plant. But perbincangan with friends help make it easier...."*
S4	*"I like this activity very much....we can create anything we like....use modern way to plant in water... And also use technology"*
S5	*"I like because planting in way safe energy. This is new to me"*
S6	*" Before, tak suka tanam pokok. But this activity makes planting interesting and fun....the modules help a lot..."*
S7	*"I like this activity because we think together...I don't have do alone...we can kongsi...share ideas...choose best way to do the project...."*
S8	*"I like the doing part....setting the trough....the pump....and controller...then the spinach....and all*

production and observation of the process showed that they were successful in setting up the aqua hydrophonics system.

Interview Schedule Administered on Students: Statement on e-EE i-Agro Sheets.

The exercises were done on the e-EE i-Agro worksheets by the students either in the class or at home using the LiveWorkSheet (LWS) application. They can take their time, but needs to be completed within a stipulated time. This aims to train the students to be more focused and responsible for their own learning and to encourage self- efficacy. As

Table 5. Students Statement on e-EE i-Agro Sheets based on Interview Schedule

Source (Students)	Statement
S1	*"I like doing excercises in the eEE iAgro Sheets. I can try many times before I submit....if not happy can clear....happy only submit...*
S2	*"...I like it best about eEE iAgro Sheets...because can see marks immediately when finish......press submit then lastly finish button...marks "*
S3	*"e-Agro sheets very nice. Easy to use. I like it....."*
S4	*"Best sangat....when...happy with my answer.... I submit...Anyway more energy saving...dont waste time too long on computer"*
S5	*"e iAgro Sheets very nice...I can type use fon I like....can choose Malay or English,...can erase, can do again---and again untul happy with answer...i like best the marks...immediate..very good"*
S6	*"I like it because can upload sketch that we do also...can show teacher our design in the eAgro sheet"*
S7	*"I like because I can do at home...it is fun to do... Not stress...save electricity...save energy"*
S8	*"the eAgro sheet through the LWS application is easy to use...I like it....I don't have to write.. Just type and can upload our sketch design...no waste time..save energy"*

indicated fromm Table 5, findings from the interview using the instrument: interview schedule/tool, shows that all students were very happy using using the e-EE i-Agro Sheets through the LWS interactive application because it is easy and fun to use and they mentioned saving energy. This is a development with the students that is very positive that they are concern over energy effiency and energy saving. The fact that this practice will lead to better sustainability of the planet is a development that needs to be further encouraged.

Interview Schedule Administered on Teachers Pertaining to Digital Resource Support.

Based on the interviews with the teachers on the effectiveness of the digital learning modules as resource support, showed that both teachers (T1 and T2) were satisfied with them as indicated in Table 6.

Interview Schedule Administered on Teachers Pertaining to Urban Agriculture Activities.

Based on the interview administered to the teachers pertaining to urban agriculture activities, it was found that both teachers (T1 and T2) were satisfied with the learning activities on urban agriculture carried out. As indicated in Table 7, both teachers' statements were positive and agreeable to the effectiveness of the urban agriculture activities conducted.

Table 6. Teachers' Statements on EE i-Agro Sheets based on Interview Schedule

Source Teachers	Statement
T1	*"From my observation, it is obvious that the students are having so much fun when they are going through the VB-P3 project production activities. The supporting modules, MM EE i-Agro book and the EE i-Agro Sheets... Looks like it is easier for the students to follow the lesson and can be left independently to work in their groups and on their own when necessary.....* "
T2	*" I find the digital modules developed and used by the students are very effective, because the students find them simple to use, also—the CT skills emmbedded to help students in the process of design...especially the steps towards the design during the ideation untul implementation is really effective....The element of energy efficiency and energy saving element is very good and timely* *The digital EE i-Agro Sheets is really helpful and students seemed to find it... Motivating ----fun...I like that they can write and upload their design sketches. Easy for teachres like me to check... it is really a good resource..support...."*

Table 7. Teachers' Statement on Urban Agriculture Activities based on Interview Schedule

Source Teachers	Statement
T1	*"I find the activities conducted are suitable for the students......especially they live in the city...the need for reservoir crop farming-in whatever form, whether hydrophonics, acquaphnics or vertical farming....an be somthing they can identify with.... Their lives..."* *"...mostly, the students live in apartments. Limited land to do real farming on the ground... They are used to see plants in pots or containers...So when this module exposes to new ways of planting in reservoirs...they are excited that there are alternative ways to do planting even in their type of homes... so this is really good experience for them... The modules I find really effective to run activities on urban agriculture....."*
T2	*"I no doubt find the activities on the production of reservoir planting projects...very interesting and related to the real lives of the students...I am sure that they are very happy to have this knowlege and skill to later develop one for their home..."* *"... Its great also that the modules allow the students to be creative and innovative and come up with the best approach to solve the problem given to them ---I really like this..."*

5   Conclusion

Therefore, this study had discussed on the Visual Based Project Production Package (VB-P3) which involved the development of the learning modules: Energy Efficient Module of EE i-Agro (MEE i-Agro) which is a digital or a conventional guide book taht also allows the students to do their sketching in there; and the digital Energy Efficient i-Agro Worksheets or *e-EE i-Agro Sheets* which allows students to do their ideation, and answer some questions on reservoir crop system or aquaphonics farming. In this digital system they can also upload their sketches on the system that they design.The whole learning process related to the design and development of the reservoir crop system or the aquaphonics Energy Efficient i-Agro (urban agriculture/urban farming) was based on the Computational Thinking IPDAA approach. The CT-IPDAA approach involved the process of reimagining using CT skills which involved the elements of imagining, pattern recognition, decomposition, abstraction, and algorithm. This approach had successfully helped the students to produce a creative and innivative Energy Efficient aquaphonics system (EE i-Agro system).

The CT approach used was effective in conducting the production project of the Design and Technology (RBT) subject for elementary 5. The modules created as well as the approach embedded was seen to be able to improve the problem-solving skills of the students. The use of the two modules had increased students'confidence in condcuting the activities both in the clssroom and on their own. The digital worksheets or the eEE i-Agro Worksheets had increased students' motivation to complete the exercises given by the teacher. The immediate response on the scoring made students more motivated to complete the tasks assigned to them. This finding is supported by the study conducted by Lee [21] which found that students learn faster when technology-assisted learning was used. This project was important as the production of the *Energy Efficient urban agriculture of EE i-Agro system* project can inculcate environmental sustainability and the importance energy efficiency and energy savings early in students' lives. This practice of environmental sustainability should be nurtured [22–24] in schools. This project had not only successfully achieved the learning outcomes of the topic but also inculcated the students' interest in energy efficiency, environmental sustainability and foster CT skills across STEM.

Acknowledgment. This research was supported by Tan Sri Leo Moggie Chair, Institute of Informatics and Computing in Energy (IICE), Universiti Tenaga Nasional (UNITEN). The authors would like to thank the Chair for funding this publication.

References

1. Hadi, S.A., Susantini, E., Agustini, R.: Training of students' critical thinking skills through the implementation of a modified free inquiry model. J. Phys. Conf. Ser. **947**(1), 012063 (2018)
2. Wormmack, A.: The Power of Imagination: Unlocking Your Ability to Receive from God. Harrison House Publishers, Tulsa (2019)
3. Ismail, A. et al.: Sains Insani eISSN : [0127–7871] Pembentukan Pemikiran Kreatif dan Kritis : Hubungannya Dalam, no. August (2020)

4. MOE. KSSR: curriculum standards document assessment and year five design and technology (1st ed; Curriculum Development Division, Ed.). Ministry of Education Malaysia, Putrajaya (2017).[2]
5. Lucas, B.: Teaching and assessing creativity in schools in England. Impact J. **7**(September), 5–8 (2019)
6. Wing, J.M.: Computational thinking's influence on research and education for all Influenza del pensiero computazionale nella ricerca e nell'educazione per tutti. Ital. J. Educ. Technol. **25**(2), 7–14 (2017)
7. Ubaidullah, N.H., Mohamed, Z., Hamid, J.: Improving novice students' computational thinking skills by problem-solving and metacognitive techniques **20**(6), 88–108 (2021)
8. Voogt, J., Fisser, P., Good, J., Mishra, P., Yadav, A.: Computational thinking in compulsory education: towards an agenda for research and practice. Educ. Inf. Technol. **20**(4), 715–728 (2015)
9. Yadav, A., Hong, H., Stephenson, C.: Computational thinking for all: pedagogical approaches to embedding 21st century problem solving in K-12 classrooms. TechTrends **60**(6), 565–568 (2016)
10. Zaman, H.B., et al.: Integrating computational thinking (CT) with English across STEM. UKM, Bangi (2019)
11. Shanmugam, L., Yassin, S.F., Khalid, F.: Enhancing students' motivation to learn computational thinking through mobile application development module (M-CT). Int. J. Eng. Adv. Technol. **8**(5), 1293–1303 (2019). https://doi.org/10.1017/CBO9780511781629.020
12. Zaman, H.B.: Computational Thinking (CT) across STEM model in teaching English amongst elementary school children in Kedah, Malaysia. Digital Transformation Landscape in the Fourth Industrial Revolution (4IR) era. In VIIS 2018. IVI, UKM, Bangi (2018)
13. Asarani, U.H.M., Yassin, S.F.M.: Pengintegrasian Pemikiran Komputasional Dalam Aktiviti Pengaturcaraan Dan Robotik. Int. J. Educ. Pedagog. **2**(2), 124–133 (2020)
14. MOE. Info Media. BPPDP Bil. (2) March - April edition. Education Policy Planning and Research Division, MOE (2019)
15. Zhang, L.C., Nouri, J.: A systematic review of learning computational thinking through scratch in K-9. Comput. Educ. **141** (2019)
16. Carlborg, N., Tyrén, M., Heath, C., Eriksson, E.: The scope of autonomy when teaching computational thinking in primary school. Int. J. Child-Computer Interact. **21**, 130–139 (2019). https://doi.org/10.1016/j.ijcci.2019.06.005
17. Angeli, C.: Computational thinking education: Issues and challenges. Comput. Hum. Behav., p. 106185 (2020). https://linkinghub.elsevier.com/retrieve/pii/S074756321930397
18. Fagerlund, J., Häkkinen, P., Vesisenaho, M., Viiri, J.: Computational thinking in programming with scratch in primary schools: a systematic review. Comput. Appl. Eng. Educ. **29**(1), 12–28 (2021)
19. Haseski, H.I., Ilic, U.: An investigation of the data collection instruments developed to measure computational thinking. Inf. Educ. **18**(2), 297–319 (2019). https://www.mii.lt/informatics_in_education/htm/infedu.2019.14.htm
20. Zaman, H.B., Ahmad, A. (eds.): Teknologi Fusion dan Pemikiran Komputasional bagi Kesediaan Data Terbuka. Penerbit UKM, Bangi (2020)
21. Chai, C.S. Chen, D.: A review on usability evaluation methods for instructional multimedia: an analytical framework. Instr. J. Multimedia 31(3), 231 (2004). ERIC http://www.eric.ed.gov/contentdelivery/servlet/ERICServlet?acc.no=ED501628
22. Lee, C., Yeung, A.S., Cheung, K.W.: Leaner perceptions versus technology usage: a study of adolescent English learners in Hong Kong secondary schools. Comput. Educ. **133**, 13–26 (2019)
23. Debrah, J.K., Vidal, D.G., Alzira, M., Dinis, P.: Raising awareness on solid waste management through formal education for sustainability : a developing countries (2021)

24. Othman, M., Ahmad, N., Suif, Z., Jelani, J., Munikanan, V.: Recycling waste practice in campus towards a green campus and promotion of environmental sustainability, vol. 4, no. 1, pp. 13–17 (2021)
25. Abril, A.M., Salazar-mendias, C., Valenzuela, L.R.: Sustainability consciousness and experiential learning through a native flora garden, no. March (2022)
26. Zaman, H.B.: New elements in CT learning model. Unpublished (2022)
27. Canfield, J., Smith, G.: Imagine: Ideation Skills for Improvement and Innovation Today. Blacklake Press, New York (2023)
28. Nagle, G.M.: Breakthrough Thinking Series. The Ideation Emporium of Creativity, New York (2023)
29. Kelly, N., Gero, J.: Design thinking and computational thinking: a dual process model for addressing design problems. Des. Sci. (2021). https://doi.org/10.1017/dsj.2021.7.Licens eCCBY-NC-SA4.0
30. Wang, W., Jia, Y., Yu, W.: An Aquaponics system design for computational intelligence teaching. IEEE Access, pp (99):1–1 (2020). https://doi.org/10.1109/ACCESS.2020.2976956. License CC BY 4.0
31. Othman, W.A.F.W.: Smart aquaponics system: design and implementation usingrduino microcontroller. Int. J. Res. 5(21), 645–653 (2018)

Multilingual Speech Emotion Recognition Using Deep Learning Approach

Chu Sheng Liau and Kai Sze Hong[✉]

Department of Electrical and Electronics Engineering, Faculty of Engineering and Technology,
Tunku Abdul Rahman University of Management and Technology, 53300 Kuala Lumpur,
Malaysia
hongks@tarc.edu.my

Abstract. Human emotion is an inherent part of human beings, and it is used to express their feelings to the listeners. While emotions are mostly conveyed via facial expressions, spoken words also contain emotions to reflect a speaker's emotional state. This project focused on researching and evaluating the deep neural network performance on multi-lingual speech emotion recognition on RAVDESS, EMO-DB and combination of both emotional speech databases. Methodology used in the project was divided into five steps: data collection and speech signal extraction, signal conversion, image recognition using transfer learning, result validation and implementation of trained network in graphical user interface (GUI). The research on AlexNet and SqueezeNet in transfer learning was carried out by training the networks using different number of maximum epochs, learning rate and image augmentations. The research showed that AlexNet provided the higher validation accuracy than SqueezeNet at 66.20% during training the combined RAVDESS and EMO-DB databases. As for the testing data, the trained model obtained an F1-score of 0.6253 on testing 264 sample data.

Keywords: Signal Conversion · Transfer Learning · Validation Accuracy · F1-Score

1 Introduction

1.1 Research Background

Emotion is an integral part of human beings as an indicative sign of a person's current feeling, and it is expressed via facial expressions and speech. People often experience different kinds of emotions such as sadness, happiness, anger, surprise and many others, therefore understanding one's emotional state can help to benefit one's mental well-being. For example, providing counselling to people who are in need of psychological assistance and recommending suitable music or songs based on their current emotion.

Emotion is easier to discern by facial expressions which is a visual information that is perceivable by human eyes. Speech emotion, is an auditory information that needs to be listened carefully by human ears in order to understand the emotions within.

H. Badioze Zaman et al. (Eds.): IVIC 2023, LNCS 14322, pp. 526–540, 2024.
https://doi.org/10.1007/978-981-99-7339-2_43

1.2   Problem Statement

Nowadays, many people are using music streaming platforms such as Spotify and YouTube to listen to the music for stress relief. The recommendation system in both applications is based on the users' frequently played songs or music, showing them their possible preferences. However, these applications lack the speech emotion recognition feature that recommends the suitable types of music and songs.

1.3   Research Objectives

This project aims to research and develop a speech emotion recognition system using deep learning approach. Secondly, the current existing works on multi-lingual emotion recognition will be researched. Third aim is to evaluate and fine-tune the neural networks to be suited for multi-lingual speech emotion recognition.

1.4   Scope and Contribution

Many researches on speech emotion recognition are only mono-lingual, which only one language is focused. This project is multi-lingual, involving two languages of speech emotions to be trained on and recognized. This project focuses on the speech emotion recognition of German and Northern American English languages. Deep learning neural network for recognition would be trained and tested using MATLAB software. This research study will enable us to detect emotions from different language speakers.

2   Literature Review

Several research works on the field of speech emotion recognition had been conducted by researchers. Various methodologies were used in previous works such as MFCC and spectrograms for audio feature extraction; CNN, RNN and SVM etc. for speech emotion classification based on the features extracted from speech signal input. The accuracy and performance of emotion recognition varied with many factors such as the deep neural networks, emotional speech database used and feature selection.

2.1   Existing Speech Databases

EMO-DB

EMO-DB is one of the publicly available databases with emotional speech. It is a German-language database consisting of 10 selected actors recording speeches with 7 variants of emotions including neutral, anger, fear, joy, sadness, disgust and boredom, in a well-equipped anechoic chamber of the Technical Acoustics Department, Technical University of Berlin, Germany [1]. An anechoic chamber is a special room used for performing antenna measurement for its effectiveness of energy radiation in the desired directions, and it is highly crucial that the room must be free from surrounding environment that may affect the measurements [2].

The EMO-DB database contains 800 speeches, with 10 different sentences each spoken by the 10 actors (5 males and 5 females) to simulate 7 different emotions together with second versions of these utterances [1].

RAVDESS

RAVDESS, or the Ryerson Audio-Visual Database of Emotional Speech and Song in full, is a validated multi-modal database of emotional speeches and songs [3]. RAVDESS dataset is one of the audio-visual datasets that offers a large number of datasets for emotion classification, which contains a total of 7356 recordings with 3 modality formats: audio-visual, video-only and audio-only produced by 24 gender-balanced professional actors (12 males and 12 females) vocalizing lexically-matched statements in neutral Northern American accent.

RAVDESS dataset contains recordings with 8 simulated different emotions, namely neutral, calm, happy, sad, angry, fearful, disgust and surprised. Inside the dataset, all files are properly labelled and named using a 7-part numerical identifier to distinguish each recording. One of the features that makes RAVDESS stands out from other emotional speech datasets is the presence of emotional intensity. Except neutral, the remaining 7 emotions were recorded with normal and strong intensity to portray the different degree of emotion intensity in real-life situations [3].

Comparison of Different Emotional Speech Databases

Table 1 summarizes the difference between EMO-DB and RAVDESS databases in terms of their languages, number of emotions contained and number of audio recordings.

Table 1. Summary of EMO-DB and RAVDESS databases.

Databases	EMO-DB	RAVDESS
Language	German	English
Number of emotions	7	8
Number of audio recordings	800	1440
Source of recordings	Studio recording	Studio recording

Multi-lingual

The next research involving the field of speech emotion recognition was CNN-based SER proposed by Huang, Dong, Mao and Zhan [14]. Huang et al. [14] proposed using semi-CNN to learn the affect-salient features of speech signals for SER and the accuracy was evaluated on four public emotional speech databases, which are Surrey Audio-Visual Expressed Emotion Database (SAVEE), EMO-DB, Danish Emotional Speech Database (DES) and Mandarin Emotional Speech Database (MES) using 5-fold cross validation. Experiments showed that these four databases yielded high performance of salient features with respect to speaker variations and environment disturbances comparing to spectrogram, acoustic features, Teager Energy Operator (TEO) and Local Invariant Features (LIF) [14].

According to Han, Yu and Tashev [15], the emotion recognition using deep neural networks (DNNs) and extreme learning machine (ELM) to learn the emotional information from low-level features demonstrated an improvement of 20% in accuracy as compared to other state-of-the-art deep learning approaches. Interactive Emotional Dyadic Motion Capture (IEMOCAP) database was adopted for evaluating their proposed method. The results reported as had outperformed the Hidden Markov Model (HMM) and open-source emotion and effect recognition toolkit (OpenEAR) for both unweighted (40.2% to 48.2%) and weighted accuracy (45.1% to 54.3%). ELM and kernel ELM (KELM) had equal performance and outperformed SVM by 5%. In a paper investigating the methods of SER published by Kerkeni et al. [16], recurrent neural network (RNN) classifier was implemented in EMO-DB and Spanish emotional speech database (INTER1SP) and was compared to multivariate linear regression (MLR) and SVM classifiers. In the research, they reported a superior accuracy of 90.05% using RNN classifier with combination of MFCC and modulation spectral features (MSFs) in INTER1SP database compared to EMO-DB with 58.51% accuracy [16]. On the other hand, Hossain & Muhammad (2019) elaborated the emotion recognition using deep learning approach from emotional big data [19].

2.2 Speech Front-End Feature Extraction

Feature extraction is an essential part of the majority of deep learning applications. It is analogous to how human brains recognize something by learning to differentiate the features, deep learning networks recognize or classify objects by extracting and "learning" their important features and getting output with desired results.

Mel-Frequency Cepstral Coefficients (MFCCs)

MFCC is one of the most popular acoustic feature extraction techniques in various speech recognition tasks as it has an advantage of being less complicated in the implementation of feature extraction algorithm [4, 5]. MFCC is modeled after the human hearing system describing the hearing mechanism of human ears assuming that human ear is a good speaker recognizer [6]. In mel-frequency scale, frequencies below 1000 Hz are linearly spaced and above 1000 Hz are logarithmically spaced, hence replicating the non-linear nature of human auditory frequency response [6].

In speech emotion recognition applications, the number of MFCCs taken for feature extraction is usually 13 which contains important acoustic information from human vocal tract. Vocal tract can be understood as a filter response for the sound produced by vibrations.

Spectrogram

Spectrogram is a visual representation of frequency spectrum at an instant of speech duration and is visualized by a graph of frequency versus time, in a form of scaled coloured image. Spectrogram is one of the most commonly used feature extractors because it maps the raw audio data to a more organized representation giving detailed information about the speech signal [7].

Shen et al. [8] used mel-spectrogram as inputs for conditioning WaveNet in natural text-to-speech synthesis. In this paper, Shen et al. [8] also stated that mel-spectrograms are more lossy than linear spectrogram due to more discarded audio information, but offer simpler and low-level acoustic representations of speech signal. Figure 2 shows an example of mel-spectrograms of 8 different speech emotions from RAVDESS database plotted using MATLAB.

2.3 Deep Learning Neural Networks

Artificial neural networks (ANNs) are computational processing architectures which the core idea was inspired from the living organisms' biological nervous system, such as the human brain. ANNs are primarily made up of a large number of interconnected "neurons" or computational nodes, working together to learn from the input in order to optimize the final output.

Convolutional Neural Network (CNN)
CNN is a type of deep learning neural network with many interconnected neurons that can perform self-optimization via learning. It is widely used in image pattern recognition by converting patterns into a feature vector and then passing through the hidden layers to obtain output [9]. CNN in general has three types of layers, namely convolutional layer, pooling layer and fully-connected or dense layer, in which they are concatenated together to become a CNN architecture [9].

AlexNet
AlexNet is a type of CNN focusing on image classification. It was named after Alex Krizhevsky, who created AlexNet and won a top-5 test error rate of 15.3%, topping the first runner-up error rate of 26.2% together with his teammates in ImageNet Large Scale Visual Recognition Challenge (LSVRC)-2012 competition, and was described as the first CNN to win ImageNet.

3   Methodology

3.1   Overview of Execution of Speech Emotion Recognition

The five main steps involved in the execution of speech emotion recognition were: Data collection and signal extraction, Signal conversion, Image recognition using transfer learning, Result validation andImplementation of trained network.

  The development of speech emotion recognition was done using MATLAB Signal Processing Toolbox, Deep Network Designer Toolbox and App Designer Toolbox.

3.2   Data Collection and Signal Extraction

This was the first step in the whole process of execution of speech emotion recognition, which was the data collection. The emotional speech databases used in this project were RAVDESS and EMO-DB. Data collection was done by loading and reading the audio files in WAV format in MATLAB, as depicted in Fig. 1.

  After that, MATLAB Signal Processing Toolbox was used for displaying the audio signals and this was where the audio processing was carried out. The variables holding the audio information of the audio files were then imported into the application so that the signals could be displayed. The speech signal extraction was also carried out at this stage, in which the region of interest (ROI) of each speech signal was extracted using the panner function. The purposes of the extraction process are to remove the undesired silent parts at the beginning and ending parts of the speech signals, and reduce the number of samples. By reducing the number of samples, this helps to simplify the training process later by extracting only the spoken part where the emotional information lies. Once the extraction was done, the ROI signals were exported into a MATLAB-specific module file (.mat) to store them to allow accessibility of the signal variables from the module.

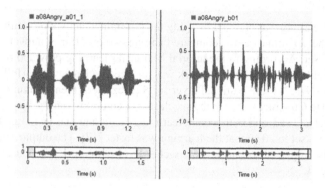

Fig. 1. Extraction of ROI signal using panner function.

3.3 Signal Conversion

The extracted ROI signals were in the form of row vector. They were converted into mel-spectrograms, the audio spectrograms scaled to mel scales because they displayed clearer power intensity at lower frequencies where most of the power is aggregated. These mel-spectrograms were treated as the input images used for training the deep learning network. The mel-spectrograms of ROI signals were plotted in multiple figures of subplots and colourmap of the spectrograms was set to "jet", which provided RGB representation to the power intensities at various frequencies. The plots of spectrogram were then exported into the current file directory.

Folders of all 6 emotion classes were created to store the cropped images in emotion categories. Images were renamed so that the file names contained the database type and the actor number. Figure 2 shows an example of a speech signal converted into RGB spectrogram.

3.4 Image Recognition Using Transfer Learning

This was the most important step of speech emotion recognition and it took the most time, since it was required to continuously fine-tune the deep network in order to improve the accuracy. Throughout the process, some problems might arise and it was necessary to carry out troubleshooting constantly.

Fig. 2. Speech signal in the form of RGB spectrogram.

Transfer learning was adopted by using the pre-trained network to train the spectrograms, and the performance was compared among two pre-trained networks – AlexNet and SqueezeNet. According to the tutorial of transfer learning provided by MATLAB, the last learnable layer of a deep network was replaced with a new one (fully-connected layer for AlexNet, 2D convolutional layer for SqueezeNet), then the number of classes was changed to 6 in order to match the six classes of emotions - angry, disgusted, fearful, happy, neutral and sad, and both weight learn rate factor and bias learn rate factor of the new layer were set to 20 so that the learning was faster [17]. The output (classification) layer was also replaced to match the six classes of emotions [17]. The illustration is shown in Fig. 3.

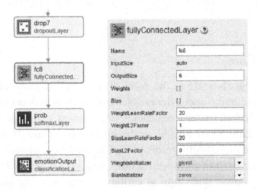

Fig. 3. Last learnable layer (left) and its parameter configuration for transfer learning (right).

Before commencing the transfer learning of the pre-trained network, the input images were imported. In the import option, the percentage of validation data that could be split from the total number of input data was entered. It is a common practice to allocate a higher percentage of training data than the validation data, since training data are emphasized in the training session. In this project, the portion of validation data was set to either 20% or 30%, with the remaining training data being 80% or 70%, respectively.

Once the input images were imported into the network designer, the training parameters were set such as the network's learning rate, maximum epochs, validation frequency and batch sizes before the training begins. Various parameters were adjusted and experimented for observing the training performance, such as learning rate, maximum epochs, batch size etc. A few trained networks with the best weights were exported and saved in the directory to be used for identifying the speech emotions in the testing images.

3.5 Result Validation

Before the transfer learning process, a portion of random images were separated as the testing images. These testing images were used for validating the training results by letting the trained network to identify the emotions represented by the mel-spectrograms. Testing images were manually selected in a random manner and relocated into a separate folder with six different subfolders for each emotion. The same step was repeated for other different emotions.

The image was resized using image resizing function into a dimension of $227 \times 227 \times 3$. This was because the trained network took the input data in this dimension. After this, the trained network was loaded and the testing image was read for classification. Confusion matrix was plotted to evaluate the neural network performance on recognizing speech emotion of all testing images.

3.6 Implementation of Trained Network

The trained network was implemented using a graphical user interface (GUI) application designed using MATLAB App Designer Toolbox to allow the users to interact with the system to recognize the speech emotions in a more user-friendly approach. The GUI (as depicted in Fig. 4 and Fig. 6) consisted of a few buttons to load audio file, generate mel-spectrogram and classify emotion, text fields to display file path and speech emotion and an axes object to display the mel-spectrogram of the chosen audio recordings to be classified.

As depicted in Fig. 5, the user first chooses the speech audio recordings in WAV format from the RAVDESS or EMO-DB datasets. Once chosen, its full file path is displayed in the text field and its corresponding emotion is shown in another text field as well. The next step is to generate the mel-spectrogram of the selected audio file since the trained network takes RGB spectrogram image as the input, and it will be displayed in the axes object located on the right-hand side. In the final step, by clicking on the "Classify" button, the application starts to initiate speech emotion recognition process, in which the trained network loaded inside the application will perform inference on the loaded audio file. After it is done, the predicted speech emotion will be displayed in another text field located next to the actual emotion text field.

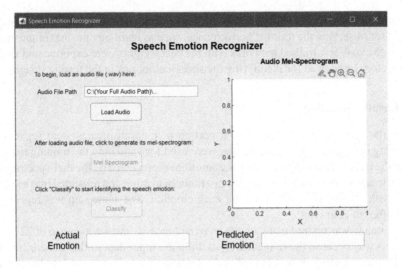

Fig. 4. GUI of speech emotion recognizer.

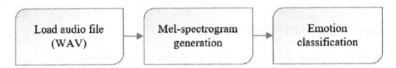

Fig. 5. Processes of speech emotion recognizer GUI.

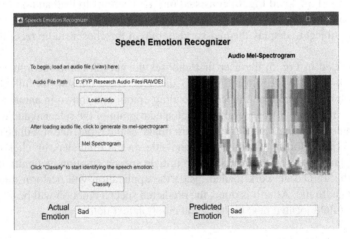

Fig. 6. Emotion recognition in speech emotion recognizer GUI.

4   Results and Discussion

4.1   Combination of RAVDESS and EMO-DB

Two pre-trained deep networks were used for training spectrogram inputs generated from RAVDESS and EMO-DB emotional speech database, and the results between different networks were compared. The networks used were AlexNet and SqueezeNet which were readily available in MATLAB Deep Network Designer Toolbox.

During the training process, the image augmentations used were:

- Image rotation range: $-15°$ to $15°$
- Random horizontal and vertical pixel translation: -5 to 5
- Random reflection axis: X

4.2   Maximum Epochs

Summary of the training results with changing epochs for AlexNet and SqueezeNet:

Table 2. Table of comparison of RAVDESS and EMO-DB combined training results with different maximum epochs using AlexNet and SqueezeNet.

	AlexNet		SqueezeNet	
Learning rate	0.0001		0.0001	
Maximum epochs	50	100	50	100
Batch size	36		36	
Training/validation (%)	70/30		70/30	
Validation accuracy (%)	61.57	62.50	52.78	55.09

4.3   Learning Rate

Summary of the training results with changing learning rate for AlexNet and SqueezeNet:

4.4   Image Augmentation

Summary of the training results with and without image augmentations for AlexNet and SqueezeNet:

Overall, the network trained with higher number of epochs gave higher validation accuracy for both AlexNet and SqueezeNet using the combination of RAVDESS and EMO-DB databases. From Table 2, higher number of epochs yielded higher validation accuracy because it was trained more times than with lower number of epochs. Based on Tables 3 and 4, observations could be made on the trend of validation accuracy with respect to learning rate and the use of image augmentations. Lower learning rate gave higher validation accuracy, since a lower learning rate indicates that the network is

Table 3. Table of comparison of RAVDESS and EMO-DB combined training results with different learning rate using AlexNet and SqueezeNet.

	AlexNet		SqueezeNet	
Learning rate	0.0002	0.0001	0.0002	0.0001
Maximum epochs	30		30	
Batch size	36		36	
Training/validation (%)	70/30		70/30	
Validation accuracy (%)	59.72	63.43	37.04	47.22

Table 4. Table of comparison of RAVDESS and EMO-DB combined training results with and without image augmentations using AlexNet and SqueezeNet.

	AlexNet		SqueezeNet	
Learning rate	0.0001		0.0001	
Maximum epochs	50		50	
Batch size	36		36	
Image augmentation	No	Yes	No	Yes
Training/validation (%)	70/30		70/30	
Validation accuracy (%)	66.20	61.57	61.57	52.78

learning at a slower rate, although slow to converge to an optimal point, lower learning rate helps to ensure no any local minima is lost during training [18]. Higher learning rate speeds up the learning process, however it is prone to missing some local minima, causing the point to oscillate which leads to reduced accuracy [18]. The absence of the image augmentation caused the training curve to converge faster, speeding up the increase rate in training accuracy. Nevertheless, training without applying image augmentation made the model become vulnerable to overfitting problem as it tends to memorize the network due to low variance in training data samples.

4.5 Testing Results

Among all the training results tabulated in Tables 2, 3 and 4, AlexNet with a learning rate of 0.0001, 50 maximum epochs, without image augmentations produced the highest validation accuracy of 66.20%. The testing image data was provided to the trained network with the highest validation accuracy, which was 66.20% to verify the emotion recognition results on the combined RAVDESS and EMO-DB testing data.

A total of 264 combined RAVDESS and EMO-DB testing data samples distributed among 6 classes of emotions were used in the evaluation of trained neural network performance. The confusion matrix was plotted as shown in Fig. 7.

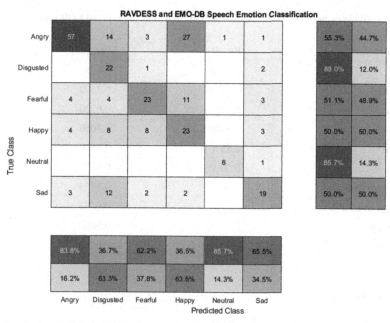

Fig. 7. Confusion matrix of RAVDESS and EMO-DB speech emotion classification.

A total of 264 combined RAVDESS and EMO-DB testing data samples distributed among 6 classes of emotions were used in the evaluation of trained neural network performance. From the confusion matrix plotted, the class "Disgusted" had the highest of 88.0%, which had predicted correctly 22 out of 25 samples of class "Disgusted", with 1 as "Fearful" and 2 as "Sad". Then followed by class "Neutral" with inference accuracy of 85.7%, which had correctly predicted 6 out of 7 samples. The classes of emotions with lowest inference accuracy were "Happy" and "Sad", both having predicted 50.0% (23 out of 46, and 19 out of 38 samples, respectively) of their testing samples correctly.

According to Table 5, the model had an accuracy of 0.5682 (56.82%) and F1-score of 0.6253. From the confusion matrix in Fig. 11, the combination of RAVDESS and EMO-DB suffered from significant class imbalance. Accuracy metric might provide misleading result given the fact that it does not consider the class imbalance, hence F1-score is the more suitable metric in this case for model evaluation. As seen in Table 6, there was a mixture of classes with low recall and high precision, and vice versa. Since the recall and precision also affected F1-score, there were some classes with low recall but high precision, for example, class "Angry", "Fearful" and "Sad", and the opposite one like "Disgusted" and "Happy", this contributed to the decreased overall model performance on the combined data.

Table 5. Table of metrics of confusion matrix for RAVDESS and EMO-DB speech emotion.

Class of emotion	Recall	Precision
Angry	0.5530	0.8380
Disgusted	0.8800	0.3670
Fearful	0.5110	0.6220
Happy	0.5000	0.3650
Neutral	0.8570	0.8570
Sad	0.5000	0.6550
Average recall		0.6335
Average precision		0.6173
Accuracy		0.5682
F1-score		0.6253

5   Conclusion

In this study, speech emotion recognition was transformed into an image classification problem by converting the extracted ROI signals into RGB mel-spectrograms. For the training process, both AlexNet and SqueezeNet were used for recognizing the spectrograms generated from the RAVDESS and EMO-DB emotional speech databases via transfer learning. After going through the experiments, it was observed that in overall, AlexNet performed better than SqueezeNet in terms of validation accuracy obtained via training process with the combination of RAVDESS and EMO-DB databases that contained both English and German languages, giving the highest validation accuracy of 66.20%.

Moving on to the testing results, the model with the highest validation accuracy was selected and was tested on its corresponding testing data samples. The model tested on the combination of RAVDESS and EMO-DB yielded an inference accuracy of 56.82%. As for the F1-score metric, the combination of RAVDESS and EMO-DB with a score of 0.6253.

5.1   Future Recommendations

Some recommendations can be done in order to improve the performance of speech emotion recognition. This includes using emotional speech databases with higher number of audio samples to increase the number of training data to minimize the occurrence of overfitting during the network training process. Furthermore, piecewise learning rate scheduling can be implemented prior to training by setting reduction factor for initial learning rate for a set of epoch intervals to provide a more adaptive training process which can improve the recognition performance. Lastly, the number of training data can be adjusted before initiating the training process to ensure all classes of emotion have balanced amount of data samples, which aids to improve the training performance.

Acknowledgements. The authors would like to thanks Tunku Abdul Rahman University of Management and Technology for providing computing resources to run these experiments. Special thanks are given to the permission to use open access database (RAVDESS and EMO-DB) in our experiments.

References

1. Burkhardt, F., Paeschke, A., Rolfes, M., Sendlmeier, W., Weiss, B.: A database of German emotional speech. In: Proceedings of Interspeech 2005, vol. 5, pp. 1517–1520 (2005)
2. Rodriguez, V.: Basic rules for indoor anechoic chamber design [measurements corner]. IEEE Antennas Propag. Mag. **58**(6), 82–93 (2016)
3. Livingstone, S.R., Russo, F.A.: The Ryerson audio-visual database of emotional speech and song (RAVDESS): a dynamic, multimodal set of facial and vocal expressions in North American English. PLoS ONE **13**(5), e0196391 (2018)
4. Ghule, K.R., Deshmukh, R.: Feature extraction techniques for speech recognition: a review. Int. J. Sci. Eng. Res. **6**(5), 2229–5518 (2015)
5. Dave, N.: Feature extraction methods LPC, PLP and MFCC in speech recognition. Int. J. Adv. Res. Eng. Technol. **1**(6), 1–4 (2013)
6. Alim, S.A., Rashid, N.K.A.: Some Commonly Used Speech Feature Extraction Algorithms. From Natural to Artificial Intelligence - Algorithms and Applications (2018). undefined/state.item.id
7. Dörfler, M., Bammer, R., Grill, T.: Inside the spectrogram: Convolutional Neural Networks in audio processing. In: 2017 12th International Conference on Sampling Theory and Applications, SampTA 2017, vol. 1, pp. 152–155 (2017)
8. Shen, J., et al.: Natural TTS synthesis by conditioning WaveNet on MEL spectrogram predictions. In: ICASSP, IEEE International Conference on Acoustics, Speech and Signal Processing - Proceedings, vol. 2018-April, pp. 4779–4783 (2018)
9. O'Shea, K., Nash, R.: An introduction to convolutional neural networks. arXiv preprint arXiv: 1511.08458 (2015)
10. Krizhevsky, A., Sutskever, I., Hinton, G.E.: ImageNet classification with deep convolutional neural networks. Commun. ACM **60**(6), 84–90 (2017)
11. Stolar, M.N., Lech, M., Bolia, R.S., Skinner, M.: Real time speech emotion recognition using RGB image classification and transfer learning. In: 2017 11th International Conference on Signal Processing and Communication Systems (ICSPCS), pp. 1–8. IEEE (2017)
12. Lech, M., Stolar, M., Best, C., Bolia, R.: Real-time speech emotion recognition using a pretrained image classification network: effects of bandwidth reduction and companding. Front. Comput. Sci. **2**, 14 (2020)
13. Zeng, Y., Mao, H., Peng, D., Yi, Z.: Spectrogram based multi-task audio classification. Multimedia Tools Appl. **78**(3), 3705–3722 (2019)
14. Huang, Z., Dong, M., Mao, Q., Zhan, Y.: Speech emotion recognition using CNN. In: Proceedings of the 22nd ACM International Conference on Multimedia, pp. 801–804 (2014)
15. Han, K., Yu, D., Tashev, I.: Speech emotion recognition using deep neural network and extreme learning machine. In: Interspeech 2014 (2014)
16. Kerkeni, L., Serrestou, Y., Mbarki, M., Raoof, K., Mahjoub, M.A.: Speech emotion recognition: methods and cases study. In: ICAART (2), vol. 20 (2018)
17. MATLAB: Transfer learning with deep network designer (2023). https://www.mathworks.com/help/deeplearning/ug/transfer-learning-with-deep-network-designer.html

18. Zulkifli, H.: Understanding Learning Rates and How It Improves Performance in Deep Learning (2018). https://towardsdatascience.com/understanding-learning-rates-and-how-it-improves-performance-in-deep-learning-d0d4059c1c10

19. Hossain, M.S., Muhammad, G.: Emotion recognition using deep learning approach from audio–visual emotional big data. Inf. Fusion **49**, 69–78 (2019)

Covid-19 Detection Using Coughing Sounds with Mel-frequency Cepstral Coefficients and Long Short-Term Memory

Jia Chong Lim and Kai Sze Hong[✉]

Department of Electrical and Electronics Engineering, Faculty of Engineering and Technology, Tunku Abdul Rahman University of Management and Technology, 53300 Kuala Lumpur, Malaysia
hongks@tarc.edu.my

Abstract. As there are a lot of limitations on current existing approach in screening of COVID-19 infection, an efficient approach must be introduced to the healthcare application as soon as possible in order to inhibit the spreading chain of COVID-19 around the world. Human can listen to audio file, but could not interpret the audio signal precisely. However, computers with deep learning algorithm could do so while handling huge amount of data. Therefore, the main focus of this research project is to develop a deep learning model in detecting COVID-19 infection through the analysis of coughing sound, Long Short-Term Memory (LSTM) is used as the deep learning neural network in this research project. It is an improved version of recurrent neural network (RNN) and it is specialized in processing time-series data which is also known as audio signals. As a result, the aim of this research project is to build a LSTM model with Mel-Frequency Cepstral Coefficients (MFCCs) feature as a diagnostic tool for COVID-19 infection. In order to achieve this, Coswara database is utilised as the source of coughing dataset, the coughing dataset is then go through the pre-processing process and hence employed for the model learning and training. Lastly, the trained model has achieved an accuracy of about 58% and its feasibility was evaluated with an unseen test dataset based on the classification report metrics.

Keywords: Audio Augmentation · Speech Enhancement · Speech Classification

1 Introduction

The outbreak of COVID-19 has occurred since March 2020 until today, it possess the strong ability of spreading nature which have infected nearly 600 million people worldwide and causing around 6.5 million death by far [1]. 600 million is a very terrible figure as it can be imagined in a scenario of approximately 1 people has infected in every 10 people around the world. As the COVID-19 is highly transmittable from one to another and it is possesses with the characteristic of long incubation period which leads to several necessary measures have been taken from the government to curb the spread of virus in the country. For example, many countries have implemented the border restriction to prohibit the entry from foreigners such that most countries are mandatory to isolate the immigrants for fourteen days and the required expenses are at their own, thus travelling, business and many other related fields have influenced by this measure. Not only that, daily activities also have been affected as remoting has become the new norm in the aspect of studying and working due to social distancing is needed. Even the vaccines for COVID-19 have been studied and developed, it is still unable to curb the spreading of COVID-19 efficiently around the world.

With the evolution of artificial intelligence (AI), the computers and machines are capable of detecting, processing, and classifying whatever information that have fed in. Consequently, AI have been widely applied in the biological field especially in image and speech recognition. For instance, cancer and Alzheimer's disease could be diagnosis by implementing image and speech processing respectively and following by neural network algorithms. As the existing method for COVID-19 detection is using the polymerase chain reaction (PCR) and reverse transcriptase polymerase chain reaction (RT-PCR) which are inefficient in term of cost and time, therefore COVID-19 screening using coughing recognition and deep learning has been studied and proposed as an alternative efficient approach. This research topic is extremely important as it allows for contactless diagnosis and thus the COVID-19 chain can be break effectively.

2 Problem Background

Restraining the outbreak of COVID-19 is primarily depends on two critical factors which are the effectiveness of the vaccines developed and the efficiency in screening of COVID-19. In this research, the primary goal is to replace the current existing method of COVID-19 diagnosis by developing a more efficient approach as there are numerous limitations in the existing method. First of all, PCR and RT-PCR is an expensive tool for COVID-19 diagnosis which cost above RM100, hence it has further increased the living expenses burden of folks as they are suffering in the working field due to large scale layoffs worldwide [2]. Other than that, these diagnosis methods are time consuming as the patients have to go to particular medical centre for screening while facing the dilemma of long queue as well as the participation of medical professionals are required [3].

Also, approximate 24 h is needed for the result of PCR test to be released, hence it is time inefficient. This might lead to self-quarantine is compulsory for everyone as long as the result have not released. Furthermore, social distancing has become the new norm or measure in the society such as population is restricted in enclosed area such as lift and public transportation, the long queue for COVID-19 diagnosis is happened during the outbreak period which is actually violates the practice of social distancing and may lead to the mass infection, thus the spreading chain of COVID-19 would be further speed up [2].

Apart from PCR test, test kits have also widely used for COVID-19 screening during the outbreak of COVID-19 pandemic, although its cost is much lower than the PCR and RT-PCR tests but the down side is it possesses relatively lower accuracy as well. However, it also facing a dilemma of shortages in many countries [5]. Besides, the invention of test kits is not eco-friendly as it could be easily disposed in the surrounding after used while it is still stained with the saliva of that user.

It can be seen that quarantine centre for COVID-19 pandemic is overcrowded and definitely has violated the practice of social distancing as well. Not only that, manpower is not sufficient in handling the patients that suffer from the outbreak of COVID-19 pandemic. This is because people are not willing to carry the RT-PCR test when the symptoms is appeared as the cost of RT-PCR is expensive and its process is inconvenient. Consequently, early diagnosis of COVID-19 cannot be accomplished effectively which leads to the overcrowded in the quarantine center. Furthermore, many studied have also shown that the RT-PCR testing may not be optimal as the false-positive rates is considered high [3]. Therefore, a clean, cheap and efficient diagnosis tool has to be developed for the real healthcare application as soon as possible to curb the outbreak of COVID-19 pandemic.

Other than that, image processing as an approach in screening COVID-19 infection has widely studied recently, specifically is the X-ray method and CT scans method. Nevertheless, some issues that have mentioned earlier are still existing such as patients still have to go to specific medical center for X-ray or CT scans process which is time consuming and would also increase the load of medicals' staff. This is because approaches of image processing cannot be undergo contactless. Besides, process of X-ray or CT scans probably takes more time as compared to RT-PCR test, this would leads to the same problem of long queue, which violating the measure of social distancing. In addition, patients are not able to repeatedly undergo the process of COVID-19 detection through the methods of X-ray and CT scan as these approaches would impact the organ's functionality as they having the ionizing capability. On the other hand, the DNN approached proposed by Rumana Islam in the article entitled "A study of using cough sounds and deep neural networks for the early detection of Covid-19" achieved an overall accuracy of 89.2%, 97.5%, and 93.8% using time-domain, frequency-domain, and mixed-domain feature vectors [14].

In this paper, the major contributions of this work are summarized as follows:

- GoldWave software is utilised for the Coswara dataset to remove any silent portion of the coughing samples in ensuring good quality input data is provided to the classifier, also signal resampling is needed as the sampling frequency of dataset is varied.
- We further augment the Coswara data sample so that a larger dataset is formed by randomly looping over the existing dataset.
- Make any necessary modification on the neural network architecture by referring to the existing works, including [8] and [9].

3 Proposed Method

In this section, we will details the proposed method that we applied to complete this research project.

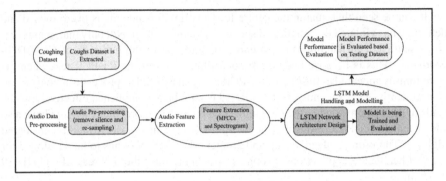

Fig. 1. Overall Framework of Designed System

In Fig. 1, it shows the overall framework of the implemented system in detecting the Covid-19 infection from coughing samples. Each step would be briefly described in sub-sections below.

3.1 Coughing Dataset Collection and Distribution

Firstly, the coughing audio is manually sorted into two classes which name as "Healthy" and "Covid". In the very first moment, there are total of 1,689 coughing samples with healthy label and 673 coughing samples with positive label are being extracted from Coswara and hence 1,689 and 673 coughing samples are sorted into "Healthy" and "Covid" classes respectively. However, only specific length between 4 to 6 s of the coughing samples could be further processed due to the capabilities of code algorithm which leads to the size of the dataset is being decreased slightly. This is because the extracted coughing samples is varying from 0 s to 30 s, where most of the coughing samples is fall between 4 to 6 s. After that, some of the audio samples are actually distorted and some of them are irrelevant to coughing such as singing sample or others, hence they are considered as unusable dataset and being removed as well. On the other hand, some samples with the length of longer than 6 s have gone through pre-processing such that preserve the only the important audio signal to the length of 5 s, so that the dataset now is being increased and robust. Lastly, the total number of dataset including healthy and Covid classes is 980 samples, where both healthy and Covid classes having the same number of samples which is 490 samples respectively, and they are further distributed to training dataset, validation dataset and testing dataset with 414 samples, 46 samples and 30 samples respectively for each classes. The brief block diagram to describe the flow is shown in Fig. 2.

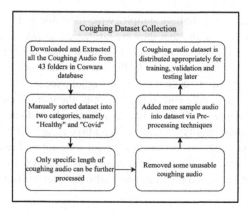

Fig. 2. Flow of coughing audio dataset is being collected and processed

3.2 Signal Pre-Processing and Feature Extraction

In signal pre-processing, some error is raised up due to several of the coughing samples are having with too short duration, specifically is the audio length of 0 s and 1 s. This is because some of the coughing samples are recorded without any signal waveform that can be observed as shown in Fig. 3 and Fig. 4, they are corresponded to the coughing sample with 0 s and 1 s respectively. Thus, these kind of samples have to be rejected and removed from the dataset since they do not provide any useful information and behave like an error data.

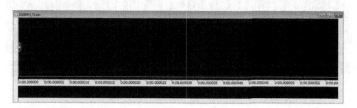

Fig. 3. Coughing sample with 0 s from Coswara

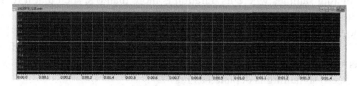

Fig. 4. Coughing sample with 1 s from Coswara

After that, there are also coughing samples with distortion and some of them are actually irrelevant samples, meaning that they are not the coughing samples. The uploaded coughing sample being distorted may due to several reasons, where one of the most common reasons is the issue regarding to the devices that used for recording such as microphone, distortion might occur if the input signal exceeds the maximum level that the recording device can handle and so on. Whereas, there are irrelevant audio samples such as song audio sample inside the Coswara dataset, which do not have the characteristics of coughing signal. In short, both type of audio data are definitely not appropriate to be included in the coughing dataset for model training and testing later due to it might reduce the reliability of the dataset and affect the model performance. Each audio example for distorted audio and the irrelevant audio samples are illustrated as Fig. 5 and Fig. 6 respectively.

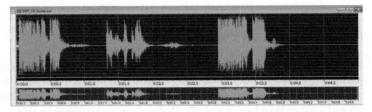

Fig. 5. Waveform of noisy and distorted coughing sample

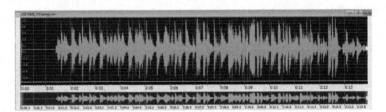

Fig. 6. Waveform of irrelevant audio sample (song)

Afterwards, in order to increase the size of coughing dataset, pre-processing is needed for the coughing samples where its duration is more than 6 s, such that it removed the silent portion of the audio sample as the silent portion is useless and contribute nothing for the model training. Not only the silent portion is contributing nothing, but it also increased the model training process which leads to the time inefficient and the memory of GPU is wasted on the Google Colaboratory. One of the coughing audio with long duration of zero signalling is depicted as Fig. 7.

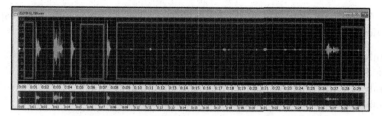

Fig. 7. Removing silent portion of a coughing sample

From Fig. 7, it could be observed that there is only about 5 s with the useful signal waveform from the original audio's length of 30 s. This pre-processing can be done by using GoldWave software. By doing so, the model training process now is becoming more time efficient as well as memory efficient. Last but not least, all the dataset now are resampling to 15 kHz for standardisation and all of them having a duration between 4 s to 6 s which considered as reasonable length as there is enough important coughing pattern or characteristics can be extracted and learnt by the training model. The brief block diagram to describe the flow is shown in Fig. 8.

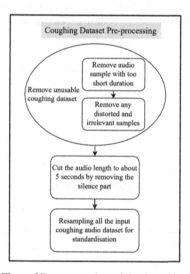

Fig. 8. Flow of Pre-processing of the Coughing Dataset

In feature extraction, MFCC feature is selected to be extracted from the audio signals among all the other audio's features as it is able to perform excellently in the field of audio recognition. Before the MFCCs can be extracted from the pre-processing input coughing dataset, some configuration or setting has to be set so that the MFCCs can be extracted successfully, which are the number of audio samples in one frame, the length of the FFT (Fast Fourier Transform) window to be used for computing the power spectrum, the number of filter that used in the mel-frequency filter bank for computing the MFCCs and the number of Mel-frequency cepstral coefficients (MFCCs) to be extracted in one frame. All of them have set in this research project as follows with their respective annotation.

- Number of audio samples in one frame, config.step = 375
- Length of the FFT window, nfft = 2048
- Number of filter that used in mel-frequency filter bank, nfilt = 26
- Number of MFCCs to be extracted in one frame, nfeat = 13

The above setting has been configured for the MFCCs to be extracted in this work as they are the common values to be used according to some related works [11, 12].

3.3 Neural Network Architecture of LSTM

LSTM network architecture is used as a classifier to learn a vector representation of a patient's coughing sequence in order to detect Covid-19 infection from coughing pattern analysis. LSTM is chosen to be implemented instead of CNN and RNN is attributed by the fact that LSTM is able to overcome the vanishing gradient problem and able to learn long-term dependencies which CNN and RNN could not, this is because LSTM stores data information for a long period and hence it can remember the past data in memory easily. Consequently, it is specialized in speech recognition field.

The basic working principle of a general LSTM network architecture is shown in Fig. 9.

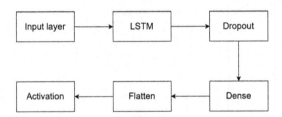

Fig. 9. Working principle of LSTM network architecture [13]

The brief block diagram to describe the design flow of the LSTM network architecture is shown in Fig. 10.

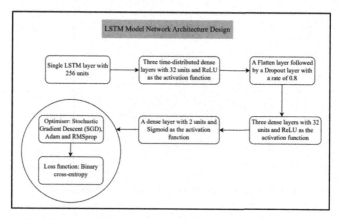

Fig. 10. Flow of the LSTM model network architecture design

3.4 Performance Evaluation on the Trained Model

Before the performance of trained model being evaluated, the augmented dataset are well allocated for the testing dataset. In this works, there are 60 coughing samples which is the unseen data that used for the performance evaluation on the trained model, where 30 samples are come from healthy class and Covid class respectively for the dataset balancing. Moreover, MFCCs is extracted from the test dataset as it is required for the trained model to do prediction for them and classify them into either healthy class or Covid class.

After all the test dataset have been predicted to their respective class, now the model performance can be evaluated. In this works, there are two different type of performance metrics that are utilised to evaluate the model performance based on the predicted coughing dataset, which are the classification report and the confusion matrix. Classification report always display in the form of values or number which includes the metrics of precision, recall, f1-score and accuracy. Whereas, confusion matrix always display in the form of illustration for better visualisation and understanding which involves the information of true positive, false positive, true negative and false negative for the test samples.

4 Experimental Results

First of all, the data allocation for both classes are displayed with pie chart as shown in Fig. 11. It indicates the data is equally allocated for both classes, where each class having 460 samples.

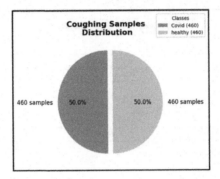

Fig. 11. Coughing samples distribution across classes

After that, the average duration of coughing samples in both classes are illustrated with bar chart as shown in Fig. 12. It indicates the average duration of sample is 5.351 s and 5.476 s for Covid class and healthy class respectively. These two charts are very crucial as it ensured the model to be trained later will not tend to over-fitting scenario. This is because the model may bias to one of the classes if the coughing sample in one class is more than the other class or the average duration of coughing sample in one class is longer than the other class, as these cases would lead to the number of extracted MFCCs in both classes in huge difference.

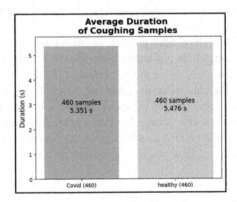

Fig. 12. Average duration of coughing samples in both classes

On the other hand, Fig. 13, Fig. 14, Fig. 15, Fig. 16 and Fig. 17 show the time series plot in sample, time series plot in second, fourier transforms, filter bank coefficients and MFCC respectively of 1 sample for each class for visualisation comparison.

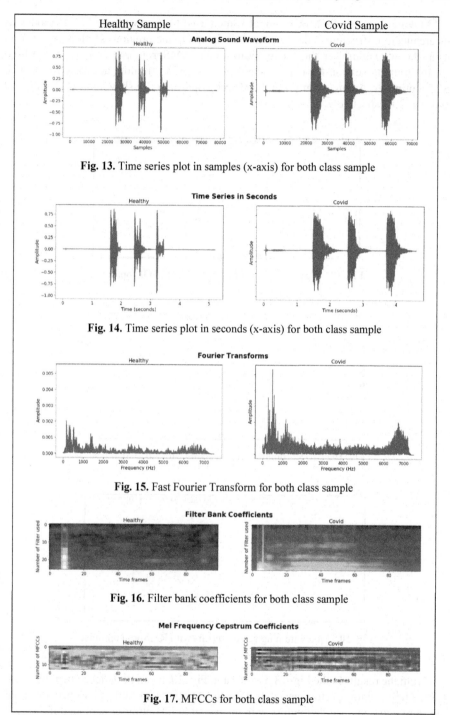

Fig. 13. Time series plot in samples (x-axis) for both class sample

Fig. 14. Time series plot in seconds (x-axis) for both class sample

Fig. 15. Fast Fourier Transform for both class sample

Fig. 16. Filter bank coefficients for both class sample

Fig. 17. MFCCs for both class sample

Moving forward, the MFCCs input is then used to train with the LSTM model, as its architecture structure is designed and explained in the previous section. Apart from using the SGD optimiser, the Adam optimiser and RMSprop optimiser are also utilised for the training session for experimental purposes. The training accuracy result with SGD optimiser, Adam optimiser and RMSprop optimiser are shown in Fig. 18, Fig. 19 and Fig. 20 respectively.

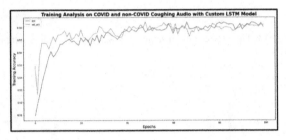

Fig. 18. Model training across epochs with SGD optimiser

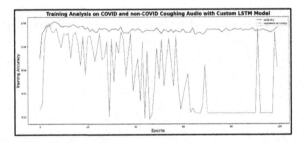

Fig. 19. Model training across epochs with Adam optimiser

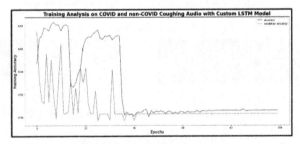

Fig. 20. Model training across epochs with RMSprop optimiser

From the results in the Fig. 18, Fig. 19 and Fig. 20, it can be deduced that the model has the best training performance when the SGD optimiser is utilised. Hence, the graph of training loss and validation loss with the use of SGD optimiser is plotted in Fig. 21.

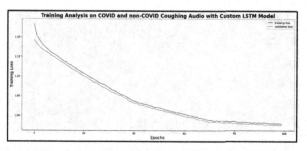

Fig. 21. Model loss across epochs with SGD optimiser

From the Fig. 21, it shows that the SGD optimiser is the best fit with the LSTM neural network in training the MFCCs input as the training accuracy is increasing across the epoch, meanwhile the training loss is decreasing across the epoch. Most importantly is the training curve and validation curve is closed to each other, meaning the model is not tend to over-fitting scenario.

Lastly, after the trained model is built, the test dataset plays a vital role in evaluating its performance. This is because test dataset is the unseen data for the trained model, and hence it is often used for evaluating the model performance before making a conclusion on the trained model or officially proposed the trained model to the society. The output result of confusion matrix and classification report is shown in Fig. 22 and Fig. 23 respectively.

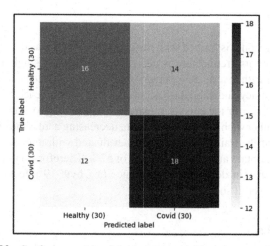

Fig. 22. Confusion matrix of the trained model based on test dataset

From the result of confusion matrix and classification report, the relatively high misclassification has performed by the trained model can be inferred as the model's accuracy is only about 57% as shown in Fig. 23. The relatively high misclassifications may due to some causes including the model has misclassified the healthy sample that with coughing symptom into the Covid class or misclassified the Covid sample that

```
[119] print(classification_report(y_true=y_true, y_pred=y_pred))

              precision    recall  f1-score   support

           0       0.57      0.53      0.55        30
           1       0.56      0.60      0.58        30

    accuracy                           0.57        60
   macro avg       0.57      0.57      0.57        60
weighted avg       0.57      0.57      0.57        60
```

Fig. 23. Classification report of the trained model based on test dataset

without any symptom into healthy class. This misclassification may attributed by some factors, such as the smaller size of dataset used for model training, quality of the dataset which leads to the poor MFCCs has been extracted as the input of LSTM classifier as well as the LSTM network architecture that might not be efficiently in differentiating the distinct features between the classes. Therefore, it is very crucial in designing an integrated LSTM network architecture that is well fit with the MFCCs inputs so that the features can be distinguished for both classes. Nevertheless, the model is said being evaluated successfully as the metrics result as shown in classification report is much closed with the training accuracy of the model. In other words, a passable performance of Covid-19 detection model is built successfully which is able to detect Covid-19 coughing sound with an accuracy of above 55%.

5 Conclusion

As a conclusion, a model is trained with the extracted MFCCs as the input of the LSTM neural network, and its architecture is designed as follows, a single LSTM layer with 256 neurons along with several dense layers. The model is said to be trained successfully as the training accuracy and validation accuracy is tallied with each other such that both curves are increasing over the epochs, meanwhile the training loss and validation loss is closed with each other such that both curves are decreasing across the epochs. Moreover, the performance of the trained model is then evaluated with unseen samples, which is 60 test dataset and obtain an overall accuracy of 57%. Therefore, a practical model with passable performance in detecting the presence of Covid-19 infection using human's coughing sounds is built successfully.

5.1 Future works

There are some future improvement that can be modified in this research project so that the model accuracy can be further enhanced. Firstly, a larger dataset could be obtained through other database such as ComParE and Sarcos dataset, so that the training dataset do not need to augment by randomly and repeatedly using the same samples within a limited dataset. Moreover, adding a filter such as Chebyshev filter to the input coughing dataset before the MFCCs extraction, this is to ensure all the extracted MFCCs is in good quality. Additionally, getting the best fit of LSTM neural network architecture in training the input MFCCs features, this is because an appropriate neural network architecture that well fit with the input MFCCs features would extremely improve the model performance. Apart from that, evaluate the trained model by splitting the test dataset, so that a larger test dataset can be performed without the restriction of GPU memory. In this way, the testing accuracy is more precise and accurate as the size of dataset used is larger. Last but not least, after the evaluation on the trained model, the true label and predicted label of every test samples are exported to a file such as.csv file, this provides a convenient way to analyse the model's predictions on every single test sample. Consequently, the accuracy of model's prediction could be further boosted by doing analysis on the prediction result of test samples.

Acknowledgement. The authors would like to thanks Tunku Abdul Rahman University of Management and Technology for providing computing resources to run these experiments. Special thanks are given to the permission to use COSWARA open access database in our experiments.

References

1. WHO Coronavirus (COVID-19) Dashboard | WHO Coronavirus (COVID-19) Dashboard With Vaccination Data. Covid19.who.int (2022). https://covid19.who.int/. Accessed 05 Sept 2022
2. Sharma, N., et al.: Coswara - a database of breathing, cough, and voice sounds for COVID-19 diagnosis. In: Proceedings of the Annual Conference of the International Speech Communication Association, INTERSPEECH (2020)
3. Nassif, A.B., Shahin, I., Bader, M., Hassan, A., Werghi, N.: COVID-19 detection systems using deep-learning algorithms based on speech and image data. Mathematics **10**(4), 25 (2022)
4. Covid: Liverpool testing trial sites doubled after queues on first day - BBC News (2020). https://www.bbc.com/news/uk-england-merseyside-54853677. Accessed 05 Sept 2022
5. Usman, M., Wajid, M., Shamim, M.Z., Ahmed, A.: On the possibility of using Speech to detect COVID- 19 symptoms: an overview and proof of concept (2020)
6. Covid-19 quarantine centres at 60% occupancy, says official | Free Malaysia Today (FMT). Bernama (2021). https://www.freemalaysiatoday.com/category/nation/2021/06/11/covid-19-quarantine-centres-at-60-occupancy-says-official/. Accessed 07 Sept 2022
7. Ishak, M.: Pesakit COVID kategori 3 di PKRC MAEPS semakin ramai. bharian (2021). https://www.bharian.com.my/berita/nasional/2021/05/817268/pesakit-covid-kategori-3-di-pkrc-maeps-semakin-ramai. Accessed 07 Sept 2022
8. Khriji, L., Ammari, A., Messaoud, S., Bouaafia, S., Maraoui, A., MacHhout, M.: COVID-19 recognition based on patient's coughing and breathing patterns analysis: deep learning approach. In: Conference of Open Innovation Association, FRUCT, p. 7 (2021)
9. Pahar, M., Klopper, M., Warren, R., Niesler, T.: COVID-19 cough classification using machine learning and global smartphone recordings. Comput. Biol. Med. **135**, 104572 (2021)
10. Kanti, T., Mishra, S., Panda, G., Chandra, S.: Detection of COVID-19 from speech signal using bio-inspired based cepstral features. Pattern Recognit. **117**, 13 (2021)
11. Al Bashit, A., Valles, D.: MFCC-based Houston Toad Call Detection using LSTM. In: 2019 22nd IEEE International Symposium on Measurement and Control in Robotics: Robotics for the Benefit of Humanity, ISMCR 2019, September 2019, p. 7 (2019)
12. Fayek, H.: Speech processing for machine learning: filter banks, mel-frequency cepstral coefficients (MFCCs) and what's in-between (2016). https://haythamfayek.com/2016/04/21/speech-processing-for-machine-learning.html. Accessed 24 Apr 2023

13. Hassan, A., Shahin, I., Alsabek, M.B.: COVID-19 detection system using recurrent neural networks. In: Proceedings of the 2020 IEEE International Conference on Communications, Computing, Cybersecurity, and Informatics (2020)
14. Islam, R., Abdel-Raheem, E., Tarique, M.: A study of using cough sounds and deep neural networks for the early detection of Covid-19. Biomed. Eng. Adv. **3**, 100025 (2022)

Enhancing Diabetes Prediction and Classification Using the Bidirectional Neighbor Graph Algorithm

Bashar Hamad Aubaidan, Rabiah Abdul Kadir[(✉)], and Mohamad Taha Ijab

Institute of Visual Informatics, Universiti Kebangsaan Malaysia, 43500 Bangi, Malaysia
P103708@siswa.ukm.edu.my

Abstract. The global prevalence of diabetes, a chronic health condition with diverse implications, necessitates improved prediction and classification methods. In this research, we propose a novel framework employing the bidirectional neighbor graph (BNG) algorithm to enhance diabetes prediction. By leveraging graph-based semi-supervised learning, we compare BNG with existing systems, thereby improving data structure modeling. The BNG algorithm addresses missing data and aims to optimize predictions for individuals with diabetes. This innovative approach holds promise for advancing diabetes research and creating more accurate prediction models for this condition. The methodology establishes a network connecting nodes to their nearest neighbors in both forward and backward directions. The evaluation of the model performance reveals an AUC (Area Under the Curve) score of approximately 0.86, demonstrating its efficacy in distinguishing true and false positive values across diverse classification thresholds. Moreover, BNG models effectively capture comprehensive and distinct features from the input data, resulting in improved classification performance. Additionally, the BNG method showcases computational efficiency, making it highly suitable for large-scale applications.

Keywords: Graph-based methods · Bidirectional Neighbor Graph ·
Classification · Feature Extraction · Machine Learning

1 Introduction

Medical data analysis is a vital area of research that employs machine learning techniques to identify and predict various medical conditions. However, analyzing medical Medical data analysis is an important field of study that utilizes machine learning techniques to detect and predict various medical conditions. However, analyzing medical data presents challenges due to limited data availability and complex interactions between variables. The utilization of Electronic Health Records (EHR) has led to a significant increase in medical datasets in the biomedical domain, offering numerous opportunities to enhance healthcare services. In recent years, there has been a notable surge in researchers and practitioners focusing on developing approaches encompassing machine learning, data

H. Badioze Zaman et al. (Eds.): IVIC 2023, LNCS 14322, pp. 557–567, 2024.
https://doi.org/10.1007/978-981-99-7339-2_45

mining, software development, and support. Medical datasets inherently exhibit problematic aspects, including missing data, and limitation. Consequently, addressing these challenges becomes crucial for leveraging the potential of medical datasets to improve healthcare services [1–3]. [4] This paper highlights the benefits of utilizing the Bidirectional Neighbor Graph for faster identification of the shortest path. It specifically focuses on its applicability in medical datasets, which often involve intricate relationships among variables. Additionally, we introduce a novel approach for imputing missing values in medical datasets based on the bidirectional neighbor graph. This method effectively addresses the issue of missing feature entries without relying on additional heuristics. It enables efficient and parallelizable computation using modern machine learning frameworks. By considering both the shortest and second shortest paths in the graph, the bidirectional neighbor graph-based imputation method offers a more reliable and precise estimation of missing values. Ultimately, this approach enhances performance compared to traditional imputation methods in medical datasets by effectively capturing complex interactions and leveraging graph-based computation [5, 6].

2 Related Work

In the medical field, there is a growing demand for efficient machine learning methods to handle imbalanced datasets with missing values. This has led to extensive research efforts to explore various approaches to tackle these challenges. Some of the proposed approaches include a bidirectional preference-based search approach, an improved frame-work for classifying Pima diabetes using imbalanced data with missing values, and an analysis of missing data in predictive model studies using machine learning. [7–9] The K-nearest neighbors (KNN) algorithm is widely used for handling missing data, computing a weighted mean of the variable based on initial k observations. However, alternative approaches like bidirectional neighbor graph imputation exist for managing missing data. [10, 11] The Bidirectional Neighbor Graph (BNG) is a powerful graph-based algorithm with applications in network analysis, social network modeling, recommendation systems, and image recognition tasks. BNG represents data points as nodes in a graph and establishes connections between each node and its nearest neighbors in both forward and backward directions. [12] This unique characteristic allows BNG to capture intricate relationships and dependencies within the data, leading to more accurate and efficient analysis. Researchers have shown that BNG excels in scenarios where data exhibit non-linear patterns and complex interactions. [13] The BNG algorithm's semi-supervised learning capabilities make it particularly valuable when dealing with limited labeled data, as it can leverage both labeled and unlabeled data points to improve predictive performance. In conclusion, the Bidirectional Neighbor Graph's powerful graph-based methodology aligns perfectly with the intricacies of medical datasets, making it a highly suitable choice for improving and streamlining data analysis in the medical domain [14, 15].

3 Methodology

3.1 Data Collection

Data collection refers to the procedure of gathering relevant information or data for a research project. In the specific case of a machine learning project focused on predicting diabetes in patients from Pima, India, data collection involves acquiring a dataset that contains pertinent details about the patients, including their medical history, demographics, and clinical measurements. The authors of the project obtain the dataset from Kaggle, specifically the Pima Indian's diabetes dataset, which comprises data from 768 patients. Subsequently, the collected data undergo preprocessing to prepare them for analysis. This preprocessing stage may encompass tasks such as data cleaning, handling missing values, and scaling or normalizing the features. The proper execution of data collection and preprocessing is of utmost importance to ensure the accuracy and dependability of the machine learning models employed for predicting diabetes in Pima Indian patients. [16] The methodology is as follows: prepare the dataset, followed by data pre-processing such as dealing with missing values and categorical values, imputation, and standardization. Feature selection will be performed using a variety of tools. Lastly, the classifiers' performance before and after feature selection will be further evaluated. The Pima Indian Diabetes dataset, commonly referred to as the Pima dataset, is a popular benchmark dataset used in diabetes research and machine learning. It focuses on a specific population group called the Pima Indians, who are a Native American group residing in Mexico and Arizona, USA. In this research, our focus is to analyze the Pima Indian Dataset with advanced algorithms to work effectively with graphs. The dataset was downloaded from Kaggle (https://www.kaggle.com/uciml/pima indians-diabetes-database). [17] The Pima Indians have been identified as having a high incidence rate of diabetes mellitus, making them a significant group for studying the disease and its impact on global health. Researching the Pima Indians can provide insights into diabetes prevalence, risk factors, and potential interventions. Additionally, studying this population is particularly relevant for addressing the healthcare needs of underrepresented minority or indigenous groups [18] The dataset consists of health-related measurements and information collected from Pima Indian females aged 21 years and older. These measurements include features such as glucose levels, insulin levels, blood pressure, body mass index (BMI), and diabetes pedigree function. The dataset is widely used for developing and evaluating machine learning models to predict the onset of diabetes based on these features. Table 1 Represents Sample a Dataset The dataset has 9 columns and 768 rows, with 500 non-diabetic cases and 268 diabetic cases. The binary classification outcome variable takes values of 0 or 1, where 0 indicates a negative test for diabetes and 1 implies a positive test.

This Table 1 represents a dataset with 768 rows and 9 columns. Each row represents an individual's information, such as the number of pregnancies, glucose levels, blood pressure, skin thickness, insulin levels, BMI (Body Mass Index), diabetes pedigree function, age, and the outcome (whether the individual has diabetes or not). Note that some values are missing (NaN) in certain columns. By focusing on the Pima Indians, researchers aim to better understand the factors contributing to the high incidence of diabetes within this population and potentially develop targeted interventions to improve

Table 1. Represents an example of a dataset with 768 rows and 9 columns.

Pregnancies	Glucose	BloodPressure	SkinThickness	Insulin	BMI	DiabetesPedigreeFunction	Age	Outcome
0	6.0	148.0	72.0	35.0	NaN	33.6	5	0
1	1.0	85.0	66.0	29.0	NaN	26.6	31	1
2	8.0	183.0	64.0	NaN	NaN	23.3	32	0
3	1.0	89.0	66.0	23.0	94.0	28.1	21	1
4	NaN	137.0	4.0	35.0	168.0	43.1	33	0
...	...	...	...	...	...	...	...	0
763	1.0	11.0	76.0	48.0	18.0	32.9	63	0
764	2.0	122.0	7.0	27.0	NaN	36.8	27	0
765	5.0	121.0	72.0	23.0	112.0	26.2	3	1
766	1.0	126.0	6.0	NaN	NaN	3.1	47	0
767	1.0	93.0	7.0	31.0	NaN	3.4	23	1

their health outcomes. The dataset provides a valuable resource for studying diabetes and developing predictive models that can aid in early detection and intervention for individuals at risk of developing the disease. [16, 18] The specific features included in the Pima Indian Diabetes dataset are not mentioned in the text provided. Table 2 Represents Feature Description However, commonly known features typically included in this dataset are: Pregnancies: Number of times pregnant Glucose: Plasma glucose concentration after 2 h in an oral glucose tolerance test Blood Pressure: Diastolic blood pressure (mm Hg) Skin Thickness: Triceps skinfold thickness (mm) Insulin: 2-h serum insulin (mu U/ml) BMI: Body mass index (weight in kg/(height in m)^2) Diabetes Pedigree Function: Diabetes pedigree function (a measure of the diabetes genetic influence).

Table 2. Represents Feature Description

Feature	Description	Data type	Range
Preg	Number of times pregnant	Numeric	[0, 17]
Gluc	Plasma glucose concentration at 2 h in GTIT	Numeric	[0, 199]
BP	Diastolic Blood Pressure (mm Hg)	Numeric	[0, 122]
Skin	Triceps skin fold thickness (mm)	Numeric	[0, 99]
Insulin	2-h Serum insulin (μU/ml)	Numeric	[0, 846]
BMI	Body mass index (weight in kg/(height in m)^2)	Numeric	[0, 67.1]
DPF	Diabetes pedigree function	Numeric	[0.078, 2.42]
Age	Age in years	Numeric	[21, 81]
Outcome	Binary value indicating non-diabetic (0)/diabetic (1)	Factor	[0, 1]

3.2 Prepressing

Pre-processing refers to the manipulation of data through a series of operations or transformations in order to prepare it for analysis. Within the field of machine learning, data preprocessing holds great importance as it significantly impacts the performance and accuracy of models developed using the data. Common techniques involved in preprocessing include eliminating errors and inconsistencies in the data, addressing missing values through imputation or exclusion of corresponding data points, standardizing or normalizing the data to ensure consistent ranges across features, and converting categorical variables into numerical representations for utilization in numerical models. The ultimate objective of pre-processing is to ready the data in a manner that streamlines the learning process of machine learning algorithms and simplifies their identification of patterns and relationships within the data.

3.3 Algorithm Proposed

The methodology framework proposed in this study comprises a set of clearly defined steps that encompass data preprocessing and modeling. The initial step involves conducting an extensive literature review and gathering the necessary data for the research. This literature review serves to clarify the research objectives, scope, and analytical methods. The Indian PIMA dataset, which contains medical data from Indian women in Pima, is utilized for data collection and for developing machine learning models that are tested in the research. This phase is crucial for establishing research findings, ensuring their relevance, and providing benchmarks for comparison with other studies in the field. In the second phase of the machine learning process, important preprocessing steps, such as normalization, removal of duplicates and outliers, handling of missing values, and division of datasets into training and test sets, are performed.

Tier 1: Normalization is an essential preprocessing procedure in machine learning, which involves scaling numerical data. Its significance in improving algorithm performance cannot be overstated, as it centers the data and ensures they have a similar range. Various techniques for normalization exist, such as using the z-score, scaling the data to a specific range, or scaling the data to have unit length. In our preprocessing framework, we prioritize the z-score method as the initial normalization step. Evaluating the impact of normalization on the model's performance and selecting the appropriate method based on the dataset and task at hand are crucial. Thus, it is always advisable to recognize normalization as a vital step in certain cases.

Tier 2: The identification and elimination of duplicate and outlier data points play a crucial role in dataset manipulation. Outliers have the potential to greatly skew the overall distribution of the dataset, usually resulting from errors in data entry or comments. Similarly, the removal of duplicate observations is important to ensure accuracy and uniqueness. By eliminating these outliers and duplicates, the risk of biased results can be minimized, and the quality of any analysis or modeling can be improved. Various standard methods such as sorting, filtering, and deduplication can be employed to detect and remove duplicates. By employing these techniques, one can confidently ensure the integrity and dependability of the dataset.

Tier 3: One method for addressing missing data in a dataset involves employing a bidirectional neighbor graph. This technique entails constructing a graph in which each variable is represented as a node, and the edges signify connections between them. By leveraging these relationships between variables, the missing values can be estimated. However, it is important to exercise caution as the accuracy of the imputed data relies on the reliability of these relationships. Additionally, it is crucial to take into account any other factors that might influence the missing values (Fig. 1).

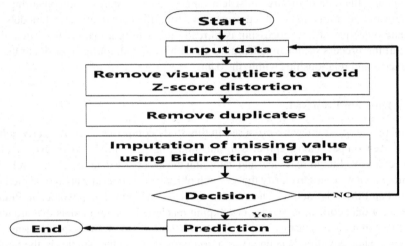

Fig. 1. Flow chart algorithm model to address missing values and predict diabetes.

4   Results and Dissection

The study aimed to evaluate the effectiveness of the bidirectional neighbor graph algorithm in computer vision tasks, specifically image and object recognition, and further optimize an SVM model with a Radial Basis Function (RBF) kernel for predicting diabetic outcomes. The research utilized a diabetes dataset, which was transformed into a graph representation using a sophisticated algorithm. Each data point in the dataset was represented as a node in the graph, and edges were created between nodes based on their similarity. The features selected for the case study included variables such as pregnancies, glucose levels, blood pressure, skin thickness, insulin levels, BMI, diabetes pedigree function, and age. Table 1 provides an overview of the diabetes dataset used in the research, highlighting these chosen features, along with the sample size and the minimum, median, and maximum values for each feature. The dataset consisted of 768 instances, with varying values for each feature. The "Pregnancies" feature ranged from 0 to 17, with a median of 3. The "Glucose" feature had a minimum value of 0, a median of 117, and a maximum of 199. Similarly, the "Blood Pressure" feature ranged from 0 to 122, with a median value of 72. The "Skin Thickness" feature varied between 0 and 99, with a median of 23. Regarding the "Insulin" feature, the dataset showed a minimum value of 0 and a maximum value of 846, with a median of 30.5. The "BMI" feature had a range of 0 to 67.1, with a median value of 32. The "Diabetes Pedigree Function" feature ranged from 0.078 to 2.42, with a median of 0.3725. Lastly, the "Age" feature varied between 21 and 81, with a median age of 29. These features provide crucial insights into the characteristics and distribution of the dataset used in the case study. Understanding the range and distribution of each feature is vital for analyzing and interpreting the results accurately. The bidirectional neighbor graph algorithm and the SVM model with an RBF kernel were utilized to predict diabetic outcomes based on the dataset's features. By transforming the dataset into a graph representation and considering the labels of neighboring nodes, the algorithm assigned labels to each node. The label assignment was determined through a majority or weighted vote, considering the distances between the nodes. The results of the study demonstrated the effectiveness of the bidirectional neighbor graph algorithm in computer vision tasks, specifically image and object recognition. By leveraging the graph representation and similarity metrics such as Euclidean distance or cosine similarity, the algorithm successfully assigned labels to each data point, providing accurate predictions. Furthermore, the SVM model with an RBF kernel was optimized for predicting diabetic outcomes. The combination of the SVM model and the transformed dataset allowed for robust predictions, considering the complex relationships between the features. The optimization process aimed to enhance the model's performance and accuracy in predicting diabetic outcomes. In conclusion, the study's results highlight the effectiveness of the bidirectional neighbor graph algorithm in computer vision tasks and the optimization of an SVM model with an RBF kernel for predicting diabetic outcomes. By transforming the dataset into a graph representation and leveraging the similarities between data points, accurate predictions were achieved. The selected features, as outlined in Table 3 summarizes the selection of characteristics for the diabetes dataset, played a significant role in understanding the dataset's characteristics and distribution. The findings of this research contribute to the field of computer vision and offer insights into improving predictive models for diabetic outcomes.

Table 3. Summarizes the selection of characteristics for the diabetes dataset.

Features Selection	Case study	Min	Median	Max
Pregnancies	768	0	3	17
Glucose	768	0	117	199
Blood Pressure	768	0	72	122
Skin Thickness	768	0	23	99
Insulin	768	0	30.5	846
BMI	768	0	67.1	32
Diabetes Pedigree Function	768	0.078	0.3725	2.42
Age	768	21	29	81

The heatmap of the confusion matrix illustrates the counts of predicted classes that correspond to the actual courses. The diagonal cells of the matrix indicate the number of correctly identified positive and negative instances, while the non-diagonal elements represent incorrect identifications in terms of positive and negative instances. Figure 2 exhibits a heatmap representation of the confusion matrix derived from a diabetes prediction model, demonstrating the comparison between predicted and actual classes. The intensity of colors on the heatmap signifies the degree to which the predicted classes align with the actual classes. The diagonal cells of the matrix correspond to true positives (TP) and true negatives (TN), while the non-diagonal cells represent false positives (FP) and false negatives (FN). These findings of this research contribute to the field of computer vision and offer insights into improving predictive.

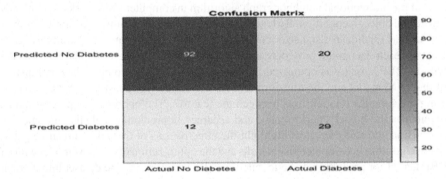

Fig. 2. Confusion matrix to evaluate the performance of the model.

The graphical representation of a binary classifier's performance at different thresholds is depicted by the ROC (Receiver Operating Characteristic) curve. This curve showcases the trade-off between the true positive rate (TPR) and the false positive rate (FPR) for various cut-off points. Figure 3 displays the ROC curve effectively, demonstrating how the classifier performs in distinguishing between true and false positives at different thresholds. Specifically, the ROC curve illustrates the classifier's ability to differentiate between actual positives and false positives, where the X-axis represents the rate of false positives, and the Y-axis represents the rate of true positives. An AUC score of approximately 0.86 serves as a measure of the overall performance of the model. AUC scores range from 0 to 1, with 1 indicating perfect classification and 0.5 representing classification that is no better than random chance. The notable AUC score of about 0.86 indicates the model's capacity to accurately distinguish between true positives and false positives across various classification thresholds, demonstrating its effectiveness in this specific scenario. Therefore, the ROC curve and AUC score provide compelling evidence that the model proficiently classifies diabetes datasets.

In future studies, it would be beneficial to further explore the performance of our proposed system in comparison with well-established machine learning techniques, notably the Random Forest algorithm and the Bidirectional Neighbor Graph (BNG) algorithm, in handling datasets with missing values. Missing data is a common challenge in real-world datasets, and the ability of a model to handle missing values effectively

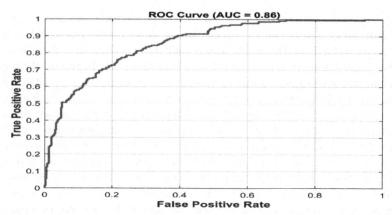

Fig. 3. Visualization of the performance of a binary classification with different classification thresholds.

can significantly impact its practical utility. Random Forest has shown robustness in various scenarios and has been employed as a benchmark in many machine-learning tasks. By comparing our system with Random Forest, we can gain valuable insights into our approach's relative strengths and weaknesses when dealing with data instances containing missing values. This analysis will not only help validate the effectiveness of our system but also provide a clearer understanding of its potential for real-world applications. Furthermore, the Bidirectional Neighbor Graph (BNG) algorithm, known for its ability to capture complex data relationships and handle missing values, presents an exciting alternative for comparison. By contrasting our system with the BNG algorithm, we can explore the nuances of handling missing data in both methods, leading to a deeper understanding of their respective capabilities. This comparative analysis would evaluate key performance metrics such as accuracy, precision, recall, F1-score, and computational efficiency on benchmark datasets with varying degrees of missingness. Additionally, exploring the impact of different missing data imputation techniques in combination with our system and the algorithms mentioned above would provide a comprehensive assessment of their robustness in real-world scenarios. By addressing the crucial challenge of missing data, our future studies aim to not only validate our system's effectiveness but also contribute to the broader field of machine learning by providing insights into the strengths of our approach relative to established methods, thus paving the way for its broader adoption in practical application.

5 Conclusion

In conclusion, this conference paper focuses on predicting diabetes in Peruvian patients using machine learning techniques, specifically leveraging the bidirectional neighbor graph algorithm. The study emphasizes the importance of data collection and pre-processing, with a specific focus on the bidirectional graph representation and the absence of missing values. By utilizing the bidirectional neighbor graph algorithm, we effectively handle missing values within the diabetes dataset of Pima Indians. This approach ensures that all data points are represented as nodes in the graph, and edges are created based on their similarity. The absence of missing values allows for a comprehensive analysis and accurate predictions. The results demonstrate the effectiveness of the bidirectional neighbor graph algorithm in analyzing the diabetes dataset and improving the accuracy of machine learning models for diabetes prediction. This technique, coupled with proper data pre-processing and graph construction, enables more reliable predictions by considering the labels of neighboring nodes. Moving forward, further studies can explore the performance and generalizability of the bidirectional neighbor graph algorithm on different datasets and medical domains. Additionally, research can focus on refining the algorithm to optimize the prediction accuracy and expand its applications. In summary, this conference paper concludes that the bidirectional neighbor graph algorithm, when applied to predicting diabetes in Peruvian patients, effectively handles missing values and enhances the accuracy of machine learning models. The absence of missing values within the graph representation ensures a comprehensive analysis, emphasizing the significance of this technique in improving predictive models for medical diagnosis.

References

1. Bania, R.K., Halder, A.: R-Ensembler: a greedy rough set based ensemble attribute selection algorithm with kNN imputation for classification of medical data. Comput. Methods Programs Biomed. **184**, 105122 (2020)
2. Bania, R.K., Halder, A.: R-HEFS: rough set based heterogeneous ensemble feature selection method for medical data classification. Artif. Intell. Med. **114**, 102049 (2021)
3. Wang, X., et al.: Exploratory study on classification of diabetes mellitus through a combined Random Forest Classifier. BMC Med. Inform. Decis. Mak. **21**(1), 1–14 (2021)
4. Zhu, C., Idemudia, C.U., Feng, W.: Improved logistic regression model for diabetes prediction by integrating PCA and K-means techniques. Inform. Med. Unlocked **17**, 100179 (2019)
5. Alić, B., Gurbeta, L., Badnjević, A.: Machine learning techniques for classification of diabetes and cardiovascular diseases, pp. 1–4. IEEE (2017)
6. Sisodia, D., Sisodia, D.S.: Prediction of diabetes using classification algorithms. Procedia Comput. Sci. **132**, 1578–1585 (2018)
7. Galand, L., Ismaili, A., Perny, P., Spanjaard, O.: Bidirectional preference-based search for state space graph problems, pp. 80–88 (2013)
8. Vijayan, V.V., Anjali, C.: Prediction and diagnosis of diabetes mellitus—a machine learning approach, pp. 122–127. IEEE (2015)
9. Roy, K., et al.: An enhanced machine learning framework for type 2 diabetes classification using imbalanced data with missing values. Complexity **2021**, 1–21 (2021)
10. Andaur Navarro, C.L., et al.: Systematic review identifies the design and methodological conduct of studies on machine learning-based prediction models. J. Clin. Epidemiol. **154**, 8–22 (2023)
11. Razavi-Far, R., Chakrabarti, S., Saif, M., Zio, E.: An integrated imputation-prediction scheme for prognostics of battery data with missing observations. Expert Syst. Appl. **115**, 709–723 (2019)
12. Bai, B.M., Mangathayaru, N., Rani, B.P.: An approach to find missing values in medical datasets, pp. 1–7 (2015)
13. Ahmedt-Aristizabal, D., Armin, M.A., Denman, S., Fookes, C., Petersson, L.: Graph-based deep learning for medical diagnosis and analysis: past, present and future. Sensors (Basel) **21**(14), 4758 (2021)

14. Barbiero, P., Vinas Torne, R., Lio, P.: Graph representation forecasting of patient's medical conditions: toward a digital twin. Front. Genet. **12**, 652907 (2021)
15. D'Auria, D., Moscato, V., Postiglione, M., Romito, G., Sperlí, G.: Improving graph embeddings via entity linking: a case study on Italian clinical notes. Intell. Syst. Appl. **17**, 200161 (2023)
16. Learning, U.M.: Pima Indians diabetes database. kaggle.com/uciml/pima-indians-diabetes-database (2016)
17. Kibria, H.B., Nahiduzzaman, M., Goni, M.O.F., Ahsan, M., Haider, J.: An ensemble approach for the prediction of diabetes mellitus using a soft voting classifier with an explainable AI. Sensors (Basel) **22**(19), 7268 (2022)
18. Chang, V., Bailey, J., Xu, Q.A., Sun, Z.: Pima Indians diabetes mellitus classification based on machine learning (ML) algorithms. Neural Comput. Appl. **35**, 1–17 (2022)

Feature Selection Techniques on Breast Cancer Classification Using Fine Needle Aspiration Features: A Comparative Study

Shahiratul A. Karim[✉], Ummul Hanan Mohamad, and Puteri N. E. Nohuddin

Institute of Visual Informatics, Bangunan Akademia Siber Teknopolis,
Universiti Kebangsaan Malaysia, 43600 Bangi, Malaysia
p105766@siswa.ukm.edu.my

Abstract. Breast cancer remains a prevalent invasive cancer in women as it ranks as the second leading cause of cancer-related death among women. It poses a significant global medical challenge due to its substantial increase in cases over the last decade. Early detection of breast cancer is vital; hence the development of computer-aided diagnosis (CAD) systems is crucial in assisting pathologists to accurately interpret and diagnose the tumor. Feature selection plays a significant role in CAD as it involves choosing the most relevant and informative features from the original dataset to improve the performance of the system. Thus, this study focuses on evaluating various feature selection methods on fine needle aspiration (FNA) features which are adapted from Wisconsin Diagnostic Breast Cancer (WDBC) dataset from UCI Repository. The analysis involved five feature selection techniques; Information Gain (InfoGain), Correlation Feature Selection (CFS), Fast-Correlation Based Filter (FCBF), Consistency and Relief-F with three different machine learning classifiers including Logistic Regression (LR), Support Vector Machine (SVM) and Random Forest (RF) with 10-fold cross-validations. Based on the experimental outcomes, it was observed that FCBF with LR classifier surpassed other FS techniques (ACC = 0.9718 and AUC = 0.993) with 7 features. On the other hand, Relief-F outshined other FS with both classifiers of SVM (ACC = 0.9772 and AUC = 0.971) and RF (ACC = 0.9684 and AUC = 0.991). This study validated that the Relief-F technique exhibited supremacy over other FS techniques. However, the task of identifying important features from high-dimensional data remains a significant obstacle in intelligent diagnosis. Henceforth, it is essential to dedicate further efforts to the development of CAD systems using efficient feature selection techniques to maximize the performance and effectiveness of diagnostic models.

Keywords: Breast Cancer · Feature Selection · FNA features · Machine Learning

1 Introduction

Breast cancer is a major health concern that affects people all over the world. It is the second most frequent disease among women, with a high mortality rate and severe disease [1]. According to the World Health Organization (WHO), more than 2.3 million

H. Badioze Zaman et al. (Eds.): IVIC 2023, LNCS 14322, pp. 568–582, 2024.
https://doi.org/10.1007/978-981-99-7339-2_46

women worldwide were diagnosed with breast cancer in 2020, with 685,000 deaths [2]. In 2023, an estimated 353,510 new cases of breast cancer would be diagnosed in women, while 2,800 new cases diagnosed in men [3]. Breast cancer tumors occur when cells abnormally grow and invade the surrounding tissues of the body. They typically arise in either the ducts or the lobules. Breast cancer symptoms include the presence of a lump or thickening in the breast, changes in size or shape, dimpling of the skin, redness, pitting, changes in the appearance of the nipple, and abnormal discharge from the nipple [4]. Breast tumors can be malignant or benign [5]. Malignant tumors are threatening because they grow quickly and spread to other tissues, yet benign tumors are not fatal since they are tiny and remain within their boundaries. However, the prompt detection of cancer ensures effective treatment and increases the chances of survival for the patients [6].

Various conventional techniques are utilized in the detection of breast cancer, such as mammography, ultrasound, and magnetic resonance imaging [7]. They commonly identified and localized abnormalities within the breast and subsequently analyzed by medical experts for diagnostic purposes. Another alternative approach to achieve precise detection of breast cancer is breast cancer classification using Fine Needle Aspiration (FNA) features. FNA is a minimally invasive procedure that involves the extraction of cellular material from suspicious breast masses using a thin needle [8]. FNA features encompass a diverse set of cellular and morphological characteristics, such as cell size, shape, nuclear features, and architectural patterns which serve as valuable indicators of malignancy. Machine learning algorithms are commonly employed to analyze these features and classify breast lesions into malignant or benign categories, providing critical information for treatment planning and patient management. The utilization of FNA features in breast cancer classification holds great promise for enhancing diagnostic accuracy, reducing unnecessary biopsies, and facilitating timely and personalized patient care [9].

Consequently, there is a pressing need for computer-aided diagnosis (CAD) methods, which exhibit remarkable efficacy in the prediction process. CAD methods hold immense potential as invaluable tools to support radiologists [10]. Figure 1 shows the block diagram of CAD in breast cancer diagnosis.

In CAD, the process involves image pre-processing, segmentation, extracting important features from medical images, selecting the most relevant features, and using classification algorithms to diagnose the tumor into categories; benign or malignant. Feature extraction identifies patterns, textures, and structures within the images, while feature selection helps in choosing the most informative features. Subsequently, classification algorithms are employed to assign a diagnosis based on the selected features [11]. CAD systems aim to automate and enhance the diagnostic process, empowering healthcare professionals to make more informed decisions and improve patient outcomes.

This research focuses on enhancing the precision of breast cancer prediction through the investigation of different techniques for selecting relevant features and evaluating their effectiveness. The remaining sections of the paper are organized as follows. Section 2 discusses related research that closely aligns with the current study. Section 3

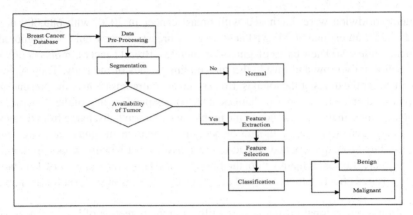

Fig. 1. Block diagram of CAD breast cancer.

provides a concise overview of the dataset, feature selection techniques, machine learning algorithms and performance measures employed in this research. Section 4 presents the results, subsequently, Sect. 5 concludes the paper.

2 Related Works

Breast cancer has emerged as a prominent cause of mortality among women in recent years. The diminished survival rate of breast cancer can primarily be attributed to the intricacies involved in the diagnostic procedure and the delayed detection thereof. Timely identification of the disease in its initial stages is pivotal in impeding its advancement and mitigating associated risks. The prompt detection and subsequent treatment of breast cancer considerably enhance the prospects of survival [12, 13]. Therefore, it is essential to utilize machine learning and deep learning techniques properly, considering all aspects of the workflow, from using efficient image processing tools to selecting appropriate features and applying suitable validation methods.

2.1 Existing Feature Selection Techniques for Breast Cancer Diagnosis

There are many research works studied the feature selection technique to select relevant features in diagnosing breast cancer. They used FNA features in datasets available in UCI Machine Repository such as Wisconsin Breast Cancer Original (WBC), Wisconsin Diagnostic Breast Cancer (WDBC) and Wisconsin Prognostic Breast Cancer (WPBC). For instance, in a study conducted by [14], a correlation feature selection (CFS) has been studied on the WDBC dataset with several machine learning classifiers such as Logistic Regression (LR), Support Vector Machine (SVM), Random Forest (RF), Naïve Bayes (NB), Decision Tree (DT) and k-Nearest Neighbours (kNN). The study found that SVM is the preferable algorithm for prediction as it performs relatively good with an accuracy of 96.5% if a clear separation between classes is present in the dataset and the dataset is high dimensional. Subsequently, RF also gave better results alongside SVM with higher accuracy of 96.5% without any normalization of dataset values. In the same year,

[15] also conducted a study with the same feature selection technique with additional Recursive Feature Elimination (RFE) and Univariate (SelectKBest method) using an RF classifier. They selected 5 out of 33 features and achieved the highest accuracy of 95.32% on CFS, subsequently 94.15% on SelectKBest and RFE. CFS also has been utilized in [16] where the authors proposed a hybrid of various meta-learning models (constituted of SVM, kNN, DT, RF, LR, Gradient Boost (GB), XgBoost, AdaBoost, Multi-layer Perceptron (MLP)) and Artificial Neural Network (ANN). Initially, they evaluated the relevancy of features using CFS, RFE-Cross Validated (RFECV) and tree-based feature selection and chose CFS with the highest accuracy of 96.49% where 16 out of 33 features were selected. The output of a combination of various meta-learning models was used as input features for ANN giving 98.74% of accuracy and 98.02% of F1-score. RFE was also used in [17] on WDBC to evaluate the features using GB, SVM, LR, NB, RF, and ANN. They implemented ten-fold cross-validation to improve the tuning of algorithm hyperparameters and robustness in the model. From the experiments, RF gave the best accuracy of 98.83% and the least accuracy of 91.22% by kNN. Deep learning algorithms ANN reached an accuracy of 99.73%.

Some recent works have employed Principal Component Analysis in diagnosing breast cancer using FNA features. PCA is a statistical technique used for dimensionality reduction and data exploration. It is commonly applied to datasets with high-dimensional features to identify the most significant patterns and capture the most important information. In [18], PCA has been used to find the most important features and found that there are 12 important features and 2 of them are redundant. Hence, the authors used the top 10 features of RF and DT classifiers. It is shown that RF performs better than DT and it achieved an accuracy of 97.52% and 93.64% by using the top 10 and 6 features respectively. Besides, [19] also studied PCA with additional feature selection techniques; supervised learning Relief algorithm and unsupervised learning AutoEncoder on WDBC and WBCO. By using SVM as a classifier, the Relief algorithm has achieved 99.91% of accuracy while AutoEncoder and PCA have shown lower accuracy.

Similarly, [20] used PCA on MLP and Convolutional Neural Network (CNN) on WDBC and SEER2017 dataset. They chose 15 out of 21 features and found that MLP gave an accuracy of 99.1% while CNN achieved 96.4% on the WDBC dataset whereas the accuracy of MLP was 89.3% and CNN 88.3% on the SEER2017 dataset. In addition, [21] implemented PCA and transformed WDBC dataset into 11 features and achieved 99.67% accuracy using Neural Network (NN) classifier. On the other hand, the authors also conducted a study in the same year [22] using univariate feature selection (Chi2) on the LR classifier. They used 16 features of the dataset which gave an accuracy of 98.50%. Besides, Chi2 feature selection is also utilized with CART, LR, kNN, SVM, RF, and Stacking classifiers [23]. They selected the top 20 features and achieved maximum accuracy of 97.2% on the stacking classifier. Another type of univariate feature selection; SelectKBest also used in [21] using classifiers SVM, LR, DT, and CNN. They utilized 10 features and all four classifiers have shown good performance where the CNN classifier achieved the highest accuracy of 98%.

There are other feature selection techniques also used in diagnosing breast cancer on WBCO, WDBC, and private data. For example, [24] used the STrong Relevant Algorithm of Subset Selection (STRASS) and Minimum Redundancy Maximum Relevance (mRMR) feature selection techniques and NN classifier. The proposed method has shown reduced drastically computing time. Besides, [25] employed genetic algorithms (GA) simultaneously in the selection of features and classification. They removed redundant and irrelevant features during 50% of the generation and formed suboptimal features which lead to achieving an accuracy of 97.07% for the WBC dataset and 95.08% for the WDBC dataset. Similarly, the GA technique also selected relevant features in [26] with the kNN classifier. The proposed method achieved high accuracy with selected features and optimization (k) value for the classifier.

Within the scope of the recent works, three classifiers have been chosen to investigate throughout this work: LR, SVM, and RF with the selected features chosen by several feature selection techniques discussed in the next section.

3   Materials and Methods

3.1   Source of FNA Data

The data of this study is Wisconsin Diagnostic Breast Cancer (WDBC) dataset which is acquired from UC Irvine (UCI) Machine Learning Repository [27]. The dataset contains 569 cases diagnosed whether as benign; the tumor is non-cancerous or malignant; the tumor is cancerous. Several features or characteristics computed from a digitized image of FNA of a breast mass describe the cells present in breast cancer samples. The original dataset contains 10 features where each feature derived its mean, standard error, and max, yielding 30 features in total. Table 1 shows the list of features and their brief description.

Table 1. List of features in the WDBC dataset.

Feature Name	Feature Description
Radius	The average distance from the center to points on the parameter of the tumor
Texture	Variations gray-scale levels
Perimeter	Length of the tumor boundary
Area	The area occupied by the tumor
Smoothness	Local variation in radius lengths
Compactness	The compactness of the tumor shape
Concavity	The severity of concave portions of the tumor contour
Concave points	Number of concave portions of the tumor contour
Symmetry	Symmetry of the cell nucleus
Fractal dimension	The complexity of the tumor boundary

In the dataset, 30 features are real values while the class of the tumor is a categorical variable; 'B' is benign, and 'M' is malignant. The count data for Benign is 357 and 212 for Malignant.

3.2 Comparison of Feature Selection Techniques

Feature selection (FS) is an essential aspect of intelligent diagnosis in identifying the most vital features for target representation in CAD models. The FS techniques can be categorized into three groups [28, 29]; filter, wrapper, and embedded method. (1) the filter method which operates independently of the machine learning classifier selects features effectively based on their correlation with the target label, avoiding overfitting, though it may incur some redundant selections. Conversely, the wrapper method uses learning algorithms to pick the best feature subset, allowing for potential feature interactions but increasing computation time. The embedded method where simultaneously performs feature selection and target classification to enhance the accuracy and effectiveness of the system. FS techniques have been widely explored in diverse fields, including target recognition [30], bioinformatics [31, 32], and industrial applications [33, 34].

In pursuit of the objectives of this paper, this study utilized five prominent and well-established feature selection approaches: Information Gain (InfoGain), Correlation Feature Selection (CFS), Fast Correlation Based Filter (FCBF), Consistency, and Relief-F.

Information Gain (InfoGain): In the context of feature selection, information theory is widely employed to assess the quality of features by measuring their uncertainty and relationships. Entropy and mutual information play key roles in quantifying the uncertainty of random features and the association between discrete features, respectively. The entropy $H(X)$ can be defined [35] as

$$H(f_i) = -\sum p(f_i) \log(p(f_i)) \tag{1}$$

and mutual information can be defined as

$$I(X; Y) = H(X) - H(X|Y) \tag{2}$$

where $H(X|Y)$ is the conditional entropy of X given the value of Y which measures the remaining uncertainty of X after knowing Y.

Correlation Feature Selection (CFS). CFS [36] calculates the merit of the feature subset and uses a correlation-based heuristic to find a feature subset that captures the most relevant information about the target class while avoiding redundant or duplicate information. Merit can be calculated as

$$Merit(S) = \frac{k\overline{r_{cf}}}{\sqrt{k + k(k-1)\overline{r_{ff}}}} \tag{3}$$

where $\overline{r}_{cf}$ is the mean feature class correlation and r_{ff} is the average feature-feature correlation. CFS employed symmetrical uncertainty [37] to obtain the feature-class correlation and feature-feature correlation.

Fast Correlation Based Filter (FCBF). FCBF is another method that simultaneously considers feature-class correlation and feature-feature correlation [38]. It selects features highly correlated with class labels based on a predefined threshold. Subsequently, it identifies redundant features and retains those most relevant to the class labels. FCBF selects a subset of features (X) that have a strong correlation with the class label C which is determined by a predefined threshold θ. It calculates the symmetric uncertainty (SU) [50] between the feature set and the class labels C as follows:

$$SU(X, C) = \frac{2 \times I(X; C)}{H(X) + H(C)} \qquad (4)$$

where $I(X; C)$ is the mutual information between feature set X and class labels C.

Consistency. Consistency is a measure proposed by [39]. It focuses on the ratio of samples correctly recognized using majority voting. The consistency measure is fast, capable of handling noise, and effectively removes redundant or irrelevant features. Assuming a subset $\{s_0, s_1, \ldots, s_n\}$ of features, a measure U that evaluates each subset S_i. The monotonicity condition requires the following:

$$S_0 \supset S_1 \supset \ldots \supset S_n \Rightarrow U(S_0) \leq U(S_1) \leq \ldots \leq U(S_n) \qquad (5)$$

Relief-F. Relief-F was proposed by [40] that focuses on distinguishing instances from different classes. It identifies the nearest instances of each class to calculate the feature score to evaluate the relevance of a feature. Feature score $W(f_i)$ can be defined as:

$$W(f_i) = \frac{1}{c} \sum_{j=1}^{l} \left(-\frac{1}{m_j} \sum_{x_r \in NH(j)} d(X(j, i) - X(r, i)) + \sum_{y \neq y_j} \frac{1}{h_{jy}} \frac{p(y)}{1 - p(y)} \sum_{x_r \in NM(j,y)} d(X(j, i) - X(r, i)) \right) \qquad (6)$$

where $NH(j)$ and $NM(j, y)$ and are the nearest instances of x_j and in class y with their sizes m_j and h_{jy} respectively whereas $p(y)$ is the ratio of instances in class y.

The choice of FS technique for breast cancer classification using FNA data depends on specific characteristics such as a measure of feature relevancy, computational constraints, the interpretability of selected features, and the robustness of the technique. These criteria have been compared and discussed in Table 2.

3.3 Supervised Machine Learning Classifier

The incorporation of machine learning in various fields like image processing [50], computer vision [51] edge computing [52] and the Internet of Things (IoT) [53] has played a vital role in advancing technologies. In this study, supervised machine learning models have been utilized to classify breast cancer tumors: Logistic Regression (LR), Support Vector Machine (SVM), and Random Forest (RF).

Logistic Regression (LR). LR is a widely employed and well-established supervised learning algorithm designed specifically for binary classification tasks. The fundamental objective is to identify a clear-cut decision boundary within the input feature space that effectively separates data instances into positive class and negative class. The specialized activation function known logistic response function is expressed in Eq. 7 with its parameters described in Eq. 8.

Table 2. Comparison of feature selection techniques

FS technique	InfoGain	CFS	FCBF	Consistency	Relief-F
Robustness and generalization	Tends to be sensitive to data imbalances and might not generalize well to new datasets	Robust to some extent but it may struggle with redundant or collinear features	Known for its robustness and suitability for diverse datasets and real-world applications	Offers robustness by considering multiple subsets of data	Generally robust and can handle noisy datasets effectively
Interpretability	It does not provide insights into the specific relationship between features and classes. However, it identifies the most informative features	Offers some interpretability which highlights features that are highly correlated with the target class	Provide partial interpretability but lacks a complete understanding of feature-class relationships	While it focuses on frequently selected features, the interpretability of specific feature-class associations might be limited	The selected features can be interpretable due to their neighborhood-based evaluation, giving insights into local feature importance
Computational efficiency	Computationally efficient as it requires calculating the entropy of features	Efficient for datasets with a small number of features, but it can become computationally expensive for high-dimensional data	Specifically designed for large datasets, making it computationally efficient even with numerous features	It may require more computation when dealing with large datasets or complex feature spaces	Relatively efficient for high-dimensional datasets since it only evaluates the feature relevance in the local neighborhood
Selection of relevant features	Measures the ability of features to discriminate between classes based on their entropy. It selects features that have the highest information gain	Relies on the correlation between features and class labels. It selects features with a high correlation to the target class	Selects features based on their correlation with class labels	Measures the ability of features to be consistently selected across different data subsets. Features that appear frequently are considered more relevant	Evaluates the relevance of features by comparing the feature values of neighboring instances. It focuses on features that can discriminate between instances of different classes
References	[35, 41, 42]	[36, 43, 44]	[38, 45]	[39, 46, 47]	[40, 48, 49]

Support Vector Machine (SVM). SVM is also a supervised learning algorithm that serves both classification and regression tasks. SVM is suitable for smaller datasets, though it demands more processing time. It can be trained using stochastic gradient descent (SGD) [54] as defined in Eq. 9.

$$\frac{dA}{d\beta} = \sum_{i=1}^{N} \begin{cases} \text{if } (p^i y^i < 1) y^i X^i \\ \text{else} 0 \end{cases} \tag{9}$$

where the expression/tests whether the point (x_i, y_i) is closer to the margin than a pre-defined threshold. If so, it will adjust by adding it with the corresponding sign y_i. This process encourages the model to push the point further away from the decision boundary in subsequent iterations.

Random Forest (RF). Random Forest (RF) is an ensemble model employing numerous decision trees to make predictions [55]. Each decision tree provides a prediction for input data and RF aggregates these predictions ultimately selecting the most voted result as the final prediction. RF generates diverse trees by selecting the best feature from a random subset of features in order to reduce overfitting risks [56]. Mathematically, the prediction of the RF can be expressed as:

$$RF(x) = mode(\{f_1(x), f_2(x), \ldots, f_T(x)\}) \tag{10}$$

where T is the number of decision trees in the RF and $f_T(x)$ represents the prediction of the T-th decision tree for the input data.

3.4 Evaluation Measure

Evaluation measure is a vital aspect of evaluating the effectiveness and proficiency of a model or system. It provides quantitative insights into how well the model performs in achieving its objectives. These measures are crucial in various fields including machine learning which constitute accuracy, sensitivity, specificity, and other relevant metrics to gauge the model's predictive capabilities.

Accuracy. Accuracy is a crucial evaluation metric that signifies the proportion of correctly predicted labels out of the total labels by a classifier. This can be mathematically expressed as shown in Eq. 11.

$$Accuracy(ACC) = \frac{TP + TN}{TP + TN + FP + FN} \tag{11}$$

Sensitivity. Sensitivity which is also known as recall measures the classifier's ability to correctly identify benign samples. The formula for sensitivity is given in as follows:

$$Sensitivity(SEN) = \frac{TP}{TP + FN} \tag{12}$$

Specificity. Conversely, specificity measures the classifier's ability to identify malignant samples correctly. The formula for specificity is as follows:

$$Specificity(SPE) = \frac{TN}{TN + FP} \tag{13}$$

where True Positive (TP) represents correctly predicted benign samples, True Negative (TN) for correctly predicted malignant samples, False Positive (FP) for incorrectly predicted benign samples, and False Negative (FN) for incorrectly predicted malignant samples.

In this study, besides using the previously mentioned metrics, the Receiver Operating Characteristic (ROC) graph area under the curve (AUC) also have been evaluated. By incorporating the ROC graph and AUC as additional evaluation measures, the study gained further insights into the model's discrimination power and its capacity to distinguish between benign and malignant tumors.

4   Results and Discussions

This section presents the results of data analysis applied to the WDBC dataset. The performance of the feature selections of InfoGain, CFS, FCBF, Consistency, and Relief-F with three classifiers LR, SVM, and RT were analyzed using evaluation measures discussed in Sect. 3. Each experiment utilized 10-fold cross-validation techniques. Subsequently, the selection of relevant features is also discussed for each FS technique.

4.1   Performance of Feature Selection Techniques

The experiment results of the performance of each FS technique with LR, SVM, and RF classifiers are presented in Tables 3, 4, and 5 respectively. Each experiment utilized 10-fold cross-validation techniques.

Table 3. Performance of FS technique with LR classifier

FS technique	AUC	ACC	SPE	SEN
InfoGain	0.975	0.953	0.956	0.953
CFS	0.989	0.968	0.964	0.968
FCBF	0.993	0.972	0.964	0.972
Consistency	0.994	0.963	0.959	0.963
Relief-F	0.972	0.948	0.947	0.948

Based on Table 3, it can be observed that FCBF with LR classifier has achieved performance in terms of ACC with 97% with a higher AUC value. Followed by Consistency with a slightly lower ACC 96% and the highest AUC value. However, Relief-F has the least ACC with other measures stated above which interpreted that it identified benign and malignant samples incorrectly with the LR classifier.

Table 4. Performance of FS technique with SVM classifier

FS technique	AUC	ACC	SPE	SEN
InfoGain	0.966	0.974	0.958	0.974
CFS	0.956	0.967	0.946	0.967
FCBF	0.946	0.958	0.935	0.958
Consistency	0.954	0.963	0.946	0.963
Relief-F	0.971	0.977	0.965	0.977

According to Table 4 and Table 5, it can be noticed that various FS techniques have good performance in terms of ACC with > 95% with SVM and RF classifiers.

Table 5. Performance of FS technique with RF classifier

FS technique	AUC	ACC	SPE	SEN
InfoGain	0.990	0.966	0.955	0.967
CFS	0.987	0.956	0.947	0.956
FCBF	0.991	0.954	0.944	0.954
Consistency	0.991	0.961	0.956	0.961
Relief-F	0.991	0.968	0.958	0.968

Notably, Relief-F stands out as the algorithm with the highest ACC and AUC with these classifiers. Relief-F also demonstrates superiority in SPE and SEN which gave insights into the great ability of Relief-F to identify benign and malignant samples correctly. FCBF and Consistency also achieved the same for AUC with RF classifier.

4.2 Relevant Features for Breast Cancer Classification Using FNA Data

Relevancy is a critical aspect of feature quality evaluation in data analysis. It refers to the significance of a feature in contributing meaningful information to the prediction task which evaluates a strong relationship with the diagnosis of breast cancer. From the data analysis, the relevant features have been selected and listed in Table 6 according to the feature number in the WDBC dataset. In this table, ranking-based FS techniques such as InfoGain and Relief-F showed 10 top-ranked features.

Table 6. Features selected from FNA data

FS technique	No. of features selected	Features number
InfoGain	10	23, 24, 21, 28, 8, 3, 4, 1, 7, 14
CFS	11	2,7, 8, 14, 19, 21, 23, 24, 25, 27, 28
FCBF	7	23, 28, 11, 2, 25, 29, 19
Consistency	7	7,13, 21, 22, 27, 28, 29
Relief-F	10	21, 28, 23, 22,1,3,8, 24, 4,7

In accordance with Table 6, it can be observed that some feature numbers: 21, 23, 24, 28, and 29 (*radius_worst, perimeter_worst, area_worst, concave points_worst, symmetry_worst*) showed the highest relevancy among 7 top ranked features for various FS. Besides, some of the features such as 2 (*texture_mean*) and 7 (*concavity_mean*) also can help diagnose the tumor. It can be decided that the shape and textural features give the most crucial information to diagnose breast cancer based on FNA features correctly.

5 Conclusion

In conclusion, this study presents a comparative study of several feature selection techniques in breast cancer classification using fine-needle aspiration (FNA) features collected from the WDBC dataset. This study shows the feature selection (FS) procedure plays a crucial role in handling high-dimensional datasets to enhance the interpretability of the model. Relevant and important features are selected using five feature selection techniques: InfoGain, CFS, FCBF, Consistency, and Relief-F with three classifiers: LR, SVM, and RF. The results show that the Relief-F technique exhibited superior over other FS techniques as it gave an outstanding performance in accuracy, specificity, and sensitivity which revealed the ability to identify benign and malignant samples correctly. Shape and textural features such as radius, perimeter, area, concavity, and texture give significant information in diagnosing breast cancer correctly using FNA features. This study also contributes to the advancements in breast cancer diagnosis research by offering a systematic approach to identify and prioritize relevant features. Future research directions could focus on exploring more sophisticated feature selection techniques such as deep learning-based methods or hybrid approaches to further enhance classification accuracy. Investigating the combination of different imaging modalities could offer valuable insights into a comprehensive understanding of breast cancer.

Acknowledgement. This study is supported by grant TAP-K021917 from Universiti Kebangsaan Malaysia.

References

1. Amin, S., Ewunonu, H., Oguntebi, E., Liman, I.: Breast cancer mortality in a resource-poor country: a 10-year experience in a tertiary institution. Sahel Med. Jr. **20**(3), 93–97 (2017)
2. Vy, V.P.T., Yao, M.M.-S., Le, N.Q.K., Chan, W.P.: Machine learning algorithm for distinguishing ductal carcinoma in situ from invasive breast cancer. Cancers **14**(10), 2437 (2022). https://doi.org/10.3390/cancers14102437
3. Siegel, R.L., Miller, K.D., Wagle, N.S., Jemal, A.: Cancer statistics, 2023. Cancer J. Clin. **73**(1), 17–48 (2023)
4. Yadav, R.K., Singh, P., Kashtriya, P.: Diagnosis of breast cancer using machine learning techniques - A survey. Comput. Sci. **218**, 1434–1443 (2023)
5. Oskouei, R.J., Kor, N.M., Maleki, S.A.: Data mining and medical world: breast cancers' diagnosis, treatment, prognosis and challenges. Am. J. Cancer Res. **7**(3), 610–627 (2017)
6. Khamparia, A., Bharati, S., Podder, P., et al.: Diagnosis of breast cancer based on modern mammography using hybrid transfer learning. Multidim. Sys. Sig. Process **32**(2), 747–765 (2021)
7. Kuhl, C.K., et al.: Mammography, breast ultrasound, and magnetic resonance imaging for surveillance of women at high familial risk for breast cancer. J. Clin. Oncol. **23**(33), 8469–8476 (2005). https://doi.org/10.1200/JCO.2004.00.4960
8. Shafique, R., et al.: Breast cancer prediction using fine needle aspiration features and up-sampling with supervised machine learning. Cancers (Basel) **15**(3), 1–21 (2023)
9. AhmedMedjahed, S., Ait Saadi, T., Benyettou, A.: Breast cancer diagnosis by using k-nearest neighbor with different distances and classification rules. Int. J. Comput. Appl. **62**(1), 1–5 (2013)

10. Drukker, K., Sennett, C.A., Giger, M.L.: Automated method for improving system performance of computer-aided diagnosis in breast ultrasound. IEEE Trans. Med. Imaging **28**(1), 122–128 (2009). https://doi.org/10.1109/TMI.2008.928178

11. Guo, Z., et al.: A review of the current state of the computer-aided diagnosis (CAD) systems for breast cancer diagnosis. Open Life Sci. **17**(1), 1600–1611 (2022)

12. Sharma, D., Kumar, R., Jain, A.: A systematic review of risk factors and risk assessment models for breast cancer. In: Marriwala, N., Tripathi, C.C., Kumar, D., Jain, S. (eds.) Mobile Radio Communications And 5g Networks. LNNS, vol. 140, pp. 509–519. Springer, Singapore (2021). https://doi.org/10.1007/978-981-15-7130-5_41

13. Hassan, N.M., Hamad, S., Mahar, K.: Mammogram breast cancer CAD systems for mass detection and classification: a review. Multimed. Tools Appl. **81**(14), 20043–20075 (2022). https://doi.org/10.1007/s11042-022-12332-1

14. Ara, S., Das, A., Dey, A.: Malignant and benign breast cancer classification using machine learning algorithms. ICAI **2021**, 97–101 (2021)

15. Raj, S., Singh, S., Kumar, A., Sarkar, S., Pradhan, C.: Feature selection and random forest classification for breast cancer disease. In: Satpathy, R., Choudhury, T., Satpathy, S., Mohanty, S.N., Zhang, X. (eds.) Data Analytics in Bioinformatics: A Machine Learning Perspective, pp. 191–210. Wiley (2021). https://doi.org/10.1002/9781119785620.ch8

16. Han, L., Yin, Z.: A hybrid breast cancer classification algorithm based on meta-learning and artificial neural networks. Front. Oncol. **12**, 1–9 (2022)

17. Mridha, K.: Early prediction of breast cancer by using artificial neural network and machine learning techniques. IEEE CSNT **2021**, 582–587 (2021)

18. Ray, S., Alghamdi, A., Alshouiliy, K., Agrawal, D. P.: Selecting features for breast cancer analysis and prediction. In: ICACCE 2020 (2020)

19. Haq, A.U., et al.: Detection of breast cancer through clinical data using supervised and unsupervised feature selection techniques. IEEE Access **9**, 22090–22105 (2021)

20. Mehedi Hasan, Md., Rakibul Haque, Md., Jahangir Kabir, M.Md.: Breast cancer diagnosis models using pca and different neural network architectures. In: International Conference on Computer, Communication, Chemical, Materials and Electronic Engineering (IC4ME2) (2019)

21. Khuriwal, N., Mishra, N.: Breast cancer diagnosis using deep learning algorithm. In: International Conference on Advances in Computing, Communication Control and Networking, ICACCCN 2018, pp. 98–103 (2018)

22. Khuriwal, N., Mishra, N.: Breast cancer diagnosis using adaptive voting ensemble machine learning algorithm. Eng. Infinite Conf. IEEMA **2018**, 1–5 (2018)

23. Basunia, M.R., Pervin, I.A., Al Mahmud, M., Saha, S. Arifuzzaman, M.: On predicting and analyzing breast cancer using data mining approach. In: IEEE Region 10 Symposium, TENSYMP 2020, pp. 1257–1260 (2020)

24. Algarni, A., Aldahri, B. A., Alghamdi, H. S.: Convolutional neural networks for breast tumor classification using structured features. In: International Conference of Women in Data Science at Taif University, WiDSTaif 2021, pp. 1-5 (2021).

25. Zemouri, R., et al.: Breast cancer diagnosis based on joint variable selection and constructive deep neural network. Middle East Conf. Biomed. Eng. MECBME **2018**, 159–164 (2018)

26. Bhardwaj, H., Sakalle, A., Tiwari, A.: Breast cancer diagnosis using simultaneous feature selection and classification: a genetic programming approach. In: IEEE Symposium Series on Computational Intelligence, SSCI (2018)

27. Abed, B.M. et al.: A hybrid classification algorithm approach for breast cancer diagnosis. In: IEEE Industrial Electronics and Applications Conference, IEACon, pp. 269–274 (2017)

28. Wolberg, W., William, M., Olvi, S., Nick, S.: Breast Cancer Wisconsin (Diagnostic) - UCI Machine Learning Repository (1995)

29. Li, J., et al.: Feature selection: a data perspective. ACM Comput. Surv. **50**(6), 1–45 (2017). https://doi.org/10.1145/3136625

30. Ang, J.C., Mirzal, A., Haron, H., Hamed, H.N.A.: Supervised, unsupervised, and semi-supervised feature selection: a review on gene selection. IEEE/ACM Trans. Comput. Biol. Bioinform. **13**(5), 971–989 (2016)

31. Zhao, S., Zhang, Y., Xu, H., Han, T.: Ensemble classification based on feature selection for environmental sound recognition. Math. Probl. Eng. **2019**, 4318463 (2019)

32. Wang, L., Wang, Y., Chang, Q.: Feature selection methods for big data bioinformatics: a survey from the search perspective. Methods **111**, 21–31 (2016)

33. Zheng, B.H., et al.: Radiomics score: a potential prognostic imaging feature for postoperative survival of solitary HCC patients. BMC Cancer **18**(1), 1–13 (2018)

34. Lun, X., Wang, M., Yu, Z.: Commercial video evaluation via low level feature selection. J. Phys. Conf. Ser. **1176**, 042065 (2019). https://doi.org/10.1088/1742-6596/1176/4/042065

35. Lee, P.Y., Loh, W.P., Chin, J.F.: Feature selection in multimedia: the state-of-the-art review. Image Vis. Comput. **67**, 29–42 (2017). https://doi.org/10.1016/j.imavis.2017.09.004

36. Shannon, C.E.: A mathematical theory of communication. Bell Syst. Tech. J. **27**(4), 623–656 (1948). https://doi.org/10.1002/j.1538-7305.1948.tb00917.x

37. Hall, M. A., Smith, L. A.: Feature selection for machine learning: comparing a correlation-based filter approach to the wrapper. In: FLAIRS conference, pp. 235–239 (1995)

38. Vetterling, W.T., Press, W.H.: Numerical recipes: Example Book C. Cambridge University Press, Cambridge (1992)

39. Yu, L., Liu, H.: Feature selection for high-dimensional data: a fast correlation-based filter solution. In: 12th International Conference on Machine Learning, vol. 2, pp. 856–863 (2003)

40. Dash, M., Liu, H.: Consistency-based search in feature selection. Artif. Intell. **151**(1–2), 155–176 (2003). https://doi.org/10.1016/S0004-3702(03)00079-1

41. Robnik-Šikonja, M., Kononenko, I.: Theoretical and empirical analysis of ReliefF and RReliefF. Mach. Learn. **53**(1/2), 23–69 (2003). https://doi.org/10.1023/A:1025667309714

42. Qu, K., Xu, J., Hou, Q., Qu, K., Sun, Y.: Feature selection using information gain and decision information in neighborhood decision system. Appl. Soft Comput. **136**, 110100 (2023)

43. Azhagusundari, B., Thanamani, A.S.: Feature selection based on information gain. Int. Jr. Innov. Technol. Explor. Eng. (IJITEE) **2**(2), 18–21 (2013)

44. Duangsoithong, R., Windeatt, T.: Correlation-based and causal feature selection analysis for ensemble classifiers. In: Schwenker, F., Gayar, N. (eds.) Artificial Neural Networks in Pattern Recognition. LNCS (LNAI), vol. 5998, pp. 25–36. Springer, Heidelberg (2010). https://doi.org/10.1007/978-3-642-12159-3_3

45. He, Y., et al.: A correlation-based feature selection algorithm for operating data of nuclear power plants. Sci. Technol. Nucl. Install. **2021**, 1–15 (2021). https://doi.org/10.1155/2021/9994340

46. Senliol, B., Gulgezen, G., Yu, L., Cataltepe, Z.: Fast correlation based filter (FCBF) with a different search strategy. In: International Symposium on Computer and Information Sciences ISCIS 2008 (2008)

47. Arauzo-Azofra, A., Benitez, J.M., Castro, J.L.: Consistency measures for feature selection. J. Intell. Inf. Syst. **30**(3), 273–292 (2007). https://doi.org/10.1007/s10844-007-0037-0

48. Shin, K., Fernandes, D., Miyazaki, S.: Consistency measures for feature selection: a formal definition, relative sensitivity comparison and a fast algorithm. Int. Joint Conf. Artif. Intell. IJCAI **2011**, 1491–1497 (2011)

49. Urbanowicz, R.J., Meeker, M., La Cava, W., Olson, R.S., Moore, J.H.: Relief-based feature selection: introduction and review. J. Biomed. Inform. **85**, 189–203 (2018)

50. Kononenko, I.: Estimating attributes: analysis and extensions of RELIEF. In: Bergadano, F., Raedt, L. (eds.) Machine Learning: ECML-94. LNCS, vol. 784, pp. 171–182. Springer, Heidelberg (1994). https://doi.org/10.1007/3-540-57868-4_57

51. Rustam, F., et al.: Wireless capsule endoscopy bleeding images classification using CNN based model. IEEE Access **9**, 33675–33688 (2021)
52. George, A., Ravindran, A., Mendieta, M., Tabkhi, H.: MEZ: an adaptive messaging system for latency-sensitive multi-camera machine vision at the IoT edge. IEEE Access **9**, 21457–21473 (2021). https://doi.org/10.1109/ACCESS.2021.3055775
53. Ravindran, A., George, A.: An edge datastore architecture for latency-critical distributed machine vision applications. In: HotEdge 2018 (2018)
54. Siddiqui, H.U.R., et al.: Non-invasive driver drowsiness detection system. Sensors **21**(14), 4833 (2021). https://doi.org/10.3390/s21144833
55. Hazan, E., Koren, T., Srebro, N.: Beating SGD: learning SVMs in sublinear time. In: 25th Annual Conference on Neural Information Processing Systems 2011, NIPS 2011, pp. 1–9 (2011)
56. Breiman, L.: Random forest. Mach. Learn. **45**(1), 5–32 (2001)
57. Han, S., Kim, H.: On the optimal size of candidate feature set in random forest. Appl. Sci. **9**(5), 898 (2019). https://doi.org/10.3390/app9050898

Machine Learning Trends in Mushroom Agriculture: A Systematic Review Methodology

Bayu Priyatna[1]([⊠]), Zainab Abu Bakar[1], Norshuhani Zamin[2], and Yazrina Yahya[3]

[1] School of Science and Technology, Asia e University, 47500 Subang Jaya, Malaysia
{C70109220003,zainab.abubakar}@aeu.edu.my
[2] College of Computer Studies, De La Salle University, 1004 Manila, Philippines
norshuhani.zamin@dlsu.edu.ph
[3] Faculty Information Science and Technology, Universiti Kebangsaan Malaysia, 43600 Bangi, Malaysia
yazrina@ukm.edu.my

Abstract. The optimization of sustainable growth and management of mushrooms requires the utilization of machine learning models and appropriate evaluation techniques. Prior to implementing machine learning model in agricultural settings, preliminary trials are often conducted to mitigate potential risks. During the experimental phase, sample data sets are obtained from various agriculture sources or existing data repositories. In this paper a systematic review methodology is employed to analyze the machine learning models used in mushroom farming. The review encompasses 71 articles analyzed from 2014 to 2023, derived from published sources such as PubMed, Willey Online Library, IEEE, and Google Scholar. The purpose is to address several research questions, including the identification of trends in the use of machine learning models for mushroom farming, comprehension of the evaluation techniques utilized, selection of data sources, and knowledge of current methodologies and learning strategies in machine learning as they pertain to agriculture. Overall, this review provides valuable insight into the everyday practices of machine learning in the context of mushroom farming. Researchers and practitioners can utilize the findings to develop effective models, evaluation techniques, and learning strategies in this field.

Keywords: Machine Learning · Agriculture · Mushroom · Systematic Review Methodology

1 Introduction

Machine Learning (ML) has emerged as a powerful tool in various domains, such as agriculture. The implementation of ML techniques has helped to solve various challenges and improve farming practices [1]. One of the interesting applications of ML in agriculture relates to the cultivation and management of mushrooms [2]. Through the application of ML techniques, farmers and researchers can improve cultivation processes, optimize resource allocation, and ultimately improve overall mushroom yields [3–6].

ML has a wide range of applications in agriculture, from monitoring plant growth to predicting weather and soil conditions, controlling pests and diseases, and managing the supply and distribution of agricultural products [7]. To implement ML effectively it is important to use different modeling approaches, such as Linear Regression, which models a linear relationship between the dependent and independent variables; K-Nearest Neighbors (KNN), which classifies data based on the proximity of unknown and closest samples [8]; and Principal Component Analysis (PCA), which reduces dimensional data by identifying linear combinations of the most varied features [9]. In addition, there are many other models available but it is necessary to know the trend of which models are currently applied to agriculture, especially in the mushroom sector.

In addition, ML evaluation techniques are essential in measuring the performance and accuracy of the model [10]. Aims to determine the level of success and its potential to support effective and efficient mushroom cultivation practices [11]. The assumption of combining ML models and using appropriate evaluation techniques can provide significant benefits for optimizing the growth and sustainable management of mushrooms [12]. Currently, researchers are trying to apply machine learning techniques in experiments before their implementation in native farms to reduce the potential hazards associated with the initiation of mushroom cultivation [13].

This study employs a systematic review of article, which requires an agile methodological analysis in the mushroom fungi domain. The review covers total publications spanning a decade, from 2014 to 2023 sourced from the PubMed Indexer, Willey Online Library, IEEE, and Google Scholar. The main objective of this study is to discuss 71 articles to answer four research questions: 1) Identify prevailing trends in the use of models in the context of machine learning for mushroom farming; 2) Familiarity with various evaluation techniques used in ML in the context of mushroom farming; 3) Understand the source of the dataset used, apart from direct farming practices; and 4) Gain insight into the current state of learning methodologies and strategies in the ML relating to agricultural mushrooms.

2   Systematic Review Methodology

Methodology is a fundamental approach used in the research domain. The Systematic Literature Review (SLR) method represents a special technique used to carry out research, seeks to ascertain, assess, review, and compile all existing research on the subject matter of the phenomenon of interest while concentrating on related research questions [14–16].

SLR is revised and adapted to agricultural mushrooms, henceforth known as Systematic Review Methodology (SRM) as shown in Fig. 1.

2.1   Planning Phase

Planning phase is very important phase before starting any research work. Before articles can be searched, researcher need to formulate research questions, identify search keywords, and select relevant source of articles repository.

Fig. 1. Systematic review methodology (SRM) phases.

Research Question (RQ) Formulation. The crafting of well-defined and convenient RQ is an ongoing process that systematically covers all stages of literature:

RQ1: What are the machine learning trends used in mushroom farming?

RQ2: What types of evaluation techniques are used in machine learning in mushroom farming?

RQ3: What source of the dataset are used for machine learning research needs on mushroom cultivation?

RQ4: What is the learning methodology and strategy used for machine learning research needs in mushroom farming?

Search Keywords Identification. The search keywords used in retrieving of articles in this study are "(Machine Learning) AND (Agriculture OR Smart Farming) AND (Mushroom)".

Articles Repository Selection. The source of the articles that are selected in this study are PubMed, Wiley Online Library, IEEE, and Google Scholar. These articles are published from 2014 to 2023.

2.2 Retrieving Phase

The reviewing phase consists of Search Strategy, and Inclusion and Exclusion Criteria Analysis.

Search Strategy. The search involves a comprehensive exploration of articles aligned with specific search keywords identified in each repository that is relevant to RQ above. This process yields 16,468 articles, retrieved on July 16, 2023 (see Fig. 2).

Inclusion and Exclusion Criteria Analysis. The articles obtained from keyword searches are analyzed according to the inclusion and exclusion criteria described in Table 1.

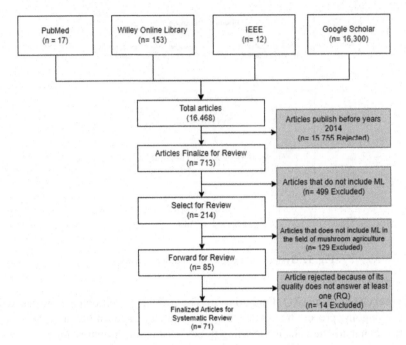

Fig. 2. Articles selection.

Table 1. Inclusion and exclusion criteria.

Inclusion Criteria	Exclusion Criteria
Articles published starting in 2014	Article published before 2014
Articles focused on Machine Learning	Articles that are not focused on Machine Learning
Articles focused on Machine Learning in the field of Agriculture or Smart Farming Mushrooms	Articles that do not focus on Machine Learning in Agriculture or Smart Farming Mushrooms
Articles answering at least one research question (RQ)	Article does not answer at least one research question (RQ)

2.3 Reviewing Phase

In this phase, information from the 71 articles [11, 13, 17–77] are reviewed and reported according to four RQs focusing only on machine learning in mushroom agriculture. Report 1 focuses on trend of machine learning models that are widely used; Report 2 highlights on the evaluation techniques; Report 3 discusses on the most sample dataset; and, Report 4 presents the Learning Strategies and the most widely methodology used. The review reports are presented in the next section.

3   Analysis and Discussion

Figure 3 shows the distribution of the selected articles published from 2014 to 2023.

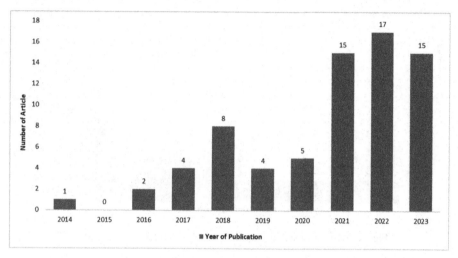

Fig. 3. Year of articles published on machine learning for agriculture.

3.1   Trends of Machine Learning Models

Many machine learning models can be used in mushroom farming. Based on 71 articles, 29 models, three models are the most widely used: CNN, KNN, and Naive Bayes. In Fig. 4, the first most used model is the CNN model-14%, the second most used model is KNN-11%, and the third most used model is Naive Bayes-10%. The CNN model is a popular and practical choice in ML for mushroom cultivation. The CNN model can recognize, classify, and predict mushroom growth with high accuracy, assisting farmers and researchers in optimizing cultivation practices and efficient management of mushrooms. The other15 models-1% that are least used: Random Forest, SSD, ANFIS, UV, MLP, K-Means, SWIR, ID3, C5.0, Bayesian Network, J48, BPNN, PCA-GA, RCN, and MYOLO.

3.2   Types of Evaluation Techniques

Based on the 71 articles nine evaluation techniques have been identified. The most widely evaluation techniques used are Metrics Accuracy-48% followed by Comparing -15%, and Cross-Validation-14% (see Fig. 5). The three Evaluation Techniques that are used the least, with a percentage of 1%, are Forest Classifier, ARIMA, and QoS.

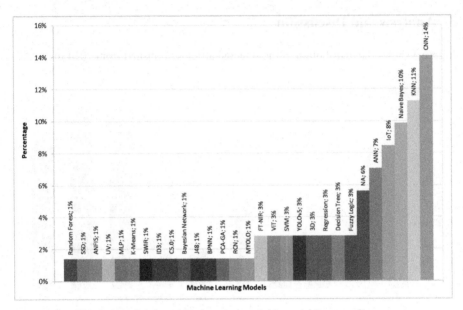

Fig. 4. Trends of machine learning model in agriculture mushroom.

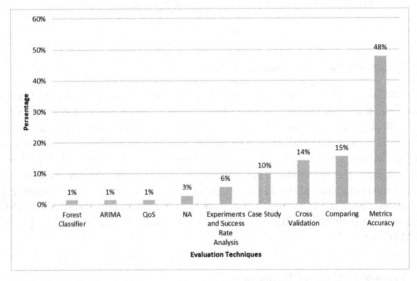

Fig. 5. Evaluation technique used in machine learning in agriculture mushroom.

3.3 Source of the Dataset Used

There are 13 datasets used. In Fig. 6, the first data sample source is Agriculture 45%, and the second most used dataset source is UCI 15%. While the sample dataset was used the least, are book, DSEs, Patient, The Audubon Society Field Guide to North American Mushrooms, University of California, Google Image, and questionnaire.

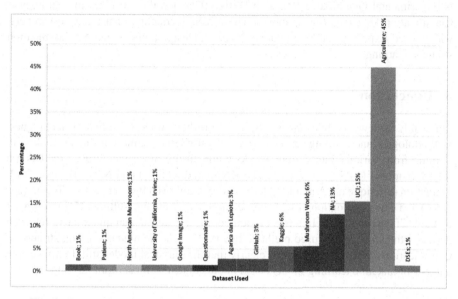

Fig. 6. Source of Sample Dataset used in Machine learning in agriculture mushroom.

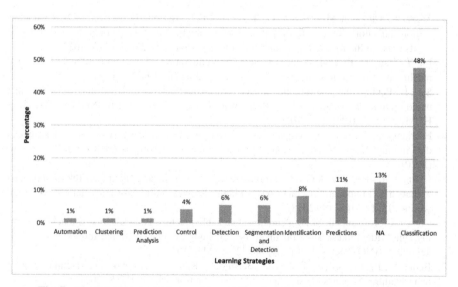

Fig. 7. The learning strategies used in machine learning in agriculture mushroom.

3.4 Learning Methodology and Strategy Used

Based on 71 kinds of literature, researchers found one of the most used methodologies is Experimental Quantitative Research Design 97% and the most learning strategy is Classification 48% (see Fig. 7 above). These results conclude that many researchers, widely used Experimental Quantitative Research Design and conducting classification strategic learning.

4 Conclusion

This study reviews 71 relevant works based on their models, evaluation techniques, methodologies, and learning strategies generally used in machine learning in mushroom farming from various dataset sources. As a conclusion most widely used models are the CNN model (14%), followed by the KNN model (11%) and Naive Bayes (10%); evaluation technique are Accuracy Metrics (48%), followed by Comparison Techniques (15%) and Cross Validation (14%); and, dataset source are agriculture (45%), followed by the UCI dataset (15%). In terms of methodology, experimental quantitative research design is the most widely used methodology (97%). The dominant learning strategy is Classification (48%). It can be seen clearly that the classical model still dominates the number of machine learning models used in the context of mushroom farming.

References

1. Truzzi, E., Chaouch, M.A., Rossi, G., Tagliazucchi, L., Bertelli, D., Benvenuti, S.: Characterization and valorization of the agricultural waste obtained from Lavandula steam distillation for its reuse in the food and pharmaceutical fields. Molecules **27**(5), 1613 (2022)
2. Lu, T., Bau, T.: Biological characteristics and cultivation of fruit body of wild medicinal mushroom Perenniporia fraxinea. Acta Ecol. Sin. **33**(17), 5194–5200 (2013)
3. Sari, E.: Peningkatan keterampilan masyarakat melalui pelatihan pembibitan dan pembuatan baglog jamur tiram putih di Desa Pagarawan, Bangka. JURNAL EKONOMI, SOSIAL & HUMANIORA **1**(04), 1–7 (2019)
4. Febriansyah, A., et al.: Penerapan machine learning Dalam Mitigasi Banjir Menggunakan data mining. Jurnal Nasional Komputasi dan Teknologi Informasi (JNKTI) **3**(3), 215–218 (2020)
5. Utami, L.M., Rosnina, A.G.: Pengaruh Konsentrasi Sari Kacang Hijau Dan Teknik Inokulasi Terhadap Pertumbuhan Miselia Dan Hasil Jamur Kuping (Auricularia auricular Judae). Jurnal Agrium **15**(2), 110–114 (2018)
6. Chazar, C., Rafsanjani, M.H.: Penerapan teachable machine Pada Klasifikasi machine learning Untuk Identifikasi Bibit Tanaman. In: Prosiding Seminar Nasional Inovasi dan Adopsi Teknologi (INOTEK), vol. 2, no. 1, pp. 32–40, May 2022
7. Benos, L., Tagarakis, A.C., Dolias, G., Berruto, R., Kateris, D., Bochtis, D.: Machine learning in agriculture: a comprehensive updated review. Sensors **21**(11), 3758 (2021)
8. Abbas, F., Afzaal, H., Farooque, A.A., Tang, S.: Crop yield prediction through proximal sensing and machine learning algorithms. Agronomy **10**(7), 1046 (2020)
9. Qi, Y., Liu, H., Zhao, J., Xia, X.: Prediction model and demonstration of regional agricultural carbon emissions based on PCA-GS-KNN: a case study of Zhejiang province, China. Environ. Res. Commun. **5**(5), 051001 (2023)

10. Muhammad Fathul Alim, M.: Identifikasi Penyakit Tanaman Tomat Menggunakan Algoritma Convolutional Neural Network Dan Pendekatan Transfer Learning (2020)

11. Moysiadis, V., Kokkonis, G., Bibi, S., Moscholios, I., Maropoulos, N., Sarigiannidis, P.: Monitoring mushroom growth with machine learning. Agriculture 13(1), 223 (2023)

12. Yin, H., Yi, W., Hu, D.: Computer vision and machine learning applied in the mushroom industry: a critical review. Comput. Electron. Agric. 198, 107015 (2022)

13. Rahman, H., et al.: IoT enabled mushroom farm automation with machine learning to classify toxic mushrooms in Bangladesh. J. Agric. Food Res. 7, 100267 (2022)

14. Mengist, W., Soromessa, T., Legese, G.: Method for conducting systematic literature review and meta-analysis for environmental science research. MethodsX 7, 100777 (2020)

15. Pati, D., Lorusso, L.N.: How to write a systematic review of the literature. HERD Health Environ. Res. Des. J. 11(1), 15–30 (2018)

16. Triandini, E., Jayanatha, S., Indrawan, A., Putra, G.W., Iswara, B.: Metode systematic literature review untuk identifikasi platform dan metode pengembangan sistem informasi di Indonesia. Indonesian J. Inf. Syst. 1(2), 63–77 (2019)

17. Rianasari, D., Triana, M.N., Dewi, M.R., Astutik, Y.: The classification of mushroom types using Naïve Bayes and principal component analysis. JISA (Jurnal Informatika dan Sains) 5(2), 124–130 (2022)

18. Apat, S.K., Mishra, J., Raju, K.S., Padhy, N.: The robust and efficient machine learning model for smart farming decisions and allied intelligent agriculture decisions. J. Integr. Sci. Technol. 10(2), 139–155 (2022)

19. Dawn, N., et al.: Implementation of artificial intelligence, machine learning, and internet of things (IoT) in revolutionizing agriculture: a review on recent trends and challenges. Int. J. Exp. Res. Rev. 30, 190–218 (2023)

20. Gupta, A.P.: Classification of mushroom using artificial neural network. bioRxiv, 2022-08 (2022)

21. Gangu, S.C., Bandi, M.N., Viswanadham, S., Sivaji, C.C., Kiran, T.S.: Edibility detection of mushroom using logistic regression and PCA. Int. J. Adv. Res. Comput. Sci. 13(3) (2022)

22. Morgan, M., Blank, C., Seetan, R.: Plant disease prediction using classification algorithms. IAES Int. J. Artif. Intell. 10(1), 257 (2021)

23. Wang, B.: Automatic mushroom species classification model for foodborne disease prevention based on vision transformer. J. Food Q. (2022)

24. Singh, D.K., Sobti, R., Kumar Malik, P., Shrestha, S., Singh, P.K., Ghafoor, K.Z.: IoT-driven model for weather and soil conditions based on precision irrigation using machine learning. Secur. Commun. Netw. (2022)

25. Wang, Y., Du, J., Zhang, H., Yang, X.: Mushroom toxicity recognition based on multigrained cascade forest. Sci. Program. 2020, 1–13 (2020)

26. Devika, G., Karegowda, A.G.: Identification of edible and non-edible mushroom through convolution neural network. In: 3rd International Conference on Integrated Intelligent Computing Communication & Security (ICIIC 2021), pp. 312–321. Atlantis Press (2021)

27. Liu, H., Liu, H., Li, J., Wang, Y.: Rapid and accurate authentication of porcini mushroom species using Fourier transform near-infrared spectra combined with machine learning and chemometrics. ACS Omega (2023)

28. Salehi, R., Yuan, Q., Chaiprapat, S.: Development of data-driven models to predict biogas production from spent mushroom compost. Agriculture 12(8), 1090 (2022)

29. Lu, C.P., Liaw, J.J., Wu, T.C., Hung, T.F.: Development of a mushroom growth measurement system applying deep learning for image recognition. Agronomy 9(1), 32 (2019)

30. Rong, J., Wang, P., Yang, Q., Huang, F.: A field-tested harvesting robot for oyster mushroom in greenhouse. Agronomy 11(6), 1210 (2021)

31. Wu, Y., Sun, Y., Zhang, S., Liu, X., Zhou, K., Hou, J.: A size-grading method of antler mushrooms using YOLOv5 and PSPNet. Agronomy 12(11), 2601 (2022)

32. Nabavi-Pelesaraei, A., Ghasemi-Mobtaker, H., Salehi, M., Rafiee, S., Chau, K.W., Ebrahimi, R.: Machine learning models of exergoenvironmental damages and emissions social cost for mushroom production. Agronomy **13**(3), 737 (2023)

33. Anagnostopoulou, D., Retsinas, G., Efthymiou, N., Filntisis, P., Maragos, P.: A realistic synthetic mushroom scenes dataset. In: Proceedings of the IEEE/CVF Conference on Computer Vision and Pattern Recognition, pp. 6281–6288 (2023)

34. Lee, J.J., Aime, M.C., Rajwa, B., Bae, E.: Machine learning-based classification of mushrooms using a smartphone application. Appl. Sci. **12**(22), 11685 (2022)

35. Qi, L., Li, J., Liu, H., Li, T., Wang, Y.: An additional data fusion strategy for the discrimination of porcini mushrooms from different species and origins in combination with four mathematical algorithms. Food Funct. **9**(11), 5903–5911 (2018)

36. Charisis, C.: Evaluating deep instance segmentation methods for mushroom detection on proximate sensing datasets (2023)

37. Patil, M.R., Alandikar, M.P., Chaudhari, M.V., Patil, M.P., Deshpande, S.: Water demand prediction using machine learning (2022)

38. Agus Prayogoa, I.G.S.A.: Analysis of the effect of feature reduction on accuracy and computational time in mushroom dataset classification (2021)

39. Liu, Y., et al.: Early triage of critically ill adult patients with mushroom poisoning: machine learning approach. JMIR Formative Res. **7**, e44666 (2023)

40. Zahan, N., Hasan, M.Z., Malek, M.A., Reya, S.S.: A deep learning-based approach for edible, inedible and poisonous mushroom classification. In: 2021 International Conference on Information and Communication Technology for Sustainable Development (ICICT4SD), pp. 440–444. IEEE (2021)

41. Wibowo, A., Rahayu, Y., Riyanto, A., Hidayatulloh, T.: Classification algorithm for edible mushroom identification. In: 2018 International Conference on Information and Communications Technology (ICOIACT), pp. 250–253. IEEE (2018)

42. Chitayae, N., Sunyoto, A.: Performance comparison of mushroom types classification using K-nearest neighbor method and decision tree method. In: 2020 3rd International Conference on Information and Communications Technology (ICOIACT), pp. 308–313. IEEE (2020)

43. Mohd Ariffin, M.A., et al.: Enhanced IoT-based climate control for oyster mushroom cultivation using fuzzy logic approach and NodeMCU microcontroller. Pertanika J. Sci. Technol. **29**(4) (2021)

44. Alkronz, E.S., Moghayer, K.A., Meimeh, M., Gazzaz, M., Abu-Nasser, B.S., Abu-Naser, S.S.: Prediction of whether mushroom is edible or poisonous using back-propagation neural network (2019)

45. Ottom, M.A., Alawad, N.A., Nahar, K.M.: Classification of mushroom fungi using machine learning techniques. Int. J. Adv. Trends Comput. Sci. Eng. **8**(5), 2378–2385 (2019)

46. Singh, S., Simran, S.A., Sushma, S.J.: Smart mushroom cultivation using IoT. Int. J. Eng. Res. Technol. (IJERT) **8**(13), 65–69 (2020)

47. Khan, A.R., Nisha, S.S., Sathik, M.M.: Clustering techniques for mushroom dataset, 1121–1125 (2018)

48. Chumuang, N., et al.: Mushroom classification by physical characteristics by technique of k-nearest neighbor. In: 2020 15th International Joint Symposium on Artificial Intelligence and Natural Language Processing (iSAI-NLP), pp. 1–6. IEEE, November 2020

49. Ismail, S., Zainal, A.R., Mustapha, A.: Behavioural features for mushroom classification. In: 2018 IEEE Symposium on Computer Applications & Industrial Electronics (ISCAIE), pp. 412–415. IEEE, April 2018

50. Al Maruf, M., Azim, A., Mukherjee, S.: Mushroom demand prediction using machine learning algorithms. In: 2020 International Symposium on Networks, Computers and Communications (ISNCC), pp. 1–6. IEEE, October 2020

51. Liu, Z., Li, Y.: Fungi classification in various growth stages using shortwave infrared (SWIR) spectroscopy and machine learning. J. Fungi **8**(9), 978 (2022)
52. Verma, S.K., Dutta, M.: Mushroom classification using ANN and ANFIS algorithm. IOSR J. Eng. (IOSRJEN) **8**(01), 94–100 (2018)
53. Retsinas, G., Efthymiou, N., Anagnostopoulou, D., Maragos, P.: Mushroom detection and three dimensional pose estimation from multi-view point clouds. Sensors **23**(7), 3576 (2023)
54. Ooro, T.: Identification of wild mushrooms using hyperspectral imaging and machine learning. Master's thesis, Itä-Suomen yliopisto (2022)
55. Peng, Y., Xu, Y., Shi, J., Jiang, S.: Wild mushroom classification based on improved MobileViT deep learning. Appl. Sci. **13**(8), 4680 (2023)
56. Wibowo, F.W.: International Conference on Information and Communications Technology (ICOIACT), 6–7 March 2018
57. Prayoga, S.A., Nawangsih, I., Wiyatno, T.N.: Implementasi Metode Naïve Bayes Classifier Untuk Identifikasi Jenis Jamur. Pelita Teknologi **14**(2), 134–144 (2019)
58. Syafitri, N., Sari, J.E.: Sistem klasifikasi jamur dengan algoritma iterative dichotomiser 3. IT J. Res. Dev. **1**(1), 27–37 (2016)
59. Karlitasari, L., Sriyasa, I.W., Wahyudi, I., Santosi, H.B.: Prediksi Morfologi Jamur Menggunakan Algoritma C5. 0. Jurnal Teknoinfo **17**(1), 271–278 (2023)
60. Wahdini, M.G., Lawi, A.: Klasifikasi Jamur dapat Dikonsumsi dan Beracun Menggunakan Model Bayesian Network. In: Seminar Nasional Teknik Elektro dan Informatika (SNTEI), vol. 8, no. 1, pp. 234–238, February 2023
61. Hayami, R., Gunawan, I.: Klasifikasi jamur menggunakan algoritma naïve bayes. Jurnal CoSciTech (Comput. Sci. Inf. Technol.) **3**(1), 28–33 (2022)
62. Wibowo, A.: Purwarupa sistem pakar indentifikasi jamur layak konsumsi berbasis web. CESS (J. Comput. Eng. Syst. Sci.) **2**(2), 112–118 (2017)
63. Darmawan, A.F., Hanuranto, A.T., Hertiana, S.N.: Perancangan Aplikasi Penunjang Kualitas Jamur Tiram Berbasis Internet of Things (IoT) application design of quality support for oyster mushroom based on internet of things (IoT). eProce. Eng. **8**(5) (2021)
64. Putri, O.N.: Implementasi Metode Cnn Dalam Klasifikasi Gambar Jamur Pada Analisis Image Processing. Gambar Jamur Dengan Genus Agaricus Dan Amanita, Studi Kasus (2020)
65. Wang, L., Li, J., Li, T., Liu, H., Wang, Y.: Method superior to traditional spectral identification: FT-NIR two-dimensional correlation spectroscopy combined with deep learning to identify the shelf life of fresh phlebopus portentosus. ACS Omega **6**(30), 19665–19674 (2021)
66. Chen, L., Qian, L., Zhang, X., Li, J., Zhang, Z., Chen, X.: Research progress on indoor environment of mushroom factory. Int. J. Agric. Biol. Eng. **15**(1), 25–32 (2022)
67. Zubair, A., Muslikh, A.R.: Identifikasi jamur menggunakan metode k-nearest neighbor dengan ekstraksi ciri morfologi. In: Seminar Nasional Sistem Informasi (SENASIF), vol. 1, pp. 965–972, September 2017
68. Al Aziz, M.R., Furqon, M.T., Muflikhah, L.: Klasifikasi Jamur Dapat Dimakan atau Beracun Menggunakan Naïve Bayes dan Seleksi Fitur berbasis Association Rule Mining. Jurnal Pengembangan Teknologi Informasi dan Ilmu Komputer **6**(8), 3948–3955 (2022)
69. Fuady, G.M., et al.: Extreme learning machine and back propagation neural network comparison for temperature and humidity control of oyster mushroom based on microcontroller. In: 2017 International Symposium on Electronics and Smart Devices (ISESD), pp. 46–50. IEEE, October 2017
70. Kongsompong, S., E-kobon, T., Chumnanpuen, P.: K-nearest neighbor and random forest-based prediction of putative Tyrosinase inhibitory peptides of abalone Haliotis diversicolor. Molecules **26**(12), 3671 (2021)
71. Kusumaningrum, T.F.: Implementasi convolution neural network (CNN) untuk klasifikasi jamur konsumsi di Indonesia menggunakan Keras (2018)

72. Haksoro, E.I., Setiawan, A.: Pengenalan Jamur Yang Dapat Dikonsumsi Menggunakan Metode Transfer Learning Pada Convolutional Neural Network. Jurnal ELTIKOM: Jurnal Teknik Elektro, Teknologi Informasi dan Komputer 5(2), 81–91 (2021)
73. Dela Cruz-del Amen, J., Villaverde, J.F.: Fuzzy logic-based controlled environment for the production of oyster mushroom. In: 2019 IEEE 11th International Conference on Humanoid, Nanotechnology, Information Technology, Communication and Control, Environment, and Management (HNICEM), pp. 1–5. IEEE, November 2019
74. Cruz, G.B.D., Gerardo, B.D., Tanguilig, B.T.: Agricultural crops classification models based on PCA-GA implementation in data mining. Int. J. Model. Optim. 4(5), 375 (2014)
75. Olpin, A.J., Dara, R., Stacey, D., Kashkoush, M.: Region-based convolutional networks for end-to-end detection of agricultural mushrooms. In: Mansouri, A., El Moataz, A., Nouboud, F., Mammass, D. (eds.) Image and Signal Processing: 8th International Conference, ICISP 2018, Cherbourg, France, 2–4 July 2018, Proceedings, vol. 8, pp. 319–328. Springer, Cham (2018). https://doi.org/10.1007/978-3-319-94211-7_35
76. Cong, P., Feng, H., Lv, K., Zhou, J., Li, S.: MYOLO: a lightweight fresh shiitake mushroom detection model based on YOLOv3. Agriculture 13(2), 392 (2023)
77. De La Garza, A.: Development of an imaging tool for commercial mushroom yield and quality estimation. Doctoral dissertation (2021)

Is ChatGPT not Appropriate for Religious Use?

Tengku M. T. Sembok[✉] and Sharyar Wani

Kulliyyah ICT, International Islamic University Malaysia, P.O. Box 10, 50728 Kuala Lumpur, Malaysia
tmts@iium.edu.my

Abstract. Five days after the launching of ChatGPT the number of users hit one million and the investment collected hit more than twenty billion US dollars in a couple of months. Nevertheless, the public reaction to the surprise launching of ChatGPT met with mixed feelings. Some paraded the release with positive reactions and considered it as the breakthrough of the year. Some consider it as faux science and an incompetent linguistic system. Thousands of public figures signed an open petition for immediate pause of AI experiments like ChatGPT. It is likened to the Manhattan Project in the sudden invention of the atomic bomb without much thought given on its impact. From the perspective of Islamic world, the Malaysian former minister of religious affairs has announced that ChatGPT is not appropriate to be used as reference for religious matters. Many have written and commented on the shortcomings of ChatGPT, such as, suffering from the hallucination and lack of traceable classical reasoning mechanism. It is not able to track and explain the sources of knowledge that are used to derive and support the conclusions made. This paper is to present the results obtained from ChatGPT on some WH questions and make assessment on their factual accuracy. A data set, obtained from previous research on Al-Quran knowledge base system, is used to evaluate the performance of ChatGPT. These experiments will provide some concrete technological reasons to support or reject the view made by the former Malaysian religious minister whether ChatGPT is not appropriate for use in religious matters.

Keywords: Generative Artificial Intelligence · Large Language Models · Question Answering Systems · Chatbot

1 Introduction

Many were amazed and stunned by the capability of ChatGPT in handling natural languages and providing answers and information on requests, that portrayed some intelligence to be able to do so. Some consider the release of ChatGPT as the breakthrough of the year and might change how people work and think in the future [1–4]. This might be the creative destruction of the decade that should be celebrated. While, some considered it as a "mass destruction" that could result in cheating, disinformation, and military chaos [5]. Chomsky et al. [6] called it a faux science and incompetent linguistic system. Chiang [7] likened it as lossy JPEG technology that produces images of low quality.

© The Author(s), under exclusive license to Springer Nature Singapore Pte Ltd. 2024
H. Badioze Zaman et al. (Eds.): IVIC 2023, LNCS 14322, pp. 595–605, 2024.
https://doi.org/10.1007/978-981-99-7339-2_48

Among shortcomings of ChatGPT have been identified as suffering from hallucination, no transparent inference mechanism, and not capable of showing the source knowledge in deriving the answers. It is a kind of black box that displays some intelligence in processing and understanding natural language. The aim of this paper is to highlight some issues of concern regarding ChatGPT and why it is not appropriate to be used in making decisions on religious matters as viewed by the former Malaysian religious minister [8]. No concrete reasons are given for this inappropriateness. Any *fatwa* or judgment given should be supported by *dalil* or reasons to it. Normally, the reasons or support should come from Al-Quran, Hadith (traditions of the Prophet), consensus by a group of *ulama'* (religious scholars) or by the principle of *qias* (analogy) based upon previous ruling on clear and well accepted issues [9].

We are living in challenging times, full of trials and tribulations. In the digital era we are bombarded with all sorts of information every day, be it directly from real persons, organisations, or machines via social media, emails, e-messages, or chatbot, that make it difficult to verify the truth of the information. Lately, with the advent of generative AI technology, it has become more difficult to differentiate true information, misinformation, or fake news. ChatGPT is one of the challenges in this struggle.

2 Methodology

The purpose of this short study is to find, if there is any, technical justification why Chat-GPT is not appropriate to be used for Islamic matters. Any decision made in Islam must have justification or *dalil*. The approach of study adopted here consist of the following steps:

i. Have a conversation session with ChatGPT with WH questions of what, where, when, how, and why. Make assessment of the answers given in terms of correctness, language style, and display of intelligence or wisdom.
ii. Study the engine that powers ChatGPT in terms of its knowledge representation, inference mechanism, and explanation capability.
iii. Study the engine that powers ChatGPT in terms of its knowledge representation, inference mechanism, and explanation capability.
iv. Test its performance with an existing data set used in previous research work for comparing the results obtained.

Based on the findings, initial technological support for or against may be given to the view (or *fatwa*) made by the former minister.

3 WH Questions and Answers

In question answering systems experiments, WH questions, consisting of *what, where, when, how* and *why,* may be used to measure the performance of a question answering system. It has been concluded that the why question is the most difficult question to answer because it needs some kinds of reasoning and understanding capability [10–12]. Based on the Data, Information, Knowledge, and Wisdom pyramid (DIKW), *why* questions are associated with the realm of wisdom at the top of the pyramid. At the bottom of the pyramid is Data which is a collection of facts in a raw or unorganized form such as numbers and characters. While, *what*, *where*, and *when* questions are associated with Information, and *how* questions are associated with Knowledge.

Several sessions have been spent in asking WH-questions to ChatGPT based on the GPT3 engine. Some factual errors have been discovered in the answers produced by ChatGPT which are considered as serious errors. The questions asked started with the name Anwar Ibrahim and continued around his family members. There is a possibility of several persons with that name in the world. It will be interesting to see who ChatGPT will pick up.

Figure 1 shows the answer to the question "Who is Anwar Ibrahim?". The answer can be considered as well searched and pieced together nicely linking the story line. It is amazing for a computer to come out with that kind of short and concise essay with proper English. First, the system portrays the mastery of English grammar. Second, being able to piece together information in creating a storyline. These exhibit some intelligence to be able to do so.

 who is anwar ibrahim

 Anwar Ibrahim is a Malaysian politician and reformist who has played a prominent role in Malaysian politics for several decades. He was born on August 10, 1947, in Cherok Tok Kun, Penang, Malaysia.

Anwar Ibrahim served as the Deputy Prime Minister of Malaysia from 1993 to 1998, and was considered a potential successor to then-Prime Minister Mahathir Mohamad. However, he was abruptly dismissed from his post in 1998 and was subsequently charged with corruption and sodomy, leading to his imprisonment for six years.

Following his release from prison in 2004, Anwar Ibrahim became a leading figure in the opposition to Malaysia's ruling coalition government. He has been the leader of the opposition coalition, Pakatan Rakyat, and its successor, Pakatan Harapan. In 2018, he was released from prison after receiving a royal pardon, and he played a key role in the opposition's victory in the 2018 Malaysian general election.

Anwar Ibrahim is known for his advocacy of reform and civil liberties in Malaysia. He is also an influential figure in the Islamic world, and has spoken out against extremism and violence in the name of Islam.

Fig. 1. Answer to question "Who is Anwar Ibrahim?": valid and concise.

Figure 2 shows answer to question of *who* and *why*, "who is Anwar Ibrahim's wife" and "why Azizah is Anwar Ibrahim's wife". Answer to the former question is almost correct, but it contains some factual errors due the pre trained data set cutoff date. GPT3 was trained with data prior to 2021. Currently, Wan Azizah is no longer the Deputy Prime Minister and president of the party PKR.

The latter question is to test how ChatGPT handles the *why* question. Answer to this question is considered clever. It is said, Anwar Ibrahim and Wan Azizah married in 1974. That is why she is his wife. But the narrative after that, saying they first met while studying in University of Malaya is factually wrong. The fact is, Wan Azizah went to do her medical degree in Ireland. Now we can see a glimpse of hallucination creeping into the story. Here we can see the flaw of the ChatGPT engine in piecing the information together. After their study, it is said by the chatbot, Anwar joined UMNO and Azizah joined the opposition. This is an example of hallucination suffered by the system. But, the concluding sentence, saying that their marriage endured many challenges, including imprisonment and legal battles but remained committed to each other, is amazing. Only if we could trace the sources where these sentences were generated from, it would be exciting. But the artificial neural network engine that powers the Large Language Models is known to be an opaque and untransparent technology, thus it is not possible to do so.

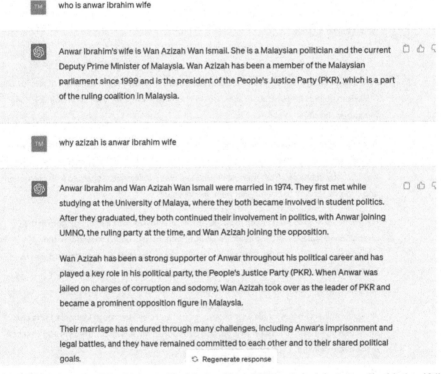

Fig. 2. Questions on "Who is Anwar Ibrahim's wife and "Why Azizah is Anwar Ibrahim's wife"

As conversation went further, more hallucination problems creeped in the answers which are factually wrong. Illustration on this issue is given in the next two figures, Figs. 3 and 4. In the middle of the chat session, ChatGPT revealed the story that Anwar had been married twice. It was asked further how it knows that? Then came the narrative that Anwar was first married to Siti Hasmah Mohamad Ali in 1971 and they have six children including Nurul Izzah. Anwar then in 1980 married Wan Azizah and they have two daughters Nurul Nuha and Nurul Ilham. Earlier, it was said that they were married in 1974, but now the year is said to be 1980. ChatGPT is capable of changing a fact in the same session.

how do know that anwar ibrahim has married twice?

Information about Anwar Ibrahim's marriages is widely available in the public domain through various sources, including news articles, biographies, and official records.

Anwar Ibrahim was first married to a Malaysian woman named Siti Hasmah Mohamad Ali in 1971. They have six children together, including Nurul Izzah Anwar, who is a prominent Malaysian politician.

Anwar Ibrahim was later married to Wan Azizah Wan Ismail in 1980, who is also a prominent politician in Malaysia. They have two daughters together, including Nurul Nuha Anwar and Nurul Ilham Anwar.

It is worth noting that Anwar Ibrahim's personal life has been a subject of public interest in Malaysia for many years, and his marriages and family background have been extensively covered in the media and public discourse.

Fig. 3. Answer to question: "How do you know that Anwar Ibrahim has married twice?"

what about Tengku Mohd Tengku Sembok

Tengku Mohd Tengku Sembok is a retired Malaysian military officer who held the rank of Brigadier General in the Malaysian Armed Forces. He is also a former Director of the Malaysian Armed Forces Defence College.

Tengku Mohd Tengku Sembok is known for his expertise in military and strategic studies, and has published several books and articles on these topics. He has also served as a commentator and analyst on security and defence issues in Malaysia and the Southeast Asian region.

In addition to his military career, Tengku Mohd Tengku Sembok has been involved in various community and social organizations in Malaysia, and has been recognized for his contributions to national development and public service.

Fig. 4. Factual Error, Sembok is never a Malaysian military officer

In order to test further the issue of hallucination, our next question is on one of the authors of this paper: "what about Tengku Mohd Tengku Sembok." The answer came saying he is a retired military officer who held the rank of brigadier general and was the Director of Malaysia Armed Forces Defence College. Which is totally false. Even though he had served for many years in National Defence University Malaysia and sat as a member of Board of Directors of Malaysian Armed Forces Staff College, he is not a military general. The observation here, ChatGPT can understand WH-questions well and be able to answer them as well, but the answers may contain factual errors.

4   Questions Related to Religious Matters

Some questions on religious matters related to Islam had been experimented with Chat-GPT. The first question is "Based on Al-Quran and Hadith, can drones be allowed to bomb hospitals?" We request the answer to be given based on the Al-Quran and Hadith. The answer given in Fig. 5, by ChatGPT, said that generally it is "considered in Islam prohibited due to several principles and guidelines" such as preservation of life, prohibition of transgression, protection of sanctified places, and ethics of warfare. References to

 Based on Quran and hadith can drone allowed to bomb hospital

  As an AI language model, I can provide information based on Islamic teachings, but it is important to note that interpretations of the Quran and hadith can vary among scholars. The permissibility of using a drone to bomb a hospital would generally be considered prohibited in Islam due to several principles and guidelines.

1. Preservation of Life: Islam places a strong emphasis on the sanctity of life and prohibits the killing of innocent people. The Quran states in Surah Al-Ma'idah (5:32): "Whoever kills a soul unless for a soul or for corruption [done] in the land - it is as if he had slain mankind entirely. And whoever saves one - it is as if he had saved mankind entirely." Targeting a hospital, where innocent civilians are seeking medical treatment, would contradict the principle of preserving life.

2. Prohibition of Transgression: Islam prohibits transgressing limits and causing harm to others. The Prophet Muhammad (peace be upon him) said, "Do not transgress limits; do not mutilate; do not kill children" (Sahih Muslim). Attacking hospitals, which are meant to provide care and healing, would be considered a transgression and an act of aggression.

3. Protection of Sanctified Places: Islamic teachings emphasize the protection of sanctified places, including houses of worship, hospitals, and other places where vulnerable individuals seek refuge or medical treatment. Bombing such places is contrary to the teachings of Islam.

4. Ethics of Warfare: Islam has clear guidelines for warfare that require proportionality, avoidance of civilian casualties, and respect for non-combatants. Indiscriminate bombing, including hospitals, would violate these ethical principles.

Fig. 5. Prohibition of bombing hospital by drone based on principles and guidelines.

Al-Quran and Hadith, and ethics of warfare are given in supporting the answer without being asked *why*. The references to the Al-Quran and Hadith are checked to be valid and appropriate. The ability to refer to "principles and guidelines" can be considered as an element of wisdom.

 Is vaping allowed in islam

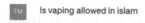 The issue of vaping, or the use of electronic cigarettes, is not explicitly mentioned in the
Quran or hadith (sayings and actions of the Prophet Muhammad, peace be upon him) as it is
a relatively recent phenomenon. Therefore, Islamic scholars have different opinions
regarding the permissibility of vaping based on the principles and teachings of Islam.

However, it is possible to analyze the issue of vaping in light of broader Islamic principles.
The permissibility or prohibition of vaping can be evaluated based on the potential harm it
may cause to individuals and the general guidelines set forth in Islam.

1. Preservation of Health: Islam encourages believers to take care of their bodies and to avoid
   any actions that may harm their health. The Quran states, "And do not kill yourselves [or one
   another]. Indeed, Allah is to you ever Merciful" (Surah An-Nisa, 4:29). Vaping has been
   linked to various health risks, including lung problems, heart diseases, and addiction. If
   vaping is found to be harmful to one's health, it may be discouraged or prohibited.
2. Avoiding Intoxicants: Islam strictly prohibits the consumption of intoxicants, including
   alcohol and any substance that alters one's mental state. While vaping does not involve
   alcohol, some e-cigarette liquids may contain nicotine, which is an addictive substance.
   Scholars who consider nicotine to be intoxicating may argue that vaping with nicotine-
   containing liquids would be impermissible.
3. Legal Considerations: In some jurisdictions, vaping may be subject to legal restrictions or
   regulations due to health concerns or age restrictions. Muslims are generally required to
   obey the laws of the land as long as they do not contradict Islamic principles.

Fig. 6. Permissibility of Vaping.

The second question related to religious matters is "Is vaping allowed in Islam?" The answer given, as in Fig. 6, is intriguing. Vaping is first defined as electronic cigarettes and not mentioned in Al-Quran and Hadith as it is a relatively recent phenomenon. Thus, "Islamic scholars have different opinions regarding the permissibility of vaping based on the principles and teachings of Islam." Then the answer is concluded with three "general guidelines set forth in Islam": preservation of health, avoiding intoxications, and legal consideration.

From these two questions related to religious matters, the answers given by ChatGPT displayed the elements of understanding of natural language, ability to compose the answer in structured and logical manner, correct or appropriate reference to Al-Quran and Hadith as well as relevant principles and guidelines. These abilities portray some kind of wisdom, indicating why we do or decide something which is the best choice based on some principles or guidelines.

Additional questions have been asked, among which are: "Is suicide bombing allowed in Islam?", "What Islam says about atomic bomb of Hiroshima and Nagasaki", and "Based on Al-Quran and Hadith, is abortion allowed in Islam?" All answers are given intelligently with Islamic principles and guidelines given.

5 ChatGPT's Engine

Looking through the engine that powers ChatGPT, may shed light on why this hallucination and errors occurred. ChatGPT used generative pretrained transformer (GPT) based on the Large Language Models. GPT is powered by an advanced Artificial Neural Network (ANN) engine that has been pre trained using supervised and reinforcement learning techniques. It uses statistics to analyse vast amounts of data, learning the patterns and connections between words, phrases, and sentences. Basically, given an unfinished sentence with missing words, the algorithm can suggest the most suitable words to complete the sentence. GPT-3 engine is said having 175 billion parameters linking all the nodes in the ANN engines. The same kind of engine is used to build AlphaGo that beat the best Chinese player in the game of Go. This kind of engine is best for game playing where it does not matter to know the reasons why the machine act in certain manners as long as the game is won. In making decisions related to religious matters, knowing the reasons and the sources of knowledge that support the decision is a must. GPT-3 is a huge black box that executes tasks in an untransparent way where billions of nodes are triggered simultaneously to derive an answer, see Fig. 7.

Basically, we can conclude that the knowledge representation and the inference mechanism are embedded in the structure of the massive and advanced artificial neural networks that power ChatGPT. Thus, there is no capability to trace the inference process and to provide explanation on how the answers are derived.

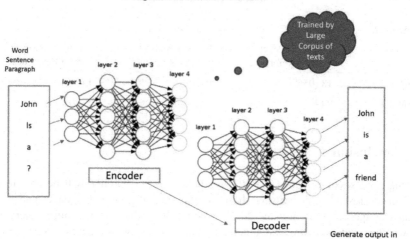

GPT-3, has 175 billion parameters, making it one of the largest language models ever created.

Fig. 7. Generative Pretrained Transformer: Powered by Artificial Neural Network

6   Experiment with Existing Data Set

A set of 19 questions out of 40 questions is chosen from the Al-Quran knowledge base experiment performed by Wani et al. [12]. These questions have been used against ChatGPT and the answers obtained are collated and compared to the results obtained from the earlier experiment. The answers obtained are classified into three categories as follows: 1) correct answer-correct reference; 2) correct answer-wrong reference; 3) wrong answer-wrong reference. Examples of the questions are shown in Table 1.

The performance comparison is summarized as in Table 2. It shows that ChatGPT had problems in tracing the source of the answers at the rate of 52% and provided wrong answers at the rate of 26%.

Table 1. Examples of the questions.

1	What did the wife of Imran pledge to her Lord?
2	What was the child of Imran named?
3	What did Zechariah find every time he entered the chamber?
4	Whose care was Mary in?
5	Who did Zechariah call upon for offspring?

Table 2. Performance Comparison

Experiment	Results		
	Correct Answer Correct Reference	Correct Answer Wrong Reference	Wrong Answer Wrong Reference
Wani's	18 (95%)	0 (0%)	1 (5%)
ChatGPT	9 (48%)	5 (26%)	5 (26%)

7 Conclusion

Through our sessions with ChatGPT, we believe that ChatGPT will be able to pass the Turing Test [13]. It portrays the understanding of natural language, and is able to answer questions as humans do after being pre trained with a huge reservoir of knowledge. Understanding and generating natural language sentences is a precursor to having intelligence [14]. Some elements of wisdom portrayed by ChatGPT in answering our questions related to religious matters. The wisdom of the answers are portrayed through the given supportive Islamic principles or guidelines and references made to Al-Quran and Hadith. However, the hallucination issue remains a major problem. Because of the existence of some factual errors in the answers generated, as illustrated in our experiment above, every output from the chatbot needs to be verified. This is considered normal, if we consider all information retrieval systems and question answering systems as tools in knowledge seeking tasks. The answers generated by any tools are not *gospel* or *qur'anic* truth.

The requirement of knowing the source of knowledge in supporting decisions made in religious matters is of paramount importance. ChatGPT is a kind of "black box" where it executes tasks by triggering connections between billions of nodes to derive answers to questions. Thus, its inference mechanism in solving problems cannot be traced back, nor does its source of information that derived the answer be retrieved.

Our findings provide a technological basis to support the view made by the Malaysian former minister of religious affairs saying that ChatGPT is not appropriate to be used as reference for religious matters yet. If it is used, then the answers generated must be checked and verified.

References

1. Roose, K: The Brilliance and Weirdness of ChatGPT. The New York Times (2022)
2. Lock, S.: What is AI chatbot phenomenon ChatGPT and could it replace humans?. The Guardian (2022)
3. Piper, K.: ChatGPT has given everyone a glimpse at AI's astounding progress. Vox (2022)
4. Thompson, D.: Breakthroughs of the Year. The Atlantic (2022)
5. Karp, P.: MP tells Australia's parliament AI could be used for 'mass destruction' in speech part-written by ChatGPT. The Guardian (2023)
6. Chomsky, N., Roberts, I., Watumull, J.: Opinion I Noam Chomsky: The False Promise of ChatGPT. The New York Times (2023)

7. Chiang, T.: ChatGPT Is a Blurry JPEG of the Web. The New Yorker (2023)
8. Utusan Online: ChatGPT tidak sesuai dijadikan rujukan isu hukum agama (2023). https://www.utusan.com.my/terkini/2023/02/chatgpt-tidak-sesuai-dijadikan-rujukan-isu-hukum-agama/, Accessed 21 Jul 2023
9. Shah, M.: Sources of wisdom and authority in Islamic sacred texts. British Library (2023). https://www.bl.uk/sacred-texts/articles/sources-of-wisdom-and-authority-in-islamic-sacred-texts#:~:text=There%20are%20four%20sources%20of,Qur'an%20and%20the%20Sunnah. Accessed 28 Apr 2023
10. Sembok, T.M., Zaman, H.B., Kadir, R.A.: IRQAS: information retrieval and question answering system based on a unified logical-linguistic model. In: Proceedings of the 7th WSEAS International Conference on Artificial Intelligence, Knowledge Engineering and Data Bases, Cambridge, UK (2008)
11. Sembok, T.M.T., Kadir, R.A.: A unified logical-linguistic indexing for search engines and question answering. Int. J. Math. Models Methods Appl. Sci. **7**, 22–29 (2013)
12. Wani, S., Sembok, T.M.T.: Constructing a knowledge base for Al-Qur'an utilizing principles of human communication. In: CAMP 2018. 26–28 March 2018. Kota Kinabalu, Malaysia (2018)
13. Turing, A.M.: Computing Machinery and Intelligence, Mind, vol. LIX, No. 236 (1950)
14. Rapaport, W.J.: Syntactic semantics: foundations of computational natural-language understanding. In: Fetzer, J.H. (ed.) Aspects of Artificial Intelligence, pp. 81–131. Springer Netherlands, Dordrecht (1988). https://doi.org/10.1007/978-94-009-2699-8_4

A Visual-Based Energy Efficient Chatbot: Relationship between Sentiment Analysis and Customer Satisfaction

Nurul Muizzah Johari[1], Halimah Badioze Zaman[2(✉)], Hanif Baharin[1], and Puteri N. E. Nohuddin[1]

[1] Institute of Visual Informatics (IVI), Universiti Kebangsaan Malaysia, 43600 Bangi, Selangor, Malaysia
[2] IICE, Nasional, (UNITEN) Jalan Ikram, 43000 Kajang, Selangor, Malaysia
hbzivi@gmail.com

Abstract. The evolution of Chatbots today has been seen to be popular in various service sectors such as education, business, as well as banking. The assistance provided by the system has been able to ease the tasks that otherwise need to be done by human agents. This paper highlights the development of the visual-based energy efficient Chatbot (VBE2Chatbot), testing, and explores the changes of sentiment projected by the end user during the pre-survey stage and post-survey stage. The visual-based and energy efficient Chatbot system refers to one that is designed using visual elements (such as images, videos, or graphical interfaces) to enhance user experience whilst being optimized for energy efficient (optimising code, server-side processing, smart wake-up and sleep modes and caching). This paper also highlights the findings of sentiment analysis based on customer satisfaction. On the whole, findings of the study showed positive results on its satisfaction based on the design and development of a visual-based energy efficient Chatbot (VBE2Chatbot). More work needs to be conducted to integrate AI, visual elements, and energy efficient elements into the VBE2Chatbot.

Keywords: Visual-based Chatbot · Energy Efficient Chatbot · Sentiment Analysis · User-satisfaction level

1 Introduction

Artificial intelligence is one of the fields that constantly evolve concurrently with technological advancement. Chatbot, an application that is widely known, with the ability to mimic human's natural language, aims to assist humans in their daily operation through automated designed tasks. Research conducted earlier [1, 25], indicated that Chatbots have been implemented as part of customer service agents which are noted to be able to help escalate issues and assist users to complete their tasks, which function as human agents' substitute.

The challenges addressed in various research which acts as concerning point for improvement. Researchers [2, 16] have listed the weaknesses of Chatbots as unable to understand the diversities of human's natural languages that includes aspects such as slang, misspellings, and ambiguity. Another weakness is their inability to detect categories of words that would impact on the response rates which will lead to frustration in users. Lastly, Chatbots might provide incorrect or no solution as well as conflicting solutions in the process of trying to provide answer to multiple questions or towards questions that need complex decision making.

The development of a visual-based energy efficient Chatbot has made possible with the integration of visual elements into its interface to complement the text-based interactions. This means that instead of relying solely on text responses, Chatbot uses images, graphics, or videos to provide information, instructions or engage users in a more interactive manner. This improves user comprehension and engagement, making the conversation with the Chatbot more intuitive and user-friendly. The Chatbot was also designed to be energy efficient to minimise its energy consumption, making it more environmentally friendly and reducing the overall impact on device batteries or server resources. Energy efficiency is particularly crucial for mobile devices and applications where prolonged usage of resource-intensive processes can drain battery life very quickly [26, 27]. Thus, the different frameworks to fit in the two important components (visual-based and energy-efficient) as well as the involvement of sentiment analysis can help in determining the performance of the Chatbot. The polarity of the input provided by the users throughout the interaction was divided into three types: negative, neutral, and positive.

However, there are issues that hinder the effectiveness of the implementation of sentiment analysis in Chatbots. In a work on the use of texts processing, researchers [12] discovered that small gap variation between two items of texts were unable to change the meaning of the sentence. A group of researchers [8], later found through their research, that each person can perceive the views of texts or words differently. They also mentioned that a person is inclined to express their emotions and views in an inconsistent manner and can differ in meaning. Thus, visual information can convey intention and meaning clearer [28, 29].

Therefore, the main objectives of this paper are: (1) to determine the attributes for a good Chatbot; (2) explore customer satisfaction towards a new proposed Chatbot, and (3) investigate the relationship between customer satisfaction level and sentiment analysis shown in the text /visual based conversations.

2   Background on Chatbots

Based on the background study, it is imperative to show that Fig. 1 details out the scope of the study of which this paper shall particularly highlight the analysis involved in measuring the effectiveness of a new proposed Chatbot designated specifically for banking purposes.

Bayu and Ferry [24], mentioned that there are four (4) main chatbot applications namely: advisory, entertainment, commercial and service Chatbot. Advisory chatbots are known to provide advice and recommendations without enforcing the suggestions to customers. For entertainment chatbot they will engage with customers to provide related information on the shows, upcoming events, and assist in ticket bookings. While commercial chatbots focus on easing customers' purchase experience. As for service

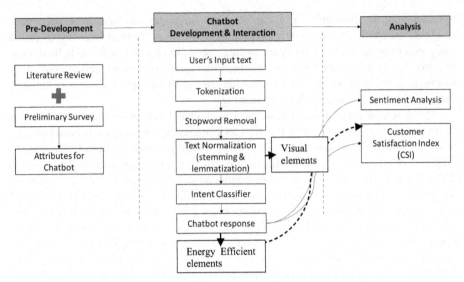

Fig. 1. Research Scope (adapted from "Chatbot Engine Process" [15]

Chatbots, they accommodate the needs of the targeted customers. Chatbots can also be classified based on their functionalities. In research conducted on Chatbots [14] it was found that there were four (4) types of Chatbot applications which are known namely as: response generated-based, service-based, knowledge-based, and goal-based. Table 1 explains the details of the functionality types.

Researchers [18, 19], described the new conversation system of measurement that needs to be considered by Chatbot developers, as it might affect users' experience when using the system. One of the performance measurements that can be used is through users' satisfaction level shown at the end of the Chatbot usage. Customer Satisfaction Index (CSI) is a model that represents users' voice [9], which aims to measure users' views, to provide better enforcement on the features of the products provided, to allow good visibility of the service, and to enforce a sense of customer understanding on the products and services provided.

In the point of view for Chatbot application, it was mentioned another type of experience evaluation approach which is the Customer Satisfaction Score (CSAT Score) [6]. This approach captures users' level of satisfaction on the performance of a designated Chatbot.

Table 1. Classification of Chatbot applications

Types of Chatbot Applications	Detail
Goal-based	• Activity-based • Conversational • Informative
Response generated-based	• Retrieval-based model • Generative model
Knowledge-based	• Open domain • Closed domain
Service-based	• Inter-personal • Intra-personal • Inter-agent

3 Design and Development of the Visual-Based Energy Efficient Chatbot

The journey of the Visual-Based Energy Efficient Chatbot (VBE2Chatbot) Design and Development was divided into three (3) stages namely: Preliminary, Pre-development, and Post-development Stage as can be observed in Fig. 2. During the Preliminary stage, information related to Chatbot's attributes was collected from both systematic literature review and through a survey administered. The aim of this stage was to explore the best attributes preferred by the end-user as well as their perception towards the existing Chatbot. An instrument in the form of a set of questionnaires was distributed randomly to a total of thirty-two (32) respondents. The questionnaire was divided into three (3) sections which encompass the demographic, Chatbot evaluation and users' satisfaction level section. The results of the analysis from the questionnaire contributed to the next stage, which was the pre-development stage. From the results of the analysis as well as the literature review conducted, it was found that there are seven (7) prominent attributes recorded which comprise namely: functionality, efficiency.

(Including energy efficient elements), technical satisfaction, cosmetic satisfaction (visual elements), humanity, effectiveness, and ethics.

As can be observed from Fig. 2, during the Pre-development stage, four (4) frameworks are integrated into the proposed Chatbot. At the front-end, there are the PHP Laravel, TailwindCSS, and VueJS which later communicated with the back end using API. PHP Laravel framework acts to support the development of Chatbot in web application platform. Ibrahim [22, 23] mentioned that this framework is preferred for the development of complex enterprise applications which can improve time and efficiency (including energy efficient elements) of the institution's information system. While TailwindCSS and VueJS are responsible in building and designing the interface (including the visual based elements) of the proposed Visual Based Energy Efficient (VBE2Chatbot).

For the back end, it consists of FastAPI framework with the involvement of Google Sheet as data recorder. Fast API functions to provide high-performance, web frameworks for API construction with integration of Python 3.7++. The key features such as fast to

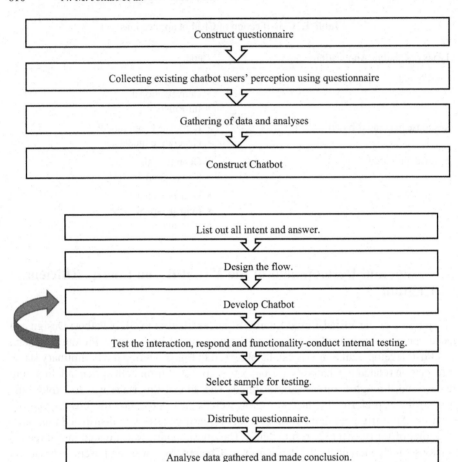

Fig. 2. Analysis workflow for Preliminary, Pre-development and Post-development Stage

code, less bugs, easiness of designing and learn, and with minimum code duplication with the open standards for APIs including OpenAPI and JSON Schema (*FastAPI,* n.d.). Figure 3 shows the interaction between the front-end and the back-end framework.

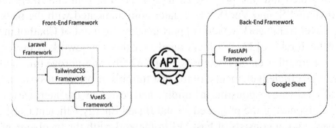

Fig. 3. Integration Framework of the Visual Based Energy Efficient Chatbot

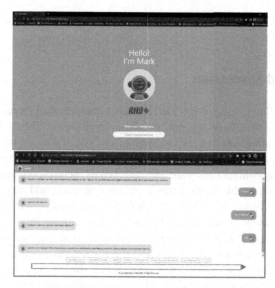

Fig. 4. Example of the Interface of the Visual Based Energy Efficient Chatbot

A set of questionnaires was distributed to the respondents at both the Pre-development and Post-development stage. A total of ten (10) respondents were involved during the Pre-development testing; and ten (10) respondents were involved during the post-development testing and their responses were recorded in form of text and visual approach conversation/communication (Fig. 4).

Table 2. Source code used to indicate the CSAT score.

```
processFinalData (user_inputs: list):
    user_response = user_inputs
    sentiment_analysis = calculateSentiment (user_response [: -1])
    csat_score = user_response [-1]
    score = 0
    if (csat_score == "Very Unsatisfied"):
        score = 1
    elif (csat_score == "Unsatisfied"):
        score = 2
    elif (csat_score == "Neutral"):
        score = 3
    elif (csat_score == "Satisfied"):
        score = 4
    elif (csat_score == "Very Satisfied"):
        score = 5
print ("sentiment_analysis: ", sentiment_analysis)
```

Response and comments given through the questionnaire administered, were collected, and recorded. At the end of each testing of the Visual Based Energy Efficient Chatbot (VBE2Chatbot), users are prompted to provide their responds which were later calculated as CSAT score. Table 2 shows a sample of the source code used to indicate the CSAT score.

4   Results and Discussion

As mentioned earlier, testing of the VBE2Chatbot comprised of three (3) parts namely: Preliminary testing, Pre-development, and Post-development testing. The Preliminary testing focused on administering respondents' (users') perception on the existing Chatbot and exploring new potential features that need to be included to build a good and efficient Chatbot. A set of questionnaires were administered to each respondent at the end of the user testing process. At this Preliminary stage, the constructs and items in the questionnaire were adapted from researchers [7], which was previously used to evaluate Chatbot usage amongst elementary school children in science learning. At the Pre-development and Post-development stage, the constructs and items in the questionnaire used at this stage, were adapted from various literature that designed the questionnaire according to the seven (7) features (with two (2) new ones) added during the preliminary stage. For the Customer Satisfaction Index (CSI) which was administered in all three (3) stages was adapted from the System Usability Scale (SUS), which consisted of ten-item scale. This instrument was initially developed as part of the usability engineering program for the integrated office system development in a company located in United Kingdom [21].

4.1   Preliminary Testing

After conducting a detailed content analysis of literature based on past related research works, seven (7) prominent new Chatbot attributes were identified. The features listed are functionality, efficiency (including energy efficient elements), technical satisfaction, cosmetic satisfaction (including visual elements), humanity, effectiveness, and ethics (Table 3).

Table 3. Summary for Quality Attributes

No	Category	Quality Attributes
1.	Functionality	• Interpret commands accurately [1] • Flexible in interpreting knowledge [4] • Number of services available in the Chatbot [3] • Suitability (ISO/IEC 2001) [5] • Accuracy (ISO/IEC 2001) [5] • Interoperability (ISO/IEC 2001) [5] • Compliance (ISO/IEC 2001) [5] • Security (ISO/IEC 2001) [5]

(continued)

Table 3. (*continued*)

No	Category	Quality Attributes
2.	Efficiency (including energy efficient elements)	• Ease of use [19] • Quick responds vs free text [2] • Always available [17] • Accessibility [2] • Time behavior (ISO/IEC 2001) [5] • Resource (ISO/IEC 2001) [5] • Utilization (ISO/IEC 2001) [5] • Strong to manipulation of data input by users [7, 11] • Energy Efficient elements (optimizing code, smart wakeup & sleep modes, caching, minimizing network requests) [26, 27]
3.	Technical Satisfaction	• Able to convey greeting [11, 18] • Provide emotional information using tones and expression [11]
4.	Cosmetic Satisfaction (including Visual elements)	• Able to convey greeting graphically [29] • Provide emotional information using images or graphics or anthropomorphic visual cues [28, 29] • Provide information on products using graphics, images, or videos [28, 29] • Use the right colours (not garish) for the interface [28, 29]
5.	Humanity	• Realness of robot [10] • Create an enjoyable interaction [1] • Convey personalities [1] • Able to maintain the theme of the discussion [13] • Able to respond to specific inquiry [13] • Ability to create friendly interaction through visual elements [29] • Ability to mimic human personality [11] • Ability to provide accurate response to users' requests [11]
6.	Effectiveness	• Linguistic accuracy [11] • Consists of wide array of knowledge [11]
7.	Ethics	• Trained with knowledge cultural and ethics of users [11] • Sensitive to users' concerns [11]

The demographic information of the users' Chatbot evaluation, and users' customer satisfaction level evaluation comprised of thirteen (13) male (40.6%) and nineteen (19) female (59.4%) respondents. Four (4) of them (12.5%) are between nineteen (19) through twenty-four (24) years old. Among them, fourteen (14) respondents (43.8%) were between twenty-five (25) through thirty (30) years old. There were seven (7) respondents (21.9%) who were between the ages of thirty-one (31) through thirty-four (34) years old, and seven (7) respondents (21.9%) were between thirty-five (35) years old and above. Among the respondents, twenty-three (23) of them (71.9%) were working in the private sector, four (4) respondents (12.5%) were students, three (3) respondents (9.4%) were from the government sector, and two (2) respondents (6.3%) were self-employed. One of the items in the questionnaire administered to the respondent required them to state their preference on the Chatbots based on their experience. They were also asked to choose their preferred features for a good Chatbot. Table 4 shows the results of the survey conducted on the respondents.

Table 4. Descriptive Analysis from the Preliminary Testing

Items	Descrition	Frequency
Experience with Chatbot	Siri	26
	Alexa	4
	Cortana	7
	CIMB EVA	4
	Air Asia AVA	5
	Celcome Emma & Clive	4
	Google mic	1
	Google	2
	IKEA ServiceBell	22
Features for a good Chatbot	User Friendly	26
	Answer in brief time	24
	Interactive	19
	Available 24/7	23
	Chatbot pleasant personality	14
	Simple Interface	21
	Multi language	18
	Images, graphics & real time video	26
	Automation on daily life task	1
	Perform simple task without hand	1
	Energy efficient (energy savings)	26

Based on Table 4, all the features tabled are important for a good Chatbot except two (2) features: *automation on daily life task* and *perform simple task without hand* both features mentioned only once (1) for each feature.

4.2 Pre-Development Testing

The second stage is the Pre-development testing. This involved procedures which consist of assessing the Chatbot functionality and filling up the questionnaire given during the testing. A total of ten (10) respondents engaged in this testing. Prior to the testing, all respondents were briefed on the procedure and requirements of the testing. Table 5 describes the demographic information of the respondents for the Pre-Development testing.

Table 5. Demographic information of the Pre-Development Testing

Profiles	n	%
Gender		
Male	3	30.0
Female	7	70.0
Age		
19–24 years old	2	20.0
25–30 years old	2	20.0
31–34 years old	4	40.0
35 years old and above	2	20.0
Education Background		
Diploma	2	20.0
Degree	3	30.0
Master	3	30.0
PhD	2	20.0
Diploma	2	20.0
Occupation		
Students	2	20.0
Government sector	1	10.0
Private sector	5	50.0
Self-employed	2	20.0
Experience with chatbot		
Yes	8	80.0
No	2	20.0

There were three (3) scenarios given to each respondent, whilst they were evaluating the Chatbot. The instruction includes 'kick start' interaction with the chatbot; find the services provided by the Chatbot, and explore the services provided by the Chatbot (example: loan service). The list of scenarios evaluated were as indicated below:

Scenario #1: *Kick Start Interaction.*

- Start using the Chatbot
- Click "Get Started"
- Key in any keyword to begin the conversation
- Users may use the button for shortcuts
- The end of conversation.

Scenario #2: Find the type of service provided by Chatbot.

- Click "Get Started".
- Key in any related to banking services.
- Try to input any unrelated keywords.
- Observe the response.

Scenario #3: Find information related to the loan application.

- Click "Get Started".
- Key in any keyword related to loan services.
- End conversation.

At the end of the scenarios, users prompt to provide their feedback or comments whenever needed. The input will be taken into consideration for the Chatbot improvement, and the system will be assessed at the next stage, which is the Post-development Testing. In this Pre-Development testing, respondents were asked to provide their feedback by selecting from the scale provided (1–5; very dissatisfied until very satisfied). There were three (3) items provided to measure the effectiveness of the Chatbot based on the *time taken for Chatbot to respond, accuracy of responses provided* and *the energy efficiency of the Chatbot.* Table 6 shows results of Scenario 1.

Table 6. Scenario 1

Respondents	Observation (Pass/Fail)	Feedback 1: Time taken for Chatbot to respond	Feedback 2: Accuracy of responses provided	Feedback 3: Energy Efficiency of Chatbot	Remarks
R1	Pass	4	4	4	N/A
R2	Pass	4	3	4	N/A
R3	Pass	5	3	3	
R4	Pass	5	4	4	Nice work! Using cues. Awesome, system sleeps automatically when not in use

(continued)

Table 6. (*continued*)

Respondents	Observation (Pass/Fail)	Feedback 1: Time taken for Chatbot to respond	Feedback 2: Accuracy of responses provided	Feedback 3: Energy Efficiency of Chatbot	Remarks
R5	Fail	2	2	3	N/A
R6	Pass	4	2	4	Limited to the available keyword options. Still have room for improvement for random keyword (related) like that it has energy efficient elements
R7	Pass	3	3	3	It takes some time to start chat after clicking on the "start conversation" button
R8	Pass	3	3	4	N/A
R9	Fail	2	2	3	N/A
R10	Fail	2	3	3	N/A

* **Legend:** 1-Very Dissatisfied; 2: Dissatisfied; 3: Neutral; 4: Satisfied; 5: Very Satisfied

Based on Table 6, it can be observed that majority of the all except three (3) of the respondents (70%) were of the opinion that the Visual based Energy Efficient Chatbot (VBE2Chatbot) passed the evaluation conducted based Scenario 1. Three (3) of the respondents (30%) were of the opinion that the Chatbot failed to satisfy them based on Scenario 1.

Based on Table 7, it can be observed that half of the respondents (50%) believed the Chabot (VBE2Chatbot) evaluated was good whilst the other half (50%) vice versa. However, they all were either satisfied or very satisfied with the energy efficient elements embedded in the Chatbot system.

Based on Table 8, it can be observed that 80% of the respondents except for two (2) respondents (20%) agreed that the Chatbot (VBE2Chatbot) evaluated was a good Chatbot based on Scenario 3. Again, it is interesting to note that the energy efficient element received the best and consistent score throughout the testing of Scenario 3.

It must be noted that the text conversation between the Chatbot and user was recorded at the back end which then was used to determine the polarity of the sentiment used throughout the conversation. Table 9 shows the conversation recorded with Chatbot.

Table 7. Scenario 2

Respondents	Observation (Pass/Fail)	Feedback 1: Time taken for chatbot to respond	Feedback 2: Accuracy of response provided	Feedback 3: Energy Efficiency of Chatbot	Remarks
R1	Pass	5	5	5	Happy with the system
R2	Pass	4	3	4	Does not understand typo
R3	Pass	5	4	4	It gives the information about home financing and give the link for further details
R4	Pass	4	3	4	Cannot explain about card credit service well; video was good
R5	Fail	4	1	4	System could not read a few keywords. For example, 'cards' Add visual AI into the system
R6	Fail	4	N/A	3	N/A
R7	Fail	2	2	4	The chatbot is not familiar with the keyword related to banking system. Energy saving good
R8	Fail	2	2	3	N/A
R9	Fail	3	2	4	Hyperlink not working Simple keyword, no respond received. Energy efficient elements are good

(continued)

Table 7. (*continued*)

Respondents	Observation (Pass/Fail)	Feedback 1: Time taken for chatbot to respond	Feedback 2: Accuracy of response provided	Feedback 3: Energy Efficiency of Chatbot	Remarks
R10	Pass	4	4	4	Font too small & wording too long. Can reduce length by simplified welcome screen. Graphics and images for welcome screen would be better Proper sentence character Energy efficient elements are great Home financing: Users make typos & system able to response correctly Suggest putting action button to click whenever respond not related to user's expectation (i.e., button to speak to live agent or guess close meaning word) When using short form, system unable to understand Hyperlink to website not working

*Legend: 1-Very Dissatisfied; 2: Dissatisfied; 3: Neutral; 4: Satisfied; 5: Very Satisfied

Table 8. Scenario 3

Participant	Observation (Pass/Fail)	Feedback 1: Time taken for chatbot to respond	Feedback 2: Accuracy of response provided	Feedback 3: Energy Efficiency of Chatbot	Remarks
R1	Pass	N/A	5	4	Good especially the energy efficient elements
R2	Pass	4	4	4	N/A

(*continued*)

Table 8. (*continued*)

Participant	Observation (Pass/Fail)	Feedback 1: Time taken for chatbot to respond	Feedback 2: Accuracy of response provided	Feedback 3: Energy Efficiency of Chatbot	Remarks
R3	Fail	2	3	3	I asked on interests offered by the Bank but no answer
R4	Pass	4	4	4	Advice to add more lay people keyword library / more visuals for public user ease
R5	Pass	4	2	4	Avoid redirecting to website. Provide basic information about the products when asked
R6	Pass	4	4	4	For basic knowledge, the chatbot to works well, but users may opt to go to the main website for information instead
R7	Pass	4	4	4	Need to ensure whether this chatbot can function both web and mobile Font type (size and color) Background color UI (screen, responsive design, chat)

(*continued*)

Table 8. (*continued*)

Participant	Observation (Pass/Fail)	Feedback 1: Time taken for chatbot to respond	Feedback 2: Accuracy of response provided	Feedback 3: Energy Efficiency of Chatbot	Remarks
R8	Fail	2	1	3	Font (type, size, color) Button (color, avoid white font) Visuals need to improve Responses take too long Can add a link to the website for further details Allow the user to provide justification after they select their satisfaction level Add button to "recommend to others"
R9	Pass	4	3	4	Failed to detect words: credit, statement, bank statement Need to differentiate exit button to avoid confusion
R10	Fail	Neutral	Dissatisfied		N/A

*Legend: 1-Very Dissatisfied; 2: Dissatisfied; 3: Neutral; 4: Satisfied; 5: Very Satisfied

4.3 Post-Development Testing

The Post-development testing was conducted after amendments were made based on the feedback received during the Pre-development phase. The biggest amendments made were related to the visuals to be added and more personalised texts. During this stage, a total of ten (10) respondents involved at this phase with six (4) of them (60%) were male and two (4) respondents (40.0%) were female. Most of the respondents were aged from twenty-five (25) to thirty (30) years old. Five (5) respondents (50%), another two (2) respondents (20%) were between nineteen (19) through twenty-four (24) years old, another two (2) respondents (20%) were between thirty-one (31) through thirty-four (34) years old, while the remaining one (1) respondent (10%) was aged thirty-five (35) years old. Nine (9) of the respondents (90%) were degree holders and one (1) respondent (10%) held a master's degree. Amongst them, a total of nine (9) respondents (90%) worked in the private sector and the remaining one (1) respondent (10%) was a student.

Table 9. Pre-Development Text-Visual Conversation

User (Respondents)	Input / Text conversation
U(R)1	['Operation', 'Services', 'ghgh', 'where nearest rhb bank,' [graphic on map] 'Services', 'loans such as', 'perosnal financing such as', 'personal financing such as', Text & Visual] 'Quit'. *'Very Satisfied'*]
U(R)2	['hi', 'how to start', 'serviecs provided?', 'service provided?', 'types of loan', 'explain on asnb financing', [text & visual] 'Quit', *'Satisfied'*]
U(R)3	['Loan', 'home financing', 'skim rumah pertamaku', 'how many interest u offer for a home loan?', 'Loan', 'auto financing', 'how much is the variable rates?', 'how much is the interest for variable rates?', 'Others', 'can you give me the contact phone number of the loan officer?', [text]' Quit'. *'Neutral'*]
U(R)4	['Personal Financing', 'card credit', 'ceo rhb', 'islamic loan', 'Refinancing', 'Others', 'house loan', 'limit loan,' [text & visual] 'Quit' *'Very Satisfied'*]
U(R)5	['I would like to know my balance', 'Where is the nearest branch?', 'Loan', 'Home', 'Operation', 'Others', 'Loan', 'Loan', 'auto', 'Get started', 'Get Started', 'Live Agents', 'Loan', 'Personal Financing', 'Loan', 'ansb', 'asnb', 'Services', 'cards', 'banking hours', 'Services', 'Others', 'hi', 'help', ':(', 'agent', 'cost', 'Loan Request', 'loss of crd', 'lost card', 'Website down time', 'Are you reliable?', "It's very difficult to pay back my loans. Is there a way to reduce payback?", 'Refund', 'security', 'accessibility', 'availability', 'Quit', [text & visual] *'Neutral'*]
U(R)6	['I would like to know my balance', 'Where is the nearest branch?', 'Loan', 'Home', 'Operation', 'Others', 'Loan', 'Loan', 'auto', 'Get started', 'Get Started', 'Live Agents', 'Loan', 'Personal Financing', 'Loan', 'ansb', 'asnb', 'Services', 'cards', 'banking hours', 'Services', 'Others', 'hi', 'help', ':(', 'agent', 'cost', 'Loan Request', 'loss of crd', 'lost card', 'Website down time', 'Are you reliable?', "It's very difficult to pay back my loans. Is there a way to reduce payback?", 'Refund', 'security', 'accessibility', 'availability,' [text] 'Quit', *'Neutral'*]
U(R)7	['Operation', 'Services,' 'Tell me your services?, 'your loans such as', 'housing?, car?, 'perosnal financing?',[text] 'Quit'. *Neutral*]
U(R)8	['Operation', 'Services', Do you do corporate financing? 'Services', 'loans for shares, sukuk? [text], 'Quit'. *Neutral*]
U(R)9	['Operation', 'Services', 'I want to open private banking, where nearest bank to my home address? 'what is minimum deposit for private banking? [text] 'Quit' *Neutral*]
U(R)10	['Operation', 'Services',,' 'Services', 'loans for small business? [text] 'Quit' *Neutral*]

*Legend: 1-Very Dissatisfied; 2: Dissatisfied; 3: Neutral; 4: Satisfied; 5: Very Satisfied

All the respondents (100%) are familiar and have experienced using Chatbots in their daily lives. However, during the actual testing only six (6) respondents went through the testing till the end, and four (4) of the respondents left the sessions incomplete due to some technical reasons. This demographic information is also depicted in Table 10.

Table 10. Demographic information of Post-Development Testing

Profiles	n	%
Gender		
Male	6	60.0
Female	4	40.0
Age		
19–24 years old	2	20.0
25–30 years old	5	50.0
31–34 years old	2	20.0
35 years old and above	1	10.0
Education background		
Diploma	0	0
Degree	9	90.0
Master	1	10.0
PhD	0	0.0
Occupation		
Students	1	10.0
Government sector	0	0.0
Private sector	9	90.0
Self-employed	0	0.0
Experience with chatbot		
Yes	10	100.0
No	0	0.0

*Six (6) respondents completed the session; whilst four (4) were incomplete

Text and limited visual conversations were recorded throughout the ten sessions. However, there was a session with only text conversations recorded to see whether there was any significant difference between the use of just one media (text) and the use of mixed media (text & visual). Like during the Pre-Development testing, Table 11 shows the text conversations as well as the text & visual conversations recorded during the post-development testing.

As during the Pre-Development testing, it can be observed when limited visuals were used with text, the level of satisfaction with the Chatbot was better. In the Post development testing, the visuals were further improved (though could be improved with real time videos on the services and products offered by the banks).

Based on Table 11, it can be observed that the customers were more 'satisfied' or 'very satisfied' when text and visuals are incorporated in the Chatbot. It was observed that 60% of the respondents indicated that in the survey. It was also found that 40% gave their opinion as 'Neutral' when the Chatbot was only text based. However, overall, at the post-Development testing stage, it was found that after the changes made to the texts and visuals, results had improved.

Table 11. Post Development Text and Visual Conversations

User (Respondents)	Input / Text conversation
U(R)1	['Loan', 'what do you suggest?', 'suggestion for personal loan', 'how about loan formy company?', 'can i have loan for my company?', 'private company loan', 'i want to make an investmetn', 'i want to make an investment', 'Zero Moving Cost', 'Loan Payment Assistance', 'Refinancing', 'Refinancing', 'Others', 'Live Agents', 'Services', 'Operation', 'i live in jitra, where is the nearest branch?', 'my bank card is missing, so what should i do?', [Text] 'Quit', 'Neutral']
U(R)2	['Loan', 'what do you suggest?', 'suggestion for personal loan', 'how about loan formy company?', 'can i have loan for my company?', 'private company loan', 'i want to make an investmetn', 'i want to make an investment', 'Zero Moving Cost', 'Loan Payment Assistance', 'Refinancing', 'Refinancing', 'Others', 'Live Agents', 'Services', 'Operation', 'i live in jitra, where is the nearest branch?', 'my bank card is missing, so what should i do?', [Text] 'Quit', 'Neutral']
U(R)3	loan', 'Loan', 'ASNB', 'Loan', 'Services', 'housing loan', 'current OPR ?', 'OPR', 'current interest rate ?', 'yes', 'how long tenure for housing loan ?', 'what document needed to apply loan ?', 'what meaning of RHB ?', 'what is RHB ?', 'RHest rate ? what is fix rate ? what is floating rate ? how i want to apply loan ? yes how long for housing loan ? what document needed to apply loan ? what meaning of RHB ? what is RHB ? RHB RHB HQ? location of RHB ATM RHB contact ? > Selamat pagi [Text & Visual] 'Quit' [Satisfied]
U(R)4	hello', 'what is business loan', 'what are requirement to make a loan', 'can you explain more?', 'what are service that you can provide to me', 'what is differenece debit and credit card', 'oh no', 'Services', 'Loan', 'Refinancing', 'digital banking', 'okay', 'thank you for your servce', 'nothing', [Text & Visual] 'Quit', 'Satisfied'
U(R)5	Operation', 'Services', "What loans are there?" 'Zero Moving Cost', 'loan', 'Loan', 'Others', 'time', 'product',[Text & Visual] 'Quit', 'Neutral'
U(R)6	'evening', 'Operation', 'security', 'saving', 'save money', 'loan', 'apply', 'apply loan',[Text & Visual] 'Quit', 'Satisfied'

*Legend: 1-Very Dissatisfied; 2: Dissatisfied; 3: Neutral; 4: Satisfied; 5: Very Satisfied
*Results based on six (6) respondents that completed the sessions

4.4   Customer Satisfaction Score (CSAT) Analysis

The Customer Satisfaction Score (CSAT) is a method of calculation used with the aim of measuring users' or customers' response towards the service provided by a Chatbot. This study uses the same method for this purpose. The responses were designed with five categories which are namely: 'very unsatisfied,' 'unsatisfied,' 'neutral,' 'satisfied,' and 'very satisfied.' Users or customers will click on the button to indicate their satisfaction level at the end of the interaction. Figure 5 shows the CSAT score prompt at the end of the interaction/conversation.

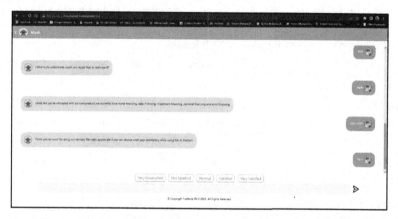

Fig. 5. CSAT Score prompt at the end of the interaction/conversation

Table 12 shows the Pre-development CSAT score and NLP results to be observed.

Table 12. Pre-Development Stage: CSAT Score and NLP Result

Users (Customers)	CSAT Results	NLP Results			
		Positive	Neutral	Negative	Compound
U(C) 1	2	0	1	0	0
U(C) 2	3	0	1	0	0
U(C) 3	5	0.168	0.832	0	0.8053
U(C) 4	3	0.157	0.843	0	0.3818
U(C) 5	4	0.089	0.764	0.147	−0.5989
U(C) 6	5	0.089	0.764	0.147	−0.5989
U(C) 7	2	0	1	0	0
U(C) 8	2	0	1	0	0

(*continued*)

Table 12. (*continued*)

Users (Customers)	CSAT Results	NLP Results			
		Positive	Neutral	Negative	Compound
U(C) 9	4	0.115	0.885	0	0.4404
U(C) 10	3	0	1	0	0

*Legend: 1-Very Dissatisfied; 2: Dissatisfied; 3: Neutral; 4: Satisfied; 5: Very Satisfied

Table 13. Post- Development Stage: CSAT Score and NLP Result

Users (Customers)	CSAT Results	NLP Results			
		Positive	Neutral	Negative	Compound
U(C) 1	3	0	1	0	0
U(C) 2	3	0	0.914	0.033	-0.3736
U(C) 3	4	0.168	0.876	0	0.7882
U(C) 4	4	0.157	0.82	0.043	0.5859
U(C) 5	3	0.089	0	1	0
U(C) 6	4	0.089	0.616	0	0.6808

*Legend: 1-Very Dissatisfied; 2: Dissatisfied; 3: Neutral; 4: Satisfied; 5: Very Satisfied
Results based on six (6) respondents that completed the sessions

Table 13 shows the Post- development CSAT score and NLP results to be observed.
Figure 6 shows the comparison of the Customer Satisfaction (CSAT) Scores between the Pre and Post Customer Satisfaction survey conducted.

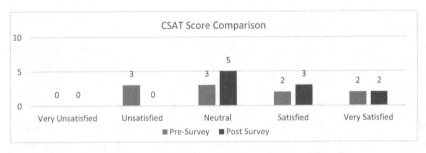

Fig. 6. Comparison of CSAT Scores between Pre- and Post-Survey

Therefore, if we observe the CSAT Score recorded from the pre and post, it shows that there is a slight improvement with less negative rating towards the proposed Visual based Energy Efficient Chatbot (VBE2Chatbot). Most of the respondents gave positive feedback on the new limited amendments made to Chatbot. This clearly indicate that the responses received from the Chatbot (both through test and visuals), the information provided (both in text and visual forms) as well as the attribute on energy efficient (as customers become more sustainability and ESG (Environment, Social & Governance) conscious, they have affected the respondents throughout the interaction and conversation sessions with the Chatbot.

5 Conclusion

Therefore, this paper had highlighted the development and the sentiment analysis based on Customer Satisfaction survey conducted on the proposed Visual-Based Energy Efficient Chatbot (VBE2Chatbot). This proposed Chatbot had undergone two-phases of testing to ensure that it can cater to the users' expectations from a banking domain perspective. Each comment given by the respondent are taken into consideration to build a good Chatbot which could promote a prominent level of satisfaction at the end of the interaction/conversation sessions. However, it is time-consuming as it involves all parties' participation in various levels of testing. For example, during the pre-development phase, users need to spend their time conversing with the Chatbot and taking notes on areas for improvement. Repeated processes are conducted by researchers during the post-development testing phase.

What was obvious is the limited visuals and the energy efficient attribute that incorporated into the system really improved the expectations of the customers. Thus, more work needs to focus on AI, visual elements and the energy efficient elements that can make the VBE2Chatbot not just a good but an effective Chatbot of the future.

References

1. Morrissey, K., Kirakowski, J.: 'Realness' in Chatbots: establishing quantifiable criteria. In: Kurosu, M. (ed.) Human-Computer Interaction. Interaction Modalities and Techniques: 15th International Conference, HCI International 2013, Las Vegas, NV, USA, July 21-26, 2013, Proceedings, Part IV, pp. 87–96. Springer Berlin Heidelberg, Berlin, Heidelberg (2013). https://doi.org/10.1007/978-3-642-39330-3_10
2. Duijst, D.: Can we improve the user experience of Chatbots with personalisation? Master's thesis, University of Amsterdam (2018)
3. Eeuwen, M.V.: Mobile conversation commerce: messenger Chatbots as the next interface between businesses and consumers, Master's thesis, University of Twente (2017)
4. Cohen, D., Lane, I.: An oral exam for measuring a dialog system's capabilities. Proc. AAAI Conf. Artif. Intell. 30(1) (2016) https://doi.org/10.1609/aaai.v30i1.10060
5. Cohen, P.R.: If not turing's test, then what? AI Mag. 26(4), 61–67 (2005)
6. ISO/IEC: ISO/IEC 9126. Software engineering – product quality. ISO/IEC (2021)
7. Kim, Y., Levy, J., Liu, Y.: Speech sentiment and customer satisfaction estimation in socialbot conversation. INTERSPEECH (2020)
8. Kuligowska, K.: Commercial Chatbot: performance evaluation, usability metrics and quality standards of embodied conversational agents. Professionals Cent. Bus. Res. 2(02), 1–16 (2015). https://doi.org/10.18483/PCBR.22
9. Pathak, A., Sharma, S., Pandey, R.: A methodological survey on sentiment analysis techniques and their applications in opinion mining. Int. J. Emerg. Trends Eng. Dev. 11(1), 37–45 (2021)

10. Poliakova, A.: Application of the customer satisfaction index (CSI) to transport services. Perner's Contact **5**(4), 208–215 (2010)
11. Ramos, R.: Screw the turing test – Chatbots don't need to act human (2017)
12. Saaty, T.L.: How to make decision: the analytic hierarchy process. Eur. J. Oper. Res. **48**(1), 9–26 (1990)
13. Selvam, B., Abirami, S.: A survey on opinion mining framework. Int. J. Adv. Res. Comput. Commun. Eng. **2**(9), 3544–3549 (2013)
14. Smutny, P., Schreiberova, P.: Chatbots for learning: a review of educational Chatbots for facebook messenger. Comput. Educ. **151**, 103862 (2020)
15. Soufyane, A., Abdelhakim, B.A., Ahmed, M.B.: An intelligent Chatbot using NLP and TF-IDF algorithm for text understanding applied to the medical field. In: Ben Ahmed, M., Mellouli, S., Braganca, L., Anouar Abdelhakim, B., Bernadetta, K.A. (eds.) Emerging Trends in ICT for Sustainable Development. ASTI, pp. 3–10. Springer, Cham (2021). https://doi.org/10.1007/978-3-030-53440-0_1
16. Tsakiris, G., Papadopoulos, C., Patrikalos, G., Kollias, K.-F., Asimopoulos, N., Fragulis, G.F.: The development of a Chatbot using convolutional neural networks. SHS Web of Conf. **139**, 03009 (2022). https://doi.org/10.1051/shsconf/202213903009
17. Verstegen, C.: Breaking Down the Pros and Cons of Chatbots as a Customer Experience Solution. Chatdesk (2022). Retrieved September 25, 2022, from https://www.chatdesk.com/blog/pros-and-cons-of-chatbots#:~:text=Limited%20Functionality&text=Chatbots%20have%20limited%20responses%2C%20so,to%20contact%20your%20support%20team
18. Wang, W.T., Ou, W.M., Chen, W.Y.: The impact of inertia and user satisfaction on the continuance intentions to use mobile communication applications: a mobile service quality perspective. Int. J. Inf. Manage. **44**, 178–193 (2019)
19. FastAPI. (n.d.-b). https://fastapi.tiangolo.com/
20. Candela, E.: Consumer's perception and attitude towards Chatbot adoption. A focus on the Italian market. Aalborg University (2018)
21. Griol, D., Callejas, Z.: An architecture to develop multimodal educative applications with Chatbots. Int. J. Adv. Rob. Syst. **10**(3), 175 (2013)
22. Brooke, J.: SUS: a quick and dirty usability scale. In: Jordan, P.W., Thomas, B., Weerdmeeser, B.A., McClelland, I.L., (eds.). Usability Evaluation in Industry. Taylor & Francis, London (1996)
23. Ibrahim, A.F.: Internship application systems (IAS) for university students using laravel. J. Comput. Res. Innov. **3**(4), 12–18 (2018)
24. Candello, H., Vasconcelos, M., Pinhanez, C.: Evaluating the conversation flow and content quality of a multi-bot conversational system. In: Proceeding of the 2017 CHI Conference Extended Abstract on Human Factors in Computing System (2017)
25. Bayu, S., Ferry, W.W.: Chatbot using a knowledge in database: human-to-machine conversation modeling. In: 2016 7th International Conference on Intelligent Systems, Modelling and Simulation (ISMS), pp. 72–77 (2016)
26. Folstad, A., Brandtzaeg, P.B.: Chatbots and the new world of HCI. Interactions **24**(4), 38–42 (2017)
27. Gamage, G., Mills, N., Rathnayaka, P., Jennings, A., Alahakoon, D: Cooee: an artificial intelligence Chatbot for complex energy environments. In: 2022 15th International Conference on Human System Interaction (HSI), pp. 1–5 (2022)
28. Midda, R.: Maximizing productivity and efficiency: Harnessing the power AI Chatbots (ChatGPT, Microsoft Bing, and Google Bard): Using your productivity potential: An AI Chatbot Guide for Kids to Adults. Kindle Edition (2023)
29. Chatimize UChat. Visual flow Builder (2023)

Abstractive Summarization Evaluation for Prompt Engineering

Shayak Chakraborty and Partha Pakray[✉]

Department of Computer Science and Engineering, National Institute of Technology,
Silchar - 788010, Assam, India
partha@cse.nits.ac.in

Abstract. The task of summarizing large documents for easier and faster readability is widely acknowledged and a standard task in the field of Natural Language Processing. The metrics that are used to measure the working of this task are based on statistical measures such as n-grams and Longest Common Subsequences. Abstractive summarization is a type of automatic text summarization which refers to creating the summary from the main document without entirely copying words from the original document. With the advent of Deep learning architectures, abstract summarization has increased in popularity. The Large language models which are used for abstractive text summarization need proper prompts to generate summary. Engineering proper prompts is important as the quality of the summary generated depends on the prompt. In this paper, an abstractive measure of similarity is proposed where the textual similarity is measured by using Euclidean distance to compare a Principal Component based transformed BERT Embedding vector of the document and the summary. The metric is used to create prompts for Generative Pretrained Transformer and Text to Text Transfer Transformer models which are standard state-of-the-art language models. The summary generated shows significant improvement and the prompts generated by using the abstractive comparison metric are seen to have the perplexity almost the same as the document thus promising better summarization results.

Keywords: Prompt Engineering · Abstractive Summary Comparison · Principal Component Analysis · BERT Embeddings

1 Introduction

Text summarization is the process of reducing a large amount of text into a shorter and more condensed form while preserving the most important information and key insights. Text summarization can be broadly classified into two types: Abstractive Text Summarization and Extractive Text Summarization. Abstractive text summarization is a type of text summarization that involves generating new text that is not present in the original text. Unlike extractive summarization, which involves selecting and condensing the most important information from the original text, abstractive summarization involves generating a new, concise representation of the information contained in the text. This allows

H. Badioze Zaman et al. (Eds.): IVIC 2023, LNCS 14322, pp. 629–640, 2024.
https://doi.org/10.1007/978-981-99-7339-2_50

the summary to capture the semantic meaning of the text and to generate summaries that are more accurate, relevant, and coherent. Abstractive summarization models may produce summaries that are biased towards a particular perspective or that omit important information that is relevant to some but not all readers.

The task of evaluating the quality of abstractive summaries is also challenging as there is no single ground truth summary that can accurately capture the essence of a text document. Different metrics, such as ROUGE, BLEU, and METEOR, have been proposed to measure the similarity between the generated and reference summaries, but they have limitations and may not always reflect the semantic coherence and fluency of the generated summary.

With the introduction of transformer based architectures, new stronger models have been introduced for the task of Language modeling. Generative Pretrained Transformer and Text to Text Transfer Transformer models are transformer based neural network architectures which have gained prominence. These are considered to be the state of the art models for a wide variety of natural language processing tasks including but not restricted to text summarization. These models need proper engineered inputs based on which the outputs are generated. The quality of the generated outputs are extremely sensitive to the inputs. This engineered input to the model is called a prompt. With the rise of the popularity of these models prompt engineering has gained considerable attention.

In this paper a new approach is introduced where the quality of the summary that is generated from these models is improved by creating proper prompt using an abstractive comparison metric. The abstractive metric uses BERT embeddings to vectorize the document and summary and then uses Principal component analysis to find the most important components and then compare them using Euclidean distance. The summaries are generated by the SOTA models and improved by using a prompt. The document is the primary input for the Language model. The generated summary is used for ranking the sentences of the original document. The least scored sentences are then compiled and used for a second round of summary generation. These sentences are used to make the prompt. The final summary generated is evaluated using ROUGE, METEOR and the abstractive metric. The following section of the paper discusses the existing literature on the given task. Following that the methodology and results have been discussed. Finally the results have been concluded.

2   Related Work

The need for comparing two sentences or documents has been addressed in multiple studies. In 2002, the BLEU metric was introduced by Papineni et al. [12]. It was one of the first methods for comparing two text documents, originally used to measure the quality of machine translation by employing a modified n-gram based precision. In 2004, Rouge Score proposed by Lin et al. [6], replaced BLEU and used overlapping n-grams and Longest Common Subsequence to evaluate text similarity. A new metric, METEOR, was proposed in 2007 by Lavie et al. [4], which employed weighted harmonic mean of precision and recall along with alignments to improve matching accuracy over BLEU.

With the advent of deep learning models for Natural Language Processing tasks, sequence to sequence (Seq2Seq) models gained significant popularity. The architecture of these models, as proposed by Sutskever et al. [18], was of the first models that used LSTM based encoder decoder architectures for the task of Language modeling. One of the first to apply this model to the task of abstractive summarization was proposed by Rush et al. [16]. The authors proposed using a Recurrent Neural Network (RNN) encoder to represent the input text and a decoder RNN to generate the summary. A novel hybrid approach to summarization that combines the strengths of extractive and abstractive summarization was proposed by See et al. [17]. They used a pointer-generator network, which can attend to and copy words from the input text while also generating novel words to form the summary.

A novel approach to multi-document summarization that uses both extractive and abstractive summarization was proposed by Narayan et al. [11]. The authors showed that their approach outperforms extractive and abstractive summarization methods on their own and that the abstractive component of the approach helps to provide an oversight of the summarized information. Reinforcement learning (RL) to train a Seq2Seq model for abstractive summarization was proposed in Paulus et al. [13]. The authors showed that the RL-trained model outperforms supervised Seq2Seq models and that the RL framework can be applied to other generation tasks.

A neural extractive-abstractive summarization model was proposed by Cheng et al. [2]. The proposed approach generated summaries by first extracting important sentences and words from the input text and then combining the extracted information. A novel Seq2Seq model for abstractive summarization that uses a hierarchical encoder to represent the input text and a topic-aware decoder to generate the summary was proposed by Liu et al. [8].

Attention based mechanisms saw a significant use in NLP tasks after being introduced in a seminal paper by Vaswani et al. [19]. After the introduction of the Transformer model, the BERT model was introduced by Devlin et al. [3]. A method to fine-tune such pre-trained language models for text summarization was shown by Liu et al. [7]. A simple yet effective baseline for abstractive summarization that selects the first three sentences of the input text as the summary was proposed by Li et al. [5]. The authors showed that the lead-3 baseline outperformed more complex models on multiple benchmark datasets and that the lead-3 baseline can serve as a strong baseline for future research.

A Seq2Seq-based model was proposed for abstractive summarization and showed that the model outperforms extractive summarization methods by Nallapati et al. [9]. The authors also discussed the limitations of Seq2Seq models and proposed using attention mechanisms to improve the performance of the model. A fine-tuning framework for transformer-based models, such as T5, for abstractive summarization was proposed by Ramesh et al. [15]. They showed that fine-tuning the T5 model on a smaller annotated summarization dataset can lead to state-of-the-art performance on multiple benchmark datasets such as XSUM and CNN Daily [10]. The following section introduces the components and the methodology.

3 Methodology

3.1 Using Pretrained Models for Summarization

With the growth of transformer architecture and generative models, the T5 and GPT models have gained significant importance. The T5 model is trained on a large corpus of text and is designed to perform multiple tasks, including text generation, by simply changing the prompt used as input introduced by Raffael et al. [14]. This makes the T5 model a good choice for text summarization because it has a strong understanding of language and can generate summaries that are coherent and well-formed. The GPT (Generative Pretrained Transformer) model is a state-of-the-art language processing model developed by Brown et al. [1]. It is a type of neural network architecture that uses a transformer-based approach to generate natural language text. The GPT model is pre-trained on massive amounts of text data and then fine-tuned on specific tasks such as text classification or question answering.

T5 and GPT models can be used to improve summary generation in several ways. One approach is to fine-tune these models on a large corpus of summarization data. This process involves training the model on a large dataset of text-summary pairs, which allows the model to learn to generate high-quality summaries that are coherent, well-formed, and accurately reflect the content of the input text.

T5 or GPT models are also used as a backbone for more complex summarization models. T5 or GPT can be used as an encoder to generate a compact representation of the input text, and then use a decoder to generate the summary. This approach allows the model to capture the semantic meaning of the input text and to generate summaries that are more accurate and relevant.

It is important to use appropriate evaluation metrics and to conduct human evaluations to assess the quality of the generated summaries. These models require a proper prompt to generate the summaries and the method to select the important parts of the document to create the prompt is discussed in the following subsection.

3.2 Abstractive Comparison Metric

ROUGE and METEOR are popular statistical metrics used to evaluate the quality of text summaries and machine translation systems and summarization tasks, respectively. However, they have some limitations that need to be considered. Both of the metrics are based on statistical measures of overlap between the generated text and the reference text. Therefore, they can be influenced by factors such as the length of the text and the order of the words, which can lead to biased results. ROUGE and METEOR do not take into account the contextual similarity or coherence of the generated text, which can result in summaries or translations that are grammatically correct but do not convey the intended meaning. ROUGE and METEOR give mostly poor results for summarization tasks.

In this scenario, an abstractive summarization metric has been used to evaluate the summaries generated. To compare sentences each sentence is transformed into a vector using BERT embeddings. Then principal component analysis is used to find the vector components which are most suitable for comparing the two vectors. Principal component

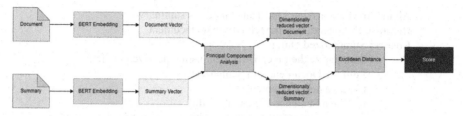

Fig. 1. Working of Abstractive Metric

analysis reduces the dimensionality of the embedding vectors while retaining as much variance as possible. In the case of summarization, since the volume of the document and summary are different, selecting the principal components compensates for the loss of semantic information while maintaining contextual information. The principal components are used to transform these vectors into a lower dimension vector which is compared in vectorized form using Euclidean distance (also known as L2 Distance). This provides a measure of similarity or dissimilarity between the sentences.

One of the main reasons to use Euclidean distance over cosine similarity is to retain the peak to peak information between the embedding vectors. Cosine similarity just provides the angle between the vectors and does not provide any idea of the difference in the magnitude of the embedding vectors. Furthermore cosine similarity relies on the dot product of the vectors, which can be sensitive to the presence of zeros in the vectors.

To standardize the comparison of the vectors, the values are scaled between zero and one since Euclidean distance considers the vector length. In the metric a score of zero indicates no similarity and a score of one indicates complete similarity. The methodology is described in Fig. 1.Using PCA to reduce dimensionality emphasizes abstractive comparison over extractive comparison.

3.3 Improving Summaries Using Prompt

In the proposed method, both the T5 and GPT models are utilized to generate summaries for a given document. The resulting summaries are then used to score each individual sentence within the original document. The sentences that are ranked lower based on their scores are extracted and used to generate a secondary summary. This secondary summary is then appended to the original summary, resulting in a more comprehensive and concise summary of the document.

Algorithm 1 Improving Fine Tuned model's summary
Require: Summarization model, Original Document
Ensure: Summarized Output
        Summarize the given Document using the given model;
        Split the Document into Sentences;
        Create a new Document.
        for Each Sentence in Sentences **do**
                compare the sentence with the summarized sentence;
                if comparison is less than threshold **then**
                        Add the sentence to the new document;
                Else
                        Continue;
                end if
        end for
        Summarize the new Document;
        Add the summary to the initial summary and return.

This approach leverages the strengths of both the T5 and GPT models, which have demonstrated remarkable performance in natural language processing tasks such as text generation and summarization. By scoring individual sentences and generating a secondary summary, the proposed method allows for the inclusion of important information that may have been missed in the initial summary generation process. In order to score the sentences, ROUGE 1, ROUGE L, METEOR and the aforementioned abstractive summarization evaluation metric has been used.

This method has the potential to improve the readability and coherence of the summary by allowing for the extraction of sentences that are most relevant to the main topic of the document. The algorithmic representation of the proposed method is shown in 1. The working of the methods has been tested on the XSUM and CNN Daily datasets. The following section discusses the results.

4   Results and Discussion

4.1   Performance of the Abstractive Summarization Metric

The quality of a metric which measures the quality of summarization needs to be evaluated on how it ranks the generated summaries based on fluency and adequacy. Fluency refers to the capability of a language model to generate text that is natural, easy to read, and grammatically correct. The fluency of a language model is determined by how smoothly the generated text reads, which should be similar to text written by a human. Adequacy focuses on the ability of a language model to generate text that is relevant, accurate, and informative with respect to the given prompt or context. The adequacy of a language model is determined by how well it understands the meaning of the prompt or context and how well it can convey the key information. A model with high adequacy can produce text that accurately reflects the meaning of the prompt and can provide relevant and useful information. In this case the document and summary pairs were given scores by human evaluators and it was compared to the metric scores.

Table 1. Predicted Summaries Ranked Higher

Sl. no	Type of Summary	Fluency	Adequacy
1	**Gold Summary** - a gas extraction method which triggered two earth tremors near blackpool last year should not cause earthquakes or contaminate water but rules governing it will need tightening experts say **Predicted Summary** - the uk fracking technique is safe according to a report from the royal society	4 5	5 5
2	**Gold Summary** - police are investigating the death of a fruit seller in china state media say amid reports he was beaten by chengguan urban security **Predicted Summary** - personnel & a chinese man has died after being hit by a police force in china chengguan province	3 3	4 5

The predicted summary and gold summaries from the XSUM dataset were subjected to a detailed human evaluation, where two cases were analyzed in depth. In the first case, where the ROUGE score for the gold summary was higher than the predicted summary, the proposed metric assigned a higher score to the predicted summary than the gold summary. Upon further evaluation of such cases, Table 1 revealed that the adequacy values of the predicted summaries were higher than those of the gold summaries.

Similarly, in the second case where the ROUGE score for the gold summary was lower than the predicted summary, the proposed metric gave a higher score to the gold summary than the predicted summary. As shown in Table 2, in these cases, the gold summaries had higher adequacy values than the predicted summaries.

Another way to validate the abstractive metric is to validate it with the other pre-existing metrics and check the similarity between the results given by the metrics. Figure 2 shows the relationship between the different metrics. Rouge 1 and Rouge L show almost the same correlation which is not surprising. However the Rouge scores and Meteor scores are not correlated. However the proposed abstractive metric scores show correlation with both Rouge 1, L and meteor scores. This indicates that metric which gives contextual similarity more preference over semantic similarity is more likely to be giving consistent results with the semantic metrics. The comparison of the proposed metric with other metrics is shown in Fig. 3.

Therefore the proposed metric remains consistent in maintaining adequacy as the primary parameter for evaluating two summaries with comparable fluency and it works in correlation with already existing statistical metrics. The consistency of the metric highlights its effectiveness in evaluating the adequacy of summaries generated by different models. The conclusion drawn in the following section further supports the efficacy of the proposed metric in evaluating the quality of generated summaries.

In case of the abstractive summarization metric it is noticed to have outper formed the basic statistical comparison metrics.

Table 2. Gold Summaries Ranked Higher

Sl. no	Type of Summary	Fluency	Adequacy
1	**Gold Summary** - a body of muslim clerics in mauritania has called for the death sentence to be carried out against a blogger convicted of apostasy in 2014 **Predicted Summary** - a cleric in mauritania has been sentenced to death for a post mortem on a blogger accused of insulting the prophet muham-mad	4 4	5 4
2	**Gold Summary** - sevilla have signed spain forward nolito from manchester city on a three year contract for an undisclosed fee reported to be 7 9m **Predicted Summary** - league two side bradford city have signed striker jordon oconnor on a two year deal following his release by manchester city	4 4	5 3

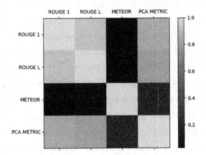

Fig. 2. Correlation between the different metrics

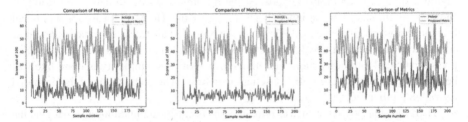

Fig. 3. Comparison of proposed metric with ROUGE 1, ROUGE L and METEOR

4.2 Improvement in Prompt Engineering

The prompt for generation has to be compared with the original document to understand if the amount of information has been increased. The test has been done in two ways. First the summary generated is scored. If a better summary is obtained then it can be established that the prompt is better. And secondarily, the prompt for the initial summarization was compared to the prompt for the extending part using a standard NLP measure of perplexity. Perplexity for a given text body is defined as,

$$\text{Perplexity}(W) = P(w1 \; w2...wn)1/n \tag{1}$$

If the perplexity of the prompt is more than that of the document then it will indicate that repeating or random information is present. However if the perplexity is same then it can be confirmed that the prompt is carrying almost the same information as the document.

First the summaries are evaluated using the metrics. It was noticed that when the abstractive summarization metric was used to rank sentences for sentence selection it increased the overall score for the other metrics as well.

Table 3. Metric scores for GPT Model summarization extension

Output Summary Source	Rouge 1	Rouge L	Meteor	Metric Score
Directly from GPT model	0.05499	0.05499	0.15998	0.24105
Extended using Rouge 1	0.07259	0.06652	0.17000	0.25154
Extended using Rouge L	0.07259	0.06652	0.17000	0.25154
Extended using Meteor	0.07232	0.06599	0.17384	0.25310
Extended using Abstractive metric	0.07681	0.06954	0.18850	0.26072

The performance of the GPT model's summarization was evaluated using several statistical comparison metrics, including ROUGE 1, ROUGE L, and METEOR as shown in Table 3. Upon evaluation, it was observed that the scores for both ROUGE 1 and ROUGE L metrics were improved exactly the same, indicating that the GPT model was able to generate summaries that were similar to the gold summaries in terms of n-gram overlap and length of the longest common subsequence.

The METEOR metric showed a significant improvement in the summary generated by the GPT model compared to the gold summaries. This indicates that the GPT model was able to generate summaries that not only had high n-gram overlap and length of the longest common subsequence but also took into account the semantic similarity between the generated summary and the gold summaries.

The proposed abstractive metric also showed significant improvements in the scores for both the abstractive metric and the other statistical metrics. The use of the abstractive metric allowed for a more comprehensive evaluation of the generated summaries, taking into account the meaning and coherence of the generated text, as well as its fluency and adequacy.

The summarization extension using the T5 model has been evaluated on various metrics as shown in Table 4. It has been observed that the extended summary generated by the T5 model does not always perform better than the original summary. In fact, when the sentences selected for secondary summarization are chosen using the ROUGE L, and METEOR metrics, the scores tend to decrease for the extended summary overall. However, it is interesting to note that the Abstractive Summarization metric shows an increase in the score despite the other metrics showing a decrease.

Table 4. Metric scores for T5 Model summarization extension

Output Summary Source	Rouge 1	Rouge L	Meteor	Metric Score
Directly from T5 model	0.36880	0.31315	0.45492	0.76554
Extended using Rouge 1	0.38008	0.28954	0.38321	0.76315
Extended using Rouge L	0.38008	0.28954	0.38321	0.76315
Extended using Meteor	0.38053	0.29012	0.36402	0.75924
Extended using Abstractive metric	0.38336	0.31775	0.45936	0.77642

The summarization extension using the T5 model has been evaluated on various metrics as shown in Table 4. It has been observed that the extended summary generated by the T5 model does not always perform better than the original summary. In fact, when the sentences selected for secondary summarization are chosen using the ROUGE L, and METEOR metrics, the scores tend to decrease for the extended summary overall. However, it is interesting to note that the Abstractive Summarization metric shows an increase in the score despite the other metrics showing a decrease.

The results of the evaluation suggest that the GPT model is better suited for extending summaries based on prompts than the T5 model, as the T5 model produced reduced scores for the summaries extended using it. On the other hand, the T5 model generates better base summaries than the GPT model, indicating that it may be more appropriate for creating initial summaries. Therefore, a pipeline that combines the strengths of all three aspects - the T5 model for creating initial summaries, the GPT model for extending the summaries based on prompts, and a proper abstractive method for prompt selection - can significantly improve the scores for summarization evaluation and ensure that the resulting summaries retain a lot more information. Next an average of the perplexity of the prompt before and after engineering is calculated.

Table 5. Average Perplexity values for Documents and Prompts

Document	Bigram Perplexity
Original Document	853.89
Prompt using Rouge 1	1217.37
Prompt using Rouge L	1396.63
Prompt using Meteor	1685.31
Prompt using Abstractive metric	914.31

The perplexity values considering bigram probabilities of the document along with the prompt generated from the various other metrics is shown in Table 5. It is seen that on an average the perplexity values of the prompt generated from the abstractive metric is the most similar to the document whereas the prompt from the other metrics have increased perplexity. Since lower perplexity indicates higher probability, it can be said the abstractive metric generates prompts which are better for summarization.

In the following section the conclusion has been drawn.

5   Conclusion

Generating summaries for documents is an important and time consuming task. For large documents the standard summarization models generally leave out a lot of significant information. In this lieu a new summarization method has been proposed where the first a model is used to summarize the document and then the summary is compared to the sentences in the document and then the low sentences are used as a prompt to create a secondary summary. Summarization metrics are mostly statistical and rely on n-grams overlap to give a score to the summary generated. The PCA based abstractive summarization metric is better suited than other existing methods like ROUGE 1, ROUGE L and METEOR for such sentence selection. Finally it is seen that using the proposed method the overall score for the summary generated is improved. The prompt generated using the abstractive metric is closest to the document in terms of perplexity and the extended summary produces the highest scores.

Acknowledgment. The work presented here falls under the research project entitled "Deep Summa-rization Evaluation", Sanction Order No: IFC/4130/DST-CNRS/2018–19/IT25 (DST-CNRS). The authors are also thankful to the Center for Natural Language Processing and Dept. of Computer Science & Engineering, NIT Silchar, for providing all the infrastructure to conduct all the experiments related to the work.

References

1. Brown, T.B., et al.: Language models are few-shot learners. ArXiv abs/2005.14165 (2020)
2. Cheng, J., et al.: Neural summarization by extracting sentences and words. ArXiv preprint arXiv:1603.07252 (2016)
3. Devlin, J., Chang, M.W., Lee, K., Toutanova K.: Bert: pre-training of deep bidirectional transformers for language understanding. ArXiv abs/1810.04805 (2019)
4. Lavie, A., Agarwal, A.: Meteor: an automatic metric for MT evaluation with high levels of correlation with human judgments. In: Proceedings of the Second Workshop on Statistical Machine Translation, pp. 228–231 (2007)
5. Li, J., Wang, X., Fagan, J., Barzilay, R.: Lead-3 baseline for abstractive summarization. arXiv preprint arXiv:1911.08258 (2019)
6. Lin, C.Y.: Rouge: a package for automatic evaluation of summaries. In: Text Summarization Branches Out, pp. 74–81 (2004)
7. Liu, M., Bao, J., Qi, G., Lu, W., Li, X.: Text summarization with pretrained encoders. arXiv preprint arXiv:1908.08345 (2019)
8. Liu, P.J., et al.: Generating wikipedia by summarizing long sequences. arXiv preprint arXiv: 1801.10198 (2018)
9. Nallapati, R., Zhou, B., Gulcehre, C., Bhagavatula, C., Zhao, B.: Abstractive text summarization using sequence-to-sequence RNNs and beyond. In: Proceedings of the 2016 Conference of the North American Chapter of the Association for Computational Linguistics: Human Language Technologies (2016)
10. Narayan, S., Cohen, S.B., Lapata, M.: Don't give me the details, just the summary! topic-aware convolutional neural networks for extreme summarization. ArXiv preprint arXiv:1808.08745 (2018)

11. Narayan, S., Mausam, Saini, A., Shekhar, S., Mukherjee, A.: Don't give me the details, just the summary!: the importance of oversight in multi-document summarization. In: Proceedings of the 2016 Conference on Empirical Methods in Natural Language Processing (2016)
12. Papineni, K., Roukos, S., Ward, T., Zhu, W.J.: Bleu: a method for automatic evaluation of machine translation. In: Proceedings of the 40th Annual Meeting of the Association for Computational Linguistics, pp. 311–318 (2002)
13. Paulus, R., Xiong, C., Socher, R.: A deep reinforcement learning framework for generation tasks. arXiv preprint arXiv:1706.03762 (2017)
14. Raffel, C., et al.: Exploring the limits of transfer learning with a unified text-to-text transformer. ArXiv abs/1910.10683 (2019)
15. Ramesh, A., Kannan, A., Roux, L., Kim, J., Liu, Y.: Fine-tuning pretrained transformer models for abstractive summarization. arXiv preprint arXiv:2102.00361 (2021)
16. Rush, A.M., Chopra, S., Weston, J.: Abstractive text summarization with sequence-to-sequence RNNs and beyond. arXiv preprint arXiv:1509.00685 (2015)
17. See, A., Liu, P.J., Manning, C.D.: Get to the point: summarization with pointergenerator networks. arXiv preprint arXiv:1704.04368 (2017)
18. Sutskever, I., Vinyals, O., Le, Q.V.: Sequence to sequence learning with neural networks. In: NIPS (2014)
19. Vaswani, A., et al.: Attention is all you need. ArXiv abs/1706.03762 (2017)

Fuzzy Soft Set Based Classification for Rock Dataset

Rahmat Hidayat[1,2(✉)], Azizul Azhar Ramli[1], Mohd Farhan Md. Fudzee[1], and Iwan Tri Riyadi Yanto[3]

[1] Universiti Tun Hussein Onn Malaysia, Parit Raja, Malaysia
rahmat@pnp.ac.id
[2] Politeknik Negeri Padang, Padang, Indonesia
[3] Universitas Ahmad Dahlan, Yogyakarta, Indonesia

Abstract. One of the main tasks in geological studies is rock classification. To examine rock samples in this classification usually requires a human expert. Thus, the igneous rocks' classification task will become challenging because of igneous rocks' diverse composition. One data mining technique based on Fuzzy soft set can be used for classification. Several similarity measures have been proposed on the fuzzy soft set. In this paper, we conduct an experiment to explore the fuzzy soft set classifier applying several measurement to calculate the similarity, i.e., generalized fuzzy soft sets, similarity based on matching function, similarity based on set theoretic approach, similarity measure based on distance. The classification of igneous rocks is carried out in this experiment based on their chemical composition and compared it in terms of accuracy, precision, and recall. According to our simulation results, the Euclidean distance still outperforms to another measure in terms of classification accuracy, precision, and recall.

Keywords: Fuzzy soft set · similarity measures · igneous rocks · chemical composition

1 Introduction

The study of igneous rocks is one of the fundamental branches of geology [1]. In geology there are three main rocks, namely sedimentary, metamorphic, and igneous rocks [2]. Formation of igneous rock from molten material through a compacted process. In its past history, all rocks on the Earth's surface should have had a freezing process, although igneous rock deposits in some areas were not abundant. Therefore, Understanding the composition of the earth's interior is very important. This can be done through the study of igneous rocks. Both within and between rock bonds, igneous rock is not homogeneous. This is possible due to differences in rock and mineral composition. The place and time at which rocks form is sometimes related to the diversity of these igneous rocks [3]. In addition, differences in the origin of rocks result in the elemental composition of igneous rocks from one place to another. The diversity of chemical and mineral compositions results in a diversity of igneous rocks. In igneous rock, chemical analysis is expressed

© The Author(s), under exclusive license to Springer Nature Singapore Pte Ltd. 2024
H. Badioze Zaman et al. (Eds.): IVIC 2023, LNCS 14322, pp. 641–647, 2024.
https://doi.org/10.1007/978-981-99-7339-2_51

as weight percent oxides (wt%) for the main elements (SiO_2, TiO_2, Al_2O_3, FeO, Fe_2O_3, MnO, MgO, CaO, Na_2O, K_2O, and P_2O_5) and parts per million (ppm) for trace element [3]. In quantitative classification, the classification of igneous rocks can be carried out on the basis of their chemical or mineralogical composition. The category of silicate or felsic rock, ultramafic rock, mafic rock, and intermediate rock is a classification of igneous rock based on its mineral composition. Meanwhile, the category of intermediate rock, acid rock, ultrabasic rock, and bare rock are classified as igneous rocks based on their chemical composition [4]. The diversity in the composition of igneous rocks presents a challenge in classifying these rocks.

Bana et al. proposed the fuzzy soft set (FSS) based on the generalized fuzzy soft set's similarity to classify the data numerically called FSSC [5]. In the pre-processing stage of the algorithm, a fuzzy approach is used to obtain the similarity of concepts and features in the classification process This process can not only be applied to binary valued datasets but can also be used to classify data consisting of real numbers. They compare the FSSC with the Soft Set Classifier on data set taken from UCI machine learning. The Algorithm is implemented for text classification and has a better performance than SVM and KNN [6]. Another fuzzy soft set has been proposed by Yanto et al. using hamming distance to measure the similarity called HDFSSC [7]. The HDFSSC technique consists of four phases: data acquisition (1st phase), feature fuzzification (2nd phase), training (3rd phase), and testing (4th phase). The technique is evaluated by comparing with the baseline fuzzy soft set classifiers, including FSCC using the data taken from the Mammographic Image Analysis Society (MIAS) with good results.

Measurement of similarities has an essential role in the Classification using FSS [8, 9]. The similarity measure is a measure to find out how similar the two data objects are. The similarity measure in the context of data mining is the distance to dimensions that represent object features. If this distance is small, it can be interpreted that the two objects have a high degree of similarity, and if there is a considerable distance, then both objects have a low level of similarity. The similarity is subjective and is very dependent on the domain and application. There are many similarity measures of the soft set, and FSS have been studied, i.e., generalized fuzzy soft sets, similarity based on matching function, similarity based on set-theoretic approach, and similarity measure based on distance. Another distance is based on new similarity measures of FSS, where the usage of this distance measure in this research is more reasonable [10]. However, not all similarity measure has been exploration to know the performance for Classification. We conduct experiments to explore the similarity measure of generalized fuzzy soft sets, similarity based on matching function, similarity based on set-theoretic approach, and similarity measure based on distance on the rock dataset.

2   Fuzzy Soft Set (FSS)

Maji et al. define and apply the fuzzy soft set concept, hereinafter referred to as FSS in decision making problems. It is known that a convenient tool for representing concept uncertainty is provided by fuzzy sets using partial membership. In the definition of a FSS, substitute for sharp subsets uses fuzzy subsets. Thus, each soft set can be treated as a FSS [11]. In addition, on the basis of an analogy such as a soft set, it can be seen easily that each FSS can be viewed as a fuzzy information system. In such systems, data tables with entries included in the unit interval [0,1] represent the FSS. Suppose that E is the set of parameters that have relations with objects in a non-empty universe denoted by U, the set of powers of U is denoted by P(U) and $A \subseteq E$. Then, the parameterized family of the subset U is called the soft set [12, 13]. A soft set of U can also be interpreted as a pair of f:E → P(U) maps. The definition is based on the consideration that set of ε-approximate elements of the soft set or set ε-elements of the soft set, rather than a (crisp) set. Meanwhile, in FSS Theory, shows the power of all fuzzy subsets. Furthermore, a fuzzy soft set over is a pair, with is mapping represented by. Thus, the substitute for subset U is the fuzzy subset in universe U. Example 1 is given as an illustration.

Example 1. A description of the attractiveness of the shirt to be purchased is given against the given parameters stated in the FSS (F, E). Suppose that the set of all the shirts being considered is represented by $U = \{x_1, x_2, x_3, x_4, x_5\}$. Next, the aggregate of all fuzzy subsets of U is represented by $P(U)$ and the colorful, bright, cheap, and warm parameters are expressed in terms of the set $E = \{e_1, e_2, e_3, e_4\}$. Let

$$\underline{F}(e_1) = \{x_1/0.5, x_2/0.9, x_3/0.0, x_4/0.0, x_5/0.0\}$$

$$\underline{F}(e_2) = \{x_1/1.0, x_2/0.8, x_3/0.7, x_4/0.0, x_5/0.0\}$$

$$\underline{F}(e_3) = \{x_1/0.0, x_2/0.0, x_3/0.0, x_4/0.6, x_5/0.0\}$$

$$\underline{F}(e_4) = \{x_1/0.0, x_2/1.0, x_3/0.0, x_4/0.0, x_5/0.0\}$$

and the family $E(e_i)$ with $i = \{1, 2, 3, 4\}$ of $P(U)$. Table 1 is given as a form of FSS representation.

Table 1. FSS representation

(U, E)	e_1	e_2	e_3	e_4
x_1	0.5	1.0	0	0
x_2	0.9	0.8	0	1.0
x_3	1	0.7	0	0
x_4	1	0	0.6	0
x_5	0	0	0	0.3

3 Similarity and Distance Measure

There are several measurement models within the scope of data clustering and grouping, one of which is the similarity between the two entities [12]. Several researchers have carried similarity measurement between fuzzy number, fuzzy sets, and vague sets.

Recently we found that the similarity measure of soft set and fuzzy fine set has also been investigated [13]. In this paper, the FSS was measured based on similarity, i.e., generalized fuzzy soft sets, similarity based on matching function, similarity based on the set-theoretic approach, and Similarity measure distance. Lets $U = \{x_1, x_2, \ldots, x_n\}$ be a universe set, $E = \{e_1, e_2, \ldots, e_m\}$ be a parameter set. Assume that the fuzzy soft set (F, A) and (G, B) have the same parameter set, $A, B \subset E$. The similarity between two generalized fuzzy soft set is defined as follows

$$d_1((F, A), (G, B)) = \max_i \left(1 - \frac{\sum_{j=1}^n |F(e_i)(x_j) - G(e_i)(x_j)|}{\sum_{j=1}^n |F(e_i)(x_j) + G(e_i)(x_j)|} \right). \tag{1}$$

The following provides a definition of similarity based on the set-theory approach presented in the formula

$$d_2((F, A), (G, B)) = \max_i \left(\frac{\sum_{j=1}^n F(e_i)(x_j) \wedge G(e_i)(x_j)}{\sum_{j=1}^n F(e_i)(x_j) \vee G(e_i)(x_j)} \right). \tag{2}$$

On the basis of the set-theory approach, similarities are also defined in terms of form

$$d_3((F, A), (G, B)) = \frac{\sum_{i=1}^n F(e_i) \cdot G(e_i)}{\sum_{i=1}^n (F(e_i)^2 \vee G(e_i)^2)}. \tag{3}$$

Meanwhile, on the basis of the distance, similarity measure by Munjandar et al. can be defined as

$$d_4((F, A), (G, B)) = \min T_i((F, A), (G, B)), \tag{4}$$

where $T_i((F, A), (G, B)) = \frac{1}{1+d_\infty^i}$, d_∞^i is the distance between the e-approximations $F(e_i)$ and $G(e_i)$ which is $d_\infty^i = \max_j |F(e_i)(x_j) - G(e_i)(x_j)|$.

Another distance-based similarity measure for the fuzzy soft set is explored by Feng et al. called new similarity measures of FSS based on hamming and Euclidean distance as a distance measure. The Hamming and normalize distance in FSS are using Eqs. (5) and (6).

$$d_5((F, A), (G, B)) = \frac{1}{mn} \sum_{i=1}^m \sum_{j=1}^n |F(e_i)(x_j) - G(e_i)(x_j)| \tag{5}$$

and

$$d_6((F, A), (G, B)) = \frac{1}{mn} \left(\sum_{i=1}^m \sum_{j=1}^n |F(e_i)(x_j) - G(e_i)(x_j)|^2 \right)^{\frac{1}{2}} \tag{6}$$

4 Methodology

In this research, methodology consists are data collection, observation stage and laboratories stage. Data collection and observation stage is in the form of data collection in the field, in the form of lithology selected after detailed geological mapping of the meticulous area in Yogyakarta. Data collection in the form of igneous rock retrieval for petrographic analysis and chemistry. Laboratories stage is divided into sample preparation stages, in the form of making thin incisions of rocks for the study of petrography and chemical analysis of rocks (main oxides, trace elements, and rare soil elements) with XRF (X-ray fluoresces) and ICP-OES (Inductively Coupled Plasma optical emission spectrometry) devices by PT laboratories. Main Intertek Service. Petrographic observations were made in the Hard-rock Laboratory, with the Olympus CX-31P polarizing microscope.

The steps of the classification algorithm that is learning (training) and classification step. Before the two steps are done, first applied fuzzification and formation of the FSS. This step is used to obtain the feature vector for all data, be it training and testing datasets. The set model for each class in fuzzy soft is obtained at the training step The data will be learned based on the data class group [7]. The Learning step is to determine the center of each class that exists. If data $U = \{u_1, u_2, \ldots, U_N\}$, there is C class of data with n_r; $r = 1, 2, \ldots, K$ data of each class where $\sum_{r=1}^{K} n_r = N$, and E be the set of parameters, $A \subseteq E, A\{e_i, i = 1, 2, \ldots, m\}$. Suppose F_{C_r} is the set of fuzzy soft sets of the r-th class. Then the center vector of the class is denoted as P_{C_r} can be defined as

$$P_{C_r} = \frac{1}{n_r} \sum_{j=1}^{n_r} \mu_{C_r(e_i)}(u_1), \tag{7}$$

where $i = 1, 2, \ldots, m$ and $r = 1, 2, \ldots, k$.

The classification is used to label the unknown data to the target class. The new data of the training step results will be used to determine the classes in the new data measuring the similarity of two sets of fuzzy soft sets acquired in the class center vector and new data. This comparative study uses the formula for similarity measure as follows:

$$S\left(F_{P_{C_r}}, F_G\right) = 1 - d_i\left(F_{P_{C_r}}, F_G\right). \tag{8}$$

where d_i is the similarity and distance measure that have been discussed i.e., generalized fuzzy soft sets, similarity based on matching function, similarity based on set-theoretic approach and similarity measure based on distance, respectively.

After the value of the similarity for each class is obtained then it will look for which class label is appropriate for new data F_G by determining the maximum value of the result of measuring similarity for all classes. The class label is;

$$label_{clas} = \arg\left[\max_{r=1}^{k} S\left(F_{P_{C_r}}, F_G\right)\right]. \tag{9}$$

5 Result and Discussion

There are 11 features in this real world dataset collected from Mount Wungkal, Godean, Yogyakarta, Indonesia.namely Titanium dioxide (TiO_2), Silicon dioxide (SiO_2), Iron (II) oxide + Iron(III) oxide ($FeO + Fe_2O_3$), Aluminum oxide (Al_2O_3), Magnesium oxide

(MgO), Manganese(II) oxide (MnO), Sodium oxide (Na_2O), Calcium oxide (CaO), Phosphorus pentoxide (P_2O_5), Class Label, and Potassium oxide (K_2O). MATLAB version 7.14.0.334 (R2012a) was used to develop this experiment. Windows 10 operating system with an Intel Core i3-3217U CPU @ 1.80Ghz, and a total main memory of 8G RAM is used to run this algorithm. The dataset is divided into two sets of data used for training and testing where each experiment is carried out randomly in the process of separating the dataset. A total of 80 times were carried out in this experiment, with the percentage of training and testing being 80% and 20%, respectively. With this algorithm, the experiments conducted focus on calculation (precision, accuracy, recovery), and the experimental results are presented in Table 2. Based on Table 2 it can be seen that in igneous rock classification, fuzzy soft set has good performance.

Table 2. The experiment results

Methods	Accuracy	Precision	Recall
set theoretic approach	0.5833	0.7000	0.6000
Similarity distance	0.3667	0.4500	0.6000
Matching function	0.6000	0.5500	0.7500
Generalized fuzzy soft set	0.8000	0.8000	0.7500
Euclidean distance	0.8667	1.0000	0.8500

6   Conclusion

In this research, we conducted experiments on six different similarity-deductors to obtain the classification accuracy of the fuzzy soft set classification algorithm. In terms of which algorithm is better used to classify igneous rock based on its chemical analysis. This is done on the basis of the chemical composition of the igneous rock which is a fundamental characteristic. Furthermore, the classification will become a quantitative classification. It is clear from the simulation results that the best performance is for fuzzy classifier based on the Euclidian distance. The more generalized Euclidian distance of fuzzy soft set is one of the Future works.

References

1. Joseph, S., Ujir, H., Hipiny, I.: Unsupervised classification of Intrusive igneous rock thin section images using edge detection and colour analysis. In: 2017 IEEE International Conference on Signal and Image Processing Applications (ICSIPA), pp. 530–534 (2017)
2. Rangel, D.N., Reyes Santiago, O., Rodríguez, A.N., Rojas, A.F., González, E.A.P.: Correlation between morphometric parameters and geology of igneous and metamorphic basins in Colombia. In: 2020 Congreso Internacional de Innovación y Tendencias en Ingeniería (CONIITI), pp. 1–6 (2020)

3. Bai, Z., Zhong, H., Hu, R., Zhu, W., Hu, W.: Composition of the chilled marginal rocks of the panzhihua layered intrusion, emeishan large igneous province, SW China: implications for parental magma compositions, sulfide saturation history and Fe–Ti oxide mineralization. J. Petrol. **60**(3), 619–648 (2019)

4. Schön, J.H.: Chapter 1 - rocks—their classification and general properties. In: Schön, J.H. (ed.) Physical Properties of Rocks, vol. 65, pp. 1–19. Elsevier (2015)

5. Handaga, B., Herawan, T., Deris, M.M.: FSSC: an algorithm for classifying numerical data using fuzzy soft set theory. Int. J. Fuzzy Syst. Appl. **2**(4), 29–46 (2012)

6. Handaga, B., Deris, M.M.: Text categorization based on fuzzy soft set theory. In: Murgante, B., Gervasi, O., Misra, S., Nedjah, N., Rocha, A.M.A.C., Taniar, D., Apduhan, B.O. (eds.) ICCSA 2012. LNCS, vol. 7336, pp. 340–352. Springer, Heidelberg (2012). https://doi.org/10.1007/978-3-642-31128-4_25

7. Yanto, I.T.R., Saedudin, R.R., Lashari, S.A., Haviluddin, H.: A numerical classification technique based on fuzzy soft set using hamming distance. In: Advances in Intelligent Systems and Computing, vol. 700, pp. 252–260 (2018)

8. Handaga, B., Mat Deris, M.: Similarity approach on fuzzy soft set based numerical data classification BT - software engineering and computer systems, pp. 575–589 (2011)

9. Singhal, N., Verma, A., Chouhan, U.: An Application of Similarity Measure of Fuzzy Soft Sets in Verndor Selection Problem (2018)

10. Feng, Q., Zheng, W.: New similarity measures of fuzzy soft sets based on distance measures. Ann. Fuzzy Math. Informatics **7**(4), 669–686 (2014)

11. Rehman, N., Ali, A., Park, C.: Note on fuzzy soft sets and fuzzy soft lattices. Rev. la Real Acad. Ciencias Exactas, Fis. y Nat. - Ser. A Mat., **113**(1), 41–48 (2019)

12. Cross, V., Mokrenko, V., Crockett, K., Adel, N.: Using fuzzy set similarity in sentence similarity measures. In: IEEE International Conference on Fuzzy Systems, vol. 2020 (July 2020)

13. Majumdar, P., Samanta, S.K.: Generalised fuzzy soft sets. Comput. Math. with Appl. **59**(4), 1425–1432 (2010)

A Diabetes Prediction Model with Visualized Explainable Artificial Intelligence (XAI) Technology

Yanfeng Zhao[1], Jun Kit Chaw[1(✉)], Mei Choo Ang[1], Marizuana Mat Daud[1], and Lin Liu[2]

[1] Institute of Visual Informatics, The National University of Malaysia (UKM), Bangi, Malaysia
p117631@siswa.ukm.edu.my, {chawjk,amc,marizuana.daud}@ukm.edu.my
[2] College of Information Engineering, Henan Vocational University of Science and Technology, Zhou Kou, China
1090511629@qq.com

Abstract. Diabetes is a group of non-communicable diseases (NCD) that cannot be cured by current medical technologies and can lead to various serious complications. Significantly reducing the severity of diabetes and its associated risk factors relies on accurate early prediction. Some machine learning algorithms have been developed to assist in predicting diabetes, but their predictions are not always accurate and often lack interpretability. Therefore, further efforts are required to improve these algorithms to achieve the level of clinical application. The aim of this paper is to find a high-performance and interpretable diabetes prediction model. Firstly, the dataset is subjected to necessary preprocessing, including missing value imputation using K-nearest neighbors (KNN) and data balancing using adaptive synthetic sampling (ADASYN). Then, with 10-fold cross validation, the predictive performance of six machine learning algorithms is compared in terms of accuracy, precision, recall, and F1 score. Finally, the prediction results are globally and locally explained using SHapley Additive exPlanations (SHAP) and Local Interpretable Model-agnostic Explanations (LIME). The experimental results demonstrate that the eXtreme Gradient Boosting (XGBoost) algorithm provides the best predictive performance. The visualized eXplainable Artificial Intelligence (XAI) techniques offer valuable explanatory information, helping healthcare professionals and patients better understand the risk and prediction results of diabetes.

Keywords: Diabetes Prediction · Machine learning · eXplainable AI · LIME · SHAP

1 Introduction

Diabetes is a group of non-communicable diseases (NCD) caused by chronic metabolic disorders. Its main symptom is high blood glucose levels (BGL) due to the body's inability to produce or properly use insulin, a hormone that regulates BGL. Diabetes is a major global public health issue, affecting hundreds of millions of people. According to the latest report from the International Diabetes Federation (IDF), the global prevalence of diabetes in adults aged 20 to 79 was estimated to be 9.8% in 2021, with approximately 537 million people affected. It is projected that by 2045, the global diabetes prevalence will rise to 11.2, with an estimated 784 million patients [1]. Unfortunately, there is currently no medical intervention that can completely cure diabetes, leading patients to often suffer from serious complications such as cardiovascular diseases, kidney failure, blindness, and amputations. Early detection and prevention of diabetes are widely recognized as crucial in slowing down the progression of diabetes and reducing the risk of complications.

Machine learning (ML) exhibits significant potential in predicting diabetes based on patient data, as it can analyze extensive datasets and uncover patterns that may elude human observation. Numerous studies have utilized ML algorithms, including random forest, decision trees, support vector machines, and neural networks [2], to forecast or diagnose diabetes using clinical and demographic data. Regrettably, these algorithms are scarcely employed in clinical practice. Some studies have reported subpar accuracy due to inappropriate model selection and inadequate data preprocessing [3, 4]. Furthermore, certain studies, despite achieving commendable predictive performance, have neglected to provide reasonable explanations for the prediction results [5]. Consequently, this lack of interpretability has engendered a distrust in these algorithms as they prove challenging to comprehend.

The objective of this study is to develop a diabetes prediction model by integrating ML algorithms with visualized explainable artificial intelligence (XAI) techniques. The model not only achieves high performance but also offers insights into the factors contributing to diabetes episodes. The study employs targeted data preprocessing techniques, such as the K-nearest neighbors (KNN) method for missing value imputation and the adaptive synthetic sampling (ADASYN) method for dataset balancing. To identify the most suitable algorithm for diabetes prediction using the PIMA Indian diabetes dataset (PIDD), six popular machine learning algorithms are compared using cross-validation. The extreme gradient boosting (XGBoost) algorithm, demonstrating the best performance, is further examined using shapley additive explanations (SHAP) and local interpretable model-agnostic explanations (LIME) techniques to provide global and local explanations for its predictions. This research offers a solution that improves the accuracy and reliability of diabetes prediction models while providing valuable insights for disease forecasting. This can assist clinical practitioners and researchers in developing more effective prevention and treatment strategies, ultimately enhancing the quality of life for diabetes patients.

The remaining sections of this paper are organized as follows. Section 2 presents a review of related work on diabetes prediction and interpretable ML methods. Section 3 elaborates on the research methodology, including the data preprocessing steps and modeling approaches. Section 4 discusses the experimental results and provides visual explanations of the prediction results using SHAP and LIME. Finally, Sect. 5 summarizes the paper and discusses future research directions.

2 Related Works

After extensive analysis of experimental data, it has been observed that implementing proper data pre-processing techniques and selecting suitable machine learning (ML) algorithms can enhance the accuracy of prediction models [6]. In a study by Chen et al. [7], mean interpolation was employed to handle missing values in PIDD, and a k-means clustering algorithm was utilized to eliminate misclassified data. However, the class imbalance issue in the dataset was not addressed. Another approach described in [8] involved balancing the dataset using SMOTE techniques, performing feature selection, and employing SVM-RBF kernels for classification, which resulted in improved prediction performance.

To enhance prediction accuracy, some studies have explored the use of hybrid algorithms. Ahmed et al. [9] combined support vector machines, artificial neural networks, and fuzzy logic to predict diabetes, achieving an accuracy rate of nearly 95% on a 30% test set. Building upon these insights, [10] employed an isolation forest for outlier removal, employed SMOTETomek for class balancing, and developed an integrated model for diabetes diagnosis with an impressive accuracy of 96.74%. However, it is worth noting that many of these studies primarily focused on improving the performance of the prediction models, often neglecting the interpretability aspect of the employed algorithms.

In order to address this challenge, researchers have explored the use of XAI techniques to provide explanations for model decision-making processes, facilitating understanding of their functioning. Common XAI methods in the literature include Fuzzy Rule-Based Systems [11, 12] and feature extraction-based models [13,14]. Additionally, more easily interpretable models such as decision trees or linear models have been employed. However, these models often lack intuitive interpretation methods, making it difficult to convey their meaning effectively to physicians and patients. Moreover, the adoption of interpretable machine learning algorithms frequently involves sacrificing predictive performance, thereby limiting their practical application in clinical settings.

In recent years, visual interpretation of black-box models has emerged as a prominent area of XAI research. Visualized XAI techniques, such as LIME and SHAP, have shown effectiveness in interpreting a wide range of machine learning and deep learning models. These methods provide visual explanations, enhancing the interpretability of the models and facilitating their comprehension by medical professionals and patients alike. In the field of predicting gestational diabetes mellitus, [15] and [16] have developed ML models using different methods. They have effectively employed the SHAP technique to visualize both global and local interpretations, significantly enhancing the credibility and acceptability of their models. Similarly, in another study by [17], a prediction model was proposed based on common factors associated with diabetes, such as blood glucose, BMI, age, and insulin. The LIME technique was utilized to identify the key attributes and the prediction rules of diabetic organization. In line with the approach presented in this paper, [18] and [19] have integrated the LIME and SHAP frameworks to develop a visualized XAI approach that explains how the model generates final prediction results. This integration allows for a comprehensive understanding of the underlying decision-making processes, thereby improving transparency and interpretability. Our work further extends their work by providing a comprehensive explanation of the predictive models from both global and local perspectives. Additionally, it delves into the implied meaning of the discriminative features to examine how diabetes is predicted with our proposed model. This work also shows how XAI models can augment the predictive model to provide trust and confidence in their predictions.

3 Proposed Methodology

To achieve both high-performance and interpretable diabetes prediction models, this paper aims to integrate the strengths of previous studies and utilize more appropriate and effective techniques in three key stages: data preprocessing, model development and validation, and model interpretation. The overall framework of the proposed approach is illustrated in Fig. 1.

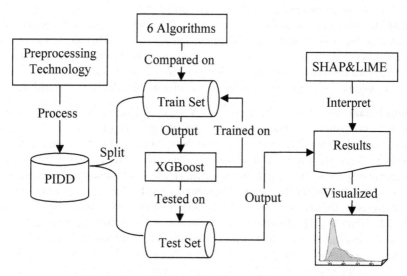

Fig. 1. Overall framework of the proposed approach

3.1 Date Preprocessing

The primary objective of this study was to explore viable solutions that strike a balance between predictive performance and interpretability of the model, rather than solely focusing on achieving high accuracy. To achieve this, we utilized the publicly available PIDD dataset, comprising only 768 samples. The dataset includes eight characteristic variables (such as the number of pregnancies, BMI, insulin levels, age, etc., of patients) and one target variable. Upon conducting exploratory data analysis, it was observed that the dataset exhibited various issues, including missing values, outliers, and data imbalances. Ignoring these issues and directly building a prediction model would inevitably yield implausible results. As a result, it was imperative to perform necessary data pre-processing steps. Here, we outline the essential pre-processing steps:

A. Missing Value Imputation.   Although the PIDD dataset initially appears to have no null values, zero values in the characteristic variables 'Glucose', 'BloodPressure', 'BMI', 'SkinThickness', and 'Insulin' are unlikely to occur in surviving patients. Thus, treating these zero values as missing values and performing appropriate imputation is necessary. We chose not to use the median imputation based on target values, as described in [6], despite its higher predictive performance. This decision was influenced by two factors: the significant number of missing values in 'SkinThickness' (29.6%) and 'Insulin' (48.7%), and the fact that target value-based imputation would overestimate predictive performance, which is not feasible in real clinical practice where future outcomes are unknown. Instead, we employed the following approach:

Median imputation: For 'Glucose', 'BloodPressure', and 'BMI', which had fewer missing values, we utilized median imputation. This involved replacing the missing values with the median value of each respective characteristic variable.

KNNImputer: For 'SkinThickness' and 'Insulin', which had a higher percentage of missing values, we applied the KNNImputer method [20]. This technique identifies k samples in the dataset that are spatially or structurally similar to the missing value samples and calculates the mean of the k neighbors for interpolation. In this study, we assigned weights as the inverse of the distance to give more influence on nearby domains.

B. Data Balancing.   The PIDD dataset consisted of 268 samples diagnosed with diabetes and 500 samples without diabetes, resulting in a data imbalance. Considering the small sample size of the dataset, the Synthetic Minority Oversampling Technique (SMOTE) is a commonly used algorithm for data balancing. However, SMOTE may introduce overlapping categories by interpolating minority class samples between majority class samples. ADASYN is an improvement over SMOTE because it adaptively generates different numbers of new samples for different minority class samples based on the data distribution [21]. The abbreviated algorithm works as follows: first, the dataset's imbalance is evaluated using Eq. (1) and compared to a set threshold. If the imbalance is lower than the threshold, the synthetic samples are generated using Eq. (2) on the basis of calculating the number of synthetic samples for each minority class sample x_i.

$$d = \frac{m_s}{m_l} \tag{1}$$

where m_s and m_l represent the quantities of minority class samples and majority class samples respectively, and $d \in (0,1]$.

$$s_i = x_i + \lambda(x_{zi} - x_i) \tag{2}$$

where x_i is an instance in the minority class, $(x_{zi} - x_i)$ is the difference vector in the feature space, and λ is a random number between 0 and 1.

Although tree-based classification algorithms do not necessarily require data normalization, we performed this step in order to compare the predictive performance of multiple ML algorithms. Additionally, after populating the missing values, we removed extreme outliers from the dataset, resulting in a final sample size of 722 for the development and validation of the prediction model.

3.2 Model Development and Validation

After data preprocessing, the dataset was split into a training set comprising 70% of the data and a test set comprising the remaining 30% to facilitate the development, training, and validation of the proposed model.

A. Algorithm Selection. To select the best performing prediction algorithm, we reviewed relevant literature and identified Logistic Regression (LR), Gaussian Parsimonious Bayes (NB), K-Nearest Neighbor (KNN), Decision Tree (DT), Support Vector Machine (SVM), and XGBoost as potential candidates. We evaluated these six algorithms separately by training them on the training set and using 10-fold cross-validation to obtain accuracy, precision, recall, and F1 scores. Based on these metrics, XGBoost was identified as the best performing algorithm.

XGBoost [22] is an improved version of the gradient boosting algorithm that is known for its simplicity, speed, and excellent results. As show in Eq. (3), its loss function comprises two components: the loss of the gradient boosting algorithm and a regularization term.

$$L(\Phi) = \sum_{i=1}^{n} l(y_{i'}, y_i) + \sum_k \Omega(f_k) \tag{3}$$

where n represents the number of training samples, l represents the loss of a single sample, $y_{i'}$ and y_i respectively represent the predicted value and true label value of the model for the training sample. The regularization term is used to describe the complexity of the model as follows:

$$\Omega(f_k) = \Upsilon T + \frac{1}{2}\lambda||w||^2 \tag{4}$$

where γ and λ are hyperparameters, w is the vector formed by the values of all leaf nodes of the decision tree, and T is the number of leaf nodes.

B. Model Training and Testing. For the XGBoost algorithm selected, the hyperparameters need to be fine-tuned to achieve optimal prediction performance. We empirically set candidate values for the hyperparameters "learning_rate", "min_samples_split", "max_depth", "subsample", and "n_estimators", respectively. The Grid Search with Cross Validation method is then utilized to search for the best combination of these parameters to construct the final prediction model. The resulting model is trained on the training set, and the final model with optimal parameters is validated on the test set. In addition to calculating accuracy, precision, recall, and F1 scores, the ROC curve of the model is plotted, and the AUC value is calculated to provide a more objective evaluation of the model's performance.

3.3 Model Interpretation

As mentioned earlier, we employed a combination of SHAP and LIME techniques to provide both global and local explanations for the final model. These techniques allowed us to visualize and interpret the model's predictions comprehensively.

A. SHAP Technique: SHAP is an additive explanation model based on cooperative game theory that can provide explanations for the output of any machine learning model [23]. Given that x_i represents the ith sample, x_i^j represents the jth feature of the ith sample, y_i represents the predicted value of the model for that sample, and y_{base} represents the baseline of the entire model (typically the mean of the target variables for all samples), the SHAP value follows the following equation:

$$y_i = y_{base} + f\left(x_i^1\right) + f\left(x_i^2\right) + \cdots + f(x_i^k) \tag{5}$$

where $f(x_i^j)$ represents the SHAP value of x_i^j, which indicates the contribution of the jth feature in the ith sample to the final prediction value y_i. A positive $f(x_i^j)$ value implies that the feature has a positive effect on the predicted value, while a negative value suggests a negative effect. This provides a more detailed understanding of how each feature influences the prediction outcome compared to conventional feature importance measures that only indicate the importance of a feature.

B. LIME Technique. Unlike delving deep into the inner workings of the model, LIME focuses on understanding how the output of a black box model changes by applying slight perturbations to the input data. It achieves this by training an interpretable model specifically around the point of interest, which is the original input [17]. The representation of data in LIME is defined as follows:

$$\exp(x) = argmin_{g \epsilon G} L(f, g, \pi_x) + \Omega(g) \tag{6}$$

Here, g represents the explanatory model for a given instance x. The approximation of the original model f and the model g is compared by minimizing the loss function. $\Omega(g)$ represents the model complexity of g, and G encompasses all potential explanatory models. The neighborhood of x is defined by π_x. By determining the model g, the neighborhood range size π_x, and the model complexity $\Omega(g)$, the model f can be made interpretable by minimizing the loss L.

4   Results and Discussions

The proposed method was implemented and tested in the Python 3.9 integrated environment. This section aims to present the experimental results of algorithm selection, model validation, and visual model interpretation, along with a concise discussion.

4.1   Performance Comparison of Different ML Algorithms

During the algorithm selection stage, the classification results of six machine learning (ML) algorithms were analyzed to determine their prediction performance. True positive (TP), true negative (TN), false positive (FP), and false negative (FN) results were extracted and used to calculate and compare the performance of the algorithms. Metrics such as accuracy, precision, recall, and F1 score were utilized to evaluate their effectiveness. Higher values of these metrics indicate superior prediction performance.

Table 1 compares these performance metrics, using the default parameter settings for each algorithm for fairness. The XGBoost algorithm achieves accuracy of 0.90/0.90, precision of 0.84/0.92, recall of 0.95/0.80 and F1 score of 0.89/0.84 on the training and test sets respectively. Although the KNN algorithm achieves equal or better results in some metrics, overall the XGBoost algorithm still has a clear advantage. On average, compared to the KNN algorithm, which has the second highest overall performance, the XGBoost algorithm improved by 2.9% in accuracy, 6.7% in precision, 3.6%% in F1 score, and only slightly decreased in recall by 1.1%. These metrics highlight the advantages of using the XGBoost algorithm for the diabetes classification problem. Based on these findings, the XGBoost algorithm was selected as the preferred model for further analysis and modeling.

Table 1. Performance comparison of different ML algorithms

Algorithms	Accuracy		Precision		Recall		F1 Score	
Dataset	Train	Test	Train	Test	Train	Test	Train	Test
LR	0.74	0.77	0.73	0.63	0.76	0.64	0.72	0.62
NB	0.75	0.81	0.76	0.70	0.78	0.73	0.75	0.70
KNN	0.85	**0.90**	0.77	0.88	**0.95**	**0.82**	0.83	**0.84**
DT	0.83	0.85	0.80	0.80	0.83	0.79	0.81	0.78
SVM	0.78	0.84	0.81	0.72	0.79	0.80	0.77	0.75
XGBoost	**0.90**	**0.90**	**0.84**	**0.92**	**0.95**	0.80	**0.89**	**0.84**

4.2   Test Results of the Final Model

First, 1080 candidate combinations of hyperparameters (433310) were generated for the selected XGBoost algorithm. By applying a 10-fold cross-validation technique, 10800 fits were obtained. These fits were then used as input for automatic parameter tuning using the GridSearchCV tool. The optimal parameter combination was found to be: learning_rate = 0.2, max_depth = 5, min_samples_split = 0.2777777777778, n_estimators = 100, sub-sample = 1.0. Subsequently, the XGBoost model, employing this optimal parameter combination, was validated on the test set. The obtained results were as follows: accuracy of 0.89, precision of 0.84, recall of 0.86, and F1 score of 0.85. Although these scores are slightly lower than those achieved on the training set, we consider this difference reasonable. Overall, the prediction performance remains excellent.

To further validate the usefulness and accuracy of the proposed algorithm, we employed the area under the curve (AUC) and receiver operating characteristic (ROC) curve. Figure 2 displays the ROC curve for the final model, demonstrating that the parameter-tuned XGBoost algorithm achieved an AUC value close to 0.97, indicating a significantly high area under the ROC curve. Additionally, we evaluated the risk differentiation ability of the model by calculating the Kolmogorov-Smirnov (KS) value.

The KS value represents the maximum difference between the cumulative distribution of good and bad samples. A larger cumulative difference signifies a stronger risk differentiation ability, resulting in a higher KS metric. In our final model, the KS value is close to 0.81, indicating that the proposed algorithm excels in risk differentiation.

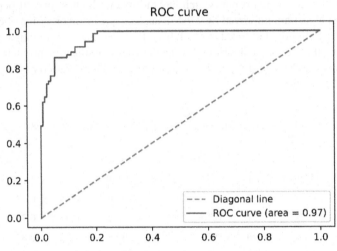

Fig. 2. ROC curve of the final model

It is worth mentioning that the PIDD dataset is characterized by a small sample size and comprises only eight predictor variables. This limitation hinders the potential for further enhancements in prediction performance. It is also possible that better prediction results could have been achieved by employing the ensemble models [24]. it is crucial to emphasize that our primary objective did not revolve around maximizing performance metrics alone. Therefore, we did not deliberately select a better dataset or an ensemble method in this particular context.

4.3 Visualized Model Explanation

In this study, we aimed to determine the importance of each feature and provide an explanation for the role of these features in influencing specific decisions. Both global and local representations of the feature impact are presented and discussed in detail.

A. Global Explanation.
The global interpretation aims to demonstrate how features contribute to a given dataset within a specific algorithm. In this study, the permutation importance of the features is utilized to fulfill this purpose. As depicted in the Fig. 3, the XGBoost algorithm highlights Glucose as the most influential feature, followed by BMI, SkinThickness, Age, PedigreeFunction, and Insulin, in descending order. Conversely, BloodPressure and Pregnancies are deemed the least significant features. The summary plot provides additional valuable information, with the y-axis representing feature importance rankings

and colors denoting low to high feature values. The x-axis showcases Shapley values, and the jittering of the overlapping points upward on the y-axis allows for visualizing the distribution of Shapley values for each feature. Figure 4 reaffirms the ranking of feature influence seen in Fig. 3, revealing a corresponding increase in diabetes risk with higher levels of blood glucose, BMI, and age. Such a conclusion aligns perfectly with existing medical knowledge.

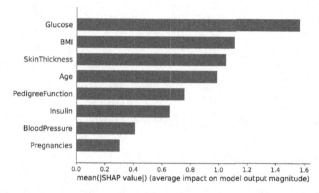

Fig. 3. The permutation importance of the features for the final model

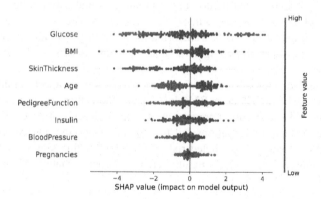

Fig. 4. The summary plot for the final model

The dependence plot illustrates the impact of an individual feature on the variability in the predicted outcome of a model. It provides insights into how a single feature influences the model's output by comparing the SHAP value of that feature with the feature values across the entire dataset. Figure 5 visualizes the changes in predictions as the Glucose feature varies. It is evident that the Glucose value exhibits a near-linear relationship with its corresponding SHAP value, indicating that higher Glucose levels are associated with an increased risk of being predicted to have diabetes. Additionally, the color-coded dots represent the distribution of another feature, Insulin, throughout the range of Glucose values. Notably, there is a clear tendency for the Insulin value to rise as the blood glucose levels increase.

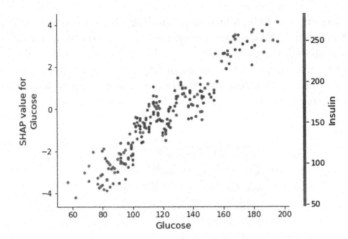

Fig. 5. The dependence plot of Glucose and Insulin for the final model

B. Local explanation.

Local explanation is employed to elucidate the contribution of each feature to the predicted values in a specific test dataset. Figure 6 showcases the SHAP force plot for a sample from the test dataset. The width of the color bar in the plot represents the magnitude of a feature's contribution to the predicted values. Red indicates a positive contribution, while blue signifies a negative contribution. The summation of contributions from all features results in the transformation of the target variable from its baseline value (the average value of the target variable across all records) to the final predicted value.

In this case, the factors that escalate the risk of developing diabetes, ranked in order of importance, are higher Glucose, BMI, Insulin, and SkinThickness values. Conversely, being 26 years old and having 0 pregnancies diminish the risk of developing diabetes. However, the negative contributions fail to counterbalance the positive contributions adequately. As a result, the predicted risk of diabetes for this sample is higher (with a predicted value of 2.58), signifying an increase of approximately 2.5 units from the baseline value.

Fig. 6. The SHAP force plot of a specific sample

LIME is another model-agnostic method for local explanation. It can display the positive and negative impact of each feature on decision-making, helping doctors understand why the model makes certain predictions. Figure 7 presents the LIME plot for a specific sample from the test dataset. In the plot, blue represents features that decrease the risk of diabetes, while orange represents features that increase the risk. It is evident that the probability of having diabetes for this sample is 0.82. The features that elevate the risk of diabetes, in order of importance, are Glucose, BMI, SkinThickness, and Age. On the other hand, the features PredigreeFunction and BloodPressure decrease the risk of diabetes. Pregnancies and Insulin, however, do not significantly affect the predicted outcome.

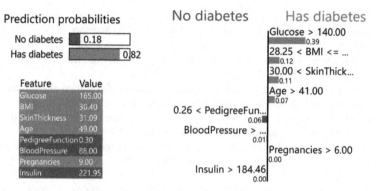

Fig. 7. The LIME tabular explainer of a specific sample

Interestingly, based on the visualized explanation results, we drew the inference that the majority of diabetic patients in the PIMA dataset were type 2 diabetic. This inference was drawn from the positive correlations observed between BMI, skin thickness, age, and insulin with the diabetes prediction results in both global and local interpretations, which aligns with the characteristics of type 2 diabetes. Conversely, indicators such as BMI, skin thickness, age, and insulin are likely to exhibit negative associations with predictive outcomes for type 1 diabetes. Although we couldn't find specific evidence supporting this conclusion in the existing literature, it has been endorsed by several physicians.

5   Conclusion

This study conducted data pre-processing and compared the prediction performance of six ML algorithms using cross-validation techniques. Based on the findings, a diabetes prediction model was developed using the XGBoost algorithm, which achieved high performance and interpretability. The results demonstrate that the final model achieved high performance with an accuracy, precision, recall, F1 score, and AUC value of 0.89, 0.84, 0.86, 0.85, and 0.97, respectively. These impressive results were obtained by fine-tuning the optimal parameters using the GridSearchCV technique. To enhance the interpretability of the prediction results, the proposed model employed SHAP and LIME techniques for global and local explanation. These techniques serve as powerful tools for physicians to assess the accuracy of prediction models. Moreover, it highlights the significant potential of these model-independent interpreters in providing visualized explanations for any ML model.

Acknowledgement. The authors would like to thank the Universiti Kebangsaan Malaysia for support-ing this work through Geran Galakan Penyelidik Muda (GGPM-2022-063) and re-search incentives TAP-K024478.

References

1. International Diabetes Federation., IDF Diabetes Atlas, 10th edn., International Diabetes Federation (2021). https://diabetesatlas.org/data/en/world/ (Accessed 06 May 2023)
2. Al Sadi, K., Balachandran, W.: Prediction model of type 2 diabetes mellitus for Oman prediabetes patients using artificial neural network and six machine learning Classifiers. Appl. Sci., **13**(4) (2023). https://doi.org/10.3390/app13042344
3. Sisodia, D., Sisodia, D.S.: Prediction of diabetes using classification algorithms. Procedia Comput. Sci., **132**(Iccids), 1578–1585 (2018). https://doi.org/10.1016/j.procs.2018.05.122
4. Mahboob Alam, T., et al.: A model for early prediction of diabetes. Informatics Med. Unlocked **16**, 100204 (2019). https://doi.org/10.1016/j.imu.2019.100204
5. Tiwari, P., Singh, V.: Diabetes disease prediction using significant attribute selection and classification approach. J. Phys. Conf. Ser., **1714**(1) (2021). https://doi.org/10.1088/1742-6596/1714/1/012013
6. Kibria, H.B., Nahiduzzaman, M., Goni, M.O.F., Ahsan, M., Haider, J.: An Ensemble app-roach for the prediction of diabetes mellitus using a soft voting classifier with an explainable AI. Sensors 22(19) (2022). https://doi.org/10.3390/s22197268
7. Chen, W., Chen, S., Zhang, H., Wu, T.: A hybrid prediction model for type 2 diabetes using K-means and decision tree. In: Proceedings of IEEE International Conference on Software Engineering and Service Sciences ICSESS, vol. 2017(61272399), pp. 386–390 (2018). https://doi.org/10.1109/ICSESS.2017.8342938
8. Ramesh, J., Aburukba, R., Sagahyroon, A.: A remote healthcare monitoring framework for diabetes prediction using machine learning. Healthc. Technol. Lett. **8**(3), 45–57 (2021). https://doi.org/10.1049/htl2.12010
9. Ahmed, U., et al.: Prediction of diabetes empowered with fused machine learning. IEEE Access **10**, 8529–8538 (2022). https://doi.org/10.1109/ACCESS.2022.3142097
10. Fitriyani, N.L., Syafrudin, M., Alfian, G., Rhee, J.: Development of disease prediction model based on ensemble learning approach for diabetes and hypertension. IEEE Access **7**, 144777–144789 (2019). https://doi.org/10.1109/ACCESS.2019.2945129
11. Aamir, K.M., Sarfraz, L., Ramzan, M., Bilal, M., Shafi, J., Attique, M.: A fuzzy rule-based system for classification of diabetes. Sensors **21**(23) (2021). https://doi.org/10.3390/s21238095
12. El-Sappagh, S., Alonso, J.M., Ali, F., Ali, A., Jang, J.H., Kwak, K.S.: An ontology-based interpretable fuzzy decision support system for diabetes diagnosis. IEEE Access **6**, 37371–37394 (2018). https://doi.org/10.1109/ACCESS.2018.2852004
13. Kocbek, S., Kocbek, P., Gosak, L., Fijačko, N., Štiglic, G.: Extracting new temporal features to improve the interpretability of undiagnosed Type 2 diabetes Mellitus Prediction models. J. Pers. Med. **12**(3) (2022). https://doi.org/10.3390/jpm12030368
14. Hao, J., Luo, S., Pan, L.: Rule extraction from biased random forest and fuzzy support vector machine for early diagnosis of diabetes. Sci. Rep. **12**(1), 1–12 (2022). https://doi.org/10.1038/s41598-022-14143-8
15. Du, Y., Rafferty, A.R., McAuliffe, F.M., Wei, L., Mooney, C.: An explainable machine learning-based clinical decision support system for prediction of gestational diabetes mellitus. Sci. Rep. 12(1), 1–14 (2022). https://doi.org/10.1038/s41598-022-05112-2

16. El-Rashidy, N., ElSayed, N.E., El-Ghamry, A., Talaat, F.M.: Prediction of.gestational diabetes based on explainable deep learning and fog computing. Soft. Comput.Comput. **26**(21), 11435–11450 (2022). https://doi.org/10.1007/s00500-022-07420-1

17. Nagaraj, P., Muneeswaran, V., Dharanidharan, A., Balananthanan, K., Arunkumar, M., Rajkumar, C.: A prediction and recommendation system for diabetes mellitus using XAI-based lime explainer," International Conference on Sustainable Computing and Data Communication Systems ICSCDS 2022 - Proc.eedings, pp. 1472–1478 (2022). https://doi.org/10.1109/ICS CDS53736.2022.9760847

18. Tasin, I., Nabil, T.U., Islam, S., Khan, R.: Diabetes prediction using machine learning and explainable AI techniques. Healthc. Technol. Lett., 1–10 (2022). https://doi.org/10.1049/htl2.12039

19. Assegie, T.A., Karpagam, T., Mothukuri, R., Tulasi, R.L., Engidaye, M.F.: Extraction of human understandable insight from machine learning model for diabetes prediction. Bull. Electr. Eng. Informatics **11**(2), 1126–1133 (2022). https://doi.org/10.11591/eei.v11i2.3391

20. Zhao, X., Jiang, C.: The prediction of distant metastasis risk for male breast cancer patients based on an interpretable machine learning model. BMC Med. Inform. Decis. Mak.Decis. Mak. **23**(1), 74 (2023). https://doi.org/10.1186/s12911-023-02166-8

21. Technique, A.O., et al.: DAD-Net : Classification of Alzheimer ' s Disease Using Neural Network, pp. 1–21 (2022)

22. Noorunnahar, M., Chowdhury, F.A., Mila, A.H.: A tree based eXtreme Gradient Boosting (XGBoost) machine learning model to forecast the annual rice production in Bangladesh, pp. 1–15 (2023). https://doi.org/10.1371/journal.pone.0283452

23. Nohara, Y., Matsumoto, K., Soejima, H., Nakashima, N.: Explanation of machine learning models using shapley additive explanation and application for real data in hospital. Comput. Methods Programs Biomed. 214 (2022). http://10.0.3.248/j.cmpb.2021.106584

24. Kumari, S., Kumar, D., Mittal, M.: An ensemble approach for classification and prediction of diabetes mellitus using soft voting classifier. Int. J. Cogn. Comput. Eng. **2**, 40–46 (2021). https://doi.org/10.1016/j.ijcce.2021.01.001

Author Index

Printed in the United States
by Baker & Taylor Publisher Services